Computer Numerical Control Machines and Computer Aided Manufacture

Computer Numerical Control Machines and Computer Aided Manufacture

P Radhakrishnan
Ph.D., FIE, CE
Director, PSG Institute of Advanced Studies
Avinashi Road, Coimbatore
Tamil Nadu

Publishing Globally

NEW AGE INTERNATIONAL (P) LIMITED, PUBLISHERS
LONDON • NEW DELHI • NAIROBI
Bangalore • Chennai • Cochin • Guwahati • Hyderabad • Kolkata • Lucknow • Mumbai
Visit us at www.newagepublishers.com

Published by New Age International (P) Ltd., Publishers
First Edition: 2012
Reprint: 2018

GLOBAL OFFICES

- **New Delhi** **NEW AGE INTERNATIONAL (P) LIMITED, PUBLISHERS**
  7/30 A, Daryaganj, New Delhi-110002, (INDIA)
  Tel.: (011) 23253771, 23253472, **Telefax:** 23267437, 43551305
  E-mail: contactus@newagepublishers.com • Visit us at www.newagepublishers.com
- **London** **NEW AGE INTERNATIONAL (UK) LTD.**
  27 Old Gloucester Street, London, WC1N 3AX, UK
  E-mail: info@newacademicscience.co.uk • Visit us at www.newacademicscience.co.uk
- **Nairobi** **NEW AGE GOLDEN (EAST AFRICA) LTD.**
  Ground Floor, Westlands Arcade, Chiromo Road (Next to Naivas Supermarket)
  Westlands, Nairobi, KENYA, **Tel.:** 00-254-713848772, 00-254-725700286
  E-mail: kenya@newagepublishers.com

BRANCHES

- **Bangalore** 37/10, 8th Cross (Near Hanuman Temple), Azad Nagar, Chamarajpet, Bangalore- 560 018
  Tel.: (080) 26756823, **Telefax:** 26756820, **E-mail: bangalore@newagepublishers.com**
- **Chennai** 26, Damodaran Street, T. Nagar, Chennai-600 017, **Tel.:** (044) 24353401, **Telefax:** 24351463
  E-mail: chennai@newagepublishers.com
- **Cochin** CC-39/1016, Carrier Station Road, Ernakulam South, Cochin-682 016, **Tel.:** (0484) 2377303, **Telefax:** 4051304
  E-mail: cochin@newagepublishers.com
- **Guwahati** Hemsen Complex, Mohd. Shah Road, Paltan Bazar, Near Starline Hotel, Guwahati-781 008,
  Tel.: (0361) 2513881, **Telefax:** 2543669, **E-mail: guwahati@newagepublishers.com**
- **Hyderabad** 105, 1st Floor, Madhiray Kaveri Tower, 3-2-19, Azam Jahi Road, Near Kumar Theater, Nimboliadda Kachiguda, Hyderabad-500 027, **Tel.:** (040) 24652456, **Telefax:** 24652457
  E-mail: hyderabad@newagepublishers.com
- **Kolkata** RDB Chambers (Formerly Lotus Cinema) 106A, 1st Floor, S N Banerjee Road, Kolkata-700 014
  Tel.: (033) 22273773, **Telefax:** 22275247, **E-mail: kolkata@newagepublishers.com**
- **Lucknow** 16-A, Jopling Road, Lucknow-226 001, **Tel.:** (0522) 2209578, 4045297, **Telefax:** 2204098
  E-mail: lucknow@newagepublishers.com
- **Mumbai** 142C, Victor House, Ground Floor, N.M. Joshi Marg, Lower Parel, Mumbai-400 013
  Tel.: (022) 24927869, **Telefax:** 24915415, **E-mail: mumbai@newagepublishers.com**
- **New Delhi** 22, Golden House, Daryaganj, New Delhi-110 002, **Tel.:** (011) 23262368, 23262370, **Telefax:** 43551305
  E-mail: sales@newagepublishers.com

ISBN: 978-81-224-3397-5
C-18-03-11227

Printed in India at Ajit Printing Press, Delhi.
Typeset at In-house, Delhi.

NEW AGE INTERNATIONAL (P) LIMITED, PUBLISHERS
7/30 A, Daryaganj, New Delhi-110002
Visit us at **www.newagepublishers.com**
(CIN: U74899DL1966PTC004618)

Dedicated to

- my mother
- my wife
- management of PSG Institute of Advanced Studies and
- my students

PREFACE

Manufacturing has been recognized as the main engine for economic growth and creation of wealth of a country. The share of manufacturing in GDP has been stagnating a low level for over two decades in India. The major reasons for the reduced level of contribution by manufacturing has been the inability of the country to build and maintain competitiveness needed to meet the global challenges as well as to develop a larger domestic market through low cost production. Competitiveness will be enhanced only if our manufacturers are able to produce products of global quality at lower costs. Automation through computer aided manufacture is one strategic approach to achieve this. This book is primarily designed to introduce the concepts and tools of computer aided manufacture to students, engineers, managers and technical supervisory personnel.

Machine tool industry is a strategic industry, forming the backbone of many if not most of the major sectors of industrial activity in a country in the traditional manufacturing context. The machine tool industry in India has played and will continue to play a key role in enhancing competitiveness and enabling development of quality and excellence in the output of the manufacturing industry and of the Indian economy as a whole. In India, the machine tool industry supports the strategic development and growth of the automotive, the white and brown goods, the capital goods industries as well as strategic sectors such as defense, railways, aerospace, etc. Based on current trends and emerging demands, the computer numerically controlled (CNC) segment is emerging as a key driver of growth for the machine tool industry in India. A significant portion of this book is therefore devoted to CNC machine tools.

India requires a large number of designers, CNC operators, programmers and supervisory personnel to meet the growing population of CNC machine tools in the country. The major emphasis in this book is on CNC. However, CNC cannot be treated in isolation though it is the largest segment of the computer aided manufacturing system. An attempt has been made in this book to introduce robots and coordinate measuring machines, though the coverage is not as comprehensive as in the case of CNC machines.

I hope that this book will address to a long felt need of users and programmers of CNC machines apart from students who wish to pursue a career in CNC technology.

—P. Radhakrishnan

CONTENTS

1 COMPUTER AIDED MANUFACTURE

1.1 INTRODUCTION

Manufacturing is the activity of producing components, products, and systems and therefore is one of the most important engineering activities. The economic prosperity of a nation is directly linked to the manufacturing capabilities of the nation. The gross national product of the nation depends to a large extent on the output from its manufacturing industries. The prosperity of the nation and the quality of life of the people depend on the manufacturing capability. Any technological advancement requires corresponding improvement in manufacturing know how. Engineers and economists give hence manufacturing considerable importance.

The share of manufacturing in the Indian exports is low compared to developed countries. There are many reasons for this situation. Indian engineering goods are generally inferior in design and quality and costly compared to global standards. Further Indian companies often default as far as delivery dates are concerned. All these deficiencies are due to the fact that the Indian manufacturing has not kept pace with the developments in other countries. The level of automation in Indian manufacturing needs improvement. Industrial processes which rely more on manual labour are generally inefficient, costly, error-prone, and slow to respond to market changes and are invariably technologically inferior to their counterparts in advanced countries. The products manufactured by companies with low levels of automation do not have consistency as far as quality and performance are concerned.

Globalization and liberalization of Indian economy has thrown great challenges to Indian manufacturing industries. Till a decade ago, they had a captive market and could sell what they could produce at the prices they quote. Today the situation has changed a lot. No longer they have a captive market. Their products have to compete with superior products, which are lower in cost and higher in quality and performance. The result is that the Indian manufacturing base is steadily shrinking and the market share of manufacturing in gross domestic product (GDP) declines.

A way out of this situation is more automation. Automation can be of two types–hard automation and flexible automation. Hard automation is employed in conventional transfer lines and special purpose machine tools using pneumatic, hydraulic, electro-pneumatic, electro-hydraulic devices. The productivity of conventional manual machine tools can be considerably increased by automation using pneumatic control (low cost automation) and hydraulic control. While such automation practices help to reduce the cost, they are not flexible enough to respond quickly to product changes. Flexible automation uses computers and microprocessors, which can be reprogrammed depending on the changing requirements. Hence they are more suitable in today's manufacturing situation. Of late manufacturing industries increasingly make use of machinery and equipment which are computer controlled and hence programmable. Numerically controlled machines, coordinate measuring machines and robots which are used in engineering manufacture are examples of such equipment. The manufacturing activity which uses computer controlled equipment is called computer aided manufacturing.

1.2 COMPUTER AIDED MANUFACTURE

Computer aided manufacture covers a wide spectrum of activities. At the lowest level, automation of individual processes or a group of processes can be achieved by microprocessors, programmable logic controllers (PLC) and micro-controllers. Computers or microprocessors can control manufacturing equipment like machine tools, welding machines, assembly machines etc. The type of control which is used in machine tools is called computer numerical control (CNC). CNC also may involve the use of programmable logic controller (PLC). A flexible-manufacturing cell may consist of one or more machine tools in which a higher level of computer controlled automation is built in. Flexible inspection systems using co-ordinate measuring machines (CMM), CNC CMM's and computer vision systems used in flexible manufacturing are also part of computer aided manufacturing. Robots and computer vision are extensively used in materials handling, welding, painting, inspection etc which are also manufacturing activities. Flexible manufacturing systems integrate all the above together to form an integrated manufacturing system.

1.3 ADVANTAGES OF COMPUTER AIDED MANUFACTURE

The advantages of computer aided manufacture can be many. Some of them are briefly mentioned below:

(i) Computer aided manufacture reduces manual labour. There is a misconception that the Indian labour is cheap. This is true in terms of per hour cost. But by world standards the Indian labour is less productive and hence are more costly compared to labour in other countries. Therefore the Indian products which involve manual labour need not necessarily be cheaper.

(ii) Manual work lacks consistency whereas computer controlled or programmable equipment is always consistent as far as output and quality are concerned.

(iii) There is less rejection and rework. Rejection if at all may be due to uncontrolled technological parameters like material variability, process changes, wear of tools etc.

(iv) Product changes can be easily incorporated.

(v) Delivery of the products can be confidently assured.

(vi) The manufacturing equipment can accept the CAD data directly. For example, a CNC machine control system can generate the manufacturing program using a CAD file with a limited number of instructions by the operator at the machine console itself. Similarly a rapid prototyping machine can produce a component directly from CAD data.

(vii) The time elapsed between the conceptualization of a product and its realization and subsequent introduction to the market is called product development lead time. The lead-time in manufacture is considerably reduced in computer aided manufacture.

(viii) Computer aided manufacture helps-to achieve higher production rates with less labour.

(ix) Cost savings can accrue due to increased manufacturing efficiency.

(x) Enterprise resource planning (ERP) operations like planning, process design, and inventory control, scheduling, machine loading, assembly and shipping are also controlled by computers today. Thus computer aided manufacture helps to integrate all the operations of a manufacturing company.

(xi) Since the production rate is more, fewer machines and less factory space is needed for a given production volume.

1.4 TYPICAL EXAMPLES

Many examples can be quoted to demonstrate the superior advantage of computer aided manufacture when compared with manual manufacture. A typical example is that of a plastic injection molding die. Before the widespread introduction of CAM, dies were produced in a die sinking machine followed by grinding and manual polishing. The process was not only time consuming but required several iterations and modifications to obtain the desired product. Today dies are milled directly using the data from the CAD model. Advanced features like NURBS surfaces and high speed CNC systems enable even very complex surfaces to be realized accurately. High speed CNC machining centers can mill the cavity on the dies in the hard condition of the die and have practically eliminated the need for a secondary polishing operation because of its capability to produce excellent finish in the die cavity. If the finish is to be improved further, the die manufacturers can use CNC EDMs with micro pulsing capability which can produce excellent finish. The process change due to the introduction of CAM and the time saving are illustrated in Fig. 1.1.

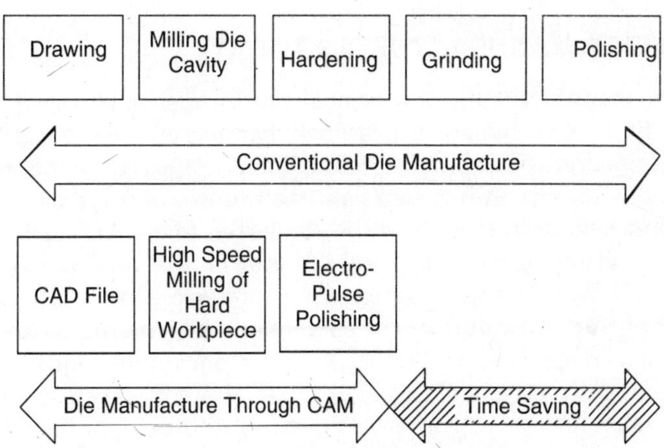

Fig. 1.1 Steps in Die Making

Another example cited here is that of an exhaust manifold of an automobile. Figure 1.2 shows the CAD model of an exhaust manifold. The reader can see that the geometry of the external surface and the internal cavity (not shown in the model) are complex. The tools required for manufacturing the part using sand casting (pattern and core box) can be milled accurately in a machining center directly using the CAD data. This process not only saves considerable time but also produces accurate castings.

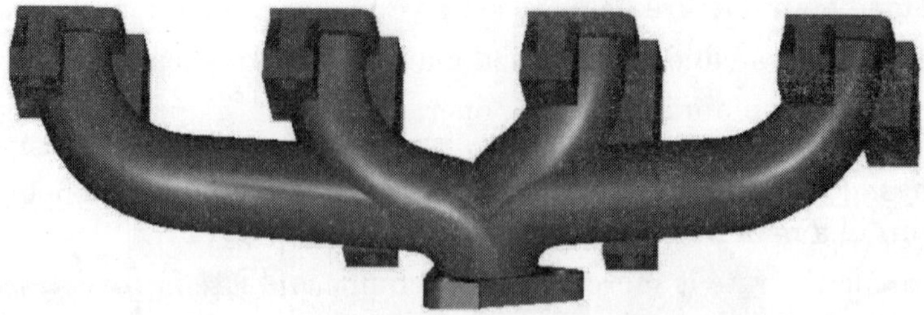

Fig. 1.2 Exhaust Manifold

1.5 TECHNOLOGIES RELATED TO CAM

There are several constituent technologies in (CAM). Some of them are:

(i) Computer Numerical Control
(ii) CAM software
(iii) Robotics
(iv) Flexible manufacturing
(v) Computer Aided Process Planning
(vi) Enterprise resource planning
(vii) Product life cycle management

This book is primarily devoted to CNC and CAM software though some of the other technologies are also introduced briefly.

1.6 COMPUTER AIDED MANUFACTURING TODAY

The steps involved in manufacturing in a typical machine shop are graphically represented in Fig.1.3. Much of the new designs are presently carried out using computers. Sometimes components are reengineered from existing components or parts using reverse engineering concepts. Mechanical or laser scanning can capture the geometric data of a part for reverse engineering. This point cloud data can then be converted to a CAD model using appropriate software. The CNC program to run the machine tool or the production equipment can be developed from the CAD model using programming software. Optionally a gantry loader or a robot can do the loading and unloading of the component. The manufactured part is inspected using a coordinate measuring machine (CMM). The programme required for operating the CNC CMM can be created directly from the CAD file. Today software packages are available to manage the entire product life cycle. Even work piece handling can be entirely automated right from raw material storage to final shipping. Thus the manual effort involved in manufacture can be reduced to a minimum using computer-aided manufacture.

Many of the technologies used in the machines are closely related to computer numerical control (CNC). CNC machines are therefore very vital to the manufacturing today. One of the interesting factors evident from the illustration in Fig. 1.3 is the seamless data transfer possible from design to manufacture. CAD data can be used to create CNC programs as well as programs for the inspection of the component. The data can also be used to program robots.

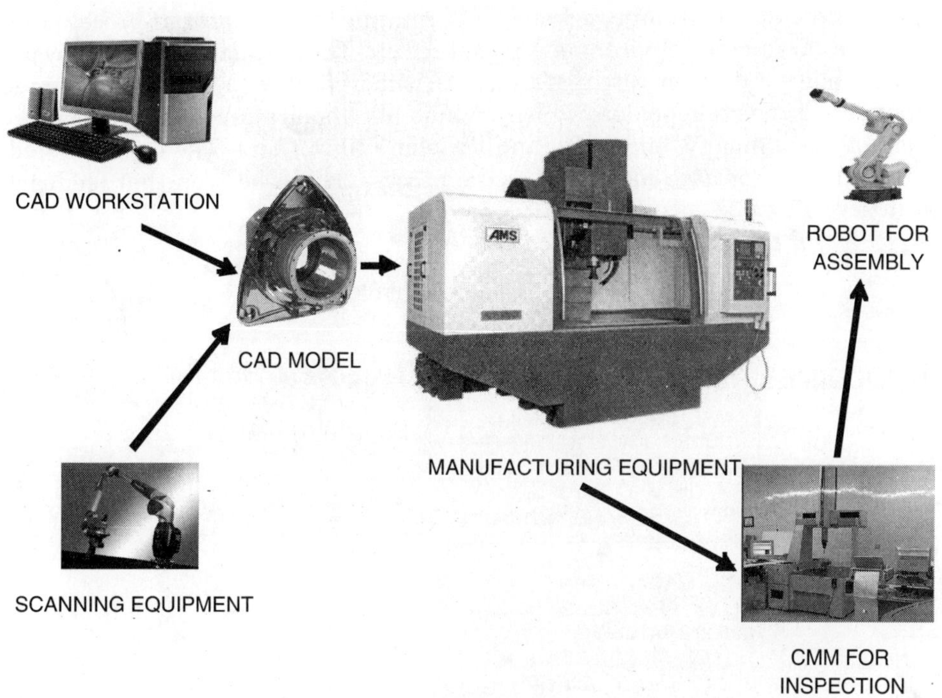

Fig. 1.3 Product Design and Manufacture Using CAM

Industries like automotive, aircrafts and die and mould use computer aided manufacture extensively. Computer aided manufacture helps mass customization. The job shops derive the benefit of both flexibility and increased production rate through computer aided manufacture. Even transfer lines use CNC today to achieve flexibility and re-configurability in the event of product changes.

The factors relevant to a manufacturing process are shown in Fig. 1.4. The component to be processed, the target cost of manufacture and its end use determine the approach to the design of the manufacturing process. A variety of manufacturing options and tools may be available for the engineer to manufacture a component. This is usually carried out at the planning stage. However, the manufacturing engineer has to make appropriate decisions to fine tune the process depending on the situation. A thorough knowledge of the capability of the machine, process, process parameters, process- process parameter interaction, tools, and performance of tools is needed for optimizing the manufacturing operation. Well laid out shop floor practices, operator safety issues and consideration for environmental aspects are also critical for efficient management of the manufacturing operations. The output of a manufacturing operation can be quantified in terms of production rate, yield, cost, quality and throughput.

A systems approach will be helpful to achieve optimum performance, output and efficiency in a manufacturing operation. Figure 1.5 illustrates the manufacturing process system. The inputs to the process are both technical as well as management. Target cost, CAD models, drawings, material data, tool data, work instructions (process plan, inspection plan), tooling sheets, production rate etc may form part of the technical inputs. The management involvement constitutes planning, organization, coordination and control. The process requires knowledge of materials, process variables, process knowledge relating to tool-material-process interaction, tool life, machine parameters, environmental aspects, etc. The output is measured by production rate, quality, yield, production rate, safety etc. Ultimately any process is evaluated by the value it provides to the stakeholders which include all who are involved in the process-from shareholders of the company, end users and suppliers to workers. The output is fed back to the input to make appropriate correction in the process. It can be seen that feedback is very important in several ways:

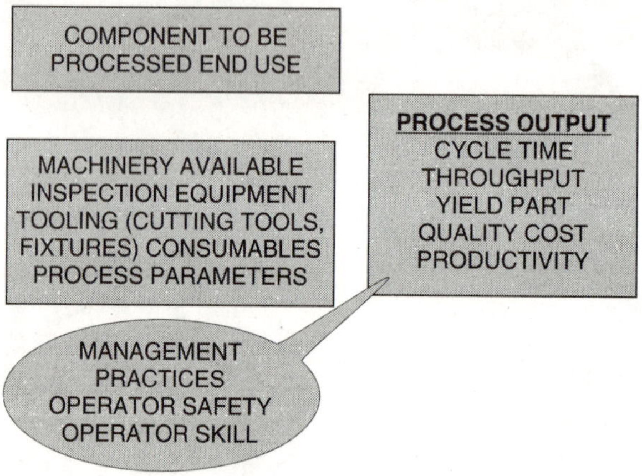

Fig. 1.4 Factors Relevant to a Manufacturing Process

- Monitoring and stabilizing the system
- Controlling deviations
- Optimizing the yield

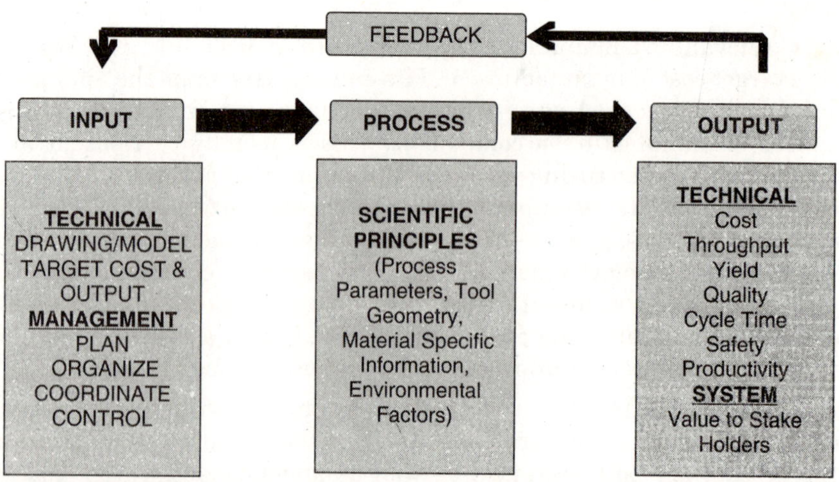

Fig. 1.5 A Systems Approach to Manufacturing Processes

1.7 SIGNIFICANCE OF CNC IN MANUFACTURING

CNC has significantly impacted engineering manufacture today. This is evident from the replacement of conventional machines by CNC machines in many of the machine shops. Most of the manufacturers of machine tools have switched over to the production of CNC machines from conventional machine tools. CNC machines constitute a major portion of machine tools manufactured today. Next chapter reviews the development of CNC as well as some basic CNC concepts.

1.8 ORGANIZATION OF A CNC MACHINE TOOL SYSTEM

A CNC Machine tool consists of:

- Mechanical structure consisting of base, column, slides, work table etc.
- Mechanical drive components like main spindle, ball screws, linear guideways, etc.
- Auxiliary elements like automatic tool changer, tool magazine, tool offset device, measuring probes, coolant system, lubricating system, pallet changer, limit switches, proximity switches, alarm indicator, chip conveyor etc.
- Main spindle motor, axis feed drive Servo motors, drive amplifiers, input/output modules and amplifiers, machine operator's pendant, machine operator's panel and integrated CNC with LCD display.
- Electrical accessories.

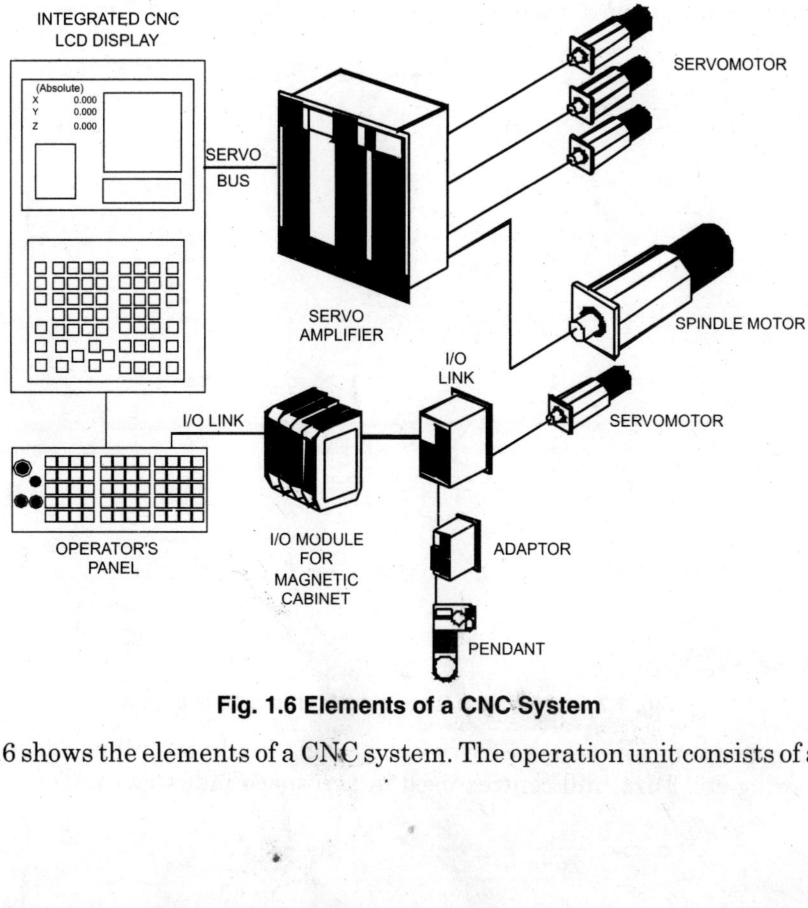

Fig. 1.6 Elements of a CNC System

Figure 1.6 shows the elements of a CNC system. The operation unit consists of an integrated

CNC with LCD display, a machine operator's panel and an operator's pendant (optional, but essential for large machines). These constitute the man machine interface. Three Servo motors are shown for three axes feed drives. The spindle motor drives the main spindle. A servo amplifier amplifies the electrical signals coming through the servo bus from the CNC. The I/O link connects the operator's panel with an additional Servo motor (optional) and control pendant (optional).

Subsequent chapters deal with the various elements of a CNC machine tool in detail.

1.9 CONVERGENCE OF MACHINE TOOLS

Manufacturing engineers are familiar with various basic machining processes like turning, boring, milling, drilling, grinding etc. Manual machines are generally designed to primarily cater to any one of these processes. For example, lathes are designed for turning and allied operations like thread cutting, drilling along the spindle axis, grooving and knurling though processing engineers may carry out many other operations with suitable tooling or attachments. A boring machine can be used for milling and drilling in addition to boring. A milling machine can be used for a variety of other machining operations other than just milling. Many axi-symmetric components may have off centre holes, milled features etc. The practice before the advent of CNC machines involved carrying out the primary machining in one machine and moving the component to other machines for subsequent operations. For example, a component with off centre holes and a milled feature as shown in Fig. 1.7 is machined first in a lathe and the subsequent machining carried out in a drilling machine and milling machine for drilling off centre holes and slot respectively. With the development of turning centres, all these operations could be done in machine without set up changes, thereby increasing productivity and accuracy.

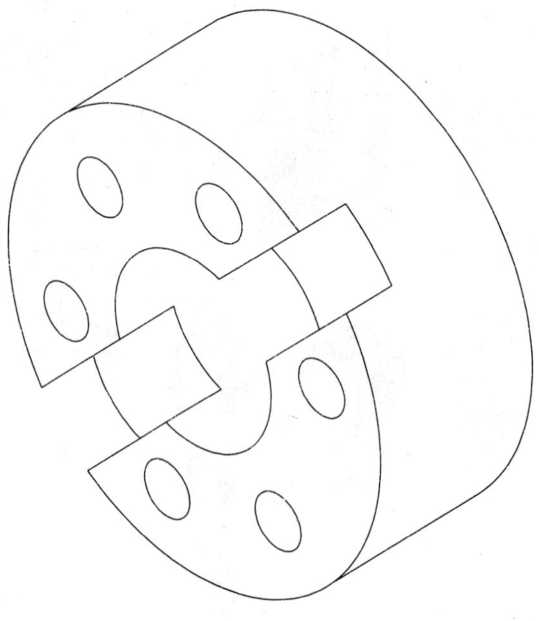

Fig. 1.7 Component Requiring Multiple Operations

Similarly machining centres can carry out various kinds of milling, drilling and allied operations, boring etc. Turn mill centres used in aerospace industry can turn and mill large components in one machine itself. Now we have fewer classes of machine tools like CNC lathes and turning centres, machining centres, etc. This has been made possible primarily due to:

- The use of multiple tools and automatic tool changing
- Positioning of tools using a program
- Manipulation of work pieces using the program
- Design of more rigid machines

This convergence is illustrated in Fig. 1.8.

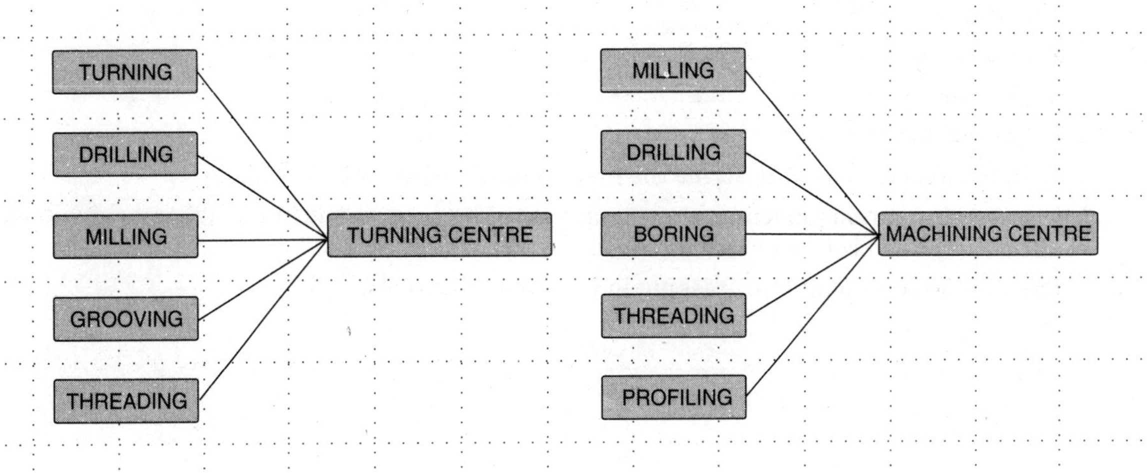

Fig. 1.8 Convergence of Machine Tools

1.10 MULTITASKING MACHINES

A new class of machines called multitasking or combo machines are now being developed. This category of machines are often tailored to machine a particular type of component. Different spindle heads designed to carry out different operations are integrated into a single machine. This approach avoids the need for multiple set ups, thereby increasing accuracy and productivity. Many machining and other manufacturing operations could be integrated into a single machine in a multitasking mode. Aerospace industry, petroleum industries and automotive industries are the major beneficiaries of multitasking concept. Since considerable engineering has to go into the development of these machines, multitasking machines cannot be used as off the shelf machines like turning centres and machining centres.

REVIEW QUESTIONS

(1) Why is computer aided manufacture more responsive to product changes?

(2) What are the benefits of computer aided manufacturing?

(3) Why do you recommend computer aided manufacturing?

(4) How does CAM help to reduce manual labour?

(5) Why should production company using computer aided manufacturing equipment operate more shifts in a day?

(6) How will the product quality be enhanced by replacing manual production by computer aided manufacture?

(7) Discuss the importance of feedback in a manufacturing operation.

(8) Study a manufacturing process and how the process could be optimized in terms of cycle time.

(9) What are the technical and system outputs in manufacturing?

(10) Why is a systems approach relevant in manufacturing?

(11) Discuss the advantages of computer aided manufacture with particular reference to the following:

- Cost of the product
- Time to market
- Consistency in quality

(12) With the aid of a sketch describe the main components of a CNC system.

(13) Discuss how various machining processes could be carried out in a single machine tool like a machining centre or turning centre.

(14) Explain the concept of multitasking in CNC machine tools.

2 CNC SYSTEMS

CNC system is the brain of the CNC machine. This chapter briefly traces the historical development of CNC technology and gives a detailed account of CNC systems and reviews some of the recent developments like open CNC.

2.1 INTRODUCTION

A CNC system is designed around one or more microprocessors and controls all the operation of the machines as well as interfaces with the external world for communications, remote diagnosis, program uploading and downloading, program management including storage, simulation, retrieval and editing. The CNC system carries out all calculations pertaining to slide movement, controls the operation of main drive and axes feed drives, creates the alphanumeric and graphics on the display device, manages operator interfaces like alarm messages and controls the operation of the programmable logic controller.

2.2 HISTORICAL DEVELOPMENT

The need for a new technology to control machine movement was felt during late 40's to meet the challenges in the production of aerospace components. The manufacture of many of these components involves several thousands of machine movements.

A major contribution to this development was made by Parsons who developed a technique to machine accurate templates to manufacture helicopter blades. This involved calculating 200 points on a curve and drilling them on a precision jig mill. He subsequently developed in 1948 a 3-D method of machining using ball end mill on a SIP jig bore and a Devlieg jig mill. The successive settings of the tool were determined using the IBM punched card reader. Parsons was later entrusted with the development of a (NC) milling machine working on the same principle. The U S Air Force was the funding agency for the NC development. The Air Force Air material Command of U.S. gave Parsons a contract for US $ 200,000. Parsons found that card reader is too slow and approached the Servomechanisms Laboratory at M I T to develop a tape reader and power drive for the proposed machine. The collaboration between Parsons and M I T ran into difficulties later. U S Air force, then, awarded a contract to M I T. The Servomechanisms Laboratory of M I T developed the first N C Machine in 1952. The patent for the concept was awarded to John T Parsons and Frank Stulen in 1958. Bendix started commercial production of NC machines. Giddings and Lewis, General Electric, IBM and Fujitsu are the companies who took interest in adopting NC technology, in its early years.

The development of the machine hardware and the programming technique called Automatic Positioning of Tools (APT) was undertaken almost simultaneously. It must also be noted here that another project undertaken at that time at M I T (Whirl-Wind Project) led to development of Interactive Computer Graphics.

Presently, all the NC machines produced are computer numerical control machines, as the NC system (or CNC system) is designed and built around one or more microprocessors. CNC machine tools now form a major part of output of machine tools in advanced countries. Table 2.1 gives the production of CNC machines in India. About 70% of machine tools manufactures in India were CNC machine tools (1655 machines). Significant among them are listed in Table 2.1.

Table 2.1 Production of CNC Machines in India during 2007-2009

Machine Tools	2007-2008		2008-2009	
	Qty	Value (in Rs. Million)	Qty	Value (in Rs. Million)
Metal Forming				
CNC	304	525.640	201	358.000
Conventional	272	1801.730	273	1878.000
Total Metal-Forming	**576**	**2327.370**	**474**	**2236.000**
Metal-Cutting				
CNC	5181	12253.800	3437	8242.000
Conventional	2673	4438.800	1910	3766.000
Total Metal-Cutting	**7854**	**16692.600**	**5347**	**12008.000**
Total Metalworking of which:	**8430**	**19019.970**	**5821**	**14244.000**
CNC is	**5485**	**12779.440**	**3628**	**8600.000**
Conventional is	**2945**	**6240.530**	**2483**	**5644.000**

(Courtesy: Indian Machine Tool Manufacturers Association)

2.3 GENERATIONS OF CNC MACHINES

There are four significant stages in the development of NC machines:

First Generation: The control system of the first generation numerically controlled machines was built with vacuum tube and associated devices. The system was bulky, consumed lot of power and reliability was poor.

Second Generation: Second generation machines were built with transistors. The size of the control elements was reduced. However, all the functions had to be realized through electronic circuits. The number of printed circuit boards was large. Since there were thousands of components and connections involved, the reliability was again poor.

Third Generation: Third generation NC machines were built with integrated circuits. The IC's with medium scale integrated improved the reliability of the system. Drive technology also made considerable progress. Thyristor controlled DC drive become popular during this period. Reliable and compact DC controllers were developed both for main drives and for the control of servo motors for axes feed drive.

The various logic functions in the early NC systems (during 50's and 60's) were realized through fixed circuitry and hence were called hard wired systems. The integration of minicomputers with NC machines that led to the development of CNC machine tools was one of the two major significant developments during mid 60's.

Initially minicomputers were interfaced with NC machine tools. This development helped to introduce the much needed flexibility. From the totally hardwired design, the design of the NC machine tools became soft wired. Instead of reading and executing programs block by block it was possible to store the program in the computer memory and execute the program. Several limitations of the NC systems were also could be overcome by CNC systems.

Program editing became much easier and several NC functions could be implemented in software. The other development was the evolution of the concept of Direct Numerical Control (DNC) technique by which several NC machine tools could be controlled from single computers. This technology enabled the NC user to by-pass the tape reader and control a number of NC machine tools from a single computer. The concept of NC data transfer from a computer or remote station using telecommunication wires was also introduced by DNC system manufacturers. A detailed description of DNC systems is provided later in this chapter.

Fourth Generation: Towards the end of 70's the computer design underwent changes and microprocessor came to be used as the CPU of computers. This change also affected the design of NC Machine tools. The designers started developing NC systems around microprocessors. This simplified the logic and control and design and instead of several PCB's in the case of NC machines, the entire control could be implemented with just one PCB for CNC machines. Initially 8 and 16 bit microprocessors were used. Later control systems with several processors (Multi-processing Systems) were introduced. The reliability of the system was considerably improved. The developments in CNC systems still continue. Today many CNC systems are based on 32 bit as well as 64 bit microprocessors. A few personal computer based CNC systems are also available in the market. Features available in modern CNC systems are discussed later in this chapter.

2.4 PRINCIPLES OF NUMERICAL CONTROL

The principle of operation of a numerical controlled machine can be explained with the help of Fig. 2.1. In a numerical controlled machine tool, the slides are driven by servo motors through re-circulating ball screw and nut assemblies. Both DC and AC servo motors are used today, the latter increasingly becoming more popular. The use of re-circulating ball screw reduces friction, backlash and wear. The low friction reduces the torque required at the motor and the lost motion through torsional deflection of the screw. Some of the high speed CNC machines are fitted with linear motors. The dynamic response of the system is also improved with the use of linear motors.

The positioning information coded in the NC program is decoded by the CNC controller and the slide is moved to the programmed position at the required feed rate. A Feedback device mounted either on the slide or on the servo motor measures the displacement or position of the slide. Feedback devices may be classified as analog or digital depending upon their output.

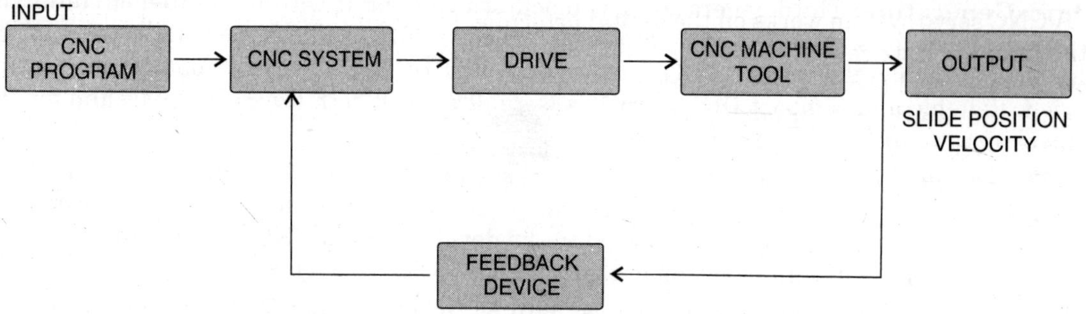

Fig. 2.1 Principle of a Numerically Controlled Machine Tool

They are also classified as linear or rotary depending upon their construction. Linear feedback devices include optical scales, inductosyn etc. Rotary feedback devices are mounted either on the ball screw or on the motor shaft and measure the slide position indirectly. Rotary encoders, optical scales, and synchro resolvers are the commonly used rotary feedback devices.

The measured and the target positions are compared and the servo system ensures that the correct positioning is achieved to make this error nearly zero. Since positioning is done electronically, it is possible to achieve accuracy and repeatability of the order of 5-10 micrometres even under heavy duty cutting conditions. Two servo loops are incorporated in feed drive - one for the position and the other for the feed. In addition to this, the selection of spindle speed is also under servo control. The principle of operation of the servo system used in a CNC Machine tool is described below.

2.4.1 Principles of Operation of a CNC Servo System

Figure 2.2 shows the block diagram of the axis drive of a CNC machine. The input to the machine is a CNC program which is a set of coded instructions to operate the machine to produce a component. The CNC system decodes this information and sends the appropriate control signals to the drive motor (servo motor). The motor drives the table through the distance specified at the stipulated feed or feed rate. The feedback transducer measures the distance moved as well as the table feed rate to compare with the input information and correction. The error drives the table until the desired position is reached. In addition, there will be a feed back control system for the main spindle drive.

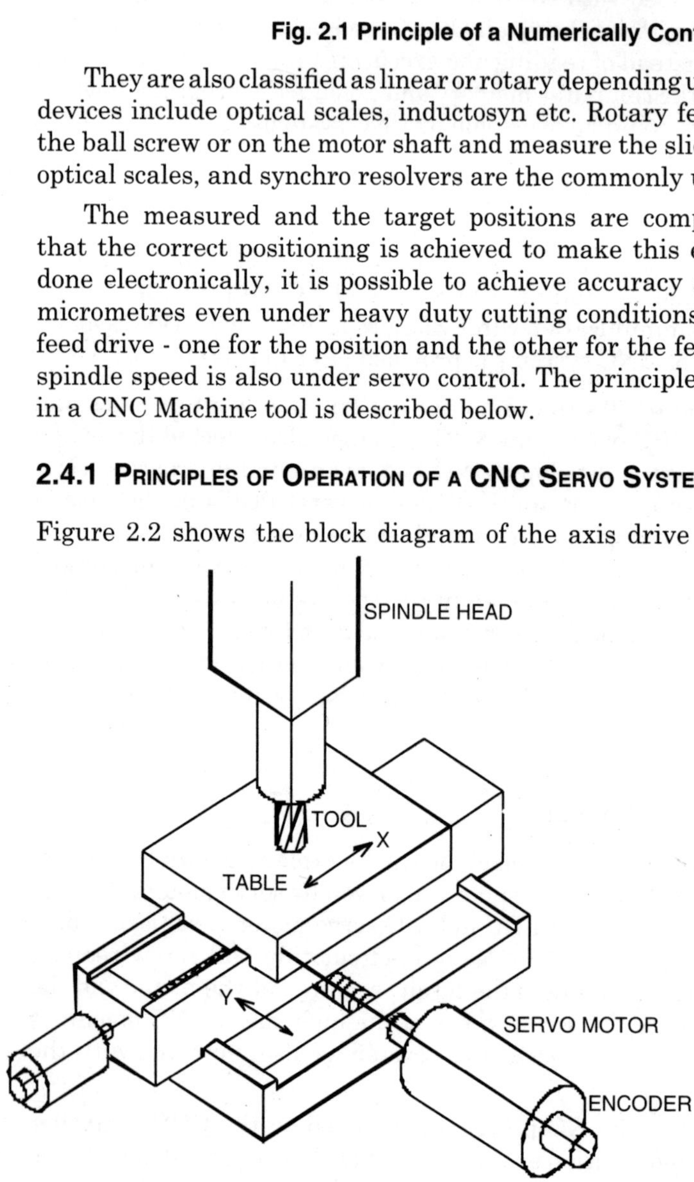

Fig. 2.2 Block Diagram of Axis Drive of a CNC Machine

A CNC servo system works on the digital principle. In a digital system, the control signal is in the form of electrical pulses. Figure 2.3 shows a typical pulse train. A pulse train will have a low voltage level (say 1.2 V) and higher voltage level (say 5 V). Low voltage level is referred to as '0' state and high voltage level '1' state. Higher voltage may be negative also. Different higher voltage levels may also be used for control purposes.

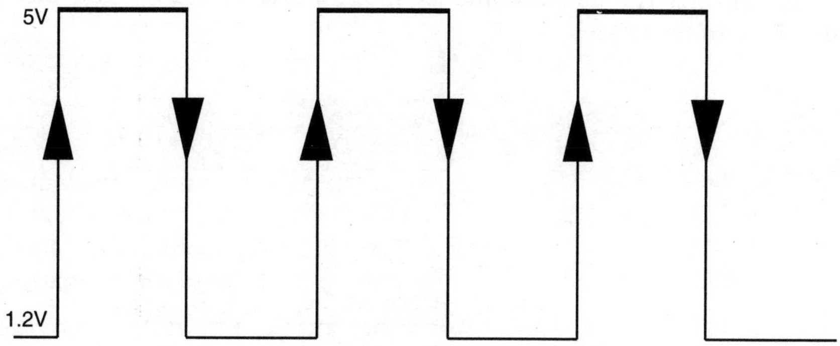

Fig. 2.3 A Typical Pulse Train

Suppose that for positioning in the Z direction, the tool has to move through a distance of 50 mm. This distance is converted into pulses one pulse for each micrometre (1/1000 of a mm). For 50 mm distance, a command signal of 50000 pulses is generated by the control system.

The resolution of the system can be improved by a factor called Command Multiply Ratio (CMR). If the feed is 0.2 mm/rev, and the spindle rpm 1000, the slide velocity required is 1000 × 0.2 = 200 mm/rev. If the pitch of the ball screw is 10 mm, the rotational speed of the z servo motor should be 200/10 = 20 rpm. The command signal (± V) from the velocity control unit will have a magnitude proportional to the speed required. Plus or minus signal denotes the rotation in clockwise or anticlockwise direction which is necessary for positive and negative movements of the table in any axis.

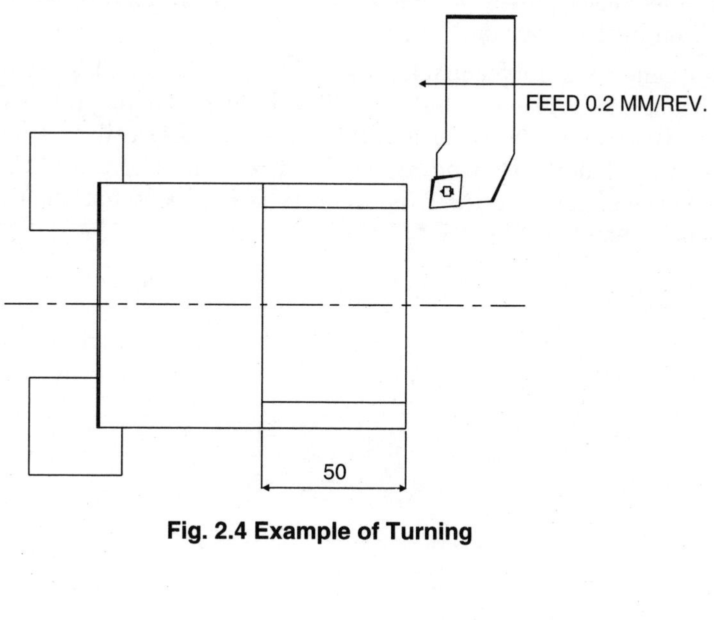

Fig. 2.4 Example of Turning

The feedback unit is a significant element of a CNC control system. The feedback involves measurement of position as well as feed velocity. In a majority of cases, the encoder which is used as the feed back device generates 2000, 2500 or 3000 pulse per revolution. This is mounted on the rear side of the axis servo motor itself. From Fig. 2.4 it can be seen that there are two servo loops in the axis drive - the outer loop for position and the inner loop for feed rate. The feedback signal for the feed rate is the pulse rate or pulse frequency. The frequency/ voltage converter converts the pulse frequency into an analog voltage and this is compared with the input signal to the motor.

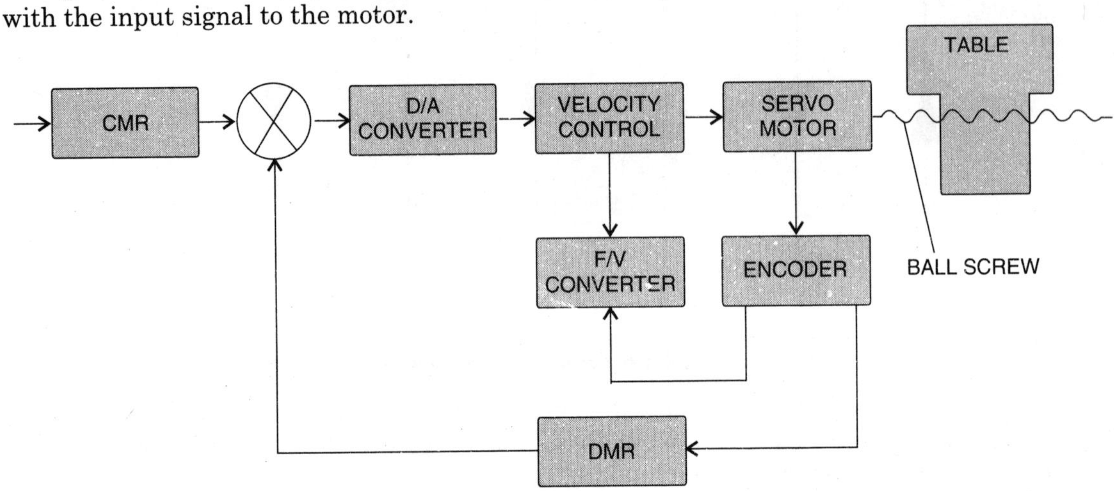

CMR - Command multiply ratio **DMR - Detect multiply ratio**

Fig. 2.5 Block Diagram of Servo Control

The outer loop is the position control circuit. The encoder generates pulses corresponding to the rotation of the motor (which is proportional to the table movement). A detect multiply ratio (DMR) is used to equalize the command pulse and the pulse generated by the encoder. The pulses corresponding to the table position are compared to (or subtracted from) the command pulse. When the feedback pulses become equal to the command pulse, the table reaches the stipulated position in the program.

The encoder generates the feedback pulses. This, in the simplest case, is done by allowing light to pass through a series of radial slits. Two light receiving stations (usually solar cells) are used (A and B). This is shown in Fig. 2.6. The two solar cells are mounted with a phase difference of ¼ wave length. Depending on the direction of rotation, the pulses from B will precede or follow the signal from A. This property is used to sense the direction of movement of the slide. This is shown in Fig. 2.7.

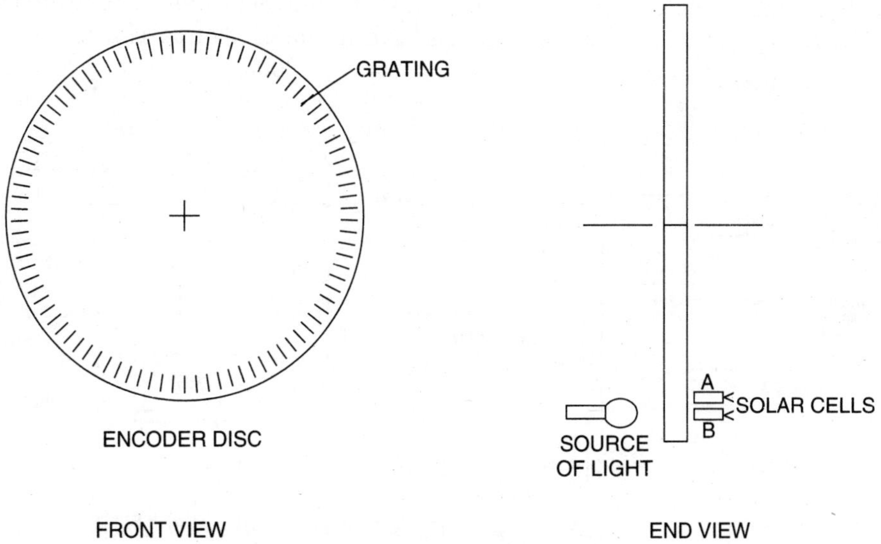

Fig. 2.6 Feedback Using Encoder

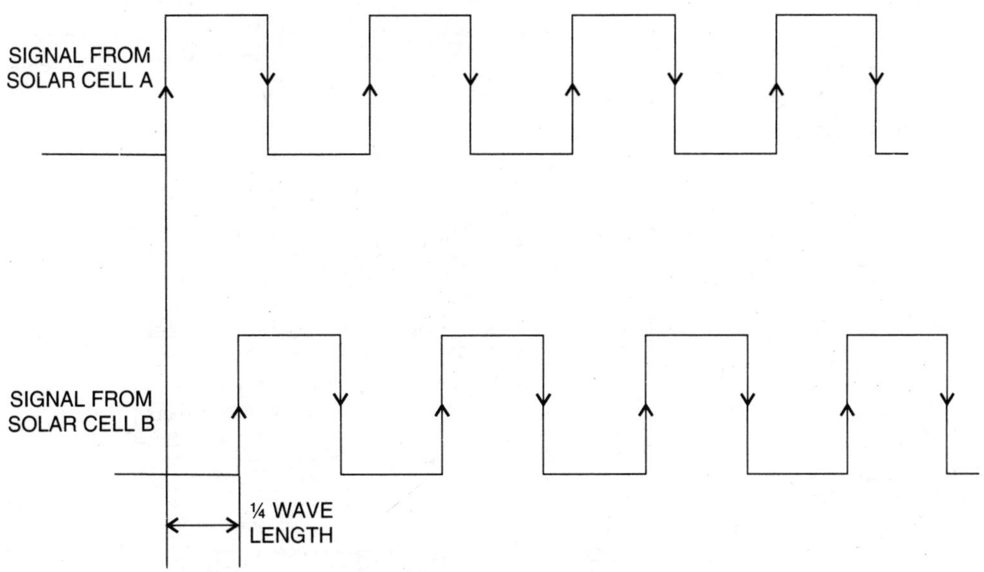

Fig. 2.7 Detection of Direction

An overview of a 3-axis CNC system is shown in Fig. 2.8. It can be seen that there are three major subsections in the CNC system. There are three major sections in a CNC control unit. The first section consists of AC Power unit, programmable machine control PCB, the magnetics cabinet, operator's panel and manual pulse generator (MPG). The master PCB has interfaces with this section and controls the positioning as well as velocity control of the 3 axis. The spindle speed control is also shown. The actuator section consists of servo motors and feed back units (encoders or linear scales).

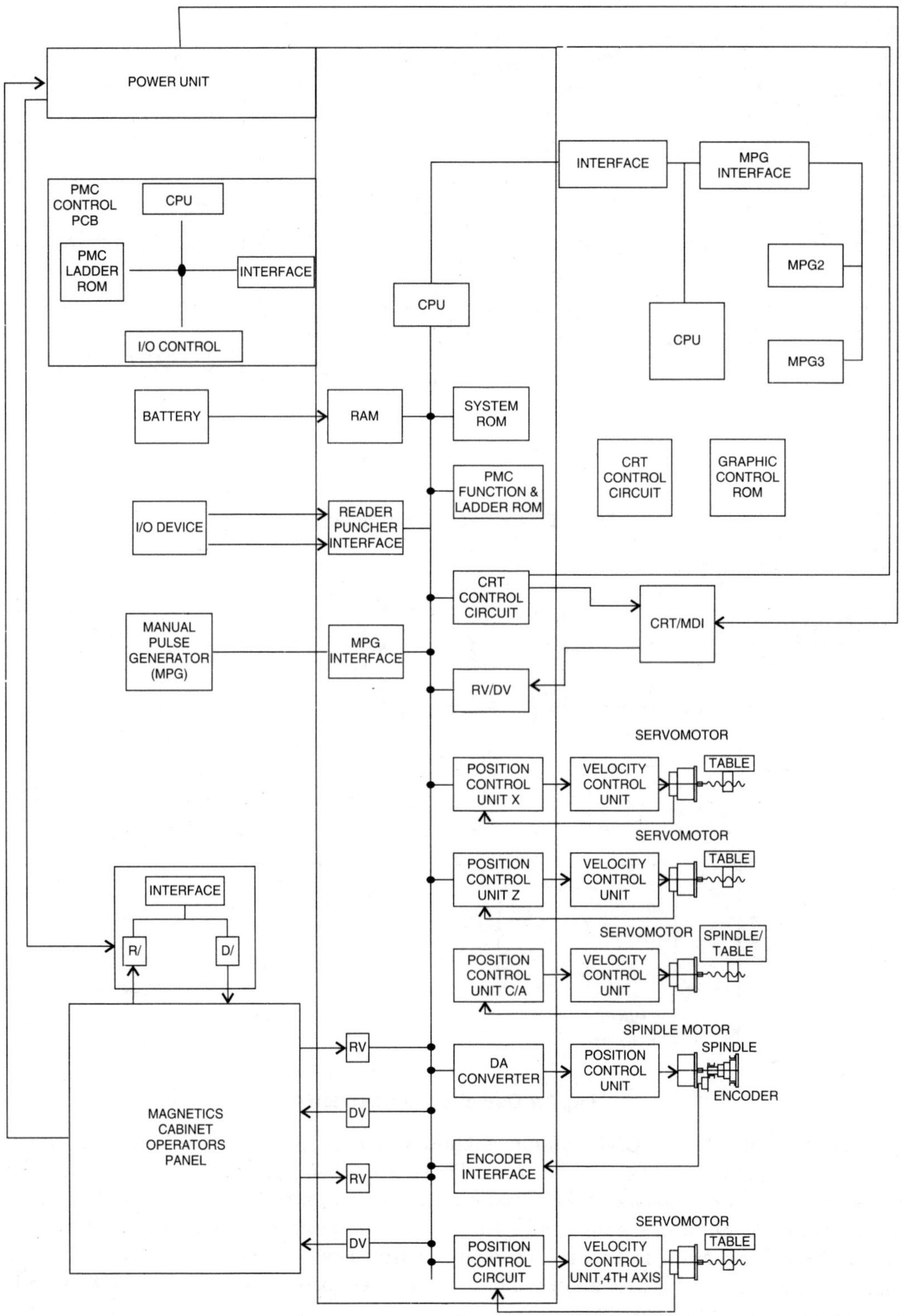

Fig. 2.8 An overview of a 3-axis CNC System

In some systems, only one encoder is used and it serves as both position and feedback unit. This is shown in Fig. 2.9. In other systems, separate feedback units for position and velocity are used. In this case, the position feedback is derived from the table position and velocity feedback is obtained from the servo motor speed. If the position feedback is obtained this way, errors due to backlash, pitch error, ball screw compliance etc. can be eliminated.

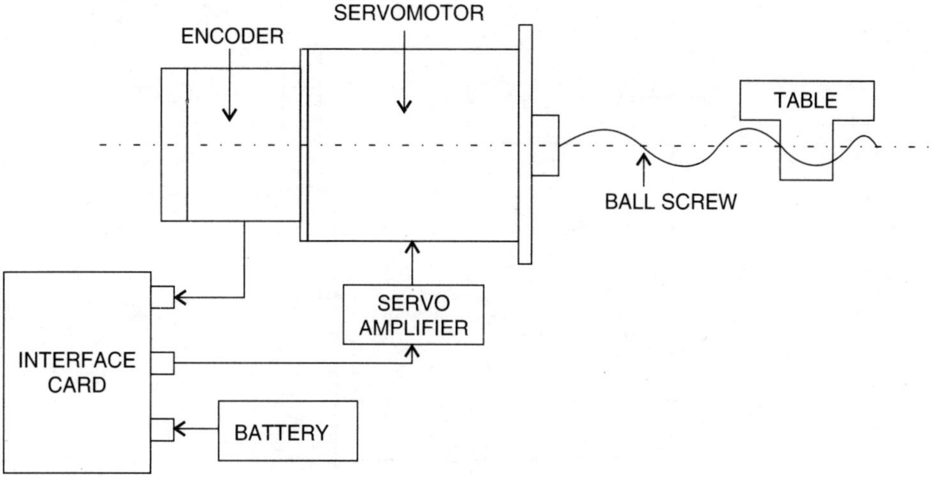

Fig. 2.9 Semi Closed Loop System

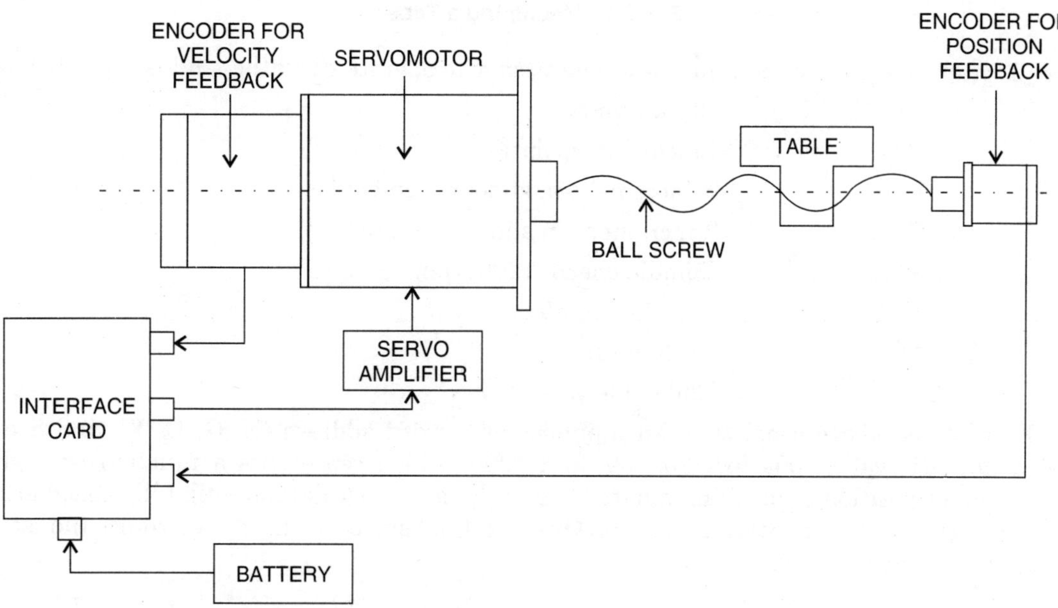

Fig. 2.10 Closed Loop System

CNC machine tools employ DC motors or AC motors which offer infinite variation of spindle speeds over a wide range of speeds. Digital technology is used in the modem AC drives. AC motors are capable of delivering high power at low base speeds. AC main drives are gradually replacing DC drives, which were dominating the CNC field till recently.

NC as described earlier is control by numbers. NC is control by information contained in a part program which is a set of coded instructions given as numbers for automatic control of a machine in a pre-determined sequence.

Figure 2.11 shows the machining a taper on a cylindrical component. To carry out this operation on a CNC lathe, we write a program block as follows:

N005 G01 U20 W-50 S1200 F0.2 M08;

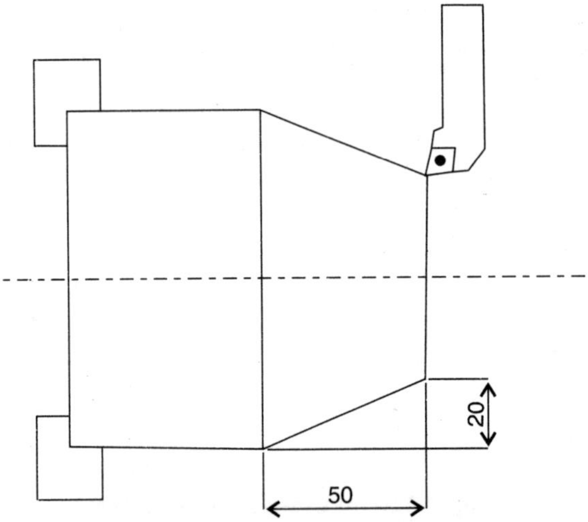

Fig. 2.11 Machining a Taper

The program block codes the information necessary to operate the lathe, and is given below:

N005	Block number
G01	Linear interpolation
U20	X increment in slide movement
W-50	Z increment in slide movement
S1200	Spindle speed, 1200, rpm
F0.2	Feed, 0.2 mm/rev
M08	Coolant on
;	End of block

Each of the above consists of an alphabet or a word address (N, G, U, W, and S etc.) and a numeric value (005, 01, 20, -50, and 1200) which represents a function or a slide displacement position or machining data. These alphanumeric data are digitally coded either in the ISO (International Standardization Organization) system or EIA (Electronics Industries Association, USA) system.

2.4.2 Coding of Information

Early NC systems coded only numeric data and they did not have any alphabetic characters. Since all the information necessary to carry out the machining operation is passed on to the control system through these coded numerical data, the control came to be known as numerical control (NC).

The numeric data given is in decimal form. For the purpose of the convenience in processing, the data is to be converted (coded) into binary form. A decimal number is represented in binary form as a power of 2.

Decimal Number	Binary Number	Binary Representation			
		2^3	2^2	2^1	2^0
1	2^0	0	0	0	1
2	2^1	0	0	1	0
3	$2^1 + 2^0$	0	0	1	1
4	2^2	0	1	0	0
5	$2^2 + 2^0$	0	1	0	1
6	$2^2 + 2^1$	0	1	1	0
7	$2^2 + 2^1 + 2^1$	0	1	1	1
8	2^3	1	0	0	0
9	$2^3 + 2^0$	1	0	0	0

To represent large number, a binary coded decimal (BCD) system is employed. For example the number 358 can be represented as:

0 0 1 1 3

0 1 0 1 5

1 0 0 0 8

There are two standards for coding, one proposed by ISO (International Standardization Organization) and the other by EIA (Electronics Industries Association of USA).

2.5 FEATURES OF CNC SYSTEMS

A CNC system can be fitted to machine tools in order to effect control over several machine functions. In order to perform these functions, a CNC system is characterized by a number of features. These functions can be broadly classified as follows:

(i) Control system features

(ii) Memory devices

(iii) Programming features

(iv) PLC features

(v) Diagnostic features

2.5.1 Control System Features

These features provide information about the characteristics of the CNC system and its capabilities. Important features are given below:

2.5.1.1 Technology of System

Currently two types of architectures are being used in CNC systems

(i) Single microprocessor based systems

(ii) Multi microprocessor based systems (Multiprocessor systems)

Single microprocessor architecture: In this type of system a 16, 32 or 64 bit microprocessor is used.

Multiprocessor architecture: This type of architecture is widely used in many CNC systems today. The control functions are carried out by a set of microprocessors, each doing an assigned task. This concept helps to implement various functions faster. Both hardware and software structures are modular thereby enhancing the flexibility of the system.

2.5.1.2 Executive Program

The executive program contains the intelligence needed to carry out different tasks in CNC system. The executive program is resident usually in EPROM/Bubble memory.

2.5.1.3 Other System Features

Other features of CNC system are:

- C R T display and alphanumeric keyboard
- M D I and operator programming
- System resolution, ex: 0.5 micron, 1 micron or 10 micron
- Feed and rapid traverse rates
- Spindle Speeds - directly programmable or through S codes
- Modes of operation like M D I, Single step, Auto etc.
- Operating controls like Jog, feedrate and spindle speed override, axis select switch, edit, reference, dry run, test mode

2.5.1.4 Axis Calibration

This is a very useful feature for obtaining higher positioning accuracy. The error in the pitch of the lead screw can be compensated with this feature.

2.5.1.5 Reversal Error (backlash) Compensation

This feature effects automatic compensation every time the slide is reversed. Error due to backlash in the lead screw can thus be minimized.

2.5.1.6 Machine Setup Data (MSD)

Machine tool parameters indicate the machine tool characteristics, specifications and functions. The contents of each parameter should be set according to the parameter list annexed to the machine. The end user must not change the contents on the parameters. This permits the machine manufacturer to use one standard control on several machine sizes and/or types.

Entering machine parameters: There are three methods of entering machine parameters

(i) Setting through parameter tape - each block contains a machine set up data code to identify the machine parameter followed by data for that parameter.

(ii) Setting data through MDI - the machine data can be input through the operator's control panel by following the procedure for the control system.

(iii) Setting data in EPROMs - machine parameters can be entered in the erasable programmable read only memories. The data is permanently stored in specific locations in the memory chip. To enter the set up data in EPROM, a PROM programmer is necessary.

2.5.2 Memory Devices

Different types of memory devices are used in storing the data in CNC machines. These include EPROMs, DRAM, CMOS RAM and off-line data storage devices. Some details of these devices are given below:

Design Application	Device	Features
Executive Program	EPROM	Non-volatile
Part Program Storage	DRAM	Semi-conductor Memory
Memory	CMOS RAM	Fast Access, Volatile
		Bubble
	Memory	Non-volatile, slow
Parameters	EPROM	Field programmable
	CMOS RAM	Battery back-up needed
Scratch Pad Ram	MOS RAM	Intermediate working
Static RAM area		
Off-line data storage	Digital Cassette Magnetic disk Floppy disk Hard disk Pen drive	

2.5.3 Programming Features

Some programming features are commonly available in most of the CNC systems. These are referred to as standard features. Some of these standard features are:

- Absolute/Incremental programming
- Decimal point programming
- Diameter/Radius programming
- Linear, circular and helical interpolation
- Multiple part program storage
- Sequence number search
- Feed /min or feed /rev programming
- Dwell programming (In block containing dwell code, there is no slide movement)
- Tool length and diameter compensation - The control has a storage area (tool buffer) for making modification to the program due to errors in tool setting length and diameters
- Position preset.

2.5.3.1 Subroutine Programming/Macro Programming

Repetitive operations can be written as subroutines and main program can call these subroutines. An example of subroutine is dressing program for a grinding wheel. The advantage of using a subroutine is that it eliminates the need for rewriting a repetitive operation, thereby saving the memory space.

2.5.3.2 Parametric Programming

Parameters are freely assigned by the control for the purpose of arithmetic calculation in a part program. Trigonometric operations are also possible with R parameters.

2.5.3.3 Canned Cycles (Fixed Cycles)

This is a powerful control feature intended to shorten the length of the part program and consequently the length of tape. Canned cycles are single block multi pass fixed cycles.

Examples: Canned cycles for rough turning and peck drilling in CNC lathes, canned cycles for drilling, boring and tapping in machining centres.

2.5.4 Programmable Logic Controller (PLC) Features

Programmable logic controller is a software oriented machine interface between the CNC system and machine tool functions such as miscellaneous functions (coolant on/off, pallet operation, spindle speed functions and tool functions). Signals from CNC to PLC are on/off type. The programmable logic controllers available today are microprocessor based units which are integrated into the CNC system. The programmable logic controllers have memory space to store interface programs.

Some of the common PLC features are listed below:

- Number of inputs and outputs 24, 32, 48 etc., (Both analog and digital)
- Memory capacity 4 k, 8 k etc,
- High speed microprocessor to execute sequence program processing time of the order of milliseconds
- Software timers and counters
- Data exchange between CNC and PLC

2.5.5 Diagnostic Features

The CNC systems have diagnostics features for faults or error conditions. Diagnostics are software programs, which check the functioning of the CNC system at various levels. Detailed use and applications of these diagnostic program are provided by the control system manufacturer. Diagnostics can be grouped as follows:

(i) Real time diagnostics

(ii) On-line diagnostics

(iii) Off-line diagnostics

(iv) Remote Diagnostics

Real Time diagnostics: DC power supply voltages, low voltage and real time clock are monitored. In case of failure of anyone of these, control system automatically assumes the emergency stop conditions shutting down the drives.

On-line diagnostics: On-line diagnostics are active during machine operation. Diagnostic messages are either readable from C R T or from LED Indicators. Program diagnostics detect programming errors (Syntax, Parity etc.).

Off-line diagnostics: It is provided in the form of tape or ROM board (PCB). Following a malfunction, the off-line diagnostic programs are to be loaded which check the different areas of the system and respond with error codes / error description on C R T Display. Diagnostics are very powerful features of CNC systems. To be productive, the system should have a low MTTR (Mean Time to Repair).

Remote diagnostics: It is now possible to send diagnostic programs through Internet to check the errors in CNC Machines. This enables manufacturer to locate faults even if the machine is located in a remote place in another country.

2.5.6 Some Modern Design Features of CNC Systems

(i) Advanced hardware architecture: Custom built very large scale integrated circuits (VLSI) are used with several functions in a single chip. This way, the benefits of reduced component count and improved reliability are realized.

(ii) Software modularity: Each function is written as a discrete module - (structured programming). Additional software features can be added at any time to upgrade the control without affecting the software.

(iii) Adaptive control: Reduces the production time by maximizing the utilization of the machine tool. It acts on measurement taken from external sensors (In-process measurement) and modifying the cutting conditions.

(iv) Conversational programming: The system featuring conversational programming are termed "user friendly" since they are designed with the operator in mind. Example of such a friendly feature is graphic display. With this feature, the operator can create the part drawing on screen and simulate the tool paths in preparation phase (Prior to machining). The operator can program in complete safety and be sure that nothing is omitted. The operator can also check the correctness of the part program on graphic display.

(v) Programming flexibility: In addition to conversational part programming language, high level language command like IF-THEN ELSE, GO TO etc., can be used to extend the programme's power. Higher mathematical functions can be used to calculate square roots, trigonometric functions etc.

(vi) DNC link: This is discussed separately in detail later.

(vii) Color graphics: This provides visual interface between the operator and CNC. Part cross sections can be highlighted. Operating and warning display can be color coded.

(viii) Machine interface: High level language (like C) is used for programming the machine logic in PC (example: GE 2000 MC) In AB8600, high level language SIPROM (System Interface-Programming) is used.

(ix) Automatic selection of cutting speeds: If we specify the tool material and work material, CNC System selects cutting speed and feed from cutting condition technology data base.

(x) Automatic selection of tools and sequencing of tools: If operation is specified, system selects corresponding tools and sequence of tools. This is knowledge based information.

(xi) Optimization of machine program: This feature will be useful for components with large number of drilling, tapping operations, etc.

(xii) Display of finished component: Today CNC systems offer a feature to display finished component dimensions. Sectioning and rotation are also possible.

(xiii) Background programming: It is a common facility now available in CNC systems. The user can run, edit and simulate another program while a program is being executed on the machine tool.

(xiv) Digital CNC: The new breed of CNC controls uses digital technology. The introduction of digital CNC has brought increased speed and precision to machine tool builders. The PC based open architecture controls incorporate such features like acceleration with jerk limitation, direct NURBS interpolation, use of high level languages, execution of large CNC programs from hard disc and increased number of zero offsets. In some of the systems the CNC and drive amplifiers are on the some board at the digital level.

2.6 A LIST OF FUNCTIONS AVAILABLE IN A TYPICAL CNC SYSTEM

The functions available in a popular CNC system are listed below:

(i)	Controlled axes	2, 3, 4, 5 etc.
(ii)	Simultaneous axes	2, 3, 4, 5 etc.
(iii)	Max. programmable dimensions	7 digits
(iv)	Linear Interpolation	
(v)	Multi-quadrant circular Interpolation	
(vi)	Thread cutting	
(vii)	Rapid traverse	
(viii)	Feed rate override	
(ix)	Rapid traverse override	
(x)	Auto acceleration and retardation	
(xi)	Exact stop	
(xii)	Dwell	
(xiii)	Reference point return	
(xiv)	Co-ordinate system setting	
(xv)	Decimal point input	
(xvi)	X axis Dia./radius programming	
(xvii)	Radius programming	
(xviii)	S, T, M codes	
(xix)	Program number display	
(xx)	Program number search	
(xxi)	Program/subprogram	
(xxii)	Program format	
(xxiii)	Optional block skip	
(xxiv)	Canned cycles	
(xxv)	No. of offsets	

(xxvi) Backlash compensation
(xxvii) Cycle start/feed hold
(xxviii) Reset
(xxix) Manual continuous feed
(xxx) Incremental feed
(xxxi) Machine lock
(xxxii) Dry run
(xxxiii) Single block
(xxxiv) Registerable programs
(xxxv) Variable tape storage length
(xxxvi) Data protect
(xxxvii) Self diagnostics
(xxxviii) Emergency stop
(xxxix) Stored stop check
(xxxx) PMC (Programmable machine control)
(xxxxi) Spindle speed
(xxxxii) T N R C (Tool nose radius compensation)
(xxxxiii) Custom macros
(xxxxiv) Run hour/part display.

2.7 CNC CONTROLLERS

A CNC machine manufacturer may use a CNC system designed and manufactured in-house or buy and fit a system from specialist manufactures like Fanuc or Sinumerik. A wide variety of CNC controllers (systems) are available today. Some of them are used by manufacturers of machines on their own machines. Systems like Fanuc, Sinumerik, Fagor, Phillips, Bosch, Num, Allen-Bradley etc. are available to be used on any machines. Generic CNC systems are available for different applications like turning machines, machining centers, grinding machines, laser cutting machines, wire-EDM, gear cutting, turret punch press, press brake, etc.

There are large number makes of CNC controllers in use today. A few of them are listed below:

(i) Acramatic
(ii) Aciera CNC
(iii) AEG
(iv) Allen Bradley
(v) Anilam
(vi) ASEA
(vii) Bendix
(viii) Bosch, 860, 880, alpha2, alpha 3, CC 100, CC 200, CC 300, CC 330 Bosch micro 5Z, 8Z, PC (PG), system 5
(ix) Boehringer B1 T, B2 T
(x) Charmilles Robofill

(xi) Cincinnati

(xii) Deckel CNC 2301, contur, FP2-FP4

(xiii) DeVlieg

(xiv) Dixi NC

(xv) Emco-Turn

(xvi) ESAB NCE 301

(xvii) FANUC, 0M, 0T, 3TF, 3M, 3TF 3T, 5M, 6MB, 6MA, 7M, 7T, 9, 10, 11, 2, 15, 20, 20A, 2000, 3000, MATE L, MATE M, MATE TS

(xviii) Fidia

(xix) GE 550, 1050, 1050HL OX, 7542, CNC2000.

(xx) Gildemeister EPL, EPM(UNI), EPM(ITY), EPM(SET), EPM II (BTR) 22

(xxi) Heidenhain TNC 135, 145, 151, 155, 355, 455

(xxii) Heller Unipro 80

(xxiii) Hurco Ultimax B M C40

(xxiv) Kongsberg NC 300, NC 2000

(xxv) MAHO 432

(xxvi) Mandelli

(xxvii) Mazak M1, M2, M32, T1, T2, T3, T4, T32

(xxviii) Meldas 5000

(xxix) NUM 560, 750

(xxx) Okuma OSP 330 D, OSP 2000, OSP3000, OSP5000

(xxxi) Olivetti Contour

(xxxii) Philips 432, 3300, 3353, 6600, 6652.

(xxxiii) Sinumerik Mate TG, PRIMO S, SPRINT T, SPRINT 3T, 3M, 5M, 5T, 6MA, 6TA, 6MB, 6TB, 7M, 7T, 520, 550C, 560K, 810, 820, 850

(xxxiv) Traub TX7, TX8, TX8D

(xxxv) Toshiba

(xxxvi) Yasnac 3000

CNC Systems available in India: The four companies manufacturing CNC system in India are:

FANUC INDIA

ACE Designers

Electro pneumatics

Electronica

2.8 SOME OF THE FEATURES AVAILABLE IN TYPICAL HIGH END CNC SYSTEM

New generations of CNC controllers are marketed periodically by CNC system manufacturers. Some of the useful and important features available in the modern CNC systems are briefly discussed in the following section.

(i) **Automatic determination of optimum tool path:** By using data that is interactively input to define the work piece contours artificial intelligence is employed to determine the optimum approach point and tool path to eliminate unnecessary tool movement. As a result, the overall machining cycle is minimized.

(ii) **Feed spindle orientation:** By the use of a digitally controlled AC spindle motor, spindle orientation is fast and precise.

(iii) **Automatic feed rate override:** Even though only one feed rate is programmed for a machining cycle such as a pocket milling, the optimum feed rate for both the in-feed direction and corner cutting is automatically determined. Also when milling pockets, the feed rate is automatically changed when machining with full cutter width and when machining with partial cutter width to maintain the optimum cutting conditions for the minimum machining time.

(iv) **Simultaneous S, M and T functions:** Simultaneous operation of different units, such as the ATC and machine table indexing, A T C and pallet changer etc. can performed to greatly reduce machine's non-cutting time.

(v) **High speed tapping:** The digitally controlled spindle motor allows spindle rotation and Z axis feed to be synchronized. This advanced design makes high speed, high precision tapping possible without the use of the floating tap holder.

(vi) **High speed cutting of complex contours:** For complex contours that require interpolation by extremely small increments, the faster processing of speed of the 32 or 64 bit processor results in a much higher vectorial feed rate than that of conventional CNC systems.

(vii) **D N C interface:** The 32 or 64 bit CNC mounted on a machine can be linked with a host computer and transmit and receive data. By DNC interface, information can be shared.

(viii) **MAP compatibility:** The 32 bit CNC controllers are designed for MAP (Manufacturing Automation Protocol) compatibility - the international communication standards to be used by equipment in an automated factory.

(ix) **Background communication:** The high speed 32 bit microprocessors can handle communications of variety of data - programs, parameters, tool data and programs with a host computer simultaneously while in automatic operation.

(x) **Absolute position detection:** If equipped with absolute position detection function, a machine does not have to return to the home position prior to beginning operation. This is especially advantageous for a machining center controlled by host computer.

(xi) **Tool life management, Tool breakage detection and recovery:** These functions resident in the individual machine's memory can be communicated with the host computer, thereby facilitating centralized tool management.

(xii) **Automatic centering:** By the use of a touch sensor mounted in the spindle, measurement of datum holes and surfaces is performed. Based on the measurement results, the work co-ordinate system is automatically shifted and machining begins.

(xiii) **Adaptive feed rate control:** By continually monitoring the load on the spindle motor and Z axis servo motor, optimum cutting conditions are maintained. When an overload condition is detected, the programmed feed rate is automatically overridden. As the cutting load becomes smaller, the feed rate will automatically return to the programmed value.

(xiv) **Process management and program layout displays:** The interconnections between processes and subprograms and processes with commonly used tools are indicated on these displays for convenient program restarts.

(xv) **Automatic tool length measurement:** Tool length can be automatically measured and registered in memory to greatly reduce tool setting time. One setting of the measurement cycle allows up to 13 tools to be automatically processed. (This process is semi-automatic for face mills and boring bars in that the tool must first be manually positioned over the measurement unit).

(xvi) **Work piece co-ordinates:** When using a tool (such as an edge finder) to establish a work piece datum point, all that is required is to enter the tool radius. The necessary calculations are performed automatically to set the work piece zero position. When the optional touch sensor is used the angular offset co-ordinates can also be set. This allows high machining accuracy to be obtained even with simple fixtures.

(xvii) **Tool path storage:** The tool path storage function can be used to store in memory the point where a tool breaks during the cutting plus the path used to retract the cutter for servicing. This allows fast and smooth program restarting.

(xviii) **Automatic cutting conditions editing:** Programmed spindle speeds and feed rate are easily altered by override keys according to actual machining conditions. By pushing an appropriate key, the programmed cutting conditions are automatically edited by the override amount on an individual tool basis.

(xix) **Modal information display:** The modal information display indicates which G, M, S, f codes are effective. This is extremely convenient for error-free restart of EIA / ISO programs.

(xx) **Deflection compensation:** Automatic compensation can be performed for the displacement at one axis in relation to another axis used as the datum.

(xxi) **In- process gauging:** During unattended machining operations a periodic checking and correction of offsets to compensate tool wear is needed. A probe mounted on the spindle or on the turret will "inspect" the work in progress and compare the dimensions on the part with the programmed dimensions. If needed, appropriate offsets are automatically incorporated.

(xxii) **Stored stroke limits:** Definition of an area on a CNC lathe or a cube on a machining centre that is safe to work within can be set by the operator. These stored stroke limits are designed to prevent collision between the cutting tool and the fixture, machine or work piece. If programming is done outside the stored stroke limits, the system interrupts the program and issues an error message.

2.9 CONTROL PANEL OF A CNC MACHINE

The control panel of a CNC machine usually consists of two distinct sections- one the CNC panel and the other the operation panel. The former is supplied by the CNC system manufacturer and the latter by the machine tool manufacturer.

2.9.1 CNC Control Panel

Figure 2.12 shows a typical control panel. This consists of a CRT display screen, and a set of assorted keys. The screen display is the window to the computer. The screen displays active programs, status of the control, current tool position, tool offsets, system parameters etc. Most of the systems will have a graphic simulation facility which may be tool path simulation or CNC program simulation which can be displayed on the screen. The CRT screen may be in color or monochrome.

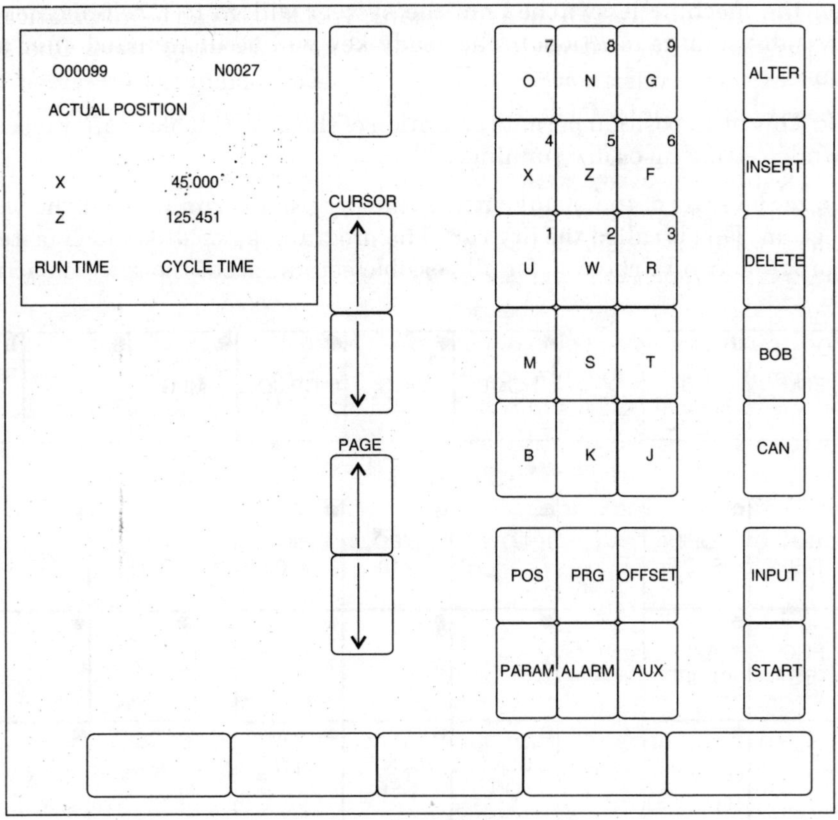

Fig. 2.12 A Typical CNC Panel

The display is controlled by keys and soft keys (which can be programmed for specific end uses). The keyboard and soft keys are used to input instructions to the control system. The programmer or the operator can use the keyboard for program input, program editing or input of parameters or offsets. The CRT also can display the errors. The user can program the system to give messages or instructions to the operator which is displayed on the CRT.

2.9.2 Operation Panel

As mentioned earlier the machine tool manufacturer designs the operation panel. Figure 2.13 shows a typical operation panel. The functions of various switches on the operation panel are briefly described below:

Zero return: This refers to the return of each axis slide to its zero position

Cycle end: A cycle means the execution of a program from start to end. Pressing M00 will end the program.

Optional Stop: M01 key will temporary stoppage of the program if the switch is in the on position. This key in the off position will ignore M01 in the program. This is also used for temporary stoppage for inspection.

Program End and Rewind: M30 switch will not only end the program but also rewind it and bring it to the start.

Ready: When the machine is switched on, the system will go to a self-diagnostic mode to check if every subsystem is functional. The ready key will be illuminated after a successful diagnostic run.

Single Block: This in on position permits operation of the program block after block. Normally this is used while setting up or dry running.

Dry run: Before the start of the metal cutting, the program is run without the work piece to verify the program. This is called the dry run. The program is executed much faster. During a dry run, the program can be checked for all possible errors except those which actually relate to cutting.

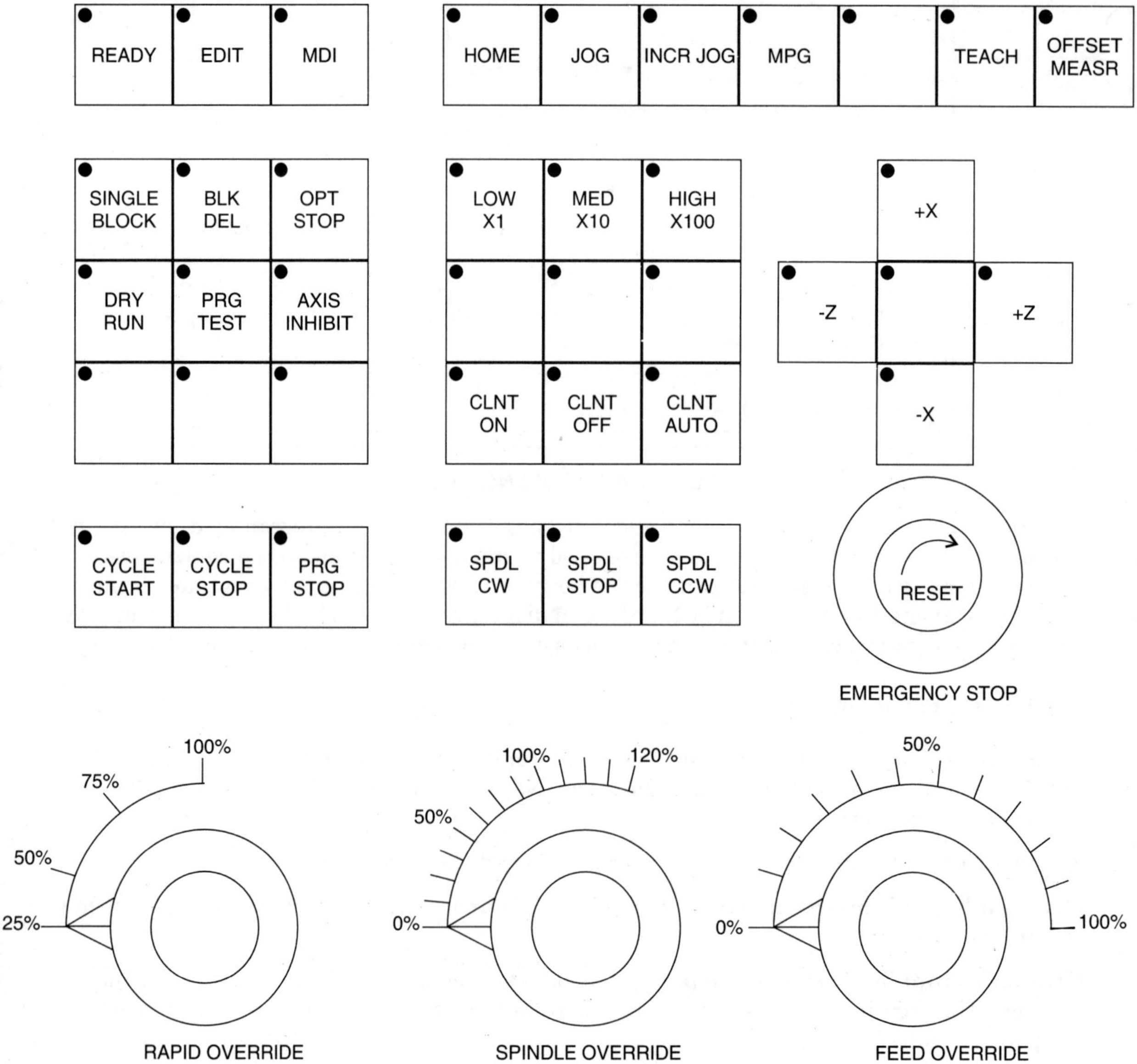

Fig. 2.13 Operator's Panel

Mode Selection: The system can work in different modes. MPG refers to manual operation of the slides by the electronic hand wheel. In jog position the slides are moved with the help of axis selection keys. The speed of slide movement can be selected by the feed selector switch. In rapid position the slides can be moved at rapid traverse rate. These are facilities for setting up the work or some minor machining manually. In MDI mode short programs input manually can be run. An example of use of this facility is for soft jaw preparation in lathes. Production runs are made in auto mode. Edit mode is used to modify an existing program.

Override: During the execution of the program the operator can change (override) the spindle speed, feed or rapid traverse by using appropriate keys.

Feed hold: Pressing this switch will stop feed movement in all axes.

Emergency Stop: A mushroom button, in distinct red color is used to stop operation of the machine in the case of any emergency.

This is a mandatory feature in all CNC machines.

2.9.3 Manual Pulse Generator

A CNC machine has an electronic hand wheel. Rotation of this wheel will generate pulses. One full rotation will generate hundred pulses. First the desired axis is selected using the axis selector switch. The range switch is used to set the distance moved for each pulse. For example, in x1 position rotation through one division will move the slide selected, (say X), through one micrometre. In x100 position on division of rotation will move the slide through 0.1 mm. The speed of movement of the slide depends on the speed with which the handle is rotated.

Figure 2.14 shows a manual pulse generator.

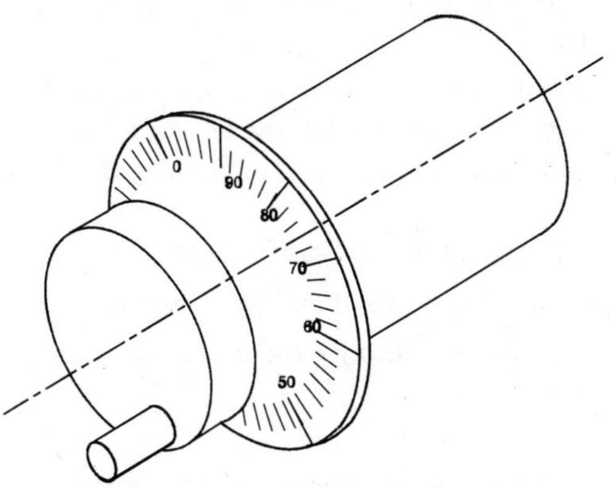

Fig. 2.14 Manual Pulse Generator

2.10 DIGITAL SERVOSYSTEMS

Current generation of CNC systems use digital servo systems. Through the use of high speed microprocessors and special integrated chips, the information on position, speed, torque and current is managed collectively and processed with great speed under digital servo control which enables high speed and high precision machining. In addition the digital servo control offers the following advantages:

(i) Full digital control- It is possible to achieve smooth, stable control without stick slip. Since there is no drift or other causes of instability, it is possible to maintain high precision.

(ii) Greater flexibility- Parameters like inertia and current limit can set to the optimum values in accordance with specific machining conditions.

(iii) Improved response to load fluctuations- During circle cutting, movement at quadrant boundaries becomes smoother.

(iv) Easier maintenance- Diagnosis and monitoring of the servo system can be performed with greater precision.

2.11 OPEN CNC

The personal computer (PC) has now become a standard component of automation. In the field of CNC technology PC is about to establish itself. The architecture of CNC systems has undergone a radical change in the recent days with the emergence of a concept called OPEN CNC. CNC systems generally use proprietary hardware and software made by CNC manufacturers themselves. In open CNCs the hardware and software can be chosen from various available standards in the market. Additionally, in open CNCs the internal data of the CNC is available for processing by any other application software.

2.11.1 Main Features of Open CNC

Open CNC has the advantage that users can exploit their familiarity with the Windows operating system. This enables the use of a large number of third party software packages like CAD/CAM software and several other application as well as development tool kits. Use of modems, Ethernet cards etc. enables the CNC machine to be connected to Internet. This also enables the machine to be a part of local area network or Intranet. Open CNC systems can have multimedia capability too.

The PC used for shop floors should be rugged to withstand the harsh shop floor environment. There is the danger of reduced reliability as hardware and software from multiple vendors is used in a PC. Another difficulty envisaged is due to the rapid obsolescence of the PC.

2.11.2 Types of PC Based Machine Tool Controllers

There are four different types of CNC control available today.

(i) Proprietary controls which are commonly used.

(ii) PC front end

(iii) Motion control card in a PC

(iv) Software based CNC

Traditional CNC controls consist of bundled hardware and software from a single vendor. This is what most CNC machine tool manufacturers currently use. The drawbacks of these systems are listed below:

(i) The proprietary systems are expensive, initially and over the operating life.

(ii) They may not be able to communicate with the other machines in the machining cell.

(iii) There is no plug and play capability.

(iv) The user is dependent upon the supplier of the CNC system for repair.

The proprietary nature of the traditional CNC controls means that volumes are low and costs are therefore high. The availability of components are limited and often they are custom-designed and manufactured. The open architecture for this configuration only comes from the support for RS-274 interface and expensive Ethernet connections.

Traditional control vendors now offer the CNC systems with a PC front end. This lets the manufacturers to install and run Windows-based applications at the control while the CNC system runs the machine tool in the background. CNC users of course get some value but at a high price. This approach though lets the manufacturer maintain a common user interface across a family of controls from the same CNC vendor, it still entails a factory trained engineer for installation and maintenance.

A CNC add-on card can implement CNC control. The card carries embedded software (firmware) that has been specially developed. The package offers choices for servo and I/O systems, PC memory, Ethernet cards and the ability to run windows applications. The motion control card or the brain is still proprietary. The vendor has to install it and handle maintenance and service.

Software-based CNC is not tied to any specific hardware and therefore can be run on any off-the-shelf hardware the customer chooses. By taking an unbundled software application approach to CNC control, the user gets maximum choice. The customer can decide who can install the software, train and support. The services of third party integrators can be availed or they can do it themselves.

With software-based CNC the manufacturer can add new hardware or software through incremental upgrades to improve machine tool productivity. Open CNC also usually includes an open API (application programming interface) for the integration of third party software. Another significant advantage of open CNC is that old machines can be upgraded using open CNC systems.

Software-based open architecture is becoming more popular due to many reasons. Apart from being an open control, the PC based CNC systems have the following specific advantages.

(i) Software based open architecture CNC machines will no longer be facing obsolescence in many years due to control.

(ii) If the CAD/CAM software is moved from one PC to another, users will be able to replace the original PC with the current generation of the PCs and reload the software-based CNC application on the new PC.

Several innovative features have been incorporated in the machine tool controllers with the advent of PC-based control. Some of them are briefly described below:

2.11.3 3D Tool Compensation and 5 Axis Tool Compensation

3D tool compensation and 5 axis tool compensation at the machine tool with gouge protection, 3D offset parallel to 3D profile, 5 axis tool compensation with gouge protection and 3D part rotation with fixture tilting compensation ect. are some features available in advanced open CNC systems.

Specialized G Codes are available in PC based CNC systems:

G61 and G64-	Buffered Look ahead spline mode
G65	Mill out rectangular pocket
G66	Mill out circular pocket
G67	Fly cut pattern

G68	Mill out rectangular pocket with fillets
G120	Mill outside square
G121	Mill outside circle or island
G122	Mill outside counter bore
G123	Mill outside ellipse pocket
G124	Mill inside ellipse pocket
G125	Mill outside slot
G126	Mill inside slot
G130	3D tool compensation with gouge protection
G131	3D offset parallel to 3D profile
G135	5 axis tool compensation with gouge protection
G140	3D part rotation and plane tilting
G141	Scale factor for X-axis only
G142	Scale factor for Y axis only
G143	Scale factor for Z axis oniy
G160	3D cylinder
G162	3D sphere
G163	3D ramped plane

PC based CNC controls provide several advanced features which are very useful to produce more accurate parts.

Dynamic feed rate option: The spindle load is sensed and feed rate is automatically increased or decreased to keep the spindle load constant. This feature enables to maintain the deformation of the machine tool-tool-work piece-fixture system at a constant level, thereby ensuring consistent accuracy.

Dynamic read ahead ability: While machining dies and molds acceleration and deceleration is too frequent, particularly when complex contours are to be produced. The dynamic read ahead facility (sometimes referred as look ahead facility) enables the computer to calculate the acceleration and deceleration requirements precisely well ahead of the execution time. There are systems available now, which can look ahead up to 180 blocks.

2.11.4 Advantages of Open CNC

Extremely fast block processing: Open CNC controllers use the latest microprocessors and hence can have the highest available clock speeds and throughput rates. This enables fast block processing.

Seamless integration with CAD system: The availability of a powerful PC enables integration of CAD and CAM more effectively. The entire modeling and manufacturing program development can be carried out on the PC controller itself.

Front-end operator interfaces: The open CNC controller is soft which enables the use to customize the system.

2.11.5 Configuration of a Typical Open CNC

Figure 2.15 shows a typical open CNC configuration. The capabilities of the PC are used as much as possible without degrading the functions, performance and reliability of the CNC. Specifically, CNC and PMC are responsible for time constraint tasks such as NC, servo control, and sequence control while personal computer is used to offer open hardware/software environments based on a general operating system.

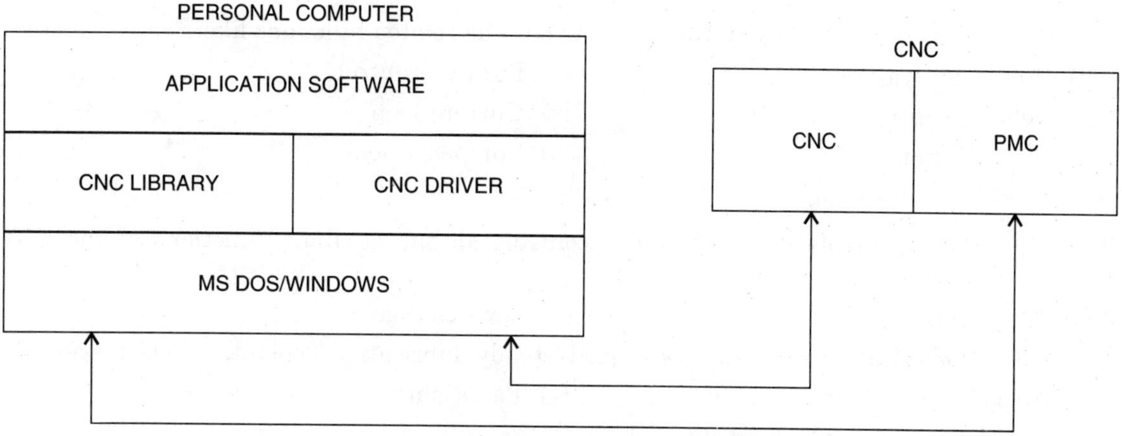

Fig. 2.15 Typical CNC Configuration

2.12 A GENERAL DESCRIPTION OF A CNC CONTROLLER

The following section is included for the benefit of readers who will be interested to know the minimum hardware and software capabilities of CNC systems and drives.

The CNC controller is broadly divided into 3 major sub systems namely the HMI (Human Machine Interface), the axes controller (servo controller) and the PLC (programmable logic controller).

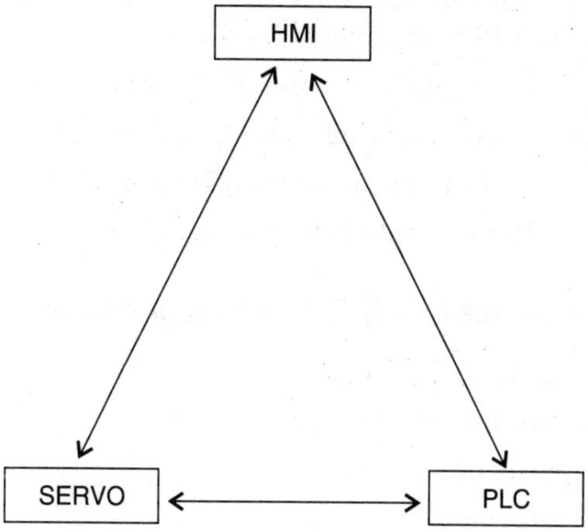

Fig. 2.16 Controller Configuration

The human machine interface (HMI) sub-system takes care of the following.

(i) Alphanumeric keyboard (for editing part program, tool offset etc)
(ii) Display (to display various screens like position, part program, tool path etc)
(iii) Part program decoding
(iv) Communication interface (RS232, RS485, CAN bus, Modbus, Ethernet and USB etc)
(v) Overall co-ordination

The servo sub-system handles all the axes and spindle related functions like:

(i) Profile generation
(ii) Position control
(iii) Velocity control
(iv) Current loop
(v) Interpolations
(vi) Compensations
(vii) Feedback processing

The PLC (programmable logic controller) controls all the auxiliary functions of the CNC machine like

(i) Tool change
(ii) Gear change
(iii) Operations chuck, turret, tailstock, quill, steady, lubrication, coolant, chip conveyor
(iv) All safety interlocks
(v) Palletising
(vi) Auto job loading/unloading etc

All the three sub-systems exchange information at a constant time interval.

2.13 GENERAL SPECIFICATIONS

The following sections give the general specifications of a digital CNC controller.

(i) Number of controllable axes: 5 + 1 spindle
(ii) Number of simultaneously controllable axes: 5
(iii) Communication between sub-systems (HMI, servo and PLC): serial digital data/dual port RAM (random access memory)
(iv) EMI (electro magnetic interference)/EMC (electro magnetic compatibility)- compatible chassis to house servo and PLC subsystem modules
(v) Fibre optic communication (digital) between CNC controller and drive
(vi) Machine monitoring (status of machine to be transferred to a server or standard PC)
(vii) Modification/reading of machine parameters/offsets by PLC
(viii) Modification/reading of offsets through part program

2.13.1 Human Machine Interface (HMI) Specification/ Features

(A) HMI Controller Specification

a. Single board computer based controller
b. RTOS (real time operating system)
c. Keyboard / mouse interface
d. SVGA controller for colour monitor

e. Industry standard hard disk
f. RS232, RS485 and Ethernet, CAN, USB and Modbus communication interface
g. DNC (distributed numerical control) for part program / parameters transfer
h. Key switch for security of data
i. To and fro transfer of part program / PLC program / parameters / offsets using USB

(B) Keyboard features
a. Membrane type alpha numeric key pad with special keys connected in a matrix format
b. Keyboard controller to scan the keys
c. Hardware debouncing for keys
d. Digital communication between keyboard and HMI
e. Completely sealed keyboard
f. EMI / EMC compatibility
g. Soft keys for screen navigation

(C) Display features
a. 15"/17" colour monitor
b. Touch screen interface

(D) Screen navigation software (to navigate through different screens)

(E) Display screens
a. Position screen
b. Tool offset screen
c. Wear offset screen
d. Setup data screen
e. Individual machine parameter screens for HMI, Servo and PLC
f. Communication interface screen
g. Part program display screen
h. PLC ladder power flow diagram screen
i. PLC input/output status screen
j. 3D tool path simulation screen
k. Tool management system screen alarms and messages screen
l. User definable screens

(F) Editing screens
a. Part program editor
b. PLC ladder/statement list editor
c. Tool offset/wear offset editor
d. Setup screen editor
e. Controller machine parameter editor
f. Drives parameter editor
g. Axes configuration editor
h. Conversational programming editor
i. Communication parameter editor
j. Password protection

(G) Part programming features
a. CAD/CAM software interface
b. Standard G and M Codes
c. Incremental/absolute
d. Inch/Metric
e. Feed/min and Feed/revolution
f. Feed rate override

g. Spindle speed override
h. Rapid traverse override
i. Plane selection
j. Linear, circular, helical, spiral and NURBS interpolation
k. Circular interpolation: radius/I, J, K vector
l. Canned cycles
m. Sub-routine programming
n. Conversational programming
o. Rigid tapping
p. Scaling
q. Tool recovery program
r. Co-ordinate system rotation
s. Dwell
t. Programmable offset setting
u. Block skip
v. Single block
w. Background editing
x. Macros
y. Cartesian and polar co-ordinate programming
z. Blue print programming
aa. Parametric programming
bb. Look ahead concept
cc. Safe zone programming
dd. Constant surface speed
ee. Set zero/program zerc
ff. Optional stop/program stop
gg. Mirror image
hh. Test run
ii. Dry run
jj. Exact stop
kk. Saving of MDI program as stored part program

(H) Compensation features

a. Tool offset / wear offset compensation
b. Tool nose radius compensation
c. Cutter error compensation
d. Pitch error compensation
e. Backlash compensation
f. Squareness error compensation
g. Thermal error compensation

(I) Diagnostic features

a. Power up diagnostics
b. On line diagnostics
c. Alarms/messages
d. PLC ladder power flow diagram
e. Context sensitive on line help
f. Powerful NC-PLC window
g. Remote diagnostics

(J) Modes of operation

a. Manual mode (reference, continuous jog, incremental jog, rapid jog, teach in)
b. Manual data input (MDI)
c. Automatic

(K) Part program parser (part program decoding software)

2.13.2 Servo Controller Specifications/Features

(A) Hardware specifications

a. Floating point DSP (digital signal processor) based controller

b. 32 bit digital command output to drive
c. Interface to encoder (or linear scale) position feedback sensor
d. Encoder signals either single ended or complementary
e. Total number of encoder interface: 6
f. 32 bit high speed counters for position information storage
g. Drive enable from servo controller itself
h. Touch probe interface
i. Watch dog timer
j. EMI / EMC compatibility
k. Multi-layer PCB
l. MPG (manual pulse generator) / HHU (hand held unit) Interface
m. Second encoder interface for all axes (number of encoder interface: 12)
n. Sensors (temperature, force, vibration) interface directly in servo controller

(B) Software features

a. 5 axes simultaneous interpolation
b. Trapezoidal / S_curve profile generation
c. Digital PID filter for all the axes
d. Command resolution: 1 micro-meter
e. Feedback resolution: 0.5 micro-meter or better
f. Axes update time: 100 micro-sec for all the axes
g. Velocity feed forward
h. Acceleration feed forward
i. Axes velocity: 1mm/min to 60 meters / min
j. Auto tuning of gain parameters
k. Auto referencing of all the axes
l. Adaptive control (on the fly changing of gain values)
m. Normal deceleration / emergency deceleration
n. Servo controller related alarms and messages
o. Touch probe interface software
p. On the fly changing of profile (for adaptive control)
q. Master-slave configuration of axes (for gantry axes)
r. Software limits
s. Tool breakage monitoring

(C) Spindle controller features

a. Spindle configuration as an axis
b. Spindle RPM: 30-10000
c. Spindle drive command: digital
d. Spindle orientation
e. Spindle oscillation for gear change
f. Number of gears: 4
g. Spindle as 'C' axis in case of lathe

2.13.3 PLC (Programmable Logic Controller) Specifications/Features

(A) Hardware specification (PLC)

a. 32 bit micro-controller based controller
b. Watch dog timer
c. 16 bit bus interface for digital/analogue input and output modules
d. Operating voltage: 24V DC
e. Total number of digital inputs: 256
f. Total number of digital outputs: 256
g. Total number of analogue inputs: 32
h. Total number of analogue outputs: 32
i. EMI / EMC compatibility
j. Communication interface between PC (personal computer) and PLC

(B) Digital input module

a. Operating voltage: 24V DC
b. 8/16/32 channel configuration
c. Optical isolation between 24V DC and 5V DC

(C) Digital output module

a. Operating voltage: 24V DC
b. 8/16/32 channel configuration
c. Optical isolation between 24V DC and 5V DC
d. Transistor output/relay output
e. Sinking type/sourcing type

(D) Analogue input module

a. 4/8 channel configuration
b. 0-20mA, 4-20mA, 0-10V, +/-10V, +/-5V, RTD Input
c. Isolation
d. Analog to digital conversion: 50Hz / 60 Hz

(E) Analogue output module

a. 4/8 channel configuration
b. 0-20mA, 4-20mA, 0-10V, +/-10V, +/-5V
c. Isolation
d. Digital to analog conversion: 50Hz / 60 Hz

(F) High speed counter input module

a. 16 bit / 32 bit counter
b. Maximum operating frequency: 200 kHz

(G) MCP: machine control panel

a. 64 keys/64 LEDs
b. Keys and LEDs connected in matrix format
c. Emergency Stop/FRO/SSO/RTO in machine control panel
d. Keyboard controller for key scanning and communication
e. Hardware debouncing for keys
f. Digital communication between keyboard and PLC

(H) Software specification

a. Scan Time: 0.25ms/K of instructions

b. Structured programming (Jump and Call Instructions)

c. Power on, time based and regular logical execution

d. Windows based application program development software (If PLC logic is to be edited in standard PC) and RTOS based application program development software if logic is to be edited in CNC controller

e. Factory logic/machine logic

f. Instructions

- Arithmetic
- Logical
- Comparison (BCD, Binary, Grey)
- Conversion (BCD to Binary, Binary to BCD)
- Shift
- Rotate
- Exchange
- Move
- Bit/byte/word/double word instructions
- Positive/negative transition inputs
- Special instruction for ATC (automatic tool change)/turret
- Digital PID filter for PLC controlled axes
- Display format: Binary, BCD, Hex

g. Timers (Software)

- ON delay
- OFF delay
- Pulse/Extended Pulse
- Variable/Constant Time Value
- Timer resolution: 1ms
- No. of timers: 128
- Enable/preset inputs
- Maximum time value: 32 bit value x 1ms

h. Counters (software)

- Up counter
- Down counter
- Up/down Counter
- No. of counters: 128
- Enable/preset/reset inputs
- Maximum count value: 32 bit value

i. Programming methods
   - Ladder diagram
   - Statement list
   - Functional flow diagram
   - Higher level languages ('C' Language)
j. PLC programming in CNC / stand-alone PC
k. Programming standard
   - IEC61131-3
l. Editor software
   - Ladder diagram editor
   - Alarms and message editor
   - Symbol and comment editor
   - Statement list editor
   - Functional flow diagram editor
   - Text editor for high level language ('C') Programming
m. Compiler software for all programming languages
n. Forcing of inputs/outputs
o. Diagnostic software
   - Power flow diagram for ladder diagram display
   - Status display of all inputs and outputs
p. Modes of operation
   - Run/stop/single step
q. Communication (If logic is built in a personal computer)
   - To upload the logic to PLC hardware
   - To download the logic from PLC
   - To monitor the logic in power flow mode
r. PLC controlled axes:
   - Maximum number of PLC controlled axes: 2

2.13.4 Drive Specifications/Features

Figure 2.17 gives a typical drive configuration of a CNC controller.

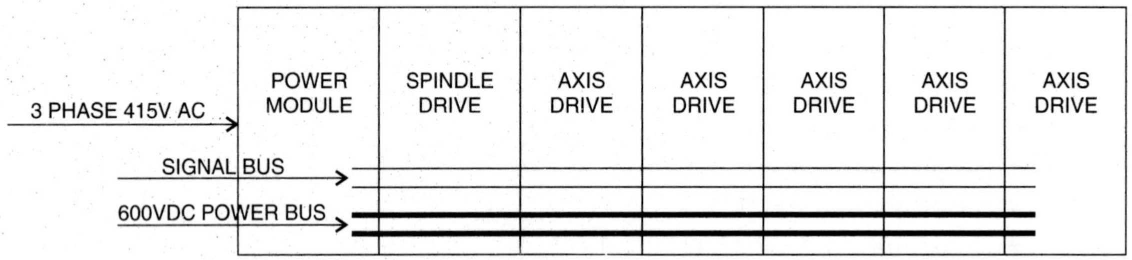

Fig. 2.17 Drive Configuration

2.13.4.1 Hardware Specifications

a. Intelligent drive
b. Digital interface (32 bit) between CNC controller and drive
c. IGBT (insulated gate bipolar transistor) power transistor based drive
d. PWM (pulse width modulated) output
e. Regenerative braking / dynamic resistor braking
f. Four quadrant operation
g. Over current protection
h. Quick acceleration / deceleration
i. Fast response to command speeds
j. Low electrical and mechanical time constants
k. Peak torque is about 4 times continuous torque
l. Common DC power supply for all the drives
m. Common signal bus for all the drives
n. Individual drive enable signals from the servo controller
o. Smooth low speed operation
p. High static stiffness
q. Drive status indications on drive: LED / LCD based display
r. Watch dog timer
s. EMI/EMC compatible chassis for housing drive module
t. Protection class: IP20
u. Cooling: self ventilation
v. Level II option: point to point positioning
w. Efficiency: > 95
x. Output frequency: 0 – 500 Hz
y. Temperature monitoring
z. Protective earth in power module as well as in all drive modules

2.13.4.2 Power Module

a. Input Power: 415V, 3 Phase AC
b. DC Bus Voltage: 600V DC
c. Over voltage / under voltage / over current protection
d. Short circuit protection

2.13.4.3 Feed Drive

a. Constant torque output for feed drives
b. Feed drive power rating (maximum): 50A
c. Short circuit protection

2.13.4.4 Spindle Drive

a. Constant power output for spindle drive
b. Spindle drive power rating (maximum): 100A
c. Short circuit protection

2.13.4.5 Software Specifications

a. Configurable drive (feed/spindle)
b. Adaptive control
c. Auto tuning of drives
d. Drive related alarms and messages display in HMI of CNC
e. Drive parametrization from the CNC controller
f. Drive service diagnostics
g. Digital PID filter for velocity control of all the axes
h. Zero adjustment, drift adjustment and speed scaling for each axes
i. Normal deceleration/emergency deceleration
j. Point to point positioning
k. Motor parameter details (identification) in drive parameters list of HMI

REVIEW QUESTIONS

(1) Describe the principle of operation of a CNC machine tool.
(2) With the help of a block diagram describe the operation of the feedback system in a CNC machine tool.
(3) What is the role of the feedback devices in a CNC machine?
(4) Describe the working principle of a 3-axis CNC system.
(5) Describe the important features available in a typical CNC system.
(6) Describe a typical CNC panel.
(7) Describe the functions available in the operator's panel of a CNC machine.
(8) Describe the classification of PC based CNC systems.
(9) What are the advantages of PC based control?
(10) Describe the working principle of a PC based CNC system.

3 CNC MACHINE TOOLS

Computer Numerical Control (CNC) is a control technology that can be applied to several general purpose, single purpose and special purpose machines. Nowadays CNC is used to control transfer machines also. Apart from machine tools like lathes, milling and boring machines, gear cutting machines, punching machines, grinding machines, spark erosion machines, CNC is widely used in laser and plasma cutting machines, turret punch press, flow forming, tube bending, electron beam welding, routing, press brake, guillotines, etc. A few popular types of CNC machines are described in this chapter.

3.1 MACHINING CENTRES

CNC technology, as mentioned in Chapter 2 was initially developed for the control of milling machines used for machining aircraft structural parts. The family of milling machines was therefore the first group of machines to be brought under CNC. Subsequently, with the development of automatic tool changer and the tool magazines, the use of separate machine tools for milling, drilling, boring etc. was replaced by a single machine, which could do all these operations. Thus the concept of machining centre was evolved. One of the greatest benefits of the machining centre was that it eliminated the necessity of multiple set-ups for completing a work piece. Thus the lead time of machining components was drastically reduced, resulting in less work-in-process (WIP) inventory. There are many other advantages in using machining centres. The machining centres are thus very important types of CNC machine tools. They are multifunction machines equipped with automatic tool changers and are capable of carrying out a variety of operations like milling, drilling, reaming, tapping, boring, counter boring and allied operations without operator intervention for change of tools.

Machining centres are classified in many ways. Most popular method is to designate a machining centre according to the orientation of the spindle with respect to the work table. They are:

(a) Horizontal spindle machining centres
(b) Vertical spindle machining centres
(c) Universal machining centres

Vertical machining centres are also classified depending on the construction of the structure of the machine. They are:

(a) C-frame machines
(b) Moving column machines
(c) Bridge type machines
(d) Double column machines
(e) Gantry type machines

Brief descriptions of common types of machining centres are given in the subsequent sections.

3.1.1 Horizontal Spindle Machining Centres

Horizontal spindle machining centres are generally single spindle machines with automatic tool changers. Some exceptions include multi-spindle machines, combination horizontal/vertical spindles etc. Horizontal spindle machining centres are generally bed type machines with the structural configuration as shown in Fig. 3.1.

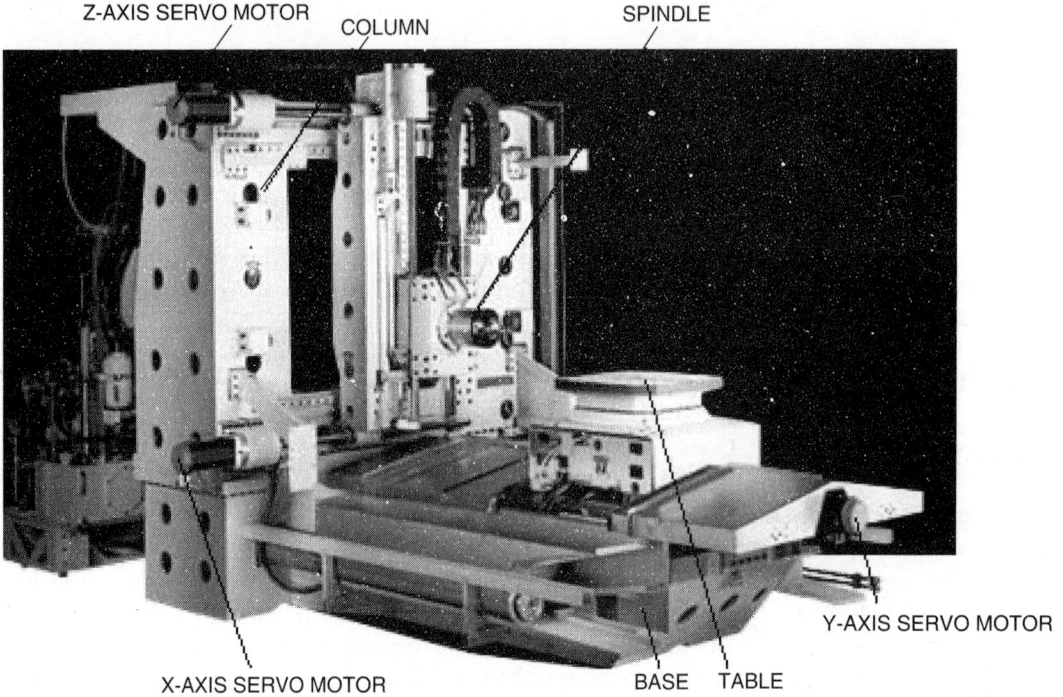

Fig. 3.1 Horizontal Machining Centre

In this type of machines X-axis traverse is provided by table or column and Y-axis traverse is provided by the up and down movement of the spindle head. The Z-axis traverse is provided by the table or column, or a ram type spindle.

The axis designation of a horizontal machining centre is shown in Fig. 3.2. The longitudinal movement of the table is the X-axis. The transverse movement is the Z axis movement. Y axis motion is obtained by the up and down movement of the spindle.

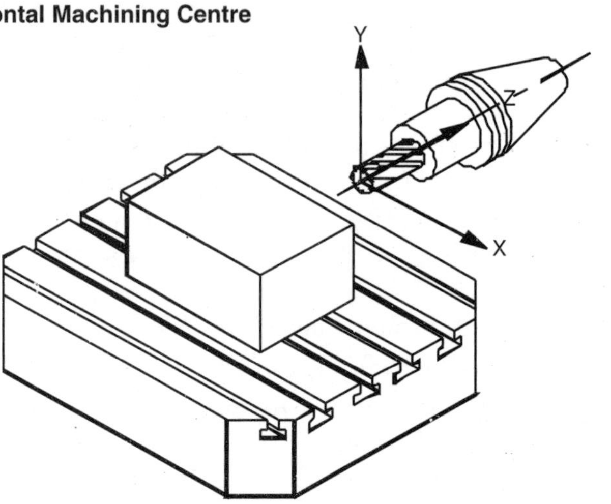

Fig. 3.2 Axis Movements of a Horizontal Machining Centre

These machines are invariably used with a rotary indexing table to facilitate multiface machining at different angles in a single set up. The axis of rotary table is parallel to Y-axis and is called 'B' axis. The rotation of the table can be used for machining contours on surfaces of work pieces located on the rotary table, if CNC control is available for B-axis.

The present day trend is to build the machines with travelling column construction with all the movements behind the tool so that the work module is independent of the basic machine. This enables choice of work holders to suit the user's requirements and also enables the use of machining centre in NC transfer lines.

Each axis of a machining centre is driven by digital AC drives:

Typical Specifications of a 3-Axis Horizontal Machining Centre

Rotary index table-size	500 × 500 mm
Rotary index table-incremental angle	5 degree automatic
Work table-lateral travel (X)	710 mm
Spindle head-vertical travel (Y)	500 mm
Saddle-cross travel (Z)	500 mm
Rapid feed rate	13,000 mm/min
Cutting feed rate	1–3,600 mm/min
Distance from spindle nose to centre of rotary index table	150–650 mm
Distance from spindle centre line to top face of rotary index table	300–700 mm (50–550 with APC)
Spindle speeds, infinitely variable	30–4,500 rpm
Spindle nose taper	ISO R397/No.50
Spindle drive motor	AC 11/7.5 kW
Total electric power	35 kVA

ATC Capacity:

No. of stored tools	40
Tool selection	Random
Max. Tool size - diameter × length	110 × 400 mm
Max. Tool weight	15 kg.

Machine Accuracy and Capability:

Linear positioning accuracy - X/Y/Z	0.01 /300 mm
Linear repeatability - X/Y/Z	± 0.003 mm
Indexing accuracy-rotary index table	± of arc sec
Max. Work load on table	10,000 N
Max. Machining thrust	10,000 N

3.1.2 Vertical Spindle Machining Centres

Vertical spindle machining centres are also bed type machines with (1) Single spindle and auto tool changers (2) Multi spindle with turret head (Turret machining centres). The structural configuration is as follows:

X-axis traverse provided by table or column

Y-axis traverse provided by the saddle or the column or ram

Z-axis traverse provided by the spindle head.

Vertical spindle machines are not suitable for large width as this increases the throat distance. For very large widths horizontal spindle configuration or bridge type configuration (double column planer type) is used.

Figure 3.3 shows a typical vertical machining centre. There are many variations of vertical machining centre. Profilers are a class of vertical machining centres which are used for large material removal involving several pocketing operations. Such machines find wide applications in aircraft industry.

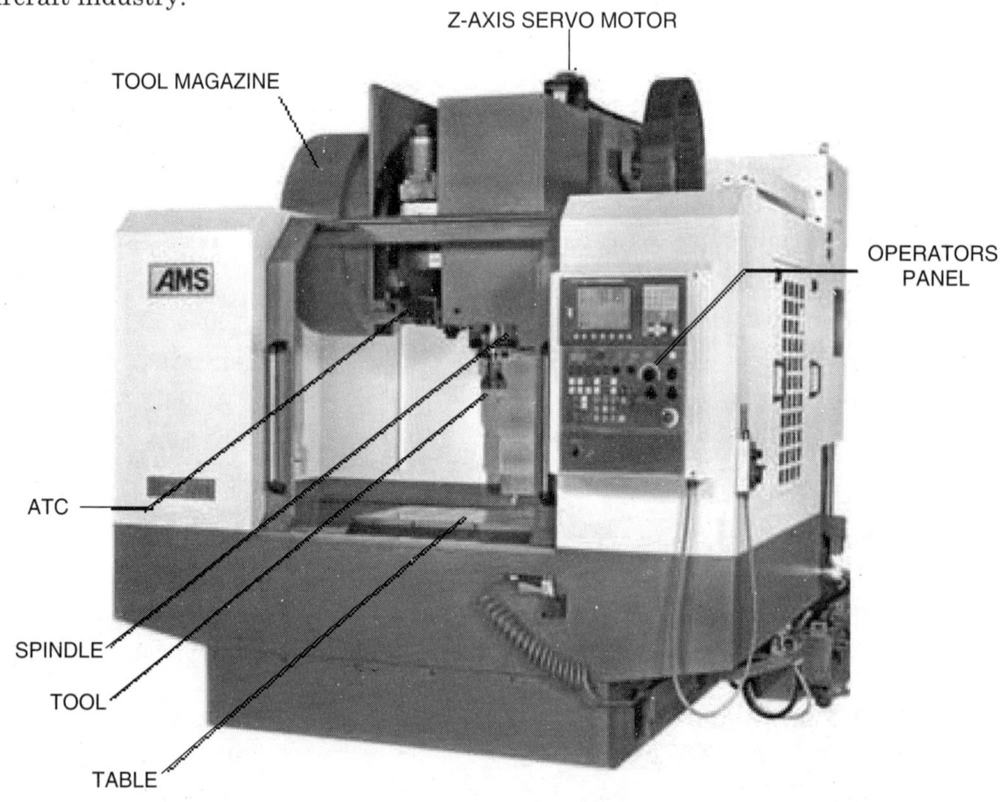

Fig. 3.3 Vertical Machining Centre

The movements of the table give X and Y axis motions in longitudinal and transverse directions respectively. The up and down movements of the spindle head give the Z axis travel. The axis movements are shown in Fig. 3.4. A rotary/index table could be used also with a vertical machining centre with the axis of the table usually parallel to 'X' axis i.e. 'A' axis.

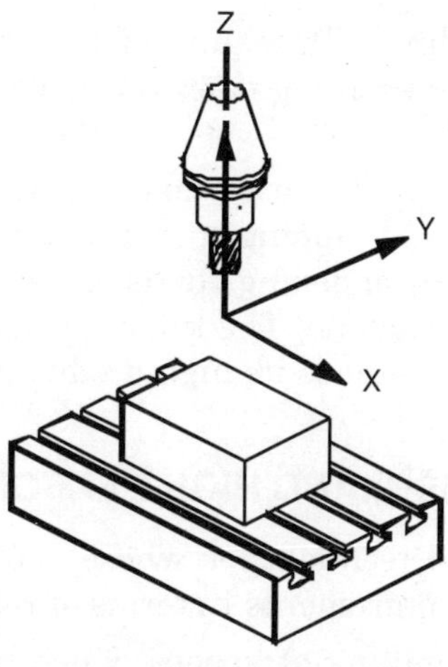

Fig. 3.4 Axis Designation of a Vertical Machining Centre

Typical Specifications of a Vertical Machining Centre

Table size	550 × 340 (mm)
X-axis travel	1000 mm
Y-axis travel	508 mm
Z-axis travel	460 mm
Magazine capacity	40 tools–60 tools (optional)
Spindle speed range	30–40,00 rpm
	60–60,00 rpm
	100–10,000 rpm
Main motor (cont/30 min. rating)	AC 7.5 HP/10 HP
Machine weight	6.5 Tonnes

3.1.3 Universal Machining Centres

These are similar to horizontal machining centres but with the spindle axis capable of tilting from horizontal to the vertical position continuously under computer control. This constitutes the fifth axis of the machine. In some cases this movement is provided by tilting of the table instead of the spindle. Such machines facilitate approach to the top surface of workpiece mounted on the table in addition to the multiple side faces in a single set up. The fifth axis facility is essential for machining of some components which require the cutter axis to be perpendicular to the surface being machined.

Recently new designs of machining centres have been introduced which can be used as either horizontal or vertical machines.

In order to save setting up time machining centres are now available with two or more pallets. It is also possible to load and machine different components depending upon the need.

3.1.4 CNC Drilling and Milling Machines

CNC drilling and milling machines are used for production drilling of holes at different co-ordinate positions in workpieces with automatic cycles consisting of X-Y positioning, rapid approach of tool to workpiece, drilling with required feed rate to the required depth and rapid retraction of tool or various types of milling operations. The automatic cycle is controlled by the CNC system.

CNC drill tap center is a special type of machine specially designed for applications involving large number of drilling and tapping operations. The special feature of this machine is that the tools are mounted on an indexing turret in front of the column of the machine. There is no separate ATC in this machine. The turret performs the loading and unloading of the tools. The advantage of this machine is its high productivity.

3.2 HIGH SPEED CUTTING (HSC) AND HIGH PERFORMANCE CUTTING (HPC)

Both HSC and HPC are advanced technologies whose potential can be fully exploited only when the tools meet demanding requirements in terms of reliability and durability.

High speed cutting refers to milling at speeds which range from 150 m/min (for super alloys) to 10000 m/min (for fibre reinforced plastics) depending on the materials of workpiece and the cutting edge and the machining parameters. The cutting speed for integral components in aircraft manufacture, which are made of aluminum alloys with tensile strength of 500 N/mm^2 ranges between 1000 to 8000 m/min. The advantages of high speed cutting include excellent quality of the machined surface, reduced cutting forces at high rates of metal removal, increased productivity, reduced costs, lower residual stresses and less distortion. Many high speed machining centres can mill hardened dies and moulds with superior finish, eliminating the need for a finishing operation either by hand or by machining (grinding/EDM).

High speed machining (HSM) helps to make more parts than cutting with slow spindle speed and low depth of cut. For example, a conventional 25 mm end mill rotating at 1500 rpm will remove 62500 mm^3 of material at a depth of cut of 12.5 mm and feed rate of 200 mm/min. A tool of the same diameter rotating at 6000 rpm with a depth of cut of 2.5 mm and feed rate of 3000 mm/min will remove 187500 mm^3 of material. High speed machining is found to reduce warping of thin sections while machining. High speed machining is capable of producing thin monolithic parts. This reduces the necessity of splitting a part to facilitate machining.

Improvements in CNC have contributed much to the popularity of high speed machining. Look ahead programming, feed forward control, etc. are some of the important features related to high speed machining. The number of blocks to be processed in high speed machining is generally large. It is therefore, desirable to compress very small blocks into a large single block that is processed in a NURBS interpolator. This approach reduces the number of blocks processed through the computer. NURBS approach will reduce the program length to 1/10th to 1/100th of the size of conventional programs. This also permits the use of high feed rates. NURBS being a continuous curve in space, the acceleration can be defined at any point without abrupt changes. This results in a smoother finish.

High speeds also call for changes in the design of spindles. The preferred spindle nose design for high speed spindles is HSK. Shrink fitting of tools is also sometimes employed. Often large diameter spindles and correspondingly larger bearings are also recommended. Typical ratings of the spindles are 30 hp at 30000 rpm to 50 hp at 20000 rpm. Composite ceramic bearings are now the standard feature of high speed spindles. The need for increased precision has compelled manufacturers to incorporate sensors for checking tool length, detecting vibration and monitor temperatures. Self-teaching adaptive controls will sample and adjust process parameters such as temperature, motion, vibration, power, speed, tool wear, tool breakage, etc. High speed spindles require better dynamic balancing for obvious reasons. High speed machines do not require large low end torque.

High speed machining is not without disadvantages. One must use right kind of tools to get the best out of HSM (hollow shank taper). Today, a wide range of tools are available for high speed machining of aluminum. Cermets and polycrystalline diamonds are widely used for solid tools and indexable inserts. It is preferable to use uncoated solid tools for machining of parts with thin ribs because of their high rigidity and sharp edges which reduce vibration and cutting forces. Materials like titanium and composites cannot be machined the HSM way. Chip accumulation is another problem to be tackled. Possibility of harmonic vibration at high speeds requires careful design as high acceleration and deceleration will lead to resonance. There is also the need to control pre-load.

3.3 TURNING CENTRES/CNC LATHES

CNC lathes are popular CNC machines and are generally classified as:

(i) Horizontal machines and

(ii) Vertical machines

3.3.1 Classification of the Horizontal Machines

(i) Chucking machines

(ii) Shaft machines

(iii) Universal machines

(iv) Mill turn centres

Some of the latest CNC lathes are twin spindle machines on which the first and second operations can be performed on the two spindles in succession. The component is removed from the first spindle after the first operation and is loaded into the second spindle for second operation, automatically.

(i) Chucking Machines: Chucking machines usually have shorter beds and a single saddle with single drum type turret which accommodates both ID and OD tools or two independent saddles with turret as shown in Fig. 3.5. Many of the present day chuckers offer optional swing-in-tail stock to facilitate shaft work. During normal working as a chucker, the tailstock is swung away from the work area. In order to facilitate simultaneous external and internal machining some chuckers are provided with two turrets. Typical components that could be machined in a chucking type CNC lathe are pump impellers, gear blanks, end covers, discs, pins, plugs, washers, flywheels, etc.

Fig. 3.5 A CNC Lathe

The spindle axis of a CNC lathe is designated as the Z axis. The tool movement along the Z axis is obtained by the longitudinal movement of the saddle. The traverse movement of the cross slide gives the X-axis movement. Thus a CNC lathe is basically a two axis machine. The axes of a CNC lathe are illustrated in Fig. 3.6.

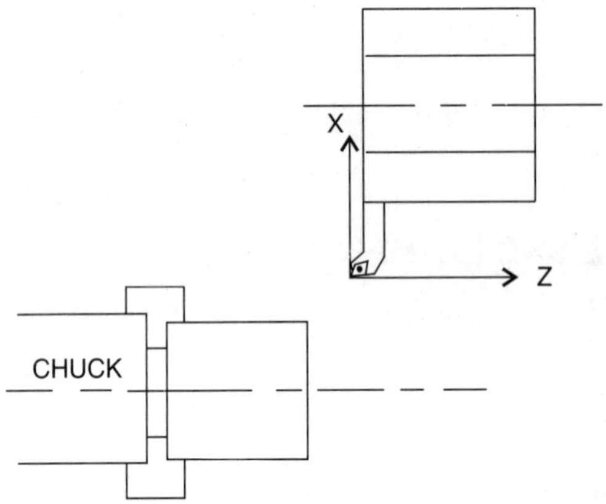

Fig. 3.6 Axes of a CNC Lathe

(ii) **Shaft Lathes:** Shaft lathes are intended mainly for between centre work. They have hydraulic or pneumatic tailstock and roller steadies for supporting the workpiece. Tooling is mainly for external working.

(iii) **Universal Lathes:** Universal lathes are suitable for both chucking and for bar work. 4-axis machines have two turrets each mounted on an independent slide and facilitate simultaneous machining with two tools.

Some lathes have rotating tools in the turret to facilitate off-axis machining such as drilling, milling, reaming, tapping, boring etc. These machines have in addition to the conventional X and Z axes, CNC control of the spindle rotation i.e. C-axis. Such machines are known as turning centres. Many cylindrical components will have cross holes, off centre holes, cam grooves (drum cams and face cams), key ways, slots etc. Machining of these features require rotating tools or live tools. The turret in a turning centre will also be provided with a servo motor to drive the tool at the required rpm. The CNC system should include, therefore, additional programming features. Figure 3.7 shows the axes of a turning centre.

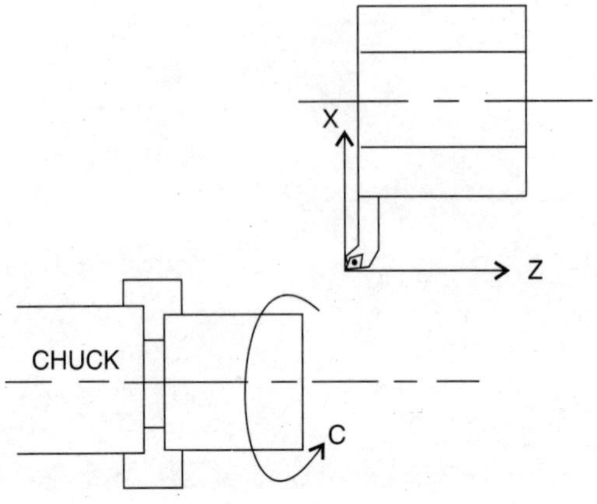

Fig. 3.7 Axes of a Turning Centre

3.3.2 Tooling and Turret Slide

The present trend is to have a single heavy drum type turret capable of accommodating both external and internal working tools. Some machines have two independent slides with one turret on each slide, one for external working tools and the other for internal tools. This arrangement will need 4-axis CNC. External and internal machining can be carried out simultaneously. Alternately both slides can be fitted with turrets carrying external turning tools to facilitate simultaneously machining of steps of the shafts from either direction. Some machines have an automatic tool changer with multi-station tool magazine and a tool clamping arrangement on a single slide. This is common in flexible turning centres. The accuracy of indexing will be about 3–4 seconds of an arc and the turret indexing time will be 0.3 to 0.5 seconds. Geneva mechanism is normally used to index the turret. A curvic coupling is used to give the necessary indexing accuracy. The tools mounted on the turret can be generally grouped into two categories:

Axial tools: Boring bars, internal threading tools, drills, taps, reamers, dies, etc. belong to this category. These tools will have their axis parallel to the Z axis.

Radial tools: Turning tools, grooving/parting tools, external threading tools, etc. belong to this category.

It is advisable that no two axial tools should be located in adjacent pockets. This is because of the possibility of the tools interfering with the work piece. If a particular tool is to be used more frequently, such tools can be located in more than one pocket. This will reduce the number of stoppages to change the tool or index the insert. Tools are identified by the pocket number in which the tools are located. For example, T04 means the tool in pocket number 4.

Linear tooling system (Platen tooling) is used in some of the less expensive CNC lathes.

There are several modules available for automating CNC turning machines and these can be employed individually or in combination. These include:

(i) Main spindle orientation and stopping

(ii) Sensor Systems for:
- Tool wear and breakage monitoring
- Machine monitoring
- Blank recognition and measurement
- Handling action monitoring
- Finished part gauging
- Sequence monitoring
- Tool measurement

(iii) Chuck changing

(iv) Chuck jaw changing

(v) Bar feed

(vi) Gantry loading equipment

(vii) Industrial robot

(viii) Handling of tool heads

(ix) Gripper changing

(x) Chip conveyor

3.3.3 Vertical CNC Lathes

These are widely used for machining heavy components. Some of these machines can also be used for milling operations. Such machines are sometimes known as turn mill centres.

Specifications of typical machines are given in subsequent sections.

(i) Typical Specifications of CNC Chucker

Capacity:	
Swing over Bed	400 mm
Swing over Cross Slide	180 mm
Max. turning diameter	165 mm
Max. weight of job	130 kg
Main Spindle:	
Spindle nose	ASA A3-6
Hole through spindle	dia. 53
Internal taper spindle	M.T.No.6
Range of spindle speed (infinitely variable)	400 to 3500 rpm
Spindle front bearing dia.	90 mm
Spindle rear bearing dia.	80 mm
Diameter of chuck	dia. 80 mm
Power	7.5 kW
Length	3100 mm
Width	3050 mm
Net Weight of the machine	3400 kg
Hydraulics:	
Tank capacity	35 litres
Pump delivery	13 lpm
Motor	1.5 kW; 1440 rpm
Coolant:	
Tank capacity	100 litres
Pump capacity	70 lpm
Motor	0.18 kW, 3500 rpm
Standard chuck size	300 mm
Tail stock spindle diameter	80 mm
Tail stock spindle stroke	80 mm
Tail stock spindle taper	MT-4

Power:

Spindle Motor	A.C. 11 kW	
A.C servo motor for	X Axis	
	Z axis	
Max. electric power consumption	30.45 kVA	
Net weight	4.5 tonnes	

(ii) Typical Specifications of CNC Turning Centres

CAPACITY:

Max. turning length	400/600 mm	
Distance between centres	550/740 mm	
Max. swing over bed	dia. 540 mm	
Max. turning diameter	dia. 300 mm	
Spindle nose/internal taper	A3-6	A3-8
Spindle dia. at front bearing	dia. 61 mm	dia. 87 mm
Chuck diameter	dia. 303 mm	dia. 354 mm
Bar capacity	dia. 53 mm	dia. 75 mm
Spindle speed	3500 ; 4800 rpm	3500 ; 4000 rpm

Spindle Motor:

Two stages gear change	11/15 kW	11/15 kW
Gear drive	18.5/33 kW	

Turret:

Type of turret/number stations	Double disk tools turret/13x3
Turret clamping force	35000 N
Tool selection	Bi-directional programming with automatic selection of shortest route
Turning tool size	OD turning: 30 mm ID boring: dia. 33 mm

X-Axis:

Travel	153 mm
Rapid traverse rate	6 m /min
AC servo motor	0.9 kW
Diameter of ball screw	dia. 38 x P6 mm

Rotating tool capacities:

Drill	Max.dia. 13 mm
End mill	Max.dia. 30 mm
Tap	Max.M10
Spindle indexing	4 deg. increment (73 divisions)
Indexing accuracy	+0.01 deg.

3.3.4 Mill Turn Centres

Mill turn centres combine the capabilities of machining centres and CNC lathes. These are manufactured with several axes. Five axis mill turn centres are widely used in aerospace industry, wind turbine industry, oil drilling industry etc.

Typical Specification of a Turn Mill Centre:

	A-13	A-16
Table diameter	dia. 1,350 mm	dia. 1, 650 mm
Max. swing	dia. 1,450 mm	dia. 3,030 mm
Max. Cutting height	1,335 mm	1,830 mm
X-/Z-axis travel	1,370/805 mm	1,780/1,370 mm
Number of tools	30 tools (rotary, ID or OD turning tools)	60 tools
Table speeds	1~350 rpm	1~330 rpm 1~300 rpm
Main motor (Cont./30 min rating)	40HP/60 HP	60 HP/80HP
Machine weight	30,500 kg	33,000 kg

3.4 CNC GRINDING MACHINES

The grinding process is unique compared to other machining processes in that there is a very heavy "tool" (wheel) wear and that the process is very sensitive to process parameters like grinding pressure, speed and feed rates and flow of coolant etc. CNC has been successfully applied to all types of grinding machines. The workpiece size control is achieved by some method of automatic wheel wear compensation included in the grinding cycle or through an interactive in-process gauging system which is interfaced with the wheel in-feed drive. CNC can be used either to regulate the machine slides to generate a workpiece or to dress the wheel to the required shape to enable plunge grinding.

3.4.1 Surface Grinding

In horizontal spindle reciprocating table surface grinding machines, in many cases, CNC is applied only to the wheel head slide (Y-axis) as the most critical operation in these machines is the depth control. Conventional hydraulic drives are retained for feed and longitudinal traverse. In some machines the cross feed is also replaced by an electric drive with a timer circuit or open loop control for feed. A closed loop control on the cross feed axis can be used directly to generate contours in the Y-Z plane while reciprocating the table in the longitudinal axis or to contour dress the wheel for plunge grinding. In some cases the table longitudinal traverse is also provided with an electric drive. By adding a fourth rotary axis, the surface grinder movements can also be used to generate involute surfaces of a gear tooth.

3.4.2 Cylindrical Grinding

In many cases CNC is provided only for wheel head slide to control diameters. In some cases CNC is provided for longitudinal traverse and wheel head traverse (3-axis) to control length of shoulders and diameter steps. Workpiece size is achieved by dressing the wheel with reference to fixed dressing point or by use of an interactive size control unit. Such machines can generate solids of revolution involving tapers, circular arcs and curved surfaces. Similar controls are available for internal grinders.

3.4.3 Tool and Cutter Grinders

CNC has been applied to complex tool and cutter grinders involving as many as eight axes. In these machines the control system is interactive with the part program residing in the memory and leads the operator step by step reducing the programming effort to the absolute minimum.

3.4.4 Profile Grinders

CNC has been used to advantage even on optical profile grinders. The control system has linear, circular and helical interpolation to generate complex contours, and has provision to dress the wheel and to compensate for wheel wear. Optics serve for tool setting, positioning the workpiece, checking wheel dressing and inspection of workpiece without removing it from the fixture.

3.5 ELECTRICAL DISCHARGE MACHINING (EDM)

3.5.1 Ram Type EDM

In this type of machine the electrode has to have the same size and shape of the counterpart of the workpiece being machined. Servo control is used to maintain the gap between the electrode and the workpiece.

3.5.2 Orbital EDM

In this type of machines, the electrode is in the form of a ball ended cutter and spins about its own axis. The relative position of the electrode and workpiece is regulated by a 3-axis CNC system to generate any three dimensional surface.

3.5.3 Wire EDM

In this type of machines, the electrode is in the form of a wire. A small hole is drilled into the workpieces and the wire electrode is threaded through the workpiece onto a take-up roll. The movement of the work table through computer numerical control in X and Y directions enable cutting the component to the required shapes. In some cases where a relief is required for the dia. or the punch being machined, a 3-axis NC is used to tilt the wire axis relative to workpiece on the contour. The direction of tilt varies with the contour and is controlled by the third axis CNC.

Some of the latest wire EDM machines have the automatic drilling and self-threading facility to enable the machines to operate untended.

Typical Technical Specification of a Wire cut EDM Machine

Travel of X and Y movements	330 × 330 mm
Travel - Z axis	135 mm
Minimum displacement when machining	1 mm
Maximum speed	0.015 m/sec
Measuring resolution	1 mm
Maximum height of workpiece	150 mm
(height with option)	(335 mm)

Max. weight of work piece	500 daN
Max.dimensions of workpiece	900 × 530 mm
Taper angle adjustable from	0' to 30' per face
Automatic wire threading	135 mm
Wire tension adjustable	from 3.5 to 30 N
Machine dimensions (height × length × width)	3335 × 1675 × 1970 mm
Weight	1930 daN
Dielectric system:	
Preliminary clearing by setting tank	
Filtration by paper filters (cartridges)	
De-ionization, with effectiveness shown by indicator lamps	
Capacity of dielectric system	300 Litres
Dimensions (h × l × w)	870 × 500 × 1610 mm
Weight (including settling tank)	170 daN
CNC:	
Memory capacity of CNC	340 kbytes
Number of programs that may be stored on Cassette	70
Total capacity per cassette	3,40,000 characters
Generator:	
Machining current	64A

3.6 PUNCHING, NIBBLING AND FORMING MACHINES

CNC has become very popular with punching and nibbling machines used for sheet metal work. Many of these machines are equipped with a turret head. These are called turret punch presses. Some of them have a plasma arc or a laser cutting for contoured patterns.

Some of the latest machines have automatic work handling, automatic tool change and automatic measuring systems interfaced with the machine.

CNC has been applied to other forming machines such as plate bending, tube bending, flow forming and stretch forming as well.

3.7 CNC GEAR CUTTING MACHINES

CNC has been applied to eliminate change gears in gear making machines. These machines use an electronic gear box which enables very accurate gear ratios to be maintained. CNC gear cutting machines are more productive compared to conventional gear cutting machines. The range of CNC gear cutting machines include:

- Gear hobbing machines
- Gear shaping machines
- Bevel gear generators
- Gear grinding machines

The following sections deal with more common machines like CNC gear *hobbing* machines and CNC gear shaping machines.

3.7.1 Gear Hobbing

The relative rotary and translatory movements of the tool and the workpiece are controlled by CNC system and can be easily programmed through key board of CNC system to facilitate quick change hobs, hob head swiveling and high speed hob spindles to make effective use of multi-start TiN coated, carbide coated or carbide insert hobs. Figure 3.8 shows the various axis movements required for a CNC gear hobbing machine.

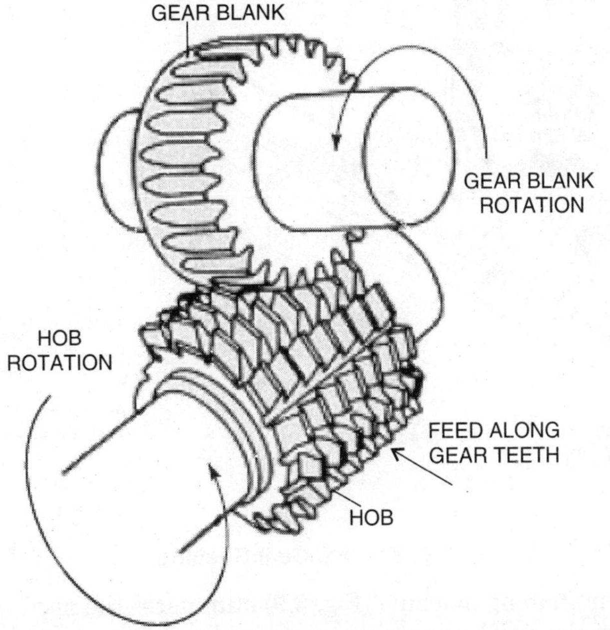

Fig. 3.8 Gear Hobbing

3.7.2 CNC Gear Shaping

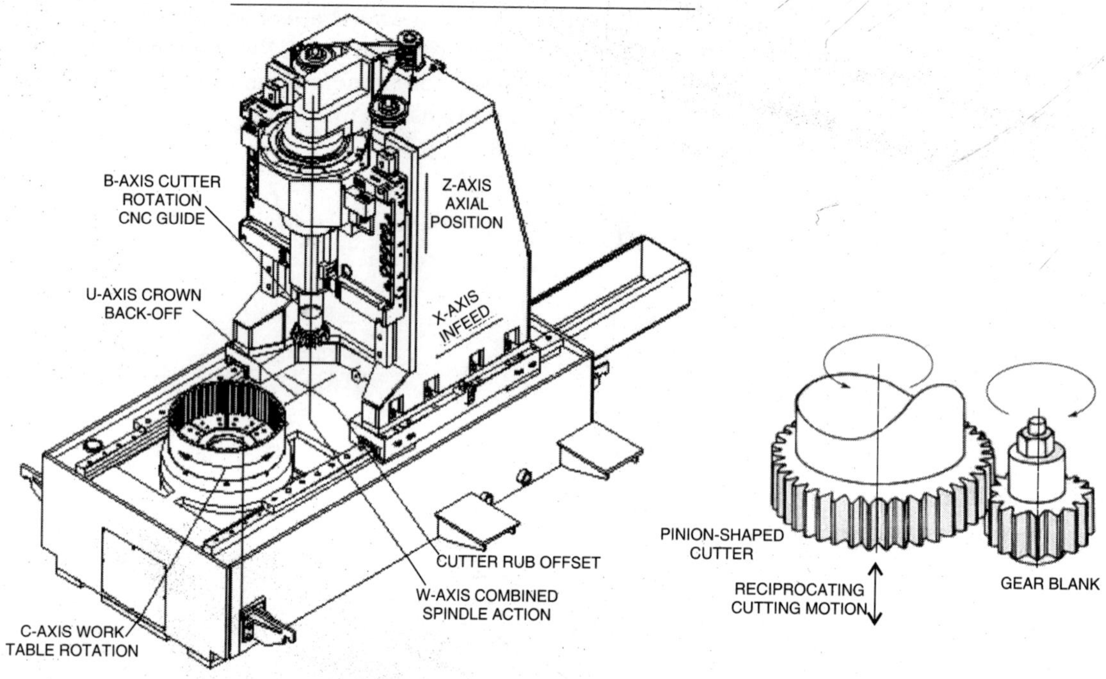

Fig. 3.9 CNC Gear Shaping

Use of CNC in gear shaping machine (Fig. 3.9) eliminates the need for change gears. CNC control is provided for the axial movement of cutter head slide, radial movement of column slide, rotary movement of cutter spindle and rotary movement of work table.

The conventional mechanical gearbox is replaced by an electronic gearbox in the case of CNC gear cutting machines. This provides very high accuracy gear ratios and hence, the gears generated by CNC machines are more accurate when compared with gears manufactured in conventional machines.

Various other types of gear cutting machines like bevel gear generators are also available with CNC.

3.8 MULTI-TASKING (COMBI) CNC MACHINES

Several new types of CNC machines which combine various functions are now being developed. For example, a CNC lathe can be provided with a grinding spindle so that parts of a component which requires grinding can be finish ground in the same set up used for turning. Machines developed on similar concept are used for many applications. Increased accuracy and reduction in machining time because of the elimination of multiple set ups are the main advantages of these machines.

3.9 LASER CUTTING AND DRILLING MACHINES

Multi-axis laser processing is a competitive method compared to conventional methods for cutting, drilling, and welding of parts in many industries, particularly in aerospace, automobile and in some other engineering industries. Greater accuracy and consistency, greater process control, flexibility for economical low volume and small lot size manufacturing, capability to machine finer details, ease with which hard materials could be machined, and higher throughput because of faster processing speeds are some of the reasons for the popularity of this process.

Laser processing concentrates laser energy to a small area and produces a narrow cut or weld with leaving a very small heat affected zone. The ability to control heat input precisely in laser processing is providing design engineers the capability to reduce the size and spacing of the features. In cutting and drilling, a high pressure inert or oxidizing gas flowing through a nozzle coincident with the beam provides mechanical energy to aid in removing the laser melted metal. The laser cut is characterized by a narrow kerf of 1-2 degrees taper. In welding a dry inert gas is used to protect the laser melted metal from the absorption of or reaction with oxygen in the atmosphere.

Laser drilling is used to produce holes as small as 0.1mm with a depth to diameter ratio of >10 (aspect ratio) and hole sat shallow angles from the surface < 10 degrees even in the toughest aerospace alloys. In aerospace applications, laser is used to drill cooling holes in turbine blades and for controlling airflow on aerofoil surfaces such as combustion liners, compressor blades and nozzle guide vanes. There are basically two types of drilling processes.

- percussion drilling
- trepanning

Of these percussion drilling is typically used for drilling holes in turbine blades. This process uses a stationary beam and one or two pulses to penetrate the thickness of the material. Trepanning involves producing a feature or a hole by contour cutting the feature shape. This process is superior to percussion drilling because of its flexibility to produce complex shapes, greater consistency, and ability to produce large holes.

3.9.1 Types of Laser Machines

There are four types of laser cutting and drilling machines.

- Fixed beam moving table systems
- Fixed beam ball transfer machines
- Hybrid systems
- Moving beam (flying optics) systems

Moving Table Laser machines: In these machines, the material to be cut is placed on the support table and the entire table is moved under the beam. The maximum size of the workpiece is limited by the size of the table.

Ball Transfer Laser Machines: These move the work material under a fixed beam over a matrix of balls or rollers that are located in the material support table. The operator loads a sheet on the table and into the clamps located in the rear of the machine. These clamps move the material in the X-axis while clamps themselves are attached to a table that moves back and forth in the Y- axis. The disadvantage of ball transfer machine is that balls may cause scratches on the work material or balls may jam.

Hybrid Laser Cutting Machines: A combination of part motion and beam motion is used to achieve the cut in this type of machine. Usually the part is moved in the X-axis while the beam is moved in the Y- axis. There are several advantages for the hybrid machine. One is that formed material can be cut. It is also possible to locate materials of different thickness that can be cut simultaneously.

Flying Optics Laser Cutting Machines: Flying optics systems cut a stationary part while the beam flies or moves above it. There are two basic designs for this type of cutting machines-gantry type and cantilever type.

Machine Capabilities: Most of the laser cutting machines uses 2000- 3500 Watt continuous wave power CO_2 laser. Various options include multiple sheet cutting, non-contact cutting, NC focusing system, auto head changer, NC gas pressure control, pipe cutting, nesting software, automatic palletization, and table guard, high pressure cutting and cutting with water assist. Maximum sheet sizes range from 1200 x 2500 to 4000 x 1500 mm or more. Amada, Trumpf, Mazak, Mitsubishi, Haco, etc are some of the well known laser cutting machines. FS-16 LB Fanuc and GE 16-M CNC are two examples of CNC systems used with laser cutting machines.

3.10 CNC TURRET PUNCH PRESS

Turret punch press is a versatile tool for sheet metal fabrication shops. These are primarily used to cut various shapes of openings in sheet metal frames of machines. Since the quantities are low, custom tooling will not be economical for such operations. Turret punch presses use standard tools for producing openings or cut outs of various shapes. Tooling for a turret punch press consists of a punch, die and stripper. The punch is located in a guide mechanism that fits in the turret. Turrets hold a variety of tools. The turret is indexed to bring different tools to the work zone depending on the program. Each punch has a corresponding die that is located under the machine table. The clearance between the punch and die depends on the thickness of the work material.

A combination of laser cutting machine and turret punch press is also now available.

3.11 CNC PRESS BRAKE

A press brake is used in fabrication shops for shaping sheet metal parts by bending process. Figure 3.10 shows a typical bending operation using a press brake. The primary parameters in bending are the bend angle, punch radius, desired inner radius of the part, the material, thickness of the material and the V-opening of the lower tool.

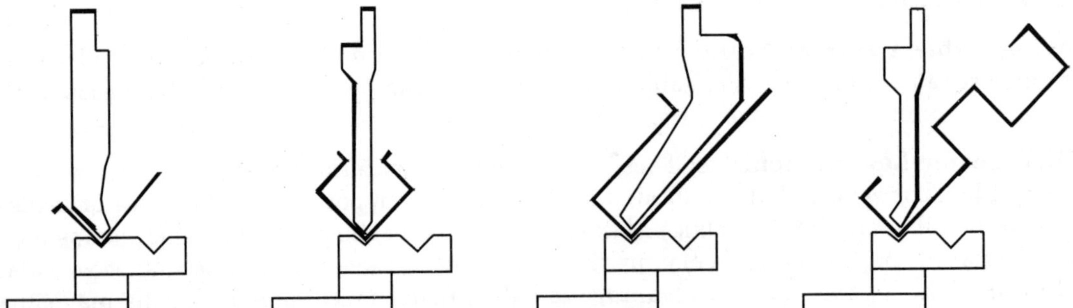

Fig. 3.10 Typical Bending Operation Using a Press Brake

Fig. 3.11 Press Brake

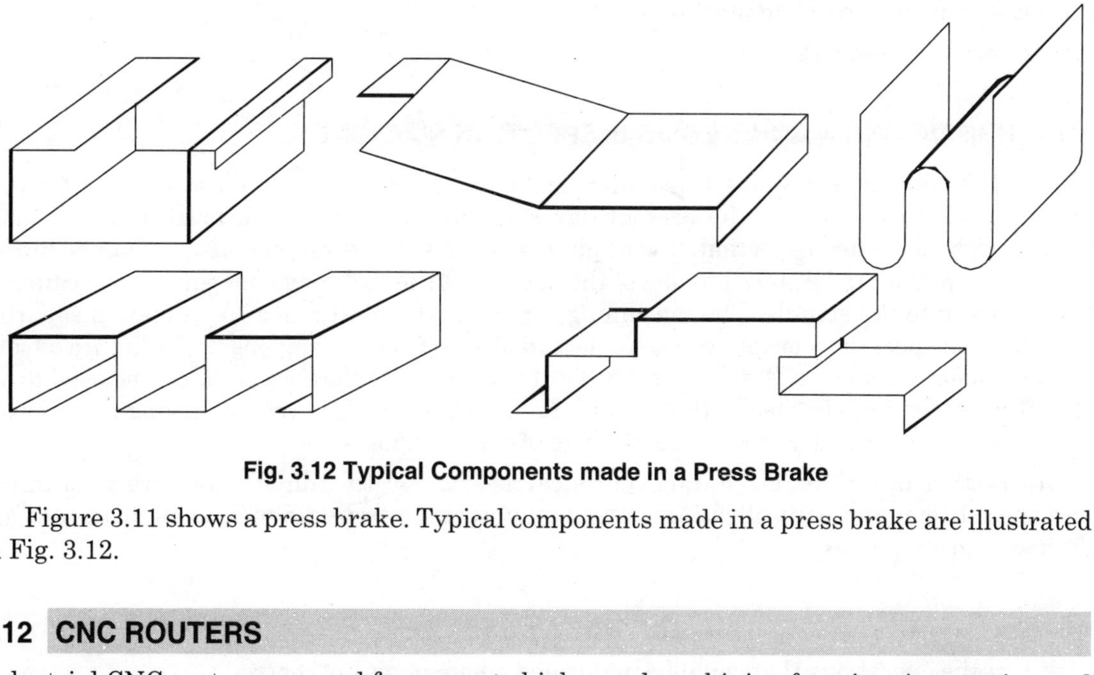

Fig. 3.12 Typical Components made in a Press Brake

Figure 3.11 shows a press brake. Typical components made in a press brake are illustrated in Fig. 3.12.

3.12 CNC ROUTERS

Industrial CNC routers are used for accurate high speed machining for trimming, cutting and shaping of plastics, composites, non-ferrous metals and wood. These machines are widely used for making large templates which are used in the aerospace industry. These machines are flat bed machines with contouring capability and are provided with high speed spindles and will have 3 or 5 axes capability. Usually a bridge type construction is adopted. Vacuum fixturing is generally used.

Specifications:

(1) Table 2500 × 1500

(2) Axes travel 3000 × 2000 × 150

(3) Feed rate up to 40 m/min.
(4) Positioning 0.01 mm unidirectional repeatability.
(5) Spindle RPM: Up to 18000 fully programmable.
(6) Control system - GE FANUC 210-i PC front end.

3.13 OTHER CNC MACHINES

Other CNC machines used in industry are:

(i) Horizontal/Vertical boring machines
(ii) Jig boring and jig grinding machines
(iii) Plano millers
(iv) CNC welding machines
(v) Assembly machines
(vi) Printed circuit board drilling machines
(vii) Tube bending machines
(viii) Electron beam welding machines
(ix) Flow turning lathes

3.14 USE OF CNC MACHINES AS INSPECTION MACHINES

Since CNC machine slides are fitted with feed-back devices, they can also be used for post process metrology. Many of the present day machines are fitted with touch trigger probes which can be used for inspection of workpiece and for setting the tool offsets. On machining centres the probe can be stored in one of the pockets of the tool magazine and can be called to be inserted into the spindle. The machining centre can be used like a co-ordinate measuring machine to inspect the workpiece. The probe can also be used to compensate for fixture offsets, thermal deformations etc. A similar probe located at a fixed reference point can be used to set the offsets of the tools located in the spindle. Such probes are also used on turning machines to set the tool offsets and for monitoring the size of the workpiece.

Inspection in a CNC machining cell is carried out by co-ordinate measuring machines and special computer controlled inspection equipment. Co-ordinate measuring machines are discussed in chapter 14.

REVIEW QUESTIONS

(1) List the operations that could be performed on a machining centre.
(2) Name and describe the two accessories, which make machining centres versatile.
(3) What are the different types of machining centres?
(4) Describe the features of a horizontal machining centre.
(5) What are the types of work-pieces that can be machined on a vertical machining centre?
(6) Describe the difference in the construction of a travelling column and fixed column machining centre?
(7) What is meant by a Universal machining centre?

(8) Describe the classification of CNC turning machines.

(9) Give typical specifications of a horizontal machining centre.

(10) What are the differences between a CNC turning centre and a CNC lathe?

(11) What is the advantage of having two tool turrets on a CNC lathe?

(12) Describe the typical operations that can be performed on a CNC turning centre.

(13) Give typical specifications of a CNC lathe.

(14) Discuss the application of computer numerical control to grinding machines.

(15) Describe a CNC wire EDM machine.

(16) Describe the special features and applications of turret punch press.

(17) What are the advantages of using CNC for gear cutting?

(18) Describe the principle of working of a CNC gear hobbing machine.

(19) Describe the principle of working of a CNC gear shaper.

(20) Discuss the application of computer numerical control for laser cutting.

(21) Describe the features of 5-axis laser machining centre.

(22) List the applications of computer numerical control for fabrication operations other than machining.

4 CONSTRUCTIONAL FEATURES OF CNC MACHINES

CNC Machines differ from conventional machines in a number of ways, whether it is the main drive, feed drive or structural elements, the approach to the CNC machine design is quite distinct from manually operated machines. This chapter describes some of the special features and their design aspects.

4.1 INTRODUCTION

High productivity, accuracy, repeatability and consistency in quality are the main advantages of CNC machines. CNC machines generally operate at higher speeds to enable efficient application of new tool materials. A CNC Machine is designed to ensure trouble free operation as it is expected to work even three shifts continuous by with perhaps a short break once in a week for routine preventive maintenance. Unlike manually operated machines, there is no need for the operator to make any adjustments in the machine during the operation. All components and subsystems that are used in building a CNC machines usually have a very high reliability, and high mean time between failures [MTBF].

The quality surface finish of the component produced in a CNC machine is very high. The structural design should therefore be vibration – free. The high speeds of operation and high metal removal rate requires very robust design to withstand high cutting forces. The special constructional features of CNC machines include rigid structural elements, infinitely variable speed and feed drive, slideways fitted with plastic inserts or linear motion systems, recirculating ball screws or linear motors for axes feed drive, automatic tool changers, tool magazines, automatic magazine changers, special rigid tool turrets etc.

The salient features of these constructional elements and the selection of some of them are discussed in this chapter.

4.2 MAIN DRIVE

A given combination of work material and tool material requires a range of cutting speeds. Since cutting speed is inversely proportional to the work or tool diameter, the spindle speeds should vary continuously in a stepless manner. In manual machines a multispeed gearbox is used to provide a number of speeds at the spindle. These speeds are selected manually. In an automatic machine like CNC machine, manual selection of speeds is ruled out. Therefore, the main drive of a CNC machine must be capable of stepless variation speeds under program control. There are two options for obtaining stepless speed variation.

(i) DC variable speed drive

(ii) AC variable speed driver

4.2.1 DC Spindle Drive

The CNC Machines produced during 1970's and 1980's mainly used DC variable speed drives. The typical speed torque characteristic of a DC drive is shown in Fig. 4.1. At low motor operating speeds the speed regulation is through increasing armature voltage from a minimum to maximum value. The field current is constant.

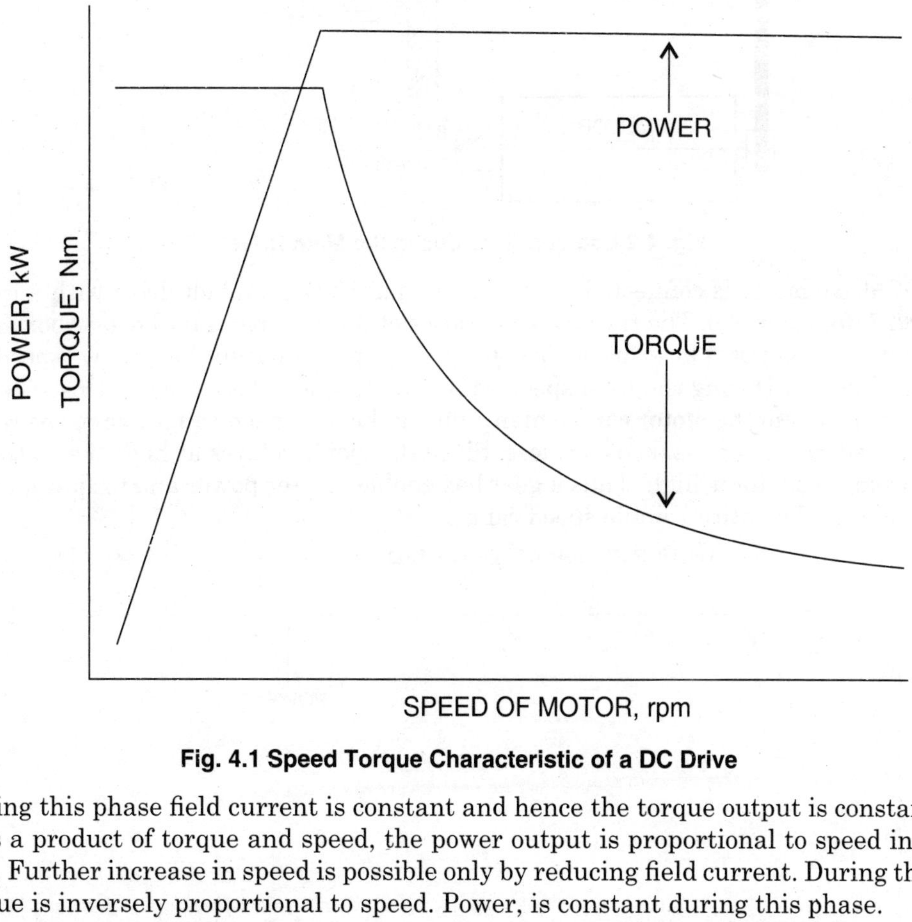

Fig. 4.1 Speed Torque Characteristic of a DC Drive

During this phase field current is constant and hence the torque output is constant. Since power is a product of torque and speed, the power output is proportional to speed in a linear manner. Further increase in speed is possible only by reducing field current. During this phase the torque is inversely proportional to speed. Power, is constant during this phase.

One disadvantage of this type of characteristic is that at low speeds, the motor output power is low. This situation is remedied by the use of a gear box. A typical drive with a gear box incorporated is illustrated in Fig. 4.2.

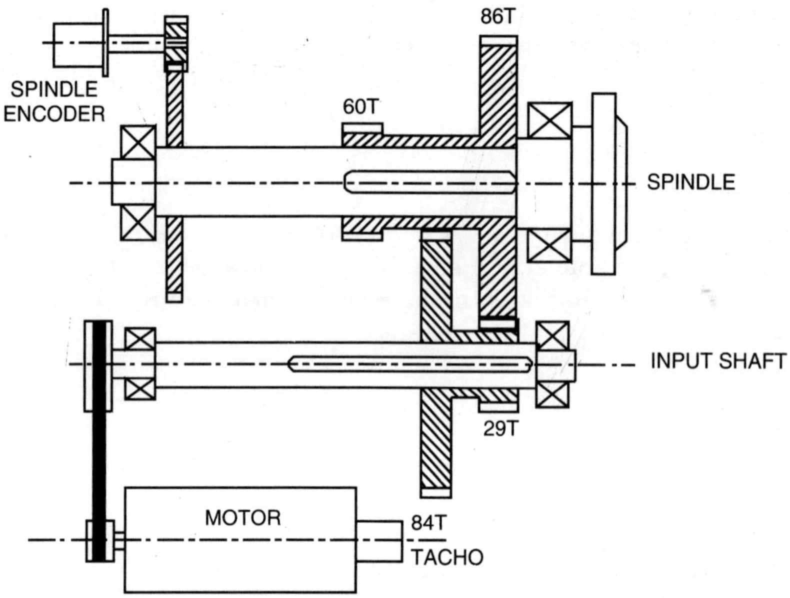

Fig. 4.2 Use of a Gear box in the Main Drive

The DC drive motor is connected to the input shaft through a belt drive with a reduction ratio of 48/27 (for example). The transmission ratios of the gear pairs in the gear box are 86/29 [reduction drive] and 60/84 [overdrive]. The torque and power output for the two speed ranges is shown in Fig. 4.3. During the high speed range the torque is less. During this speed range the power output from the motor can be high. During the low speed range, when the reduction gear is engaged, the spindle speeds are less. Since the motor rotates at high speed, the power available from the motor is high. Thus a gear box enables better power and torque availability at the spindle for the entire spindle speed range.

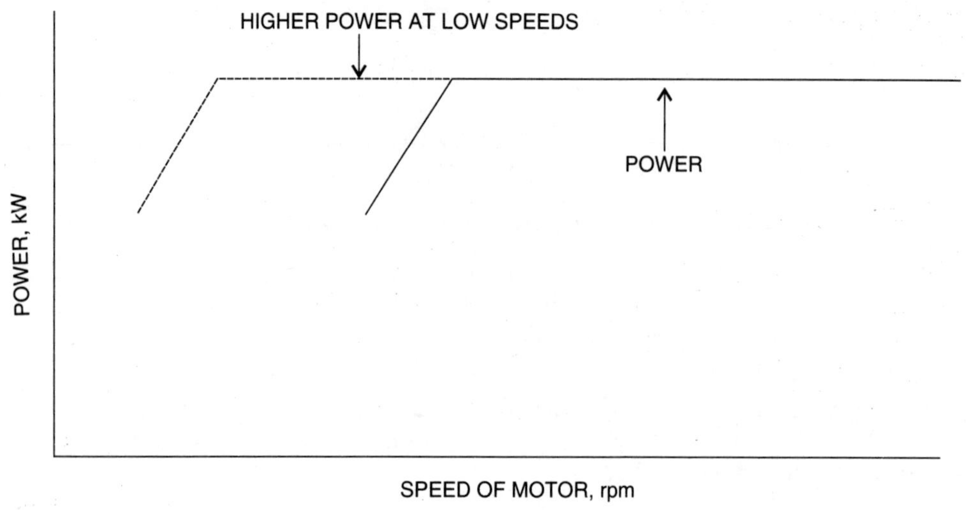

Fig. 4.3 Torque Speed Characteristic with Gear box

The gear box can be housed inside the headstock or can be mounted separately. Separate mounting isolates the vibration from the motor and gear box being transmitted to the structure of the machine.

DC motors require a separate AC motor driven fan. The air exit openings are arranged to the side on the drive and the bearing plate. A filter is provided to get clean air for cooling. The noise level is reduced by 1-2 dB when a filter is provided. Filter requires frequent cleaning to remove the dust particles. Forced cooling permits large range of speed control at full torque. The cooling air flows from the non-drive end to the drive end. Forced cooling permits large speed control range at full torque. F class insulation is used in these motors for reliable operation. This insulation allows the motor to be operated under severe climatic conditions. The motors are rugged enough to withstand high switching frequency and load surges. Built in thermal sensors in the windings ensures that the temperature does not increase beyond the permissible limits. Motors are fitted with heavy duty permanently lubricated cylindrical roller bearings.

4.2.1.1 Converters

Converters are used for the speed regulation of the motor. It contains power section with thyristors for armature and field circuit, semiconductor fuses and transformers. The converter is placed between AC reactor and motor.

The reversal of current direction is done by pulse changeover. This is helped by thyristor bridges in the armature circuit in 6 pulse anti-parallel connection. A fully controlled single phase bridge circuit is provided for field supply to permit acceleration and braking. The converter used is normally a 6 – pulse type. The unit controls the motor speed with the aid of subordinate armature current control and armature voltage-dependent field weakening circuit. The units are designed for 4 quadrant operation. Figure 4.4 shows the block diagram of the feed back control loop of a DC motor drive. A tachogenerator mounted on the motor shaft is used as the feedback device.

Digital control has replaced analog control in modern DC drives. The digital design opens up the possibilities of easy start up and servicing.

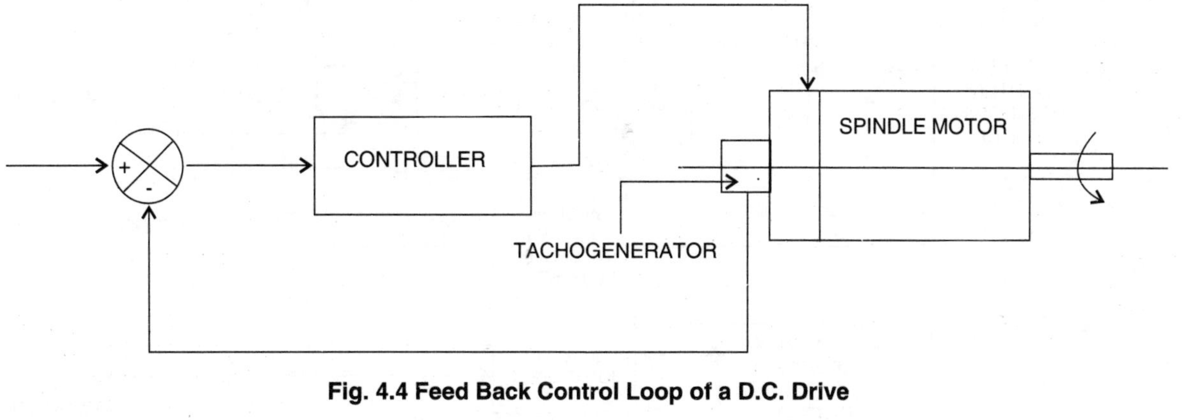

Fig. 4.4 Feed Back Control Loop of a D.C. Drive

4.2.2 AC Spindle Drive

AC spindle drives are the preferred main drive for CNC machines due to a variety of reasons:

(i) AC motors are robust and rugged and hence more reliable than DC motors under severe operating conditions including floating dust and coolant splash.

(ii) AC motors being free of brushes and other wearing parts do not require frequent maintenance.

(iii) The unique stator cooling system in AC motors result in high speed high output characteristics with compact size.

(iv) AC drives provide stable and smooth operation with reduced vibrations and noise from low speed to high speed.

Figure 4.5(a) shows a typical torque-speed and power-speed characteristics of an AC spindle motor. It can be noted that the constant power region covers a wider range. These high power motors do not require a gear box. The speed range ratio, n_{max}/n_b is of the order of 4:1 to 5:1. A higher speed range of 8:1 is possible with specially designed high power series motors. The characteristic of the high power series motor is shown in Fig. 4.5(b) for comparison.

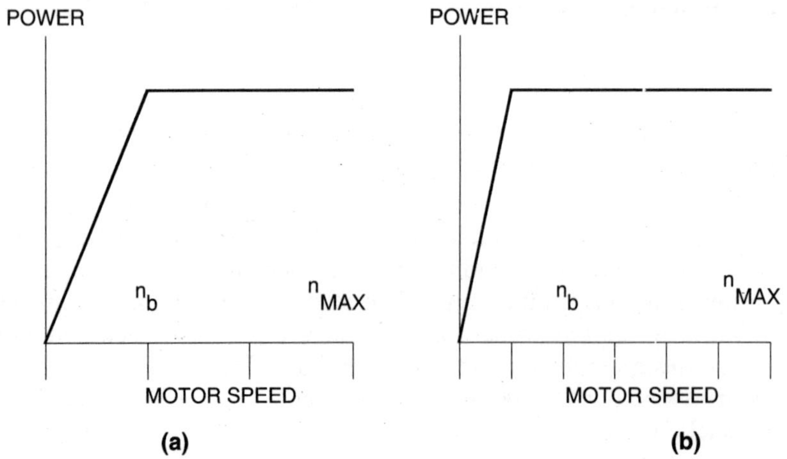

Fig. 4.5 Typical Torque-Speed Characteristics of AC Drives

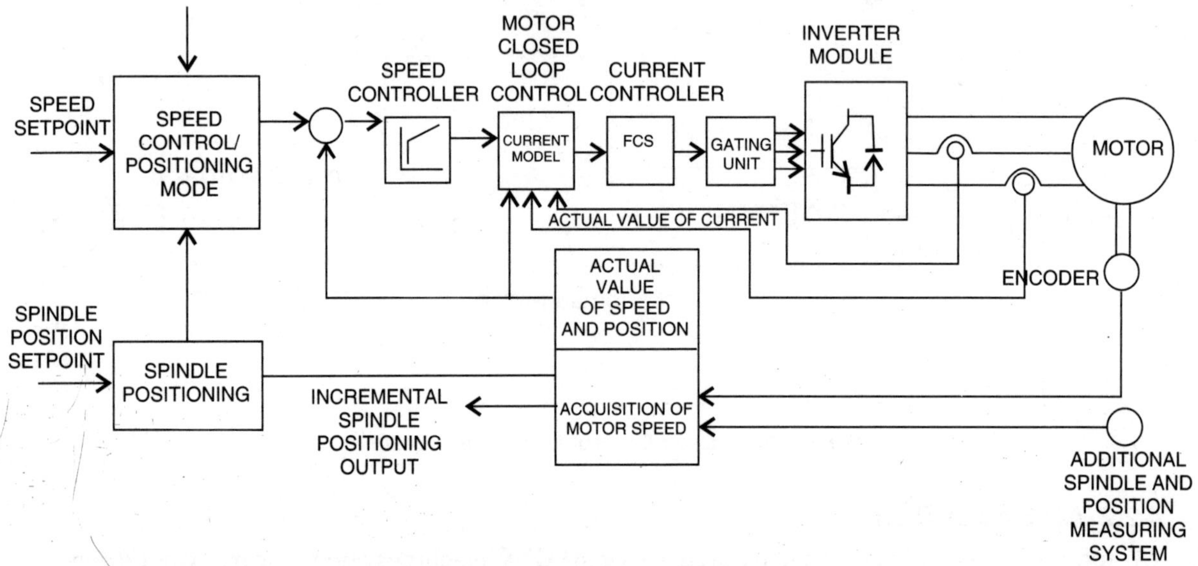

Fig. 4.6 Block Diagram of an AC Spindle Drive

A block diagram of spindle drive is shown in Fig. 4.6. Digital AC drives are preferred today because:

(i) Fast response for stable high cutting performance.

(ii) Improved acceleration and deceleration in low speed range.

(iii) Improved rigidity at spindle orientation.

(iv) Improvement in the linearity of load meter.

(v) Easy setting of maximum rpm through parameter values.

AC spindle drive for machine tools comprise a squirrel cage induction motor and transistor inverter type controller. These motors

- enable fast installation
- have high degree of safety
- are maintenance free
- enable easy setting of parameters during servicing
- save mechanical gear reductions
- are usually of robust 4 – pole designs
- have short speed and torque response time
- have low inertia

In order to reduce inertia, rotors are made hollow. The magnetic material used is usually samarium cobalt. Two thermistors integrated into the stator windings are used to protect motor from excessive temperature rise. The motors have permanently lubricated bearings. They are designed for a minimum ambient temperature of –15 degree Celsius. The service life of the bearings is 20000 hours. The bearings are grease lubricated and it is recommended that grease be renewed after 10000 hours of operation. Some of the spindle motors have separate ventilation. A fan is mounted on the non-drive end for this purpose. The normal direction of airflow is from the drive end to the non-drive end in order to keep the exhaust heat of the motor away from the machine tool. Some of the motors are water cooled. This ensures high power output with small mounting volume. Water cooled motors are less noisy.

The motor has integrated encoder with sine and cosine voltage signals for measuring the speed and rotor position. The encoder system is C-axis capable as standard. Main motor spindles work with a frequency up to 800 Hz.

The important characteristics of transistor pulse inverters are listed below:

(i) Direct connection to mains without transformer and commutating reactors.

(ii) Regenerative braking.

(iii) Digital multi processor configurations for speed and torque control.

(iv) Load and command characteristics similar to DC.

(v) High degree of safety.

Both analog and digital controls are used in converters.

Some of the recent designs of CNC machines use integral rotor spindles. Here the spindle carries the rotor of the motor and the spindle housing carries the stator. Such spindle motors are preferred for high speed operation. They are also preferred where good surface finish, accuracy and dynamic balance are required. They also have short ramp up times owing to low moment of inertia as motor is directly mounted on the spindle and as no belt transmission and gearbox are used. The constant power band of these machines is as high as 1:16. These motors also have an overload capacity of 1:2. Figure 4.7 shows an integral rotor spindle.

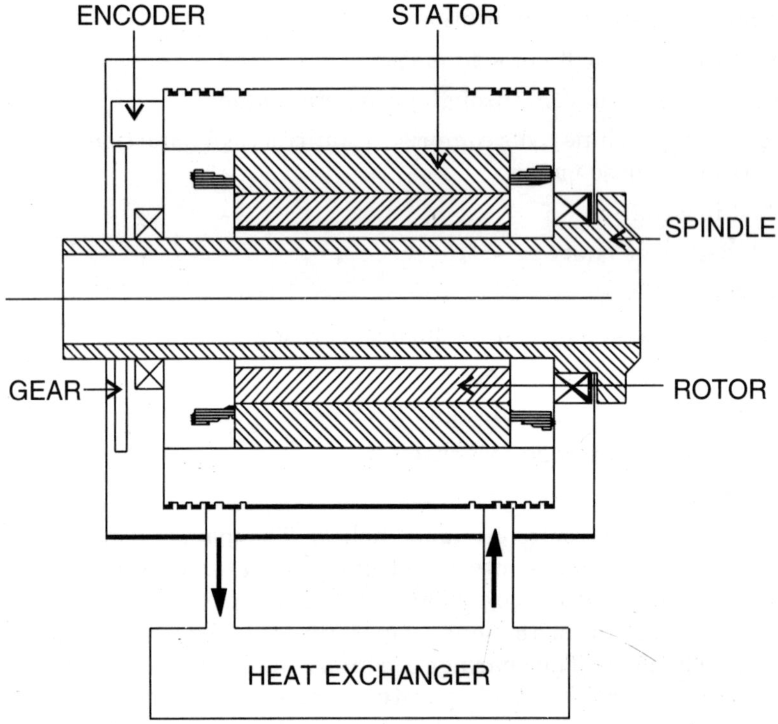

Fig. 4.7 Integral Rotor Spindle

4.2.3 Transmission Belting

Different types of transmission belting are used in CNC drives. For low speed operation, say up to 3000 rpm, it is common practice to use toothed belt. A typical toothed belt drive arrangement is illustrated in Fig. 4.8 (a). For higher speeds a poly V-belt, shown in Fig. 4.8 (b), is recommended. The advantage of this belt is low weight coupled with the capability of high speed operation. The matching profile on the pulley reduces slip. Standard V-belts are used in some CNC machines.

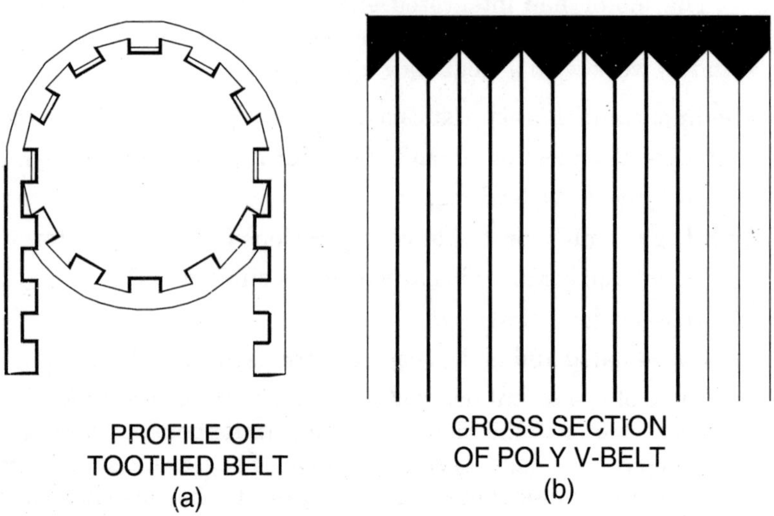

Fig. 4.8 Transmission Belts

4.3 AXES FEED DRIVES

A special distinguishing feature of a CNC machine compared to conventional machines is the individual drive for each axis. Similar arrangements are used for each axes, with variation in only ratings of motors and size of ball screws.

Figures 4.9 (a), (b), (c) show a typical axis feed drives. Fast response is one of the important functional requirements of an axis feed drive motor to satisfy continuous variation of slide velocity depending on the contour of the workpiece. This requires a low inertia servo motor. The servo motor can be directly coupled to the ball screw or can be transmitted through a toothed belt reduction drive. The belt reduction drive makes it possible to use a low torque output servo motor.

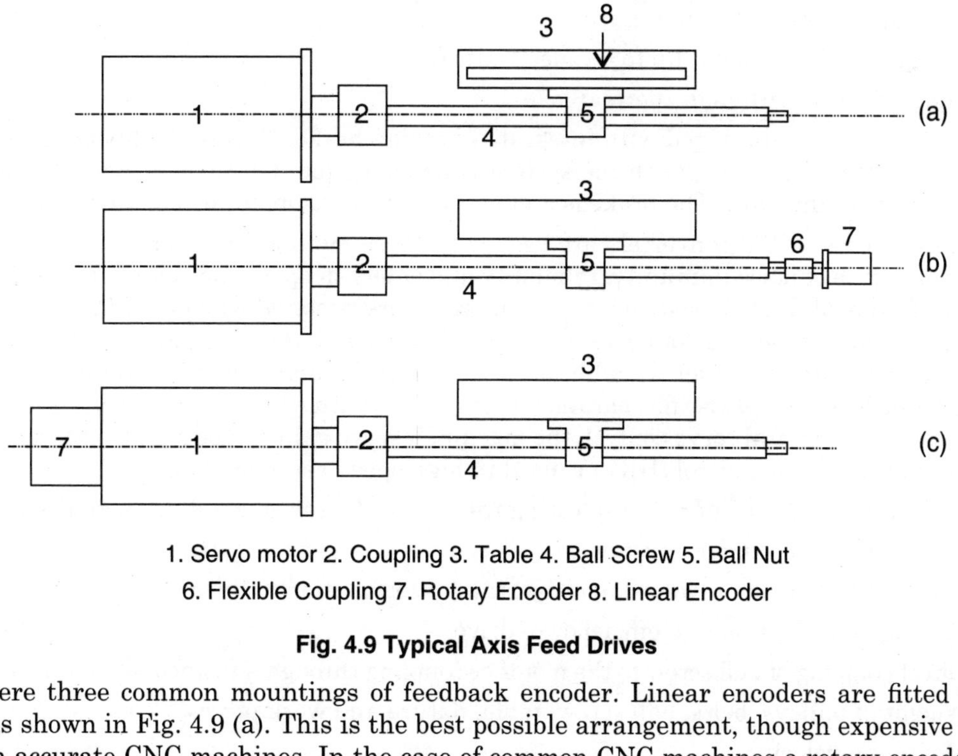

1. Servo motor 2. Coupling 3. Table 4. Ball Screw 5. Ball Nut
6. Flexible Coupling 7. Rotary Encoder 8. Linear Encoder

Fig. 4.9 Typical Axis Feed Drives

There three common mountings of feedback encoder. Linear encoders are fitted to the table as shown in Fig. 4.9 (a). This is the best possible arrangement, though expensive and is used in accurate CNC machines. In the case of common CNC machines a rotary encoder or a synchro resolver is used for feedback. A rotary encoder can be mounted at the free end of the ball screw. This is shown in Fig. 4.9 (b). The feedback device, is preferably mounted on the rear of the servo motor as shown in Fig. 4.9 (c). This makes harness design simpler. This has the advantage of simplicity in wiring.

Mounting feedback device on the servo motor has a few disadvantages. The errors due to the ball screw (pitch to pitch error, cumulative pitch error, mounting errors, torsional deflection, backlash, thermal distortion etc.) will affect the positioning accuracy. However a trade off can be achieved by using a precision class of ball screw.

Usually axis drive motors are designed with the same shaft and flange dimensions over a range of torque and are self-ventilated. The servo motors are of two categories.

(i) AC servo motor (ii) DC Servo motor

4.3.1 AC Servo Motor

AC servo motor is standard with present day CNC machine builders. The advantages of AC servo motors are:

(i) Low moment of inertia
(ii) High power/weight ratio
(iii) Constant acceleration torque up to maximum speed
(iv) Practically maintenance free, owing to permanent field excitation
(v) Light weight motor
(vi) Fast speed and torque response
(vii) High frequency response
(viii) High mean time between failure
(ix) High overload capacity, up to 4 times static torque
(x) Long life even with high thermal load

These motors are provided with integrated holding brake. This brake holds the feed axis stationary, without play, or when the system is de-energized. Permanent magnet single disc brakes are generally used. The brake is a must for the X-axis motor of a slant bed CNC lathe.

Transistorized PWM converters are used with these motors. These are of compact design with high degree of noise immunity, reliability and safety in operation. The closed loop control of digital feed modules is based on a powerful signal processor which perform the axis specific closed loop control functions for current and speed. The current and speed control are based on an easy to set state controller. In addition to excellent dynamic response characteristics, the digital closed loop control also has parametrizable filters with which mechanical resonances can be attenuated. In digital servo control, the machine's servo gain can be significantly increased. High resolution vector control (HRV) is used in high speed servo motors.

The factors to be considered in selecting the size of the servo motor are listed below:

(i) Type of motion—linear or rotary
(ii) Kinematic elements involved in converting rotary motion to linear motion
(iii) Coefficient of friction and efficiency of drive
(iv) Direct coupling of ball screw to the motor or coupling through a toothed belt reduction drive
(v) Weight of pulleys, belts, ball screw, table, fixture and work piece
(vi) Maximum velocity
(vii) Acceleration time
(viii) Maximum cutting forces

4.3.2 DC Servo Motor

Though not much used in new designs, DC servo motors could be found in old CNC machines. These are characterized by high load capacity and excellent dynamic response with low inertia. The speeds usually vary up to 3000 rpm or more. The DC servo motors are usually of permanent magnet type. This feature avoids overheating of motor windings. They are insensitive to demagnetization and provide smooth rotation even at low speeds.

Various types of converters are available to drive these motors. They normally provide a speed control range of 1:10. Transistor choppers with pulse width modulated voltage are also popular. They have quick acceleration time. The main draw back of a DC servo motor is the necessity to replace brushes as these are likely to wear out over a period of time.

4.3.3 Linear Motor

Linear motor is a recent development in CNC for axis feed drive. The advantages of linear motors include high speed and acceleration reliability and very fast response. As there is no mechanical linkage and no backlash, it is possible to achieve smooth and reversible travel at high speeds. The linear motors are superior for axes feed drive because of:

(i) Direct drive—No backlash from lead screws, ball screws, and belt drives etc.
(ii) No metal to metal contact—This eliminates wear.
(iii) Simple drive—There is only one moving part.
(iv) Length of travel—Unlimited.
(v) High velocity—Velocity can be as high as 50 m/sec.
(vi) Acceleration—High acceleration up to 10 g possible.
(vii) Smooth—The drive is smooth as there are no mechanical linkages.
(viii) Accuracy and Repeatability—positioning accuracy and repeatability can be increased to sub micrometer level if associated with appropriate feedback device.
(ix) High stiffness compared to ball screws.
(x) No maintenance—Being non-contact devices, the drive is virtually maintenance – free.
(xi) Life—Indefinite life under specified working conditions.

4.3.3.1 Working Principle

The linear motors are similar to a rotary motor whose stator and rotor have been cut along a radial plane and unrolled so that it provides a linear thrust. This results in generation of a linear force as opposed to torque in the as of a rotary motor. The linear motors can utilize the same amplifiers and controllers as rotary motors. It is also possible to make the motor in a tubular fashion.

4.3.4 Vector Drives

Vector drives are inverters that have additional specialized circuits. Those circuits receive a signal from specialized AC motors designed specifically for vector drive applications. Those specialized motors have encoders that send digital speed and position information back to the vector control. Vector drives deliver precise speed and torque control even up to zero rpm. They can deliver full load torque at zero rpm which helps to stop and hold torques at an exact position. In addition to precision position control and speed control, they can deliver high uniform torque at low speeds or maintain set speed even at high rpm. They are also easy to install and interface.

4.4 SLIDE WAYS

Precise positioning and repeatability of machine slides are the major functional requirements of CNC machines. Manual machines use guideways with metal to metal contact. This leads to a phenomenon called "stick slip" which is a kind of self excited vibration which requires to be avoided. Since CNC machines use very low positioning speeds at the end of transverse, plain metal to metal contact type guideways can not be used. Further, these are subject to wear with its attendant contribution to inaccuracy.

The requirements of a good slide way system in a CNC machine are:

(i) Low coefficient of friction at varying slide velocities
(ii) Minimum difference between static and dynamic friction coefficient. The velocity friction characteristic should have positive slope
(iii) Low rate of wear
(iv) High stiffness
(v) Sufficient damping

These requirements are met by two types of slide way systems. (i) Slide ways coated with low friction PTFE (Poly Tetra Fluoro Ethylene), (ii) Rolling friction slide ways (Linear motion systems).

4.4.1 Slide Ways with Plastic Inserts

Figure 4.10 shows the cross section of a slide way system in which plastic inserts are used. There are many materials available either in liquid from [skc-3, Moglice] or in plastic sheet form [Turcite – B]. It is found that for these coated slide ways the static coefficient of friction is very close to the dynamic coefficient of friction. With increase in speed, the dynamic coefficient of friction increases slightly and then remains constant.

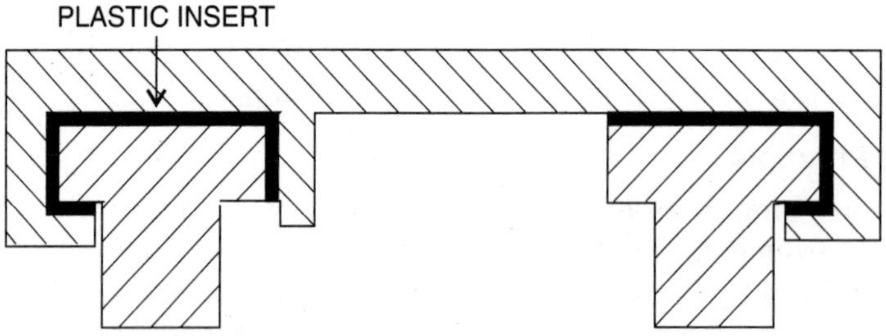

Fig. 4.10 Cross Section of A Slide way with Plastic Inserts

These inserts/composites are made of two or more materials in which one reduces coefficient of friction. The other increases strength, wear resistance and load bearing capacity. They possess self lubricating property and have a soft matrix for taking up dust or particles and to eliminate scoring. That is why, though plastic is soft, their rate of wear is low. Another significant advantage is the case with which a worn out strip can be replaced without the need for scraping or grinding of slide ways. Turcite – B is very popular which is available in sheets of 1.6 mm thick and upwards. These can be cut to the required slide and pasted on the underside of the moving slide way using a suitable adhesive. Table 4.1 gives important properties of these materials.

Table 4.1 Properties of Plastic Inserts for Guideways

	Coefficient of friction		
Lubrication	**TURCITE – B**	**Ferobestos/CA3**	**SKC – 3**
Trace Static	0.073	0.152	0.041
Dynamic	0.368	0.1427	0.040
Flooded Static	0.062	0.097	0.04

Dynamic	0.059	0.082	0.31
Bearing Pressure N/mm²	up to 140	up to 35	up to 500
Minimum sliding speed nm/min	0.01	-	0.01
Wear coefficient	0.04	0.06	0.06
(under clean lubrication Engineering Ccst)	Low	Low	High

4.4.2 Linear Motion System [LM Guideways]

Rolling elements can be used for reciprocating motion. Such guideways are linear motion systems. They have the following advantages:

(i) There is very little difference between coefficient of dynamic friction and coefficient of static friction in the case of linear motion systems. The low coefficient of friction helps to reduce the rating of the drive motor, making the axis feed drive system more compact. This feature also results in less weight, and reduction of overall cost as well as maintenance cost.

(ii) Even though internal clearance is reduced to zero to absorb vibration and shock, smooth motion is obtained.

(iii) Lubrication at very low speeds in metal to metal contact guideways is very inefficient. Rolling element bearings require only trace lubrication and therefore show comparatively very little wear even after prolonged usage.

(iv) The manufacture of the guideway is easy and quick, the sliding accuracy ensured by the accurate LM system.

4.4.2.1 Constructional Features of Linear Motion Bearings

Figure 4.11 shows a typical linear motion (LM) guideway system, which consists of a bearing block and rail. Two raceways are provided on one side of the bearing block where two rows of balls are retained and caused to recirculate by means of a retainer and two end plates.

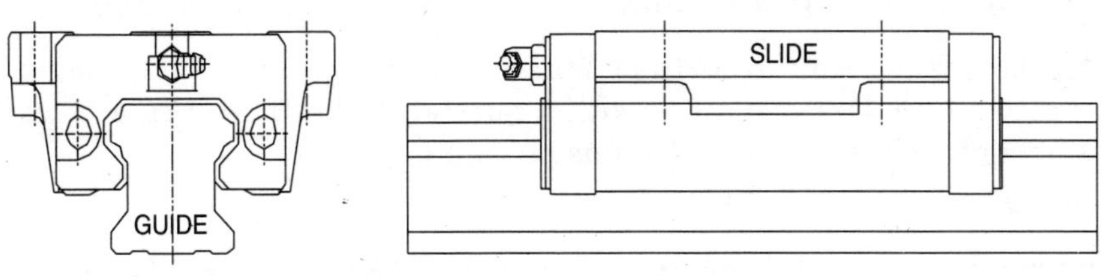

Fig. 4.11 LM Guideway System

The unit is constructed in such a manner that each of the rows of balls rolling over the rail comes in contact with the raceway at an angle of 45°. The bearing system has a high load carrying capacity.

4.4.2.2 Selection of Linear Motion Systems

As in the case of rolling element bearings, the fatigue causes the bearings to fail. This is manifested by flaking of the surface. The life of the bearing is the total travelling distance from the time of start to the time when first flaking appears either on the surface of the trackway or on the rolling elements. Bearing life may show great variation even though they are manufactured under identical conditions. Nominal life is the sum total of the maximum distance travelled without flaking by 90% of a group of bearings tested individually. The basic dynamic load rating C is the load at which the nominal life of L = 50 km for ball elements and L = 100 km for roller elements. The nominal life under applied load P is

$$L = (C/P)^3\ 50$$

Considering the effects of temperature, shock and hardness of track, the above equation is modified as:

$$L = \left\{\frac{f_H\, f_T\, f_C}{F_w} \cdot \frac{C}{P_c}\right\}^3 \cdot 50$$

where L = Nominal Life, km

C = Basic Dynamic Rating, kgf

P_C = Calculated Load, kgf

f_H = Hardness factor, 0.3 to 1

f_T = Temperature factor = 1

f_C = Contact factor, 0.6 to 1

F_W = Load factor, 1 to 3.5

The nominal life

L = $\{C/P\}^3.50$

Where C = Basic dynamic load rating, kgf

P = Load, kgf

Travelling distance per minute = $S = 2.l_S.n$ m/min.

Where

l_S = Stroke length, m

n = Number of cycles/min.

A nomogram showing the relationship between S, C/P and L_n is given in Fig. 4.12.

Example: The service life time L_h is to be obtained for a linear motion system with a basic dynamic load rating C of 4190 kgf, used with a normal load of 1140 kgf, a stroke length l_s of 1 m and a number of reciprocating operations per minute, n = 6.

Load ratio, C/P = 4910/1140 = 4.3

Travel distance/minute = $2.l_S.n$ = $2.l_S.n$ = 2.1.6 = 12 m/min.

Life can be read from the nomogram given in Fig. 4.12 as approximately 5500 hours.

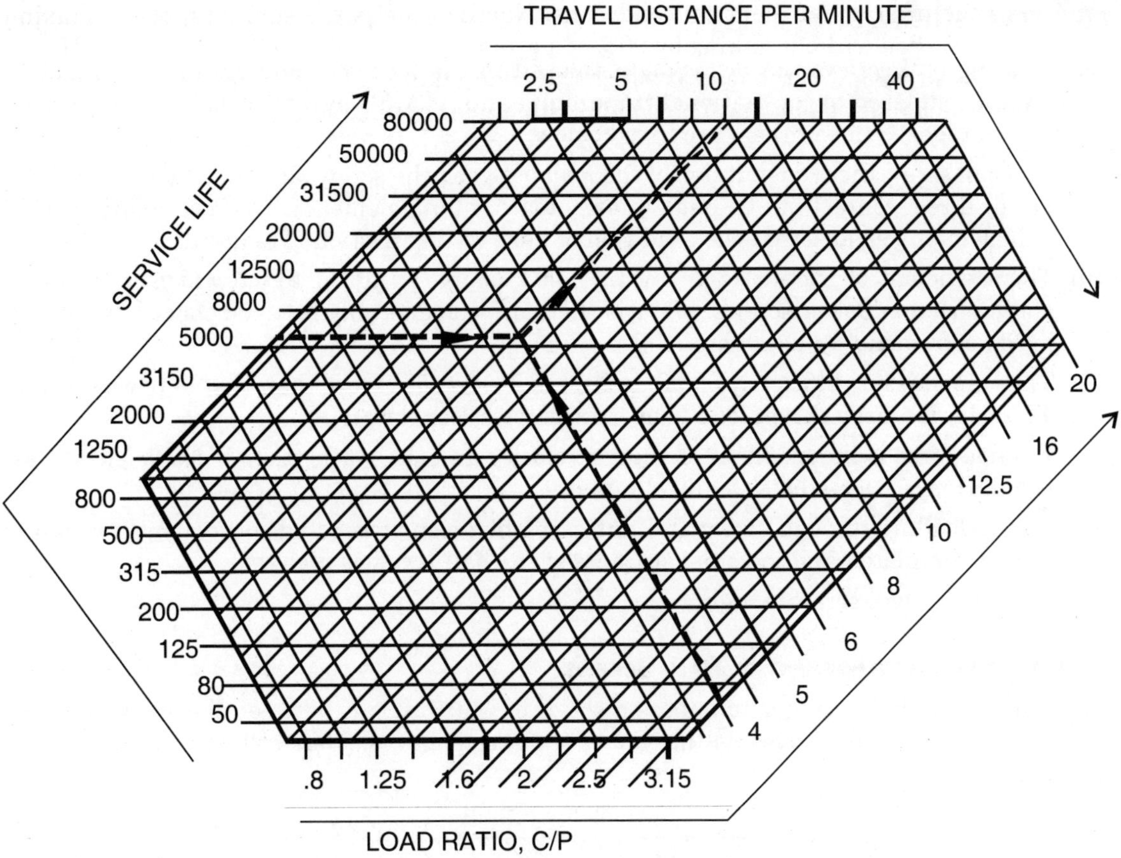

Fig. 4.12 Capacity of LM Bearings

4.4.2.3 Basic Static Load Rating Co

When a linear motion system is subjected to a large impact either in static condition or during motion a partial permanent deformation results. The basic static load rating is set as the limit of statically allowable load. This is the static load which when applied impose maximum stress and the degree of permanent deformation of the rolling bearing and that of the race is 0.0001 times the diameter of the rolling element bearings. The factor of safety (f_S) which has to be used in selection calculations will vary from application to application. Table 4.2 gives recommended values of factor of safety.

Table 4.2 Recommended Values of Factor of safety, f_s

Movement	Load condition	Limiting Value of f_s
Intermittent	Small	1.0 – 1.3
Movement	Large	2.0 – 3.0
Normal motion	Track deflection	
	Small	1.0 – 1.5
	Large	2.5 – 5.0

The condition $(C_0/P_0) >= f_S$ has to be satisfied.

4.5 BALL SCREWS

Recirculating ball screws are primarily employed in the feed mechanisms of CNC Machine tools. When compared to conventional trapezoidal and ACME screws, the ball screws provide many advantages. Some of them are listed below:

(i) In a ball screw the transmission of the load between the screw and nut is not transmitted not by direct contact but through intermediate rolling elements. The recirculation of the ball elements ensure that the condition of pure rolling friction is realized.

(ii) The coefficient of friction is as low as 0.004 compared to 0.1 to 0.5 which is typical of sliding friction power screws. Wear is therefore considerably less and there is very little need for frequent adjustments.

(iii) The transmission efficiency of ball screws is 2 – 9 times more than that of power screws. This enables large thrust load to be carried with less torque.

(iv) Friction force is independent of sliding velocity and the static friction coefficient is very small. Hence stick-slip is totally eliminated.

(v) By pre-loading the ball screw and nut assembly, clearances and consequently backlash can be eliminated and the axial stiffness of the ball screw is high.

(vi) Accuracy of ball screw is high.

4.5.1 General Arrangement of Ball Screws

The basic idea of ball screw is to impose a series of bearing balls between the screw and nut. These balls roll in the grooves as the nut or the screw moves. Thus rolling friction replaces sliding friction.

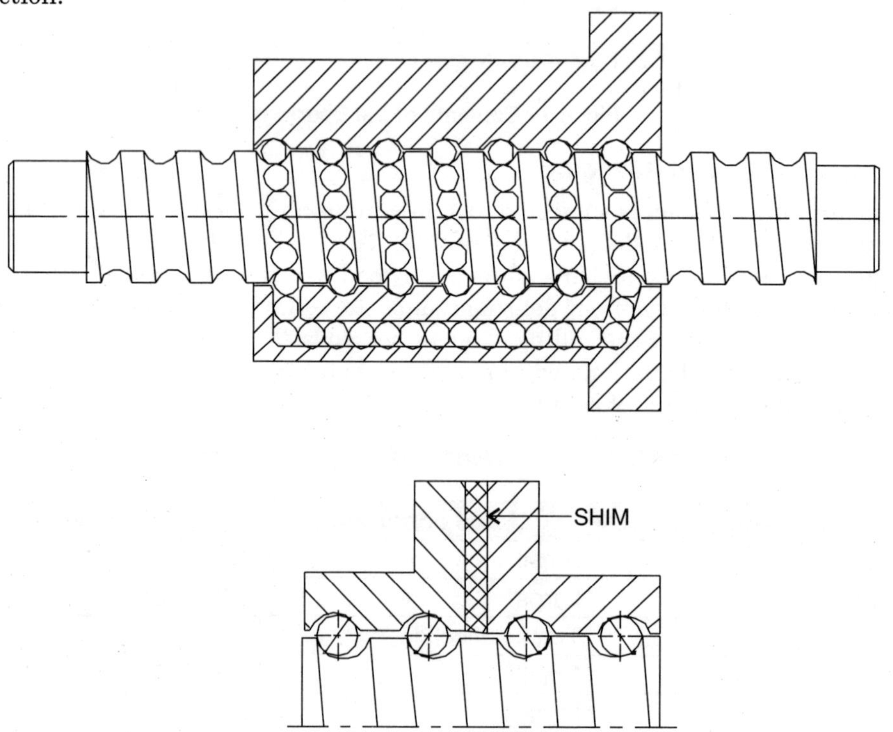

Fig. 4.13 Arrangement of a Ball Screw

Figure 4.13 shows a simplified arrangement of a ball screw. The balls rolling in the thread grooves exit at the trailing end of the nut and are picked up by the return tube inserted from the outside and are recirculated into the leading end of the nut. In some ball screws as shown in Fig. 4.13, the re-circulating path is inside the nut itself. Use of a double nut facilitates preloading. Varying the thickness of the shim, different preloads can be achieved.

The profile of the groove of the screw may be circular or gothic are as shown in Fig. 4.14. Gothic are has the advantage that any dirt that enters the screw is collected in the outer are, allowing the ball to continue to transmit torque smoothly. Circular are grooves allow little axial deformation and greater load capacity.

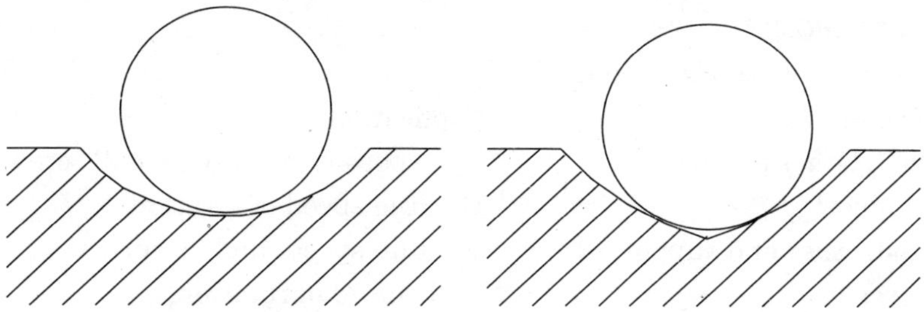

CIRCULAR ARC GOTHIC ARCH

Fig. 4.14 Profile of Ball Screws

The greater the number of balls, greater will be the frictional resistance. Therefore the use of excessive number of balls is not recommended.

4.5.2 Nut Configurations

(i) Round flanged nut with embedded tube for the return of balls.

(ii) Round cylindrical nut with embedded tube.

(iii) Small outside diameter flanged nut with outside tube.

(iv) Rectangular nuts.

Nuts can be double nut or single nut

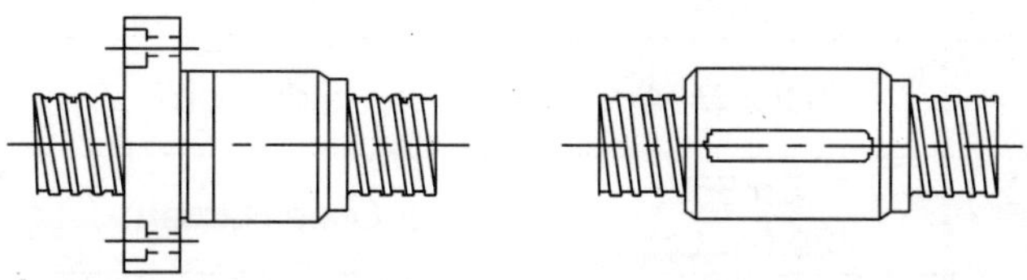

FLANGE END SINGLE NUT ROUND, SINGLE NUT

Fig. 4.15 Single Nut with Internal Recirculation

TUBE ABOVE NUT TUBE INSIDE THE NUT

Fig. 4.16 Flanged End Single Nut Configuration

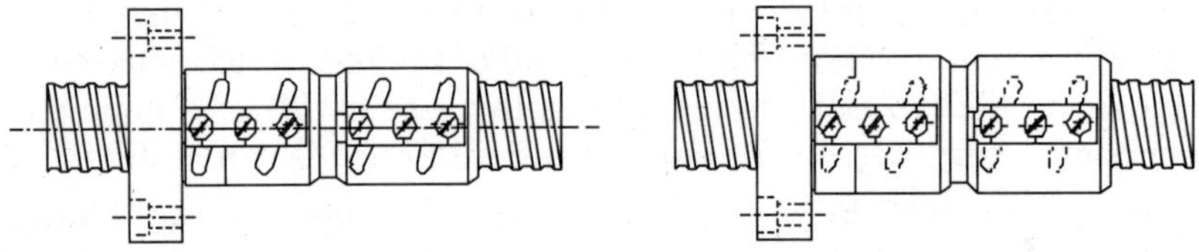

Fig. 4.17 Flange End Double Nut Configuration

4.5.3 Mounting Methods

There are four distinct methods of mounting ball screws.

Mounting Condition	Application
One end fixed, Other end free	Low speed of rotation, small screw life
Both ends supported	Medium speed of rotation
One end fixed, other end supported	Medium speed, high accuracy
Both ends fixed	High speed of rotation, High accuracy

The mounting method is determined from the point of view of design. Careful consideration has to be given to it as the supporting method has a direct relation to stiffness of the screw, critical speed, and allowable load. These factors influence the selection of the diameter of screw.

4.5.4 Materials and Heat Treatment

Table 4.3 gives the recommended materials and heat treatment for ball screw and nut. The ends of ball screws are kept soft to enable the manufacturers to carry out the required sizing.

Table 4.3 Materials and Heat treatment of Ball screw and Nut

	Material	Heat treatment	Hardness
Screw	En 19		
	En 9		
	50Cr M04	Induction	HRC 58 – 62
Nut	En 362 20 Mn Cr5	Case Harden	HRC 58 – 62
Ball	En 31 10 Cr 6	,,	HRC 62 – 66

4.5.5 Pre-Loading

A certain amount of radial and axial clearance exists in ball screws of single nut type. When thrust loads are applied, the balls and grooves are deformed slightly because the balls are pressed down to screws. Backlash is the sum of axial clearance and deformation caused by axial loading.

CNC machines should ensure precise positioning. The drive system of these machines also should have high stiffness. These requirements necessitate elimination of backlash. This is achieved by pre-loading.

The pre-load has to be specified in accordance with the required stiffness. Usually it is limited to one-third of the operating load. A high pre-load will reduce the life of the screw. A lower pre-load will result in reduced stiffness. Pre-loading is applied in general to two nuts either in tension or compression. A shim plate to achieve correct pre-loading is inserted between the two nuts or between the nut and the housing. Then they are tightened with a pre-loading bolt in the direction of compression or pulled with two pre-loading pins in the direction of tension Figure 4.18 illustrates the use of a shim for pre-loading.

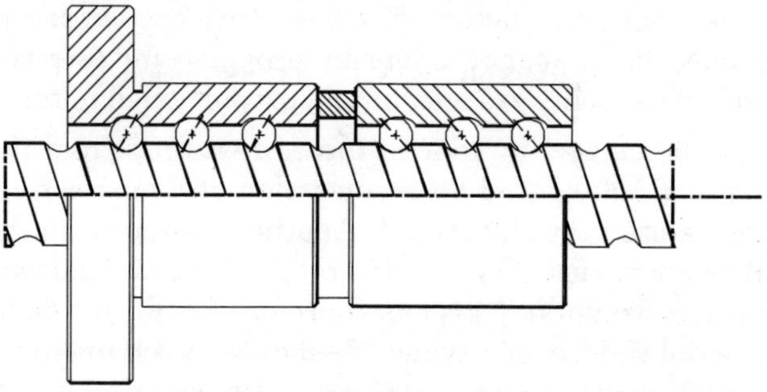

Fig. 4.18 Pre-loading of Ball Screws

A higher pre-load improves positioning accuracy and results in higher stiffness, but requires more torque to drive the screw. Too high a pre-load will result in reduced life and reduction in positioning accuracy depending on the characteristics of the servo loop. A low pre-load also results in low drag torque, low system stiffness and low positioning accuracy.

4.5.6 Accuracy of Ball Screw Drives

Various factors like the cutting processes, geometric and thermal accuracy, static and dynamic rigidity and the positioning response of the feed drives influence the accuracy of work pieces. The various sources of errors which contribute to positioning error are briefly discussed here.

Accuracy is the measure of a control system's capacity to position the slide at a desired target location specified the axis coordinate value. The desired location may lie in between two adjacent control points in the worst case. The accuracy is also influenced by the lost motion due to gear backlash, play in the screws, and deflection in the components of the mechanical positioning system. Backlash includes play in the gearing, any looseness in the bearing or bearing mounting, end play of the screw play between screw and nut, looseness in the nut mounting, and the effect of cocking of the slide. In modern machine tool design and manufacture most of these are eliminated. This is achieved by using high quality precision bearings, pre-loaded double thrust bearings at least at one end of ball screw, and two pre-loaded ball nuts to eliminate backlash between the screw and nut. Wind up and deflection are secondary sources of lost motion. Wind up is the torsional deflection of screws and deflection is the linear compression, stretching or bending of the ball screw. Deflection is a function of stiffness and load and by increasing stiffness the deflection can be reduced. The degree of accuracy and repeatability depends on the type of control system and the location of the feedback unit. Digital absolute encoders are immune to noise and are not influenced by cable capacitance. They support higher resolutions and faster motor speeds. Designers improve the accuracy and repeatability with closed loop digital systems. The mechanical errors form a statistical distribution about the target point as shown in Fig. 4.19. Hence accuracy is equal to half of resolution + 3 σ. Resolution is the range of axis movement divided by the control points usually defined by the feed back device and σ is the standard deviation of the mechanical error.

4.5.6.1 Kinematic Error

The kinematic error is attributed to ball screw pitch error, play in the feed elements, backlash, and pitch loss, which results from a shift of the balls during positioning of ball screw drives with two-point pre-loading. Pitch loss can contribute to a positioning error of 1 to 10 μm.

4.5.6.2 Cutting Force

Cutting forces in CNC machines are in the range of several kN. The effect of cutting force is distributed over the entire machine structure. The feed drive system contributes to only a small portion of the total deformation. A linear encoder can recognize and correct this deformation. The dimensions of the feed drive elements are adequately proportioned to take care of this error.

Deformation can also be caused by inertia forces resulting from the acceleration of the slide. A typical slide mass of 500 kg and an acceleration of 4 m/s^2 can result in deformations of 10 to 20 μm and is therefore very significant. Another source of inaccuracy is friction. The frictional force in guideways varies between 1% to 2% for LM guideways and 3 to 12% for sliding friction guideways. A weight of 5 kN can therefore result in a feed drive deformation of 0.25 to 6 μm. The mean axial rigidity of a typical feed drive mechanism is of the order of 100 to 200 N/μm. Frictional heat is another source of error. A typical pre-load of 3 kN will result in a frictional moment of 0.5 to 1 Nm. When the ball screw is rotating at 2000 rpm, approximately 100 to 200 W is dissipated as heat in the ball screw nut.

4.5.6.3 Type of Ball Screw Bearing

Different types of ball screw bearing arrangements have different effects on the positioning accuracy. In the case of the bearing arrangement where one end is fixed and other end floating, the ball screw will expand freely away from the fixed bearing. This is, therefore, a better arrangement. Continuous operation of the slides will alter the thermal profile on the screw and it will have effect on positioning accuracy.

Some ball screws are commercially available which allow fine adjustment without the use of shim plates.

4.5.6.4 Life and Basic Load Capacity of Ball Screws

The life of ball screw is determined by metal fatigue which leads to flaking on the balls as well as screws. It is difficult to measure such fatigue phenomenon accurately as this depends on conditions under which the ball screw is operated which can vary widely. The rated life is determined in general by a value which more than 90% of the samples can reach without flaking.

The operating life of a ball screw is given by:

$$L = \{C/(F_r.f_w)\}^3.10^6$$

Where L = Operating life, revolution

C = Basic dynamic load rating

F_r = Resultant load, kgf

f_w = Load factor (1 to 3)

Operating Condition	f_w
Smooth running without impact	1.0 to 1.2
Running with impact	1.2 to 1.5
Running with heavy impact and vibration	1.5 to 3.0

Basic load capacity indicates how much load a ball screw can withstand on the application intended. This can be divided into two groups. One is rated dynamic load when nut travels and another, is the rated static load when the nut is at rest.

Rated dynamic load, when the nut travels with load always in one direction, such a load gives 1×10^6 nut revolutions. This is the rated dynamic load, C_a.

Rated Static Load: This is the load that causes a permanent deformation of a ten thousandth of ball diameter.

4.5.7 Selection of Ball Screws

The factors influencing the selection of ball screws are load, stroke, life, accuracy, driving torque, backlash, stiffness, lead, screw diameter etc. They are all inter-related. A larger screw diameter ensures higher stiffness, but increases inertia. If the lead is fine, positioning accuracy increases and driving torque required will be small. However, this requires high rotating speeds to achieve the required positioning speed. Since smaller diameter balls are to be used, the stiffness is reduced. On the other hand, coarse lead will reduce rotational speed, increase ball size and consequently stiffness. The driving torque increases. There may be a slight reduction in the positioning accuracy.

4.5.8 Tolerances of Ball Screws (After DIN 69051)

The accuracy classes of ball screws are specified by DIN 69051. Typical accuracy classes are 5,10, 25 etc. A class 10 ball screw will have a pitch error of 0.005 mm over a length of 300 mm.

4.6 AUTOMATIC TOOL CHANGER [ATC]

The versatility of the machining centre is partly due to the ATC. An ATC picks up the tool from the magazine and keeps it ready for swapping with the tool in the spindle which is presently cutting. The tool change time [chip to chip] varies between 0.5 second in the case of some of the high speed machines to 5 seconds. ATC plays a significant role in reducing idle time in the case of a machining centre.

The tool change function is M06. Regardless of the machine tool used two conditions are necessary to perform automatic tool change correctly.

(i) Spindle must be stopped M05.

(ii) Tool changing axis must be at the home position (Machine reference. position).

A double ended arm is used for tool changing. There are a number of variations in the double ended arm. One is the design of the arm itself. The other variation is in the relative movement between arm and spindle during tool change. Quill type spindle generally move out to the arm to accept a new tool or return the previous tool.

The concept of armless ATC's is employed in some vertical machining centres. Here the magazine itself moves to withdraw the tool from the spindle and insert a new tool. This process is usually slow.

Apart from the tool changer features, programmer should take care of the following:

(i) Maximum tool diameter

(ii) Maximum tool length

(iii) Maximum tool weight

4.7 TOOL MAGAZINE

A typical CNC machining centre is equipped with a special tool magazine that stores all tools required for a machining program. It may be good practice to keep commonly used tools in the magazine all the time. A typical 16 – tool magazine is illustrated in Fig. 4.19. The capacity of a tool magazine may be as low as 12 tools and as high as a few hundred tools on special machines. A medium size machining centre will have between 40 and 60 tools. A magazine consists of a certain number of pockets in which a tool holder along with a tool is placed during set up. The tool magazine can be indexed under program control or manually to bring any pocket to a desired position or tool changing position or waiting position which is aligned with the tool changer.

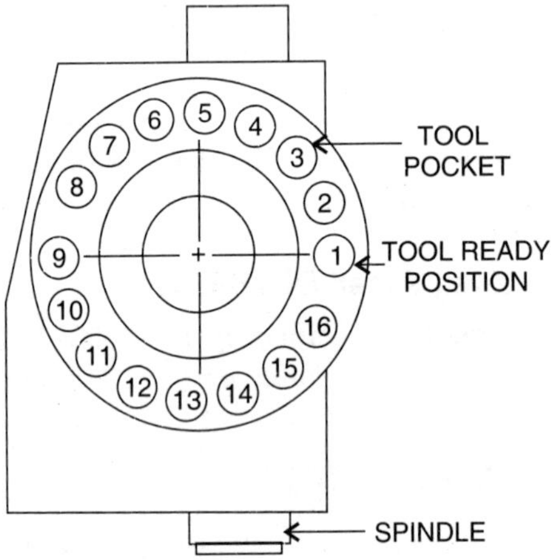

Fig. 4.19 Tool Magazine

Tool magazines should satisfy the following requirements:

(i) Tool magazines must be capable of holding enough tools needed for performing complete operations for some typical operations on the machining centres.

(ii) As the magazine gets larger and larger, the space required is more and it adds to the cost of the machine.

(iii) The interchange of tools should not interfere with the workpiece space and tool space.

(iv) The magazine should facilitate easy and safe manual exchange of tools.

4.8 WORK TABLES

One or more work tables with suitable provision for clamping of fixtures or workpieces are supplied with the machining centres. These can be tilted or indexed to present a new surface for machining. Hinges in the case of horizontal machining centre do tilting of tables. These are provided at the side of the table closest to the column and the table is tilted from the other side using a ball screw. Other designs employ a trunnion type carrier that hinges the table through a pivot running through the tables centre line. One innovative approach mounts one rotary table on top of and at 45° angle to a second rotary table. By coordinating the two rotations the unit can present the work at compound angles to the spindle.

A variety of drive systems, including Geneva mechanism for simple indexing have been used. A typical drive arrangement for a rotary table uses an AC servo motor connected to a worm drive that rotate the table on pre-loaded roller bearings. Backlash is usually taken by double lead method in which pre-loaded worm drives are combined with double pinions to the driven gear rim.

The control loop to CNC is closed by readings from a precision encoder or optical reader. Some ultra precision encoders have resolutions up to 180000 counts per revolution (1 count = 0.0002°). Rotation is halted at the end of indexing and the table is clamped hydro-mechanically.

Positioning accuracy is expressed as the plus and minus value of half the difference between the commanded angle and the angle that is actually rotated. Positioning accuracies between 10 – 15 arc seconds on a medium sized machine are usually quoted.

The work table or pallet in a horizontal machine is usually of square type with rounded or chamfered corners. The top of the table is provided with necessary T-slots, centre holes, tapped holes for locating the component or fixture. The table is either designed to have a continuous rotary motion or indexing facility. The indexing resolution is normally provided are 90°, 5°, 2.5° or 1° and is achieved by curvic couplings. The maximum permissible load depends on the size of the machine and the design of the table and related elements.

4.9 AUTOMATIC PALLET CHANGER

The setting up time and operating time of the components machined in machining centre are usually high. During set up time, the machine which will have several hundreds of Rupees of machine hour rate (MHR) will be idle. For example, if it take 2 ½ hours to set up the workpiece on a machine with ₹ 1000 MHR, a loss of ₹ 2500 will result. A solution to avoid this kind of loss is to have a second table on which the next workpiece can be set up while one component set upon one table is being machined. The worktables are called pallets. While the component on one pallet is being machined, the operator sets up the next component on the second pallet.

After completing the first component, the pallet concerned moves to the unloading position and the second pallet moves to the machining position. This will take only a few seconds. Thus the interval between finishing of one part and starting the machining of another part will be only a few seconds. The operator can now unload the finished component and then load the new component. The mechanism for changing the pallet is called an automatic pallet changer (APC). The operation of an APC is illustrated in Fig. 4.20. A machine can have 7,8 or even 32 pallets. The CNC system can be programmed to machine the component one after another. Thus APC is a very useful option for unattended manufacturing.

The pallet when transferred from the pallet changer to the machine gets located and clamped either hydraulically or mechanically. The function of pallet changer is to interchange the pallet on the machine which carries the finished component and the other pallet with the newly loaded component.

Reducing idle time by setting up one workpiece while spindle works on another can be accomplished in a number of other ways. One is travelling column and moving gantry machines that cover a bed which can accommodate two or more parts. Indexing type table is some times used to save set up time in vertical machining centres. Two workpieces are set up on the table. After one work is completed, the table is indexed in the X – direction to bring next workpiece under the spindle. The machining space is isolated so that the operator can safely unload the finished part and load a new workpiece.

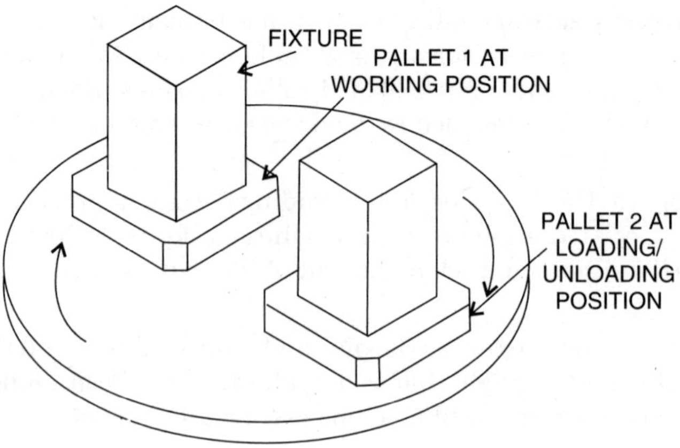

Fig. 4.20 Automatic Pallet Changer

There are two types of pallet changers:

- Rotary Pallet Changer
- Shuttle Type Pallet Changer

Figure 4.20 shows a rotary pallet changer. The principle of working of a shuttle type pallet changer has been described in chapter 7.

Palletizing is a procedure in which components are mounted in a suitable pallet off-line and then moved to the machining centre to load on it. Palletizing is widely used in FMS installations. Even when there is a variety of workpieces, palletizing is economical.

4.10 SPINDLES

A spindle in a CNC machine is used to hold and rotate on form the workpiece or hold and rotate or move a cutting tool. The requirements of spindles in a CNC machine are:

(i) High static and dynamic stiffness
(ii) High running accuracy
(iii) High axial and radial load carrying capacity
(iv) Thermal stability

Nowadays, the trend is ever-increasing spindle speeds. Hence, the above requirements should be satisfied over a wide range of spindle speeds.

Bearings used normally on CNC machine spindles are angular contact ball bearing. These bearings are used singly or two's or three's, depending on the load. The advantages of angular contact ball bearings are high speeds of operation and good axial and radial load carrying capacity. Multiple bearings reduce the overall size of the spindle as well as bearing housing. There are many designs where other types of bearings are also used. High speed spindles often use ceramic balls. The spindle is hollow to take care of bar feeding and the operation of hydraulic chuck on the clamping of the tool holder, spindle rigidity is achieved by ample pre-loading. This enables faster acceleration/deceleration and reduced vibration during high speed operation in many high speed cooling arrangements are provided both for the stator and the bearings.

4.11 BEDS AND COLUMNS

The way the machining forces are directed into the bed of the machine can have considerable influence on the accuracy, cutting forces are directed on to the bed in a loop from the spindle to the workpiece and bed and back towards the spindle. It is necessary to minimize the length of the force loop. This results in extreme rigidity and accuracy without excessive dead weight. Cast or welded box type structures are generally used for beds and columns. Large base structures can be fabricated with concrete plus resin mixture which yields high rigidity and reduced vibration.

The column is heavily ribbed to providing high static stiffness and dynamic rigidity.

The beds of CNC lathes designed generally with a slant bed configuration. This design permits closed box type construction with easy chip fall. Apart from ensuring high rigidity, this design permits a chip conveyor to be attached to transport the chip to a bin located outside the machine. The slant bed design enables the setting up or inspection of the tools on the turret, usually mounted on the rear side of the machine. Epoxy concrete and concrete mixed with other synthetic material are also used in some high precision machines. These beds have high vibration damping capacity.

4.12 TURRETS

CNC lathes are fitted with 8-12 or 16 station turrets. Figure 4.21 shows a typical tool turret which consists of a tool plate which can hold both axial [drills, boring bars, taps, dies) and radial (turning, external threading, external grooving etc.). Axial tools should not be placed in adjacent slots as it may cause interference with the workpiece.

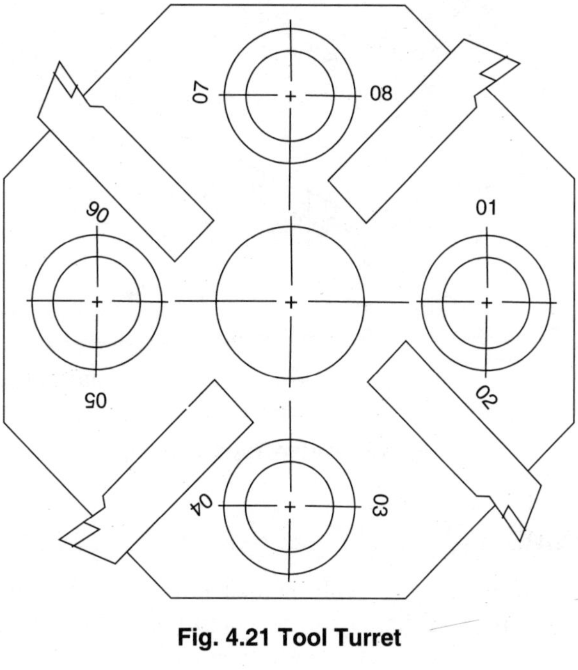

Fig. 4.21 Tool Turret

Axial tools require special adaptors. The tool plate is indexed under program control. The indexing accuracy is achieved by using a Hurth Coupling on a curvic coupling. The indexing accuracy will be of the order of two seconds of an arc. The tool positions are coded and a feedback device, usually an encoder is used to monitor tool positioning. The indexing is bi-directional to minimize indexing time.

There are different types of tool turrets:

(i) Pneumatic: These are generally used in small training machines.

(ii) Electromechanical: These are most popular. Indexing is carried out using a mechanism like Geneva mechanism. This is usually powered by a small indirection motor.

(iii) Hydro-mechanical: These are powered by a hydraulic motor. These are fast indexing and are extremely robust in design. There are rotated and locked hydraulically.

(iv) Hydraulic with AC Servo technology. These are meant for high speed operation. The rotation of turret is through an AC servo motor. They will be locked hydraulically. These are also suitable for backward turning.

In turning centres, it is required to use live tools. An AC servo motor is used to provide rotation for the tool.

4.13 PLATEN TYPE OR LINEAR TOOLING

Cost of a turret tool post is high. In order to reduce cost CNC chuckers are fitted with linear tooling. The tools are mounted on the cross slide at suitable intervals and are programmed to perform operations on the workpiece. A linear tooling arrangement is shown in Fig. 4.22.

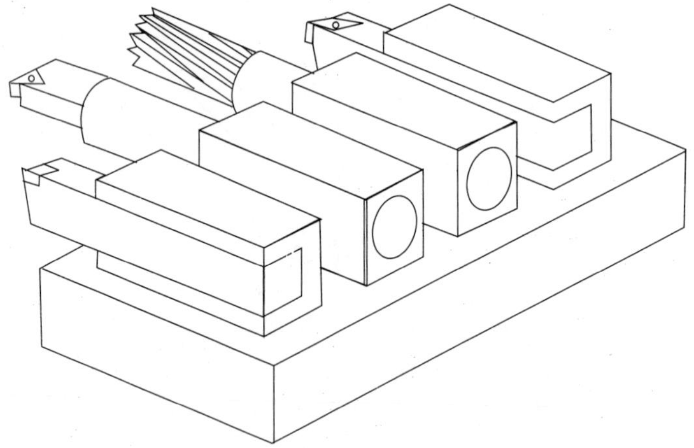

Fig. 4.22 Platen Type Tooling

4.14 CHIP CONVEYORS

CNC turning machines produce large volumes of chips which are difficult to dispose off manually. A chip conveyor is often fitted to the machine. Chips fall directly on the conveyor which transports them to a bin which later can be emptied conveniently. Chip conveyors can be mechanical or magnetic.

4.15 FEEDBACK DEVICES

The accuracy of positioning in CNC Machine tools is achieved by measuring the position/ displacement of the slide and comparing it with the commanded position in the part program. The servo system actuates the slide such that the error which is the difference between programmed position and commanded position is brought to zero. The position of the slide can be measured directly by fitting a linear transducer to the slide or indirectly by mounting a rotary transducer to the ball screw of the slide or mounting the transducer on the servo motor shaft. Direct measurement is preferred for more accurate positioning. However, today, a majority of CNC machines are designed with the feedback device mounted on the rear side of the servo motor. Any backlash in the ball screw and nut and the pitch error in the lead screw can be compensated in software. The indirect feedback is more economical and adequate for most of the CNC machine tools particularly when the ball screw used is of a higher class of accuracy. Feedback devices can be broadly classified into:

(i) Digital incremental measuring devices
(ii) Digital absolute measuring devices
(iii) Analog measuring devices

4.16 DIGITAL INCREMENTAL DISPLACEMENT MEASURING SYSTEMS

Digital measuring methods offer three fundamental advantages when applied to numerical control systems for machine tools:

(i) The measured value can be transmitted directly to a numerical data processing unit. This means that once the measurement is available in the digital form the accuracy of its further processing depends only on the number of significant figures it contains.
(ii) The data can be processed numerically right from the moment when it is originally produced (from the time when the drawings are made) to the end of the process (even to the inspection machine), without the use of any linear measurement converter, digital/ analog converter etc. It is therefore, possible to minimize the control circuitry.
(iii) It is possible to provide a numerical value for the actual position of the slide using very simple means.

One of the most important preliminary decisions that have to be made when selecting suitable components for digital processing of machine tool data is the maximum pulse-rate of the displacement data to be processed. This depends on the velocity of the machine tool slide and the magnitude of the displacement elements. To reduce idle times rapid traverse speeds of 10 to 15 m/min. or more are common. So this range must be included in the consideration. In majority of practical instances, it is necessary to use electronic components and circuits that are suitable for frequencies of 20 to 30 GHz and above. These frequencies are well within the capabilities of modern semiconductors. In practice, it is often better to design a system on the pulse rise time (switching time) instead of the frequency. The digital measuring scales become very costly when graduated to closer than 0.01mm because of high precision required in their manufacture and installation. Hence, where such extremely small displacement data have to be used (such as for jig borers) use is either made of some other method or an electronic dividing circuit.

Another factor that affects the design and selection of components is the necessity of ensuring reliable operation, even for very slow movements of slides. There are numerous ways in which it is technically possible to create digital displacement measuring system. Some basic design possibilities are as follows:

(a) Incremental and absolute measuring processes

(b) Displacement measuring systems using rotary and linear movements.

The characteristic feature of the incremental process is that the displacement elements are summed in a counter which is external to the displacement measuring unit itself. It is a fundamental requirement for this process to ensure that no extraneous information is fed into the counter. In the displacement measuring unit, the displacement elements are transformed into electrical pulses which are routed via a connecting cable to an electronic counter which must be easily capable of dealing with a counting rate of at least 30,000 pulses per second. Difficulties occur more in the pulse generating unit rather than in the electronic counter.

There are mainly two possible sources of error in these measurements:

(i) Vibration of machine tool caused by heavy cuts and unbalance vibrations. This can be transmitted to the displacement measuring unit and can generate additional pulses. If under adverse and unfavourable conditions the amplitude of the vibration exceeds about 3 to 4 micrometers, spurious pulses can be generated in the measuring system which can be registered by the counter even though the slide is stationary.

(ii) Modern machine tools often have electrical control systems incorporating numerous relays. There are also frequently a large number of inductive loads supplied with direct current (Solenoid operated valves etc. with one side of the supply earthed to the body of the machine) and these produce very undesirable switching effects, despite the low voltage on which they operate. As a result machine tool circuits carry many spurious voltages and inductive or capacitive coupling can cause these to have adverse effects on precision measurements involving electronic instruments.

Two methods are available for countering spurious pulses of the first type (due to vibration). These are as follows:

(a) Mechanical Method: The machine tool and the measuring instruments are made as stiff as possible and in addition the displacement measuring unit is arranged so that any vibrations that occur will have minimal effect upon it.

(b) Electrical Method: The displacement measuring unit is designed so that it is directional in its response. No vibrating motion can then produce a spurious increment.

The spurious pulses of the second type (induced spurious pulses) are always purely electrical phenomena. These can be eliminated as follows:

(a) Suppression of the spurious pulses at source: In this case careful suppression will be needed throughout the installation. It will be necessary to avoid inductive effects by incorporating usual circuit devices such as local surge voltage suppression on all switched inductors, spark suppression at all switch contacts, strict separation of the power and control circuit wiring from the measuring circuit wiring, independent earthing of all electronic components avoiding the body of the machine tool, and careful shielding of the measuring circuit wiring.

(b) Elimination of spurious pulses by an evaluation circuit: This can be achieved, for e.g., by giving the measuring pulses characteristics 'Signature', which differentiates them from the spurious pulses directly at the pulse source.

An important feature of the incremental measurement system is that the datum can be selected anywhere along the length of the scale and hence at any position within the working range of the machine tool. This is a major advantage of the incremental control system. It is sometimes desirable to locate the datum in some fixed position depending on the type of machine, or to arrange the datum to be variable only within certain limits. This situation is necessary for machines that perform a single stroke operation.

In every instance where advantage is to be taken of the simple free choice of datum position, care must be taken to ensure that equipment is available on the machine which will enable the initial position of the workpiece, relative to the tool, to be determined with sufficient accuracy to enable the counter to be 'set to zero' at this point. When the datum is fixed on the machine slide, this must be provided with an index mark to enable the particular tool in use to be calibrated, when the datum is determined relating to the workpieces.

4.17 INCREMENTAL ROTARY ENCODERS

The design of an incremental rotary encoder is shown in Fig. 4.23. The visible exterior of the unit includes the shaft, the flange, the rotor housing and output cable.

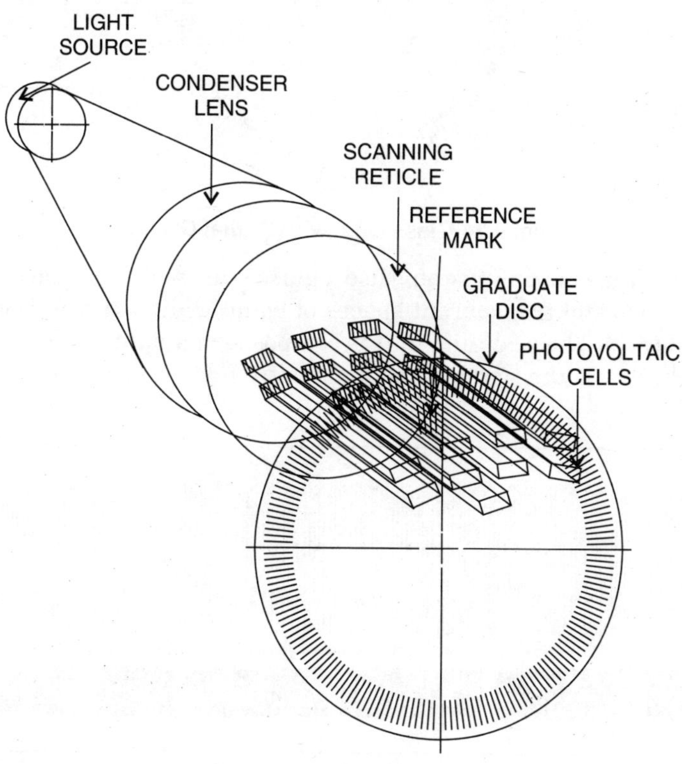

Fig. 4.23 Incremental Rotary Encoder

The shaft carries a graduated glass disc with radial grating (Fig. 4.24). The opaque lines which are about as wide as the transparent gap between them consist of chromium applied through vapour deposition process. Mounted on the flange at a small distance from the graduated disc is a scanning reticule with four small fields, each with a grating identical to that on the disc. The four fields of lines are phase shifted in relation to each other by one-fourth of the grating pitch. On both the graduated disc and the scanning reticule there is an additional reference mark either in the form of a single line for coarser graduations or a group of lines for finer graduations. All these fields are penetrated by a beam of collimated light produced by a light source and condenser lens. The beam of light is modulated during rotation of the graduated disc and falls on to solar cells which generate two sinusoidal output signals (phase shifted by 90 deg) and a reference mark signal. One signal cycle of 360 deg corresponds to the angle of rotation of one pitch of the radial grating i.e. one line and one space. The sinusoidal output signal is converted into square wave output signals with digitizing electronics. These signals are then externally interpolated to obtain 5,10,25 or 50 signal cycles corresponding to one pitch of radial grating.

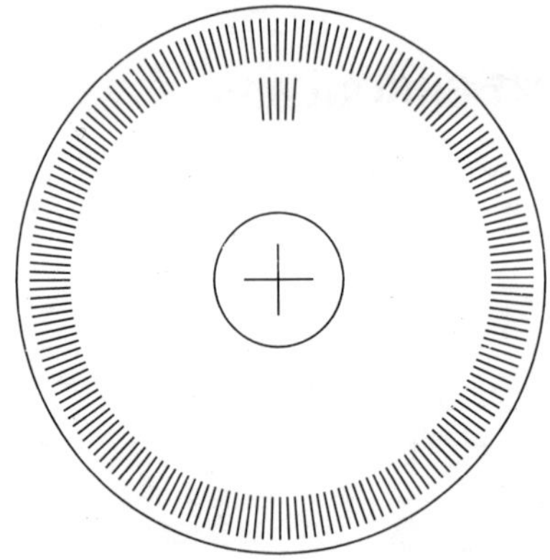

Fig. 4.24 Glass Disc with Radial Grating

Incremental linear measuring systems use a glass scale with line grating (Fig. 4.25), which consists of opaque lines and transparent spaces of equal width. One or more reference marks constitute a second tract. The scanning unit is composed of a light source, a condenser lens for collimating the light beam, the scanning reticule with index gratings and silicon solar cells.

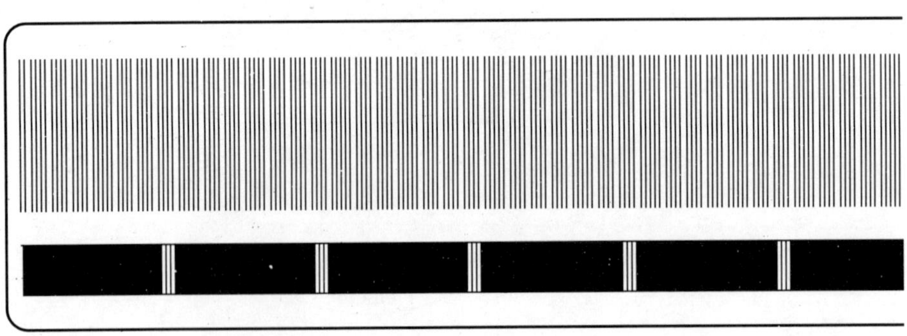

Fig. 4.25 Incremental Linear Measuring System

When the scale is moved relative to the scanning unit the lines and spaces of the scale alternately coincide with those of the index gratings. The corresponding fluctuations of light are sensed by solar cells which generate two output signals (phase shifted by 90 deg) and a reference mark signal. Using digitizing and interpolation circuitry the number of pulses for one pitch of grating can be increased by a factor of 5,10, 25 or 50.

4.18 MOIRE' FRINGES

The Moiré' fringe effect is produced when an optical grating slides in a direction at right angles to its lines over another similar optical grating with its lines inclined at a slight angle to those on the other grating. This interference fringe effect manifests itself as a pattern of light and dark alternating bands, and progressive movement one grating relative to the other causes the pattern to go through a cycle i.e., from light to dark and back again. Because these bands are, in essence, a magnified image of the pitch or spacing of the lines on the optical grating, these can be detected by a system incorporating photo electric cells and hence provide a highly accurate method of measuring small movements.

4.19 THE DIGITAL ABSOLUTE MEASURING SYSTEM

A numerical control system in which all positional dimensions are measured with respect to a common datum point is called a digital absolute system. In such a system, the transducers therefore give a direct reading of position with reference to the common datum. All position commands are given as absolute distances from that datum point (zero point). The zero point may be either a floating or a fixed point. A zero floating allows the operator by pushing a button to select arbitrarily the zero reference point at any point within the limits of machine tool table. The control unit retains no information on the location of any previous zeros.

The main advantage of the absolute system as compared with the incremental one is in cases of interruption that force the operator to stop the machine. With an absolute system, in case of an interruption like tool breakage, table is manually moved and the cause of the interruption is eliminated. When restarting the program, the table is automatically returned to its last position and the operation proceeds from the same place that it was interrupted. With an incremental system, any time the work is interrupted, before switching on again, the operator must bring the tool manually to the exact place of the last operation in which the interruption occurred.

Fig. 4.26 Absolute Rotary Encoder

Figure 4.26 shows an absolute rotary encoder. These derive the angle positions directly from the code pattern of the graduated disc and convert it into a coded signal which corresponds to one definite angle position. Multi-turn absolute rotary encoders provide electronically coded measured values not only for one but also for several revolutions. The code pattern on the disc has several tracks. The number of tracks depends upon the desired resolution and the type of code. Each track is assigned its own solar cell so that all tracks can be read simultaneously. Most frequently used code is Gray code. This is a code, which prevents gross errors in signal transfer. Gray coded measured value can be electronically converted to corresponding positions. Absolute encoders are preferred by many machine tool designers nowadays.

4.20 ELECTROMAGNETIC ANALOG POSITION TRANSDUCERS

4.20.1 Synchros and Synchro-resolvers

A synchro is an electromagnetic position transducer comprising a rotor and a stator with a number of windings (Fig. 4.27). The level of output voltage depends upon the angular position of the rotor. The peak value of the voltage induced in the rotor winding varies sinusoidally with the angle of rotation of the rotor. The voltage reduces to zero when the axis of the rotor coil coincides with the field vector of the stator.

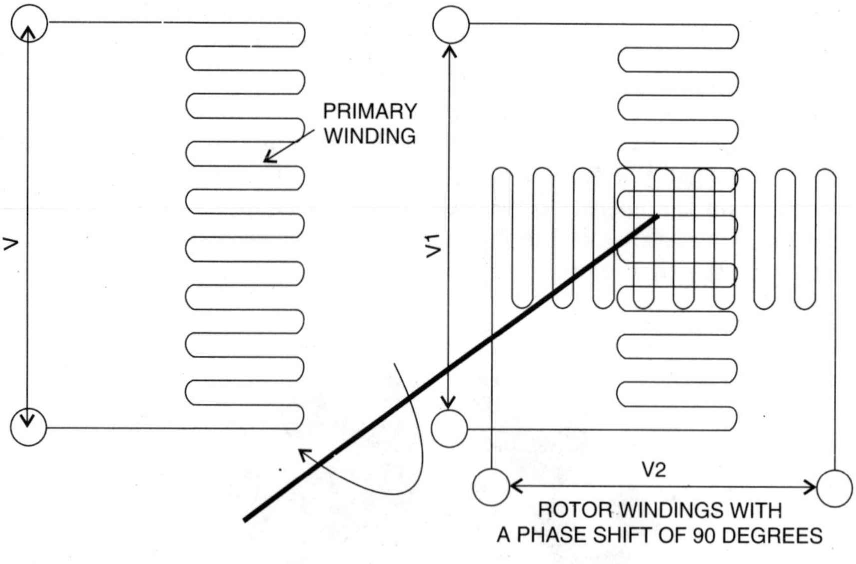

Fig. 4.27 Synchro Resolver

A synchro resolver (resolver) has the windings at exactly 90 deg to each other and resolves the voltage into two components at a phase difference of 90 deg. The peak values of these components vary sinusoidally: they, therefore, vary as sine and cosine values corresponding to the angular position of the rotor shaft. The angular position of the rotor for null depends upon the ratio of the voltages on the two stator windings – one winding is supplied with a voltage proportional to sin θ and the other winding is supplied with a voltage corresponding to cos θ where θ is the angular position of the rotor shaft.

4.20.2 Application of Synchros and Resolvers

The desired position of a machine tool slide is expressed as a linear dimension, i.e., as a coordinate in a digital form. This coordinate value is recorded in binary code on punched tape and is used as the input data for the machine control unit. The digital information passed as signal to a Digital/Analog converter. This unit converts the coordinate value from its digital form to corresponding analog form i.e., a voltage. This voltage is fed to the stator coils of the synchro. The voltage induced in the rotor and expressed, as a voltage output through the phase sensor is an error signal. It corresponds to the difference between the desired position of the rotor and its actual position. The error signal is amplified and used to initiate action by a servo motor. This drives the lead screw in a direction which will reduce the error signal to zero and the slide is at the desired position.

4.20.3 Inductosyn

The inductosyn is a precision feedback device for the accurate measurement and control of angles or linear distances with inductive coupling between conductors separated by a small air gap. Accuracy of better than one second of arc and linear accuracy of better than 0.5 microns is achieved.

There are two forms in inductosyns. Rotary form is used in precision servo systems on machine tools and other equipment as a primary signal generator for shaft digitizers. The linear form provides means for accurate control of elements moving in translation and widely used in automatic machine tool controls. Figure 4.28 shows rotary and linear and inductosyn.

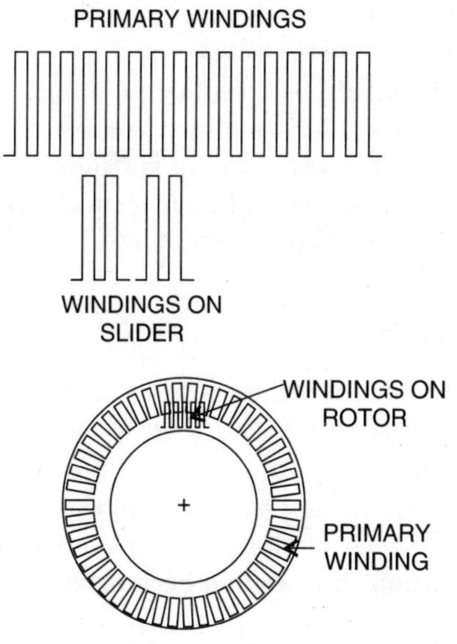

Fig. 4.28 Linear and Rotary Inductosyns

4.20.4 The Operating Principle of Inductosyn

The operating principle of inductosyn i.e., rotary inductosyn is similar to resolver. The output signal developed is a function of rotation angle and is obtained by inductive coupling between stationary and moving conductors. The principle is like gonimeter which consists of two stationary (crossed) coils would as shown in Figure 4.29. There are two rotor coils on two rotor shafts connected together as transmitter and receiver. If an AC voltage is applied to the rotary coil of the transmitter, a maximum voltage will be induced in rotary coil of the receiver when the two rotors are at the same angle with respect to their associated stators and a null voltage will occur at +90 deg from this position. As the rotor of the transmitter is turned, the induced voltage in one stator coil follows a sine curve and the voltage induced in the other follows a cosine curve. Similarly in Inductosyn the coils are metallic deposits on insulated discs or plates and are in the form of hairpin turns. In rotary inductosyn large number of poles is provided so that the stator sine and cosine voltages are in the form of sin (n θ) and cosine (n θ) where θ is the angle of rotation and n is the number of poles.

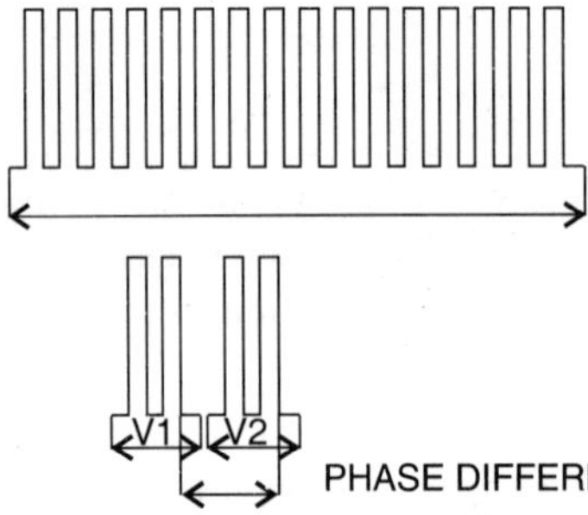

Fig. 4.29 Principle of Operation of an Inductosyn

The rotary inductosyn may be used in pairs as angular data transmitter and receiver in a similar manner to the use of resolvers or as a device for absolute angular measurement or for producing an angle in response to a control input.

The principle of linear inductosyn is similar to rotary. Here linear distances being equivalent to angles. The stator is known as slider and rotor as scale. Either slider or scale may comprise the moving element, the other being stationary. The signals are averaged over a distance corresponding to 32 to 48 cycles. In linear form the poles are at intervals of a linear distance (usually 1.25 mm) giving a distance per cycle of 1.25 mm.

4.21 LASER INTERFEROMETER

Interferometric techniques have been developed due to the demand for greater accuracy and due to inherent manufacturing errors which lead to decreased accuracy in conventional position and velocity transducers.

Conventional light sources are limited to path lengths 200 mm and traverse rates of 10 mm/sec. Because of lack of coherence of the beam and poor signal to noise ratios. The gas laser has made a major contribution in this field because of its extremely high coherence and frequency stability which enabled industrial practical interferometers to be developed with positional resolution of part in 10^6 over path lengths of several hundred metres.

The advantages of laser interferometer are as follows:

(i) Laser interferometers are being used for calibrating testing measurements of machine tools, inspection precision measurements. The measurement ranges extend up to 91.5 metres for displacement and up to 3 metres/sec for velocity.

(ii) Digital output in binary coded decimal form enables positional resolution up to 7.62×10^{-5} mm. The output in digital binary coded decimal form enables for a direct interface with an NC computer.

(iii) This can be used in wide environmental conditions and does not require highly skilled operator.

(iv) The beam can be deflected readily by means of prisms or mirrors to reach required point.

Laser interferometers are mainly used for the calibration of CNC Machine Tools.

REVIEW QUESTIONS

(1) What are the advantages of using a gear box in the spindle drive of a CNC machine tool? Sketch the torque speed characteristics with and without a gear box.

(2) Why is AC variable speed drive preferred for the main drive of a CNC machine tool.

(3) Discuss the advantages of an integral rotor spindle.

(4) What is the purpose of a spindle encoder?

(5) Sketch the torque speed characteristics of a AC spindle drive.

(6) What are the factors to be considered in the selection of the axis feed drive of a machine tool?

(7) What are the advantages of AC servo drives?

(8) What are the factors to be considered in sizing the servo motors?

(9) What are the factors to be considered in selecting the servo drive for the axis feed drive of a CNC machine? What are the advantages of digital drives?

(10) A CNC lathe has the following design specifications:

(i) Weight of the table:	2000N
(ii) Maximum chip size:	2 sq.mm in medium carbon steel
(iii) Size of ball screw:	50 mm diameter, 10 mm pitch
(iv) Maximum linear speed:	20 m/min.
(v) Maximum feed:	4 m/min
(vi) Type of drive:	Directly coupled.
(vii) Type of slide way:	fitted with Turcite-B inserts

Assume other data required and determine the rating of the servo motor.

(11) A vertical CNC machining centre has the following specifications:

(i) Feedrate:	1-60 000 mm/min.
(ii) Rapid traverse:	60 m/min.
(iii) Weight of the table:	9000 N
(iv) Maximum weight of workpiece:	3600 N
(v) Type of guideway:	L.M. system
(vi) Power of main motor:	11 kW

Assume suitable data estimate the rating of the servo motor to drive the Y-axis.

(12) What are the advantages of ball screws which make it very suitable for application in CNC machines?

(13) Explain the constructional features of a re-circulating ball screw and nut assembly.

(14) Sketch and explain the common mounting arrangement of ball screws. What are their advantages and disadvantages?

(15) How is the ball screws pre-loaded? How does pre-loading influence the friction and friction coefficient?

(16) What are the factors affecting the accuracy of feed drives?

(17) Why stick-slip is an undesirable phenomenon in axis feed drives of CNC machines?

(18) What is backlash? Why is backlash undesirable? How do you control backlash through pre-loading? What is meant by backlash compensation?

(19) Define pitch error and cumulative pitch error with reference to a re-circulating ball screw. How is pitch error compensated?

(20) Sketch the feed drive system of a CNC machine tool- in open loop and closed loop. What are the advantages of closed loop systems?

(21) Discuss the trade off between the accuracy of ball screws and accuracy of encoders in obtaining the desirable positioning accuracy.

(22) How does the size of the ball screw influence the accuracy of positioning?

(23) Sketch an axis feed drive and explain the feed back loops for position (displacement) control and feed rate control. What are the different options available for deciding the locations of the feedback devices in a axis feed drive of a CNC machine tool? What are the relative advantages and disadvantages of these options?

(24) What are the requirements of slide ways of CNC Machines? Why are plastic slide ways superior to plain metal to metal contact slide ways ?

(25) What are the benefits of LM systems?

(26) What are the common indexing mechanisms used the turrets of CNC lathes?

(27) What are the advantages of platen type tooling in CNC lathes?

(28) How are feedback devices classified?

(29) Sketch an incremental rotary encoder and explain the working principle.

(30) Sketch an incremental linear encoder and explain the working principle.

(31) How does an analog measuring device like synchro resolver differ from a digital incremental measuring device like rotary encoder?

(32) Compare the cost and position measurement accuracy of digital incremental and analog feedback devices in CNC machines.

(33) Compare the capabilities of an inductosyn and a synchro resolver.

(34) Sketch and explain the working principle of a rotary inductosyn.

(35) Describe the stages in processing the feedback signals from encoders.

(36) How is the direction of motion detected in a feedback transducer signal?

(37) How does a linear motor work?

(38) What are the significant advantages of linear motor?

(39) What are the advantages of a laser interferometer for the calibration of a CNC machine tool? How do you determine the accuracy and repeatability of positioning in a CNC machine tool?

5 PROCESS DEFINITION FOR CNC MACHINING

Process definition is a critical activity in NC programming. There are several Alternative processes possible for manufacturing a part. The programmer must explore the optimum solution and make the best use of the developments in the tooling technology to realize parts with the required quality at the lowest cost.

5.1 INTRODUCTION

In manual manufacturing the quality, accuracy and productivity depend on the skill of the operator. The consistency of these important factors is linked to the state of mental alertness or the level of fatigue of the operator. The advantage of the CNC lies in the fact that the quality, accuracy and productivity do not depend on the operator. These are determined by the machine, the process and the tools used. Proper design of the process is, therefore very important. The definition or the design of the process influences the cost of manufacture also. The aim of the programmer should be to minimize the time of manufacture and thereby minimize the cost.

5.2 FUNDAMENTALS OF METAL CUTTING

A large number of CNC machines are designed for metal cutting. Therefore it is appropriate at this stage to review some fundamental issues in metal cutting.

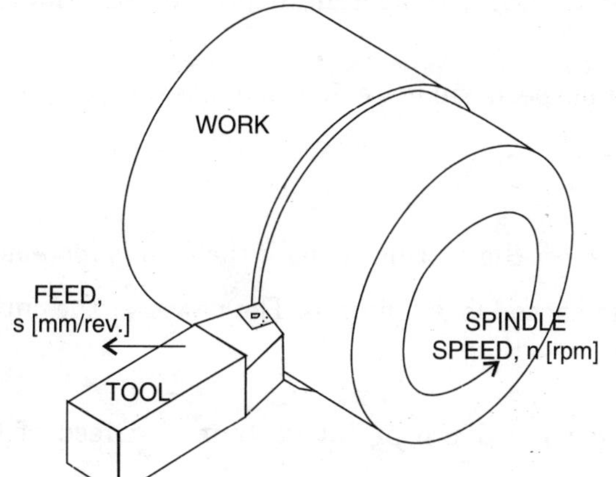

Fig. 5.1 Turning Operation

Figure 5.1 shows a typical turning operation. The important cutting parameters are the cutting speed, feed and depth of cut.

5.2.1 Cutting Speed

Cutting speed, expressed in m/min or m/sec, is the relative linear velocity between the tool and work material. The cutting speed, V is calculated using the formula

$$V = \pi\, d\, n/1000, \text{ m/min.}$$

Where d = diameter of work piece or tool, mm

n = rpm of work piece or tool, mm

Engineering components may be made out of steel, plastics, non-ferrous materials, cast iron, composites or many other materials. Similarly there are varieties of materials out of which tools are made. These include high-speed steel, various types and grades of cemented carbides, ceramics, cubic boron nitride, diamond and a variety of other special tools. There exists a range of cutting speeds for a combination of work material and tool material. Usually, cutting speeds are selected for a specified tool life. Higher the cutting speed, shorter will be the life of the tool. This is illustrated in Fig. 5.2.

Economics is an important consideration for the selection of cutting speed for rough machining. In the case of manual machining, tool cost and tool-changing cost contribute significantly to the total cost of machining, as the machine hour rate is comparatively less. Hence the economic tool life is taken between 90 to 120 m/min. In the case of transfer machines and semiautomatic machines tool setting time is more. Hence tool life may be taken as 480 and 240 minutes respectively. CNC machines are costly and therefore, their machine hour rate is high. The contribution of tool cost to the total cost of machining is not as significant as in the case of manual machines. The cutting speed for CNC machining is selected for a tool life of 15 minutes. Figure 5.2 also indicates the cutting speeds for the various types of machines.

In the case of finish machining higher cutting speeds generally yield a better surface finish. Hence cutting speeds for finish cut are 20 to 25 % higher than that of rough machining operation.

The recommended cutting speeds for turning low carbon steels are given in Table 5.1.

Example 1

Select Cutting speed for turning C15 at 4mm depth and 0.25 mm/rev. feed. Tool P20 grade carbide.

From Table 5.1 the cutting speed can be read as 310 m/min. The power required at the cutting edge is 17.1kW.

Example 2

For the above example, select the cutting speed if the feed is increased to 0.4 mm/rev.

The recommended cutting speed is 300 m/min. The power at the cutting edge is 23.4 kW.

Example 3

Select the cutting speed for a depth of cut of 4mm and feed of 0.4 mm/rev. for a coated carbide tool.

The cutting speed is 370 m/min. and the power required at the cutting edge is 29 kW. Coated carbides can be used at relatively higher cutting speeds, resulting in higher productivity.

Table. 5.1 Typical Cutting Speeds for Turning Operation

C 10

C 15

C 20

C 25

C 30

Carbide grades		Depth of cut a mm	Cutting Speed v (m/min.) and power consumption. P (kW) for feed S (mm/rev.)						Wear Criterion
			0,10	0,16	0,25	0,4	0,63	1,0	
NONCOATED CARBIDE METALS	*P 01* *P 05* *P 10*	1	430 2,7	420 3,8	410 5,3	390 7,3			VB 0.2 K 0.3
		2	400 5	390 7,1	380 9,9	360 13,5			
		4	370 9	360 13,5	350 18	340 26			
	P 10 *P 15* *P 20*	1	410 2,7	380 3,9	360 5	340 6,8			VB 0,4 K 0,3
		2	380 5,3	350 7,1	330 9	310 12,6			
		4	350 9	330 13,5	310 17,1	300 23,4	280 32	260 43	
		8			300 32	280 44	260 59	240 80	
	P 20 *P 25* *P 30* *P 40*	2		320 6,2	300 8,4	270 10,8			VB 0,5 K 0,3
		4		300 11,7	270 15,3	250 20,7	230 27	210 36	
		8			250 28	230 38	210 50	190 66	
COATED CARBIDE METALS	*TiC* *TiN* *Al_2O_3*	1		470 4,5	450 6,2	420 8,3			VB 0,4 K 0,3
		2		440 8,5	420 12	390 16			
		4		410 16	390 21	370 29	340 39	320 52	
		8			360 39	340 54	320 73	300 95	

Range of validity

Tool life T = 15 min. Tool life criterion = VB and K
Cutting speed V is recommended for round, uninterrupted cut
Basic material = drawn, skin-turned or pre-turned material

For other conditions, cutting speed v is to be multiplied by the Factor WS (cutting influence on workpiece):

Forging skin, mill scale or casting skin	WS 0.70 – 0.80
Workpieces hard to cut	WS 0.80 – 0.95
Interruption of cut (T = 10 min)	WS 0.80 – 0.90
Machine in bad condition	WS 0.80 – 0.95

Conversion factors for cutting speed v for other tool lives T:
For 30 min. = 0.8; for 60 min. = 0.6.

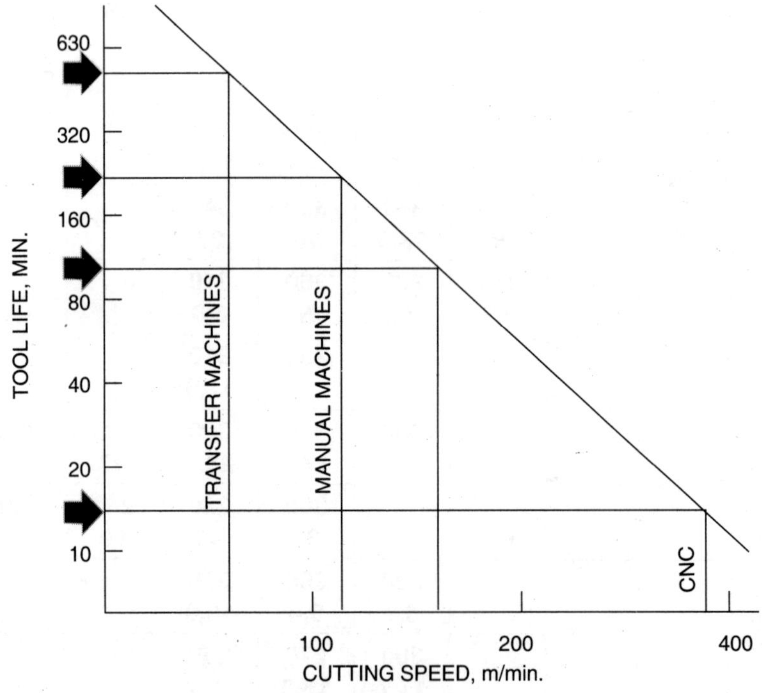

Fig. 5.2 Cutting Speed and Tool Life

5.2.2 Feed and Depth of Cut

The productivity in machining depends on the magnitudes of cutting speed (v), feed(s) and depth of cut (a). The metal removal rate is the product of v, s, and a. For roughing operations, a high depth of cut and heavy feed is selected. Care has to be taken to ensure that the adequate spindle power is available in the machine. In fact, the cutting parameters selected from the tables are to be modified to take into account not only the power available but also the nature of cut (continuous or intermittent), condition of material (hard, soft etc), rigidity of machine or fixture, slenderness of the work material etc. A large depth of cut and small feed will yield higher tool life. Doubling the depth of cut will double the power requirement but will only marginally reduce tool life where as doubling the feed will result in almost doubling the cutting force and reducing the tool life considerably.

In roughing operations a high depth of cut will result in higher metal removal rate and less time for machining, resulting in low machining cost. Increase in depth of cut does not affect tool life significantly, though there will be proportional increase in the cutting force and power required for machining. Higher feed will also reduce machining time and therefore, machining cost. Increase in feed will increase the magnitude of cutting force and hence the power required will also increase. However the increase in feed will affect the tool life significantly and this is more important. It is advisable to select a higher depth of cut and smaller feed for the same chip cross section. In finishing it is necessary to select small depth of cut and feed. This will result in small cutting force and hence less deformation for the machine tool- work-tool-fixture system so that the accuracy of the work piece is maintained at the required level.

5.3 PLANNING PROCEDURE FOR CNC TURNING

Before writing the part program it is necessary to plan the process of manufacture at micro-level. The programmer to develop a CNC program may use the following procedure as a guide. This step by step procedure outlines a systematic approach to program development.

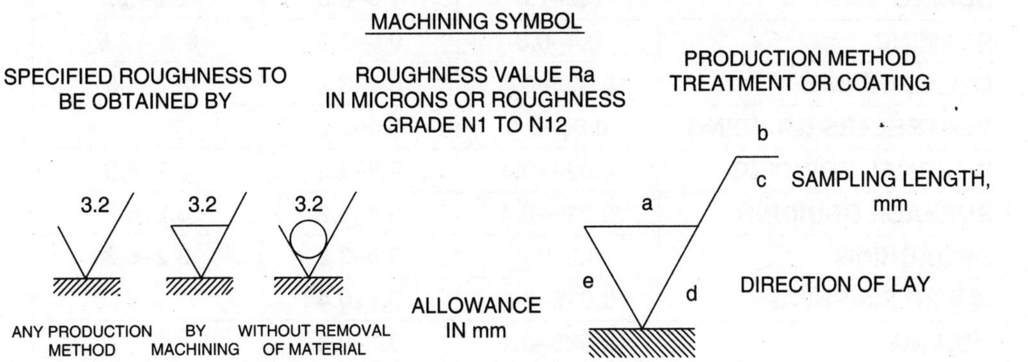

SYMBOLS USED TO DENOTE SURFACE ROUGHNESS

OLD METHOD		∇∇∇∇					∇∇∇		∇∇			∇		∼
PRESENT METHOD	IN μm	0.012	0.025	0.05	0.1	0.2	0.4	0.8	1.6	3.2	6.3	12.5	25	50
	IN GRADES		N1	N2	N3	N4	N5	N6	N7	N8	N9	N10	N11	N12

Fig. 5.3 Common Machining Symbols

The following information given in the drawing is of significant interest to the programmer.

(a) Study the drawing.

(i) Material: The machinability of the material is an important guide in selecting the cutting parameters. The hardness of the raw material and the condition of the material (forged, cast, chilled, hard skin, annealed, hardened, tempered etc) are also important.

(ii) **Surface finish:** Another information is the finish required on the various surfaces of the part. For example N7 surface finish represents a CLA value (Ra) of 1.6μm. This requires after roughing a finish machining operation usually at a higher cutting speed and small values of feed and depth of cut. N8 symbol indicates a finish of 3.2μm. This finish calls for only rough machining. Figure 5.3 shows the symbols commonly used for representing the surface finish and the corresponding roughness values, (Ra).

Table 5.2 shows the surface finish that could be achieved in different manufacturing processes.

Table 5.2 Surface Finish Obtained with Different Manufacturing Processes

SHELL MILLING	1.6–3.2	3.2–25	25–50
DRILLING	3.2–6.3	6.3–25	
PLANING & SHAPING		1.6–12.5	
FACE MILLING	0.8–1.6	1.6–12.5	12.5–50
TURNING	0.2–1.6	1.6–6.3	6.3–50
BORING	0.2–1.6	1.6–6.3	6.3–50
REAMING	0.4–0.8	0.8–6.3	6.3–12.5
CYL.GRINDING	0.025–0.4	0.4–3.2	3.2–6.3
CENTRELESS GRINDING	0.05–0.4	0.4–3.2	
INTERNAL GRINDING	0.025–0.4	0.4–3.2	3.2–6.3
SURFACE GRINDING	0.025–0.4	0.4–3.2	3.2–6.3
BROACHING	0.2–0.8	0.8–3.2	3.2–6.3
SUPER FINISHING	0.025–0.1	0.1–0.4	
HONING	0.025–0.1	0.1–0.4	
LAPPING	0.006–0.05	0.05–0.4	

(iii) **Finishing operations:** Parts may require further operations like hardening, grinding, anodizing, and plating, stress-relieving etc. The process design should also consider these operations. The programmer should consider possible distortions in the hardening process and suitable machining allowances should be left on the workpieces to be hardened. For example, if grinding is specified grinding allowance should be left on the workpiece after turning.

(iv) **Tolerances:** Internal and external functional surfaces will have tolerances. Symbols like *H6, H7, H8* etc represents internal dimensions (bearing bores, locating holes etc). *H* indicates that the minimum size of the hole is equal to the nominal size. The number 7 gives the grade of tolerance and is the difference between the maximum and minimum dimensions. For example, 20 H7 means that the minimum size of the hole will be 20.000 mm. The tolerance value for the grade 7 for 20 mm size is 21μm. Hence the maximum size of the dimension is 20.021mm. Outside dimensions will have tolerances like h6, h7, h8 etc. For outside dimensions *h* symbol indicates that the maximum permitted size on that feature is equal to the nominal size. The tolerance grades 5–8 will require finish machining after roughing. This information is also useful for setting the tools. Table 5.3 gives the IT grades of tolerances. The difference between the maximum and minimum dimensions for a given tolerance grade can be read from the table.

Table 5.3 (a) Tolerance Chart for Holes

OVER			3	6	10	18	24	30	40	50	65	80	100	120	140	160	180	200	225	250	285	315	355	400	450				
TO		3	6	10	18	24	30	40	50	65	80	100	120	140	160	180	200	225	250	285	315	355	400	450	500				
A9	N	295	300	316	333	352			372	382	414	434	467	497	560	620	680	775	855	935	1050	1180	1340	1490	1655	1805			
	G	270	270	280	290	300			310	320	340	360	380	410	460	520	580	660	740	820	920	1050	1200	1350	1500	1650			
B9	N	165	170	186	193	212			232	242	264	274	307	327	360	380	410	455	495	535	610	670	740	820	915	995			
	G	140	140	150	150	160			170	180	190	200	220	240	260	280	310	340	380	420	480	540	600	680	760	840			
C9	N	85	100	116	138	162			182	192	214	224	257	267	300	310	330	355	375	395	430	460	500	540	595	655			
	G	60	70	80	95	110			120	130	140	150	170	180	200	210	230	240	260	280	300	330	360	400	440	480			
E8	N	28	38	47	59	73			89			106		126			148			172					191			214	232
	G	14	20	25	32	40			50			60		72			85			100					110			125	135
F7	N	16	22	28	34	41			50			60		71			83			96					108			119	131
	G	6	10	13	16	20			25			30		36			43			50					56			62	68
G7	N	12	16	20	24	28			34			40		47			54			61					69			75	83
	G	2	4	5	6	7			9			10		12			14			15					17			18	20
H5	N	4	5	6	8	9			11			13		15			18			20					23			25	27
	G	0	0	0	0	0			0			0		0			0			0					0			0	0
H6	N	6	8	9	11	13			16			19		22			25			29					32			36	40
	G	0	0	0	0	0			0			0		0			0			0					0			0	0
H7	N	10	12	15	18	21			25			30		35			40			46					52			57	63
	G	0	0	0	0	0			0			0		0			0			0					0			0	0
H8	N	14	18	22	27	33			39			46		54			63			72					81			89	97
	G	0	0	0	0	0			0			0		0			0			0					0			0	0
H9	N	25	30	36	43	52			62			74		87			100			115					130			140	155
	G	0	0	0	0	0			0			0		0			0			0					0			0	0
H10	N	40	48	58	70	84			100			120		140			160			185					210			230	250
	G	0	0	0	0	0			0			0		0			0			0					0			0	0
H11	N	60	75	90	110	130			160			190		220			250			290					320			360	400
	G	0	0	0	0	0			0			0		0			0			0					0			0	0
J7	N	4	6	8	10	12			14			18		22			26			30					36			39	43
	G	-6	-6	-7	-8	-9			-11			-12		-13			-14			-16					-16			-18	-20
K6	N	0	2	2	2	2			3			4		4			4			5					5			7	8
	G	-6	-6	-7	-9	-11			-13			-15		-18			-21			-24					-27			-29	-32
K7	N	0	3	5	6	6			7			9		10			12			13					16			17	18
	G	-10	-9	-10	-12	-15			-18			-21		-25			-28			-33					-36			-40	-45
M7	N	-2	0	0	0	0			0			0		0			0			0					0			0	0
	G	-12	-12	-15	-18	-21			-25			-30		-35			-40			-46					-52			-57	-63
N7	N	-4	-4	-4	-5	-7			-8			-9		-10			-12			-14					-14			-16	-17
	G	-14	-16	-19	-23	-28			-33			-39		-45			-52			-60					-66			-73	-80
P7	N	-6	-8	-9	-11	-14			-17			-21		-24			-28			-33					-36			-41	-45
	G	-16	-20	-24	-29	-35			-42			-51		-59			-68			-79					-88			-98	-103
S6	N	-14	-16	-20	-25	-31			-38			-47	-53	-64	-72	-85	-93	-101	-113	-121	-131	-149	-161	-179	-197	-219	-239		
	G	-20	-24	-29	-36	-44			-54			-66	-72	-86	-94	-110	-118	-126	-142	-150	-160	-181	-193	-215	-233	-259	-279		
S7	N	-14	-15	-17	-21	-27			-34			-42	-48	-58	-66	-77	-85	-93	-105	-113	-123	-138	-150	-169	-187	-209	-229		
	G	-24	-27	-32	-39	-48			-59			-72	-78	-93	-101	-117	-125	-133	151	-159	-169	-190	-202	-226	-244	-272	-292		

NOTE:- G-Go; N-No go ;Tolerances in microns, 1 micron=0.001mm=$1*10^{-6}$

Table 5.3 (b) Tolerance Chart for Shafts

OVER			3	6	10	18	24	24	40	40	50	65	80	100	120	140	160	180	200	225	250	280	315	355	400	450
TO		3	6	10	18	24	30	40	50	65	80	100	120	140	160	180	200	225	250	280	315	355	400	450	500	
a9	G	-270	-270	-280	-290	-300		-310	-320	-340	-360	-380	-410	-460	-520	-580	-660	-740	-820	-920	-1050	-1200	-1350	-1500	-1650	
	N	-295	-300	-316	-333	-352		-372	-382	-414	-434	-467	-497	-560	-620	-680	-775	-855	-935	-1050	-1180	-1340	-1490	-1655	-1805	
b9	G	-140	-140	-150	-150	-160		-170	-180	-190	-200	-220	-240	-260	-280	-310	-340	-380	-420	-480	-540	-600	-680	-760	-840	
	N	-165	-170	-186	-193	-212		-232	-242	-264	-274	-307	-327	-360	-380	-410	-455	-495	-535	-610	-670	-740	-820	-915	-995	
c8	G	-60	-70	-80	-95	-110		-120	-130	-140	-150	-170	-180	-200	-210	-230	-240	-260	-280	-300	-330	-360	-400	-440	-480	
	N	-74	-88	-102	-122	-143		-159	-169	-186	-196	-224	-234	-263	-273	-293	-312	-332	-352	-381	-411	-449	-489	-537	-577	
c9	G	-60	-70	-80	-95	-110		-120	-130	-140	-150	-170	-180	-200	-210	-230	-240	-260	-280	-300	-330	-360	-400	-440	-480	
	N	-85	-100	-116	-138	-162		-182	-192	-214	-224	-257	-267	-300	-310	-330	-355	-375	-395	-430	-460	-500	-540	-595	-635	
c11	G	-60	-70	-80	-95	-110		-120	-130	-140	-150	-170	-180	-200	-210	-230	-240	-260	-280	-300	-330	-360	-400	-440	-480	
	N	-120	-145	-170	-205	-240		-280	-290	-330	-340	-390	-400	-450	-460	-480	-530	-550	-570	-620	-650	-720	-760	-840	-880	
d8	G	-20	-30	-40	-50	-65		-80		-100		-120		-145			-170			-190		-210		-230		
	N	-34	-48	-62	-77	-98		-119		-146		-174		-208			-242			-271		-299		-327		
d9	G	-20	-30	-40	-50	-65		-80		-100		-120		-145			-170			-190		-210		-230		
	N	-45	-60	-76	-93	-117		-142		-174		-207		-245			-285			-320		-350		-385		
d10	G	-20	-30	-40	-50	-65		-80		-100		-120		-145			-170			-190		-210		-230		
	N	-60	-78	-98	-120	-149		-180		-220		-260		-305			-355			-400		-440		-480		
e6	G	-14	-20	-25	-32	-40		-50		-60		-72		-85			-100			-110		-125		-135		
	N	-20	-28	-34	-43	-53		-66		-79		-94		-110			-129			-142		-161		-175		
e7	G	-14	-20	-25	-32	-40		-50		-60		-72		-85			-100			-110		-125		-135		
	N	-24	-32	-40	-50	-61		-75		-90		-107		-125			-146			-162		-182		-198		
e8	G	-14	-20	-25	-32	-40		-50		-60		-72		-85			-100			-110		-125		-135		
	N	-28	-38	-47	-59	-73		-89		-106		-126		-148			-172			-191		-214		-232		
e9	G	-14	-20	-25	-32	-40		-50		-60		-72		-85			-100			-110		-125		-135		
	N	-39	-50	-61	-75	-92		-112		-134		-159		-185			-215			-240		-265		-290		
f6	G	-6	-10	-13	-16	-20		-25		-30		-36		-43			-50			-56		-62		-68		
	N	-12	-18	-22	-27	-33		-41		-49		-58		-68			-79			-88		-98		-108		
f7	G	-6	-10	-13	-16	-20		-25		-30		-36		-43			-50			-56		-62		-68		
	N	-16	-22	-28	-34	-41		-50		-60		-71		-83			-96			-108		-119		-131		
f8	G	-6	-10	-13	-16	-20		-25		-30		-36		-43			-50			-56		-62		-68		
	N	-20	-28	-35	-43	-53		-64		-76		-90		-106			-122			-137		-151		-165		
g4	G	-2	-4	-5	-6	-7		-9		-10		-12		-14			-15			-17		-18		-20		
	N	-5	-8	-9	-11	-13		-16		-18		-22		-26			-29			-33		-36		-40		

g5	G	-2	-4	-5	-6	-7		-9		-10		-12		-14			-15			-17		-18		-20		
	N	-6	-9	-11	-14	-16		-20		-23		-27		-32			-35			-40		-43		-47		
g6	G	-2	-4	-5	-6	-7		-9		-10		-12		-14			-15			-17		-18		-20		
	N	-8	-12	-14	-17	-20		-25		-29		-34		-39			-44			-49		-54		-60		
g7	G	-2	-4	-5	-6	-7		-9		-10		-12		-14			-15			-17		-18		-20		
	N	-12	-16	-20	-24	-28		-34		-40		-47		-54			-61			-69		-75		-83		
h5	G	0	0	0	0	0		0		0		0		0			0			0		0		0		
	N	-4	-5	-6	-8	-9		-11		-13		-15		-18			-20			-23		-25		-27		
h6	G	0	0	0	0	0		0		0		0		0			0			0		0		0		
	N	-6	-8	-9	-11	-13		-16		-19		-22		-25			-29			-32		-36		-40		
h7	G	0	0	0	0	0		0		0		0		0			0			0		0		0		
	N	-10	-12	-15	-18	-21		-25		-30		-35		-40			-46			-52		-57		-63		
h8	G	0	0	0	0	0		0		0		0		0			0			0		0		0		
	N	-14	-18	-22	-27	-33		-39		-46		-54		-63			-72			-81		-89		-97		
h9	G	0	0	0	0	0		0		0		0		0			0			0		0		0		
	N	-25	-30	-36	-43	-52		-62		-74		-87		-100			-115			-130		-140		-155		
h10	G	0	0	0	0	0		0		0		0		0			0			0		0		0		
	N	-40	-48	-58	-70	-84		-100		-120		-140		-160			-185			-210		-230		-250		
h11	G	0	0	0	0	0		0		0		0		0			0			0		0		0		
	N	-60	-75	-90	-110	-130		-160		-190		-220		-250			-290			-320		-360		-400		

Tolerances of form and position are also important in designing the process of manufacture. Parallelism, perpendicularity, flatness, concentricity, circularity, cylindricity etc are often specified on the drawing depending on the functional requirements of the features. Set up, locating, clamping, process design, sequencing of the process etc will be influenced by the geometric tolerances. Figure 5.4 shows the commonly used symbols for tolerances of form and position.

	Characteristics to be toleranced	Symbol		Characteristics to be toleranced	Symbol
Tolerance of form	Straightness	—	Tolerance of form	Parallelism	//
	Flatness			Perpendicularity	⊥
	Circularity	○		Angularity	∠
	Accuracy of Profile	⌒		Concentricity	◎
	Accuracy of Surface			Symmetry	⌯
				Position	⌖

Fig. 5.4 Tolerances of Form and Position

(b) Method of holding the workpiece

Self- centering 3-jaw chucks, diaphragm chucks, collets, face drivers etc are some of the many devices used for holding and driving the work pieces in turning. Chucks are usually hydraulically operated. Sometimes pneumatic operation is also employed. A variety of standard and special jaws are used for holding the work pieces. Hard jaws are used only when the gripping surfaces are rough like the surface of a casting or a forging. Hard jaws leave an impression on the surface of the part. Hence for holding finished surfaces only soft jaws should be used.

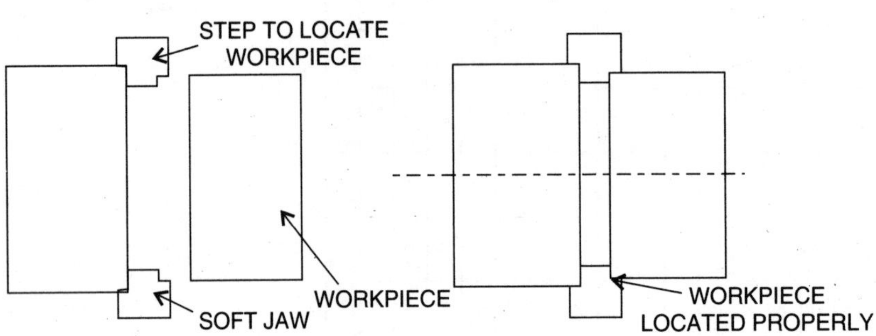

Fig. 5.5 Work Holding

Work pieces should be located axially. Axial location is achieved by turning a 4 –5 mm deep step on the jaw. The jaws are fitted to the chuck body in the desired location. A boring bar is mounted on one station of the turret of the lathe and a step of desired diameter is machined in manual data input or using the electronic hand wheel on the control panel. The diameter of the step should be equal to the holding diameter on the workpiece. This ensures uniform and firm grip on the workpiece without leaving any indentation due to clamping force. Figure 5.5 shows the chuck and jaws, soft jaws prepared and the work held in the soft jaws.

(c) **Decide on the number of set ups required to machine the component.**

In the case of components made out of rounds, cast work pieces, forged work pieces etc it may be necessary to have two end operations. These are generally referred to the first operation and second operation. In the case of bar work, the components after machining are parted off from the bar stock.

(d) **Determine the process of machining in each set up and the sequence of machining.**

(e) **Select the tools appropriate for each process.**

Wherever necessary separate tools are used for roughing and finishing operations. The tools already located on the turret should be utilized as much as possible.

(f) **Determine optional stops (M01 machining cycle interrupt stages) for checking dimension sizes wherever required.**

(g) **Decide on the additional programming codes necessary for the setting up purposes, which may not be needed subsequently during batch machining.** Corresponding blocks of program can be prefixed with block delete symbols (/).

(h) **Select the cutting speeds considering the following factors:**

- Component material
- Method of driving
- Roughing or finishing
- Rigidity of the machine
- Rigidity of the work holding fixture
- Rigidity of the work piece
- Power of main spindle motor
- Type of tool insert
- Type of cut- continuous, interrupted etc
- Use of coolant

(i) **Determine the depth of cut and feed for roughing and finishing.**

Table 5.4 shows typical cutting speed data for a tool life of 15 minutes. The power required at the spindle for the cutting conditions suggested are also giver below the cutting speed (in small point). These values assume ideal conditions of cutting and therefore require modification depending upon the actual conditions of cutting.

Example of use of the Chart.

Problem:

Select the cutting speed for rough machining a C45 work piece.

Solution: Select coated carbide tool insert. Assume that depth of cut is 2 mm and feed .25 mm per revolution. The cutting speed can be read from the table as 390 m/min. Machining under these conditions requires a power of 11 kW.

Table 5.4 (a) shows typical cutting data for machining carbon steels with carbide tools (Tool life = 15 min.). Table 5.4 (b) gives the data for machining steel with ceramic tools.

Table 5.4 (a) Typical Cutting Data for Machining Carbon Steel

Carbide Grade	Depth of cut (a) mm	Cutting Speed , V(mm/min)				
		Feed, mm/rev				
		0.16	0.25	0.40	0.63	0.8
Coated carbide	1	450 4.3	420 5.8	390 7.8		
TiC	2	420 8.1	390 11	360 16		
TiN	4	390 15	360 20	340 27	310 35	290 48
Al_2O_3	8		347 37	320 51	290 66	270 89

Note: Figures in smaller point indicates the power at spindle.

Examples of selection of Cutting Parameters:

Example: Calculate spindle speed for turning C45 of dia. 100mm using coated carbide tools.

Depth of cut = 4mm.

From the table, select a feed of 0.4mm. For this feed and depth of cut the cutting speed (V) is 340 mm/min, and the power required for machining is 27kW.

$$\text{The spindle speed, } n = \frac{1000 \times V}{\pi \times d}$$

$$= \underline{1082} \text{ rpm.}$$

For depth of cut, say 3mm the cutting speed can be selected by interpolating between 360 and 340 m/min. In this case the value is 350m/min

Depth of cut(a), mm	Cutting speed, V m/min				
	Feed, mm/rev				
	0.16	0.25	0.40	0.63	1.0
1	474	447	420		
2	442	417	392		
4	412	389	366	345	325
8		383	341	322	303

Power, $P = 0.041.\ a.\ s^{0.79}\ V$, kW.

Example:

Determine the power required to machine steel at a depth of cut of 2mm, and feed of 0.4 mm/rev.

Select cutting speed from the table = 474m/min.

$$\text{Power} = 0.041.\ a.\ s^{0.79}\ V\ \text{kW}.$$

$$= 14.6\ \text{kW}.$$

Table 5.4 (b) Cutting Data for Machining with Ceramic Tools

Depth of cut(a), mm	Cutting speed, V m/min				
	Feed, mm/rev				
	0.16	0.20	0.25	0.32	0.40
1	698	682	667		
2	651	637	623	607	594
4	607	594	581	567	554
6	583	570	558	544	532

5.4 PROCESS SHEET FOR TURNED COMPONENTS

It is desirable to prepare a process sheet systematically to document a machining process. This will help the operator and the tool setter and will serve for future references as well as for analyzing and optimizing the process. Table 5.5 shows the format for a typical process sheet.

Table 5.5 Process Sheet for Turning Operation

SL No.	Operations	Tool Tip	Tool Holder	Cutting Speed, m/min.	Spindle Speed, rpm	Feed, mm/Rev.	Remarks

5.5 PROCESS DESIGN FOR TURNING

Figure 5.6 shows a cast iron component. It has 5 mm machining allowance all over. The machining symbols indicate that only rough machining is necessary. In the first set up (first operation) a turning tool is used for facing and turning and a boring bar is used for finishing the bore. In the second set up the remaining part of the component is machined. Figure 5.7 shows the first and second operations.

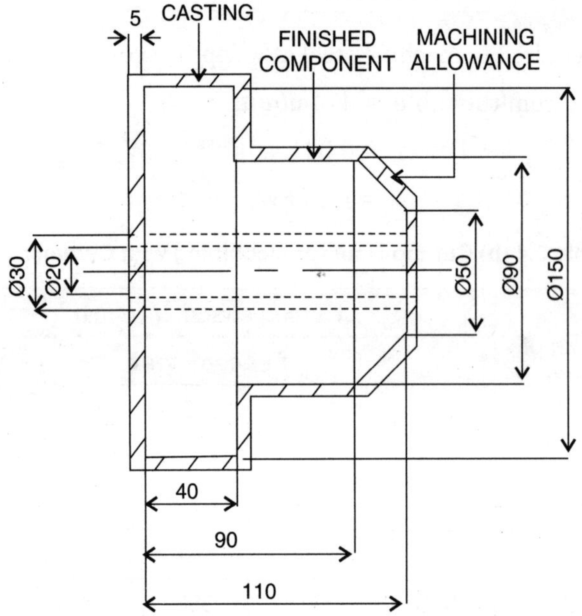

Fig. 5.6 Component to be Machined

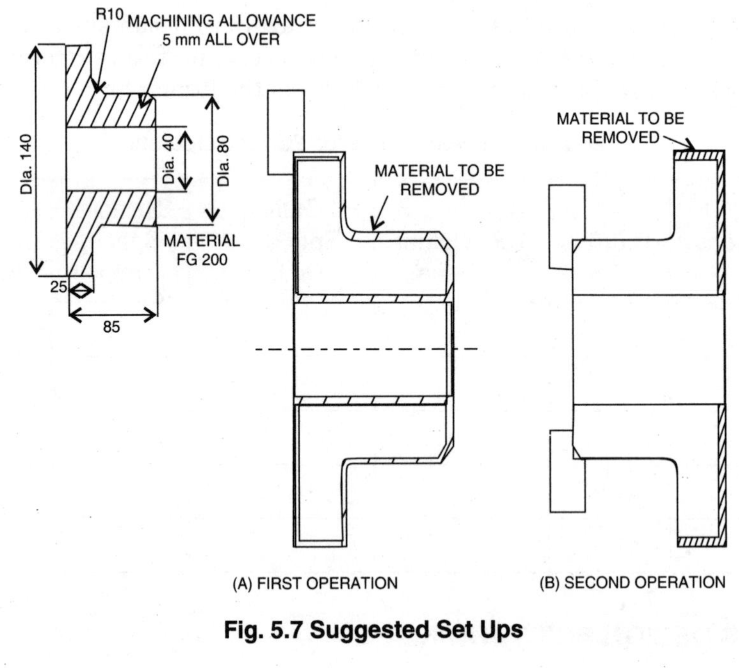

Fig. 5.7 Suggested Set Ups

5.6 PROCESS PLANNING FOR THE FIRST OPERATION

A CNC program to machine the component is written in such a way that the tool is assumed to follow the profile of the component. The first step in programming is, therefore, to determine the coordinates of the profile points of the components. The work coordinate datum (X=0, Z=0) is assumed to be located on the finished surface of the component. The coordinates are indicated in the absolute coordinate system in Fig. 5.8.

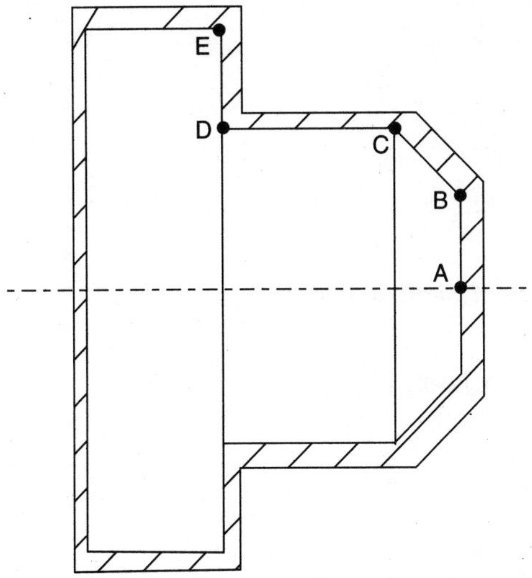

POINT	COORDINATES X (RAD)	Z
A	0	0
B	25	0
C	45	-20
D	45	-70
E	75	-70

POINT	COORDINATES X (DIA)	Z
A	0	0
B	50	0
C	90	-20
D	90	-70
E	150	-70

Fig. 5.8 Coordinates of the Workpiece

The component is held in a self-centering chuck as shown in Fig. 5.9. The boring operation is performed as follows: The tool from position 1 is moved in rapid traverse to position 2. Boring is done till the tools leaves the work (2-3). The boring bar is then withdrawn in the radial direction by a small distance (3-4) to avoid leaving a tool mark and is moved out of the work piece in rapid traverse (4-5). The tool is then moved to the initial position in rapid traverse (5-1). The next operation is turning. The turning tool is indexed to working position as shown by the initial position of the turning tool (Fig.5.10). The tool approaches the workpiece in rapid traverse (tool path 1-2 shown in dotted lines). Since the work piece is a casting, it is desirable to stop rapid traverse at a distance of 3 to 5 mm from the workpiece. Facing (2-3) is done from this point. The tool is withdrawn at rapid traverse (3-4). This is to ensure that the tool does not leave a tool mark on the finished face. The chamfer is machined in the next step (4-5). OD is then turned up to 6 (5-6) The shoulder is then faced (6-7). The tool is then taken at rapid traverse to the initial position.

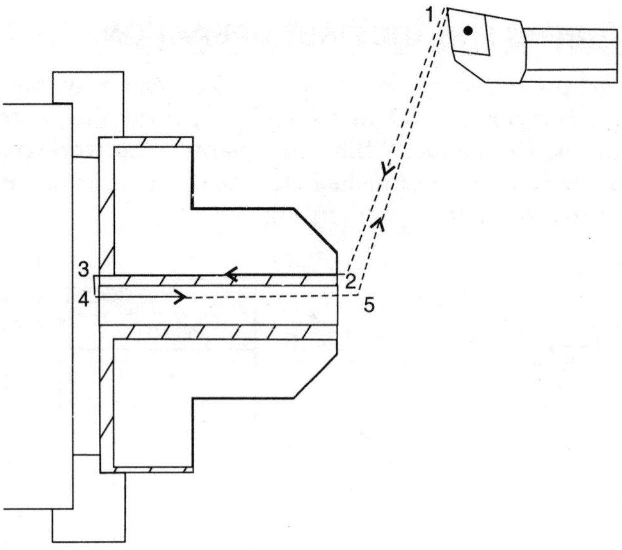

Fig. 5.9 Sequence of Steps in Boring

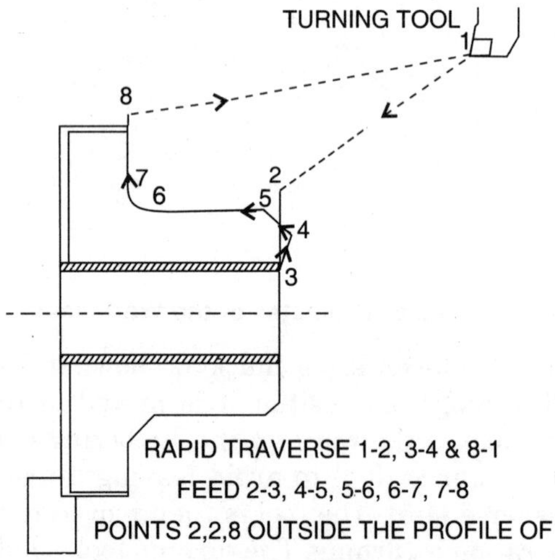

Fig. 5.10 Sequence of Steps in Turning

5.7 PROCESS PLANNING FOR SECOND OPERATION

The machining during the second operation is shown in Fig. 5.11. This operation requires only one tool. The facing operation is carried out first. This is then followed by OD turning.

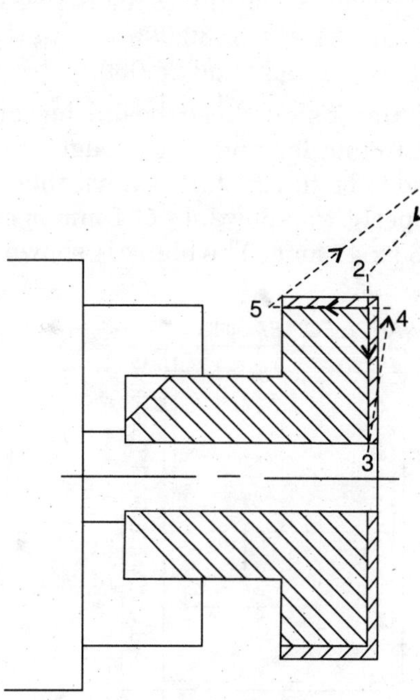

Fig. 5.11 Second Operation

5.8 EXAMPLES OF A PROCESS PLAN

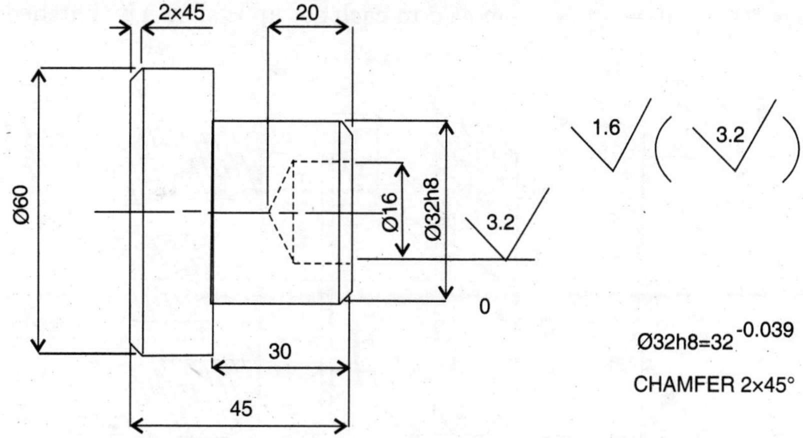

Fig. 5.12 Steel Plug

Figure 5.12 shows the drawing of a steel plug. This to be machined in a CNC lathe.

(i) Study of the drawing: The material of the component is C45, which has good machinability properties. This is to be made out of a blank cut from a round bar stock. The surface finish is shown to be 1.6 micrometers (CLA) except in the hole portion. Since the hole is shown with 3.2 micrometers (CLA) finish, it needs only drilling. The other surfaces should be finish turned. Hence there should be a rough cut pass, followed by a finish cut. Diameter 32 should be produced within h8 tolerance. The limits of dimensions read from the table of tolerances are 31.961 to 32.000. Similarly, the length dimension 25mm should be within 25+/-0.05, i.e., 24.950 and 25.050.

(ii) Selection of raw material and blank size: Since the finished diameter of the workpiece is 60mm, it is cut from a 63mm round, leaving just enough material for finish turning on the OD. The two sides are also to be finished. It is advisable to keep minimum facing allowance. If the blank is cut properly, an allowance of 1 mm is more than adequate. The blank size should therefore be ϕ63 x 47 long. The blank is shown in Fig. 5.13.

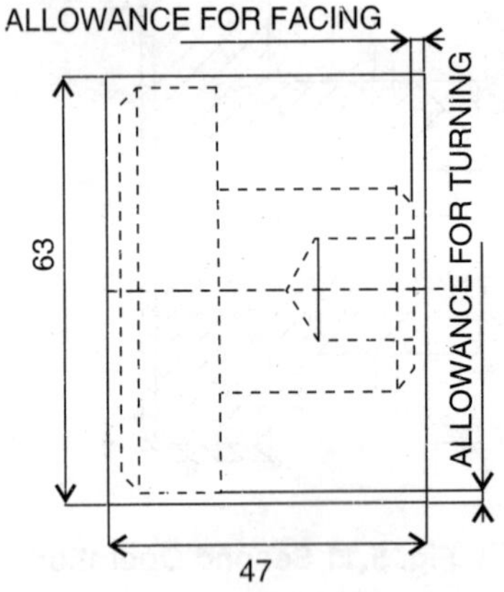

Fig. 5.13 Blank

(iii) Set up: Since both ends of the component are to be machined, two set-ups are required. We call the two set ups as first operation and second operation. Figure 5.14 shows the two operations. The material to be removed in each set up is shown by hatched areas.

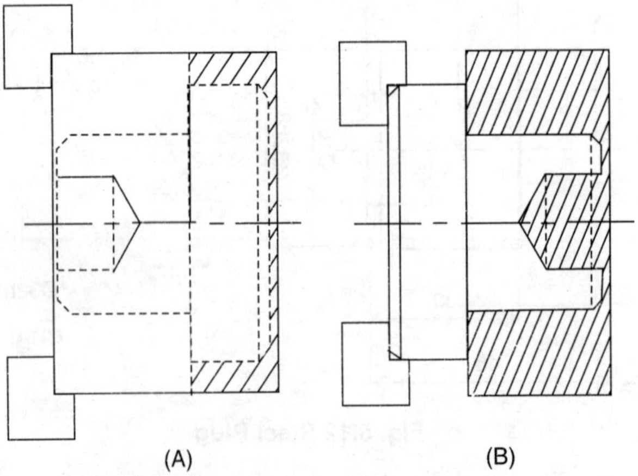

Fig. 5.14 I & II Operation Set Ups

In the first operation (Fig. 5.14(a)) the blank is held on the 63 dia. The component is held in soft jaws. It is rough faced to 0.8mm depth and OD is rough turned to 60.5 dia. to a distance of 16mm. This leaves a finishing allowance of 0.2mm on the face and 0.25mm on the dia. This will be removed in finish machining.

In the second operation, the finished dia. of 60 is chucked using soft jaws. A drilled hole is made to a depth of 21mm.(20mm from the datum)

The side is faced (Roughing at a depth of 0.8mm leaving a finishing allowance 0.2mm). OD has to be reduced from 63mm to 32. Three rough cuts of 5mm and a finish cut of 0.25mm will be necessary to get the size of 32 h8.

(iv) Soft jaws: Two sets of soft jaws – one with 63mm holding dia and another with 60mm holding dia are necessary for the I and II operations respectively. A 5-mm step is made to locate the components properly.

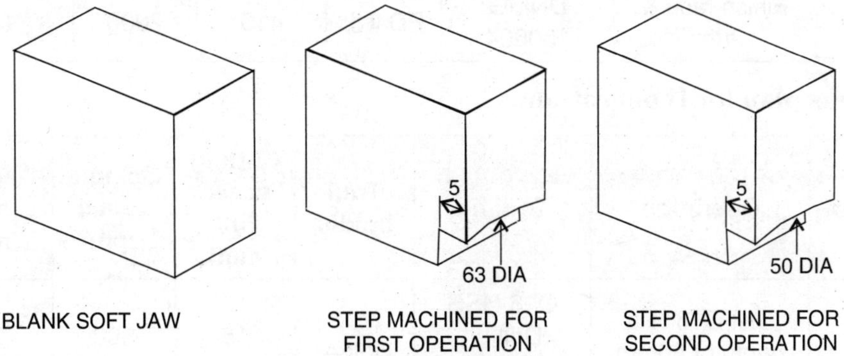

Fig. 5.15 Soft Jaw Preparation

(v) Datum Setting: Figure 5.16 shows the datum setting for both I and II operation

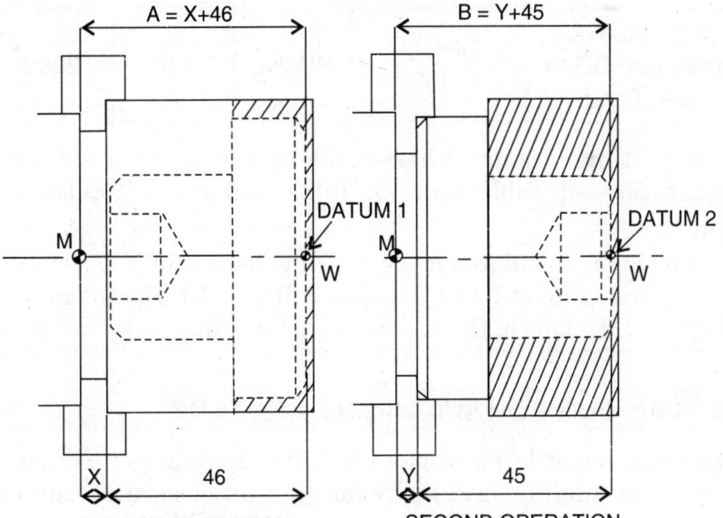

Fig. 5.16 Datum Setting

(vi) Process plan for I operation:

S.No.	Operation	Tool tip	Tool holder	Cutting speed (m/min)	Spindle speed (rpm)	Feed (mm/rev)
1	Rough face and turn to 60.5	CNMG 120412-PM	PCLNL	190	1000	0.35
2	Finish face & turn	DNMG 150604	PDJNL	410	2000	0.1

(vii) Process plan for II operation:

S.No.	Operation	Tool tip	Tool holder	Cutting speed (m/min)	Spindle speed (rpm)	Feed (mm/rev)
1	Drill Ø16 to a depth of 20mm	Ø16 HSS Drill bit (MT2)	MT2 Holder	15	300	0.2
2	Rough face & turn OD to 32.5mm	CNMG 120412-PM	PCLNL	190	1000	0.35
3	Finish turn & finish turn OD to 30+/-0.025	DNMG 150604	PDJNL	410	2000	0.1

(viii) Estimation of time: Using either simulation or manual calculation the time for machining is estimated. Table shows the full process sheet. Total cycle time is estimated to be 5 min.

(ix) Cost: The cost can be calculated if the machine hour rate of the CNC lathe is available. For a machine hour rate of ₹ 120, the cost will be ₹ 10 Often it may be necessary to go through further iterations of the process plans to reduce cost and improve productivity.

5.9 PROCESS PLANNING FOR MACHINING CENTERS

Machining Centers are versatile machines with the capability of carrying out a variety of operations. These include milling, drilling, reaming, counter-boring, counter-sinking, tapping etc. The number of operations performed in a component will depend upon the complexity of machining. The initial cost of the machining center is high and therefore the machine hour cost is also high. Another significant factor is that the cost of the work piece may be high in the case of these components. The work pieces may require long machining cycles and hence the value addition in machining may be high. Any rejection due to faulty machining will entail heavy loss and often delay in the project completion. Careful planning can reduce the cost of machining. A few tips on efficient process planning of machining centers are given in the following sections.

(a) **Study of the drawing:** The issues discussed in the case of turned components are applicable in the case of components to be machined in the machining centers also. Up to five sides can be machined in many machining centers. However a component may require a number of set ups depending upon the capabilities of the machine and complexity of the component. For each set up the work piece datum must be defined. In machining centers the facility to use the work coordinate systems is of great convenience. These can be finalized during the planning phase. For locating the component in the fixture or on the pallet will require a machined datum. The creation of the initial datum may be done on the machining center or on a conventional milling machine.

Every machining feature must be carefully studied to note the surface finish, dimensional tolerances and the tolerances of form and position, to decide on the correct sequence of operations. The amount of machining allowance available must be properly distributed among various operations particularly in the case of cast components.

(b) **Selection of workpiece origin:** The work piece origin can be located conveniently by the programmer. It is advantageous to locate it (X0, Y0, and Z0) in the top center in the case of vertical milling of prismatic components. In the case of horizontal machining centers the locating plane in the fixture can be taken as Y = 0. X and Z origin and the work coordinates can be chosen depending on the features on the face being machined.

(c) **Fixture design:** It is necessary to locate the components in a fixture that in can be clamped to the pallet. It is advisable to use standard fixture elements to fabricate a fixture rather than going for a custom built fixture. This will not only save time but also will be economical in the long run. Fixture design is discussed in detail in this chapter.

5.10 TIPS ON PROCESS DESIGN

5.10.1 Drilling and Allied Operations

(i) **Selection of cutting parameters:** Drilling, counter sinking, counter boring, reaming, tapping and etc, belong to the category of hole making processes. High-speed steel can be used for these machining operations. Carbide tipped tools or solid carbide tools are available for drilling operations. Reaming and tapping operations employ cutting speeds less than those for drilling. The spindle speed can be calculated using the formula

$$n = \frac{1000 \times v}{\pi \times d}$$

where d = Tool diameter in mm

v = Recommended cutting speed for the operation.

Table 5.6 gives the cutting speeds for drilling operations with HSS tools. The recommended cutting speeds with carbide tipped tools are given in Table 5.7.

Table 5.6 Recommended Cutting Speeds for Drilling with HSS Drills

RECOMMENDED DRILL ANGLES, SPEEDS, FEEDS AND CUTTING FLUIDS FOR DRILLING VARIOUS MATERIALS WITH HSS DRILLS								
Material	**Hardness HB**	**Point angle Degrees**	**Lip clearance angle**	**Chisel edge angle Degrees**	**Helix angle Degrees**	**Peripheral Speed**	**Feed rate mm/rev**	**Cutting Fluid**
			Degrees			m/min		
Aluminium	99 to 101	90 to 140	12 to 17	125 to 135	24 to 48	195 to 390	0.127 to 0.89	Kerosene
Brass	192 to 202	118	12 to 15	125 to 135	0 to 17	60 to 75	Heavy	Kerosene
Bronze	166 to 183	118	12 to 15	125 to 135	0 to 17	60 to 75	Heavy	Soluble oil or dry
Cast iron, Soft	126	90 to 100	12	125 to 135	24 to 32	42 to 45	Heavy	None
Cast iron, Medium	196	90 to 100	12	125 to 135	24 to 32	24 to 33	Medium	None
Cast iron, hard	293 to 302	118	10 to 12	125 to 135	24 to 32	13 to 15	Light	Soluble oil
Cast iron chilled *	402	150	5 to 7	115 to 125	24 to 32	4 to 5	Light	Lard oil and turpentine
Cast Steel	286 to 302	118	12 to 15	125 to 135	24 to 32	12 to 15	Light	Lard or Soluble oil
Copper	80 to 85	100 to 118	12 to 15	125 to 135	28 to 40	21	Light	Soluble oil
Duralumin	90 to 104	118	12	125 to 135	32 to 45	60	Medium	Kerosene
Formica	-	90 to 100	12 to 15	125 to 135	10 to 17	16	Light	None
Magnesium	-	70 to 118	12	120 to 135	10 to 30	90 to 600	0.127 to 0.9	Mineral oil
Marble	-	90 to 130	10 to 12	125 to 135	28 to 40	4.5	Light	None
Monel metal	149 to 170	118	12 to 15	125 to 135	24 to 32	15	Medium	Lard oil
Nickel pure	187 to 202	118	12	125 to 135	24 to 32	23	Medium	
STEELS:	170 to 202	118	12 to 15	125 to 135	24 to 32	33 to 37	Heavy	Soluble oil
C15,C20,C30								
C40,C50	170 to 196	118	12 to 15	125 to 135	24 to 32	24	Medium	
	196	118	12 to 15	125 to 135	24 to 32	18	Medium	
	241	125	10 to 12	125 to 135	24 to 32	15	Medium	
Tool Steels	302	125	10 to 12	125 to 135	24 to 32	12	Light	
	351	150	7 to 10	125 to 135	24 to 32	6	Light	Sulphur base oil
	402	150	7 to 10	125 to 135	24 to 32	4.5	Light	
Spring steel	402	150	7 to 10	115 to 125	24 to 32	6	Light	
Stainless steel	146 to 149	118	12	125 to 135	24 to 32	15	Medium	
Wood	ÂTD>							
Wood	Â	60	15 to 20	135	20 to 32	150	Light	None
*Use cobalt drills								

Table 5.7 Recommended Cutting speeds for drilling with Carbide tools

WORK MATERIAL	GRADE OF CARBIDE	CUTTING SPEED, m/min	Feed mm/rev.
Low Carbon Steels	P	60–90	0.25–0.4
Low Carbon alloy Steel	P	50–80	0.25–0.35
High Alloy Steel/Tool Steel	P	30–60	0.2–0.35
Stainless Steel (Ferritic)	P	30–50	0.12–0.3
Stainless Steel (Austenitic)	M	45–60	0.2–0.35
Grey Cast Iron	K	50–60	0.4–0.5
SG Iron	K	50–70	0.4–0.65
Malleable Cast iron	K	50–70	0.4–0.65
Aluminium, Malleable alloys	N	125–225	0.2–0.4
Aluminium, Cast Alloys	N	125–200	0.2–0.4
Copper and Copper Alloys (Brass & Bronze)	N	50–85	0.2–0.25
Plastics	N	50–100	0.2–0.25
Heat Resistant Alloys	S	20–30	0.1–0.2
Titanium Alloys	S	20–30	0.15–0.2

Figure 5.17 shows the drilling operation. The cutting speed in drilling is the peripheral speed of the twist drill. The cutting speed is given by the formula,

$$v = (\pi\, d\, n/1000) \text{ m/min.}$$

where d = diameter of the drill in mm

n = rpm of the drill

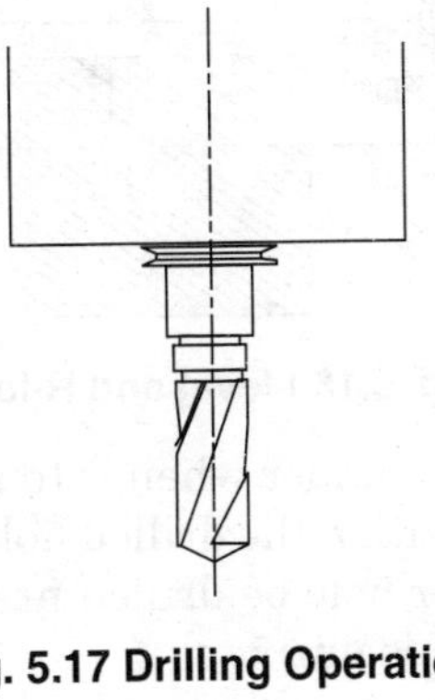

Fig. 5.17 Drilling Operation

The other machining parameter of importance is the feed rate, which is expressed in terms mm/minute in the case of machining centers. Feed rate is obtained by multiplying feed (in mm/rev.) by the rpm. The recommended feeds for drilling will be available in cutting data published by the manufacturers of cutting tools or in hand books. For rough drilling coarse feed rates are used for achieving higher productivity. For accuracy and good surface finish fine feed rates are recommended.

Example:

Calculate the spindle speed and feed rate for drilling 10mm dia. hole in cast iron.
From Table 5.6 select the cutting speed as 25 m/min. and feed 0.2 mm/rev. respectively.
Spindle speed, $n = (1000\ v)/(\pi\ d)$
Substituting the values for $v = 25$ and $d = 10$ the spindle speed n can be obtained as 800 rpm.
Feed rate = feed × rpm = 0.2 × 800 = 160 mm/min.

Feed Stroke in Drilling: Drilled holes are classified into two- blind holes and through holes. Blind holes terminate inside the material whereas through holes penetrate the material. The drill is initially positioned away from the surface of the work piece as shown in Fig. 5.18. This is called the initial level (*I*- level). The drill is then moved close to the work piece at rapid traverse, 2 to 3 mm away from the surface of the work piece (*a*). This is called *R*- level. This distance depends upon the nature of the surface (machined/cast/forged). In the case of cast components, there may be considerable dimensional variation and it may be advisable to use a larger distance to avoid possible collision between the tool and work piece. For rough cast surfaces a distance of 5 mm is recommended. In the case of machined surfaces "*a*" may be taken as 2 to 3 mm. The drilling is then commenced at the recommended feed rate till the end of the hole. Tool is then retracted at rapid traverse to the *R*- level or to the *I*- level.

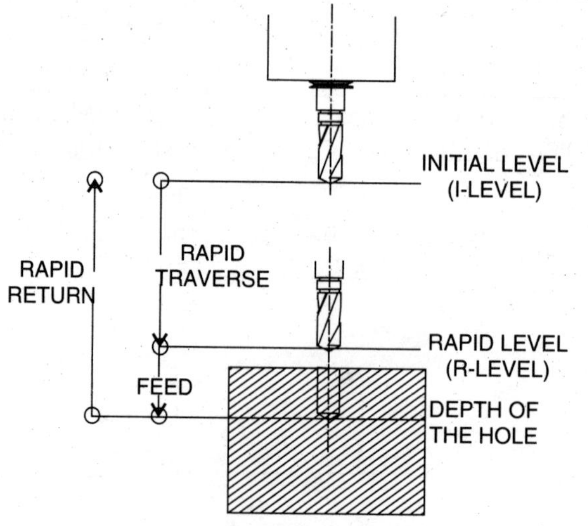

Fig. 5.18 I-level and R-level

The twist drill has a tendency to wander when it touches the work, affecting the accuracy of positioning the hole. In order to position the drilled holes correctly on the surface of the work piece it is recommended that a center hole be drilled first. A special tool bit referred to as CC drill, shown in Fig. 5.19 is used for this purpose.

In the case of through holes it is necessary that the drill completely penetrate the workpiece as shown in Fig. 5.20. The recommended value of c is $d/3$ where d is the diameter of the drill.

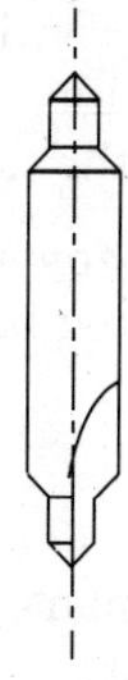

Fig. 5.19 Center Drill

Tapping: Tapping is the process of creating internal threads in holes. For tapping great care should be taken while designating the feed rate in tapping. The feed rate in the tapping operation is obtained by multiplying the pitch of the thread with the rpm. For example, to machine a M10 × 1.5 tapped hole the feed rate is 1.5 × rpm. Usually the cutting speed for tapping is less than that of drilling. Assuming a spindle speed is 250 rpm. The feed rate is then equal to 1.5 × 250 = 375 mm/min.

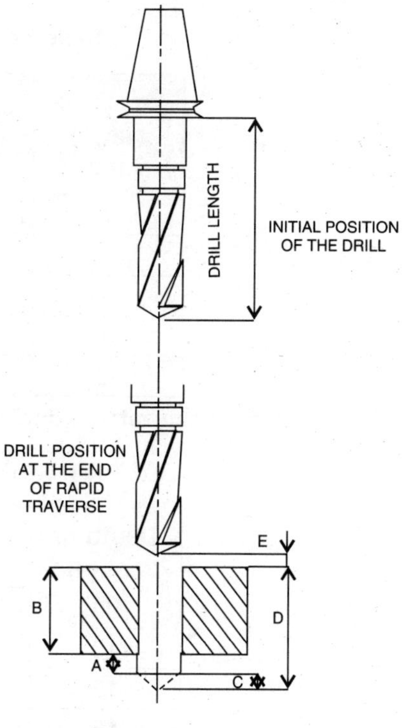

Fig. 5.20 Feed Stroke in Drilling

The programmed spindle speed and the actual spindle speed may differ slightly. The feed rate of the tap is the product of the actual spindle speed and the pitch of the thread. The machine axis feed rate is the product of the programmed speed and the pitch of the thread. While tapping, the actual feed rate of the tap and the machine feed rate may not exactly coincide. Since tap is a fragile tool, this difference will cause the breakage of the tool. This can be avoided by using a special tap holder. There are three types of tap holders:

(a) Expansion type

(b) Compression type

(c) Combination type

Generally combination type is used in machining centers. This takes care of the difference in the tap feed rate and the machine axis feed rate. The air cut stroke in tapping is usually taken to be double of that of drilling. As mentioned earlier the programmed feed rate and the actual feed rate of the tap may not match. Therefore, if the air cut stroke is small, the tap might still be engaged even after in-fed axis is retracted to its end. Machine axes will start positioning after retraction command is executed disregarding whether the tap is still engaged or not, causing the tap and the tap holder to be damaged.

In the case of recently built machining centers there is a rigid tapping option, which overcomes this difficulty. Machines with this facility can be used to tap at higher speeds without breakage of the tap.

Reaming: Although the air cut stroke can be determined in the same manner as in drilling, the in- feed stroke must be determined taking the chamfered tip contour into consideration.

5.10.2 MILLING

There are many types of milling operations performed in CNC machines. End milling and face milling are two common operations.

5.10.2.1 Face Milling

Different type of cutters is used in face milling. Table 5.8 gives the recommended cutting speeds for face milling steel.

Table 5.8 Cutting Speeds for Milling Steel

Depth of cut,(a) mm	Cutting speed, v, m/min Feed, st, mm/tooth		
	0.1	0.2	0.3
2	114	101	-
4	106	101	90
6	102	91	86
8	99	88	84
10	97	86	82

Table 5.9 gives the cutting data for face milling cast iron.

Table 5.9 Cutting Speeds for Milling Cast Iron

Depth of cut,(a) mm	Cutting speed, v, m/min Feed, st, mm/tooth		
	0.3	0.4	0.5
10	76	72	69
12	75	71	68
16	73	69	66
20	71	67	64

Example:

Select the cutting speed and calculate the spindle speed for face milling of cast iron.

Cutter diameter 250mm.

Depth of cut = 10 mm.

Select feed/tooth = 0.4mm

For depth of cut = 10 mm

$$\text{Cutting speed} = \frac{1000 \times v}{\pi \times d}$$

$$= \frac{1000 \times 72}{\pi \times 250}$$

$$= 92 \text{ rpm.}$$

Table 5.10 gives typical cutting data for face milling of steel.

Table 5.10 Cutting Data for Heavy Duty Face Milling

Cutting Speed in m/min.					
Depth of cut, mm	Feed in mm/tooth				
	0.30	0.40	0.60	0.80	1.00
	Tool Life, min				
	60	60	60	40	30
	109	104	98	93	90
12	107	102	96	91	88
14	104	99	93	88	85
16	102	97	91		

The above values are only indicative. The reader is advised to refer to the values recommended by the cutting tool manufacturers for actual programming applications.

5.10.2.2 Cutting Width for Face Milling

The maximum width of cutting when face milling should be restricted to 70–75 percent of the diameter of the face milling cutter. In some cases milling may have to be carried out over this limit. In such cases cutting conditions should be appropriately reduced. The cutter diameter and the maximum width of cut recommended are shown in Fig. 5.21.

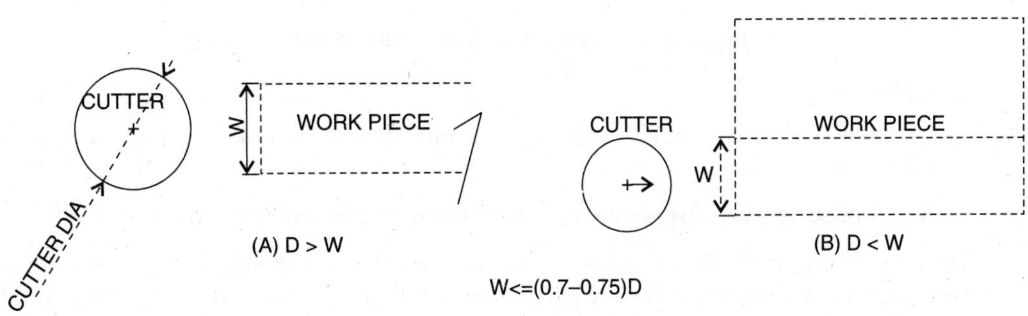

Fig. 5.21 Recommended Width of Cut in Face Milling

5.10.2.3 Air Cut Stroke in Face Milling

In face milling, air cut stroke along the Z- axis is zero. Therefore, the cutter may be fed to the starting point of cutting at rapid feed rate. Care should be taken so that the cutter may not be struck against the work piece when it is fed along the Z- axis direction in rapid feed rate after positioning along X and Y axes has been done.

5.10.2.4 Feed Stroke in Milling

The stroke through which the axis is to be fed at the cutting feed rate is the sum of cutter diameter; air cut amount and the dimension of the work piece whose surface is required to be milled. Feed stroke is calculated with respect to the center of the milling cutter. Figure 5.22 illustrates the feed stroke in face milling.

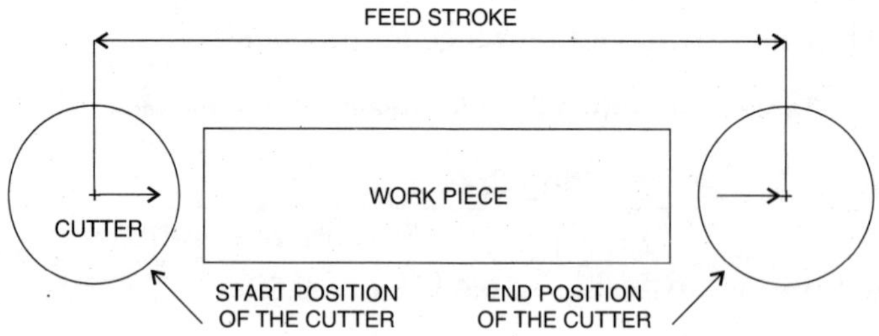

Fig. 5.22 Feed Stroke in Face Milling

5.10.2.5 Pattern of Surface Finish

When machining a surface the pattern of surface finish may be of interest to the designers. Two approaches to machining are shown in Fig. 5.23. In the first case (a) the cutter marks will be different in both the directions. In the second case (b) the feed stroke is in the same direction and the cutter marks will be similar.

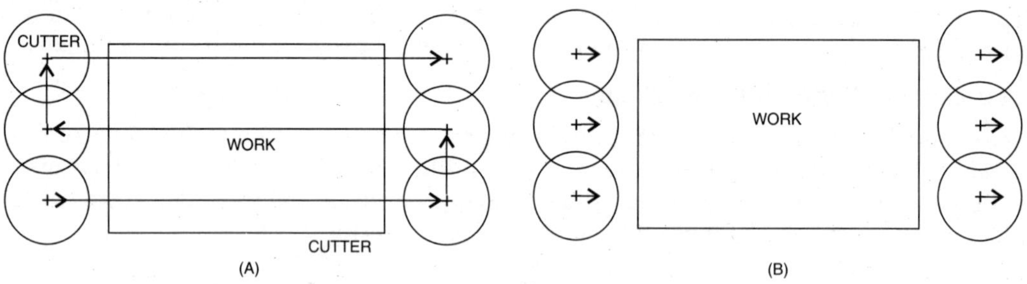

Fig. 5.23 Feed Direction and Cutter Marks

5.10.2.6 End Milling

End mills are used in several machining applications. Requirements on end milling differ according to the application.

Air cut along Z-axis: The air cut stroke can be determined in the same manner as drilling.

Air cut along X, Y axes: The cut stroke and the axis movement stroke can be determined in the same manner as face milling. However the air cut stroke in end milling is much smaller. The guidelines given for drilling can be used in the case of end milling. The recommended feeds in end milling are given in Table 5.11.

Table 5.11 Recommended feeds in end milling

Cutter Diameter in mm	feed/tooth, mm					
	0.05	0.1	0.15	0.2	0.25	0.3
12	■	■	■			
16	■	■	■			
20	■	■	■			
25	■	■	■	■		
32	■	■	■	■		
40	■	■	■	■	■	
50	■	■	■	■	■	■

The data given in Table 5.12 can be used for selecting the cutting speed for end milling applications.
(Tool – Carbide)

Table 5.12 Typical cutting speeds for end milling

Depth of cut, mm	Cutting speed, v, m/min Feed, st, mm/tooth					
	0.05	0.1	0.15	0.20	0.25	0.30
2	200	194	188	183	178	173
4	186	180	175	170	165	160
6	173	168	163	158	154	150
8	160	155	151	147	142	138
10	150	145	140	135	130	125

Example:

Select the cutting speed and calculate the spindle speed for milling a slot of 20mm wide at a depth of 4mm.

From the table, recommended feed/tooth for 20mm end mill is 0.1mm per tooth, the cutting speed is 180 m/min.

$$\text{Therefore, Spindle speed} = \frac{1000 \times v}{\pi \times d}$$

$$= \frac{1000 \times 180}{\pi \times 20}$$

$$= 2860 \text{ rpm}$$

5.10.3 Boring

The air cut stroke can be determined in the same way as in the case of drilling. Since especially close tolerances are required in most of the boring operations suitable boring tools like micro-boring bars adequate to yield the accuracy must be selected. On machines equipped with ATC the spindle taper and the magazine socket taper must be periodically cleaned to maintain the accuracy. A number of special boring cycles are provided in the CNC system. Appropriate cycle should be selected for the best results.

Process planning is critical in the case of machining center operation. Table 5.13 shows a typical process sheet.

Table 5.13 Process planning sheet for machining center operation

Component name-----------------------

Drawing number-------------------------

Sl. No	Operation Details	Tool and Tool Insert	Spindle Speed, rpm	Feed Rate, mm/min.	Remarks

5.11 EXAMPLE OF PROCESS DEFINITION OF A COMPONENT

Figure 5.24 shows the line diagram of a vertical machining centre. The table moves in X and Y directions and the up and down movement of the spindle gives the Z axis motion. According to the right hand thumb rule notation the table movements to the left and away from the column are positive.

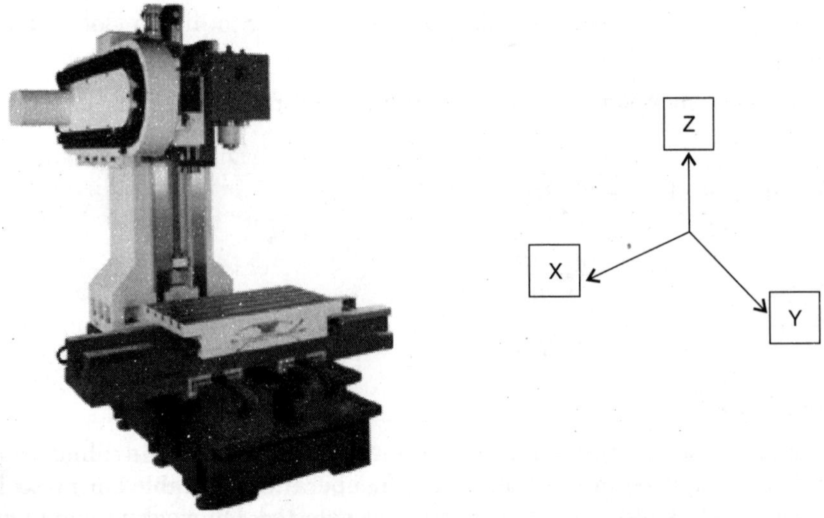

Fig. 5.24 Axes of a Vertical Machining Centre

However in programming practice, the tool is considered to move relative to the workpiece and hence the directions are redefined as:

Tool movement to the right +X

Tool movement towards the column +Y

The following example illustrates the approach to programming a simple component in a vertical machining centre. The component is shown in Fig. 5.25. The blank is of size 400 × 300 in length and width pre-machined to the shape shown. There are six M10 × 1.5-tapped holes and a centre hole of 20 H7.

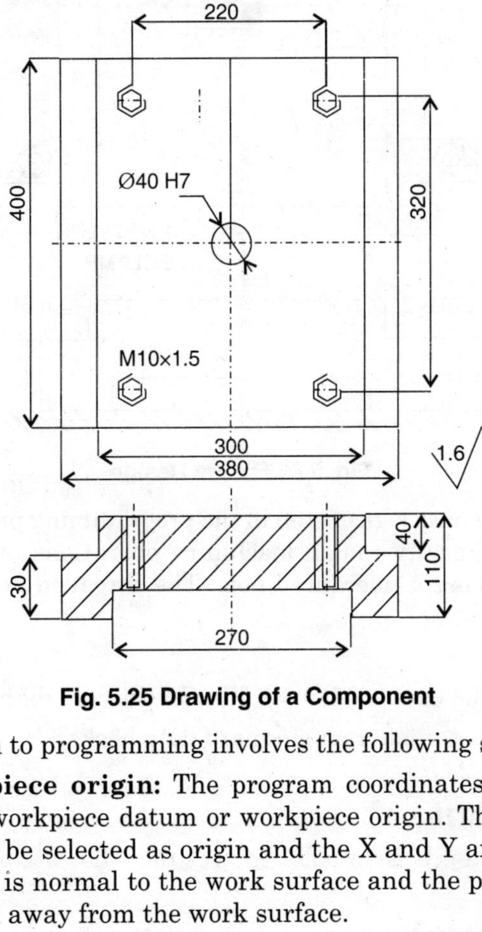

Fig. 5.25 Drawing of a Component

A systematic approach to programming involves the following steps:

(i) Setting the workpiece origin: The program coordinates are conveniently selected with reference to a workpiece datum or workpiece origin. The centre of the top surface is a suitable point to be selected as origin and the X and Y axes directions are shown in Fig. 5.26. The Z axis is normal to the work surface and the positive direction means the movement of the tool away from the work surface.

(ii) Designing the fixture: The workpiece is to be properly located and clamped to ensure that all degrees of freedom of the workpiece are arrested. The fixture must be rigid enough to withstand the static and dynamic forces encountered in cutting. Foolproof loading is another important consideration. Modular fixtures are recommended in preference to custom-built fixtures. A detailed discussion about the modular fixtures has been included in this text. A simple fixturing is shown in Fig.5.26 wherein the component is located by two flat locators at the sides. The workpiece is clamped at the top without interference to the machining operations. It may be noted that standard components are used in the fixture design, which will make the realization of the fixture faster. Thus the main aspects of fixture design like 3-2-1 location; adequate clamping and avoidance of interference with the tools while cutting have been taken care of.

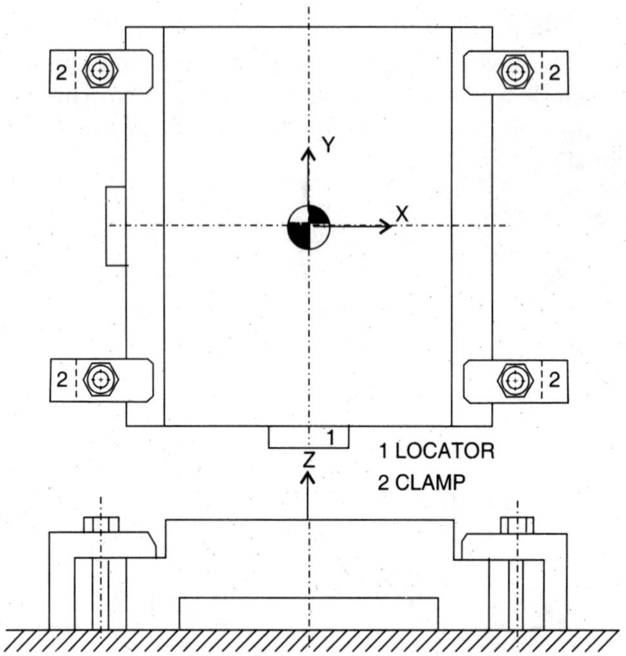

Fig. 5.26 Fixture Design

(iii) Process Design: The next logical step in the programming process is the process design. In this example there are two main machining operations to be performed viz. tapping four holes and producing a toleranced hole. The threaded holes can be realized in four operations or processes.

(i) Centre drilling

(ii) Core drilling (In the case of M10 × 1.5 in C.I the core diameter is 8.5 mm)

This data can be obtained from standard data books

(iii) Chamfering the holes

(iv) Machine tapping M10 × 1.5

The hole Ø20H7 being a precision hole requires the following processes:

(i) Centre drilling

(ii) Drill a pilot hole of Ø18

(iii) Drill a hole of Ø19.5 so that only a small allowance is left for the final boring or reaming operation.

(iv) Boring Ø20H7. Boring is preferred to reaming as boring facilities better control of dimensions in batch manufacture.

In programming the machining centres a common-sense approach is to finish all operations using a tool in one go. This is because positioning of the table will take less time than tool changing. Therefore centre drilling at all the seven locations can be done as one process. Thus there are a total of 7 processes. They are listed below in Table 5.14.

Table 5.14 Process design

PROCESS	TOOL	OPERATION
1	Centre Drill	Centre Drilling
2	Drill Ø8.5	Drilling core holes for M10 tap
3	Ø18 Drill	Pilot hole for Ø20 hole
4	Ø19.5 Drill	Final core drill for Ø20 hole
5	Ø25 Chamfering tool	Countersinking the hole
6	M10 x 1.5 Tap	Tapping
7	Ø20H7 Boring	Ø20H7 hole boring

(iv) Selection of cutting conditions: Once the processes are selected the next step is to choose the cutting conditions. The factors influencing the cutting parameters are:

Work material and its hardness
tool material
roughing or finishing feed depth of cut.

Tables of cutting speeds and feeds are available from which one can make the appropriate selection of the cutting conditions. Spindle speeds and feed rates are coupled from these data and are then tabulated as shown in Table 5.15.

Table 5.15 Process Parameter Selection

Process	Tool Pocket No.	Tool Details and Cutting Speed (m/min)	Spindle Speed rpm	Feed rate mm/min	Tool offset
N1	1	4 mm centre Drill @ 25m/min	1990	199	1
N2	2	8.5 Drill @ 25 m/min	936	187	2
N3	3	18 Drill @ 25 m/min	442	88	3
N4	4	19.5 drill @ 25 m/min	408	82	4
N5	5	25 Chamfering tool @ 20 m/min	254	51	5
N6	6	M10 x 1.5 Tap 10 m/min	318	477	6
N7	7	20H7 Boring (Carbide Tipped Tool) @ 60 m/min	955	95	7

Note:

(1) It is not necessary to name processes as N1, N2 etc. in the serial order. Similarly tool pocket numbers and offset numbers can be selected at the convenience of the programmer.

(2) In machining centres feed rate is specified instead of feed.
Feed rate = feed × rpm or feed/tooth × number of teeth of cutter × rpm.

(3) In threading feed is equal to pitch. Therefore feed rate for tapping is obtained by multiplying the pitch of the thread by the rpm of the tap.

(4) Tool length offset values corresponding to each tool are input in the memory of the CNC system in the appropriate registers.

5.12 SIGNIFICANCE OF TOOLING

Tools are very important in the operation of CNC machines. The quality and productivity in CNC operation depend to a large extent on the tools used. It is therefore very important that the programmer is aware of the best tools for various operations. Most of the machining operations are today carried out using carbide, coated carbide, ceramic, cubic boron nitride or diamond coated tool inserts. HSS tools are used only to a very limited way as the cutting speeds and feeds possible with HSS are very low compared with those possible with various other tool materials.

5.12.1 Tool Inserts

Indexable inserts are used for turning, milling, drilling, boring etc. Depending on the geometry of these inserts, they will have two, three, four, six, eight etc cutting edges. These inserts are used in conjunction with matching tool holders. After one cutting edge wears out, the insert is indexed in the tool holder to bring the next available cutting edge to working position.

The inserts are designated in many ways:

Based on the shape: Tool inserts are available in different shapes. Figure 5.27 shows the common shapes of indexable inserts for turning and milling operations. The features of the workpiece, the operations to be performed and the angle of the profile primarily determine the selection of insert shape. The nose radius and the lip angle determine the strength of the insert. Inserts of shape A, B; C, W etc are recommended for roughing operations. Shapes D, T and V are recommended for light or finishing cuts. C and W are very versatile tool inserts. There are many new shapes of inserts available now. Insert shape C is suitable for finishing particularly curved profiles where there is a possibility of the sides of the insert may interfere with the workpiece. The reader is advised to consult the catalogs of tool manufacturers for the correct selection of inserts.

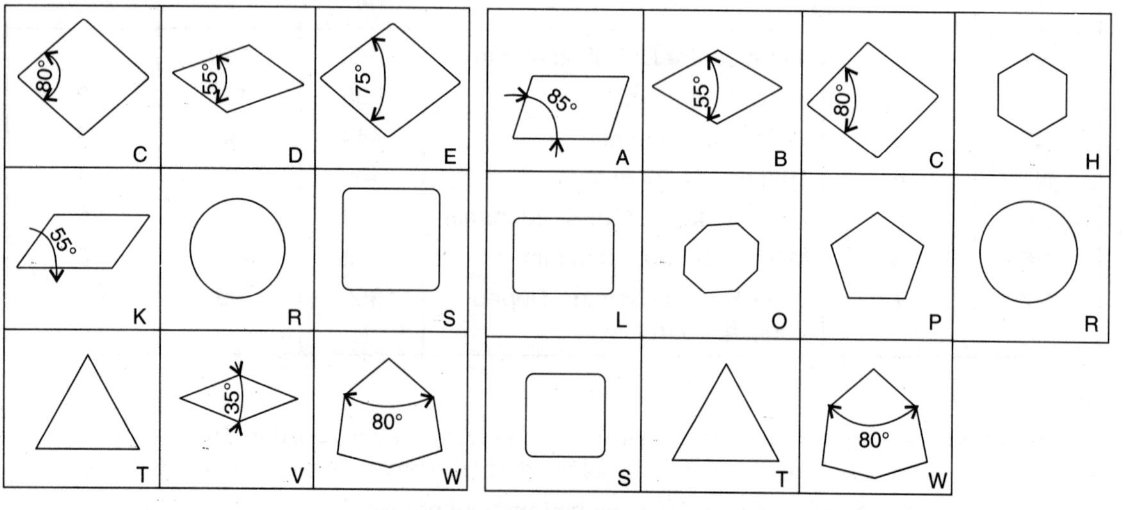

Fig. 5.27 Common Shapes of Indexable Inserts

Based on the clearance angle: The end clearance angle is another important factor. The classification number according to end clearance angle is shown in Fig. 5.28.

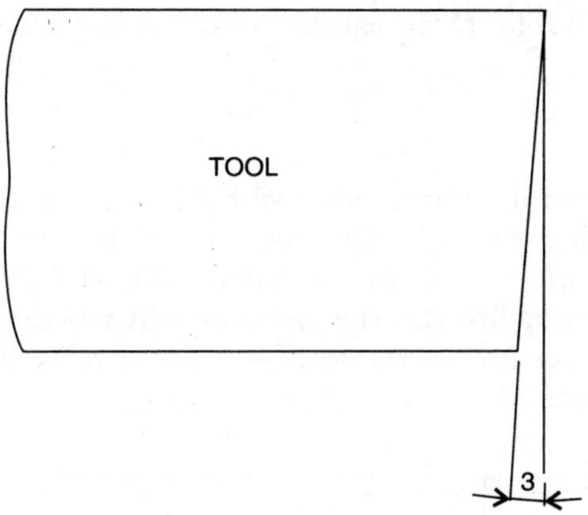

Clearance Angle (Degree)	3	5	7	15	20	25	30	0	11
Specification	A	B	C	D	E	F	G	N	P

Fig. 5.28 End Clearance Angle

Based on the dimensional tolerances: Another important factor in selecting the insert is the tolerances. Inserts are classified by characters from A to U depending on the tolerances, which may vary between 0.0005 to 0.015.

Based on the shape of the chip breaker groove and clamping method.

Chip removal is easy when the cutting is interrupted or the material is brittle. Machining ductile materials produces long continuous chips which are difficult to handle and dispose of. Further long chips will entangle with the workpieces and spoil the surface finish. Grooves on the rake face of the inserts give an additional curvature to the chip thereby breaking them.

Characters from A to W are used to designate the inserts based on the chip breaker groove and shape.

Other factors to designate a tool insert are:

- Length of the insert
- Thickness
- Nose radius
- Cutting direction
- Top rake angle (for milling inserts)
- Manufacturers Details

For example Insert CNMG 12 04 12 means:

C	80 degree rhomboidal shape
N	0 degree end clearance angle
M	Tolerance on length +/- 0.002, on thickness +/- 0.0005 mm
G	Chip breaker groove on both sides, pin clamping
12	Length of insert, mm
04	Thickness of insert, 5mm
12	Signifying the value of nose radius

The reader is advised to refer to the catalogues of the manufacturers of tool inserts for the correct designation.

5.12.2 Tool Holder

The tool inserts are mounted in appropriate tool holders. As in the case of inserts, there are standard tool holders to suit the inserts. The tool holder is designed in such a way as to give the necessary approach angle and rake angle for cutting. Figure 5.29 shows a typical tool holder used with rhomboidal roughing inserts. The insert usually sits in a cavity on a base part which provides even support and is clamped rigidly. There are several clamping schemes depending upon the design of the insert.

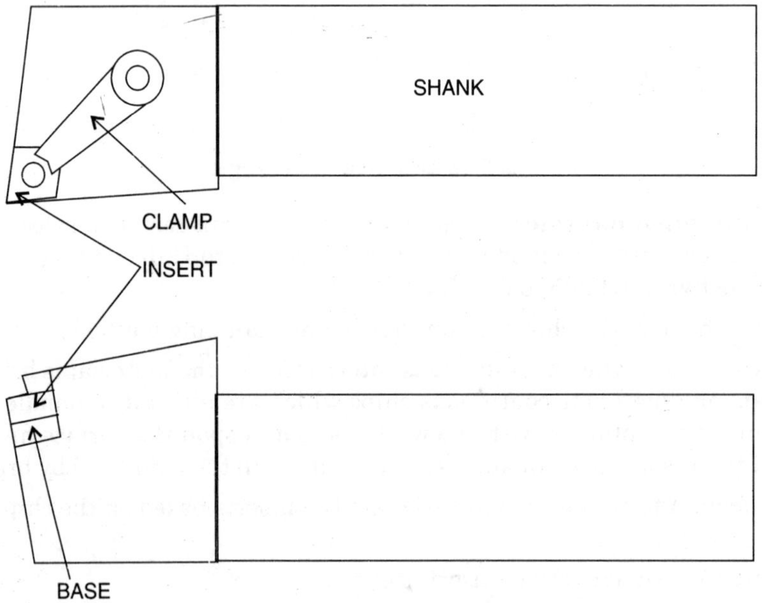

Fig. 5.29 Tool Holder

The tool holders may be left handed or right-handed. The shank of the tool holder is usually square. It is designed to take up heavy cutting forces encountered in CNC turning.

5.13 TOOL HOLDERS FOR MACHINING CENTRES

As mentioned before, machining centres employ a large number of tools and the tool holder system should enable switching of a wide range of tools in the spindle automatically. There are several standards for tool holder systems. Examples are BT, ISO, ANSI, Caterpillar, De Vlieg etc. The spindle nose of a machining centre will have a standard taper of 7/24. This is a self release taper. The taper is specified as ISO 40, ISO 50, BT 40, BT 50 etc. The tool holder should match the spindle taper.

A standard tool holder has the following basic components:

- Tapered shank
- Adapter
- Pull stud

- Slots to fit the tenons on the spindle face
- Flange

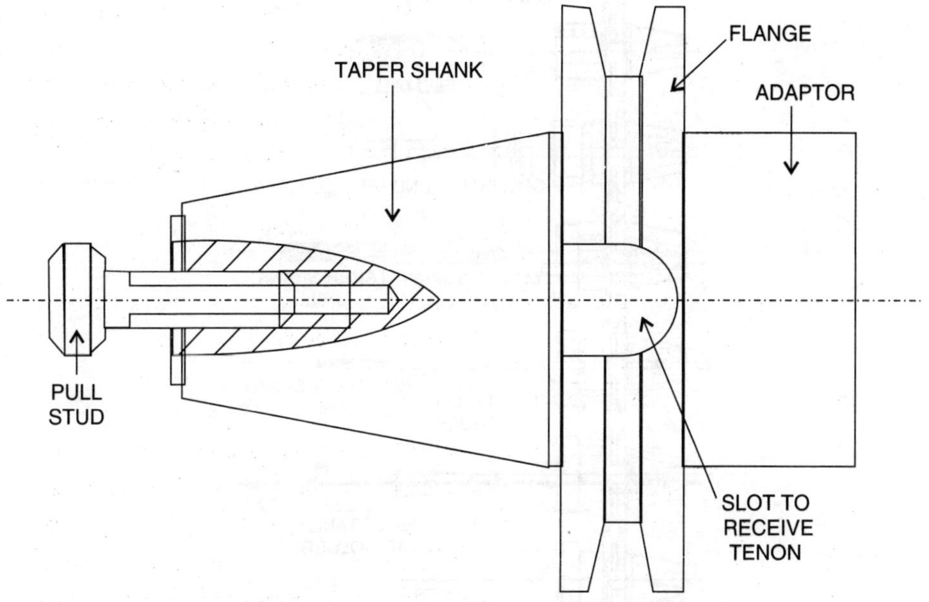

Fig. 5.30 Tool Holder for Machining Centre

A typical tool holder is shown in Fig. 5.30.The taper shank fits inside the spindle. Size 30 is used for small machines and size 60 for large machines. Size 40 and 50 are commonly used with a power range of 7.5 to 28 kW. The adaptor receives the tool and there will be provision to secure the tool in the adaptor. Some common holders are end mill holders, drill holders, Jacob chuck holders, face mill holders, tap holder etc. The pull stud allows the locking draw bar to pull the tool holder firmly into the spindle and release it automatically during tool change. There are two opposing slots on the flange to receive the tenons mounted on the face of the spindle. The taper on the tool holder, being of self release type cannot transmit torque from the spindle to the tool. The tenons provide the positive drive. The automatic tool changer grabs the tool using the flange portion. The V-groove on the flange fits with the end of tool changer arm.

In the case of high speed machining, the conventional tool holders are found to be unsuitable. Special types of tool holders like HSK tool holders are recommended for high speed machining.

5.14 TOOL HOLDER SYSTEM FOR MACHINING CENTRES

Tools are a major investment in machining centres. The productivity depends substantially on the right tool used. Hence care must be taken in choosing the right tool and the appropriate tool holder system. The tool holder system of a machining centre is standardized. Various types of holders and adaptors for a variety of machining applications are illustrated in Fig. 5.31. The choice of tools for a machining centre is very wide and only a few representative samples have been illustrated here.

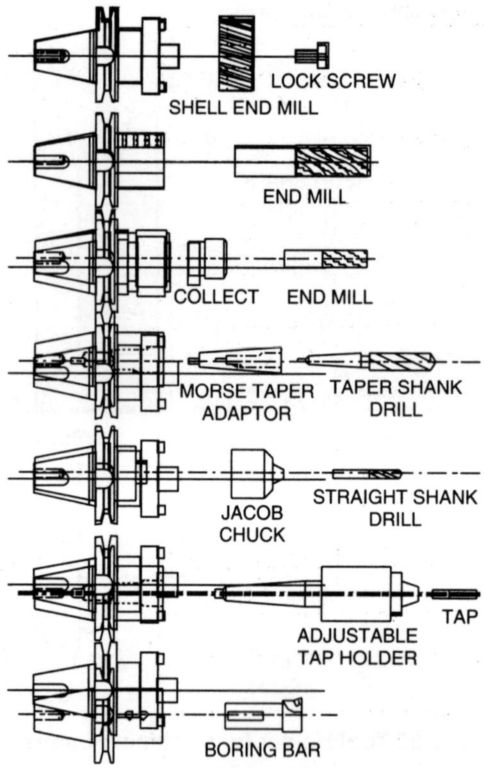

Fig. 5.31 Tool Holder System for Machining Centres

5.15 FIXTURES

A variety of fixtures are used for locating and clamping the workpieces in a machining centre. These are classified into three:

5.15.1 Standard Fixtures

These are general purpose fixtures like vices, chucks etc. They are used for non-repetitive and simple jobs or when limited number of workpieces only are to be machined. They are also used for rush jobs.

5.15.2 Custom Built Fixtures

These are specially designed for a particular workpiece if they are to be made in repeated runs in large lots. Since these are custom designed the lead time of the realization of fixture should be considered in estimating the delivery time of the part. In the case of large projects inventory of custom built fixtures may be large. Storage and retrieval of fixtures are also of importance.

5.15.3 Modular Fixtures

The present trend is to use standard off-the shelf components to design and manufacture the fixture. Since CAD libraries of these components are available, the design of the fixture as well as assembly could be completed in a short time. Once a particular production run is over, the fixture can be dismantled and the components can be used in building another fixture. The fixture inventory can be reduced considerably by using modular fixture.

5.15.4 VACUUM CLAMPING

Vacuum clamping is widely used where flat components are involved and where clamping at the top surface is to be avoided. The component is placed on the fixture table, which has pockets on the top surface. When vacuum is created in the pockets, the atmospheric pressure acting on the part securely clamps the part to the table. This method of clamping is ideal for a variety of jobs in aircraft industry.

REVIEW QUESTIONS

(1) Determine the range of spindle speeds necessary to machine the component shown in Fig. 5.12.

(2) Suggest suitable cutting speed for rough turning C20 using P20 grade carbide tool at a feed of 0.25 mm/rev. Determine the improvement in metal removal rate if a coated carbide insert is used for this purpose.

(3) Calculate the cost of manufacturing in cylindrical turning a C15 pin of diameter 72 mm to 64 mm in one pass at a feed of 0.25 mm/rev. using P20 grade carbide insert. Assume machine hour cost and tool cost. If the machining is done with a feed of 0.4 mm calculate the new cost of machining. If the machining is done with a coated carbide tool at a feed of 0.4 mm/rev. Calculate the cost of machining.

(4) What is the logic behind recommending a lower tool life in CNC machining than in manual machining?

(5) Make a detailed study of different types of tool inserts available for CNC turning.

(6) What is the significance of chip breaker grooves?

(7) Figure 5.32 shows a gear blank to be machined from EN8 steel. Discuss how the geometric tolerances will influence the process plan or the sequence of operations.

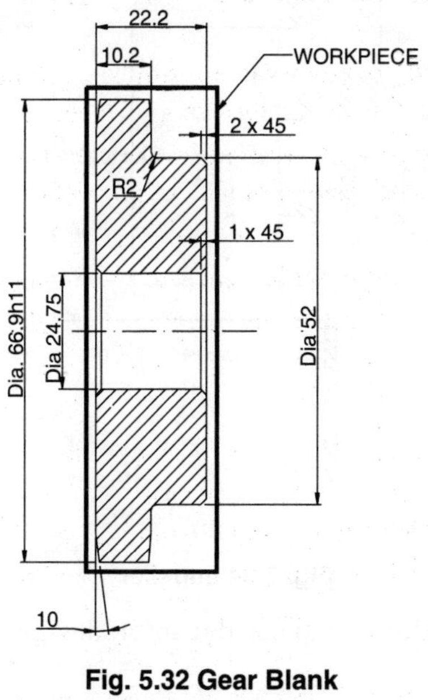

Fig. 5.32 Gear Blank

(8) Discuss why soft jaws are recommended for holding workpieces in turning? Are soft jaws the perfect answer when frequent job changes are to be handled? What problems will you encounter when jaws are reset every time?

(9) Describe the different types of chucks available for work holding in a CNC lathe.

(10) Discuss whether the statement is correct: Doubling the feed is a better way than doubling the depth of cut to double metal removal rate.

(11) Prepare a process sheet for machining the components shown in Fig. 5.33 and Fig. 5.34

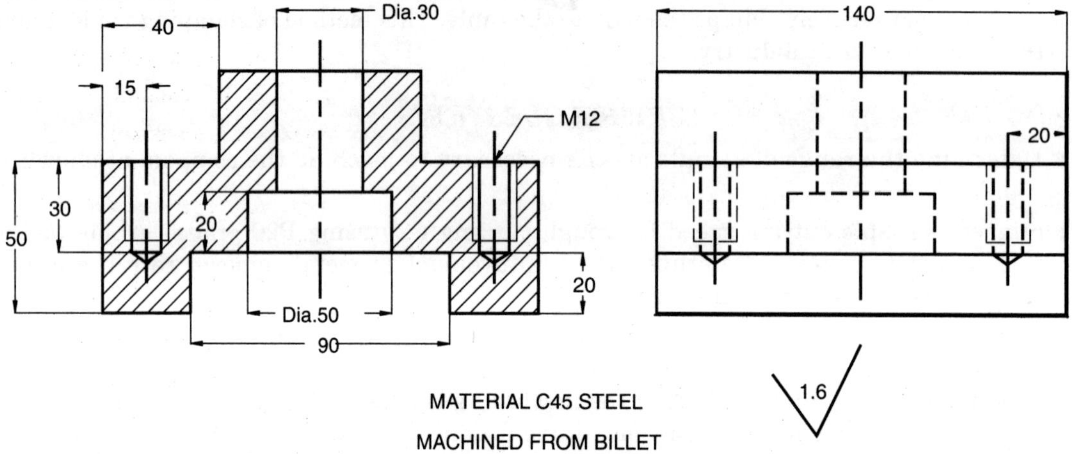

Fig. 5.33 Base

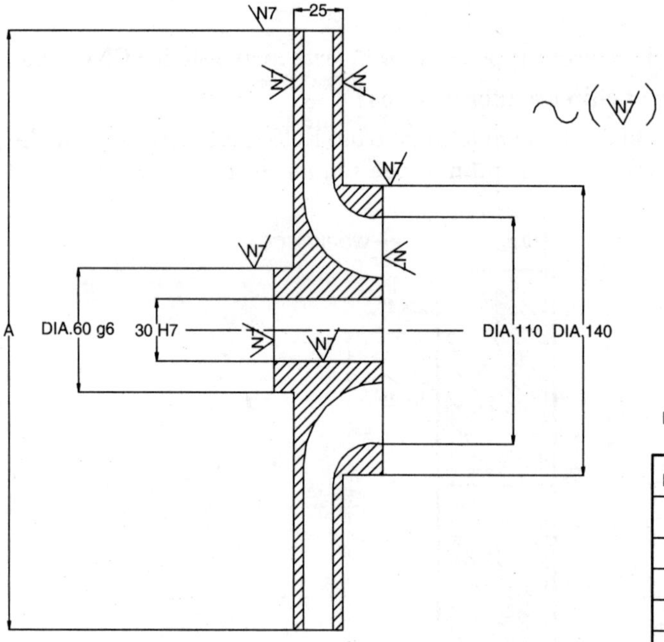

RANGE	A
1	260
2	270
3	280
4	290
5	300

Fig. 5.34 Impeller

(12) Discuss the importance of the workpiece datum in designing the process of machining in CNC machines.

(13) Why the full width of a face mill is not employed in face milling?

(14) What are the factors to be considered in determining air cut distance in drilling/milling?

(15) Prepare process plans for the components shown in Fig. 5.35 and Fig. 5.36.

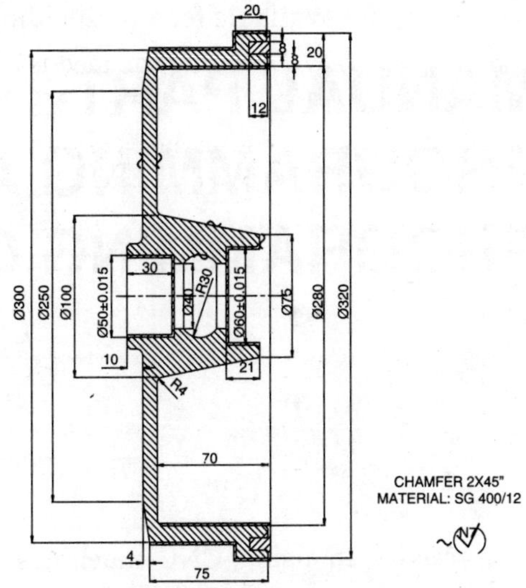

Fig. 5.35 Brake Drum

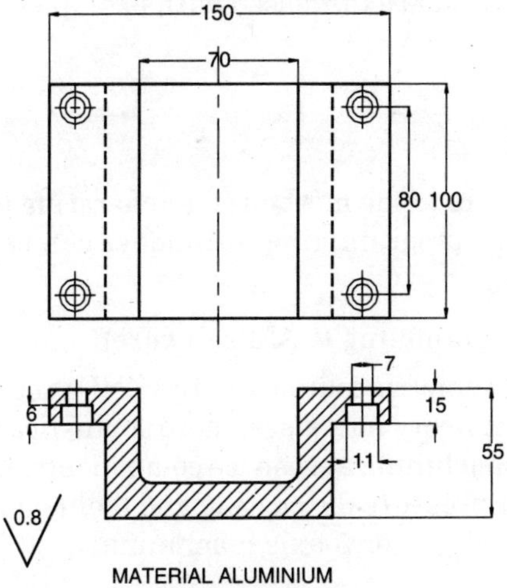

Fig. 5.36 Bracket

(16) Discuss the features of a HSK tool holder which make it suitable for high speed machining

(17) What are the advantages of designing fixtures with modular tooling elements when compared with custom built fixtures?

(18) What is the principle of working of vacuum fixtures?

Study Project

For a specified component, prepare a total machining solution including tools, fixturing, process sheet, time estimation and cost estimation. Is your estimate the optimum? If yes, justify your answer. If not, discuss how you can further reduce the cost of machining and improve productivity.

6 MANUAL PART PROGRAMMING AND PROGRAMMING OF LATHES

Programming is an important activity in using CNC machines. Programs for machining simple components can be written manually. This chapter deals with the basic principles of programming of CNC machines. The fundamental principles are explained in detail. The programming codes commonly used are discussed with examples. A few examples of programs are also given.

6.1 INTRODUCTION

The term CNC programming refers to the methods for generating instructions used to drive and control CNC machine tools. CNC programming techniques can be classified into two groups:

(i) Manual part programming

(ii) CAD/CAM based CNC programming (CAM software)

For components with little geometric complexity the CNC program can be written manually. However when geometrical complexity increases, more sophisticated programming techniques are necessary, particularly for machining aerospace components, manufacture dies and moulds for plastic injection moulding or pressure die casting and tooling for manufacturing automotive body panels. These may involve 3-, 4-, or 5-axis machining.

CNC programming has to be done in a methodical manner. The steps in programming include:

- Study of production drawing and other documents prepared by planning department
- Determination of stock size
- Study of machine tool specifications and features of control system
- Sequencing machining processes in an optimum manner
- Deciding the set ups
- Tool selection
- Selection of technological parameters like speed, feed etc.
- Tool path determination
- Preparation of working sketches and calculations if needed
- Programme preparation (manually or by computer)
- Programme transfer to the CNC

- Tool path simulation/program simulation
- Program testing-dry run, and debugging
- Manufacture of components
- Documentation for future reference

The previous chapter dealt with the planning aspects in detail. This chapter focuses on program preparation. Tool path simulation and program simulation are discussed in the chapter on CAM software.

6.2 STRUCTURE OF A PART PROGRAM

A CNC program is a series of sequential instructions related to machining a part. The instructions, usually called part programs are specified in a format the CNC system can accept, interpret and process. A part programme is written to suit a particular machine and its control system.

6.2.1 Basic Programming Terms

A small segment of a CNC program is given below:

```
N40   G90   G00      G54       X20.5   Y40.0   S2000   M03;
N50   G43   Z3.0     H02;
N60   G01   Z-40.0   F400.0;
N60   G00   Z3.0;
```

A program consists of several lines. Each line is called a block. For example, N40 G90 G00 G54 X20.5 Y40.0 S2000 M03; is a block. A block is composed of a number of words. Example: Z-40.0. A word is a meaningful combination of characters. In Z-40.0, Z, 4, 0, - are all characters.

6.2.1.1 Character

A character is the smallest unit of the CNC program. It may be:

- a digit (0 to 9)
- a letter (A to Z)
- a symbol (+, –, %, ( ) etc).

The combination of digit, letter and symbol is referred to as alphanumerical characters.

6.2.1.2 Word

A program word is a combination of alphanumerical characters creating a single instruction which will be decoded by the control system. Typical words indicate axes position, preparatory commands, speed command, feed command, miscellaneous functions etc. Each word normally begins with a capital letter followed by a number representing a program code or actual value.

6.2.1.3 Block

A block is a line of the program and is used as a multiple instruction. A block contains the data required for transferring the cutting tool from one point to the next one, including all machining instructions that must be executed either at the point or along the path between points. A block begins with a line number (optional in some systems) and ends with an end of block (EOB) symbol like ";". The lines or blocks are properly sequenced.

6.2.2 Block Format

The block format stipulates the way in which the programming instructions are coded. The format currently in wide use is the word address format. Each word starts with a letter. This is called the address. G, M, X, Y, Z, S, F etc. are addresses representing preparatory function, miscellaneous function, X axis movement, Y axis movement, Z axis movement, spindle speed and feed respectively. The letter is followed by the numerical data representing a programming code (in the case of G and M functions) or actual value (in the case of axis position, speed, feed etc).

In manual program preparation, the programmer has to determine the machining parameters and the optimal sequence of operations to be performed. Based on this sequence, the tool path is calculated and a program is written. The arrangement of the information within a block is referred to as block format.

A typical block form is:

G01 X 43.56 Z -39.52 F0.2 M08;

The letter and the number which follows it as a whole is referred to as a 'word'. The first letter of the word is the 'word address'. The word addresses in the block given above are G, X, Z, F and M. Most of the present day CNC machines use a variable block format (Ref.: EIA standard RS-273-A and RS-274-B) which is combination of word address and tab sequential formats followed earlier. In the word address format each word must be headed by a word address. The machine control unit (MCU) uses this address letter to identify the meaning of the word following this letter. In this type of format the words need not be arranged in any specific order within the block since the letter identifies the corresponding word. The address characters, currently used as per DIN 66025 are given in Table 6.1.

Table 6.1 Address characters as per DIN 66025

Character	Meaning
A	Rotation about X-axis
B	Rotation about Y-axis
C	Rotation about Z-axis
D&E	Rotation about additional axes
F	Feed
G	Preparatory function
H	Unassigned
I	Interpolation parameter
J	Interpolation parameter
K	Interpolation parameter
L	Unassigned
M	Miscellaneous function
N	Block number
O	Not used
P, Q, R	Movements parallel to X, Y and Z
S	Spindle speed

T	Tool
U, V, W	Movements parallel to X, Y and Z
X	Movement in X-axis
Y	Movement in Y-axis
Z	Movement in Z-axis

6.2.2.1 Format Notation

Control system manufacturers specify the input format in an abbreviated form as:

X +/– 5 . 3

Here X is the address, +/– denotes the direction of axis movement, 5 the maximum number of digits before the decimal point and 3 the number of digits after the decimal point. In some systems the decimal point is compulsory.

6.3 NOMENCLATURE OF THE CNC

Though there are variations, the prevailing industry trend in this respect is to follow the International Standard ISO/R841. The US standard EIA (Electronic Industries Association) document RS267 formed the basis of the ISO standard. The information in the following paragraphs pertains to the ISO standard.

6.3.1 Co-ordinate System

Fixing of the co-ordinate system is the first requirement in part programming. The co-ordinate system for designating the axes is the conventional right hand co-ordinate is shown in the Fig. 6.1. Six representations of the co-ordinate systems are shown in this figure. The relative positive directions of the axes in all cases can be fixed by using the right hand convention as shown in Fig. 6.1. All these adopt the same right hand co-ordinate system.

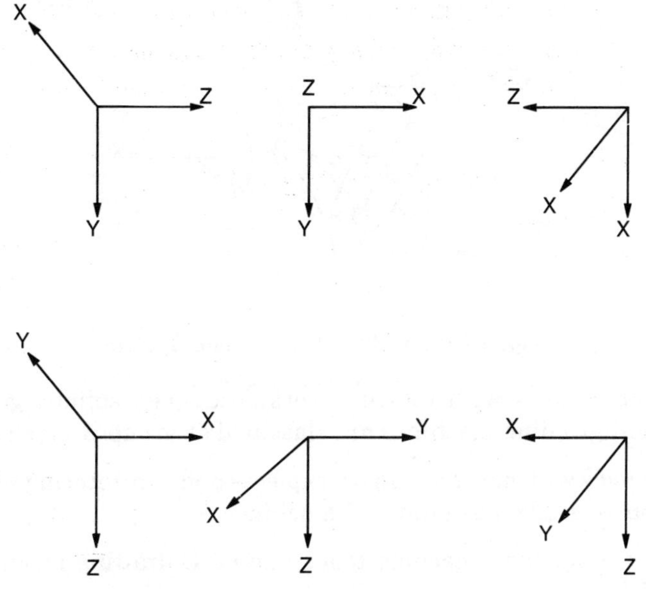

Fig. 6.1 Dispositions of Co-ordinates in Right Hand Co-ordinate System

6.3.2 Machine Types

It is convenient through not necessary, in the context of the standard, to classify the CNC machines in the following four groups:

Group I: Machine tools with rotating tools are classified as group I (i.e., Spindle providing the cutting power). Of these machines, those having vertical spindles as in vertical knee mill, drilling machines, profiling and contour mill, vertical boring mill, tapping machines etc. are grouped as I(a). The vertical spindle machines may be single column type or gantry type. Those with horizontal spindles like horizontal boring machine, horizontal machining centres etc. are grouped as I(b).

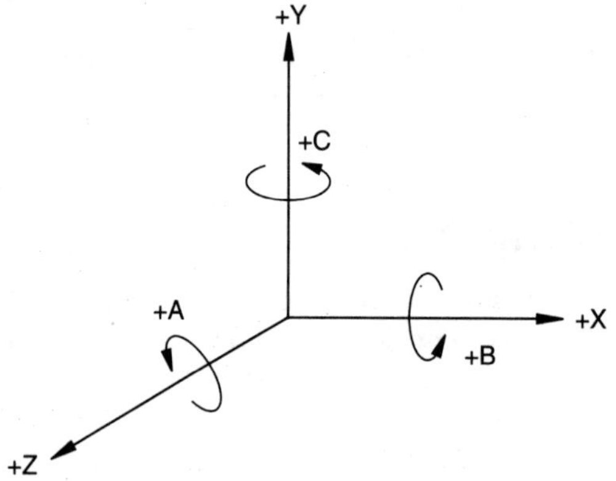

Direction for Rotary Motions

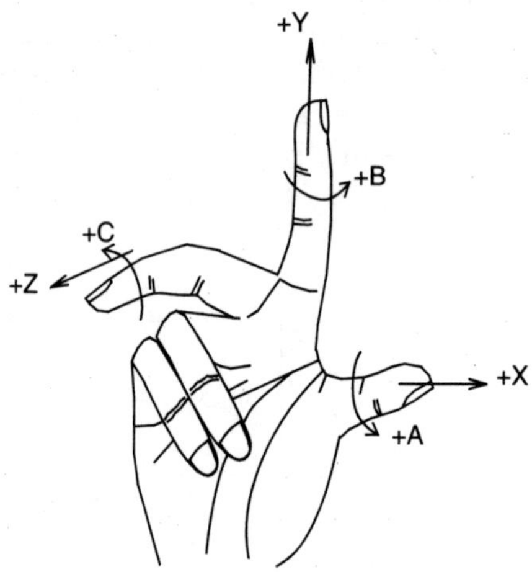

Fig. 6.2 Right Hand Co-ordinate System

Group II: All Machines tools with rotating workpieces (i.e., spindle generating surface of revolution) like lathes, grinding machines are classified as group II machines.

Group III: Machine tools with non-rotating workpieces and non-rotating tools (i.e., no spindles) like shaper, planer are classified as group III machines.

Group IV: Machines other than machine tools, like CNC drafting machine are classified as belonging to group IV.

6.3.3 Motion Designation

Z-motion shall be designated first and shall be followed by X and then Y motions.

6.3.3.1 Z-axis and Motion Designation

(a) **Location:** In case of machine groups I and II Z-axis is taken either along the spindle axis or parallel to the spindle axis. In case of machine group III and IV it is taken as the perpendicular to the work holding surface. The axis may or may not pass through the controlled point (i.e., cutting tool tip).

(b) **Z-axis Direction:** For the machine of groups I and II the cutting tools move in the negative Z direction to move a tool into the workpiece. The clearance between tool and workpiece decreases by Z-movement. For other machines the positive Z-motion increases the clearance between the work surface and the tool holder.

(c) **When there are several spindles and slides**: In such cases, one of the spindles, preferably perpendicular to the work holding surface may be chosen as the principal spindle. The primary Z-motion is then related to this primary spindle. The tool motions of other spindle quills or other slides, which are termed as secondary and tertiary motions, may be designated as U, V, W and P, Q, R respectively.

6.3.4 Rotary Motion

Axes. A, B and C, define the primary rotary motions.

(a) **Location:** These motions describe rotation about the axis X, Y and Z or about axes parallel to X, Y, Z respectively. If, in addition to the above mentioned primary rotary motions, there exist secondary rotary motions, whether parallel or not to A, B and C. They are designated as D or E.

(b) **Direction:** Positive (+) A, B and C directions are the directions which advance a right hand screw in the positive X, Y and Z directions.

In Fig.6.2 the fingers of the right hand point towards the above mentioned directions, viz., X, Y, Z; U, V, W; P, Q, R and A, B, C and are with reference to the point, movement of which is being controlled. This point is mostly the tip of the cutting tool. Many times the tool point may not be moving in the same direction, e.g., the quill of the spindle of a vertical milling machine is moving in Z-direction but not in X and Y directions. In such cases the work surface is generally moved in a direction opposite to the one intended for the tool, e.g. table of the milling machine holding the workpiece may be moved in -X and -Y directions. Such movements of machine elements say -X or -Y denoted as +X' or +Y' respectively. Primed letters are used to all motions to indicate directions for moving work surfaces instead of the tool motion which is in the opposite direction.

6.3.5 Objective of Axes Designation

The conventional mathematical right hand co-ordinate system is, in general is used to designate axes. The machine movements designated as above permit the part programmer to assume safe tool movements relative to the right hand co-ordinate system of a stationary workpiece. The programmer can thus imagine himself to be sitting on the tool and describing all the machining operations. For example,(Fig. 6.3) for moving a tool (say a ball-end mill) in a vertical milling machine from position P to position Q the part programmer specifies the movements from (5, 7, 6) to (8, 8, 5). The actual motions which take place on the machine tool are:

Movements of quill	(Z)	6 to 5. The quill goes up by one unit.
Movement of table	(X)	5 to 8. Table moves to the left by 3 units.
	(Y)	7 to 8. Table moves by one unit towards the column.

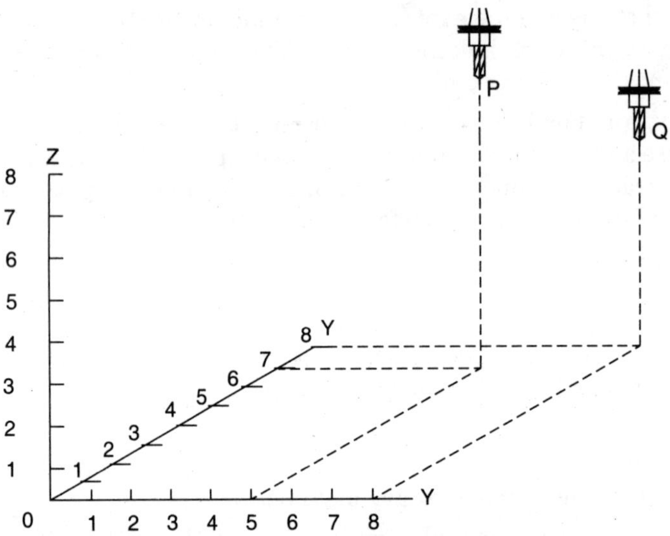

Fig. 6.3 Moving a Tool from Point P to Q

6.4 REFERENCE POINTS FOR MANUAL PROGRAMMING

(i) The Machine Datum - M: The machine datum is the origin to the co-ordinate system (See Fig. 6.4). For lathes it is on the mounting flange of the main spindle and the tuning axis. It cannot be changed by the user of the machine. It is fixed by the manufacturer and programmed into the computer memory. The point generally has the co-ordinates X = 0, Z = 0.

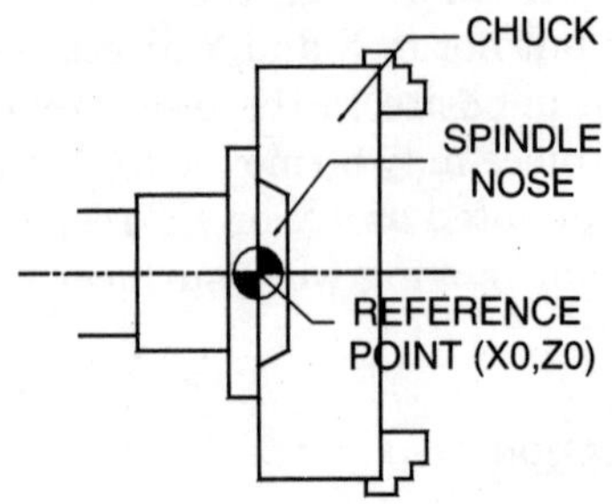

Fig. 6.4 Machine Datum of a Lathe

(ii) Machine Reference Point: The machine zero or machine reference position is the origin of the machine coordinate system. On all CNC machines, the machine zero is located at the positive end of each travel range. Figure 6.5 (a) shows the machine zero of a vertical machining center with respect to the work volume or envelope.

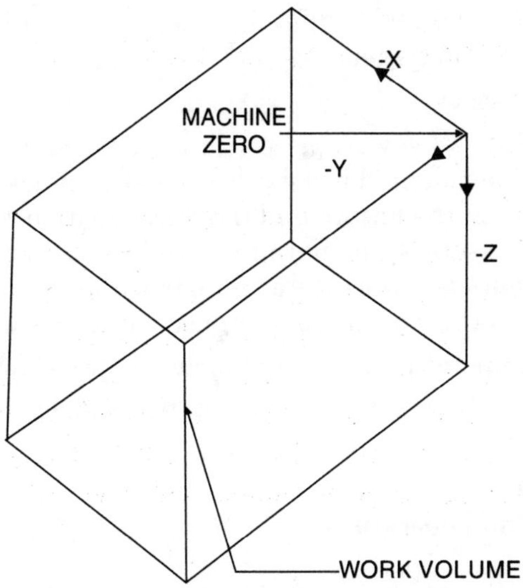

Fig. 6.5 (a) Machine Zero of a Vertical Machining Centre

During the machine set up, particularly after the power is turned on, the position of all axes has to be preset to be always the same. In modern machines this is achieved by a zero return command. Fanuc and other control systems require the machine zero return command performed at least once for automatic operation. Figure 6.5 (b) shows the machine zero in the top view of a vertical machine when looking at the table and Fig. 6.5 (c) shows the machine zero in the front view.

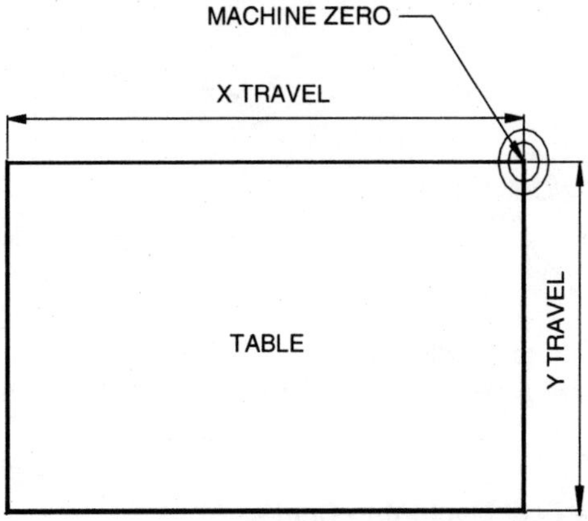

Fig. 6.5 (b) Machine Zero of a Vertical Machining Centre
Top View

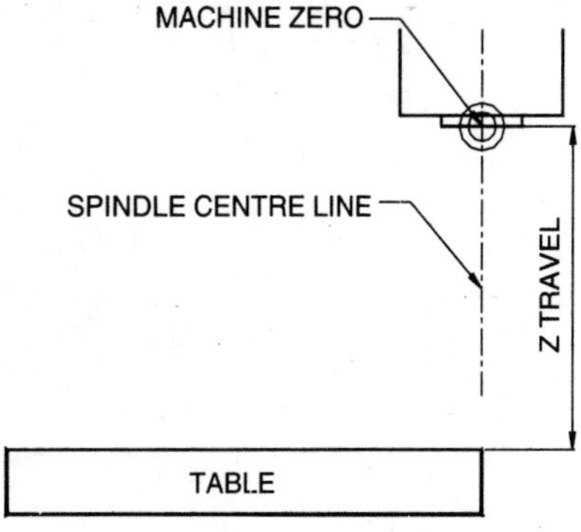

Fig. 6.5 (c) Machine Zero of a Vertical Machining Centre
Front View

A typical procedure to physically reach the machine zero position is:

- Turn the power on
- Select machine zero return mode
- Select first axis move (Z for machining Center and X for lathes)
- Repeat for all other axes

- Check the lighted in-position indicators
- Check display of position on screen
- Set display zero if necessary

(iii) Workpiece Zero-Point - W: A workpiece is located within the travel limits of a machine. Every workpiece must be mounted in a fixture, pallet or chuck depending on the situation. The location of the part in the fixture and the fixed position of the fixture with respect to the machine table are essential to guarantee consistent results and precision. It is very important to ensure that each workpiece of a particular batch is set the same way. Once the set up is established the workpiece reference point can be selected.

The workpiece reference point is commonly known as program zero or workpiece zero. In principle the workpiece zero can be selected anywhere. Three factors influencing the choice of workpiece zero are:

- Accuracy of machining
- Convenience of set up and operation
- Safety

In the case of prismatic components machined in a vertical machining centre the centre point of the top surface can be taken as the workpiece reference point. This is shown in Fig. 6.6.

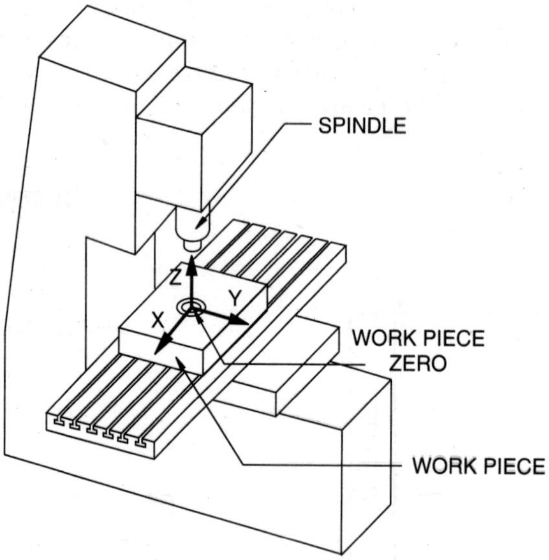

Fig. 6.6 Workpiece Reference for a Vertical Machining Center

In the case of a horizontal machining centre, the workpiece datum for Z axis can be located on the face of the workpiece facing the column. The Y-axis zero can be located on the top face of the fixture (i.e. the base of the workpiece). X axis zero can be located conveniently, say in one corner of the workpiece.

Selecting program zero for round parts or patterns (bolt circles, circular pockets etc.), the most useful program zero is at the centre of the circle as indicated in Fig. 6.7.

Program zero position can be built into the special fixtures can be used for setting up the workpieces. It must be mentioned here that a number of workpiece datum can be used in a part program.

In the case of CNC lathes program zero selection is simple. The X = 0 is generally located on the axis of rotation of the workpiece i.e. the spindle axis. As far as Z axis is concerned three positions are used:

- on the face of the chuck
- on the face of the jaw
- on the finished face of the workpiece

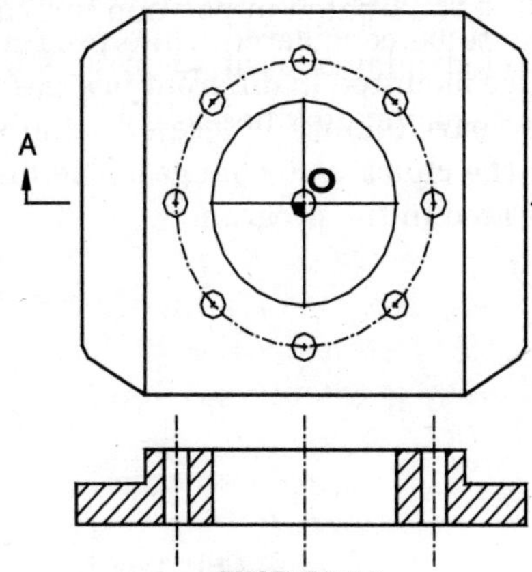

Fig. 6.7 Program Zero for Holes in a Pitch Circle

These positions are shown in Fig.6.8. In Fig. (a) the datum is on the face of the chuck (point 1). Usually this is the default datum in a lathe. In this case all coordinates of the work piece are positive. In Fig. 6.8(b) the datum is located on the face of the soft jaw (point 2). The shifting of the datum can be done in different ways. One method is to write a block of program as given below:

G59 Z0 X10.0;

In Fig. 6.8(c) the datum is located on the finished face of the work piece. The shifting of the datum can be done through a program block similar to the previous one.

G59 Z0 X110.0 ;

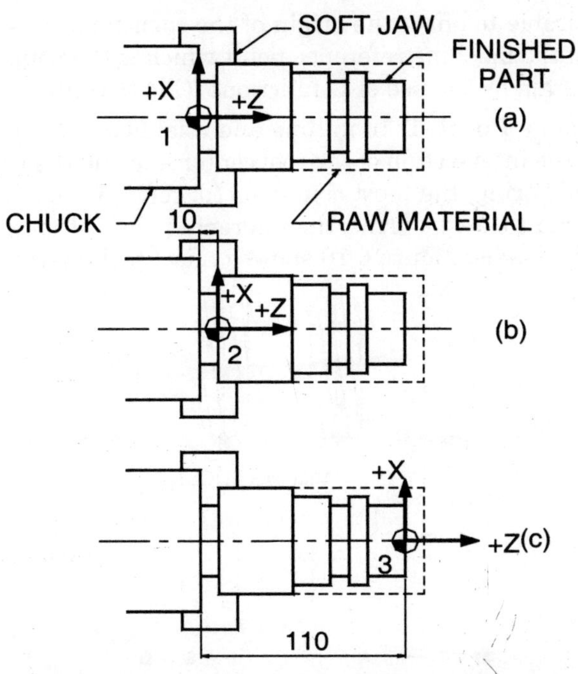

Fig. 6.8 Common Workpiece Zero Points for CNC lathes

During different machining processes various jaw positions of chucks are used and these are mounted onto the machine spindle. The distance of the face side of the workpiece from the machine datum (X1/X2/X3) differs, depending on the jaw surface which is used for chucking. This has to be considered while programming. This is indicated in Fig. 6.9 where the same workpiece mounted in different jaw positions is shown to have different values of work datum. The raw part (blank) is located axially in a shoulder. Correspondingly the position of the jaws in the chuck also changes. The distances X1 and X2 must be accurately measured and incorporated in the program.

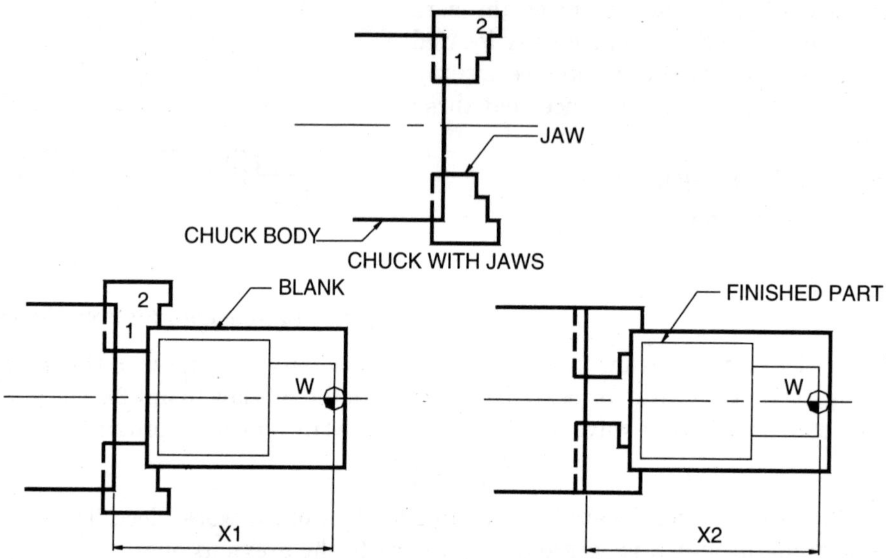

Fig. 6.9 Different Workpiece Datum Points Depending on Location in the Chuck Jaws

Therefore, it is desirable to offset the origin of the co-ordinate system into the workpiece zero point W, instead of the machine reference point which is the usual origin of the machine. It is effected in the program by the use of G-functions (G54 to G59).

(iv) Tool Post Reference Point–T: In milling and related operations the reference point of the tool is usually the intersection of the tool center line and the lowest positioned cutting tip. In turning and boring, the most common tool reference point is an imaginary point on the tool insert. For tools like drills, the reference point is the extreme tip of the tool, as measured along the Z-axis. Figure 6.10 shows typical tool reference points.

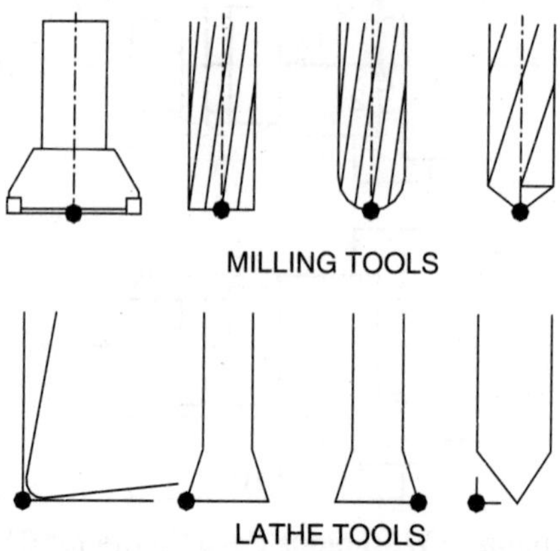

Fig. 6.10 Typical Tool Reference Points

6.5 PROGRAMMING USING ABSOLUTE VALUE/PROGRAMMING ON THE BASIS OF REFERENCE VALUES

CNC machines allow both absolute and incremental programming. The computer must be, however, informed of the method used so that the data which are put in can be properly interpreted.

G functions like G90 (Absolute dimension input) and G91 (Incremental dimension input) are used in several CNC systems for this purpose.

Dimensions of the workpiece to be turned are mostly indicated by diameters and to convert the diameter values into radius values during part programming is not only time consuming but can also introduce errors. Therefore, practically in all CNC lathes the diameter is programmed, though radius programming facility is also available in some systems.

Program Example 1

Programming using absolute value for the component shown in Fig. 6.11 with values referred to workpiece datum, W.

Points P1/P2/P3 has to be described in the absolute system, with zero point of the co-ordinate system being the workpiece datum as indicated.

				Target point
N01	G90			
N02	G01	X80	Z0	(P1)
N03	G01		Z-30	(P2)
N04	G01	X140	Z-60	(P3)

The command word G90 in the first program line causes all following X/Z inputs to be used as absolute values. This instruction will be cancelled, by the use of command word G91.

Program Example 2

With G91, the programmer uses incremental values with reference taken from the previous position of tool.

The above program in incremental format would be;

				Target point
N01	G91			
N02	G01	X10		(P1)
N03	G01		Z-15	(P2)
N04	G01	X10	Z-15	(P3)

Some CNC systems permit the use of mixed format. (Example - FANUC O-TE) In such cases, both incremental and absolute co-ordinates can be used freely in the program. Even in a single block one co-ordinate can be expressed in incremental format and the other in absolute format. In such cases, U, V and W addresses are used for designating incremental co-ordinates and X, Y, Z are used for absolute co-ordinates.

The following program line for example

N04 G01 U10.0 Z-30

can be used for moving from point P2 to P3 in the previous example.

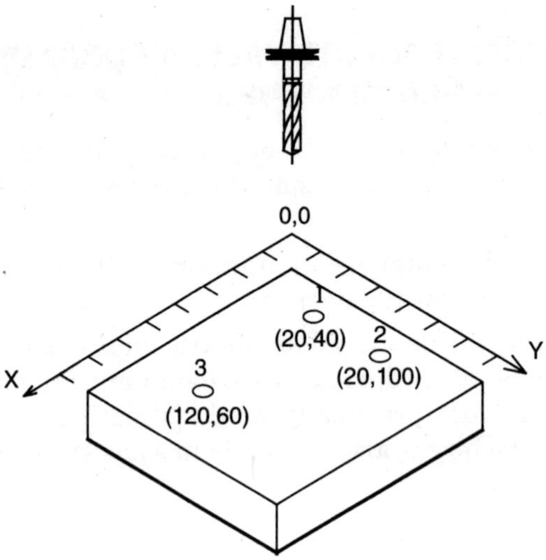

Fig. 6.11 Sample Workpiece for Program Examples 1& 2

Program Example 3

Figure 6.11 (b) shows a flat plate with three holes. Locations of the holes are:

Hole	X Coordinate	Y Coordinate
1	20.0	40.0
2	20.0	100.0
3	120.0	60.0

In **absolute** format the program for the slide movement is written as:

```
G90;
N1      X20.0      Y40.0;
N2                 Y100.0;
N3      X120.0
```

In **incremental** format, the program for the movement is written as:

```
G91;
N1      X20.0      Y40.0;
N2                 Y60.0;
N3      X100.0     Y-40.0:
```

For the convenience in programming both incremental programming and absolute programming modes can be used in a single program. For example:

```
G90;
N1      X20.0      Y40.0;
G91;
N2                 Y60.0;
N3      X120.0     Y-40.0;
```

6.6 REGISTER COMMANDS

It is necessary that the control system should be aware where the tool is located with respect to the work envelope of the machine. The method is to register the current position of the tool into the control system memory through the program using a command called position register command.

G92 Position register command in machining centers

G50 Position register command in lathes

The formats are:

G92 X....... Y......Z......

G50 X.......Z......

6.7 PROGRAM FORMAT SPECIFICATION ACCORDING TO ISO

The program format as per ISO is: N4/G2/X43/Z43....etc. This means that the block number can vary between 1 and 9999 (N0001 to N9999), preparatory function can have two digits, (G00 to G99), X-co-ordinates and Z-co-ordinates 7 digits each (e.g. 12334.567, 0987.654) etc. However, there can be exceptions to these specifications.

6.8 PREPARATORY FUNCTIONS (G-FUNCTIONS)

These are commands which prepare the machine for different modes of movement like positioning, contouring, thread cutting etc. The preparatory functions always precede the dimension word. The preparatory functions as per DIN 66025 are given in Tables 6.2 and 6.3.

Some systems also permit the use of more than one G-function in a single block.

6.9 FIXED OR CANNED CYCLES

A canned cycle is a combination of machine moves that performs any one particular machining function such as drilling, milling, boring, tapping, etc. These are described in various sections in detail in this chapter. For example, a drilling operation involves fast approach to the work piece, drill at the specified feed rate and fast return. Programming a drilling operation, therefore, involves a minimum of three blocks. A component may require several holes to be drilled. Programming each drilling individually will make the part program lengthy, requiring more memory space. Canned cycle permits coding the drilling operation as a cycle, call the cycle in the programme and position the workpiece wherever the drilling is to be carried out.

Table 6.2
Preparatory functions and their function as per DIN 660025

Function	Meaning
G00	Point to point, positioning
G01	Linear interpolation
G02	Circular interpolation, clockwise
G03	Circular interpolation, anti-clockwise
G04	Dwell

G06	Parabolic interpolation
G08	Acceleration
G09	Deceleration
G17	XY plane selection
G18	XZ plane selection
G19	YZ plane selection
G25 G29	Unassigned
G33	Thread cutting, constant lead
G34	Thread cutting, increasing lead
G35	Thread cutting, decreasing lead
G36 G39	Unassigned
G40	Tool offset cancel
G41 G42	Tool offset
G54 – G59	Linear Shift
G60	Fine positioning
G61	Medium Positioning
G62	Coarse positioning [fast]
G63	Tapping
G80	Canned cycle cancel
G81 – G89	Canned cycles
G90	Absolute dimension
G91	Incremental dimension
G92	Position pre-set
G93	Inverse time, feed rate
G94	Feed/minute
G95	Feed/revolution
G96	Constant surface speed
G97	Spindle speed

Table 6.3
G-functions of a typical CNC Lathe

Function	Format	Meaning
G00	G00 X/U Z/W S M	Linear movement at rapid traverse
G01 & G09		Straight line at feed rate
G01	G01 X/U Z/W A C R F S M*	,,
G09	G01 X/U Z/W A C R F S M	,,

G02		Circular interpolation clockwise
G03		Circular interpolation anticlockwise
G02	X/UZ/W R I K F S M	
G03	X/UX/ W R I K F S M	
G04		Dwell
G04	X S M	
G22		Subroutine call-up
G22	A P Q H	
G24,G25, G26, G27		Rapid return to tool changing point
G28		Position to reference datum point
G28	X/UX/WSM	
G33		Thread cutting block by block
G33	G33X/UZ/WFEM	
G37,G38		Tool data/parameter input
G40		Call down of tool nose radius compensation
G41		Call up of tool nose radius compensation
G53		Reference to machine zero datum
G53	XZSM	
G54-G57		Workpiece zero datum position
G59		Programmed additional zero datum shift
G59	XZSM	
G71		Longitudinal roughing cycle towards contour
G71	APQIKDFS	
G72		Face roughing cycle towards contour
G72	APQIKDFS	
G73		Contour parallel roughing cycle
G73	APQU/WI/KDFS	
G74		Longitudinal cycle with interrupted cut
G74	X/UZ/WIKDF	
G75		Facing cycle with interrupted cut
G75	X/UZ/WIKDF	
G76		Screw cutting cycle
G76	X/UZ/WIKHF/EAD	
G77		Chamfer cycle
G77	X/UZ/WIKF	
G78		Screw cutting cycle
G78	X/UZ/WIKF	

G79		Chamfer cycle opposite to spindle direction
G79	X/UZ/WIKF	
G81		Multiple cycle
G81	UWH	
G82		Threading cycle for taps or button dies
G82	Z/WF	
G83		Drilling cycle in Z-axis
G83	Z/WDHF	
G92		Speed limitation and monitoring
G92	PQ	
G94		Feed, mm/min
G95		Feed, mm/rev
G96	V	Constant cutting speed
G96		
G97		Spindle speed
G97	SVX	

6.10 ZERO-SUPPRESSION

All CNC machines are equipped with decimal point input. In order to simplify program input the leading zeros can be omitted.

e.g. 12.145 instead of 0012.145

Consecutive zeros after decimal point also need not be entered.

e.g. 12 instead of 12.000

10.4 instead of 10.400

6.11 FEED WORD (F)

Feed in turning is the advance of the tool into the workpiece for every revolution of the workpiece. In machining centers (for drilling, milling, boring etc) feed rate is used. Feed rate is the product of feed and the rpm of the tool. While feed is expressed as mm/rev. feed rate is expressed as mm/min. The calling address for feed or feed rate is F followed by a number of digits. The number of digits depends on the feed rate mode and the machine tool application. Decimal place is usually allowed.

Examples:

F0.25	Feed 0.25 mm/rev.
F500	Feed rate 500 mm/min.

A feed override switch on the control panel permits the operator to vary the programmed feed usually between 0 to 200 %.

6.12 SPINDLE SPEED WORD, S or V

The spindle speed can be specified in rpm, whereas, the cutting speed is given in m/min. The speed word allows for both cases. The spindle speed word is directly programmed in revolutions per minute. For example a speed of 450 rpm is programmed directly as:

G97 S450

As the machinability tables recommend cutting speed, a more convenient method of programming is to specify the cutting speed and this can be directly programmed using V. For example, if a facing operation or a contour turning operation is performed, the spindle speed will have to vary depending on the diameter of the workpiece being turned. It is impractical to calculate manually the spindle speeds in such cases. This task is better left to the computer. Suppose that the cutting speed is maintained at an optimum value of 250 m/min. for a facing or contour turning operation. In this case the spindle speed can be specified as

G96 V250.

The spindle speed will be automatically calculated and selected by the computer depending on the X value i.e. the position of tool tip.

A tricky situation may arise in drilling holes along the axis where X is equal to zero. The spindle speed has to be infinite in this case which is absurd. If it is desirable to specify the cutting speed for a drilling or boring operation it can be done using G97 code with diameter specified. For example,

G97V160 X20

will set the spindle speed of 160 m/min at a diameter of 20 mm. (i.e. the diameter of the drill or the bore to be machined).

The spindle speed can also be directly programmed in a block as:

N04 G01 X70.0 Z-50.5 S450 F0.3 ;

It may be necessary to specify the clockwise and counterclockwise rotation of the spindle. M03 is used to specify clockwise rotation and M04 counter clockwise rotation.

6.13 TOOL WORD, T

T function is used to denote the tool. There are differences in the tool functions for lathes and machining centres.

6.13.1 T Function for Machining Centres

Vertical and horizontal machining centres are equipped with automatic tool changers. The tool changer picks the tool from a magazine to be loaded into the spindle or replaces back a tool after machining in the magazine. Figure 6.12 shows a typical view of a tool magazine. The tool magazine may be circular or may be shaped in a zigzag form. It consists of a certain number of pockets where tool holder along with a cutting tool is placed during set up. Pockets are numbered consecutively. The magazine can be operated through the program or in the manual data input (MDI) mode. Within the travel of the tool magazine one particular position is aligned with the tool changer. It is in this waiting position, where the tool changer picks up the tool from the magazine or replaces a tool in the magazine. This is called the tool change position.

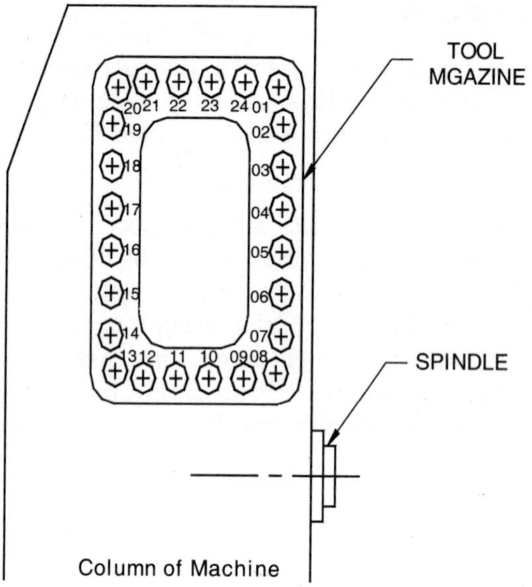

Fig. 6.12 View of a Typical 24- Tool Magazine

A command, say T04 indexes the tool magazine and brings the tool in pocket #4 to the tool changing position. Tool change is initiated by a M06 command. The ATC picks up the tool from the tool changing position, moves to the spindle, and removes the tool which has just completed machining, inserts the new tool into the spindle and returns the previous tool to the magazine. Simultaneously, the magazine will index to bring the pocket corresponding to the tool removed from the spindle to the tool changing position.

6.13.2 Lathe Tools

A typical slant bed lathe uses a hexagonal, octagonal or circular turret, which can hold external as well as internal tools. Turning centres will also have live tools driven by a servomotor. The turret accepts, generally, 8,12 or 16 tools. Figure 6.13 shows a typical tool turret. Sometimes there may be more than one turret in a machine. It is recommended that axial tools should not be located in adjacent pockets.

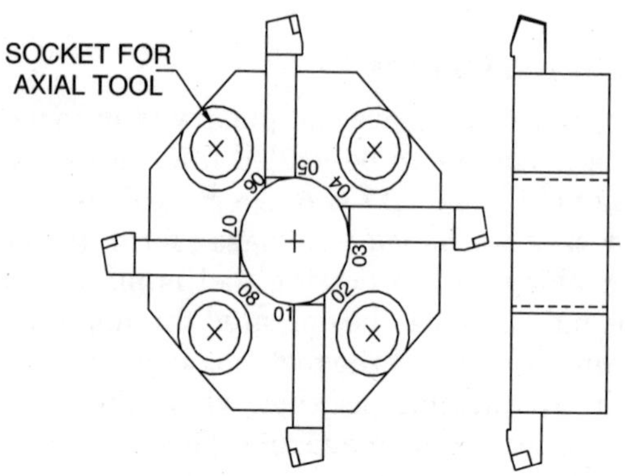

Fig. 6.13 Tool Turret

The tool number in lathes is associated with the tool length offset and tool wear offset. The general representation of a tool in lathes is T ABCD where AB is the tool station number and CD is the tool wear offset number. In general tools are referred as:

T01, T02, T03 etc.

Calling a tool, say T04 causes the turret to be indexed to bring the tool in pocket #4 to the machining position.

6.14 MISCELLANEOUS FUNCTION (M)

The address M in a CNC program block denotes a miscellaneous function. M functions control the program flow or activates some functions of the machine. This function pertains to auxiliary or switching information which does not relate to dimensional movement of the machine, such as spindle command, or coolant on/off and other functions. A list of M functions of a CNC lathe is given in Table 6.4.

There are two types of M functions

(i) Machine related functions

These control typically:

Spindle rotation, CW or CCW, stop

Gear change

Automatic tool change

Automatic pallet change

Coolant on or off

Tailstock quill movement

(ii) Program related functions

M functions are also used to control the execution of program flow.

Examples are:

Program stop

Program end

Program end with rewind of program

Optional stop

Tables 6.4 and 6.5 list the M functions of a turning machine and a machining center respectively.

Table 6.4
List of M functions of a CNC Lathe

M code	Description
M00	Program stop
M01	Optional program stop
M02	End of program
M03	Spindle rotation CW

M04	Spindle rotation CCW
M05	Spindle stop
M07	Mist coolant ON
M08	Coolant ON
M09	Coolant OFF
M10	Chuck open
M11	Chuck close
M12	Tailstock quill IN
M13	Tailstock quill OUT
M17	Turret indexing forward
M18	Turret indexing reverse
M19	Spindle orientation
M21	Tailstock forward
M22	Tailstock backward
M23	Thread gradual pull out ON
M24	Thread gradual pull out Off
M30	Program end and rewind
M41	Low gear selection
M42	Medium gear selection-1
M43	Medium gear selection-2
M44	High gear selection
M48	Feedrate override cancel OFF
M49	Feedrate override cancel ON
M98	Subprogram call
M99	Subprogram end

Table 6.5
Typical M Functions of Machining Centres

M code	Description
M00	Program stop
M01	Optional program stop
M02	End of program
M03	Spindle rotation CW
M04	Spindle rotation CCW
M05	Spindle stop
M07	Mist coolant ON
M08	Coolant ON
M09	Coolant OFF

M30	Program end and rewind
M48	Feedrate override cancel OFF
M49	Feedrate override cancel ON
M60	Automatic pallet change
M78	B-Axis clamp
M79	B-Axis unclamp
M98	Subprogram call
M99	Subprogram end

6.15 TOOL NOSE RADIUS COMPENSATION

The carbide insert used in turning operation has a certain corner radius (R) as shown in Fig. 6.14. Without the corner radius, the carbide tool tip will break or melt when working. These radii are standardized according to ISO.

$$r = 0.2/0.4/0.8/1.2/1.6/\text{etc.}$$

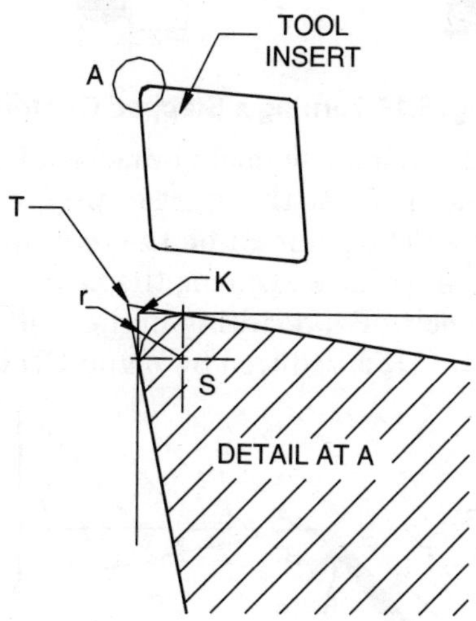

Fig. 6.14 Tool Insert

The parameters of the tool tip are defined with reference to the Fig. 6.14.

S = Centre of radius

r = Corner radius

K = Imaginary cutting point (Location of reference point)

T = Theoretical tool point

Consider turning a contour ABCD shown in Fig. 6.15. The point P is cutting while turning AB and CD and the point Q cuts while facing the shoulder BC. However, the imaginary setting point K lies on the contour. The programmed path is for the imaginary centre point and the radius of the cutting edge does not influence the workpiece contour while turning in X or Z direction.

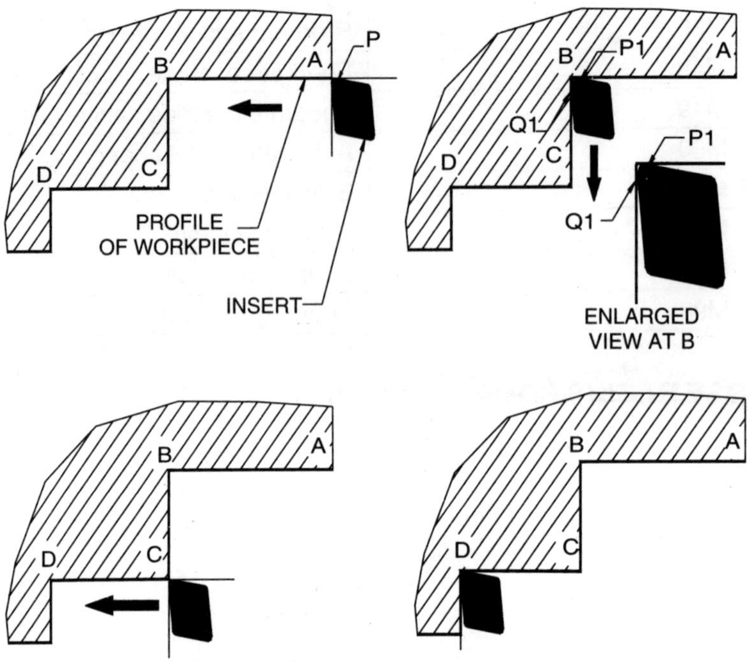

Fig. 6.15 Turning a Stepped Contour

While turning a taper or a curved profile, the tool nose radius affects the accuracy of the workpiece. This is illustrated in Fig. 6.16. At the start of profile the imaginary cutting point K coincides with the point A. The point P1 on the tool tip does the cutting up to B. When K coincides with B, P1 is at point B'. During the next block the tip moves parallel to BC and cutting is done with point P2, resulting in the shift of the taper from BC to B'C'. As a consequence, the length AB is reduced by Z and CD is increased by ΔZ.

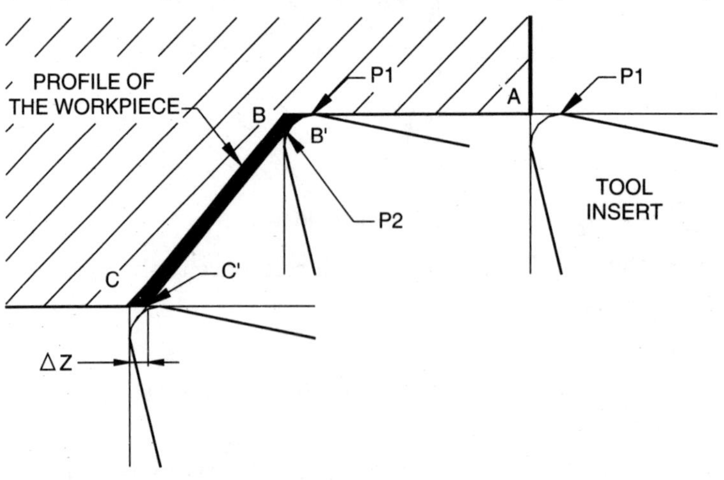

Fig. 6.16 Effect of Nose Radius of Inserts in Turning

Two methods are adopted for avoiding this error due to tool nose radius.

(i) Programming the imaginary cutting point K.

(ii) Programming the centre of the radius S.

In the present day CNC machines, the computer automatically performs this correction. The tool nose radius is programmed into the memory of the machine and the software of the machine takes care of the effect of the tool nose radius.

The cutter radius affects the profile accuracy of the workpiece in the case of milling or contouring machines. The radius may vary slightly from one cutter to another cutter of the same diameter or the cutter size may vary due to regrinding. In these machines, the centre line path of the cutter is calculated by the computer taking into account the variation of the cutter diameter. Since cutters with throwaway inserts are widely used in CNC machining, the issue of regrinding applies only to HSS cutters. The tool nose radius compensation is called up or called down by the appropriate G codes.

6.16 TOOL LENGTH OFFSET

The length of each cutting tool has to be taken into account in running a CNC program. The length of a tool used for machining can be determined on the CNC machine or away from it. This is very important as the length of travel of the slide depends on the tool length. For example, in the case of a drilling operation, the program does not take into account the length of the drill. The programmer specifies the zero datum on the machine in the Z-axis. The distance between the Z0 of the machine and Z0 of the work is the distance the tool tip has to traverse to reach the workpiece. The control system has to compute the actual distance to be traversed by subtracting the tool length from this distance. In order to carry out this calculation the tool length must be stored in the memory of the machine in appropriate registers. In the case of machining centers this information is stored in D or H registers and they are called in the program using appropriate G-functions. In the case of turning machines the tool lengths are usually associated with the tool number.

In the case of a boring tool both Z and X offsets are important. In the case of end mills the cutter radius must be available to compute the tool path either in pocketing or in profile milling. Both Z and X offsets are to be considered for turning tools. In the case of parting tools, one of the tool tip corner is referenced to measure the length.

6.16.1 On-machine Tool Length Measurement

This is usually done by the operator who places the tool in the spindle and measures the distance the tool travels from machine zero to workpiece zero. This can be done only between jobs and is definitely non-productive.

(i) Some machines have automatic tool pre-setting devices which are mounted on the machine tool itself. In the case of CNC lathes these probes will have four sensors to measure the tool offset of different kinds of tools. Sensors are often fitted with machining centres to measure the tool offset.

(ii) Another popular method in the case of lathes is to hold the blank in the chuck and jog the tool to touch the diameter and face of the workpiece. The diameter and length information can then be input into the memory of the machine. Many manufacturers prefer this method as the input of tool offset is achieved completely through software.

6.16.2 Off-machine Tool Length Measurement

Off machine tool length measurement requires a tool pre-setter which can be mechanical, optical, or electronic. The offsets are input manually or stored in programmable chips mounted on the tool holder.

In addition to the other data required for the execution of the program, tool length information also has to be input to enable the computer to calculate the tool path. In the case of the machining centres, tools are preset using a pre-setting device.

6.17 INTERPOLATION FUNCTIONS

A CNC program consists, among other codes, a series of instructions which represent movement of the tool in a specified path which may be along a straight line or along a part of a circle or a specified curve. Three common interpolation functions are:

(i) Linear interpolation
(ii) Circular interpolation
(iii) Helical interpolation

6.17.1 Linear Interpolation

Linear interpolation is used in part programming to either move the machine slides in a straight line either in the rapid traverse or feed mode. The linear movement is effected by calculating automatically a large number of intermediate points along the tool path and moving the slides from one intermediate point to another. Linear interpolation algorithms are used for computing intermediate points. Linear interpolation can be along a single axis or along two or more axes simultaneously.

6.17.2 Circular Interpolation

The programming of the slides of a machine to result in a path which is part of an arc of a circle is called circular interpolation. It is commonly used in CNC lathes, machining centers, routers, water jet and laser cutting machines, wire EDM, and other machines. The CNC system interpolates the arc to obtain a large number of intermediate points to define the tool path very precisely.

6.17.3 Helical Interpolation

Helical interpolation is an operation where a circular interpolation uses three axes simultaneously. It is a simultaneous two axes circular motion in the working plane with a linear motion along the remaining axis. A typical example of application of helical interpolation is thread milling.

6.18 SHOPFLOOR PROGRAMMING/ CONVERSATIONAL PROGRAMMING

Several CNC systems permit direct programming in manual data input mode. The following features and input procedure are common in such options:

(i) Component profile directly from drawing
(ii) Material shape and dimensions
(iii) Machine reference point and home position of the turret
(iv) Process and tool selection
(v) Machining area and selection of cutting conditions
(vi) Calculation of tool centre path
(vii) Machining time display

6.19 DETAILED DESCRIPTION OF G-FUNCTIONS OF LATHES

Codes like G01, G02 etc. used in programming are called preparatory functions and denote various control functions like the type of interpolation conducted in the control unit, plane selection, stored stroke limit, reference point specification, thread cutting, tool nose radius compensation, fixed cycles, feed specification, inch/metric selection, etc.

Typically G-functions will have the address G followed by two digits (00 to 99). Some G-functions will have three digit numbers. Example is cylindrical interpolation (G107). Table 6.6 gives a list of G-functions commonly used in CNC lathes. It is to be noted that there may be some differences in G-functions from one control system to another.

A number following address G determines the meaning of the command for the concerned block.

The G codes given in Table 6.6 are Fanuc 0 codes. There are three G code systems: A,B and C, G – code system A is standard. The users can specify the system depending on their requirements. The following points are to be noted in using G-codes.

(1) G codes of group 00 except G10 and G11 are single-shot G codes.
(2) Alarm 010 is displayed when a G code not listed in the G code list is specified or a G code without a corresponding option is specified.
(3) G codes of different groups can be specified in the same block. If G codes of the same group are specified in the same block, the G code specified last is valid.
(4) G codes are displayed for each group number.

Table. 6.6 G-Functions of CNC Lathes

G code			Group	Function
A	B	C		
G00	G00	G00	01	Positioning [Rapid traverse]
G01	G01	G01		Linear interpolation [Cutting feed]
G02	G02	G02		Circular interpolation/Helical interpolation CW
G03	G03	G03		Circular interpolation/Helical interpolation CCW
G04	G04	G04	00	Dwell
G10	G10	G10		Data setting
G11	G11	G11		Data setting mode cancel
G17	G17	G17	16	XpYp plane selection
G18	G18	G18		ZpXp plane selection
G19	G19	G19		YpZp plane selection
G20	G20	G70	06	Input in inch
G21	G21	G71		Input in mm
G27	G27	G27	00	Reference position return check
G28	G28	G28		Return to reference position
G30	G30	G30		2nd reference position return
G31	G31	G31		Skip function
G32	G33	G33	01	Thread cutting
G40	G40	G40	07	Tool nose radius compensation cancel
G41	G41	G41		Tool nose radius compensation left
G42	G42	G42		Tool nose radius compensation right

G50	G92	G92	00	Coordinate system setting, max. spindle speed setting
G52	G52	G52	00	Local coordinate system setting
G53	G53	G53		Machine coordinate system setting
G54	G54	G54	14	Workpiece coordinate system 1 selection
G55	G55	G55		Workpiece coordinate system 2 selection
G56	G56	G56		Workpiece coordinate system 3 selection
G57	G57	G57		Workpiece coordinate system 4 selection
G58	G58	G58		Workpiece coordinate system 5 selection
G59	G59	G59		Workpiece coordinate system 6 selection
G65	G65	G65	00	Macro command
G70	G70	G72	00	Finishing cycle [Other than 0-GCD]
G71	G71	G73		Stock removal in turning [Other than 0-GCD]
G72	G72	G74		Stock removal in facing [Other than 0-GCD]
G73	G73	G75		Pattern repeating [Other than 0-GCD]
G74	G74	G76		End face peck drilling [Other than 0-GCD]
G75	G75	G77		Outer diameter/internal diameter drilling [Other than 0-GCD]
G76	G76	G78		Multiple threading cycle [Other than 0-GCD]
G71	G71	G72	01	Traverse grinding [For 0-GCD]
G72	G72	G73		Traverse direct constant-dimension grinding cycle [For 0-GCD]
G73	G73	G74		Oscillation grinding cycle [For 0-GCD]
G74	G74	G75		Oscillation direct constant-dimension grinding cycle [For 0-GCD]
G90	G77	G20	01	Outer diameter/internal diameter cutting cycle
G92	G78	G21		Thread cutting cycle
G94	G79	G24		End face turning cycle
G96	G96	G96	02	Constant surface speed control
G97	G97	G97		Constant surface speed control cancel
G98	G94	G94	05	Per minute feed
G99	G95	G95		Per revolution feed
-	G90	G90	03	Absolute programming
-	G91	G91		Incremental programming
-	G98	G98	11	Return to initial level
-	G99	G99		Return to R point level

G codes are divided into the following two types.

Type	Meaning
One-shot G code	The G code is effective only in the block in which it is specified
Modal G code	The G code is effective until another G code of the same group is specified

Example:

G01	X100.0	Z2	F0.2;	(1)
			Z0;	(2)
	X125;			(3)
		Z-50;		(4)
G00	X150;			(5)

It may be noted that in blocks 2,3,4 the operating G-function is G01 but need not be specified.

Some G-codes like G00, G22, G25, G40, G80, G90, G95 and G97 are initial G codes when power is turned on. A number of G-codes can be specified in the same block. When more than one G-code of the same group is specified the G-code specified later is effective. If any g code of group 01 is specified in the canned cycle mode, the canned cycle will be automatically cancelled.

Brief descriptions of G-functions are given in the subsequent sections.

6.19.1 Positioning (G00)

G00 is positioning (in rapid traverse).

The tool moves to the specified target position with an absolute command or to a position at a specified distance from the current position with an incremental command at rapid traverse rate. As shown in Fig. 6.17. The tool moves from initial position to target position 2.

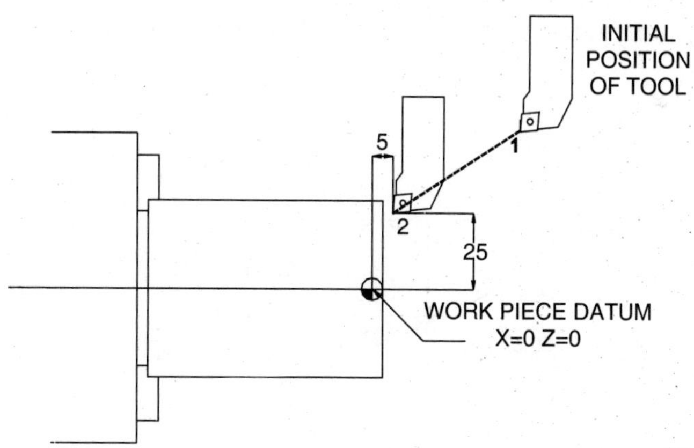

Fig. 6.17 G00

The format is:

G00 X----.--- Z----.---; Absolute format

G00 U----.---W----.---; Incremental format

For example the program block for the movement shown in Fig. 6.17 is:

G00 X100.0 Z5.0;

Positioning is done with each axis independently.

6.19.2 Linear Interpolation (G01)

Linear interpolation defines the feed movement either independently along each axis or simultaneously to produce tapered surfaces. The tool tip moves to the target position as commanded in absolute or incremental format at the specified feed. Since the feed specified by the F code remains effective until a new feed code is specified, it need not be repeated.

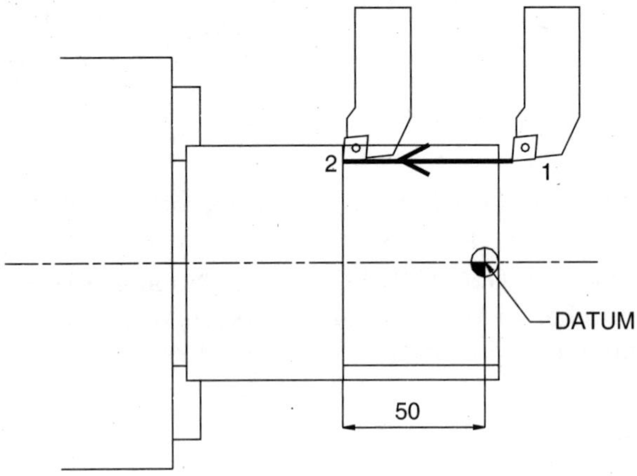

Fig. 6.18 G01

Example:

Referring to Fig. 6.18, the program to move the tool to the target point is:

G01 Z –50.0 F 0.2;

(Since there is no change in X dimension it need not be specified).

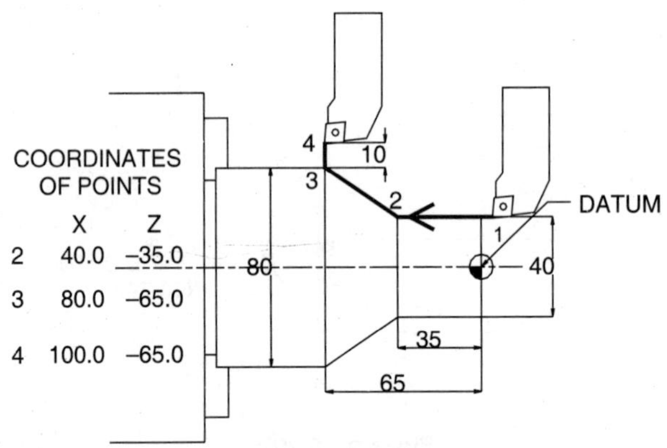

Fig. 6.19 G01- Another Example

Referring to Fig. 6.19, the tool moves first parallel to its axis to point 2 (X40, Z=–35), then to point 3 (X=80,Z= –65) and then to point 4 (X=120,Z=–65).

The program for this movement can be written as:

```
G01     X 40.0     Z-35.0     F0.2     ;
        X80.0      Z-65.0              ;
        X100.0                         ;
```

Please note that for X coordinate the diameter is specified instead of radius!

The same program can be written in incremental mode as follows:

G01		W-35.0	F0.2
	U30.0	W-30.0	
	U10.0		

The feed rate commanded is measured along the tool path.

6.19.3 Circular Interpolation (G02,G03)

This command will move the tool tip along a circular arc. G02 is circular interpolation in the CW direction and G02 is circular interpolation in CCW direction.

The format for circular interpolation is:

G02 X-----.--- Z----.--- I----K---- F----;

Where X , Z	Coordinates of target point
I	Distance from start point to arc centre along X direction
K	Distance from start point to arc centre along Z direction

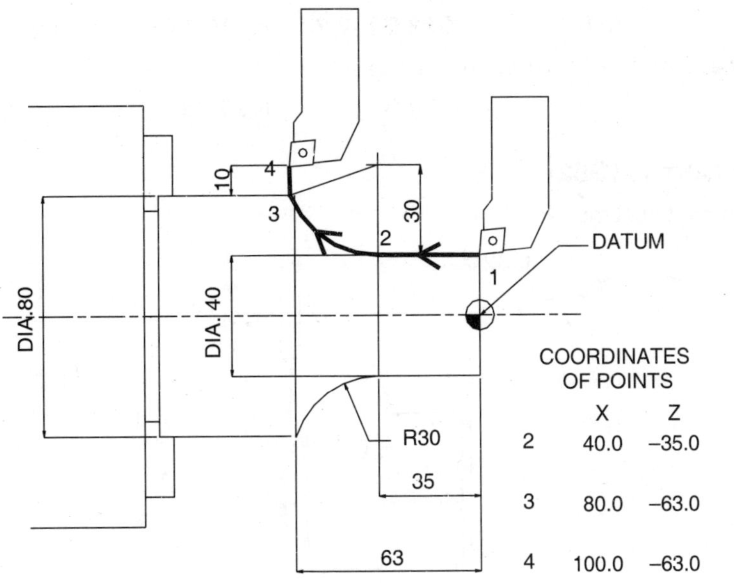

Fig. 6.20 G02

For Fig. 6.20, the tool point moves from point 2 to point 3 in circular interpolation (CW). The distance from the start point to the arc centre along the X direction ("I') is 30 mm. The distance from the start point to the arc centre along Z direction (K) is zero.

The program in absolute format is:

G02	X80.0	Z-63.0	I30.0	K0	F0.2;

The program in incremental format is:

G02	U20.0	W-28.0	I30.0	K0	F0.2;

Another possibility is to use radius programming. In this case the program can be written as:

G02	X80.0	Z63.0	R30.0	F0.2;

G03 is circular interpolation in counterclockwise direction. For Fig. 6.21 the program for the movement from point 2 to point 3 can be written as:

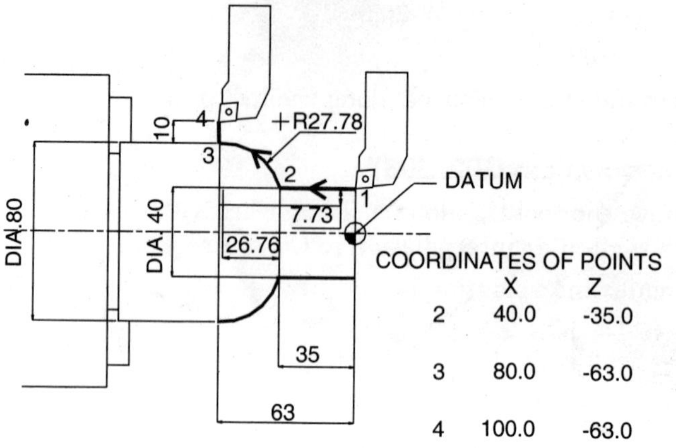

Fig. 6.21 G03

G03 X80.0 Z-63.0 I -7.73 K -26.76 F0.2;

In radius programming this can be written as:

G03 X80.0 Z-70.0 R 27.78;

6.19.4 Thread Cutting (G32)

The format for thread cutting is:

G32 X----.---Z----.---F--.----- ;

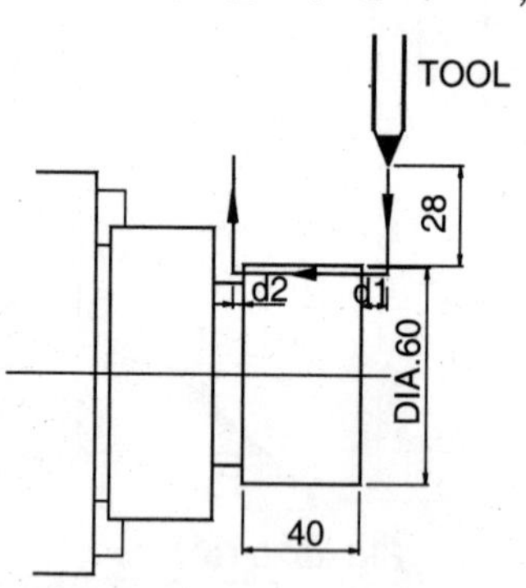

Fig. 6.22 Threading

6.19.5 Multiple Repetitive Cycles

One of the most time consuming programming task is removal of excessive stock, particularly in turning bar stock. Usually this may involve a number of passes. For roughing a complex contour this is not only time consuming but also error prone. Special cycles, also called fixed cycles (multiple repetitive cycles) enable such roughing tool path to be processed automatically. In general there are seven multiple repetitive cycles available. They are:

G71	Longitudinal turning cycle
G72	Facing cycle

G73	Contour parallel turning cycle
G70	Finishing cycle for G71,G72,and G73
G74	Peck drilling cycle
G75	Peck grooving cycle
G76	Threading cycle

Some of these cycles are shown in Fig. 6.23. Each one of them is discussed in detail in the following sections.

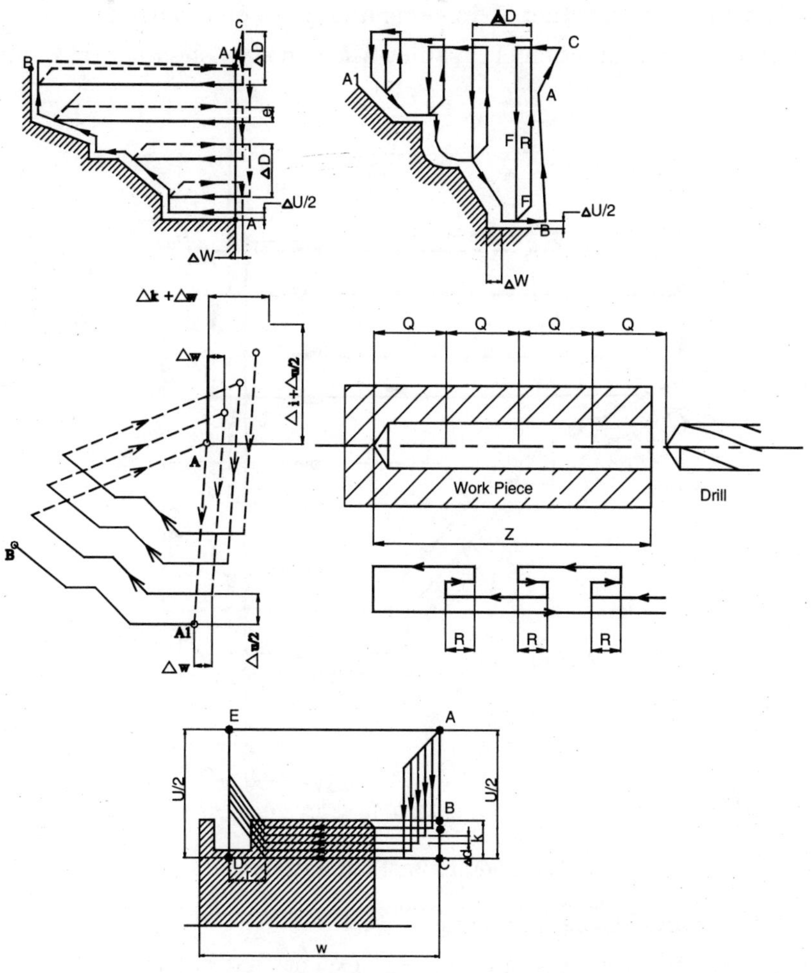

Fig. 6.23 Multiple Repetitive Cycles

6.19.5.1 G71 Longitudinal Turning Cycle

Figure 6.24 shows a longitudinal turning operation for stock removal. In this case a finished shape from A to B is to be obtained with a roughing depth of cut of ΔD and finishing allowance of ΔU/2 on the radius and ΔW on the shoulder.

Format:

G71 U (ΔD) R (e)

G71 P (ns) Q (nf) U (ΔU) W(ΔW) F(f) S(s) T(t);

Note: The contour of the finished workpiece is defined from block numbers N (ns) and N(nf)

N(ns)	Starting block number
N(nf)	Finishing block number
ΔD	Depth of cut (radial). This is to be designated without sign. The cutting direction depends on the direction of A1 -A.
e	Amount of tool withdrawal after every pass (pre-programmed).

This value can be specified by a parameter or in the program.

ΔU	Distance and direction of finishing allowance on diameter
ΔW	Distance and direction of finishing allowance on shoulder (in Z direction)

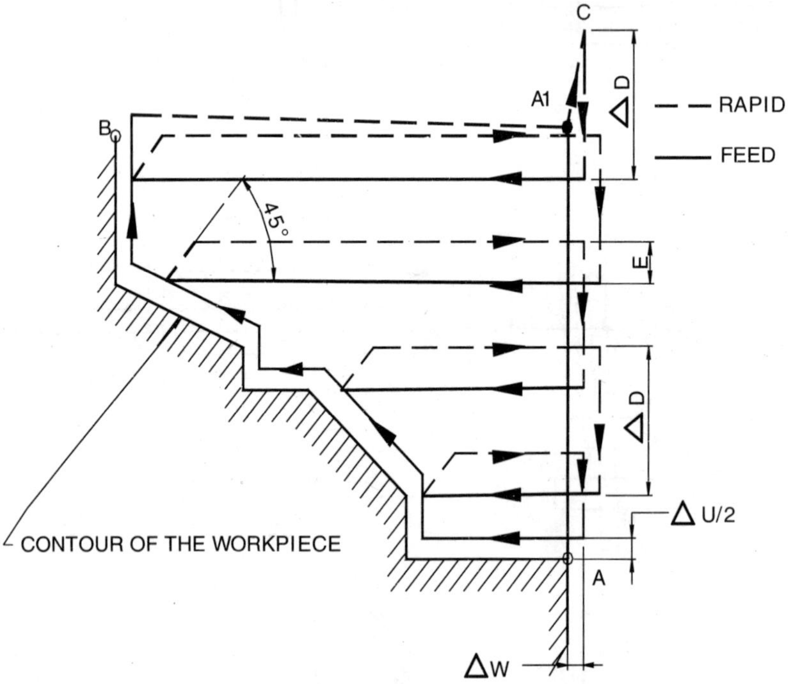

Fig. 6.24 Longitudinal Turning Cycle

6.19.5.2 G72 Stock Removal Cycle in Facing

As shown in Fig. 6.25, the cycle is similar to G71 except that cutting is made by operation parallel to X axis. The symbols used have the same meaning as in G71.

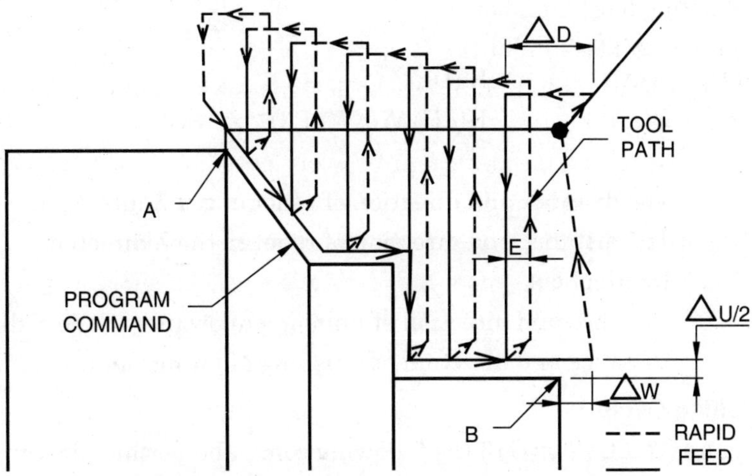

Fig. 6.25 G 72 Stock Removal Cycle In Facing

6.19.5.3 G73 Pattern Repeating (Contour Parallel Turning)

This G-function permits cutting in a fixed contour pattern repeatedly, with pattern being repeated with a displacement. By this cycle it is possible to efficiently cut workpieces whose initial surface has already been made by pre-machining, casting or forging.

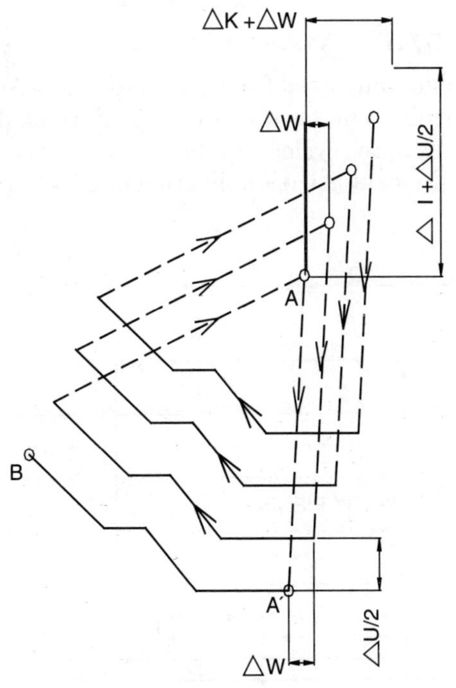

Fig. 6.26 Pattern Repeat Cycle

The pattern commanded in the program is from A to A′ to B as shown in Fig. 6.26.

Format:

G73 U(ΔI) W(ΔI) R (D);

G73 P(ns) Q(nf) U(ΔU) W(ΔW) F(f) S(s) T(t);

Where

ΔI	The distance and direction of relief in the X direction
ΔK	The distance and direction of relief in the Z direction
D	Depth of cut
ΔU	Distance and direction of finishing allowance in the X direction
ΔW	Distance and direction of finishing allowance in the Z direction

6.19.5.4 G70 Finishing Cycle

After rough cutting by G71, G72 or G73 the following command permits finishing.

G70 P (ns) Q(nf) U(ΔU) W(ΔW) ;

(ns)	Sequence number of the last block for the program of finished contour
(nf)	Sequence number of the first block for the program of finished contour
(ΔU)	Finishing allowance in the X-direction
(ΔW)	Finishing allowance in the Z-direction

When the cycle machining by G70 is completed the tool is returned to the start point and the next block is read.

6.19.5.5 Peck Drilling Cycle (G74)

This cycle along with G75 is commonly used for interrupted cuts. Apart from drilling along the Z axis, G75 can be used for turning and boring of hard materials, deep face grooving, difficult parting off operations etc. As in other cycles, the format will vary depending on the model of the CNC system. Figure 6.27 illustrates the application of G74 to peck drilling.
A typical format is:

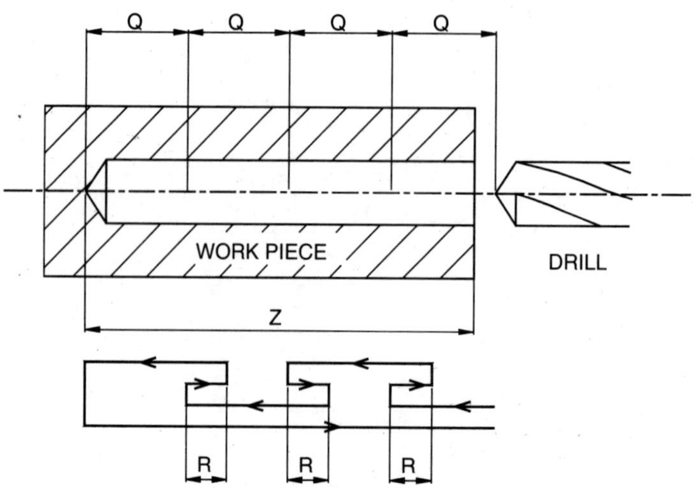

Fig. 6.27 Peck Drilling Cycle

G74 R

G 74 X(U) Z (W) P Q R F S;

First Block:

R = Return amount, mm (clearance for each cut)

Second Block:

X (U) = Final groove diameter to be cut

Z (W) = Z position of the last peck (depth of the hole)

P = Depth of each cut (no sign)

Q = Depth of each peck (no sign)

R = Relief amount after each cut (zero for face grooving)

F = Feed rate

S = Spindle speed

6.19.5.6 Groove Cutting Cycle (G75)

The G75 cycle used along the X-axis is used for operations requiring an interrupted cut, for example for breaking chips during a long or deep cutting motion.

Typical format for G75 is:

G75 R

G75 X(U) Z(W) P Q R F S ;

First Block:

R = Return amount, mm (clearance for each cut)

Second Block:

X (U) = Final groove diameter to be cut

Z (W) = Z position of the last peck (depth of the hole)

P = Depth of each cut (no sign)

Q = Depth of each peck (no sign)

R = Relief amount after each cut (zero for face grooving)

F = Feed rate

6.19.5.7 Thread Cutting Cycle (G76)

Use of simple threading G32 will involve several blocks to complete a threading operation. A multiple repetitive threading cycle G76 is recommended for programming of thread cutting. Figure 6.28 illustrates the cycle. The format for G76 is:

G76 P------ Q------R------ ;

G76 X------Z------R------P------Q------F------ ;

Where

First Block:

P = is a 6 digit data entry in pairs

Digits 1 and 2- number of finishing cuts (01-99)

Digits 3 and 4- number of leads for gradual pull out

Digits 5 and 6- angle of thread (00,29,30,55,60,80 only)

Q = Minimum cutting depth (Positive radial value-no decimal)

R = Fixed amount of finishing allowance (decimal permitted)

Second block:

X = Last diameter of thread (absolute) or the distance from start point to the last thread (incremental)

Z = End of thread along Z axis (absolute or incremental)

R = Radial difference between start and end positions of thread at Final pass (for taper threads)

P = Height of thread (Positive radial value-no decimal)

Q = Depth of first threading pass (Positive radial value-no decimal)

F = Pitch of the thread

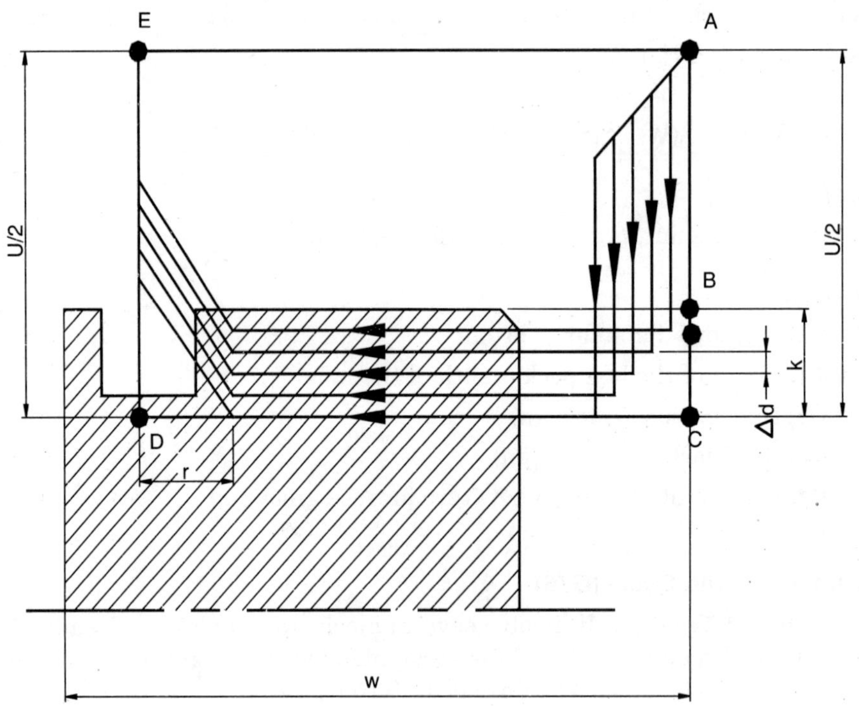

Fig. 6.28 Threading Cycle

Example:

For cutting M24 × 3 thread

G76 P010160 Q01 R0.05;

G76 X20.32 Z-40.0 R0 P1840 Q0500 F3.0;

The thread cutting insert has two cutting edges. Thread cutting is normally carried out in a number of passes. This number will depend upon the pitch and the depth of cut. Figure 6.29(a) shows two approaches to cutting of threads. In the case of tool feed normal to axis, both the edges of the insert will remove material where as in the other case only one edge is removing material. Since the former approach is prone to chatter, the latter is preferred. Even in this case depth of cut is reduced successively as shown in Fig. 6.29(b). If Δd is the initial depth of cut, the total depth of cut at the nth pass will be $\Delta d\sqrt{n}$. The material removed per cycle is thus held constant.

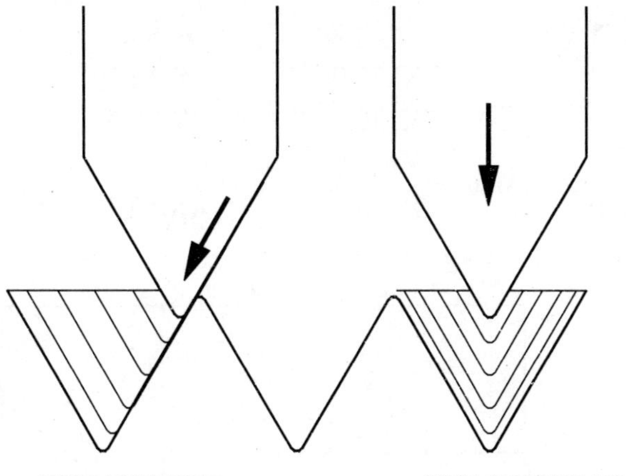

Fig. 6.29(a) Two Approaches to Thread Cutting

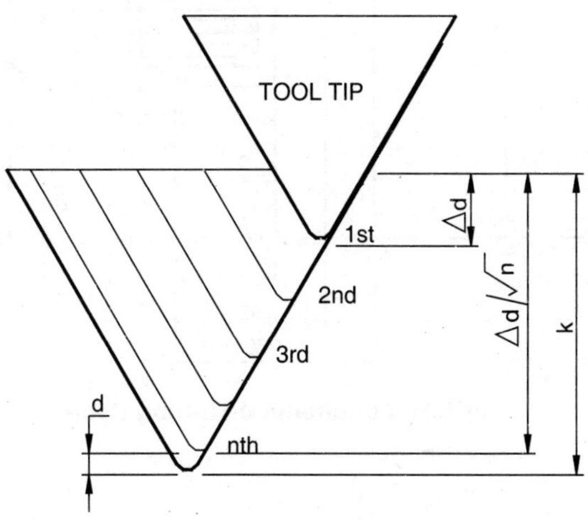

Fig. 6.29(b) Preferred Method

6.20 EXAMPLES

Figure 6.30 shows the set up of a component with work datum on the face of the chuck. The sequence of operations is also illustrated in the figure.

Longitudinal Turning Cycle (G71)

The program segment for machining the component is given below:

N010	G50	X250.0	Z160.0 ;		
N011	G00	X180.0	Z110.0 ;		
N012	G96	V250 ;			
N013	G71	U7.0	R1.0 ;		
N014	G71	P015	Q019	U4.0	W3.0f0.3;
N015		X120.0	F0.15;		
N016	G01		W-30.0;		
N017		X120.0	W-15.0;		
N018		X140.0	W-15.0;		
N019		X150.0;			
N020	G70	P015	Q019;		

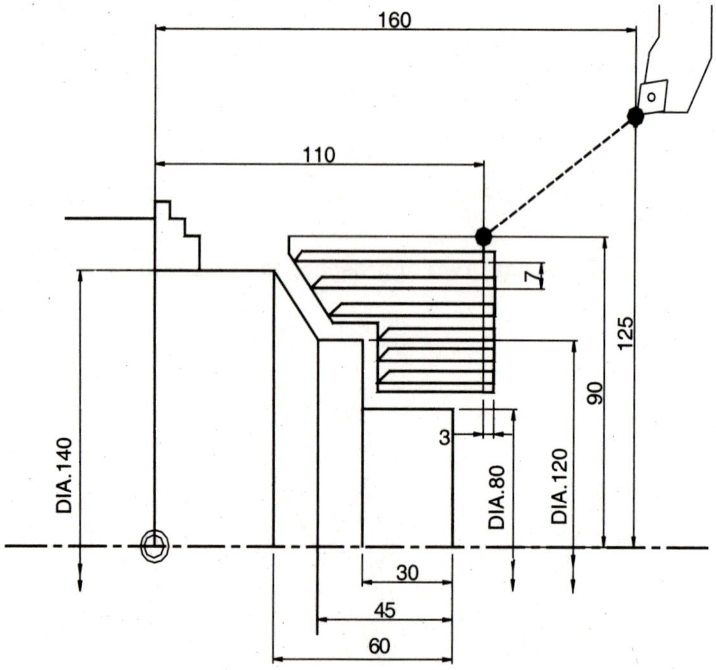

Fig. 6.30 Longitudinal Turning Cycle

Facing cycle (G72)

Refer to Fig. 6.31.

The method of machining the same contour with G72 is illustrated in this example.

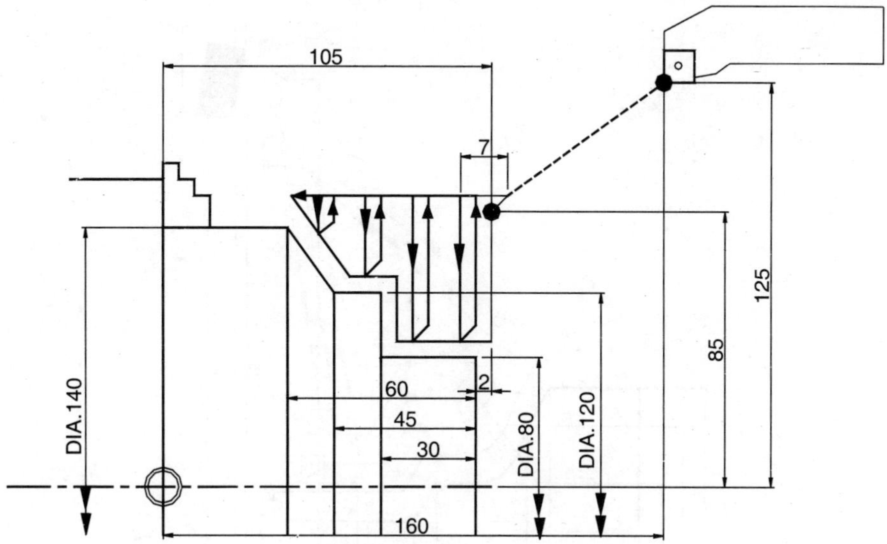

Fig. 6.31 Facing Cycle

N015	G50	X250.0	Z160.0;			
N016	G00	X170.0	Z105.0;			
N017	G96	V200;				
N018	G72W7.0		R1.0;			
N019	G72	P020	Q025	U4.0	W2.0	F0.3;
N020	G00	Z55.0;				
N021	G01	X140.0	W15.0;			
N022		X120.0	W15.0;			
N023			W15.0;			
N024		X80.0;				
N025			W32.0;			
N026	G70	P020	Q025;			

Pattern Repeating Cycle (G73)

An example of pattern repeating cycle is given in Fig. 6.32.
The program can be written as follows:

N30	G50.0	X280.0	Z180.0;			
N31	G00	X270.0	Z142.0;			
N32	G96	V280;				
N33	G73	U12.0	W15.0	R3;		
N34	G73	P35	Q39	U4.0	W2.0	F0.4;
N35	G00	X70.0	W-22.0;			
N36	G01		W-20.0;			
N37		X90.0	W-10.0;			
N38			W-20.0;			
N39	G01	X140.0	W-15.0;			
N40	G70	P35	Q39;			

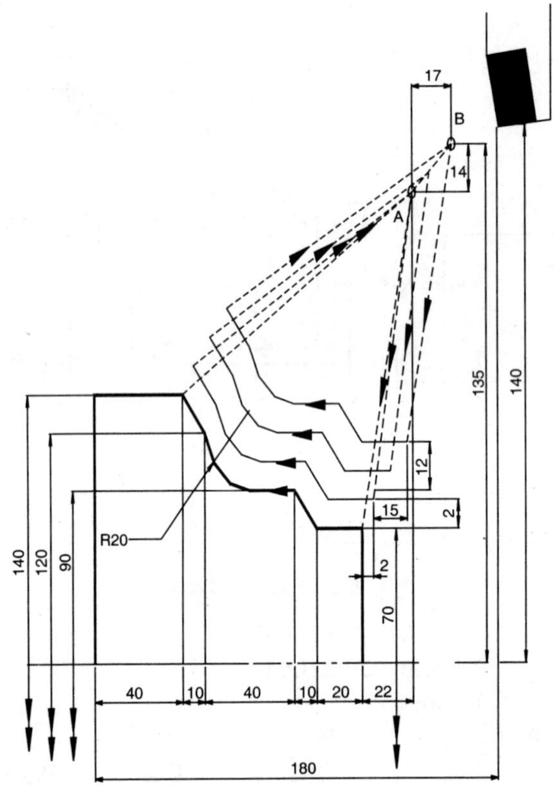

Fig. 6.32 Pattern Repeating Cycle

End face peck drilling cycle (G74)

When drilling deep holes, it is desirable to carry out the drilling in a number of sequential stages. As shown in Fig. 6.33 drilling is carried out for a certain depth (Δk), drill is then withdrawn to remove the chips, again drill through a further depth of Δk and so on until the full depth is reached. This facilitates chip breaking and avoids clogging of chips and the consequent increase in drilling forces resulting in the breakage of drills.

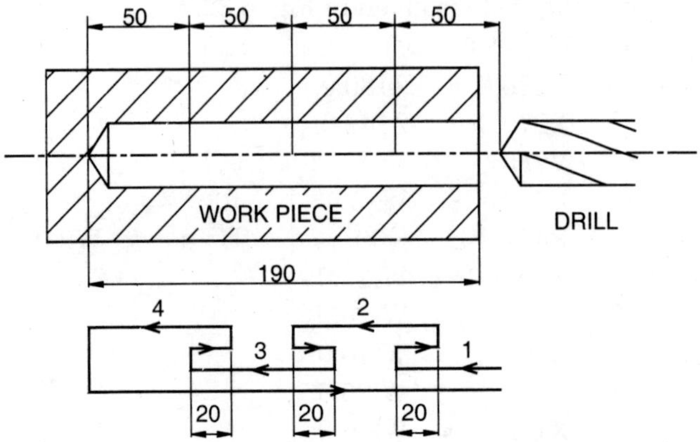

Fig. 6.33 Example of Peck Drilling Cycle

The format is:

G74	20.0;		
G74	Z190.0	Q50.0	F0.4;

6.20.1 Canned Cycles for Drilling

The canned cycles for drilling simplifies the program by replacing three or more blocks required for machining by a single block. The details of the canned cycles are given in Table 6.7.

Table 6.7 Canned Cycles for Drilling

G Code	Drilling Axis	Hole Machining Operation	Operation in the Bottom Hole Position	Retraction Operation	Application
G80					Cancel
G83	Z	Cutting Feed/ Intermittent	Dwell	Rapid	Drill/Peck Drilling
G84	Z	Cutting Feed	Spindle CW	Feed	Tapping
G85	Z	Cutting Feed	Dwell	Feed	Boring
G87	X	Cutting Feed/ Intermittent	Dwell	Rapid	Drill/Peck Drilling
G88	X	Cutting Feed	Spindle CCW	Feed	Tapping
G89	X	Cutting Feed	Dwell	Feed	Boring

6.20.2 Direct Drawing Dimension Programming

Angles of straight lines, chamfering values, corner rounding values (fillet radius) and other dimensional values can be programmed by directly inputting these values. In addition, chamfering and corner rounding can be inserted between straight lines having an optional angle. Figure 6.34 shows a profile of a work piece.

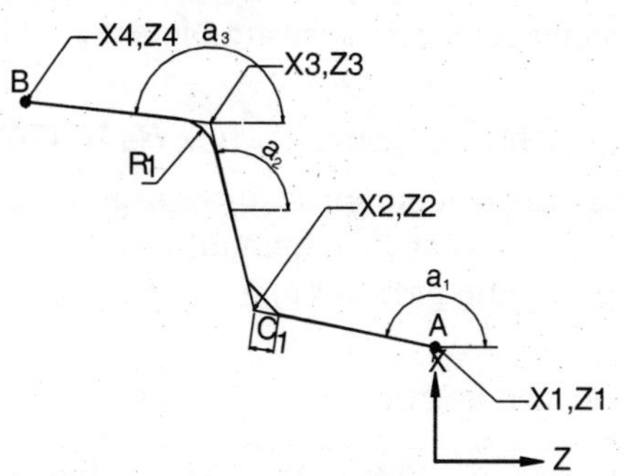

Fig. 6.34 Direct Drawing Dimension Programming

AB is the contour to be machined which consists of three line segments, a chamfer of length C1 and a fillet of radius R1.

The contour can be programmed as:

X (X2)	Z (Z2)	C (c1);	
X (X3)	Z (Z3)	R (R1);	
X (X4)	Z (Z4);		

or

A (a1)	C (c1)	;		
X (X3)	Z (Z3)	A (a2)	R (R1)	;
X (X4)	Z (Z4)	;		

Example:

Refer to Fig. 6.35.

G01	A169	C16.0	F0.2 ;
X 200.0	Z 145.0	A 104	R25.0;
X 220.0	Z 260.0;		

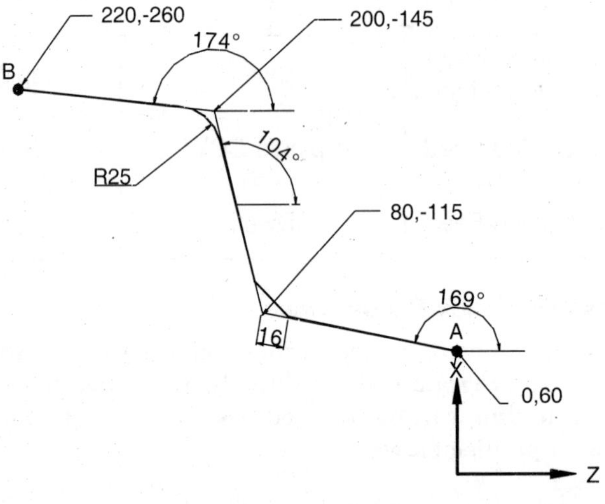

Fig. 6.35 Example for Direct Drawing Dimension Programming

6.20.3 Example of Tool Nose Radius Compensation (G40/G41/G42)

Tool inserts have different nose radii depending on their geometry. The nose radius will have significant influence on the accuracy of the component during taper turning or cutting formed shapes. It has no effect during turning parallel to X- or Z-axis. This has been discussed earlier in this chapter.

The effect of tool nose radius can be automatically compensated by G-codes G41 and G42.

G41	Offset of tool nose radius to the LEFT of the contouring direction
G42	Offset of tool nose radius to the RIGHT of the contouring direction
G40	Tool nose radius compensation cancel

6.21 CUSTOM MACROS

A custom macro is a function covering a group of instructions stored in the memory as a sub-program. The stored function is represented by one instruction so that only representative instruction need be specified to execute the function. This group of instructions is called a macro and the representative instruction is called a custom macro instruction or macro call.

Custom Macro is a powerful programming facility. Using this, the programmer can program, store, recall, and executive his own automatic cycles, family of programs etc. The user or the machine tool builder can thus create his own unique software designed to cater to the needs of a given CNC machine tool for enhanced functional expandability and customized machine tool operation. The main features of custom macros are:

(i) Variables can be used.
(ii) Addition, subtraction, multiplication, division of variables, trigonometric operations, binary and decimal transformations, etc. are possible.
(iii) Interrupt control can be carried out by an external signal.
(iv) Macros facilitate repetitive machining patterns by changing parameters.
(v) Complex part shapes can be described by mathematical equations.

The advantages of macros include reduction in programme size, reduction in programming time, reduction in the number of errors and improvement in programming productivity.

6.22 PLANNING AND PROGRAMMING PROCEDURE FOR CNC TURNING

The following procedure may be used as a guide by the programmer, by describing each step required in preparing the method of production. Before writing the part program a detailed planning procedure is required.

6.22.1 PLANNING PROCEDURE

(i) From part drawing information, check suitability of part to be machined against the machine capacity.
(ii) Determine the method of driving the component (chuck type, chuck size, type of jaw, collet, collet size, face driver, etc.)
(iii) Determine the tooling required to suit the method of machining and utilize as much as possible the tools which are permanently located in the turret set up on the machine.
(iv) Determine the sequence of machining and the tooling stations.
(v) Determine the optional stops (M01 and machining cycle interrupt stages) incorporating block delete codes (-) for checking dimensions where required.
(vi) Determine cutting speeds bearing in mind the following:
  (a) Component material, method of driving, rigidity of component.
  (b) *The tooling selected* : Tool holders with carbide inserts (coated or uncoated), the grade of the carbide insert selected, carbide drills, high speed steel drills, ceramics, etc., for roughing and finishing operations.
(vii) Determine from surface finish requirements, the cutter nose radius most suited for the finishing operations and feed rates are then decided.
(viii) Allocate tool offsets as required.

6.22.2 Programming Procedure

(i) After completing the planning sheet drawing the components to scale showing the cutter paths (a scale drawing is not mandatory where the components shape and the cutting paths are simple. A sketch may prove sufficient).

(ii) Select a component datum and dimensions in scale drawing (or sketch) with the length and diameter of cuts with reference to the component datum.

(iii) Draw a tooling layout sheet (Fig. 6.36) showing tools to be used in the program and indicate the station number for each tool.

Operation No	Operation	Tool Insert	Tool Holder
1 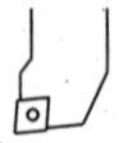	Turning		
2 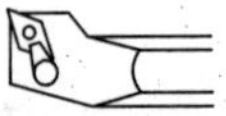	Boring		

Fig. 6.36 Tool Layout Sheet

(iv) Complete the tool layout sheet by indicating code for each tool and the grade and type of inserts to be used.

(v) Write the program and test by dry run or simulation.

6.23 EXAMPLES OF PROGRAM DEVELOPMENT

Example 1 A Casting:

Programming starts with the process of establishing method of machining. This is similar to the preparation of the process sheet in conventional machining. For example, refer to the component shown in Fig. 6.37. The raw material is a casting. The machining allowance is 5 mm all over. Figure 6.38 shows the casting drawing (shown in hidden lines) with the finished component shown in section.

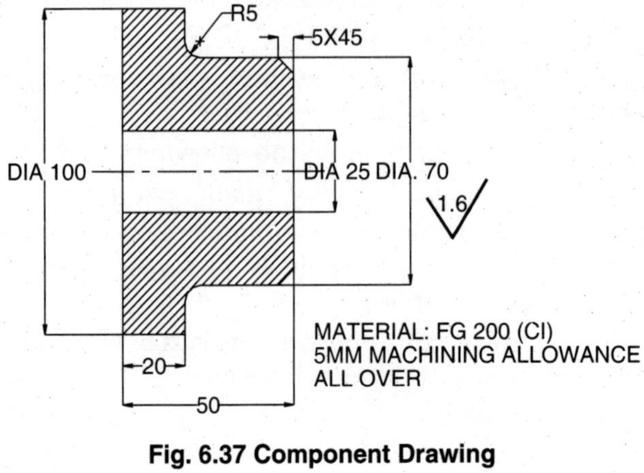

Fig. 6.37 Component Drawing

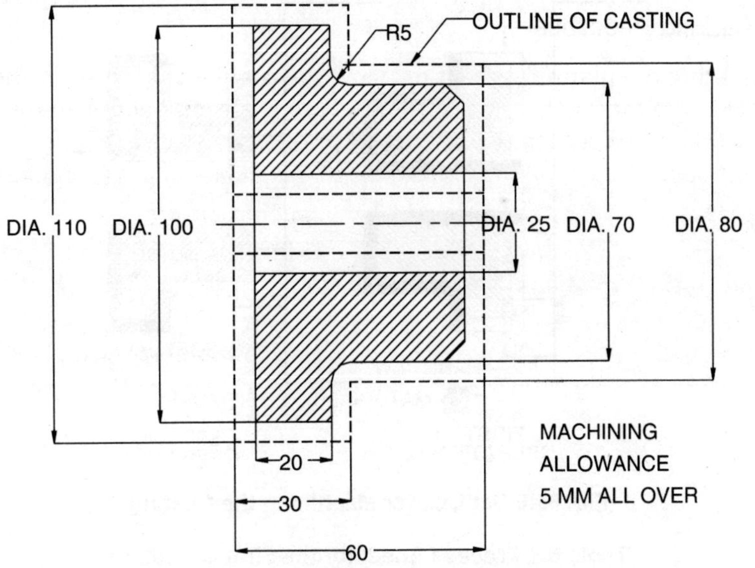

Fig. 6.38 Casting Drawing

The surfaces to be machined are shown in Fig. 6.39. The features A, B, C, D and E are machined using a facing and turning tool. The bore F is machined using a boring bar. For carrying out these machining operations, the casting is held in a chuck, the jaws being clamped on the 110 mm dia. During the second operation, the workpiece is clamped on the 70 mm diameter using soft jaws. The surfaces H and G are machined in this set up. Thus, it is necessary to have two set ups to machine the component completely. The first operation involves turning and boring. The second operation involves only turning. The two set ups are shown in Fig. 6.40. The process sheet for the first operation is shown in Table 6.7.

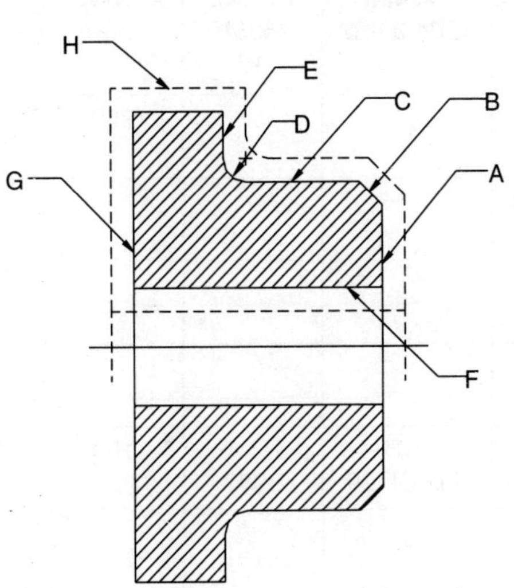

Fig. 6.39 Surfaces to be Machined

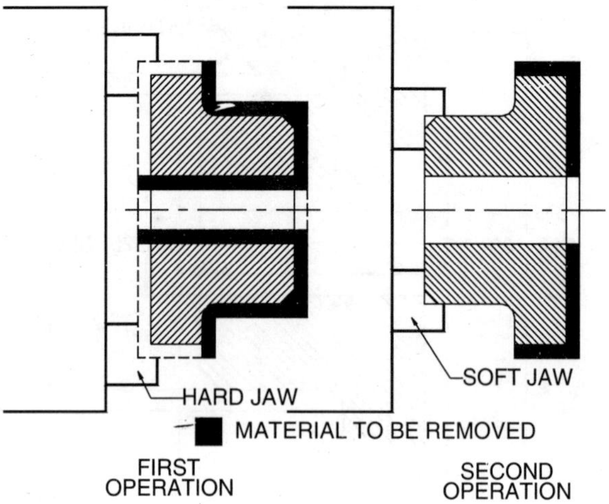

Fig. 6.40 Set Ups for Machining the Casting

Table 6.8 Process Sheet for the First Operation

Sl. No.	Operation	Tool Insert	Tool Holder	Cutting Speed (m/min)	Spindle Speed (rpm)	Feed (mm/rev)	Remarks
1	Hold Work in Chuck						
2	Index Turning Tool to position						
3	Rapid Traverse to Start of Facing						
4	Face	SCMM 1204 04-52	PCLNL 2525M 16	250		0.4	Constant Surface Speed
5	Turn Chamfer, 70 OD, Fillet, Shoulder			250		0.4	Feed during Filleting 0.2
6	Retract Turning Tool to Reference Position					Rapid	
7	Index Boring Tool to Position						
8	Rapid Traverse to Start of Boring					Rapid	
9	Boring	S10K-STFCL 09	TCM-0902	100	1000	0.2	
10	Retract to Outside the Workpiece, Return to Tool Reference Position						Rapid
11	Unload the Workpiece						

The sequence of turning operations is shown in Fig. 6.41.

Rapid Traverse	1-2
Facing	2-3
Retraction	3-4
Chamfer Turning	4-5
O.D. Turning	5-6
Fillet	6-7
Shoulder Turning	7-8
Retract to Tool Reference	8-1

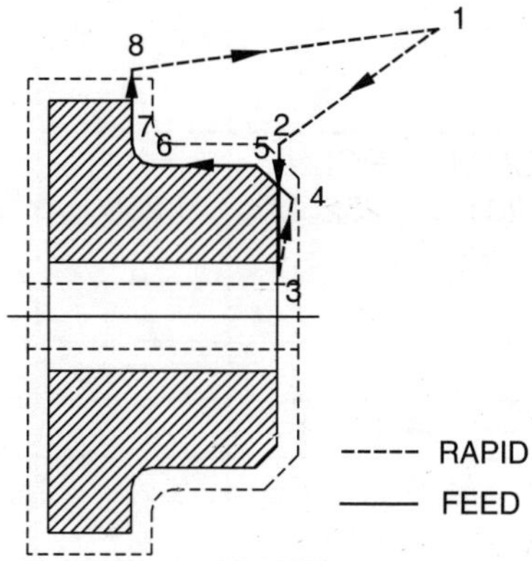

Fig. 6.41 Sequence of Turning Operations

The coordinate positions are also shown in the figure for the convenience of programming.

The sequence of boring operations is given in Fig. 6.42.

Rapid traverse to boring start	1-2
Boring	2-3
Retract (To tool avoid rubbing on finished bore)	3-4
Retract tool to outside workpiece	4-5
Retract to tool Reference	5-1

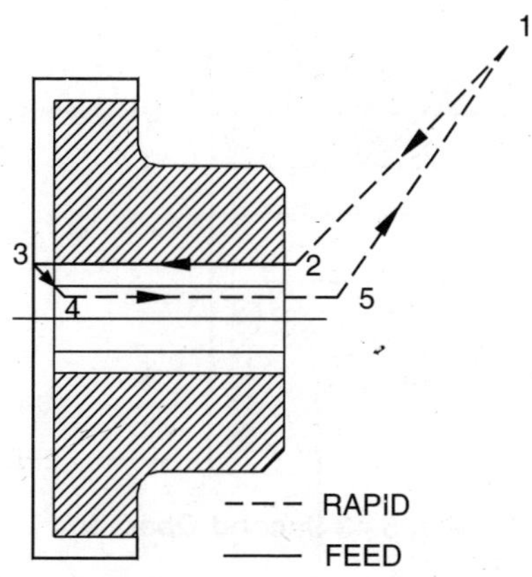

Fig. 6.42 Sequence of Boring Operations

Figure 6.43 shows the second operation which involves facing and turning the 100 mm outside diameter. The process sheet for the second operation is shown in Table 6.9.

Table 6.9 Process Sheet for Second Operation

Sl. No.	Operation	Tool Insert	Tool Holder	Cutting Speed (m/min)	Spindle Speed (rpm)	Feed (mm/ rev)	Remarks
1	Hold Work in Chuck						
2	Index Turning Tool to Position						
3	Rapid Approach to Facing						
4	Facing	SCMM 1204 04-52	PCLNL 2525M 16	250		0.4	Constant Surface Speed
5	Rapid Retraction						
6	Turning						
7	Retraction						
8	Workpiece						

The sequence of operations for the second operation is:

Bringing the turning tool to start of facing (Rapid traverse)	1-2
Facing	2-3
Retract	3-4
Turn 100 O.D.	4-5
Retract to tool reference position	5-1

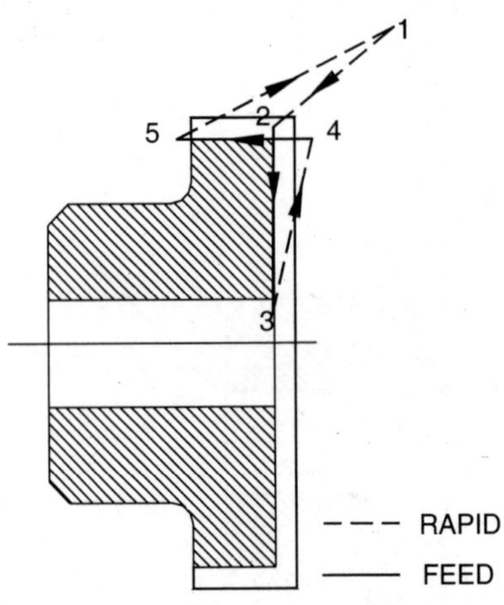

Fig. 6.43 Second Operation

The programs for first operation and the second operation are given in Tables 6.9 and 6.10.

Table 6.10 Program for First Operation

Block No.	G-Code	X Coordinate	Z Coordinate	M Code	Spindle Speed	Feed, mm/min	Remarks
N10	G28	U0	W0				Ref. Point Return
N20	G50	230.5	40.4				Workpiece Datum
N30				M03			
N40				M08			Coolant On
N50	G96				250		Constant Surface Speed
N60	G00	85.0	0				Rapid Approach
N70	G01	15.0	0				Face
N80		37.5	22.5			0.4	Retract
N90		70.0	–5.0				Chamfer
N100			–25.0				Turn 25 Dia.
N110	G02	80.0	–30.0	R5		0.2	Turn Fillet
N120	G01	115.0				0.4	Turn Shoulder
N140	G28	U0	W0				Ref. Point Return Ref. Point Return
N150				M06 T02			Boring Tool
N160				M03	S1000		1000 rpm
N170	G00	35.0	5.0				
N180	G01		–55.0			0.2	Bore
N190	G00	20.0	–45.0				Retract
N200	G00		8.0				Retract
N210		U0	W0				
N220				M09			Coolant Off
N230				M30			Program End

Table 6.11 Program for Second Operation

Block No.	G-Code	X	Z	M-code	T	Speed	Feed	Remarks
N10	G28	U0	W0					
N20					T01			
N30	G50	215.4	50.5					Datum
N40	G00	115.0	0					
N50				M03				
N60				M08				

N70	G96					250		
N80	G01	28.0					0.4	
N90	G00	70.0	4.0					
N100	G01	28.0					0.4	
N110	G28	U0	W0					
N120				M09				
N130				M30				

Example 2 A Brake Drum:

Figure 6.44 shows the drawing of a brake drum. The material of the brake drum is FG 260 which is grey cast iron of hardness of about 220-250 BHN and tensile strength 260 N/sq. mm. This material has good machinability.

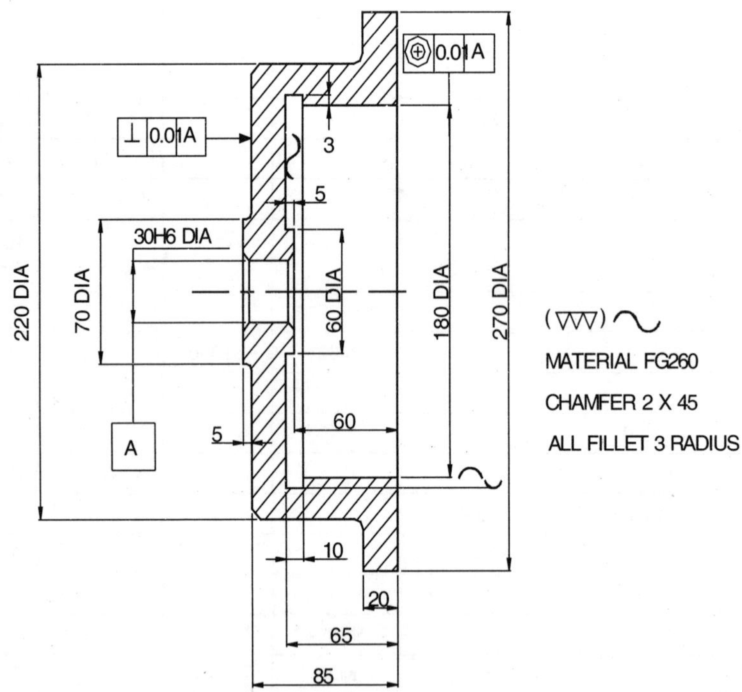

Fig. 6.44 Brake Drum

Significant features of the component are:

(i) 30 mm bore (bearing bore) and 180 mm bore are to be finish machined. Since the tolerance on the 30 bore is critical, machining of 30 bore is done in three stages—29 mm diameter, 29.5 mm diameter and 30 mm diameter.

(ii) 180 bore must be concentric with 30 bore within 0.01 mm.

The machining is carried out in two set ups.

First set up:

Rough machining of bearing bore and rim bore.
Facing the boss, semi finish machining of bearing bore and facing flange.
Finish machining the bearing bore and rim bore.

Second set up:

Facing the boss and chamfer.
Facing and turning O.D.

Figure 6.45 shows the sequence of operations involved in rough boring. The sequence of operations in facing and turning are illustrated in Fig. 6.46.

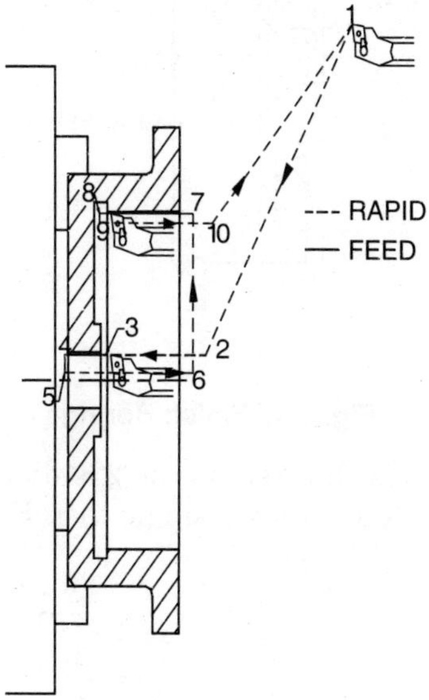

Fig. 6.45 Rough Boring

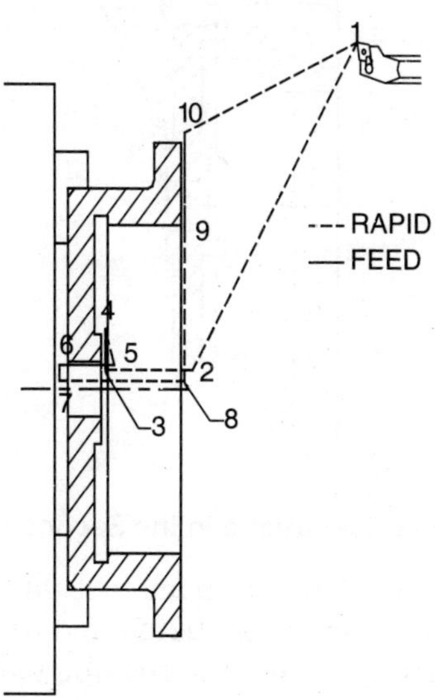

Fig. 6.46 Facing the Boss, Semi Finish Boring and Facing Flange

The finishing of the bore is done finally with a different tool. The sequence of tool movement in finishing the bore is given in Fig. 6.47. The same tool is used for chamfering the bore.

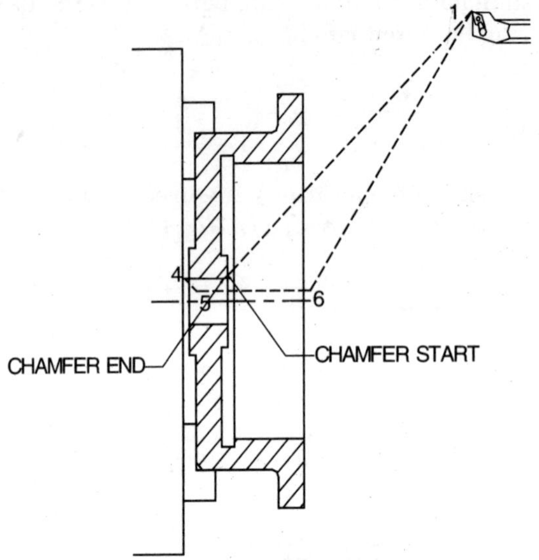

Fig. 6.47 Finish Boring

In the second set up, the drum is chucked on the 220 diameter using a soft jaw. There are two operations which can be completed with a single tool. Figure 6.48 shows the sequence of machining in the second set up.

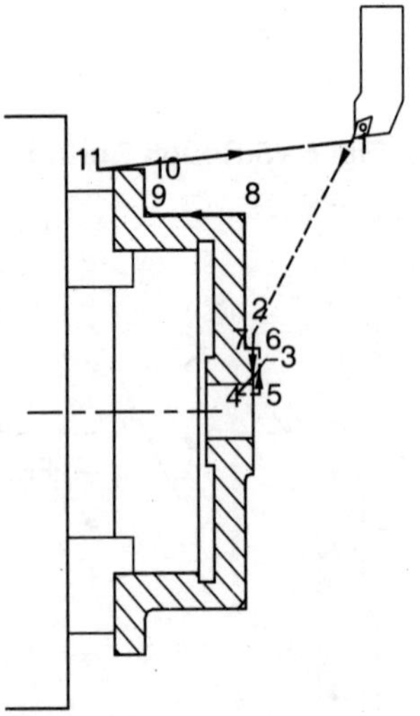

Fig. 6.48 Operations in the Second Set Up

The process sheet for the first operation is given in Table 6.12. In this set up there are only two machining operations: Rough boring (Tool 0202) and turning and facing (Tool 0101). The boring tool is mounted in tool station # 2 and the turning tool in station # 1.

Table 6.12 Process Sheet for First Operation (Drum)

Work material : FG 260

Operation number	Operation	Tool Holder	Insert	Cutting Speed (m/min)	Speed (rpm)	Feed (mm/ rev)	Depth of cut (mm)	Remarks
1	Rough Boring 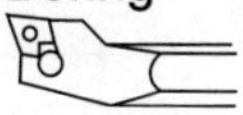	S12M-SCLCL	CNM-1204	160	1820	0.2	3.5	T0202
2	Finish Turning, semi finish boring and facing 	"	"	160		0.25		T0202
3	Finish Boring 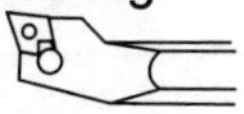	S20S-SDUCL	DCM-11T3	200	2120	0.1		T0606

The process sheet for the second operation is given in Table 6.13. There are four operations performed in this set up.

Table 6.13 Process Sheet for Second Operation

Work material : FG 260

Operation number	Operation	Tool Holder	Insert	Cutting Speed (m/min)	Speed (rpm)	Feed (mm/ rev)	Depth of cut (mm)	Remarks
1	Facing 70 mm boss chamfer 30 dia Face up to 220 dia turn 220 dia face up to 220 dia turn 270 flange 	SDUCL	DCMT 11T304-UT	160		0.25	3	T0404

The programmes for the first and second operations are given in the subsequent sections. In order to understand the purpose of each block explanations given in the bracket against each block. (They are not part of the program).

PROGRAMME FOR FIRST OPERATION

Seq. No.	Program	Description
O0009;		(Program Number)
N10	G21;	(Metric Data input)
N20	G28 U0 W0;	Home Position)
N30	G50 X------Z-----;	
N40	M06 T0202;	(Tool change, Tool No. 2, Offset Value 02)
N50	M03 S1820;	(Spindle Rotate CW at 1820 rpm)
N60	G00 X 28.0 Z 5.0 M08;	(Rapid Positioning)
N70	G01 Z-90.0 ;	(Rough Boring)
N80	G00 X 27.0	(Rapid Retraction)
N90	G00 Z 5.0	(Rapid Retraction)
N100	G00 X 180.0;	(Rapid Retraction)
N110	G01 Z-57.0;	(Boring)
N120	G00 X 178.0;	(Rapid Retraction)
N130	G00 Z5.0;	(Rapid Retraction)
/M01		
N140	G28 U0 W0;	(Home Position)
N150	M06 T0202;	
N160	G96 S 160;	(Constant Surface Speed Control Cutting Speed 160m/min)
N170	G00 X 28.0 Z 5.0;	(Rapid Positioning)
N180	G00 Z-55.0;	(Rapid Positioning)
N190	G01 X 65.0 F0.25;	(Face Boss)
N200	G00 X 29.5 Z 54.0;	(Rapid Retraction)
N210	G01 Z-95.0;	(Feed)
N220	G0 X 28.5;	(Rapid Retraction)
N230	G00 Z0 ;	(Rapid Retraction)
N240	G00 X174.0;	(Rapid Positioning)
N250	G01 X 280.0 F0.25;	(Face Flange)
N260	G97 G28 U0 W0;	(Home Position)
/M01		
N270	M06 T0606;	
N270	S2120;	
N280	G00 X 35.0 Z1.0;	(Rapid Approach)
N290	G01 X 30.0 Z-3.0 F0.1;	(Chamfer)
N300	G01 Z- 86.0;	
N310	G00 X 34.0 Z-84.0;	(Rapid Retraction)
N320	G00 X 5.0 M09;	(Rapid Retraction)
N330	G97 G28 U0 W0:	(Home Position)
N340	M30;	

PROGRAMME FOR SECOND OPERATION

Seq. No.	Program	Description
O0010;		(Program Number)
N10	G21 G97;	(Metric Data Input)
N20	G28 U0 W0;	(Home Position)
N30	M06 T0404;	(Tool Change, Tool No. 4, Offset Value 04)
N40	G96 S160;	(Constant Surface Speed Control Cutting Speed 160 m/min)
N50	G00 X 76.0 Z0;	(Rapid Positioning)
N60	G01 Z-34.0 F0.25;	(Facing)
N70	G01 X 28.0 Z-3.0;	(Chamfering)
N80	G00 X 70.0 Z1.0;	(Rapid Retraction)
N90	G00 Z0.5;	(Rapid Positioning)
N100	G01 Z-5.0 R3.0;	(Turning, Filleting)
N120	G01 X220.0 C2.0;	(Face and Chamfer)
N120	G01 X-87.0;	(Turn OD of Flange)
N130	G28 U0 W0;	(Home Position)
N140	M09;	(Coolant Off)
N150	M30;	(Program End)

REVIEW QUESTIONS

(1) Describe the steps involved in manual part programming.

(2) Explain the terms: program, block, word, character, block format.

(3) Describe the right hand coordinate system. With neat sketches mark the axes of the following machines: CNC lathe, horizontal machining centre, vertical machining centre, gear hobbing machine, internal grinding machine, wire-EDM and laser cutting machine.

(4) Discuss the different possibilities of axes nomenclature in the case of the following machines: 4-axis lathe, 4-axis vertical machining centre, and 5-axis horizontal machining centre and 5-axis vertical machining centre.

(5) Discuss the importance of machine datum and workpiece datum.

(6) What is the significance of machine reference point?

(7) Distinguish between absolute value programming and incremental value programming. What are their advantages and disadvantages?

(8) What is the role of a register command in a CNC program?

(9) What are preparatory functions? Discuss the logic of grouping them.

(10) How are spindle speeds specified in a program?

(11) Differentiate between feed and feed rate. How is the "feed" specified in a thread cutting operation?

(12) Discuss the numbering of lathe tools.

(13) What is the role of an M-function in a CNC program?

(14) Discuss the effect of tool nose radius when the turning tool
- moves parallel to only one axis.
- moves simultaneously in two axes.

(15) The profile of the workpiece has a diameter of 50 mm for 20 mm length (AB) and a taper with a length of 20 mm (BC) with diameter 80 mm at the larger end for a length of 80 mm (CD). A turning insert with a nose radius of 0.8 mm is used to cut this profile. What will be the error in the lengths of AB and CD?

(16) Determine the error while turning a semicircle of 60 mm radius with an insert of 0.4 mm nose radius if no tool nose compensation is employed.

(17) What is the need for changing tool offsets when a tool is changed?

(18) Describe various methods of determining tool length offsets.

(19) Describe various types of tool presetters.

(20) Discuss different types of interpolations and their applications.

(21) Discuss the currently used algorithms for interpolation.

(22) Write program segments for the following profiles of workpieces shown in the figures:

(23) What are the advantages of fixed cycles?

(24) With sketches explain longitudinal turning cycle.

(25) What are the situations where you will recommend G71, G72 and G73?

(26) Describe a threading cycle.

(27) Where do you use a peck drilling cycle?

(28) Where do you use subprograms?

(29) Discuss the features of custom macros in CNC programming.

(30) Prepare process sheet and write programs for the components shown below, starting with blank selection:

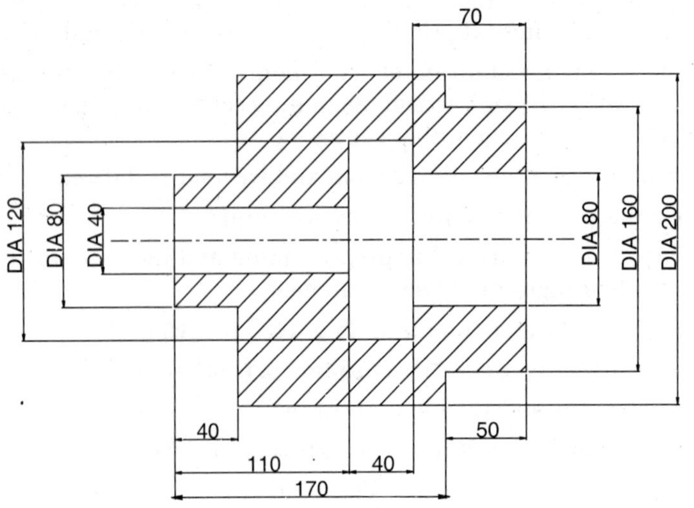

MATERIAL: CAST STEEL

Fig. 6.49 Valve Block

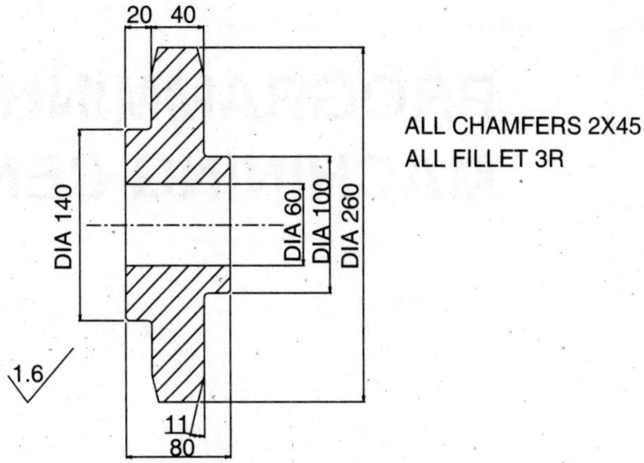

MATERIAL:20MNCr5

Fig. 6.50 Gear Blank

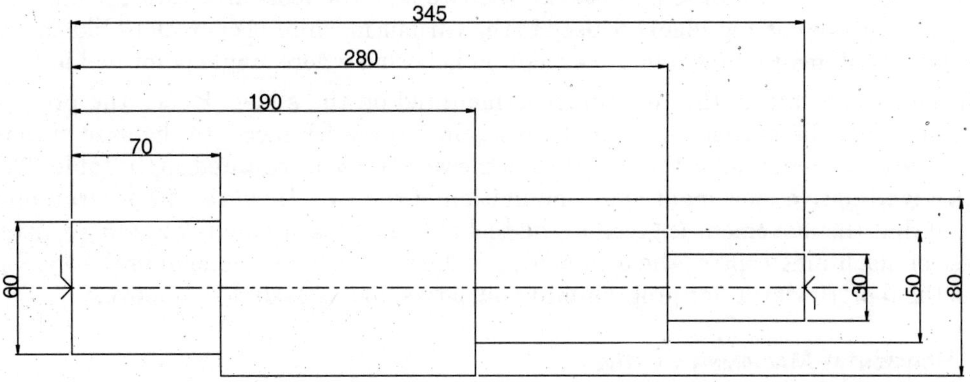

M.S. SHAFT

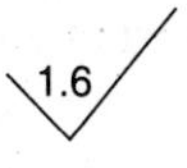

Fig. 6.51 Shaft

7 PROGRAMMING OF MACHINING CENTRES

7.1 PROGRAMMING OF MACHINING CENTRES

Programming of machining centres follows more or less the same approach as the programming of CNC lathes. A major difference between the two is in the tools used. Multipoint tools (tools with more than one cutting edge) are used in the various machining operations like face milling, end milling, drilling, tapping, etc. An exception is boring where single point tool may be used.

In the case of lathes, the tool turret is mounted on the slides. Hence the programming involves directly the movement of the tools against the work piece. In the case of machining centres, the tool is mounted in the spindle and the work piece is mounted on the table. Therefore, the effective relative movement is a combination of the two. However, in programming, it is assumed that the movement is given to the tool and the programme is written accordingly. In the case of machining centres the feed motion is derived by the movement of the work piece as well as the tool. However, for programming purposes, tool is assumed to move.

7.1.1 Horizontal Machining Centre

Figure 7.1 shows a horizontal machining centre. In the case of horizontal machining centres Y axis movement is by the up and down movement of the spindle head. Z and X axes movements are provided at the table as shown in the figure.

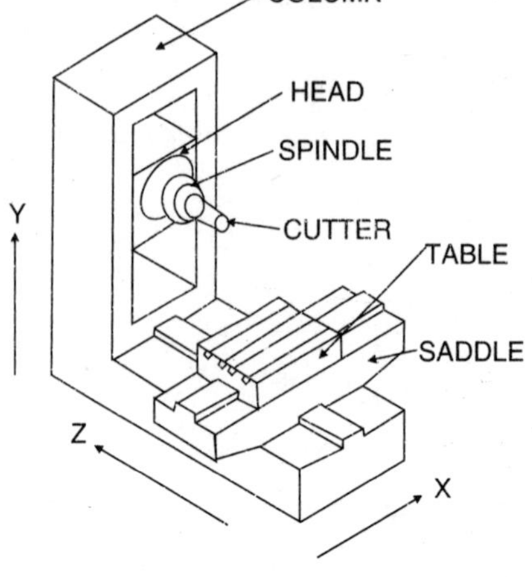

Fig. 7.1 Horizontal Machining Centre

7.1.2 VERTICAL MACHINING CENTRE

In the case of vertical machining centre, shown in Fig. 7.2, the movements of the table give X and Y axes and the Z axis is by the movement of the spindle head. The positive direction of X-axis is table moving to left (or cutter moving to the right with respect to the workpiece) and the table moving towards the operator in the Y-direction. The upward movement of the tool represents the positive Z-direction.

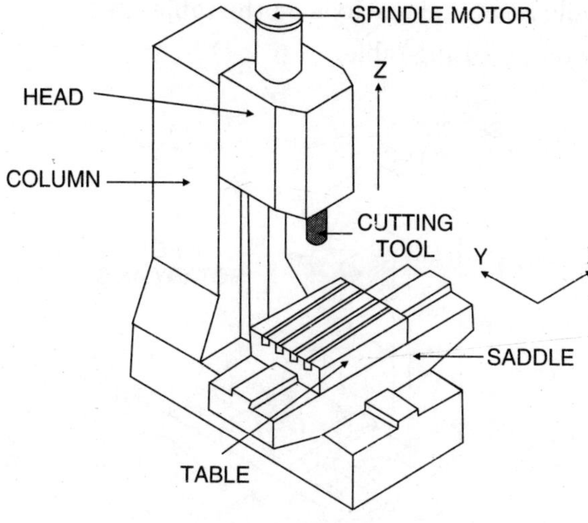

Fig. 7.2 Vertical Machining Centre

7.1.3 HORIZONTAL MACHINING CENTRE WITH B-AXIS

Machining centres can have more than three axes. For example, a four axis machining centre is shown in Fig. 7.3. The fourth axis is a rotary table. Since the rotation of this axis is with respect to Y, the axis is designated as B. A vertical machining centre can be fitted with a rotary axis which can rotate about X-axis. In this case the 4th axis is called A axis.

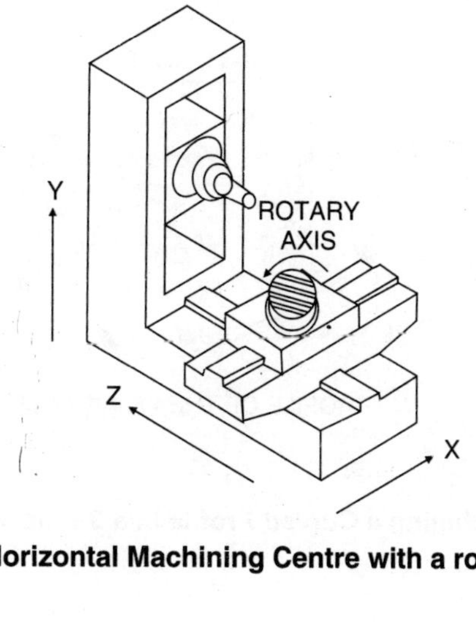

Fig. 7.3 Horizontal Machining Centre with a rotary B-Axis

7.1.4 5-Axis Machining Centre

A 5-axis machine is popularly used to machine components with doubly curved surfaces like aerospace components and dies and molds. With a five axis machine it is possible to keep the tool normal to the surface while machining. Better surface finish, higher accuracy and more productivity can be obtained using 5-axis machines. A five axis machine will have 3 translational axes (X, Y and Z) and two rotary axes. These rotary axes can be:

- Two axes on the spindle head
- One axis on the spindle head and one axis on the table
- Both the axes on the table (tilting table)

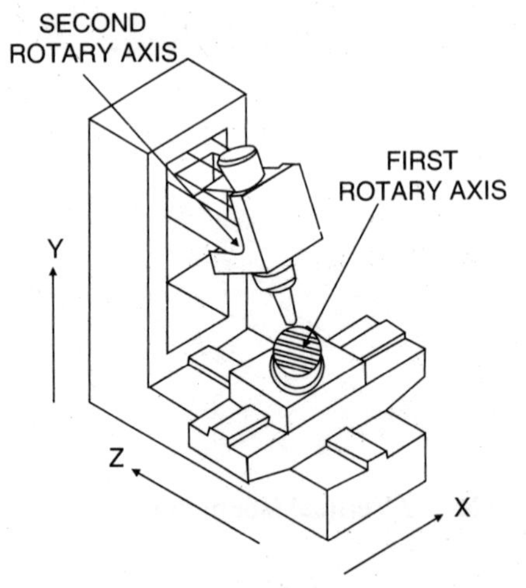

Fig. 7.4 5-Axis Machine

7.1.5 Multi Axis Machining

Figure 7.5 shows machining a work piece with a curved profile using a ball nose cutter in 3-axis machine.

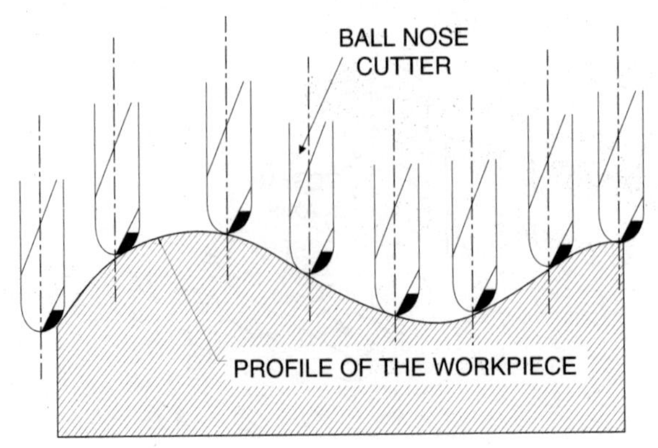

Fig. 7.5 Machining a Curved Profile in a 3-Axis Machine

Figure 7.6 shows machining the same profile using a 4-axis machine. The tool axis is to be kept normal to the surface. In the figure shown the movement of the tool is assumed to be along the Y-axis. Hence the inclination of the tool is about the Y-axis.

The machining of a doubly curved surface is shown in Fig. 7.7. A-5 axis machine is the right choice for this type of components. The normal to the surface will have inclination about X-axis (A) and about Y-axis (B). Values of X, Y, Z, A and B can be computed from the geometry of the surface machined.

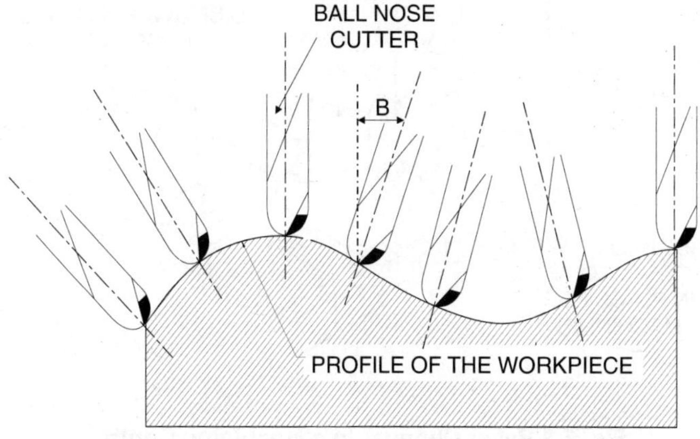

Fig. 7.6 Machining a Profile in a 4-Axis Machine

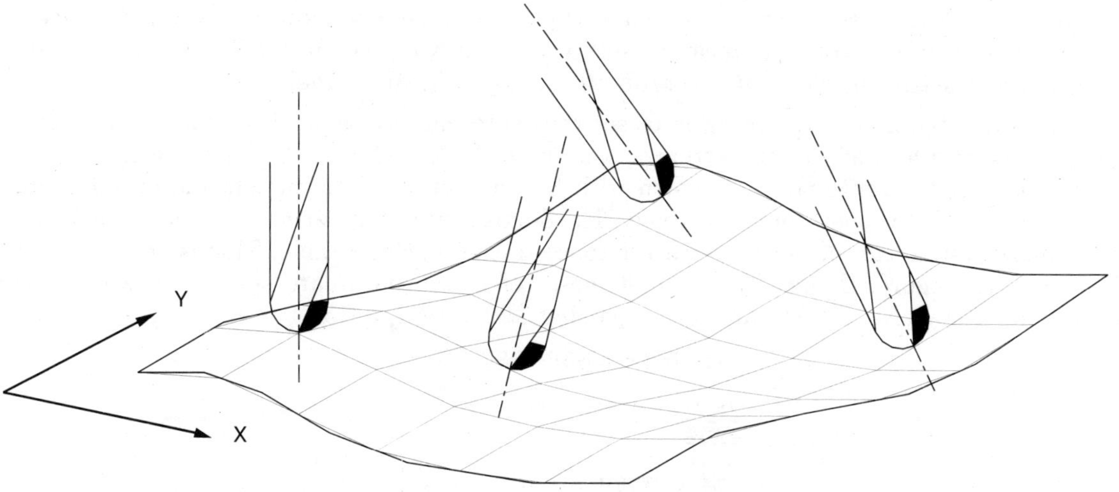

Fig. 7.7 Machining a Doubly Curved Surface on a 5-Axis Machine

7.1.6 Pallet Changer

Machining centres are used to machine large workpieces. The setting up time is usually large, which sometimes run into a few hours. It is not advisable to keep a costly machine like a machining centre idle while work piece is being set up. The usual solution for this problem is to use a pallet changer. Figure 7.8 shows a machining centre with two pallets. While machining is done on the component in one pallet, the operator can set up the next part on the second pallet. As soon as machining is complete the pallet with the finished workpiece is moved out of the machining area and the pallet on which the fresh workpiece is mounted is move to the machining area. This will reduce the idle time to one or two minutes.

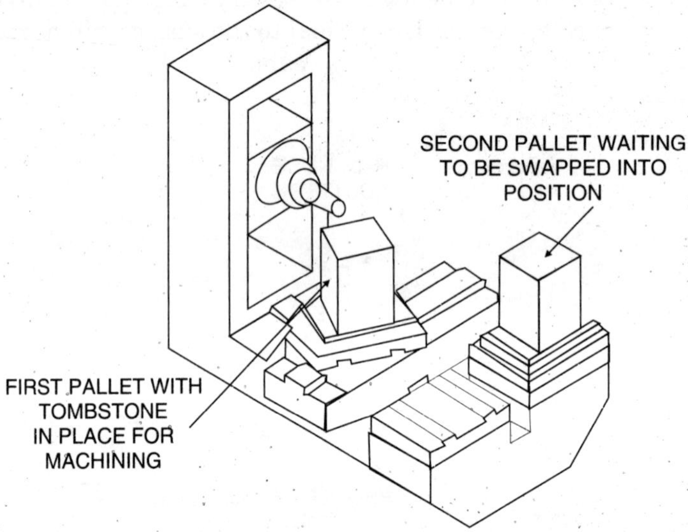

Fig. 7.8 Pallet Changer in a Machining Centre

7.1.7 Setting The Coordinate Systems of Machining Centres

A coordinate system used for machining a workpiece is called a work piece coordinate system. The workpiece coordinate system can be set in different ways—by using G92 in the program, by parameter setting or by input of coordinates using CRT/MDI panel.

The first step in programming is to set the coordinate systems. The machine reference point is usually located at the extreme positions of X, Y and Z axes. Referring to Fig. 7.9, the work piece reference point is shown with X and Y at the extreme left and at maximum distance towards the operator respectively. The Z-axis is at the uppermost position. A machine coordinate system can be set up with reference to the machine table. This is shown as X1, Y1, Z1 in the figure. Using either one of these reference coordinate systems, a work piece coordinate system X2, Y2, Z2 can be set up using G92 or G54 to G59.

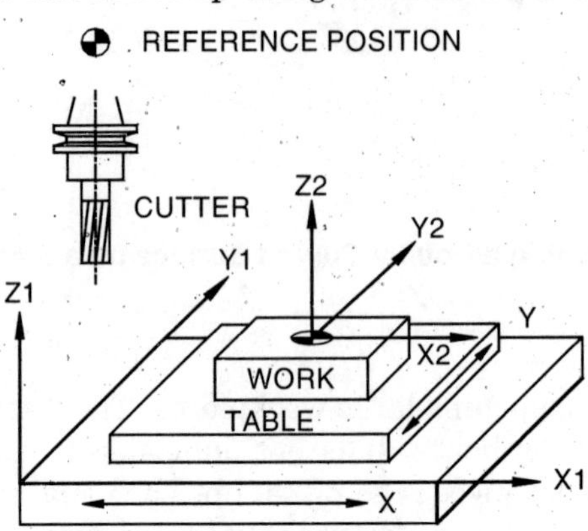

Fig. 7.9 Coordinate System Setting

7.1.7.1 Setting a Workpiece Coordinate System Using G92

A workpiece coordinate system is set so that a point on the tool such as the tool tip is at specified coordinates. Referring to Fig. 7.10 the tool tip is at X, Y, Z from the reference point on the workpiece.

G92 X Y Z;

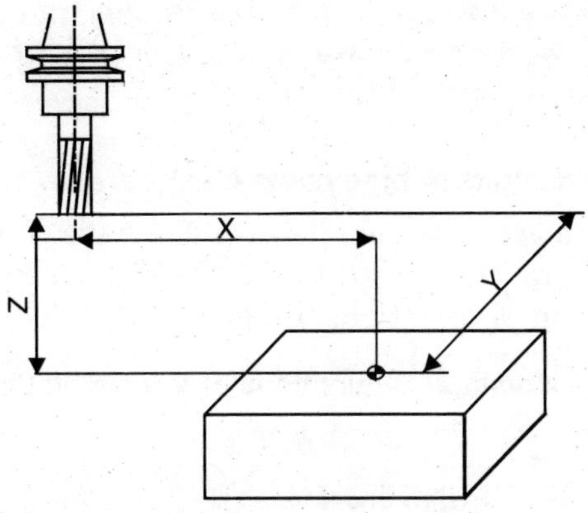

Fig. 7.10 G92

7.1.7.2 Setting Work Coordinate System Using G54-G59

G54, G55, G56, G57, G58 and G59 provide a very convenient method of specifying work coordinates as in the case of CNC lathes. The X, Y, Z coordinates corresponding to these workpiece coordinate systems are stored in the control using CRT/MDI and are called in the program when needed. These coordinate systems can be used in a single workpiece as well as in multiple workpieces.

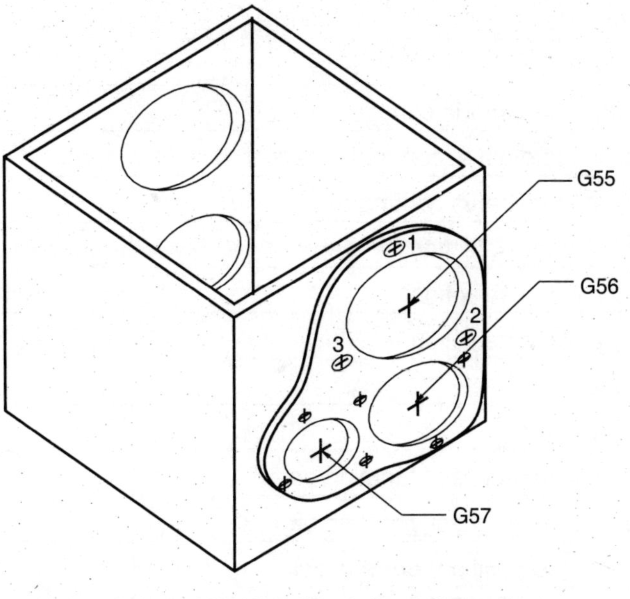

Fig. 7.11 Use of Multiple Work Coordinate Systems

Figure 7.11 illustrates use of multiple work coordinate systems on a single workpiece. There are three bores on one face of the box and these bores have associated features like threaded holes. It is common to dimension these associated features with reference to the corresponding bores. In such cases the centre of each bore can be taken as a work coordinate system and the associated features can be programmed with reference to the coordinate system. For example calling G55 in the program will shift the work coordinate system to the centre of the largest bore as shown. With this coordinate system the bore and the tapped holes 1, 2 and 3 can be machined. Similar procedure can be adopted for machining other bores and features. An example of using different work coordinate systems for machining four similar workpieces mounted on the table is discussed later in this chapter.

7.1.8 G-Functions and M-Functions in Machining Centres

As in the case of CNC lathes machining centres also will have G-Functions and M-Functions for programming purposes. Some of them will have the same meaning as in the case of CNC lathes. A list of G-Functions and M-Functions are given in Table- 7.1 and 7.2.

Table 7.1 Common G-Functions of Machining Centres

G CODE	GROUP	FUNCTION	
G00	1	Positioning	
G01		Linear interpolation	
G02		Circular interpolation/Helical Interpolation CW	
G03		Circular Interpolation/Helical Interpolation CCW	
G04	0	Dwell Exact stop	
G05		High speed cycle machining	
G09		Exact stop	
G10		Data setting	
G11		Data setting mode cancel	
G15	17	Polar coordinates command cancel	
G16		Polar coordinates command	
G17	2	XpYp plane selection	Xp: X axis or its parallel axis
G18		ZpXp plane selection	Yp : Y axis or its parallel axis
G19		YpZp plane selection	Zp: Z axis or its parallel axis
G20	6	Input in inch	
G21		Input in mm	
G22	4	Stored stroke check function on	
G23		Stored stroke check function off	
G27	0	Reference position return check	
G28		Return to reference position	

G29		Return from reference position	
G30		2nd, 3rd and 4th reference position return	
G31		Skip function	
G33	1	Thread cutting	
G37	0	Automatic tool length measurement	
G39		Corner offset circular interpolation	
G40	7	Cutter compensation cancel	
G41		Cutter Compensation left	
G42		Cutter compensation right	
G43	8	Tool length compensation + direction	
G44		Tool length compensation - direction	
G45	0	Tool offset increase	
G46		Tool offset decrease	
G47		Tool offset double increase	
G48		Tool offset double decrease	
G49	8	Tool length compensation cancel	
G50	11	Scaling cancel	
G51		Scaling	
G52	0	Local coordinate system setting	
G53		Machine coordinate system selection	
G54	14	Workpiece coordinate system 1 selection	
G55		Workpiece coordinate system 2 selection	
G56		Workpiece coordinate system 3 selection	
G57		Workpiece coordinate system 4 selection	
G58		Workpiece coordinate system 5 selection	
G59		Workpiece coordinate system 6 selection	
G60	0	Single direction positioning	
G61	15	Exact stop mode	
G62		Automatic comer override	
G63		Tapping mode	
G64		Cutting mode	
G65	0	Macro call	
G66	12	Macro modal call	
G67		Macro modal call cancel	

G68	16	Coordinate rotation	
G69		Coordinate rotation cancel	
G73	9	Peck drilling cycle	
G74		Counter tapping cycle	
G75	1	Plunge grinding cycle (0-GSC)	
G76	9	Fine boring cycle	
G77	1	Direct constant - dimension plunge grinding cycle (0-GSC)	
G78		Continuous-feed surface grinding cycle (0-GSC)	
G79		Intermittent - feed surface grinding cycle (0-GSC)	
G80	9	Canned cycle cancel/external operation function cancel	
G81		Drilling cycle, spot boring cycle or external operation function	
G82		Drilling cycle or counter boring cycle	
G83		Peck drilling cycle	
G84		Tapping cycle	
G85		Boring cycle	
G86		Boring cycle	
G87		Back Boring cycle	
G88		Boring cycle	
G89		Boring cycle	
G90	3	Absolute command	
G91		Increment command	
G92	0	Setting for work coordinate system or clamp at maximum spindle speed	
G94	5	Feed per minute	
G95		Feed per rotation	
G96	13	Constant surface speed control	
G97		Constant surface speed control cancel	
G98	10	Return to initial point in canned cycle	
G99		Return to R point in canned cycle	
G107	0	Cylindrical interpolation	
G150	19	Normal direction control cancel mode	
G151		Normal direction control left side on	
G152		Normal direction control right side on	
G160	20	In-feed control function cancel (0-GSC)	
G161		In-feed control function (0-GSC)	

Table 7.2 Common M-Functions of Machining Centres

M00	program stop
M01	optional stop
M02	end of program (no rewind)
M03	spindle CW
M04	spindle CCW
M05	spindle stop
M06	tool change
M07	mist coolant ON
M08	flood coolant ON
M09	coolant OFF
M19	spindle orientation ON
M21	tool magazine right
M22	tool magazine left
M23	tool magazine up
M24	tool magazine down
M25	tool clamp
M26	tool unclamp
M27	clutch neutral ON
M28	clutch neutral OFF
M30	end program (rewind stop)
M98	call sub-program
M99	end sub-program

7.1.9 S, T, F Functions

The manual programming of machining centres uses the variable word address block format. A typical block of program will have a similar structure as described in chapter 6.

Spindle speed (S) is generally recommended in writing programmes for machining centres. However, S could be used for cutting speed if G96 is used. The tool is addressed by the pocket in the magazine in which it is kept. For example, T 17 designates the tool in pocket number 17. Feed rate instead of feed is used in programming machining centres. Feed rate is obtained by feed in mm/revolution multiplied by the rpm of the spindle (in drilling for example). In the case of milling, feed rate is calculated by feed per tooth multiplied by the number of teeth of the cutter and rpm. In the case of tapping, feed rate is obtained by multiplying the pitch of the thread and the rpm of the tap.

7.1.10 Important Accessories of Machining Centres

The productivity of machining centres are increased by the following accessories—pallet changer, automatic tool changer and tool magazine.

7.1.10.1 Pallet Changer

As mentioned earlier in this chapter, loading and setting of work pieces in machining centres takes up considerable time. A pallet changer is used to reduce idle time to a minimum. Figure 7.12 shows a typical 2-pallet arrangement. Pallet A is in the machining position while the operator sets up the work piece on pallet B. Once the machining is over, the door of the machining centre is lifted and pallet A moves to unloading position and pallet B moves to machining position. The operator unloads the finished work piece and then loads the new job on pallet B. The pallet change is called in the program and hence is operated automatically either hydraulically or pneumatically.

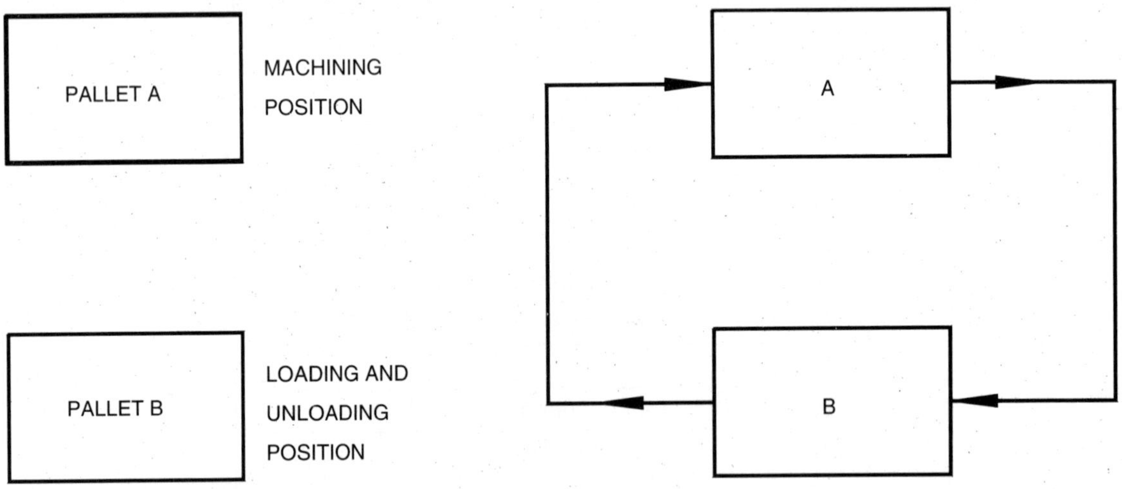

Fig. 7.12 Pallet Changing

Pallet changer is very useful for unmanned operation. Sometimes machining centres are filled with upto 32 pallets which can load or similar or different components with facilities like automatic program loading and automatic magazine change, tool breakage detection etc. The operator needs to load all the pallets and program the supervisory computer and the jobs will be machined one after the other automatically.

7.1.10.2 Tool Magazine

One of the important technical features of the machining centre is that it can carry out a number of machining operations like face milling, drilling, boring, tapping, countersinking, counterboring, threading, end milling etc. Hybrid machines like mill turn centres and more sophisticated machines like multi tasking machining could also carry out in addition turning operations. This feature reduces the number of set ups which increases both productivity and accuracy. All the tools required for machining a component can be loaded in a tool magazine which is a common accessory for a machining centre. Small machining centres can accommodate twelve to thirty two tools. Large machining centres will have magazines which can receive 40 to 100 tools or even more. More sophisticated automation enables automatic magazine change, facilitating use of more tools. There are different designs for tool magazine—drum type, carousel type, chain type etc.

Tool setting in the magazine is a time consuming activity prior to trial run of the component. Wherever magazine change facility is available, tools can be set in the magazine before hand and the idle time involved in setting the tools can be eliminated.

The following factors need be taken into consideration while loading the tools in the tool magazine:

(a) Maximum length of the tool

(b) Maximum diameter of the tool

(c) Maximum weight of the tool.

The manufacturers of the machine usually give guidelines on the above in the user manual of the machine.

7.1.10.3 Automatic Tool Changer (ATC)

ATC is a standard feature of machine tools. In programming tool is called using T function in block. For example, assume that a program segment uses T16 and the current tool in the spindle is T24. T16 is called in the program segment when T24 is used. The tool magazine indexes and brings T16 to the tool changing position. At the end of the machining with T24 and M6 command is issued. ATC picks up a tool T16 from the tool magazine from the tool changing position and moves to the spindle. The common design of ATC will have two arms. The free arm grabs the tool in the spindle (T24) and pulls it out. The ATC then indexes through 180 degrees and pushes T16 into the spindle taper. The hydraulic clamping inside the spindle grips the pull stud tightly so that the taper of the tool holder sits snug in the taper of the spindle. While this is being done, the tool magazine is indexed to bring the socket number 24 to the tool changing position to receive T24. ATC moves out of the spindle region and puts back T24 in socket number 24 and moves to its parking position waiting for the next tool change command. Figure 7.13 illustrates automatic tool change in a simple manner.

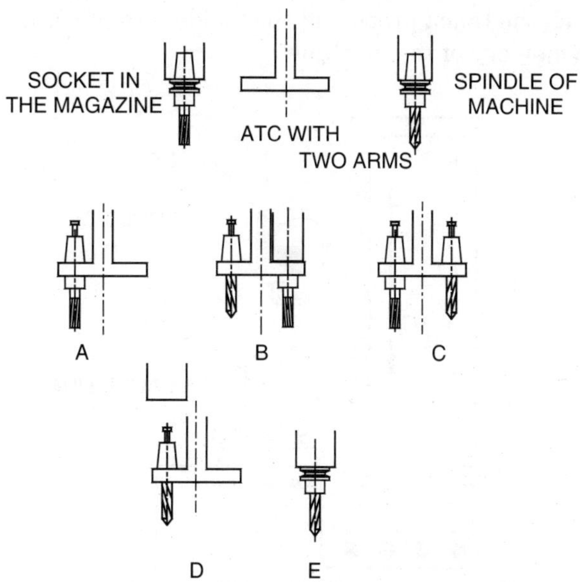

Fig. 7.13 Operation of an Automatic Tool Changer

At the top of the figure both the magazine and the spindle are shown. The spindle has a drill and it is to be replaced by an end mill. The socket carrying end mill is at the tool changing position.

The sequence of operation is as follows:

(a) ATC moves from the parking position to grab the end mill.

(b) ATC pulls out the end mill from the socket A.

(c) ATC moves to the spindle and grabs the drill and pulls it out B.

(d) ATC rotates through 180 degrees about its axis, and inserts the end mill into the spindle C.

(e) The magazine indexes and the brings the socket to receive the drill to the tool change position.

(f) ATC inserts the drill into the socket.

(g) ATC moves to the parking position.

7.1.10.4 Tool Presetter

The actual movement of the slides depends on the tool length offset. Tool presetter is used to measure the tool length offsets. There are many types of tool presetters.

(a) Mechanical tool presetter: This is the simplest type. The tool is mounted on a fixture so that the gauge line is collinear with the reference face of the fixture. The presetter has X and Z axis movements and electronic/mechanical scales attached to the slides.

(b) Optical presetter: Optical presetter will have CRT to give an enlarged view of the tool tip so that the tool offset can be determined accurately.

(c) Electronic presetter: There are many types of electronic presetters. The most sophisticated presetter measures the tool offsets and stores in a memory chip attached to the tool holder. When the tool is inserted into the spindle, the control can read the values stored and compute the corresponding slide movement.

(d) Another method is to use touch probes fitted on to the machining centre itself. The tool tip is made to touch the touch probe and the tool length offset is automatically measured and stored in the memory of the machine.

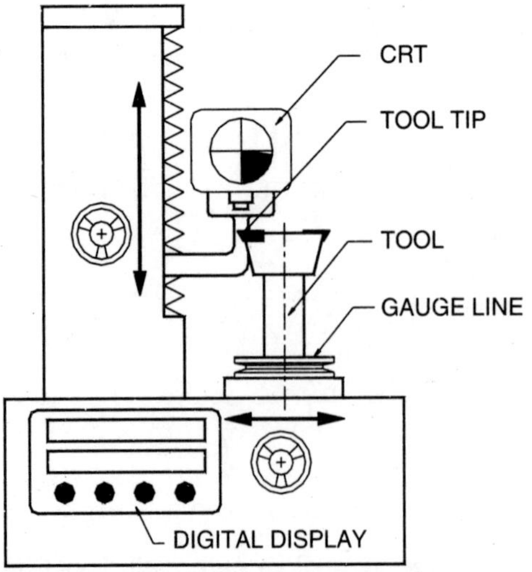

Fig. 7.14 Tool Presetting

Figure 7.14 shows a tool presetter. The tool with the holder is inserted in a socket in the spindle of the presetter. The gauge line of the tool holder will be collinear with the gauge line of the spindle of the presetter. The tool tip can be viewed through an optical system and the position of the insert is aligned with the cross hairs. The tool offset can be noted from the digital display. If the presetter is part of a flexible manufacturing cell, the offsets can be loaded into the memory of the machine tool.

7.2 INTERPOLATION FUNCTIONS

It must be clear to you from the discussion on programming of lathes that programming involves moving a tool tip from the current position to a targeted position along a straight or curved path. Though in programming, only the end points are specified, the machine control will have to calculate the intermediate points and the corresponding velocity vectors. Once the velocity vectors are estimated, the acceleration and deceleration of the slides could be computed. In the case of complex doubly curved parts like molds and dies, the accuracy of the part depends on the number of intermediate points calculated. Usually this involves considerable computation. A few mathematical techniques like DDA algorithm are available for carrying out this computation. The common interpolations in machining centers are linear, circular or helical. Some machines will have special interpolation techniques. In order to reduce computational overhead, mathematical techniques like NURBS are being adopted in some CNC systems. This section discusses some common interpolation codes with examples.

G00 Positioning (Rapid Traverse)

Cutting tools are initially located either at the tool reference point or in a predetermined position away from the workpiece. At the start of machining the tool has to be brought to a position close to the work piece. The G00 command moves a tool to the position in the workpiece system specified with an absolute or an incremental command at a rapid traverse rate.

In the absolute command, the coordinate value of the end point is programmed.

In the incremental command the distance the tool moves with respect to the previous point is programmed.

The tool is positioned for each axis at the point programmed by X, Y, Z or A, B, C or U, V, W (additional axes). Consider the following line of block:

G00 X 220.0 Y 100.0;

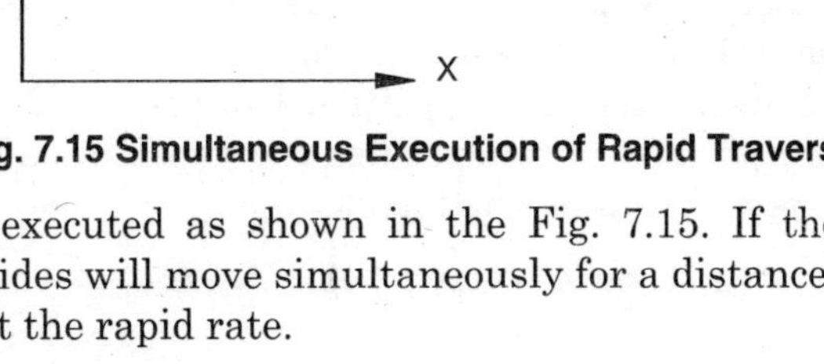

Fig. 7.15 Simultaneous Execution of Rapid Traverse

The motion will be executed as shown in the Fig. 7.15. If the rapid traverse rate is 40 m/min, the X and Y slides will move simultaneously for a distance of 100 mm and then the X–axis alone will move at the rapid rate.

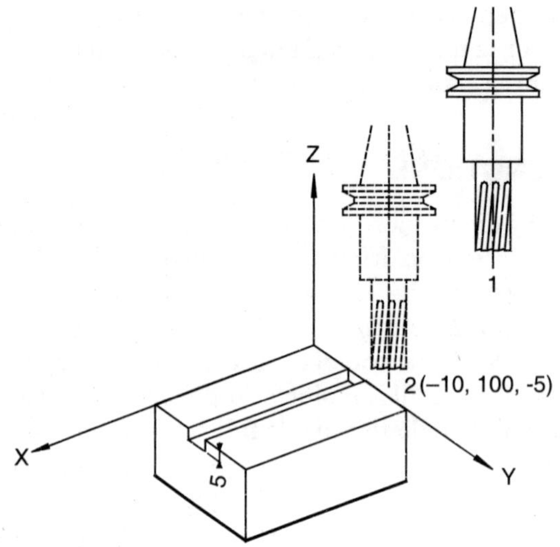

Fig. 7.16 G00 Rapid Traverse

Figure 7.16 shows the milling of a slot using an end mill. The tool initially in the reference position is brought to a position near the start point of the slot. (A little away from the work piece).

7.2.1 LINEAR INTERPOLATION

Linear interpolation involves movement of the tool tip along a line either in one axis or in more than one axis simultaneously.

Rapid Traverse (G00)

(air cutting)

The tool moves at rapid traverse to approach the workpiece. Since there is no material being cut, it is desirable that rapid traverse is performed as fast as possible. Current generation of machines have rapid traverse rates of 40 metre per minute or more. Rapid traverse is also performed while positioning movements between drilling, boring or tapping operations also. The tool is retracted from the workpiece after machining at rapid traverse.

The format is,

G00 X Y Z

X - specify end point coordinate of x axis

Y - specify end point coordinate of y axis

Z - specify end point coordinate of z axis

Figure 7.16 shows a block in which a slot is to be milled. The tool (an end mill cutter) is initially located at position 1. The start point of milling the slot is corresponding to position 2. The tool has to move in rapid traverse from position 1 to position 2. The coordinates of point 2 is (–10, 100, –5). The Z coordinate (–5) specifies the depth of cut. The program block for movement from point 1 to point 2 can be written as:

G 00 X –10.0 Y 100.0 Z–5.0;

It is a good practice to plan this movement in two blocks. In the first block, the tool is moved in X and Y directions and in the second block the tool is moved in the –Z direction.

G00 X –10.0 Y 100.0;

G00 Z–5.0;

This approach to planning the tool movement may avoid possible collision between the tool and the work piece.

Linear Interpolation at Feed (G01)

(Cutting Material)

A tool moves along a line to the specified position at the feed rate specified in F.

The feed rate specified in F is effective until a new value is specified. It need not be specified for each block.

The format is,

G01 X Y Z F;

X - specify end point coordinate of x axis
Y - specify end point coordinate of y axis
Z - specify end point coordinate of z axis
F - specify the feed rate

In the operation of the machining centre, the common practice is the use feed rate (Feedrate = feed per cutting edge x number of cutting edges of the tool x rpm of the cutter). The rpm is calculated from the recommended cutting speed for the work material-tool material combination and the diameter of the tool.

Figure 7.17 shows machining of a slot by the end mill. The tool moves from position 2 (X = –10, Y = 100 and Z = –5) to position 2 (X = 240, Y = 100, Z = –5).

The programme block can be written as:

G01 X 240.0 Y100.0 Z–5.0 F 500;

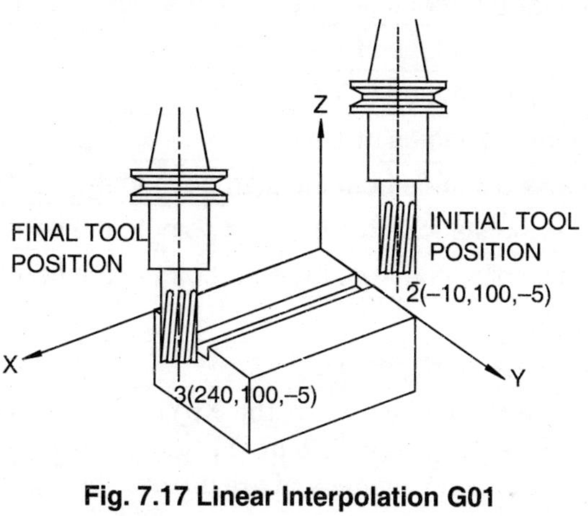

Fig. 7.17 Linear Interpolation G01

The feed rate specified in F is effective until a new value is specified. It need not be specified for each block. The feed rate commanded is measured along the tool path.

Example:

Consider the following block specified in incremental dimensions:

G91 G0 X 60.0 Y 80.0 F600.0;

The feed rate along the path of the linear interpolation is 600 mm/min. The feed rate along X axis is calculated as follows:

Length of tool path	$= (60^2 + 80^2)^{½}$	= 100 mm
Feed rate in X-direction	= 600 × 60/100	= 360 mm/min
Feed rate in Y-direction	= 600 × 80/100	= 480 mm/min

Circular Interpolation

G02 and G03 are circular interpolation functions which move the tool along a circular arc. Circular arcs can be programmed either in the XpYp plane or ZpXp plane or YpZp plane. The format is:

G17 { G02/G03} Xp-------Yp-------- { I----J---/R-------} F----;

G17 { G02/G03} Xp-------Zp-------- { I----J---/R------- } F----;

G17 { G02/G03} Yp-------Zp--------{ I----J---/R-------} F----;

Table 7.3 gives the details of the command format.

Table 7.3 Details of Command Format

Command	Description
G17	Specification of arc on XpYp plane
G18	Specification of arc on ZpXp plane
G19	Specification of arc on YpZp plane
G02	Circular Interpolation, clockwise direction (CW)
G03	Circular Interpolation, counter clockwise direction (CCW)
Xp	Command values of X axis
Yp	Command values of Y axis
Zp	Command values of Z axis
I	Xp axis distance from the start point to the centre of the arc with sign
J	Yp axis distance from the start point to the centre of the arc with sign
K	Zp axis distance from the start point to the centre of the arc with sign
R	Arc radius
F	Feed rate along the arc

Clockwise sense of rotation is defined when the XpYp plane is viewed along the negative direction of the Z axis. The arc centre is specified by the addresses I, J, K for the X, Y, and Z axes respectively. I, J and K are vector components and are *always specified as an incremental value.*

Circular Interpolation (CW) (G02)

An example of G02 is illustrated in Fig. 7.18 where a semicircular portion of the slot has to be milled. The programme block can be written in two ways as:

G02	X245.0	Y60.0 R	100.0	F315.0;	
G02	X245.0	Y60.0	I 100.0	J0	F315.0;

Figure 7.18 shows an example of G02.

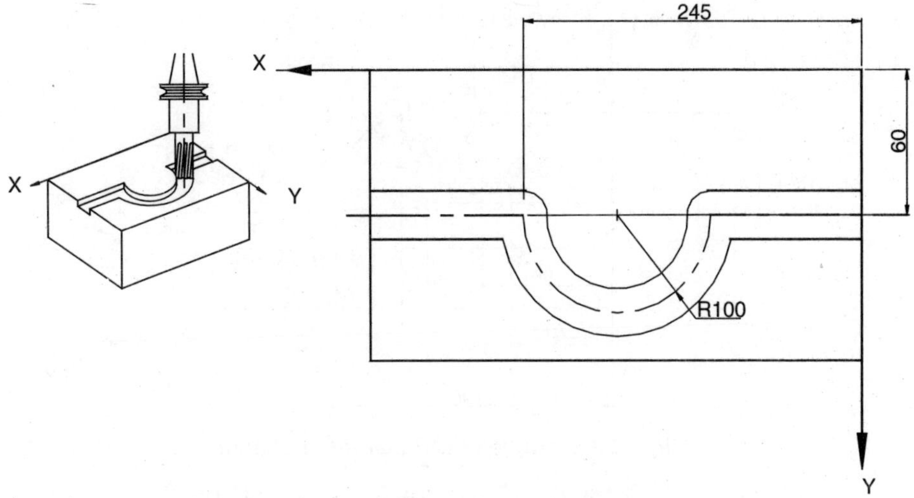

Fig. 7.18 G02 Circular Interpolation (CW)

Circular Interpolation (CCW) (G03)

An example of G03 is illustrated in Fig. 7.19 where the above semicircular portion of the slot has to be milled in a symmetrical fashion. The programme block can be written in two ways as:

G03	X245.0	Y60.0	R40.0	F315.0;	
G03	X245.0	Y60.0	I40.0	J0	F315.0;

The end point of the arc is specified by address X, Y, Z and is expressed as an absolute or incremental value according to G90 or G91.

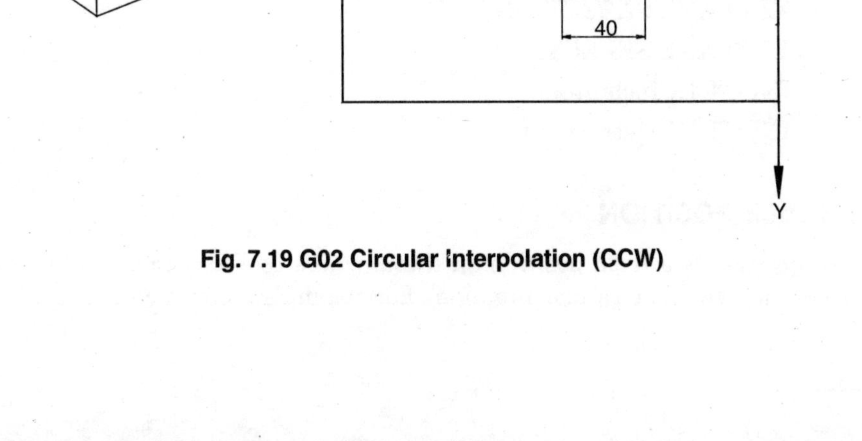

Fig. 7.19 G02 Circular Interpolation (CCW)

Example:

Figure 7.20 shows a template ABCD with two circular arc segments. The coordinates of the arc centres are (127.5, 70) and (90, 130) respectively. The programme blocks for the circular segments can be written as:

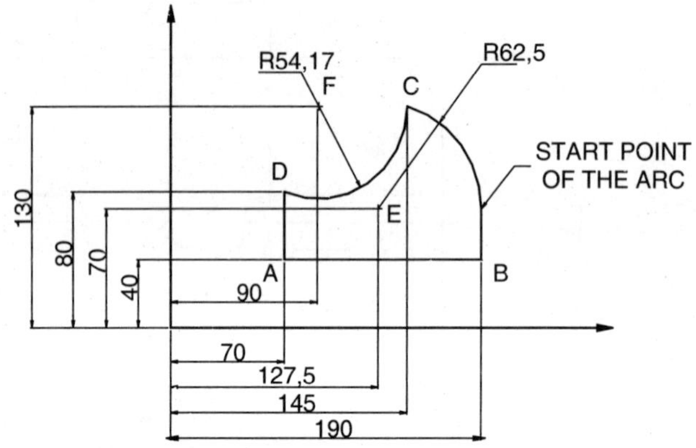

Fig. 7.20 Example of Circular Interpolation

G03	X145.0	Y130.0	R62.5	F400.0;	
G02	X70.0	Y80.0	R54.17;		

Alternatively,

G03	X145.0	Y130.0	I-62.5	J0	F400.0;
G02	X70.0	Y80.0	I-55.0	J0;	

Dwell (G04)

By specifying dwell, the execution of the next block is delayed by the specified time.

The format is,

G04 X

X - specify a time in seconds.

Dwell facility is useful in several situations. For example, while boring a stepped hole, dwell feature is used to clean up the bottom of the bore and make it square with the axis.

Plane Selection

G17, G18 and G19 are used to specify the plane on which machining is carried out.

G17	XY PLANE SELECTION
G18	XZ PLANE SELECTION
G19	YZ PLANE SELECTION
G20	INPUT IN Inch units
G21	INPUT IN Metric Units

7.3 REFERENCE POSITION

The reference position is a fixed position on the machine tool to which the tool can be easily moved by reference position return function. For example, reference position is used as a position at which tools are automatically changed. Up to four reference positions can be set in the machine coordinate system. The first reference position must be the machine zero point.

Reference Position Return Check (G27)

G27 command positions the tool at rapid traverse rate.

The format is,

G27 X Y Z

X - specify end point coordinate of x axis

Y - specify end point coordinate of y axis

Z - specify end point coordinate of z axis

If the tool reaches the reference position, the reference position return lamp lights up.

Reference Position Return (G28)

Positioning to the intermediate or reference positions are performed at the rapid traverse rate of each axis.

The format is,

G28 X Y Z

X - specify end point coordinate of x axis

Y - specify end point coordinate of y axis

Z - specify end point coordinate of z axis

Return from the Reference Position (G29)

G29 is commanded immediately following the G28 command. Positioning to the intermediate or reference positions are performed at the rapid traverse rate of each axis.

The format is,

G29 X Y Z

X - specify end point coordinate of x axis

Y - specify end point coordinate of y axis

Z - specify end point coordinate of z axis

2nd, 3rd, 4th Reference Position Return(G30)

Up to four reference positions can be specified by setting coordinates in the machine coordinate system in parameters. The first reference position must be the machine zero point.

7.4 THREADING

Constant Lead Threading (G33)

Straight threads with constant leads can be cut.

The format is,

G33 X or Y or Z F

X - specify end point coordinate of x axis

Y - specify end point coordinate of y axis

Z - specify end point coordinate of z axis

F - Pitch of thread

Cutting feed rate override is not applicable when G33 is executed.

Figure 7.21 shows thread cutting in a machining centre.

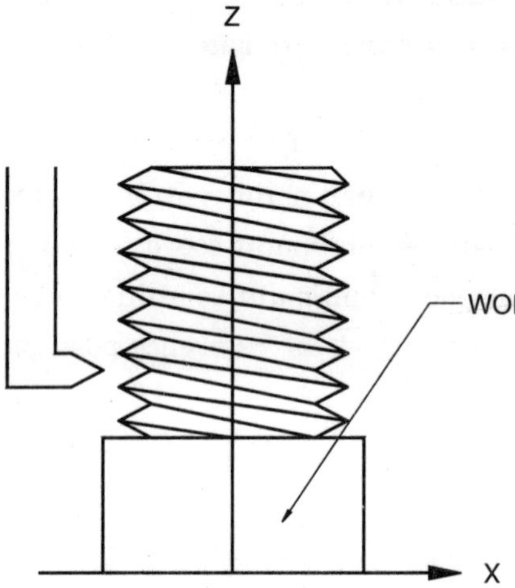

Fig. 7.21 Constant Lead Thread Cutting

For example, the programme for thread cutting with a lead of 3 mm can be written as:

G33 Z25.0 F3.0

7.5 AUTOMATIC TOOL LENGTH MEASUREMENT

Automatic Tool Length Measurement (G37)

By issuing G37 the tool starts moving to the measurement position and keeps on moving till the approach end signal from the measurement device is output. Movement of the tool is stopped when the tool tip reaches the measurement position.

The format is,

G37 X or Y or Z

X - specify end point coordinate of x axis

Y - specify end point coordinate of y axis

Z - specify end point coordinate of z axis

7.6 CORNER OFFSET CIRCULAR INTERPOLATION (G39)

When this command is specified in the G01,G02,G03 mode, corner offset circular interpolation can be executed with respect to the radius of the tool.

The format is, G39 X Y

OR

G39 I J

X - specify end point coordinate of X axis in Absolute

Y - specify end point coordinate of Y axis in Absolute

I - specify end point coordinate of X axis in Incremental

J - specify end point coordinate of Y axis in Incremental

This command can be given in offset mode, that is, only when G41 or G42 has already been specified. Whether the arc is to turn clockwise or counterclockwise, is defined by G41 or G42, respectively.

An example of corner offset circular interpolation is shown in Fig. 7.22.

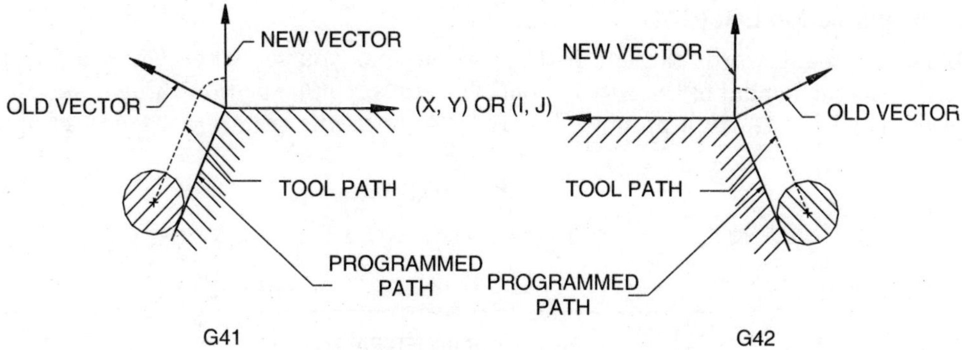

Fig. 7.22 Corner Offset Circular Interpolation

7.7 CUTTER COMPENSATION

Figure 7.23 shows a template which is milled using an end milling cutter. The actual tool path is indicated by dotted lines in the figure. In programming, the profile of the workpiece is specified. Therefore, in order to obtain the tool path the template profile has to be shifted by the radius of the tool. This is achieved by the cutter compensation function.

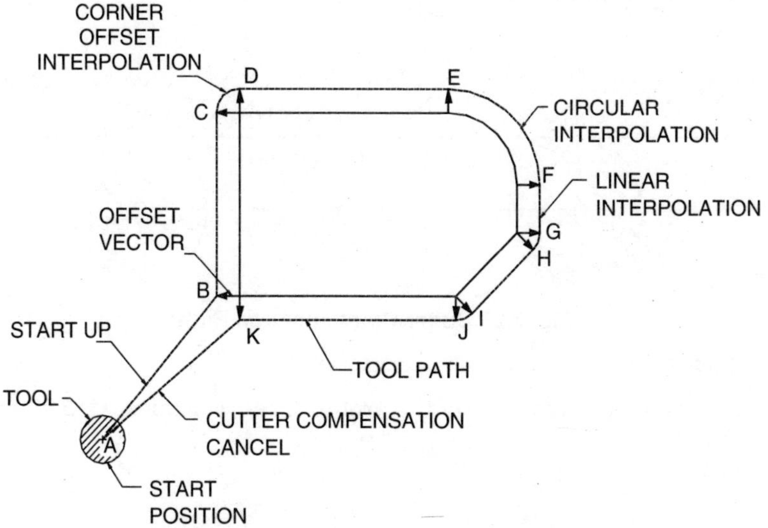

Fig. 7.23 Cutter Compensation Function

In the figure various instances of application of cutter compensation are shown. The tool starts from point A. The call up of cutter compensation moves the cutter to point B. The path B-C-D-E-F-G-H-I-J-K represents the tool path of the cutter. The cutter compensation is called off before the tool moves back to point A.

Cutter Compensation Cancel (G40)

This command changes the mode of the equipment from the cutter compensation mode to cancel mode.

Cutter Compensation Left (G41)

G41 offsets the tool towards the left of the workpiece as you see when you face in the same direction as the movement of the cutting tool. The cutter compensation value is specified after the address H with a 1-3 digit number. Figure 7.24 shows the situation where G41 applies.

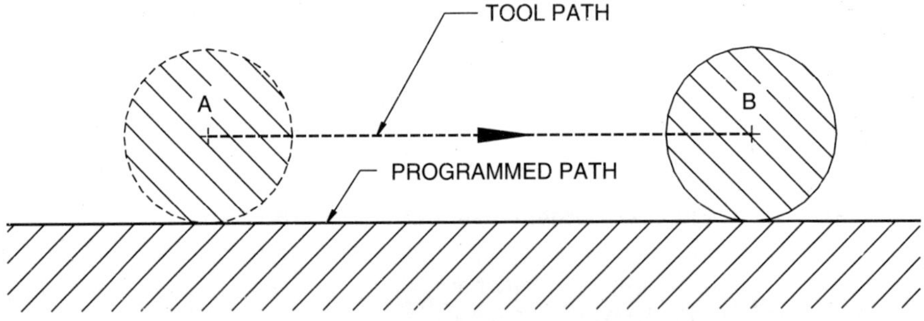

Fig. 7.24 Cutter Compensation Left

Format is: G41 X-------Y-------(or I--------J--------) H---;

Cutter Compensation Right (G42)

G42 offsets the tool towards the right of the workpiece as you see when you face in the same direction as the movement of the cutting tool.

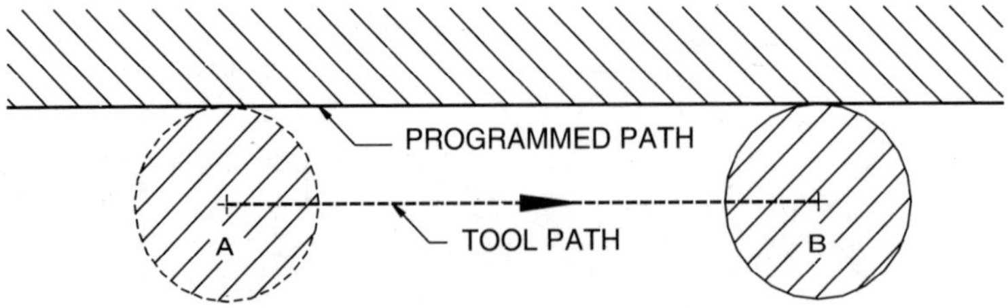

Fig. 7.25 Cutter Compensation Right

Format is: G42 X-------Y-------(or I--------J--------) H---;

When the cutter is on the right side of the profile of the workpiece G42 should be used. This is illustrated in Fig. 7.25.

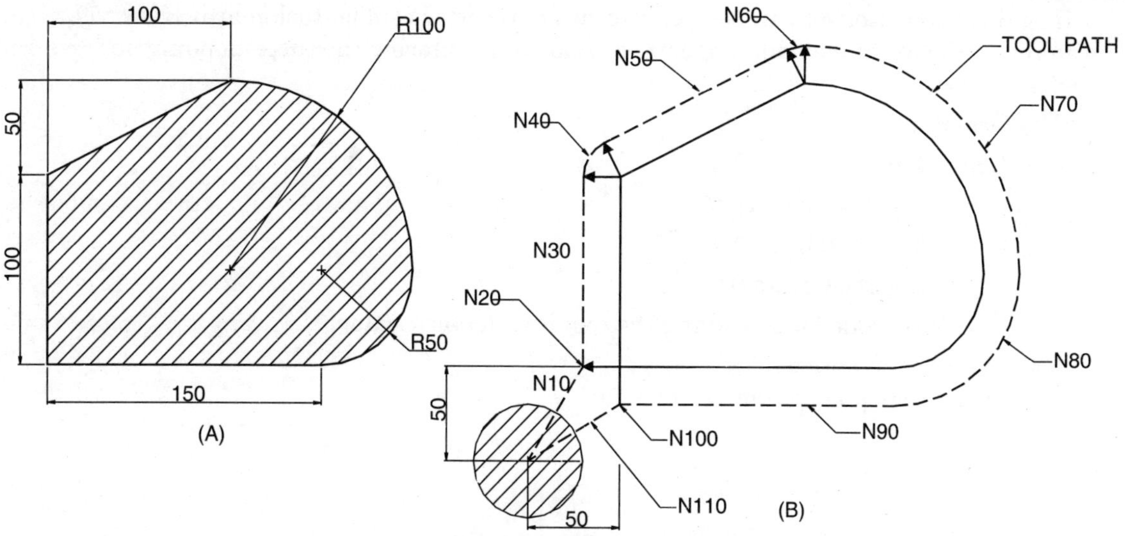

Fig. 7.26 Example for Cutter Compensation

Example:

Figure 7.26 (A) shows a template and the tool path for milling the profile of the template with an end mill is shown in Fig. 7.26 (B). The programme can be written in incremental format (G91) in Xp Yp plane (G17) as follows.

N10	G91	G17	G00	G41	X50.0	Y50.0	J100.0	H04;
N20	G01	Z-50.0	F200.0;					
N30	Y100.0	F400.0;						
N40	G39	I100.0	J50.0;					
N50	X100.0	Y50.0;						
N60	G39	I100.0;						
N70	G02	X100.0	Y-100.0	R100.0;				
N80	X-50.0	Y-50.0	R50.0;					
N90	G01	X-150.0;						
N100	G00	Z50.0;						
N110	G40	X-50.0	Y-50.0;					

Note: The tool offset is stored in memory corresponding to H04.

7.8 TOOL LENGTH OFFSET

Tool Length Offset (G43/G44/G49)

This function can be used by setting the difference between the tool length assumed during programming and the actual tool length of the tool used in to the offset memory. It is possible to compensate the difference without changing the program.

The direction of offset can be specified with G43 or G44. The tool length offset value can be stored in the offset memory and can be recalled by entering the corresponding address and number (H code).

The format is,

G43/G44 X or Y or Z H

X - offset in x axis

Y - offset in y axis

Z - offset in z axis

H - code for specifying the tool length offset value.

G43 : POSITIVE OFFSET

G44 : NEGATIVE OFFSET

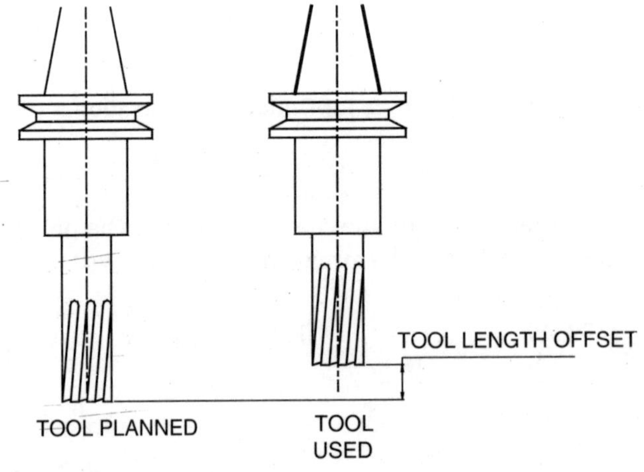

Fig. 7.27 Tool Length Offset

When G43 is specified, the offset value is added to the coordinates of the end position specified by a command in the programme. For example, if the stored value of H2 is 30 mm, the programme block:

G90 G43 Z150.0 H2;

will result in a Z movement of 180 mm. Referring to Fig.7.27, the reduction in tool length necessitates additional movement of Z slide to the extent of the tool offset.

The tool length offset is cancelled by G49 or H0.

Tool Offset(G45/G46/G47/G48)

The programmed travel distance of the tool can be increased or decreased by a specified tool offset value or by twice the offset value.

The format is, G45/G46/G47/G48 X Y Z D

X - offset in x axis

Y - offset in y axis

Z - offset in z axis

D - code for specifying the offset value.

G45 : Increase the travel distance by the tool offset value

G46 : Decrease the travel distance by the tool offset value

G47 : Increase the travel distance by twice the tool offset value

G48 : Decrease the travel distance by twice the tool offset value

G49 Tool Length Offset Cancel

After G49 is specified, the system immediately cancels the offset mode.

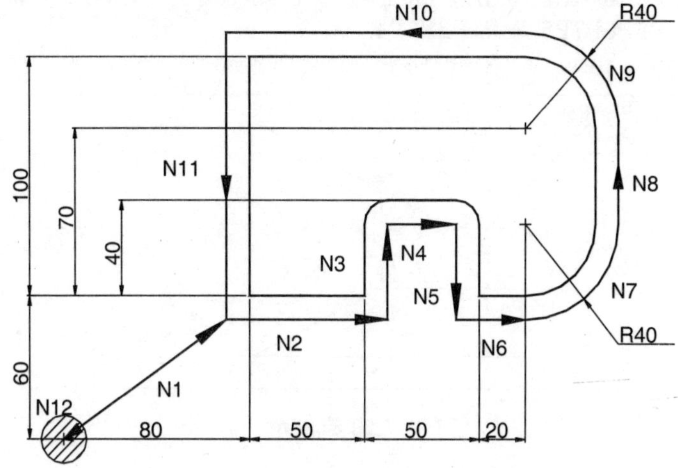

Fig. 7.28 Program Using Tool Offset

Figure 7.28 illustrates the use of this G-code. Consider the end milling operation shown in the figure.

```
N1    G91      G46       G00       X80.0     Y60.0  D01;
N2    G47      G01       X50.0     F500.0;
N3    Y40.0;
N4    G48      X50.0;
N5    Y-40.0;
N6    G45      X20.0;
N7    G45      G03       X40.0     Y40.0     J40.0;
N8    G01      Y30.0;
N9    G45      G03       X-40.0    Y40.0     I-40.0;
N10   G45      G01       X-120.0   ;
N11   G47      Y-100.0;
N12   X-80.0   Y-60.0;
```

7.9 SCALING

Scaling (G51)

A programmed figure can be magnified or reduced (scaling). The dimensions specified with X, Y, Z can each be scaled up or down with the same or different rates of magnification. The magnification rate can be specified in the program.

The format is,

G51 X Y Z P;

(X, Y, Z - Absolute command for centre coordinate value of scaling.

P - Scaling magnification)

G50; (SCALING CANCEL)

Figure 7.29 illustrates the scaling operation. Point P0 is called the scaling centre. The scaling is done from P5P6P7P8 to P1P2P3P4.

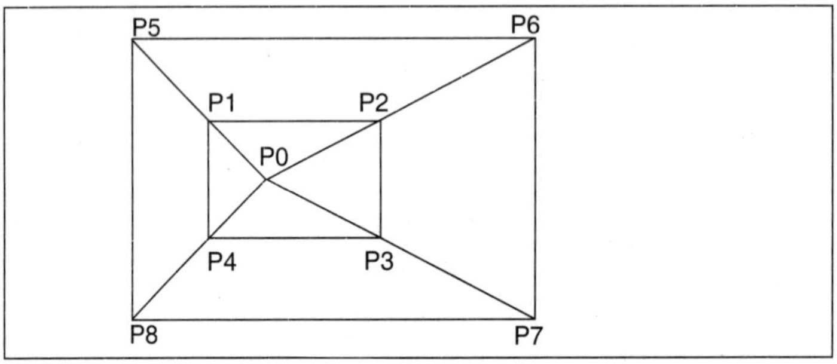

Fig. 7.29 Scaling

7.10 COORDINATE SYSTEMS

Local Coordinate System (G52)

When a program is created in a workpiece coordinate system, a child coordinate system may be set for easier programming. Such a child coordinate system is referred to as a local coordinate system.

The format is,

G52 X Y Z;

X, Y, Z - Coordinates of X, Y, Z axes

Machine Coordinate System Selection (G53)

A coordinate system with a machine zero point set as its origin is referred to as a machine coordinate system. G53 is used to select a machine coordinate system. When the tool is to be moved to a machine specific position such as tool change position, the movement can be programmed in a machine coordinate system based on G53.

7.11 CYCLES TO SIMPLIFY PROGRAMMING

Many special cycles are available for programming purposes. These are generally called fixed cycles or canned cycles. These are used to carry out a set of repetitive programming operations in machining centres like drilling, boring, tapping etc. Some cycles are commonly available in most of the CNC systems (e.g. G80-G89). Some control systems offer their own special fixed cycles. Some systems provide facilities for the users to design their own fixed cycles. The major advantages of fixed cycles are:

(i) Programme size is considerably reduced.

(ii) Programming time is also reduced, resulting in higher programmer productivity.

(iii) Errors in programming are reduced.

(iv) Less memory is required to store the programme.

High Speed Peck Drilling Cycle (G73)

This cycle performs high-speed peck drilling. It performs intermittent cutting feed to the bottom of a hole while removing chips from the hole.

The format is,

G73 X Y Z R Q F K;

X, Y	- Hole position data
Z	- The distance from point R to the bottom of the hole
R	- The distance from the initial level to point R level
Q	- Depth of cut for each cutting feed
F	- Cutting feedrate
K	- Number of repeats

When this cycle is used, chips can be removed from the hole easily, and a smaller value can be set for retraction. This allows drilling to be performed easily. The clearance d is set in parameter.

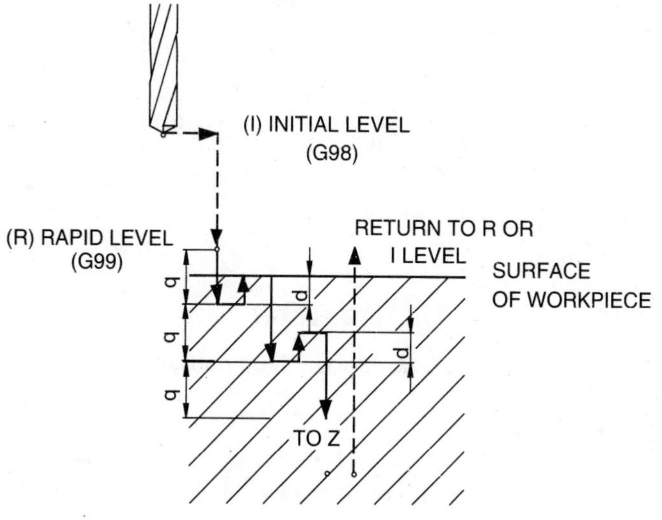

Fig. 7.30 Peck Drilling

Peck drilling is illustrated in Fig. 7.30. The drill is initially brought to a position above the point where drilling is to be done. This is called initial level or I-level. From this point drill approaches the work in rapid traverse up to R-level. Drill is then fed at the specified feed rate for a distance of *q* and then withdrawn through a distance of *d* at rapid traverse rate. Again drilling is performed for a distance of *q* and then withdrawn by a distance equal to d. This is repeated drill the desired drill depth is reached. Drill is then withdrawn at rapid traverse rate to either I-level or R level depending on the requirements.

Left Handed Tapping Cycle (G74)

This cycle performs left-handed tapping.

The format is,

G74 X Y Z R P F K;

X, Y	- Hole position data
Z	- The distance from point R to the bottom of the hole
R	- The distance from the initial level to point R level
P	- Dwell time
F	- Cutting feed rate
K	- Number of repeats

In the left-handed tapping cycle, Tapping is performed by rotating the spindle counterclockwise. When the bottom of the hole has been reached, the spindle rotates clockwise. Feedrate overrides are ignored during left-handed tapping. Before specifying G74, Miscellaneous function (M-code) should be used to rotate the spindle Counter Clockwise.

The tapping cycle is illustrated in Fig. 7.31. The tool can be taken back to either I-level or R-level. The rotational direction is reversed to facilitate the withdrawal of the tap. The feed rate should be the product of pitch x rpm.

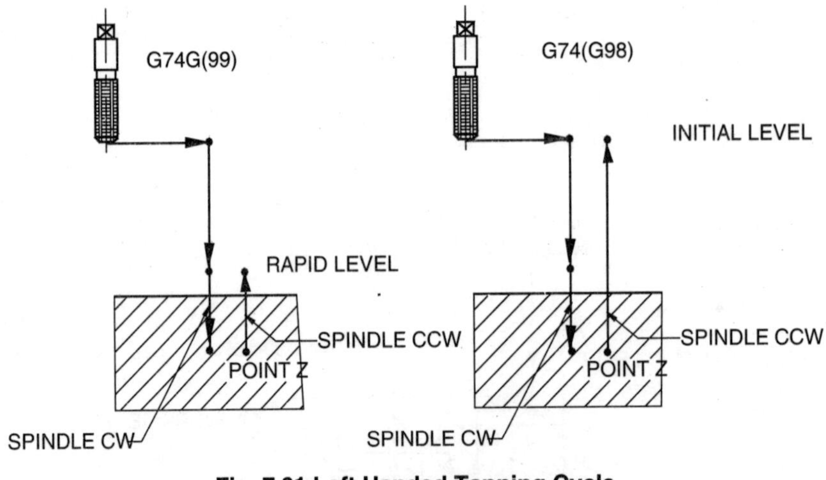

Fig. 7.31 Left Handed Tapping Cycle

Fine Boring Cycle (G76)

The fine boring cycle bores hole precisely. When the bottom of the hole has been reached, the spindle stops, and the tool is moved away from the machined surface of the workpiece and retracted.

The format is,

G76 X Y Z R Q P F K;

X, Y	- Hole position data
Z	- The distance from point R to the bottom of the hole
R	- The distance from the initial level to point R level
Q	- Shift amount at the bottom of a hole
P	- Dwell time
F	- Cutting feed rate
K	- Number of repeats

Q (shift) is a modal value retained within canned cycles. It is also used as depth of cut for G73 and G83.

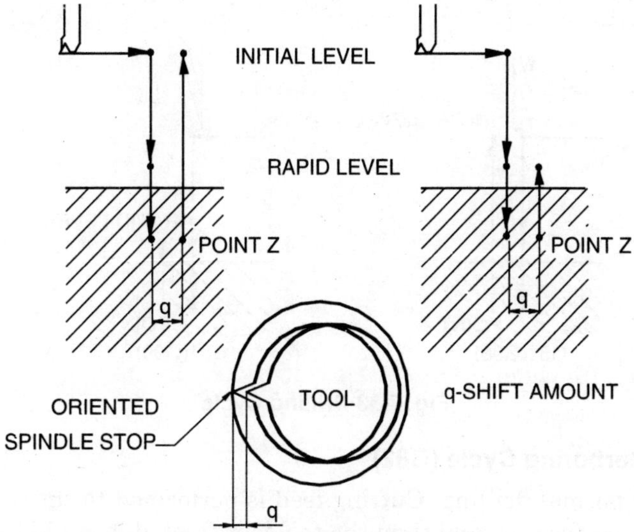

Fig. 7.32 Fine Boring Cycle

Figure 7.32 shows fine boring cycle. An example of fine boring cycle is given below:

Example:

M03	S600;								
G90	G99	X76	X250.0	Y200.0	Z-100.0	R5.0	Q5.0	P1000	F200.0;
	Y 300.0;								
	Y 400.0;								
G80	G28	G91	X0	Y0	Z0;				
M05;									

G76 will perform fine boring at locations 1 (250, 200), 2 (250, 300) and 3 (250, 400). It is sufficient to call the cycle once at location1. The function will be repeated at locations 2 and 3. It is very important to cancel the canned cycle.

Canned Cycles Cancel (G80)

All canned cycles are cancelled by G80 revert back to the normal operation of the machining centre.

G81 Drilling Cycle, Spot Drilling

This cycle is used for normal drilling. Cutting feed is performed to the bottom of the hole. The tool is then retracted from the bottom of the hole in rapid traverse.
The format is,

G81 X Y Z R F K;

X, Y	- Hole position data
Z	- The distance from point R to the bottom of the hole
R	- The distance from the initial level to point R level
F	- Cutting feedrate
K	- Number of repeats

After positioning along the X and Y axes, rapid traverse is performed to point R. Drilling is performed from point R to point Z. The tool is then retracted in rapid traverse either to I-level or to R-level. The G81 canned cycle is illustrated in Fig. 7.33. G01 group code should not be used together with G81.

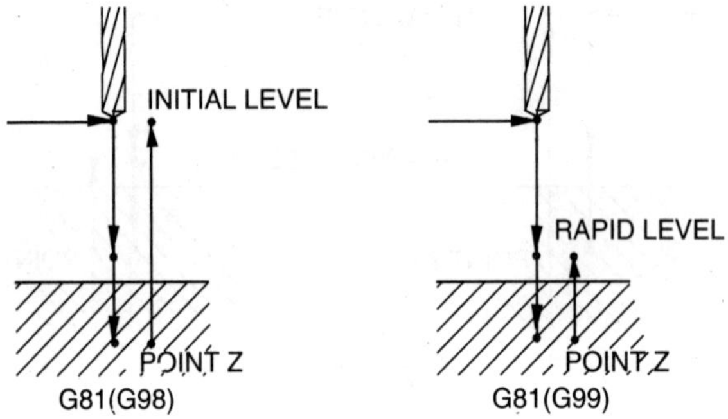

Fig. 7.33 Drilling Cycle

Drilling Cycle, Counterboring Cycle (G82)

This cycle is used for normal drilling. Cutting feed is performed to the bottom of the hole. At the bottom, a dwell is performed, and then the tool is retracted in rapid traverse. This cycle is used to drill holes more accurately with respect to depth. After positioning along X and Y rapid traverse is performed up to point R. Drilling is then performed up to Z. A dwell is performed at the bottom of the hole. The tool is then retracted in rapid traverse. Before specifying G82, an M code should be used to rotate the spindle.

The format is,

G82 X Y Z R P F K;

X, Y	- Hole position data
Z	- The distance from point R to the bottom of the hole
R	- The distance from the initial level to point R level
P	- Dwell time at the bottom of a hole
F	- Cutting feedrate
K	- Number of repeats

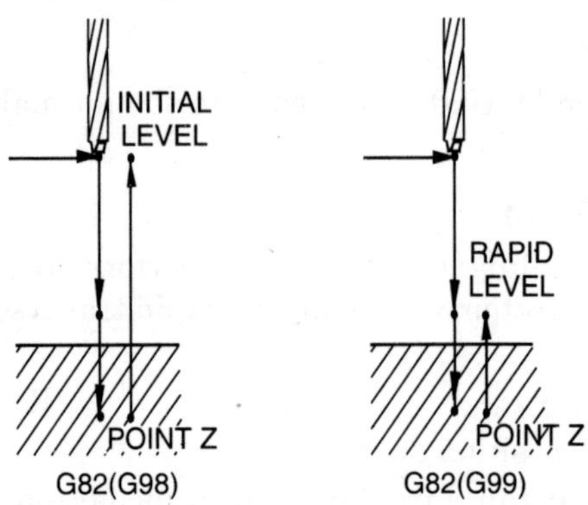

Fig. 7.34 Counterboring Cycle

The counterboring cycle is illustrated in Fig. 7.34.

Peck Drilling Cycle (G83)

This cycle performs peck drilling. It performs intermittent cutting feed to the bottom of a hole.

The format is,

G83 X Y Z R Q F K;

X, Y	- Hole position data
Z	- The distance from point R to the bottom of the hole
R	- The distance from the initial level to point R level
Q	- Depth of cut for each cutting feed
F	- Cutting feedrate
K	- Number of repeats

Q represents the depth of cut for each cutting feed. It must always be specified as incremental value.

In the second and subsequent cutting feeds, rapid traverse is performed up to a point just before where the last drilling ended and cutting feed is performed again.

Tapping Cycle (G84)

This cycle performs tapping. In this tapping cycle, when the bottom of the hole has been reached, the spindle is rotated in the counter clockwise direction.

The format is,

G84 X Y Z R P F K;

X, Y	- Hole position data
Z	- The distance from point R to the bottom of the hole
R	- The distance from the initial level to point R level
P	- Dwell time
F	- Cutting feedrate
K	- Number of repeats

In the tapping cycle, Tapping is performed by rotating the spindle clockwise. When the bottom of the hole has been reached, the spindle is rotated in reverse direction for retraction. Feedrate overrides are ignored during left-handed tapping.

Boring Cycle (G85)

This cycle is used to bore a hole.

The format is,

G85 X Y Z R F K;

X, Y	- Hole position data
Z	- The distance from point R to the bottom of the hole
R	- The distance from the initial level to point R level
F	- Cutting feedrate
K	- Number of repeats

After positioning X, Y axes, rapid traverse is performed to point R. Boring is performed from point R to point Z. *When point Z has been reached, cutting feed is performed to return to point R.*

Figure. 7.35 shows the boring cycle.

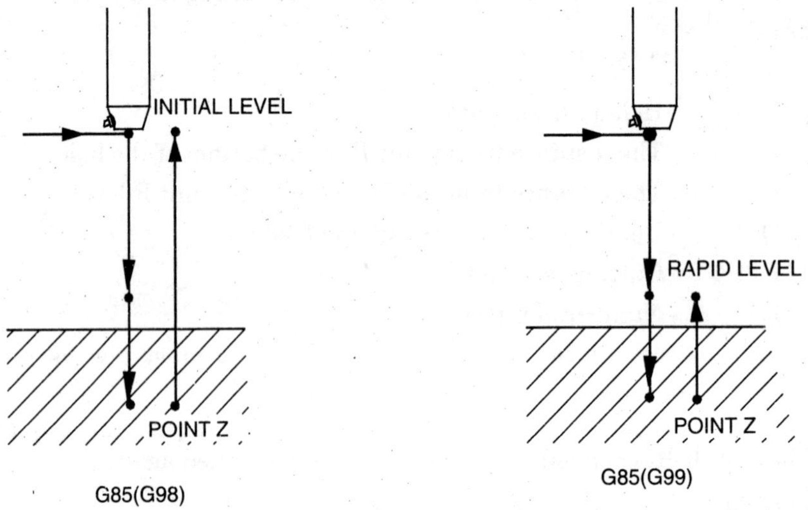

Fig. 7.35 Boring Cycle

Boring Cycle (G86)

This cycle is also used to bore a hole.

The format is,

G86 X Y Z R F K;

X, Y	- Hole position data
Z	- The distance from point R to the bottom of the hole
R	- The distance from the initial level to point R level
F	- Cutting feedrate
K	- Number of repeats

After positioning X, Y axes, rapid traverse is performed to point R. Boring is performed from point R to point Z. *When the spindle is stopped at the bottom of the hole, the tool is retracted in rapid traverse.*

Back Boring Cycle (G87)

This performs accurate back boring.

The format is,

G87 X Y Z R Q P F K;

X, Y	- Hole position data
Z	- The distance from the bottom of the hole to point Z
R	- The distance from the initial level to point R (the bottom of the hole) level
Q	- Tool shift amount
P	- Dwell time
F	- Cutting feedrate
K	- Number of repeats

After positioning the X and Y axes, the spindle is stopped at the fixed rotation position. The tool is moved in the direction opposite to the tool tip; positioning (rapid traverse) is performed to the bottom of the hole (point R). The tool is then shifted in the direction of the tool tip and the spindle is rotated clockwise. Boring is performed in the positive direction along the Z axis until point Z is reached. At point Z, the spindle stopped at the fixed rotation position again, the tool is shifted in the direction opposite to the tool tip, and then the tool is returned to initial level. The back boring operation is shown in Fig. 7.36.

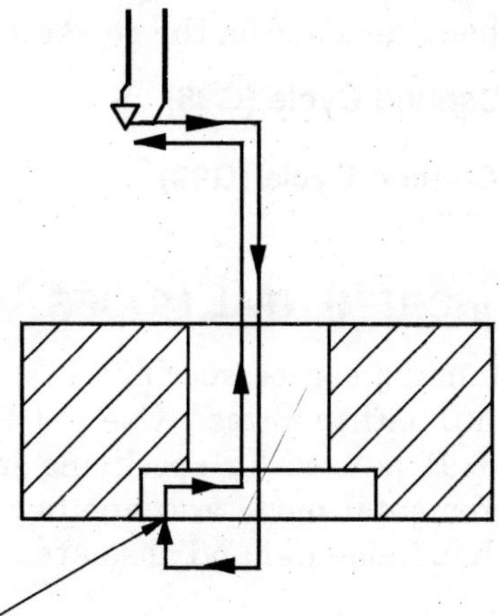

Fig. 7.36 Back Boring Operation

Boring Cycle (G88)

This cycle is used to bore a hole.

The format is,

G88 X Y Z R P F K;

X, Y	- Hole position data
Z	- The distance from point R to the bottom of the hole
R	- The distance from the initial level to point R level
P	- Dwell time at the bottom of a hole
F	- Cutting feedrate
K	- Number of repeats

After positioning X, Y axes, rapid traverse is performed to point R. Boring is performed from point R to point Z. When boring is completed, a dwell is performed, and then the spindle is stopped. The tool is ***manually*** retracted from the bottom of the hole (point Z) to point R. At point R, the spindle is rotated clockwise, and rapid traverse is performed to the initial level.

Boring Cycle (G89)

This cycle is same as G85. The difference is that this cycle performs a dwell at the bottom of the hole.

The format is,

G89 X Y Z R P F K;

X, Y - Hole position data

Z - The distance from point R to the bottom of the hole
R - The distance from the initial level to point R level
P - Dwell time at the bottom of a hole
F - Cutting feedrate
K - Number of repeats

There are two options for return of the tool after executing a canned cycle. One is to return to the rapid approach level (R-level) and another to the initial level (I-level) at which point the canned cycle starts. The choice depends on the geometry of the workpiece.

Return to Initial Level in Canned Cycle (G98)

Return to Rapid Level in Canned Cycle (G99)

7.12 ABSOLUTE AND INCREMENTAL MODES

The coordinates in programming can be specified in either incremental in absolute mode. A programme can be written in either format. Use of G90 indicates that the programme is in absolute mode. Similarly G91 is used for specifying incremental dimensions. A part of the programme can be in incremental mode and another part in absolute mode. X, Y, Z word addresses are used for both incremental and absolute modes.

G90 Absolute Command

In the absolute command, coordinate value of the end position is programmed for the tool to move.

Example:

G90 X40.0 Y75.0;

G91 Incremental Command

In the incremental command, move distance of the position itself is programmed.

Example:

G91 X-50.0 Y35.0;

7.13 SPEED AND FEED SETTING

Maximum Spindle Speed (G92)

The maximum spindle speed of the machine can be specified using G92.

The format is,

G92 S;

Feed Per Minute (G94)

The feed rate is set to inch/mm per minute.

The format is,

G94 F;

This is used together with G20 for inch and G21 for metric dimensions.

Feed Per Rotation (G95)

The feed rate is set to inch/mm per rotation.

The format is,

G95 F;

Constant Surface Speed Control (G96)

The spindle is rotated so that the surface speed is constant regardless of the position of the tool.

The format is,

G96 S; [surface speed (mm/min or inch/min)]

Constant Surface Speed Control Cancel (G97)

The spindle is rotated so that the surface speed is cancelled.

The format is,

G97 S; (spindle speed rpm)

7.14 CYCLES FOR PATTERN DRILLING

Special fixed cycles are available for drilling holes along a line or in a pitch circle.

Fixed Cycle to Drill Holes in a Pitch Circle (G34)

The format is:

G34 X--------Y--------I--------J-------K;

Where X and Y, the coordinates of the centre of the circle

I, the radius of the pitch circle (in units of 0.001mm)

J, the angle at which the first hole is located (in units of 0.001^0)

K, the number of holes

For example, let us consider drilling 6 holes on a pitch circle diameter of 125 mm. The coordinates of the centre of the pitch circle is, say 200,230

```
N20    G90;
N30    G98    G81      R4.0     F250.0;
N40    G34    X200.0   Y230.0   I125000   J30000K6;
N50    G80;
```

Fixed Cycle To Drill Holes In A Line (G35)

This cycle defines an array of points at equal intervals along a line that can be at any angle to the positive X-axis.

The format is:

G35 X---------Y-------I-------J-------K;

Where X and Y, the coordinates of the start point

I, the interval distance between the points

J, the angle between the line of holes and the positive X-axis in units of 0.001°

K, number of holes including the starting hole.

7.15 SUBPROGRAMME

If a programme contains a fixed sequence or a frequently repeated pattern, such a sequence or pattern can be stored as a subprogramme. A subprogramme can be called from a main program. A subprogramme can call another subprogramme. A subprogramme is identified by a programme number (letter O followed by a maximum of 4 digits). A subprogramme ends with M 99 code.

A subprogramme is called in the main programme by

M98 P (followed by the number of subprogramme)

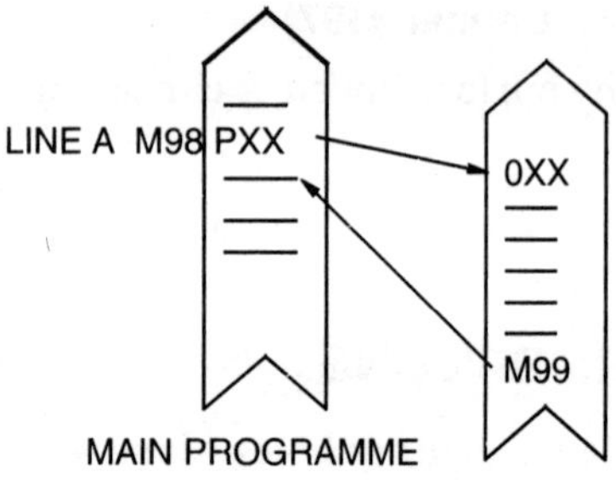

Fig. 7.37 Subprogramme

Referring to Fig. 7.37 on reading line number A the main programme branches off to the subprogramme XX whose number is identified by the address P. The control returns to the main programme on reading the end of subprogramme code M99.

7.16 EXAMPLES

Some simple examples are given in this section to familiarize the reader with programming.

Example 1

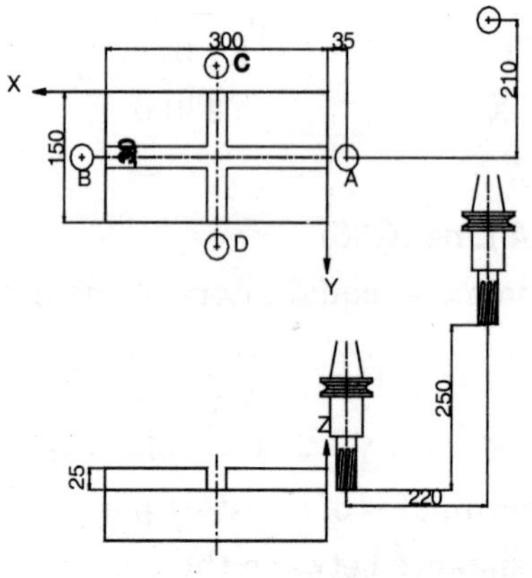

Fig. 7.38 End Milling

Figure 7.38 shows a workpiece in which two orthogonal slots are to be milled. An end mill is used in machining. The tool is brought to position A in rapid traverse and then end milling is done up to point B at a feed rate of 450 mm/min. The tool is then positioned at C and milling is done up to point D. A clearance of 20 mm between the workpiece and tool is maintained at the end of rapid approach as well as an over travel of 20 mm after milling.

N 010	G90 .	G00	X35.0	Y75.0;
N020	Z-25.0;			
N030	S700	M03;		(Position A)
N040	X335.0	F315.0	M08;	(Position B)
N050	G00	Z100.0;		
N060	G00	X150.0	Y-35.0;	
N070	Z-25.0;			(Position C)
N080	G01	Y185.0;		(Position D)
N090	G00	Z+225.0;		
N100	G00	X-255.0	Y-135.0;	
N110	M09;			
N110	M05;			

Example 2

Referring to Fig. 7.39 the X0, Y0 and Z0 are located in the centre of the top of the workpiece. Four numbers of 8 mm dia. holes are to be drilled. The drill is initially located above hole 1 and then drilling is carried out using G81 canned cycle. The process is repeated in locations 2, 3 and 4. The tool is then returned to the home position.

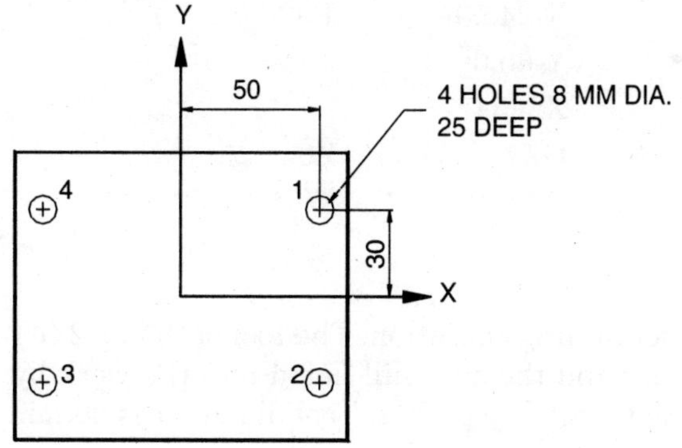

Fig. 7.39 Drilling of Holes

N 005	G00	G90	X0	Y0;	
N010	Z100.0;				
N015	X50.0	Y30.0;			
N020	G81	G98	Z-25.0	R 4.0	F200.0;
N025	Y30.0;				
N030	X-50.0;				
N035	Y30.0;				
N040	G80;				
N045	G91	G28	X0	Y0;	
N050	G28	Z0;			

Example 3

The machining involves face milling of a workpiece of size 300 × 200, shown in Fig. 7.40. The cutter diameter is 160 mm. Therefore two passes are necessary to complete the milling operation. The face milling cutter is brought to position 1 and milling is performed from position 1 to position 2. The tool is then moved to rapid traverse to position 3. Milling is done from position 3 to position 4. Care is taken to ensure that the width of cut is about 70-75% of the cutter diameter to reduce vibrations.

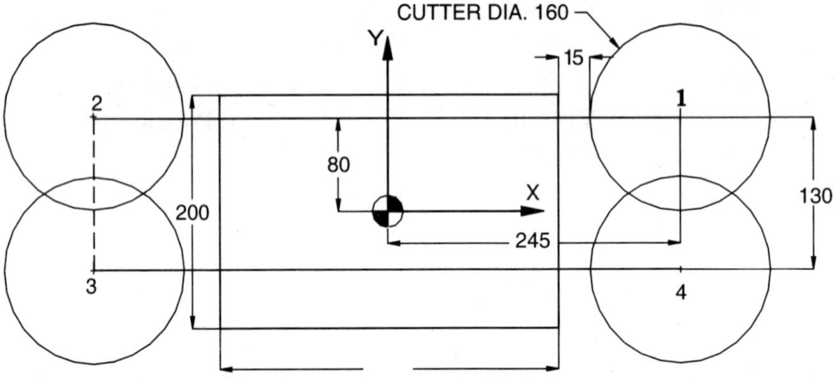

Fig. 7.40 Face Milling

N010	G00	G90	X245.0	Y80.0;
N020	Z-5.0;			
N030	G01	X-245.0	F500.0;	
N040	G00	Y-60.0;		
N050	G01	X245.0;		
N060	G91	G28	Z0;	
N070	G28	X0	W0;	

Example 4

Figure 7.41 shows a pocket milling operation. The tool path is 1-2-3-4-5-6-7-8. Initially the tool is brought above position 1 and the end mill is fed into the work by 10 mm. The tool is then moved along the tool path to mill the pocket. Tool diameter is 20 mm.

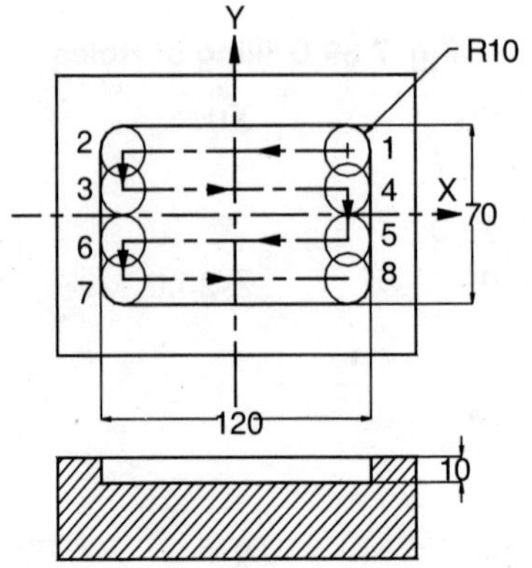

Fig. 7.41 Pocket Milling

N010	G90	G00	X50.0 Y25.0;
N011	Z10.0;		
N12	G01	Z-10.0;	
N013	X-50.0	F200.0;	
N014	Y10.0;		
N015	X50.0;		
N016	Y-10.0;		
N017	X-50.0;		
N018	Y-25.0;		
N019	X50.0;		
N020	G00	Z10.0;	
N021	G91	G28	Z0;
N022	G28	X0	Y0;

Example 5

Figure 7.42 shows a steel block with four counterbored holes. The block is pre-machined to 200 × 150 × 45 mm. 20 Diameter (H7) hole is not considered.

The process chart for the component is shown in Table 7.4.

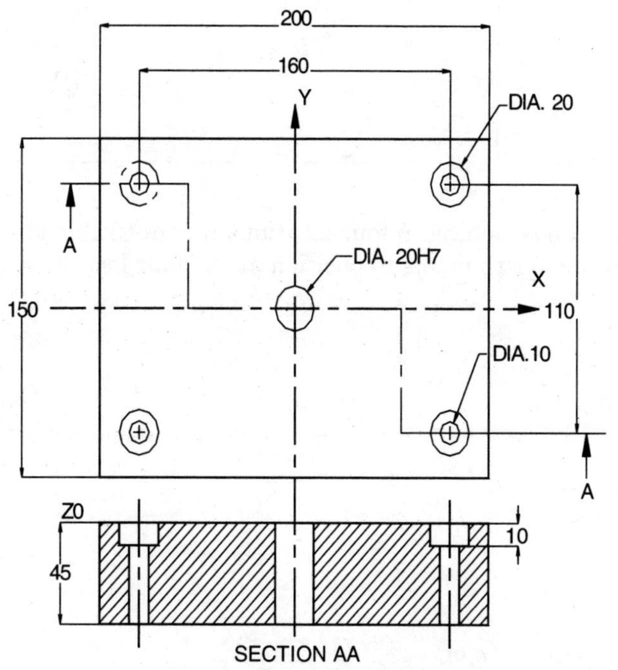

Fig. 7.42 Use of Canned Cycle

Table 7.4 Process Chart for the Component of Fig. 7.42

Sl. No.	Operation	Cutting Speed, m/min.	Spindle Speed, rpm	Feed, mm/ min	Tool	Tool Offset
1	Centre Drill	20	1250	125	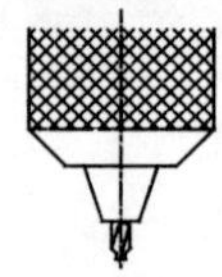	H1
2	10 dia. drill	25	800	160	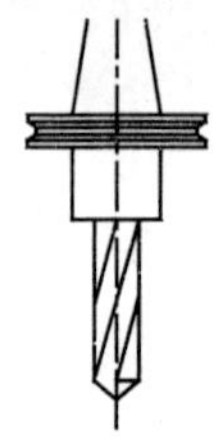	H2
3	20 dia. C'bore	25	400	80	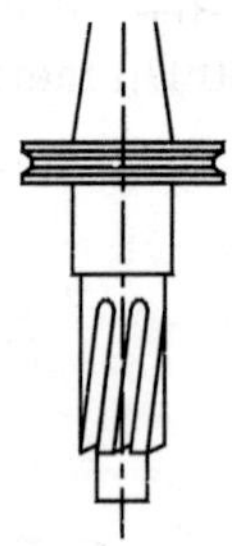	H3

Programme

Since there are repeated positioning in four locations it is desirable to use the subprogramme concept. A subprogramme for the tools to position at the four locations is given below:

Subprogramme

```
O36;
N8000    Y-55.0;
N8001    X-80.0;
N8002    Y55.0;
N8003    M99;
```

Main Programme

```
O4563;
/N100   G0    G40   G80;
/N101   G91   G28   X0    Y0    Z0;
/N102   T1;
/N103   M06;
/N104   M1;
```

```
N105   T2;
N106   G0    G90   G54     G43   X80.0   Y55.0   H1    S1250   M3;
N107   G98   G81   Z-5.0   R3.0  F125.0;
N108   M98   P36;
N109   G80   G91   G28     Z0;
N110   M6;
/N111  M1;
N112   T3;
N114   G0    G90   G54     G43   X80.0   Y55.0   H2    S800    M3;
N115   G81   G98   Z-50.0  R3.0  F160.0;
N116   M98   P36;
N117   G80   G91   G28     Z0;
/N119  M1;
N120   M6;
N121   T1;
N122   G0    G90   G54     G43   X80.0   Y55.0   H3    S400    M3;
N123   G81   G98   Z-10.0  R3.0  P500    F80;
N124   M98   P36;
N125   G40   G80   G91     G28   X0      Y0      Z0;
/N126  M1;
N127   M6;
N128   M30;
```

Example 6

An end mill can be used to bore a hole using circular interpolation. Consider the component shown in Fig. 7.43. A 100 mm bore is to be made in a CI blank as shown in the figure. It is assumed that the bore size in the blank is 92 dia. The machining allowance hence is 4 mm.

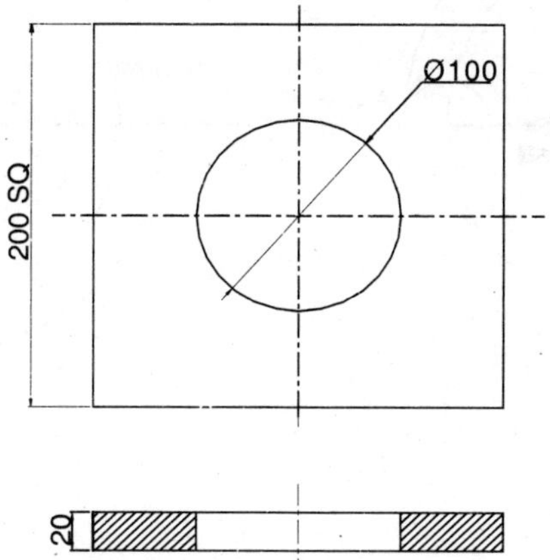

Fig. 7.43 Machining a Bore by Circular Interpolation

The blank 200 × 200 × 20 is already pre-machined. Figure 7.44 shows the set up.

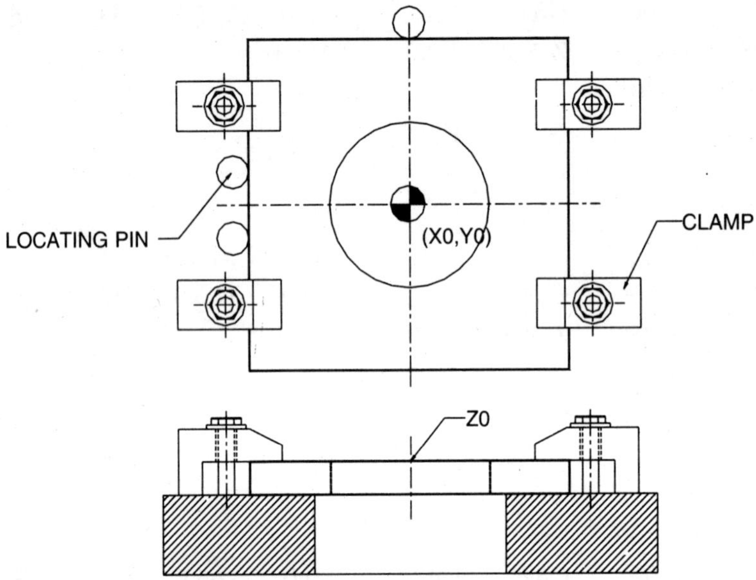

Fig. 7.44 Set Up

The workpiece is located using 3-2-1 location and clamped as shown. The centre point of the top surface is taken as the zero point of the work coordinate system.

There are two methods of planning the machining. One method is shown in Fig. 7.45 (a). The tool is taken to point where the tool touches 100 dia bore and then a circular interpolation is called. This may result in tool digging in at point the tool reaches 100 dia bore. A better method is to approach the starting point tangentially and leaving the profile tangentially as shown in Fig. 7.45 (b). The program is written for the second approach.

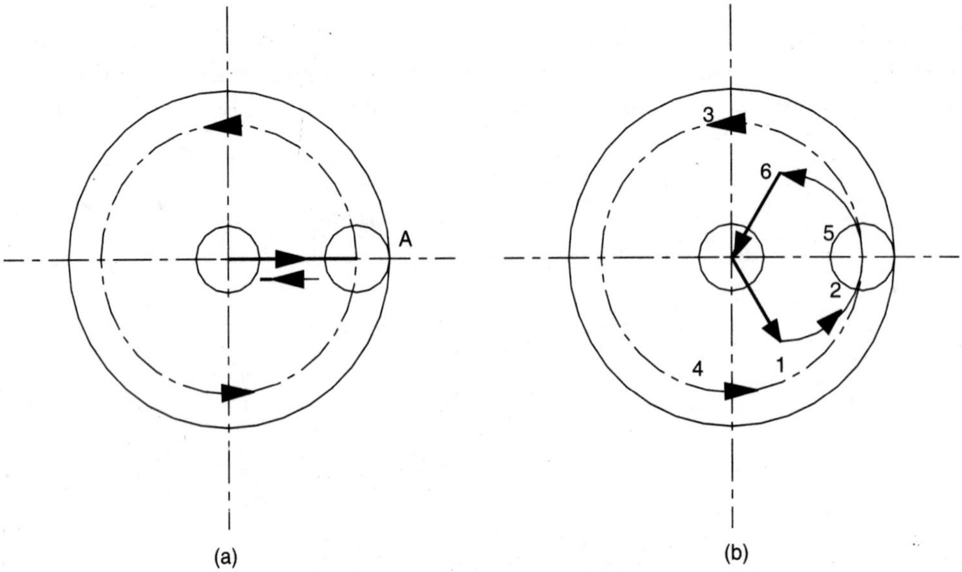

Fig. 7.45 Two Approaches for Machining

Table 7.5 Process Details

Process	Tool No.	Tool	rpm	Feed rate	Offset, H	Offset, D
1	5	20 Dia End Mill	360	124 mm/min	5	5

Program

```
O25;
N10   G0   G40   G80;
/N20  G91  G28   X0     Y0     Z0;
/N30  T1;
/N40  M6;
/N50  M1;
N60 (20 Dia End Mill);
N70   G0   G90    G54    X0     Y0     S360   M3;
N80   G43  Z-50.0 H5;
N90   Z-25.0;
N100  G1   G41    X20.0  Y-30.0 D5     F124;
N110  G3   X50.0  Y0     R30.0;
N120  G3   I-50.0;
N130  G3   X20.0  Y30.0  R 30.0;
N140  G1   G40    X0     Y0     F1200;
N150  G0   Z50.0  M5;
N160  G91  G28    Z0;
N170  T1;
N180  M6;
N190  M30;
```

Example 7

Machining of multiple pieces in one set up.

Often there will be situations where smaller workpieces will have to be machined. Machining one by one will involve waste of time. In order to increase productivity and cost of machining, many workpieces will be mounted on the table. Four similar workpieces are shown mounted on the table in Fig. 7.46.

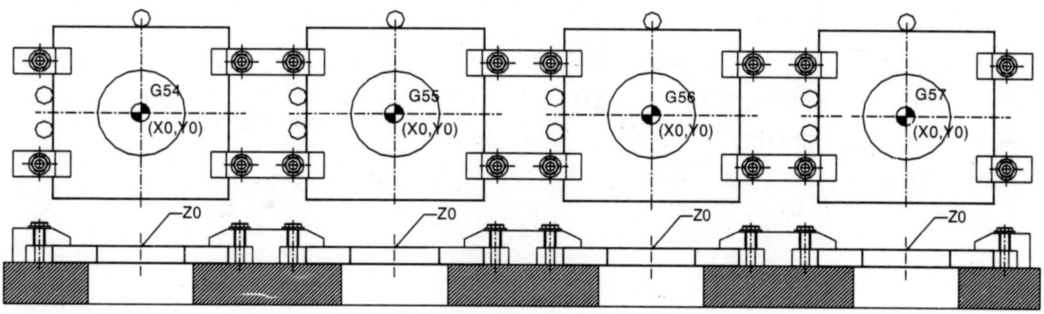

Fig. 7.46 Multiple Component Set Up

The workpiece datum (X0, Y0) of the components is set at G54, G55, G56 and G57 as shown. The program given in example 6 is written as a subprogram. The subprogram 054 is repeated with G55, G56 and G57 as workpiece coordinate systems.

Program

```
O36;
/N10    G0     G40     G80;
/N20    G91    G28     X0      Y0      Z0;
/N30    T1;
/N40    M6;
/N50    M1;
N60 (20 Dia End Mill);
N70     G0     G90     G54     X0      Y0      S360    M3;
N80     G43    Z-50.0  H5;
N90     M98    P54;
N100    G55    X0      Y0;
N110    M98    P54;
N120    G56    X0      Y0;
N130    M98    P54;
N140    G57    X0      Y0;
N150    M98    P54;
N160    G91    G28     Z0      M5;
N170    G0     G40     G80;
N180    T1;
N190    M6;
N200    M30;
```

Subprogram

```
O 54;
N200    G1     Z-25.0;
N300    G1     G41     X20.0   Y-30.0  D5      F124;
N400    G3     X50.0   Y0      R30.0;
N500    G3     I-50.0;
N600    G3     X20.0   Y30.0   R 30.0;
N700    G1     G40     X0      Y0      F1200;
N800    G0     Z50.0;
N900    M99;
```

REVIEW QUESTIONS

(1) Compare the axis designation of the following machines:
- horizontal machining centre
- vertical machining centre
- 4-axis horizontal machining centre
- 5 axis machining centre with tilting spindle heads

(2) Explain the linear and circular interpolation functions in machining centre programming.

(3) What is reference return? What are the codes used for this purpose?

(4) How are tool length offsets measured?

(5) How will you program thread cutting in machining centres?

(6) What is corner offset circular interpolation? Where is it applied?

(7) What is cutter compensation? How is cutter compensation programmed?

(8) What is meant by tool length offset? How is it programmed?

(9) What are the different work coordinate systems in machining centres? Explain with an appropriate example.

(10) What is a canned cycle? Describe a typical canned cycle.

(11) Write short notes on:
- High speed peck drilling cycle
- Left handed tapping cycle

(12) How do you programme a machining centre in absolute and incremental modes?

(13) What is a subprogramme? Give an example.

(14) Why are different boring cycles provided in a machining centre?

(15) A few components are shown below. Prepare process charts and programmes for the components.

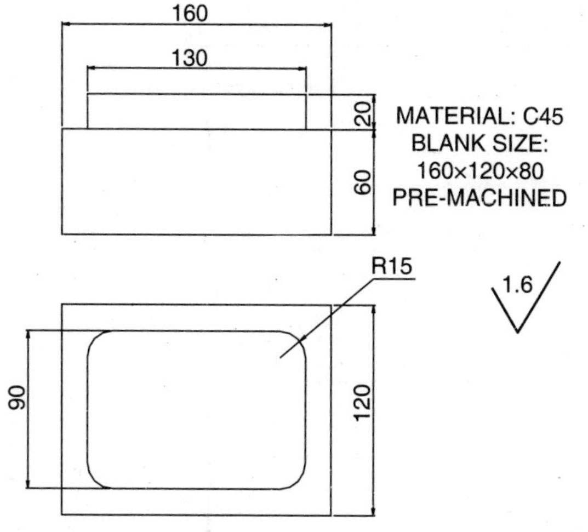

Fig. 7.47

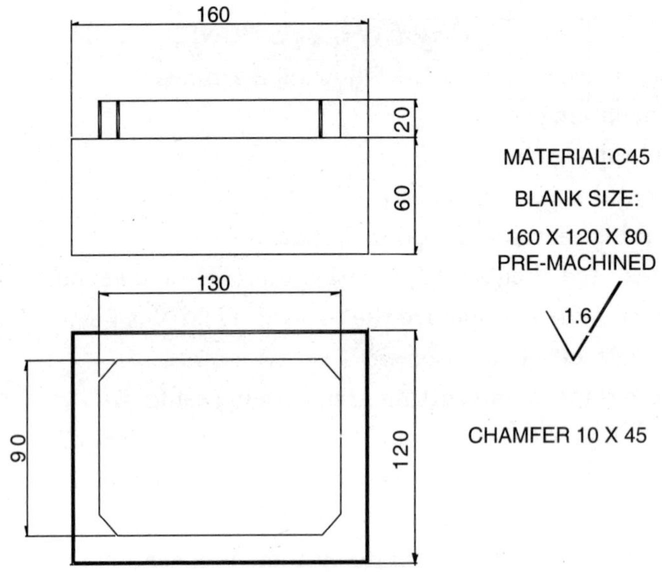

Fig. 7.48

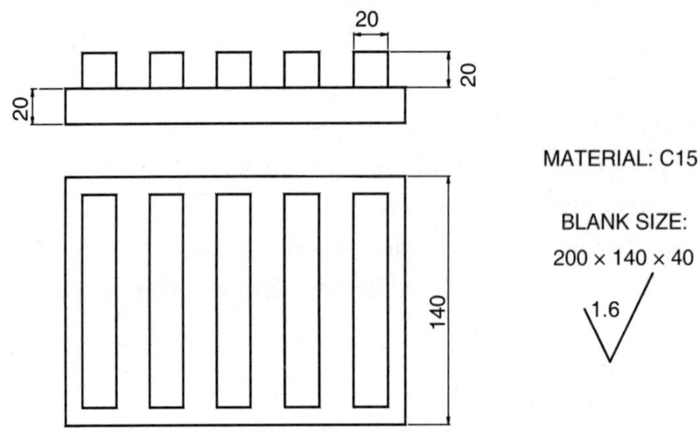

Fig. 7.49

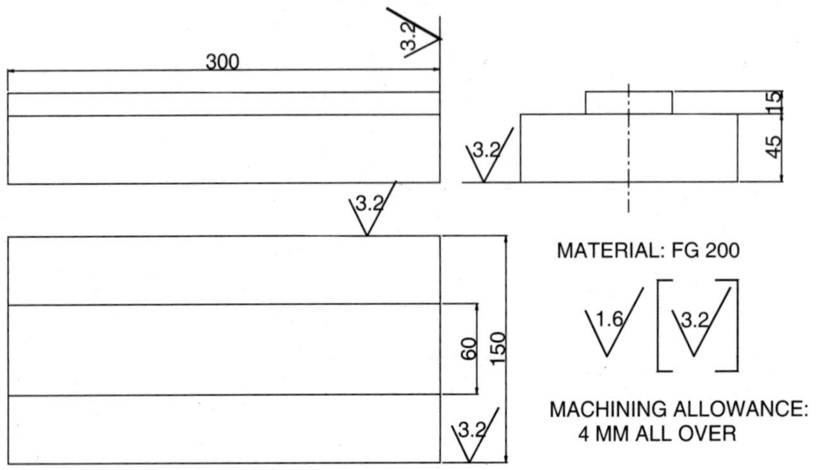

Fig. 7.50

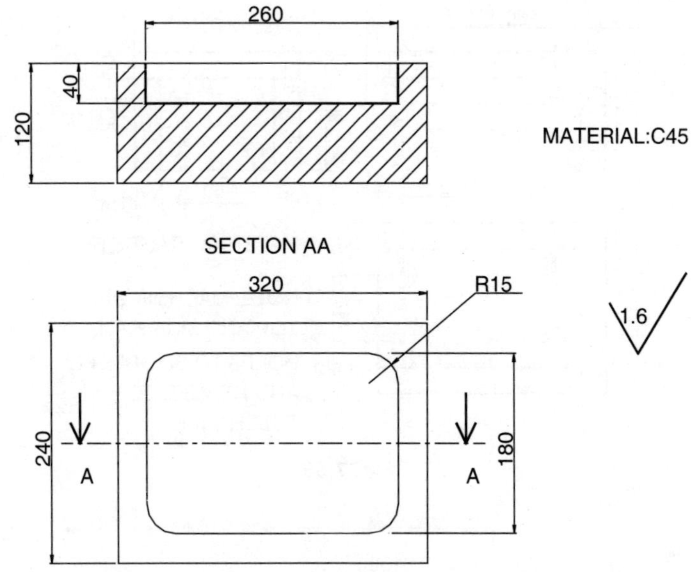

Fig. 7.51

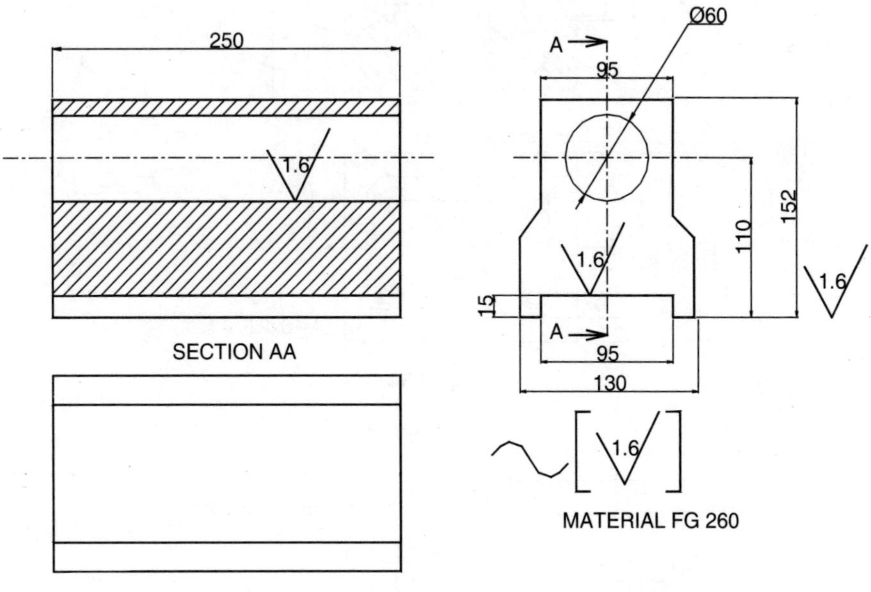

Fig. 7.52

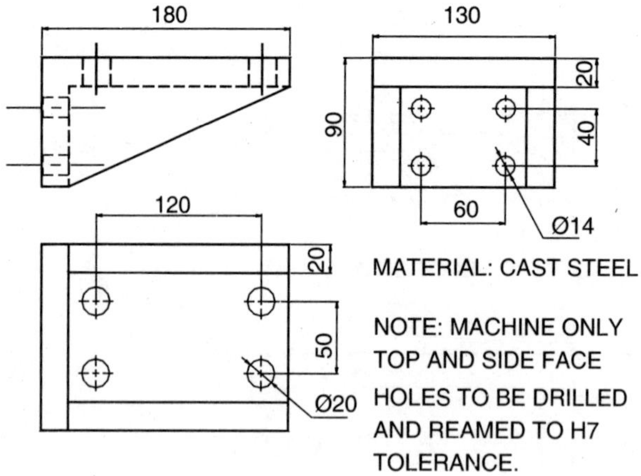

Fig. 7.53

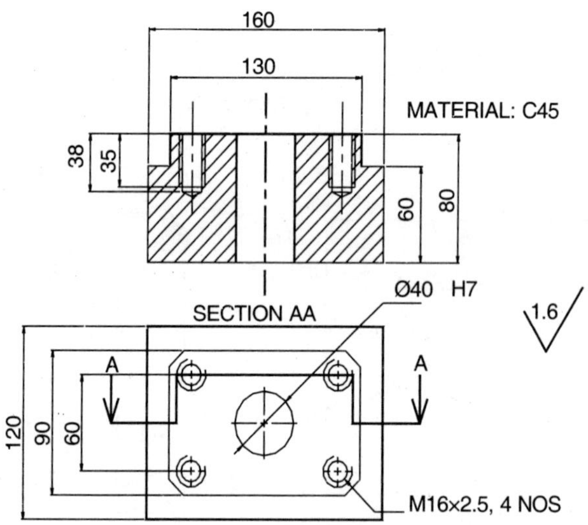

Fig. 7.54

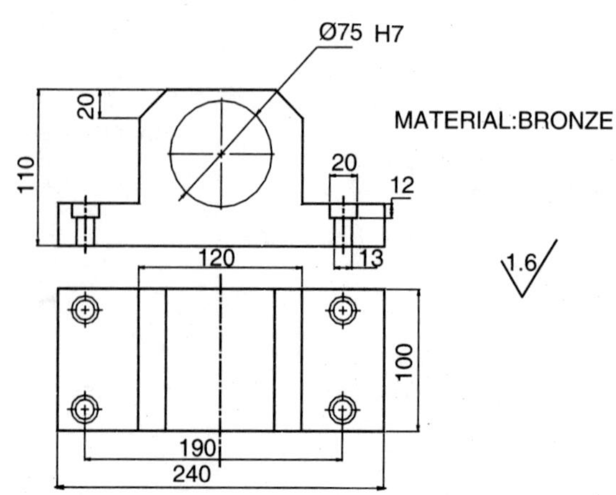

Fig. 7.55

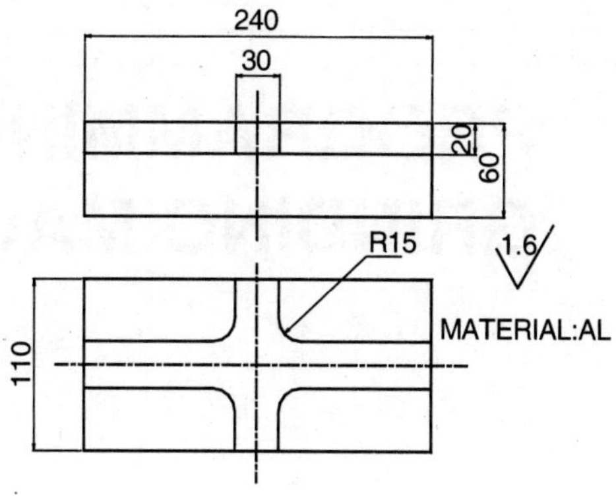

Fig. 7.56

8 PROGRAMMING OF GRINDING MACHINES

Computer numerical control has been extensively applied to many other machines. Grinding machines are widely used in machine shops. Finish and accuracy are the prime considerations in grinding. The CNC grinding machines are designed such that they are capable of providing consistent quality.

8.1 GRINDING PROCESS

Grinding is a finishing process in which material is removed by the abrasive grains embedded in a rotating cylindrical grinding wheel. There are many types of grinding processes. Cylindrical grinding machines (external, internal, universal), surface grinders, Centreless grinders, tool and cutter grinders, gear grinders etc. are available in CNC version. CNC grinding machines are now widely used in the manufacturing industries. The following sections give a brief overview of the programming concepts pertaining to cylindrical grinding. Some of the common grinding operations are illustrated in Fig. 8.1.

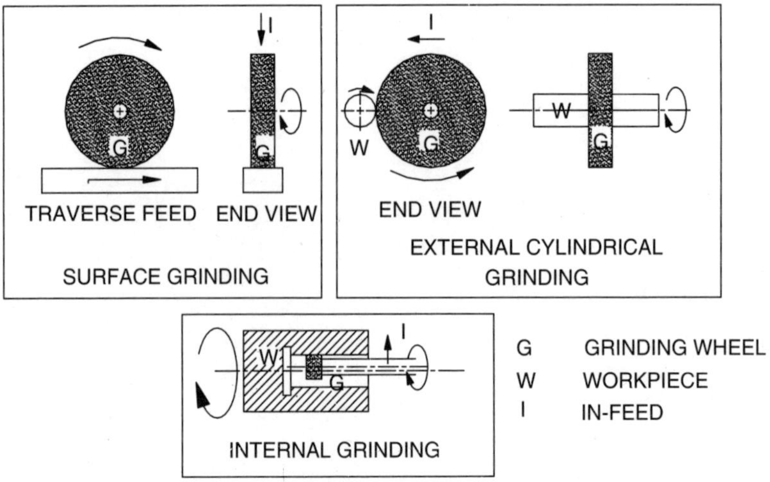

Fig. 8.1 Common Types of Grinding

Surface grinding is used to finish flat surfaces. The grinding wheel is rotated at a suitable rpm to obtain the desired grinding speed. The workpiece is mounted on a table which reciprocates.

This gives the traverse feed. The grinding wheel is mounted on a short table which is moved against the workpiece to provide the depth of grinding. This is called in-feed. If the workpiece is broader than the wheel, a lateral feed is to be provided at the end of each stroke.

Cylindrical grinding can be external or internal. In external cylindrical grinding a grinding wheel larger in diameter than the workpiece is used. In internal grinding the size of the grinding wheel is smaller than the bore ground. In external cylindrical grinding, the workpiece is mounted on a reciprocating table which gives the traverse speed.

8.2 AXES NOMENCLATURE FOR A CYLINDRICAL GRINDING MACHINE

A typical 6-Axis CNC grinding machine is shown in Fig. 8.2. This machine is capable of several operations: bore or outside-diameter grinding; cylindrical or taper grinding, blending chamfers and radius capabilities; front or back faces, etc. A common axis configuration designates the main axes as X and Z, with Y, C, A, U and W as auxiliary axes. Z-axis gives the traverse speed and X-axis in-feed.

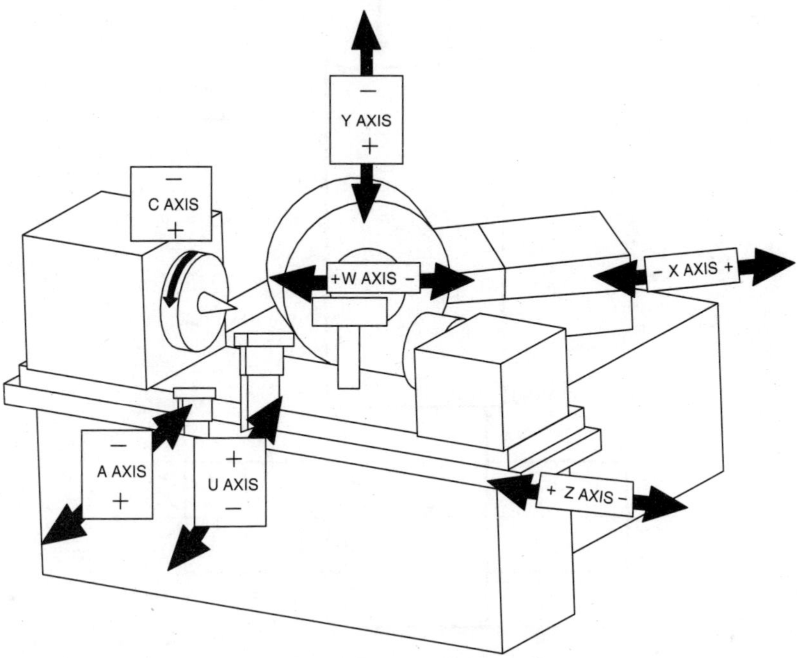

Fig. 8.2 CNC Grinding Machine

The profile of the grinding wheel can be dressed on these grinders by CNC axes dedicated specifically for dressers. Linear and circular interpolation commands are used to dress the wheel to any desired profile.

The following grinding operations are generally performed on the grinding machines:

Plunge Grinding

Traverse Grinding

Tapers

Faces

Contours

Forms

Profile dressing

8.3 PROGRAMMABLE CNC GRINDING CYCLES

Some of the common cycles are included in this section. Different controls may give alternate names to these same operations.

8.3.1 External Cylindrical Grinding Cycles

Straight Plunge Grinding

Figure 8.3 shows plunge grinding. The width of the grinding wheel is greater than the width of the workpiece and hence there is no need for traversing.

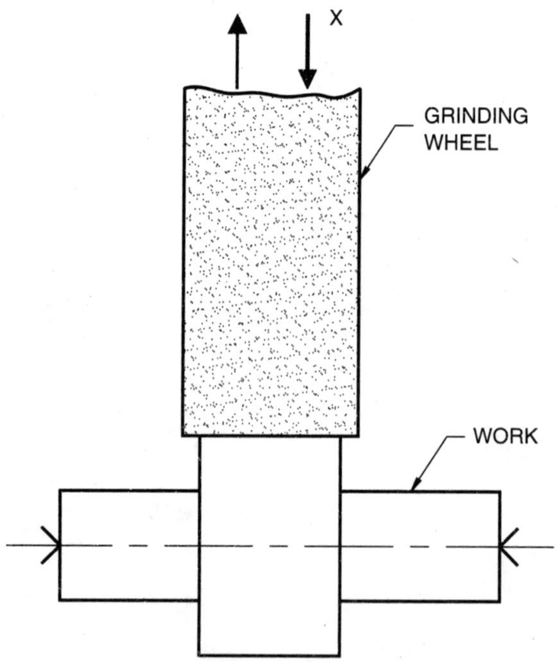

Fig. 8.3 Plunge Grinding

The format for plunge grinding is:

X---------Z----------F-------;

In practice this is a six-step cycle that moves the wheel into the workpiece in 2 axis directions, each separately—air grinding; roughing; stress-relief back-off, finish pass; final sizing and zero reset and rapid retraction. This is illustrated in Fig. 8.4.

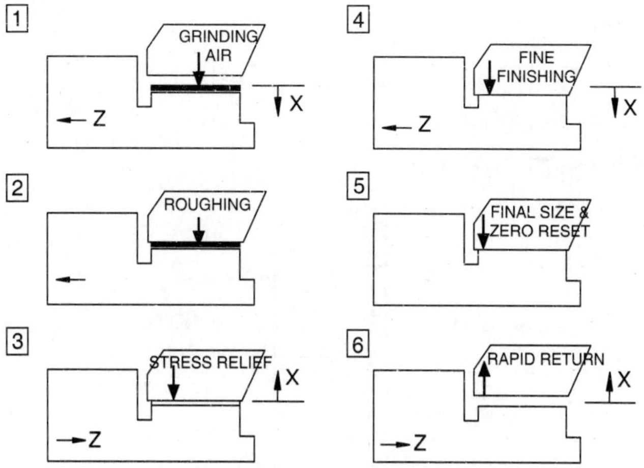

Fig. 8.4 Plunge Grinding Cycle

Angular Plunge Grinding

Figure 8.5 shows an angular plunge grinding cycle.

X---------Z--------F---------;

This plunges the wheel into the surface of the workpiece in a two-axis direction, simultaneously in an angular direction.

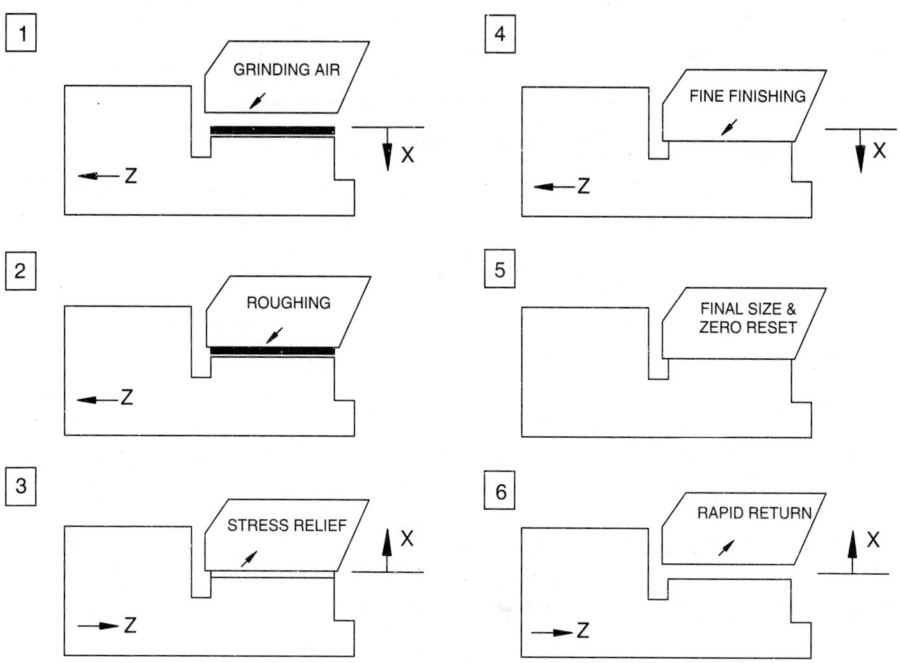

Fig. 8.5 Plunge Grinding (Angular)

Traverse Grinding

X---------Z--------F--------K---;

where K is the number of passes.

Traverse grinding is shown in Fig. 8.6.

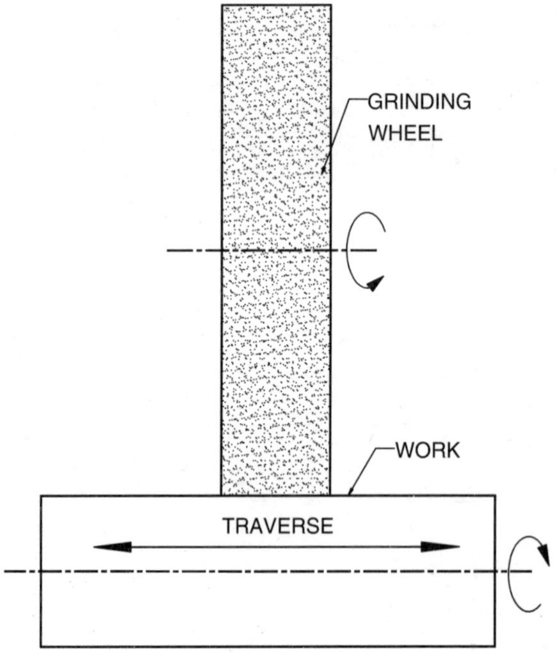

Fig. 8.6 Traverse Grinding

This is also a six-step cycle the wheel down a step cut, traverses the workpiece surface, moves in a step cut, traverses the surface by the number of passes specified, finishes, and resets to zero.

Face Grinding:

X---------Z--------F--------K---;

where K is the number of passes.

This is a six-step cycle that moves in and face-grinds with selected axis movements.

CNC Grinding Wheel Dressing

CNC profile dressers accurately move a diamond tool in a programmed tool path, enabling the generation of complex profiles on grinding wheels for machining into workpiece surfaces. Precision contour wheel dressing allows the pivoting axis of the dresser to form the smallest, deep contours into the wheel.

8.4 FEATURES OF A TYPICAL CNC GRINDING SYSTEM

Features available in a typical grinding system are given below:

8.4.1 General Features

- Number of axes 4 (2 in basic machines)
- Simultaneous traversing unto 4 axes
- Linear or circular interpolation in 2 out of 4 axis
- Input resolution: 0.01 mm, 0.001 mm or 0.0001 mm.
- Position control resolution equal to half of input resolution

8.4.2 Technological Functions

Feed rate G (94)

Feed rate is specified in 7 digits in mm/min.

0.1 to 446000 mm/min with 0.01 input resolution

1.1 to 44600 mm/min with 0.001 input resolution

1.1 to 4460 mm/min with 0.0001 input resolution

Rapid Traverse (G00)

Maximum rapid traverse will be at the maximum values of the feed rate.

Feed per revolution (G95)

G95 F------;

1.1 to 2000 mm/rev with 0.01 input resolution

0.001 to 200 mm/rev with 0.001 input resolution

0.0001 to 20 mm/rev with 0.0001 input resolution

Constant Cutting Speed (G96)

Cutting speed programmable by address S1 or S2 in 4 digits in m/min. 1 to 9999 m/min.

Thread Grinding

G33	Constant pitch
G34	Pitch linearly increasing
G35	Pitch linearly decreasing

Canned Cycles

There are four canned cycles for grinding: traverse grinding cycle (G71), traverse direct fixed dimension grinding cycle (G72), oscillation grinding cycle (G73), and oscillation direct fixed grinding cycle (G74).

Traverse grinding cycle (G71)

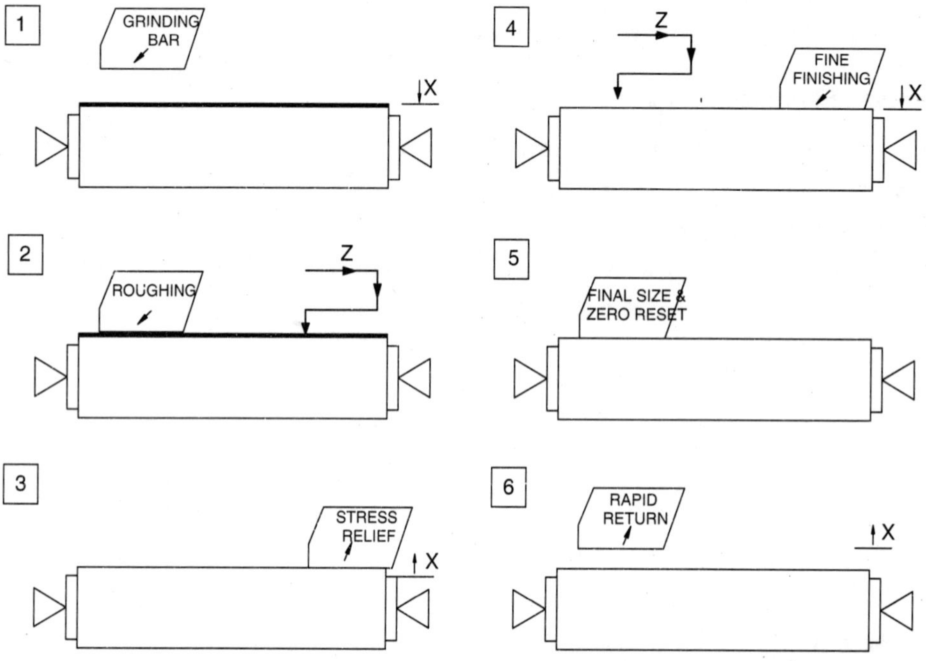

Fig. 8.7 Traverse Grinding Cycle

Figure shows the sequence of movements in a traverse grinding cycle. The format is:

G71 A------B-------W-------U-------I------K------H------;

Where A = First depth of cut

B = Second depth of cut

C = Grinding range

U = Dwell, maximum 99999.99 sec

I = Feed rate of A and B

K = Feed rate of W

H = Number of repetitions, setting value 1 to 9999.

A and B are to be specified in incremental mode. In the case of single block operation the sequence 1-2-3-4-5-6 are performed with one cycle start operation.

A = B = 0 implies spark out.

Traverse Direct Fixed Dimension Grinding Cycle (G72)

The format is:

G72 P------A--------B-------W-------U------I------K------H;

Where P = Gauge Number, 1 to 4

A = First depth of cut

B = Second depth of cut

W = Grinding range

U = Dwell time, maximum: 99999.999 sec

I = Feed rate of A and B

K = Feed rate of W

H = Number of repetitions, setting value 1 to 9999

When multistage skip operation is used, a gauge number can be specified. The method of gauge number specification is the same as multistage skip function. When the tool moves along the Z-axis to grind a workpiece if a skip signal is input, the tool returns to the Z coordinate where the cycle started after the tool reaches the end of the specified grinding area. When the tool cuts a workpiece along X-axis, if a skip signal is input, the grinding wheel stops immediately and returns to the Z-coordinate where the cycle started. The skip signal is valid during dwell also. The operation of skip signal is shown in Fig. 8.8.

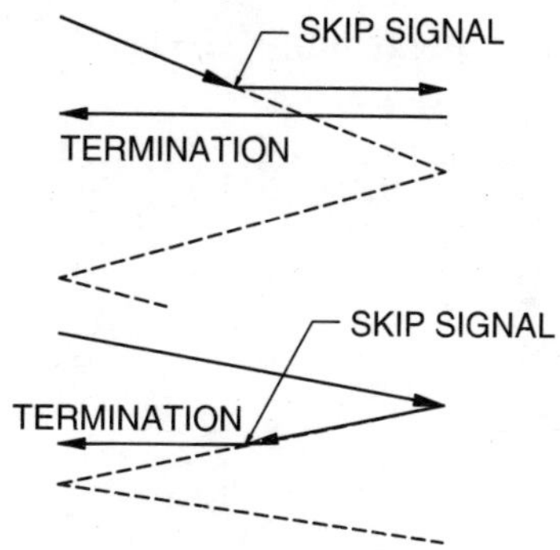

Fig. 8.8 Skip Signal

Oscillation Grinding Cycle (G73)

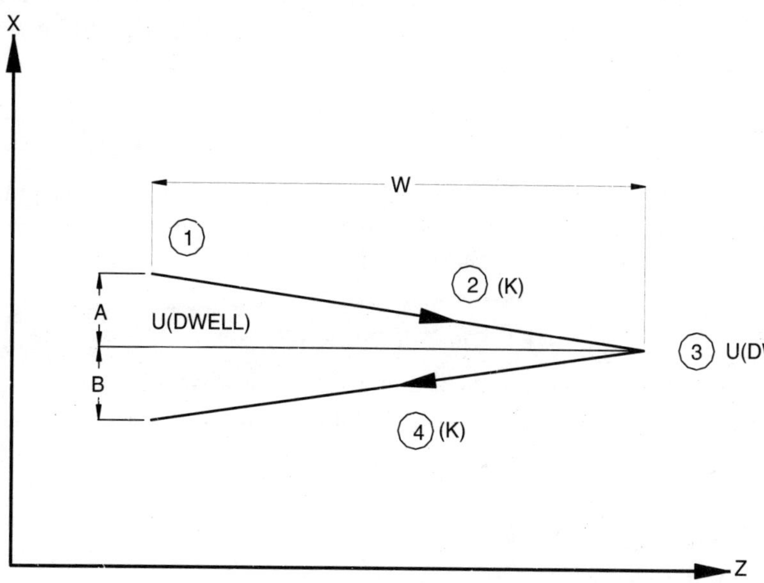

Fig. 8.9 Oscillation Grinding Cycle.

Figure 8.9 shows the sequence of movements in an oscillation grinding cycle.

The format is:

G73 A------ (B) ------W------U-----K-----H------;

Where A = Depth of cut

B = Depth of cut

C = Grinding range

U = Dwell time

K = Feed rate

H = Number of repetitions, setting value: 1 to 9999.

A and B are to be specified in incremental mode. In the case of single block operations 1-2-3-4 are performed with one cycle start operation.

Oscillation Direct Fixed Dimension Grinding Cycle (G74)

The format is:

G74 P-----A-----(B)------W------U------K-------H--------;

Where P = Gauge number, 1 to 4

A = Depth of cut

B = Depth of cut

W = Grinding range

U = Dwell time

K = Feed rate

H = Number of repetitions, setting value: 1 to 9999.

When multistage skip operation is used, a gauge number can be specified. The method of gauge number specification is the same as multistage skip function. When the tool moves along the Z-axis to grind a workpiece, if a skip signal is input, the tool returns to the Z coordinate where the cycle started after the tool reaches the end of the specified grinding area. The skip signal is valid during dwell also.

8.5 SUMMARY

This chapter gives an insight into the programming of common CNC grinding machines. For further information the reader should refer to the programming and operation manuals of well known CNC control systems like Fanuc, Sinumerik etc.

REVIEW QUESTIONS

(1) Sketch and explain the axis nomenclature of a CNC cylindrical grinder.

(2) What is the specialty of the grinding process when compared with other metal removal processes?

(3) Discuss the importance of dressing in grinding operation.

(4) What are the common grinding cycles?

(5) Discuss a grinding cycle.

9 CNC PROGRAM DEVELOPMENT USING CAM SOFTWARE

The integration of CAD and CAM has resulted in a paradigm shift in the methodology of CNC programming. Today it is possible not only to generate CNC program required to manufacture a component directly from the CAD model but also design and model the fixturing set up, design the blank, process plan, select optimum process parameters, and simulate the machining operations on the CAD/CAM workstations to ensure that the program is capable of producing acceptable components.

9.1 NEED FOR GENERATING LARGE PROGRAMMES

For many years, attempts have been made to automate the numerical control (NC) programmer's task of creating a numerical control program. Automated CNC programming has been a necessity since the beginning of numerical control. The software for automated NC programming is generally called computer aided manufacturing (CAM) software. The CAM software uses the CAD database of the component either directly or through a neutral file like STEP, IGES or DXF. CAD systems provide a complete electronic definition of a component. CAM systems have matured and offer the programmer numerous productivity tools.

Numerical control was initially developed to meet the requirements of the aerospace industries. In many cases these components are to be milled from solid billets in order to ensure structural integrity on the components. It is therefore quite common to start machining a workpiece weighing several hundred kilograms and the final component may have only a weight of a few kilograms. Figure 9.1 shows a typical aerospace structural components. In order to reduce the weight, the structures are made thin. In order to ensure that the structural member is able to withstand the heavy stresses and strains during the operation it is necessary to provide ribs. The geometry is often complex with doubly curved surfaces which necessitate 5-axis machining.

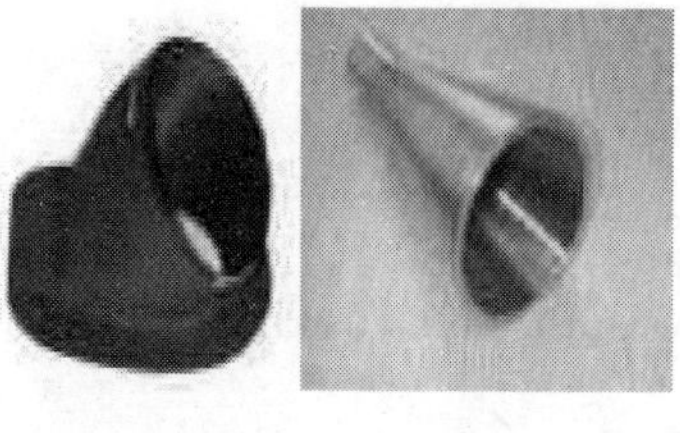

Fig. 9.1 Two Typical Aerospace Structures

Such machining operations require several thousands of blocks and it is tedious to write such complex programmes. Thus the need for developing computer techniques for NC program development was felt right from the beginning of numerical control itself.

Automotive industry needs large dies to manufacture the body panels of automobiles. The tool path is to be obtained from the CAD models which are often very complex to meet aesthetic requirements. Manually creating the programs in such cases is also very tedious and error-prone.

Plastic injection molding industry requires complex dies to be manufactured accurately. Here again the input is the CAD model of the part to be injection molded. The molds are to be manufactured with almost mirror finish. Several thousands of program blocks are to be created to manufacture a die surface. CAM packages is the only solution in such cases.

There are many other examples from engineering industry, jewellery industry etc where CAM packages find ready application.

Early softwares were developed based on surface models. Today because of the popularity of solid models the CAM softwares are designed to directly access the geometry data from CAD files or through other neutral files derived from CAD geometry.

9.2 ADVANTAGES OF COMPUTER ASSISTED CNC PROGRAMMING

Manual programming of aircraft structures is very difficult because of the sheer size and complexity of these programs. Mathematical calculations involved in 5-axis contouring is time consuming and tedious. A programmer is liable to make mistakes and detection and elimination of mistakes is a time consuming activity. Moreover writing NC codes of 20 or 30 thousand lines manually is a stupendous task.

These programming operations will involve complex calculations to determine the co-ordinate of points for the positioning of tools. Many issues like incorporation of cutter diameter compensation make these calculations very involved. Further, errors if undetected will result in enormous wastage in terms of materials and time resulting in overruns in project time and cost. The advantages of using CAM software are listed below:

(i) The data is directly accessed from CAD files

(ii) There will practically be no mistakes

(iii) The program generation is fast.

(iv) Many softwares have built in tool data and cutting data

(v) The tool path simulation facility helps to refine the program

(vi) The need for dry run is avoided and hence no loss of machine time

(vii) The lead time to produce prototypes is reduced

(viii) The program verification is another attractive feature

(ix) The operator can be trained before manufacture starts

(x) The programs can be optimized to reduce cost of manufacture.

Therefore the investment in CAM software can be easily justified. The software can be used equally well for simple and complex components. Generally software packages have modules for CNC lathes, machining Centers, Wire-EDM, Turret Punch Press, etc. Special softwares are supplied by the manufacturers of CNC press brakes, routers, laser cutting machines etc.

9.3 ORIGIN OF COMPUTER AIDED MANUFACTURING

The need for computer tools for program development was felt early in the history of NC. MIT developed APT in 50's and for a long time APT used to be the most commonly used software for computer aided NC programming. APT [acronym for **A**utomatic **P**ositioning of **T**ools) was originally developed by Massachusetts Institute of Technology. Later Illinois Institute of Technology Research Institute, Chicago developed APT further. An organization called CAM-I was carrying out developments in APT after IITRI. Depending on the computer on which APT was implemented there were several versions of APT namely, UNIAPT [Univac Computer], NELAPT [National Engineering Laboratory], FAPT [Fujitsu Fanuc], ADAPT [IBM], AUTOSPOT [IBM], CINTURN [Cincinnati Milacron], COMPACT-II [Manufacturing Data Systems International], GENTURN [General Electric], MILTURN [Metal Institute, Netherlands], NEL-APT [Ferranti], etc. Several other computer aided programming software's were also available to the programmers in sixties and seventies.

Several attempts have been made by other organizations in the industry to automate the NC programming process. CAM-I, an international consortium for advanced manufacturing, starting in 1976 spent many years trying to achieve this. Its efforts included:

- Designing an advanced NC processor
- Developing algorithms for decomposing parts into machinable subvolumes
- Capturing knowledge for machining and inspection

In the late 1980s, Automation Technology Products (ATP) developed a commercial product (Cimplex G/NC) that focused specifically on automating NC programming. Like CAM-I, ATP worked with several corporations, such as Boeing, Chrysler and Ingersoll Milling Machines, to develop this generative NC (GNC) product. Having access to a more complete product definition and an integrated solids-based NC processor motivated ATP's efforts. This product was redesigned as Manufacturing Analyst by Cimplex Corp. It imports third-party CAD data, incorporates technology to automatically recognize manufacturing features, and utilizes C++ source code for knowledge representation. This product has proven successful in niche applications but has yet to be deployed for widespread use.

Other approaches included the STRATA package offered by Spatial Technology Inc.in the late 1980s. It provided automated 2-1/2 axis machining for prismatic parts using a volume decomposition approach. The product had limited success and was repackaged as a tool kit to support the development of automated NC systems. SDRC's (Structural Dynamics Research Corp.) Generative Machining product came out in the early 90s.This provided functionality to capture machining knowledge to assist the NC planner and programmer. ICEM PART came to market in the early 90s with a product designed to automatically machine prismatic parts. Rights to this product were later sold to Tecnomatrix. It, like the other GNC products, does not appear to have captured much of the CAM market.

The approach to computer aided part programming in these softwares is as follows:

(i) **Definition of geometry [Geometry statements]:** The geometry of the component is defined with statements like POINT, LINE, PLANE, CIRCLE, CYLINDER, ELLIPSE, VECTOR, CONIC, TABCYL [Tabulated cylinder] etc. Using these statements the geometry of the component can be completely defined.

(ii) **Motion statements:** The tool assumed to around the workpiece to carry out the machining operations. Commands like GO, GODLTA, GOTO, OFFSET, TLLFT, GOLFT, GOUP, TLNDON, etc., are used to define the tool movements.

(iii) Post processor statements: It is necessary to specify the cutter details, spindle speed, feed rate, tolerances etc., and these are included in the post processor statements.

The APT processor will create a cutter location data file [CL Data file] which is basically a text file containing the co-ordinates of the points to be visited by the tool. It is necessary to modify this and convert it into a NC program to suit a particular combination of a machine tool and a control system. Since the specifications and capabilities of machine tools and the features of the control systems vary widely it is essential to develop separate post processors to create NC programs for each machine tool and control system combination.

APT was the forerunner of the present CAD/CAM technology. The developments in CAD and CAM have made this approach of program creation obsolete. The availability of inexpensive softwares on personal computers has made the CAM software affordable even to small manufacturers. Today the geometry of the component can directly be imported from the 3-D CAD model. The steps involved in the part program development using CAM softwares are described in the next section.

The advent of powerful graphic workstations and personal computer based workstations gave a fillip to the development of CAM software packages. There are several popular CAM software packages available today. Some of them are listed below:

MASTERCAM
NX CAM
PRO/Engineer
EdgeCAM
CATIA
SurfCAM
ESPRIT
VISI Series
GibbsCAM
CIMATRON
Power Series (DELCAM)
Space E
AUTO-CODE
BobCAD/CAM
CAMTEK
CAMSOFT
CVCNC
EZCAM
EUCLID
FEATURE CAM
FAPT
I-DEAS generative Manufacturing
PATHTRACE
PC-APT
SIGMA NEST

SMART CAM

TEBIS

WORK NC

VISICAM

The next section describes in detail the procedure of creating a NC program using a CAM software.

9.4 APPROACHES TO THE DEVELOPMENT OF CAM SOFTWARE

There are a few distinct approaches to automated NC program development.

9.4.1 Generative Approach (Generative NC, GNC)

This approach emulates the typical NC programming activity where the NC programmer studies the situation, applies his or her knowledge to determine the correct strategy, and creates the center line (CL) data. The key advantage to this approach is that it does capture a standard practice and applies it to each new part. Ideally, this results in a more desirable and possibly optimal NC program. Unlike the variant approach, generative NC has a large degree of freedom in determining the resultant strategy based on the best practices that are applied to each specific part.

GNC does not impede the design change process like the variant approach. Applying the process logic to a newly revised design should not result in a breakdown as long as the design is still within the scope of the captured process knowledge.

A key factor in this approach is selecting a viable "vault" to keep process knowledge in."Vault" is simply a metaphor for where and how knowledge is represented and captured. This could be a language, inference system, structures, tables, or parameters. For large investments, it is recommended that implementations using vendor's proprietary application programming language be avoided. After a while, a large amount of process knowledge captured in a proprietary language can become a liability. No one knows the language to begin with or wants to work with the language for career reasons. Choosing the wrong vault can create a knowledge repository that is very rigid, making it difficult to stay up to date with changing shop practices. Choosing a vault with object-oriented characteristics is likely to offer benefits in reuse and maintenance.

Regardless of the vault, how knowledge is augmented and stays current is a key factor. Ideally, the knowledge can grow by simply adding new rules. Given the complexity of the NC machining knowledge, a robust inference (artificial intelligence) approach has not yet made a significant impact on NC automation. Inference systems offer more promise in support roles used for specific needs, such as ordering the machining operations. They have not proven successful for defining entire NC programs for anything other than the more simplistic of the two and 2-1/2 axis parts. Today, process knowledge is probably more commonly captured in a programming language. As such, it cannot be changed to address a new shop practice as fast as a NC programmer can. This lack of agility needs to be considered, and advance notice needs to be provided to the maintenance group if the new process is to be available in a timely manner. Users must learn to adapt to the system 's deficiencies in the meantime while the new process is being developed. One advantage the generative approach has over an NC programming organization is that once it is implemented it will be consistently applied, which is not always the case with NC programs created by several NC programmers.

The generative approach captures NC process knowledge outside the resultant models. In the generative approach, parts can be reprogrammed to address process changes by just changing the process knowledge once and automatically reapplying it to each part. This differs from the variant approach where each existing program has to be manually modified to retrofit a process change because the strategies inside each program are what drive the automation in the variant approach.

9.4.2 Feature Based Approach

Unlike the part-based approach, softwares in the second category use a feature-based approach. This approach views the part as a group of interrelated features, such as pockets, holes, and cutouts. Parts in this class can vary dramatically in complexity. They may be roughed out globally but are often finished one feature at a time.

There are two approaches for automating this class of parts : (1) variant and (2) generative. For many part families, a variant approach using parametric modeling is common. For more generic parts with common features, a generative approach could be viable.

A generative approach requires the features, on which to apply machining knowledge, to first be identified. Many CAD systems allow the designer to build the part using features. These features may or may not correspond to the manufacturing features. Some CAM systems allow the NC programmer to identify the features interactively or use feature recognition to automatically recognize the features on the part.

Some success has been achieved by designing with manufacturing features that have machining knowledge associated with them. In this case, a stock definition is first specified and features (which subtract materials) are applied to the stock much like the machining process taking place. This requires a formal design discipline with certain limitations when features start to interact with each other. This works well when the design methodology lends itself to modeling the part with manufacturing features. However, if this is not the case, a more structured discipline is required, demanding a versatile engineer who accounts for both the modeling and manufacturing aspects of the part. This concurrent engineering approach can provide benefits larger than just automating NC, but the impact that design changes have on the process needs to be considered. A drawback to this approach is that the fabrication process needs to be considered is completely integrated within the design definition. However, if the fabrication process for a released part needs to change, a new part may need to be defined rather than just defining a new process for the same part. This could have effects on design authority and certification.

The interaction approach to feature identification is the most flexible and easy to implement. This approach provides a mapping of the feature to its constituent geometry, such as a pocket's entry face, walls, floor and fillets. An NC programmer simply selects which faces and edges of a part make up each feature. One drawback to this approach is that it does a poor job of identifying the volumetric shape of the manufacturing feature because it is limited to geometry on the part or stock. This shape (or material removal volume), which is required for an automated system, must be inferred.

Feature recognition uses technology to automatically determine the manufacturing features associated with a designed part. There are several issues associated with the feature recognition approach. First, it works poorly for 3D parts as compared to 2D parts due to the complexity of the geometry. Second, when common features interact, most recognizers break down. Third, feature recognition system often recognize the features based on the CAM system's criteria, not on the user's process criteria. Many systems do not allow users to define their own feature types. Finally, the feature recognition software rarely, if ever, considers the context in which the part is machined, such as the machine constraints, fixturing constraints, and part position in the setup assembly. To be accurate, the feature recognition software must mimic an NC programmer's thought process for determining the areas to machine. Today's state-of-the-art technology considers just the part in an isolated state.

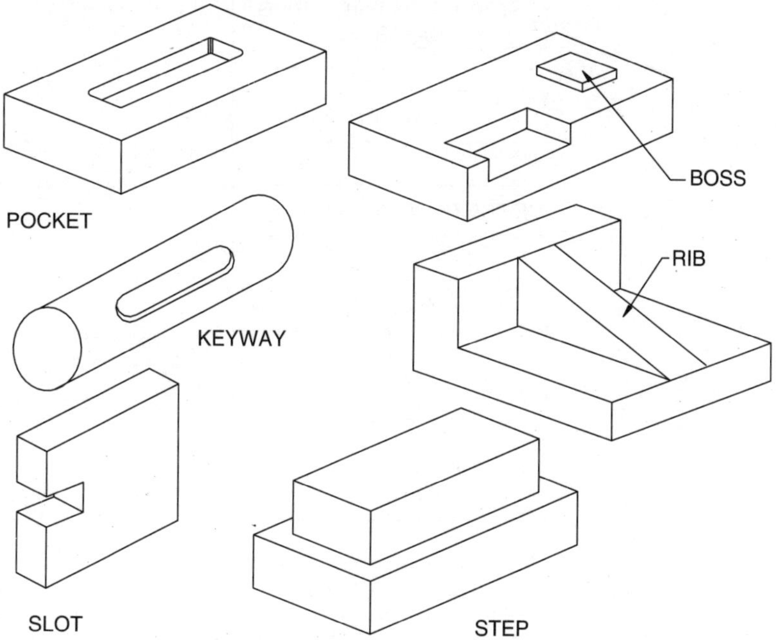

Fig. 9.2 Typical Features

A combination of the above techniques is probably the most common approach, where the designer may design with some manufacturing features, the system may automatically recognize others, and the NC programmer reviews the results and interactively identifies the rest. Some common features are shown in Fig. 9.2.

9.5 PROCEDURE FOR DEVELOPING A CNC PROGRAM USING CAM SOFTWARE

The block diagram shown in Fig.9.3 illustrates the steps involved in creating a NC program using a CAM software packages. The starting point of CAM is the CAD file. A common approach is the program creation carried out using solid models or surface models. Data for program creation can also be obtained from SAT [ACIS solids], IGES, VDA, DXF, CADL, STL, STEP or ASCII file using suitable translators.

(i) *Create a manufacturing model from the design model and the work piece.* The programmer has to decide on the shape and size of the raw work piece. This can be a forging, casting, billet or round bar depending upon the material and the production volume. The Raw workpiece is superimposed on the CAD model to obtain the manufacturing model.

(ii) *Set up the tool database.* Tools must be defined before an operation is performed. Tool libraries can be created and retrieved for a manufacturing operation. Many softwares have extensive tool libraries built-in. Alternatively, they also can be created at the time of defining the manufacturing operation.

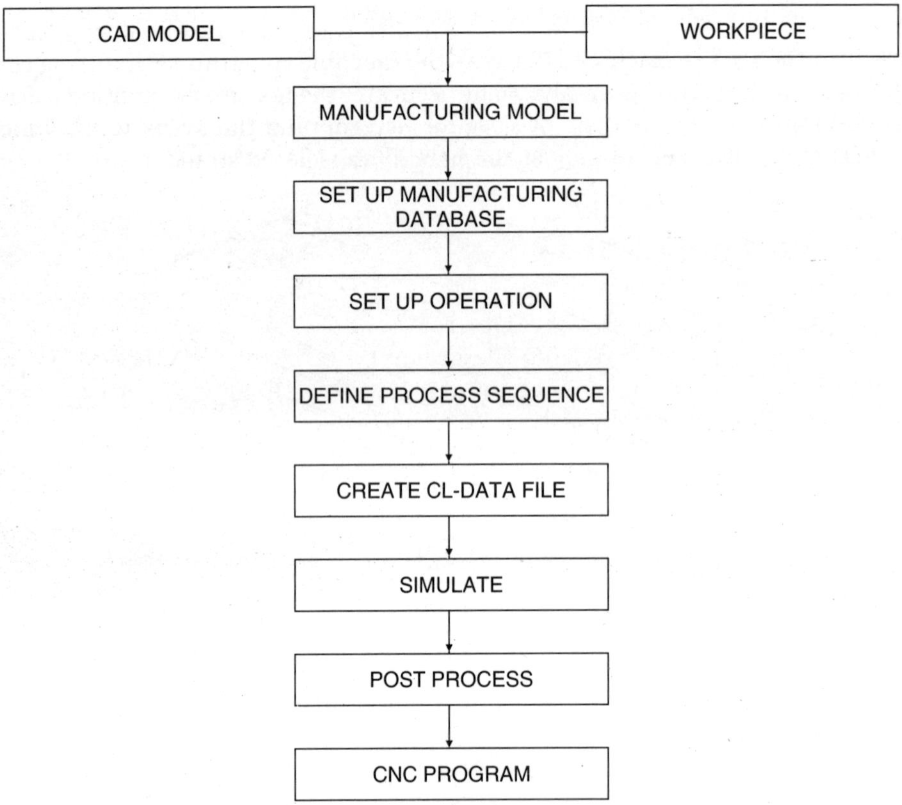

Fig. 9.3 Steps Involved in NC Program Creation

(iii) *Select the set up for the machining operation.* A component may require more than one set up to complete the machining operation.

(iv) Fixtures are necessary at each set up. Fixtures can be displayed along with the workpiece. This is to ensure that the path of the tools does not interfere with the tools. Fixtures consist of the locating and clamping elements to hold the workpiece on the machine table during the machining operation. In the case of a turning operation appropriate chucking devices should be used. Standard fixture elements can be created as a library of parts and assembled before the manufacturing operation is commenced. These are also available as standard libraries.

(v) Create a machinability database. These may also be available readily as part of the software package. Parameters like spindle speed and feed rate can be selected from the machinability databse.

(vi) Create the manufacturing operations to generate the CL data. As each manufacturing operation takes place, material is removed from the workpiece to simulate the actual manufacturing operation. This simulation is enhanced by the tool path being displayed for each operation.

(vii) If needed, the CL data can be modified by altering the operation parameters or by editing the CL data file. At this stage, the programmer should also evaluate alternative solutions to reduce the cost of machining as well as to increase the productivity.

(viii) Create a manufacturing route sheet at the end of the manufacturing session.

(ix) Post-process the CL file to create the NC program.

(x) Some of the softwares provide a facility to simulate the CNC program. This is a very useful facility and can ensure an acceptable component in the first production run itself. The details of CNC program verification software are discussed later in this chapter.

9.6 PROCEDURE OF CAM

The CAD model represents the finished product. This is used as a basis for the manufacturing operations. Features, surfaces and edges are selected on the design model as references for each manufacturing operation. Referencing the geometry of the design model sets up parametric relationship between the design model and the workpiece. Because of this relationship, when the design model is changed, all associated manufacturing operations are updated to reflect the change.

The workpiece is the raw material from which the component is obtained after the manufacturing operations. The workpiece can be bar stock, casting, billet, forging etc. It may be easily created by copying the design model and modifying the dimensions or deleting or suppressing the features to represent the real workpiece.

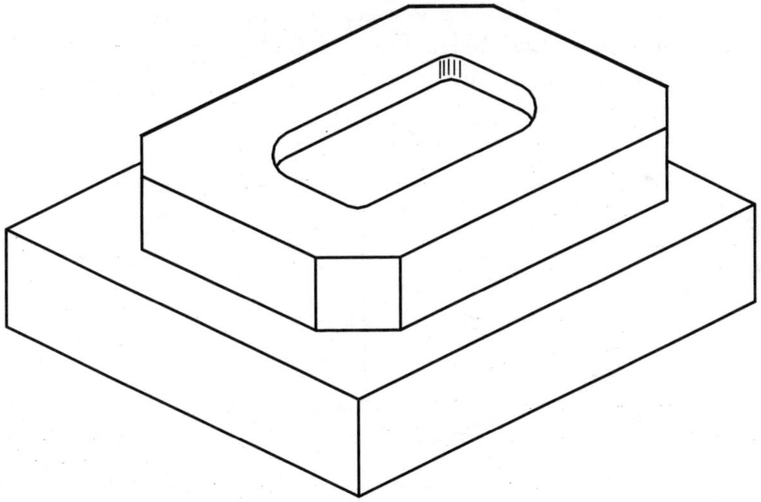

Fig. 9.4 Design model

For example consider the model of the component shown in Fig. 9.4. The raw material for this component is a cast aluminum part. It is necessary to create a datum surface on the component for initially locating it on the fixture or the machine table. This operation is often performed separately. In the case of the component shown in the figure the bottom surface can be conveniently taken as the datum. The component is to be milled on the top surface as well as the sides. Dimensions of these surfaces must be increased by the amount of material to be removed (machining allowance).

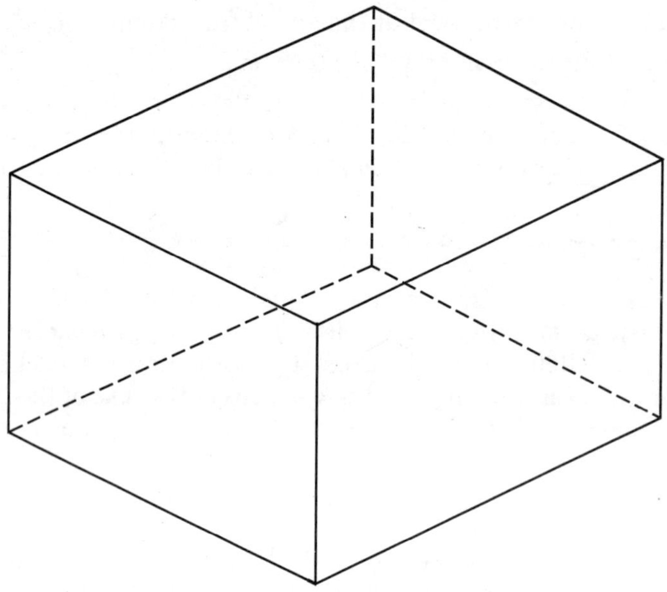

Fig. 9.5 Workpiece

The workpiece is shown in Fig. 9.5. The design model and the workpiece are then assembled together to form the manufacturing model. Figure 9.6 shows the manufacturing model. The solid lines show the design model and the dotted lines show the workpiece.

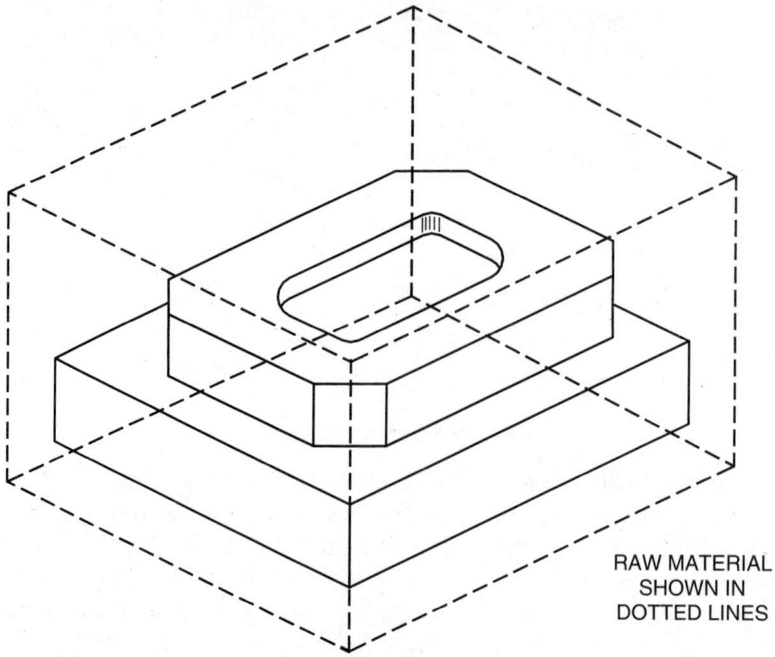

Fig. 9.6 Manufacturing model

In the case of aluminum parts for aerospace applications it may be necessary to start manufacturing from a billet. The machining allowances to be added to the envelope of the workpiece to obtain the length, breadth and the height of the billet. In the case of a turned part the raw material may be a casting or bar stock. In the former case machining allowance is to be added. It may also be necessary to eliminate dimensionally small features like threads, grooves, fillets, chamfers, holes etc., which can be created during the machining operation. In the case of bar stock the workpiece is a plain cylindrical part.

9.7 SELECTING CO-ORDINATE SYSTEM

Co-ordinate systems are vital components in manufacturing. They define the orientation of the workpiece on the machine and act as the origin of the CL data generation. The co-ordinate system can belong to the workpiece or the design model.

9.7.1 Z-Axis Orientation

During the manufacturing operations the co-ordinating systems should be oriented in such a way that the positive Z-axis points away from the holding fixture. For example Fig. 7.7 (a) shows the orientation of the Z-axis for the machining operations to be performed on the top surface of a component. The Z-axis orientation of a turned part is shown in Fig. 7.7 (b).

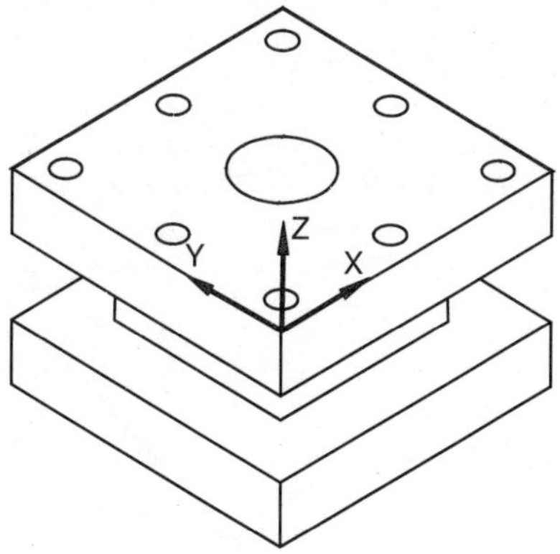

Fig. 9.7 (a) Z-axis orientation for a Prismatic Part

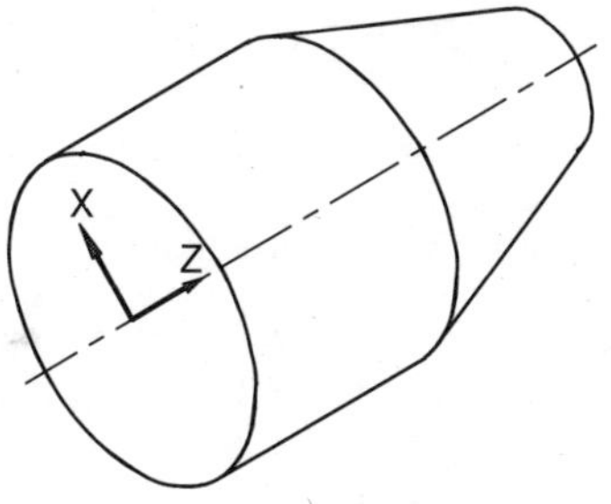

Fig. 9.7 (b) Z-axis orientation for a turned part

9.7.2 X – and Y – Axis Orientation

The orientation of X and Y axes of the operation co-ordinate system will affect the CL data file. In milling the main cut feed direction will be parallel to the X-axis.

9.7.3 Fixtures

As mentioned in the last section fixtures are parts or assemblies which help to hold and orient the workpiece during a machining operation. Fixtures can be created as and when needed.

9.8 COMMON MANUFACTURING OPERATIONS

Important manufacturing operations are discussed in this section.

9.8.1 Milling

The milling operations normally performed can be classified into a number of groups.

(i) **Volume milling:** In this case a closed volume is to be removed in the milling operation. This approach is used for rough face milling or pocket milling operations. A special feature of volume milling is that the tool will always be within the milling volume. To define the milling volume the geometry of the design model is to be intersected with the workpiece model. Typical example of volume milling is shown in Fig. 9.8.

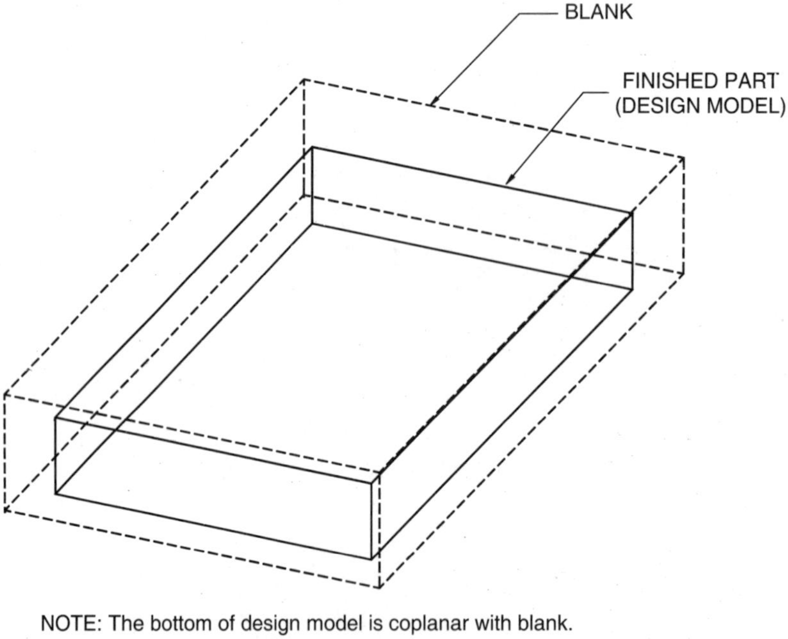

Fig. 9.8 Volume Milling

(ii) **Surface milling:** A surface of the component can be selected for the milling operation. Examples are 3-, 4- or 5-axis milling of the surfaces, profiling, pocket finishing etc. There are three types of surface milling operations:

(a) Conventional surface milling: This operation generates a tool path which will completely machine the specified surface.

(b) Trajectory milling: Certain milling operations can be performed by specifying a trajectory. Examples are milling of slots, face milling operations, and many end milling operations.

9.8.2 CNC TURNING

The approach to NC program creation in turning is different from that of milling. The procedure is briefly described in the following sections.

Co-ordinate setting

In NC turning the Z-axis is usually collinear with the turning axis. Therefore, the turning cut is sketched in the XZ plane. The typical co-ordinate setting is shown in Fig. 9.9.

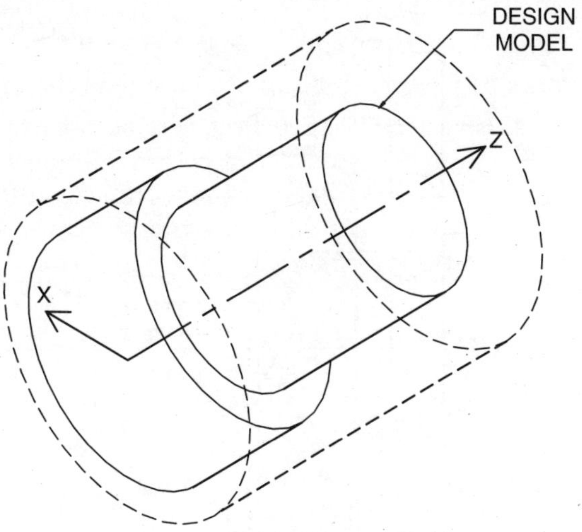

Fig. 9.9 Co-ordinate Setting in NC Turning

Defining turn profile

The profile [outline] of the workpiece is to be defined in the to generate the tool path. A CAM software provides several facilities to create the profile. Some of the common facilities are:

(i) Sketching the profile.

The profile of the cut can be sketched as shown in Fig. 9.10.

(ii) Using surfaces to define a profile

(iii) Using a curve to define a turn profile

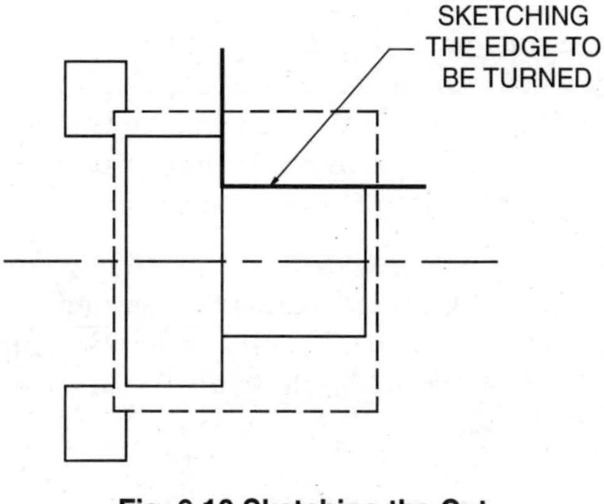

Fig. 9.10 Sketching the Cut

Stock boundary and Area Turning

It is often convenient to define the stock boundary and then create the NC sequences through the area clearance approach. Figure 9.11 (a) shows a component to be machined. The stock boundary can be defined as shown in Fig. 9.11 (b) Area turning allows the programmer to define the stock material removed graphically. The tool path will be generated by scanning this area to remove the material in step depth increments. The successive cuts for machining this area are shown in Fig. 9.11 (c).

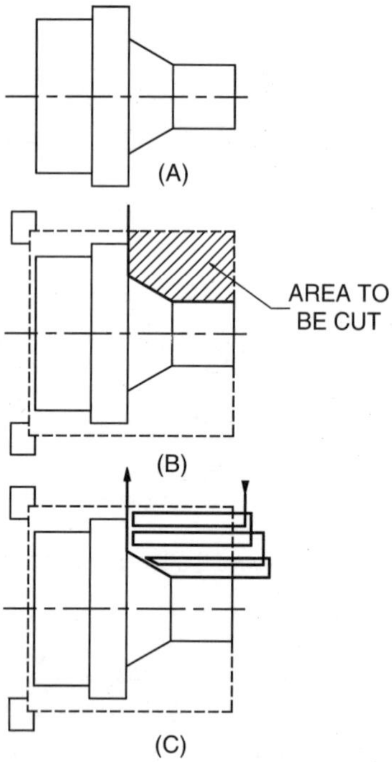

Fig. 9.11 Stock Boundary Definition and Area Turning

Profile Turning: Profile turning allows the programmer to interactively specify the cut motion trajectory. The profile can be specified as outside, inside, and face. This influences the tool orientation and location with respect to the trajectory of cut.

Groove Turning: Grooves are a common feature on turned components. This is carried out by a plunge cutting tool with a flat end and cutting edges on either side. Groove turning can be inside, outside, or on the face. When the width of the groove is more than the width of the tool, the distance between the neighbouring cuts by the step-over parameter. When the depth of the groove is large peck cycles are used in rough groove turning.

Thread Cutting: Threads commonly provided on the turned components may be external and internal – blind and through. The thread sequences are defined by sketching the first tool movement which corresponds to the major diameter of an external thread and to the minor diameter of an internal thread. The thread depth is calculated based on the pitch of the thread by a parameter THREAD_FEED.

9.8.3 Drilling Holes

Hole making NC sequences include drilling, reaming, boring, tapping etc. These operations have to be carried out both in turning machines and machining centres. A hole making NC sequence is created by selecting the cycle type and specifying the holes to drill by defining the hole sets. A hole set includes one or more hole to be drilled. Each hole set will have a drilling depth specification or countersink diameter value associated with it. A single hole making sequence may include more than one hole set enabling the programmer to drill holes with different depth specifications as well as having multiple countersink diameter values.

There are various methods of selecting the holes to be included in hole set.

(i) By selecting individual hole axis
(ii) By including all holes on a selected surface
(iii) From a hole containing the co-ordinates of the datum points
(iv) By including all datum points on a specified surface
(v) By including all holes of a specified diameter
(vi) By including individual datum points on specified surface

A CAD software may contain several types of hole making option.

Drill - standard, deep, or break chip

Face - Drill a hole with an optional dwell at the final depth to assure a clean surface at the bottom of the hole.

Bore - Bore a hole with a finish hole diameter of high precision.

Ream - Create a precision finish hole using a multi-edge reamer.

Countersink - Drill a chamfer at the entry of the hole

Tap - Drill a threaded hole.

9.9 TOOL MOTION PARAMETERS

A number of tool motion parameters are to be input to create a NC program. Some of them are:

FEED–RATE
CUTCOM (Tool compensation)
COOLANT
SPINDLE–SPEED
SPEED–SENSE
MAX–SPINDLE–RPM
SPINDLE–RANGE
CLEAR–DIST
PULL–OUT–DIST
LEAD–RADIUS
LEAD–STEP
APPROACH–DISTANCE
EXIT–DISTANCE

9.10 AUXILIARY NC SEQUENCES

These are used to create a point-to-point tool path. They can be used to specify the connecting tool motions and change tool axis orientation. The machine probe functionality can also be accessed using these sequences. Some typical auxiliary sequences are:

GO TO POINT

GO DELTA

GL HOME

FOLLOW SKETCH

9.11 DATA FILES

Cutter Location (CL) data files are generated from the cutter paths specified within the NC sequences. Each NC sequence generates a separate CL file. They can be merged together to produce a single file for the whole operation. These CL data files can be post-processed by machine specific or generic post-processors for the creation of the NC program. A sample file is shown below:

```
$$* xxx/Clfile Version 2.1
$$->MFGno/T
PARTNO CASING
$$->FEATNO/21
MACHIN/HMTMILL,600
$$->UNITS/MM
LOADTL/16
COOLNT/ON
FROM/0.00000000,0.00000000,0.00000000
SETSTART/0.00000000, 0.00000000,25,00000000
RAPID
GOTO/150.00000000, 70.00000000,70.00000000
SPINDL/RPM,600
FEDRAT/100.000000000,MMPM
CYCLE/DRILL, -5.0, 100.000000000 MMPM
RAPID
GOTO/0.00000000, 0.00000000, 0.00000000
CYCLE/OFF
SPINDL/OFF
$$->END/
FINI
```

The CL data can be used to display the tool path. This feature will help to locate errors in the program. The CL data can be edited and modified by rotation, translation, mirroring and scaling.

9.12 POST-PROCESSING

The specifications and capabilities of a CNC machine tool will vary from one to another. There are number of manufacturers of CNC control systems and each system will have a number of versions which will be different with regard to their features. The CL files require to be modified to generate a NC program from the CL data to suit a machine tool-control system combination. This procedure is called post-processing and CAM softwares usually incorporate a software module called generic post-processor for this purpose. Usually the MACHINE statement is used to select the post-processor. A GENER statement will retrieve all the necessary information about the NC machine from the database. The NC program thus created can be stored; listed or simulated on the screen for editing or modification if needed, or transferred to a CNC machine using DNC. The NC program can also be checked using a software like VERICUT.

9.13 CNC PROGRAM VERIFICATION

Creation of programs through CAM software packages is a significant development. This method eliminated the drudgery involved in writing large programs. Errors are reduced and thereby wastage is avoided. However it is still necessary to prove the program as there are so many factors which will influence the acceptability of the component. Gouging is a common problem encountered in creating complex surfaces. Improper programming may remove more material or leave material on the workpiece unremoved. Errors in geometry or tool motion statements may result in a workpiece whose dimensions after machining may not be acceptable. Dry runs and program prove out on the machine are always time consuming and costly. Hence it is desirable to simulate the machining program on the computer to verify the program.

Program verification softwares which are now available as a module of CAM software packages are a useful tool to carry out machining on the computer workstation. Since the machining is carried out in a virtual environment it is called virtual machining. This enables the programmers to visualise and modify the program until they are completely satisfied about the program. It helps to remove all moves that would have gouged the part. Cuts deeper then what is required are also detected. The experience of the users of virtual machining indicates that it is possible to straight away proceed to machining metals and usual problems encountered in machining like tool breakage, collisions and tool wear due to long run times are avoided. The tool library built into the system enables the programmers to select the tool of the actual shape and dimensions used on the shop floor for simulation.

A typical CNC program verification software will have the following capabilities:

- Capability to simulate 2, 3, 4 and 5 axis milling, 2 axis and 4 axis (synchronous) turning, Drilling, EDM etc
- It can interpret G-codes and detect errors inn the tool path and avoid scrap.
- By detecting collision between tool and work and tool and fixture it avoids possible damages due to incorrect programs
- It eliminates errors due to fast feed rates
- The software has capability to check the dimensional accuracy of the part. Distances, angles, thickness, scallop height, material volume etc can be measured.
- The part can be rotated and sectioned

- Tool path can be optimized, thereby reducing cutter wear, time for machining and lead time for development and improving finish of the part.
- It detects gouging
- Excess material if any left on the part can be detected and program can be corrected
- The program verification avoids the need for close monitoring of the machine by the operator during machining
- Operation of the machine tool itself can be simulated
- The software can be used to train employees

REVIEW QUESTIONS

(1) What is the necessity for computer aided part programming?

(2) What are the advantages of computer aided part programming?

(3) Describe the three stages in computer aided part programming.

(4) Compare the generative and feature based approach to automated CNC program development.

(5) Explain with the help of a flow diagram the steps involved in computer aided part programming.

(6) Discuss the procedure for developing a CNC program using CAM software.

(7) Distinguish between design model and manufacturing model.

(8) Discuss briefly the selection of coordinate system in CNC programming.

(9) With the aid of suitable examples, explain volume milling and surface milling.

(10) What is meant by gouging? How is it avoided?

(11) Discuss different approaches to pocket milling.

(12) Why is 5 axis milling superior to manufacture doubly curved surfaces?

(13) Discuss the procedure for program development for a turned component.

(14) Discuss the structure of a cutter location data file.

(15) Study a typical CAM package and prepare a note on the various modules available in the software.

(16) Why is post processing necessary?

(17) Discuss tool path simulation. How does program verification software differ from tool path simulation software?

(18) What are the typical capabilities of a program verification software?

APPENDIX- EXAMPLE OF MACHINING OF A PART IN PRO/MANUFACTURING

PRO/Manufacturing by PTC is a popular package for CNC program generation. In this example, the procedure for defining the various processes for machining is explained with suitable illustrations. The part is shown in Fig. 9.12.The bottom surface is the datum and it is pre-machined. All the five sides of the component need machining which involve face milling, boring and drilling.

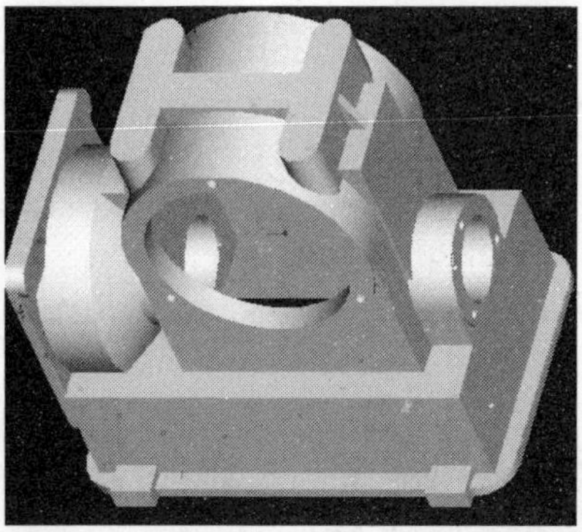

Fig. 9.12 CAD Model of the Part

The det→ailed procedure after initializing the software is described below:

Click on New

In the New dialog window, enter the name (casing) of the file

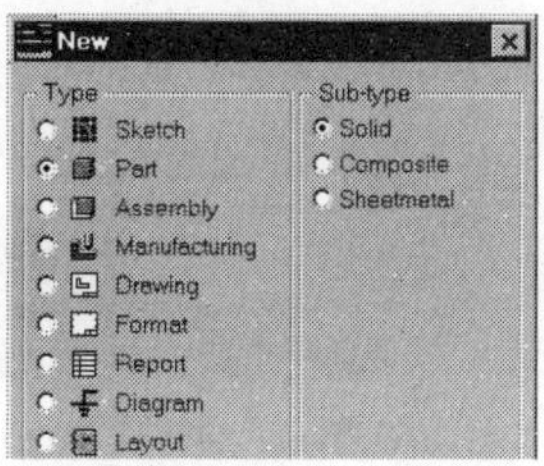

Click on part in type and solid in sub-type

Click on OK

In the part screen menu select

Feature → Create → Datum → Plane → Default

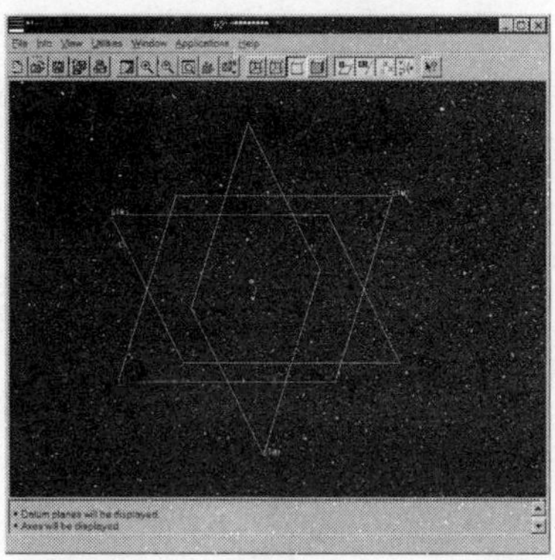

Feature

Create

Solid

Protrusion

Extrude

Solid

Done

In attributes option select One side *and* done

Select the left face of the rectangular block as Sketch Plane

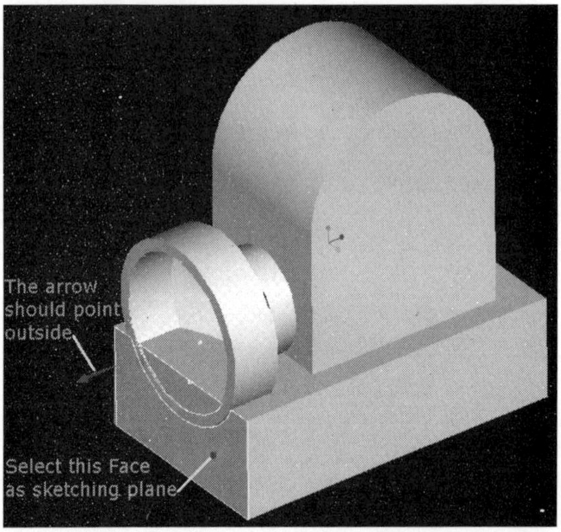

The Direction arrow should point away from the rectangular block. Otherwise Flip it and click on Ok

Click on Default *for 2D view orientation*

Draw a rectangle such that it covers the revolution we created earlier

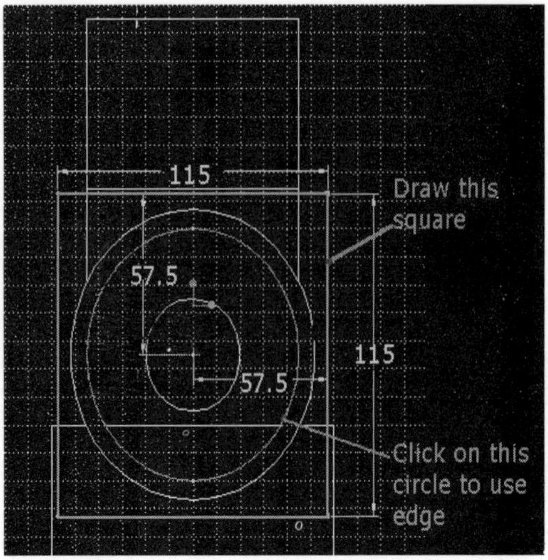

Click on GeomTools Use edge *and select the second circle from outside.*

Add the dimensions as shown and Regenerate the sketch

The system prompts "Regeneration Completed Successfully"

Select Blind *in the Depth option and click on* Done

Enter 5 *as value for depth and click on* Ok

~~Feature~~

~~Create~~

~~Solid~~

Cut

Revolution

Solid

Done

For sketch plane select DTM3

Accept the default direction by clicking ok

Select Default *for 2D view orientation.*

Click on hidden line icon in the menu bar to see the hidden lines

Click on Geomtools Use edge *and select the curves shown here (Use GeomTools Trim Corner to remove the projected curves)*

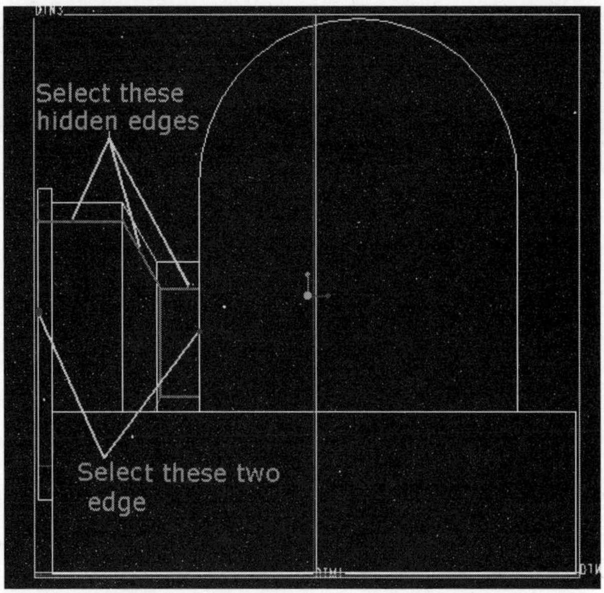

Draw a horizontal line parallel to the axis

The system prompts "Regeneration Completed Successfully"

Click on Done

Select Blind in the depth option and click on Done

Enter 90 for depth value and click on OK

Click on View → Default to view the component in 3D.

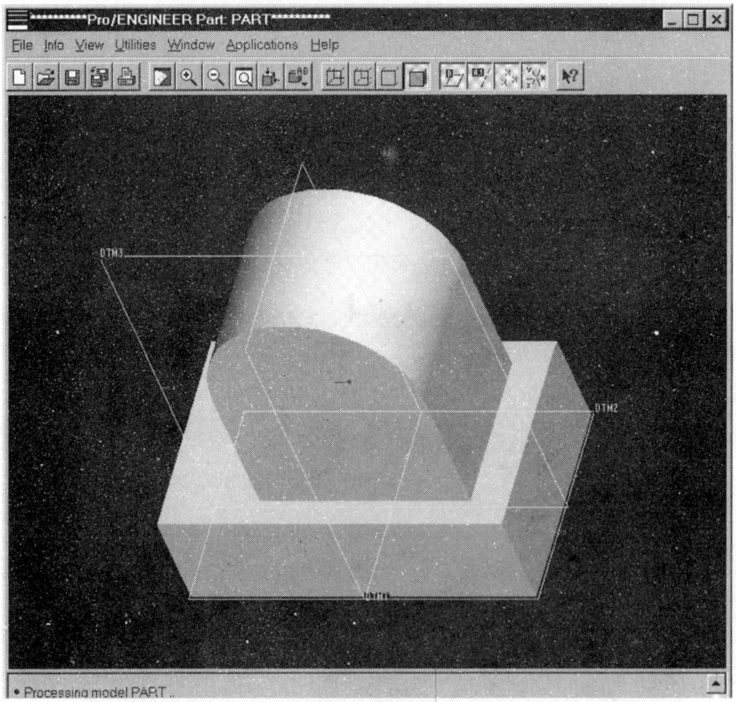

~~***Feature***~~

~~***Create***~~

~~***Solid***~~

Protrusion

Revolve

Solid

Done

In Attribute select

One side

Done

Select DTM3 as sketching plane

Accept the direction arrow by clicking ok

Click on Default for 2D view orientation

Draw the sketch and dimension it as shown

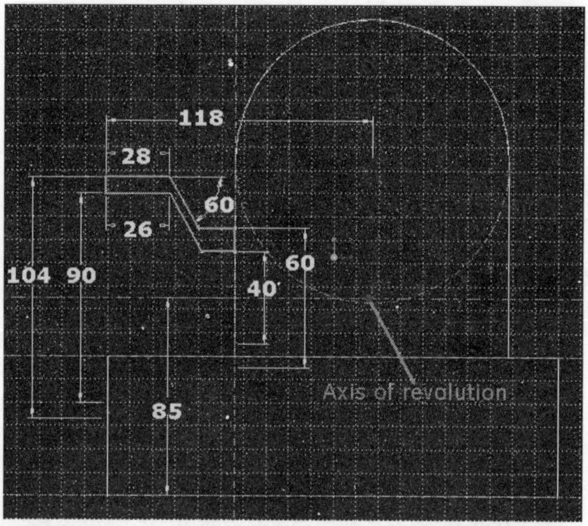

Regenerate the sketch

The system prompts "Regeneration Completed Successfully"

Click on Done

Click on 360 *(for degree of revolution) and* Done

Click on OK

Change the View to Default *by clicking* View Default

Rotate and view the component

The revolution is partly done inside the rectangular block. This can be removed later.

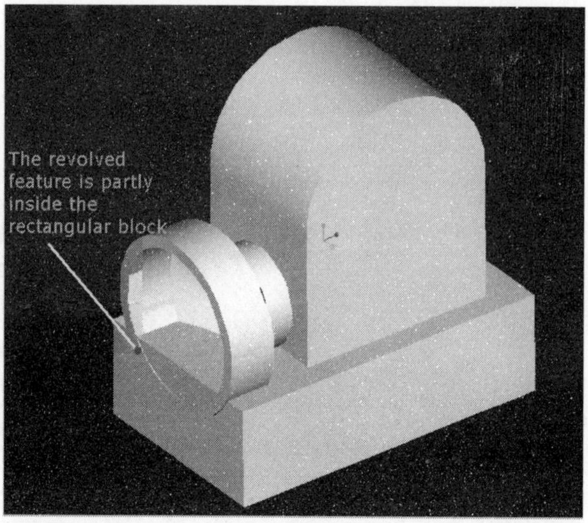

~~***Feature***~~

~~***Create***~~

~~***Solid***~~

Protrusion

Extrude

Solid

Done

In attributes option select Both sides *and* done

Select DTM3 as Sketch Plane

Click OK *to Accept the Direction*

Click on Default *for 2D view orientation*

Draw a rectangle as shown

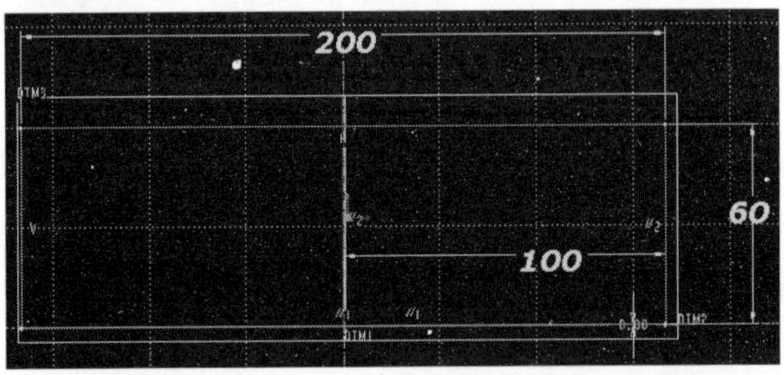

Add Dimension to the sketch

Regenerate the sketch

The system prompts "Regeneration Completed Successfully"

Click on Done

Select Blind in the depth option and click on Done

Enter 120 *for depth value and click on* OK

Click on View → Default *to view the rectangular block in 3D.*

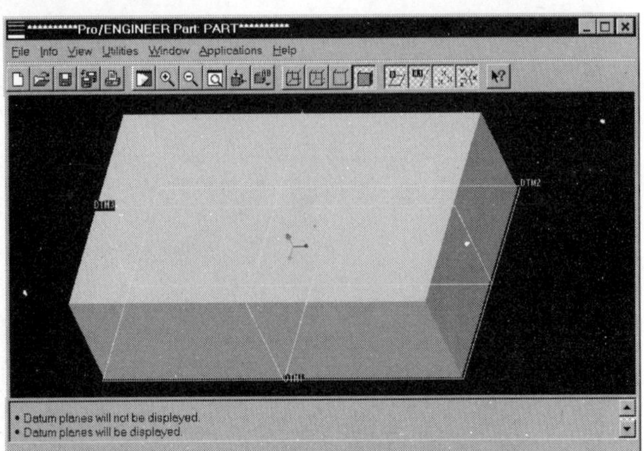

~~***Feature***~~

~~***Create***~~

~~***Solid***~~

Protrusion

Extrude

Solid

Done

In attributes option select Both sides *and* done

Select DTM3 as Sketch Plane

Click Ok *to Accept the Direction*

Click on Default for 2D view orientation

Sketch two verical lines as shown

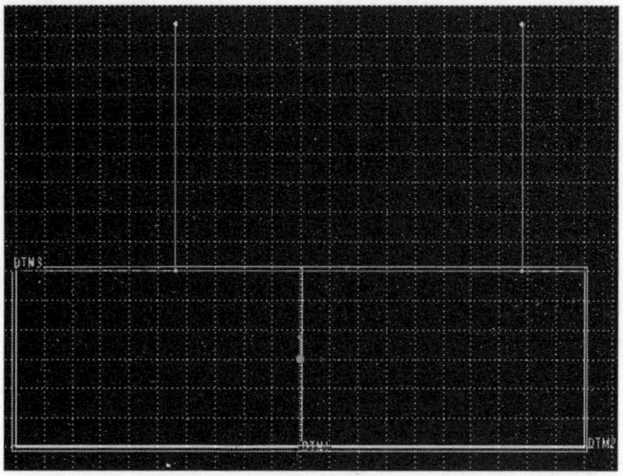

Draw a 3 Point arc (semi circle) so that end points of arc lies on end point of lines

Click on GeomTools → Use edge

Select the top horizontal edge of the block

Trim the curves to form a closed loop

Add the dimensions and regenerate the sketch

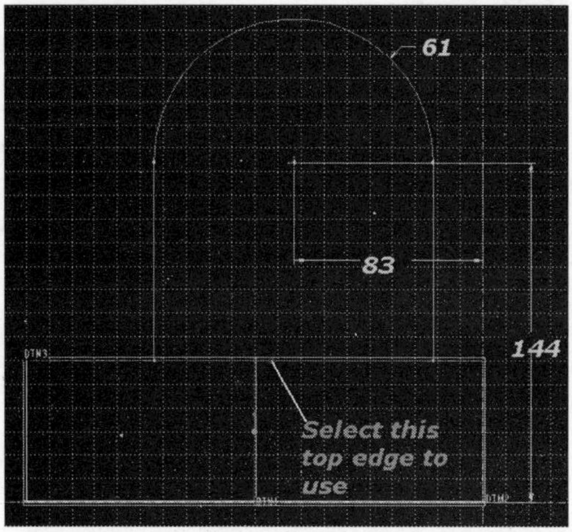

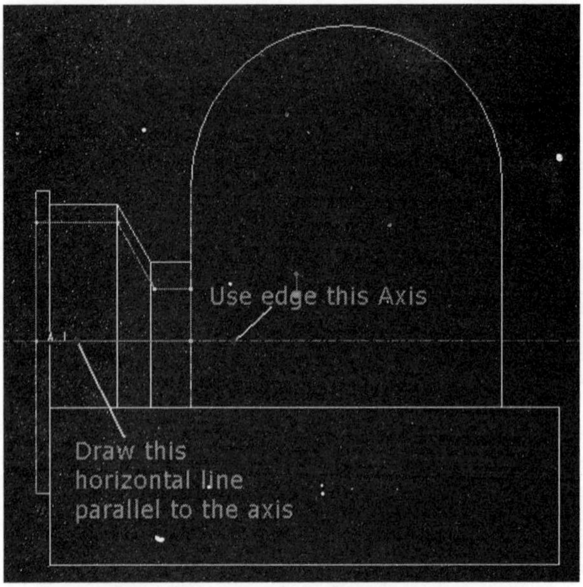

Click on GeomTools Use edge *and select the Horizontal axis (Axis 1)*

Regenerate the sketch

The system prompts "Regeneration Completed Successfully"

Click on Done

Click Ok *to accept the direction of revolution*

Click on 360 *(for degree of revolution) and* Done

Click on OK

The projected material is removed. Rotate the component and check.

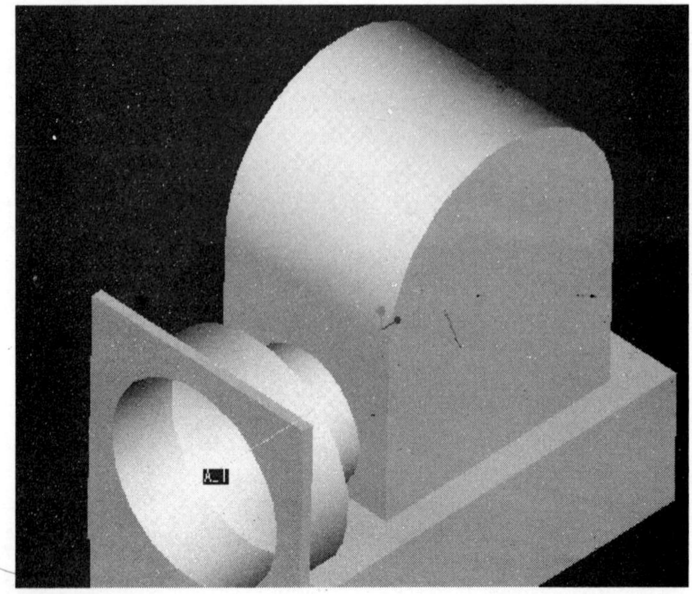

~~***Feature***~~

~~***Create***~~

~~***Solid***~~

Protrusion

Extrude

Solid

Done

In attributes option select One side *and* done

Select the Right face *of the rectangular block as Sketch Plane*

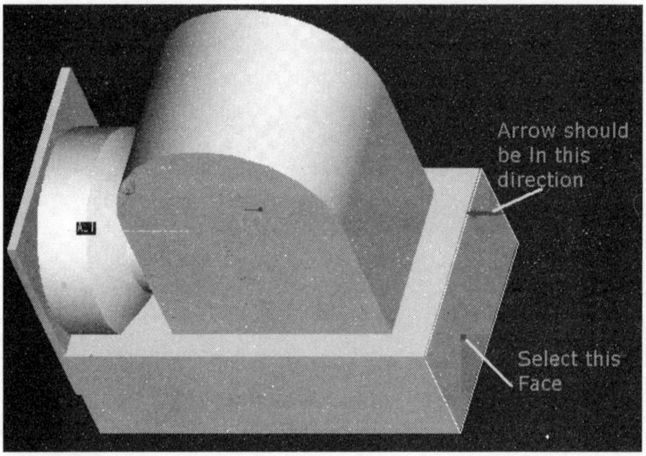

The Direction arrow should point Towards the rectangular block. Otherwise Flip it and click on Ok

Click on Default *for 2D view orientation*

Click on Sketch Arc Concentric *and select the existing circle*

Draw a semi circle as shown

Click on Sketch Line *and click on end point of arc and draw two horizontal lines as shown*

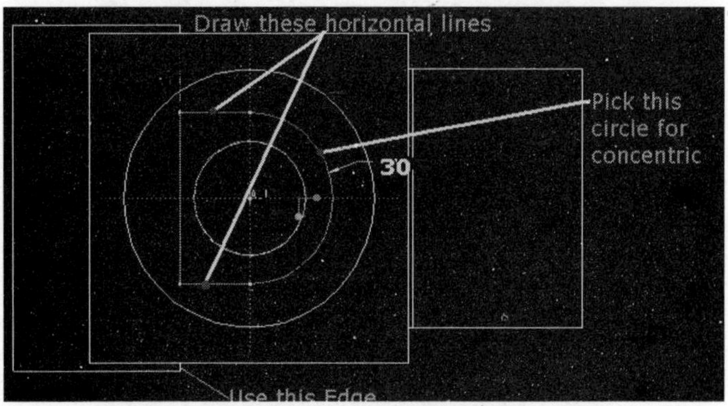

Click on done

Accept the direction of material removal by clicking ok (the arrow should point inside the sketch)

In depth option select Blind *and click on* done

Enter 2.5 *and click on* Done

Click on View Default *for default view.*

Feature

Copy

Mirror

Independent

Done

When the system prompts to select the feature,

Click on

sel by menu

Last feature

The last created feature gets selected

Click on Donesel *and* Done

Select DTM3 for the plane to mirror about

Rotate the component to see the mirrored feature

Feature

Create

Solid

Hole

Straight

Done

Select Coaxial *and click on* done

Select the axis shown (axis 4)

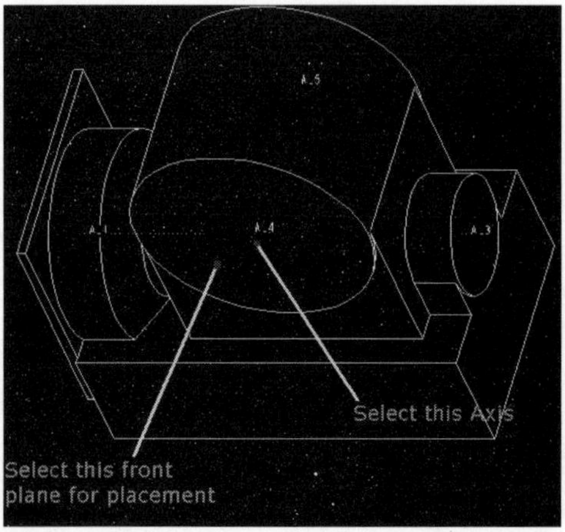

Select One side *and Click on* done

Select Thru All *in the depth option and click on* done

Enter the diameter value as 100

Click on OK

Feature

Create

Solid

Hole

Straight

Done

Select Coaxial *and click on* done

Select the axis shown (axis 3)

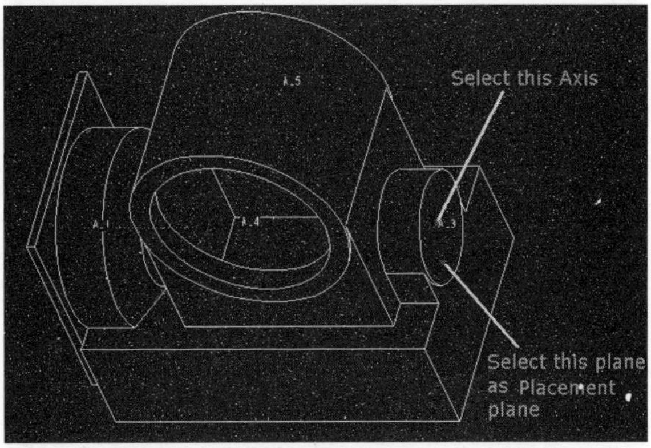

Select the Right face of the boss for placement plane

Select One side *and Click on* done

Select Thru Next *in the depth option and click on* done

Enter the diameter value as 32.5

Click on OK

Create another coaxial hole at the same axis and placement plane for 40 mm dia and 24 mm depth.

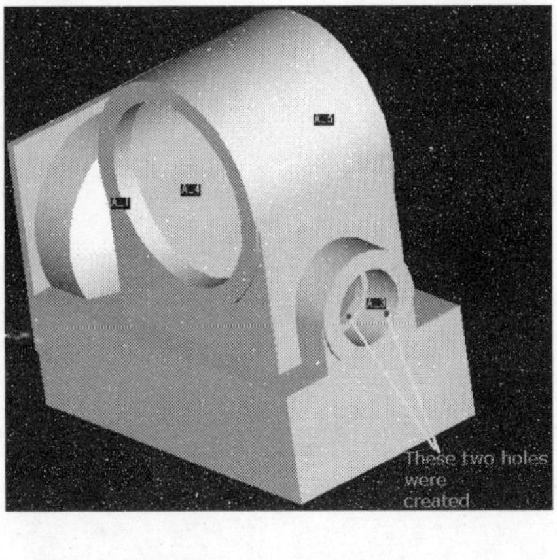

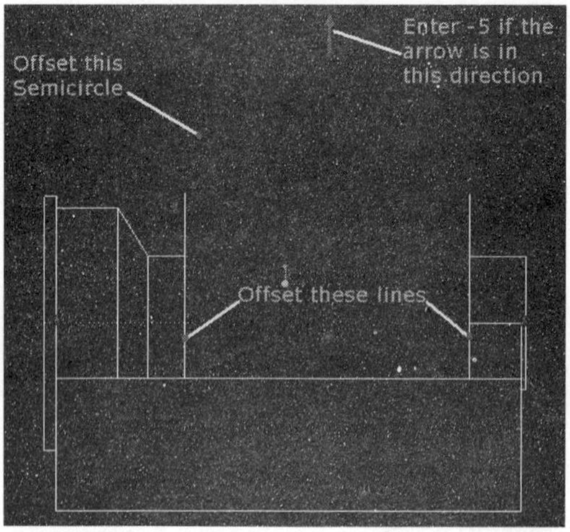

Click on Done/Return

Enter the Offset value as 5 *if the arrow points towards the component (or) –5 if the arrow points away from the component*

Similarly offset the two vertical lines inside

Draw a horizontal line

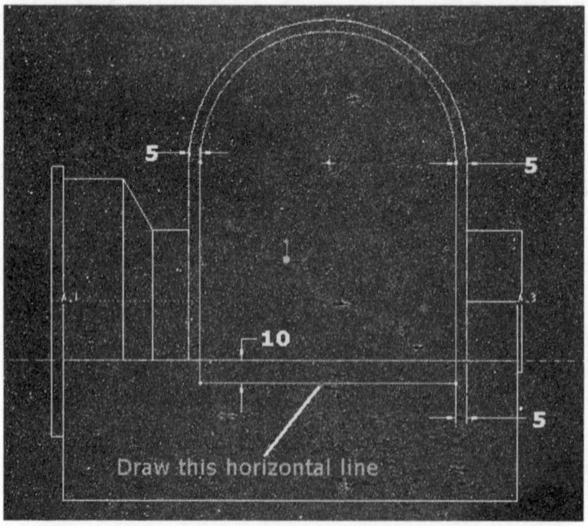

Trim the Curves to form a loop as shown

Add required Dimensions and modify them

Regenerate the sketch

The system prompts "Regeneration completed Successfully"

Click on done

Accept the direction of material removal by clicking ok (the arrow should point inside the sketch)

In depth option select Blind *and click on* done

Enter 70 *and click on* Done

Click on View Default *for default view.*

~~**Feature**~~

~~**Create**~~

~~**Solid**~~

Protrusion

Extrude

Solid

Done

In attributes option select One side *and* done

Select the Front face of the rectangular block as Sketch Plane

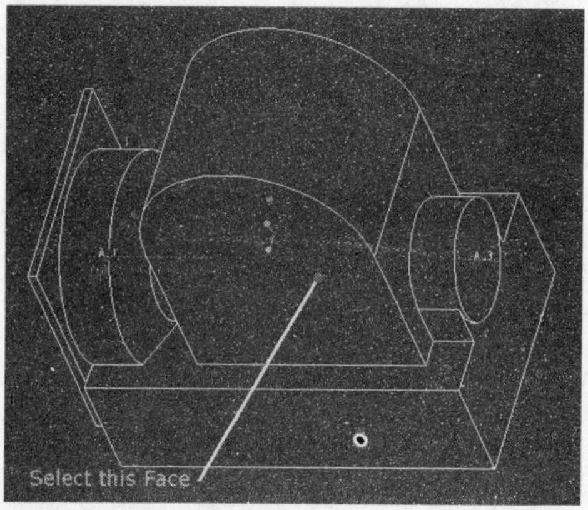

The Direction arrow should point away from the rectangular block. Otherwise Flip it and click on Ok

Click on Default *for 2D view orientation*

Create a concentric circle to the arc

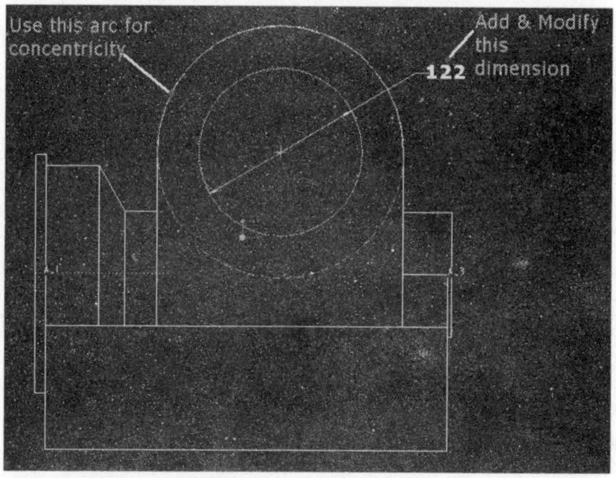

Add the dimension and modify the diameter value to 122

Regenerate the sketch

The system prompts "Regeneration completed Successfully"

Click on GeomTools Use edge *and select the Top edge of the block*

Trim the curves to get the closed profile shown

Add dimension and modify the radius to 30

Regenerate the sketch

The system prompts "Regeneration completed Successfully"

Click on done

In depth option select the Up to Surface *and click on* done

Click on View Default *for default view, so that selection of surface is easy.*

Select the surface shown

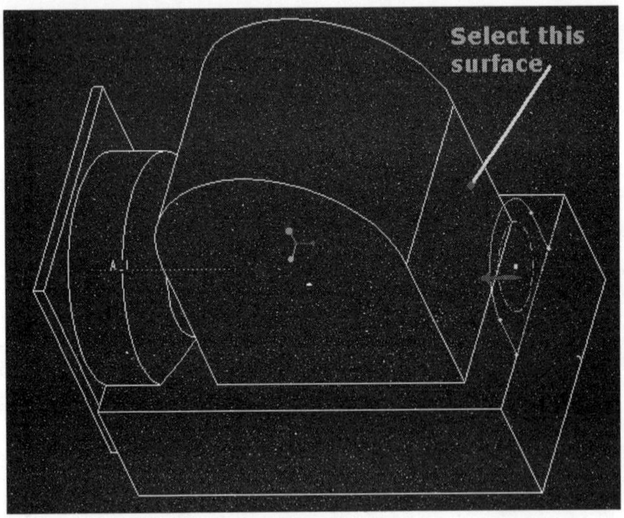

Click on OK

~~Feature~~

~~Create~~

~~Solid~~

Protrusion

Extrude

Solid

Done

In attributes option select One side *and* done

In the Sketch Plane option select UsePrev, *the previously used sketching plane will be selected*

Leave the direction arrow to point away from the block.

Click on Ok

Draw a concentric Circle to the existing arc.

Click on Sketch Circle Concentric *Click on the arc.*

Click again and Drag the mouse to draw the circle

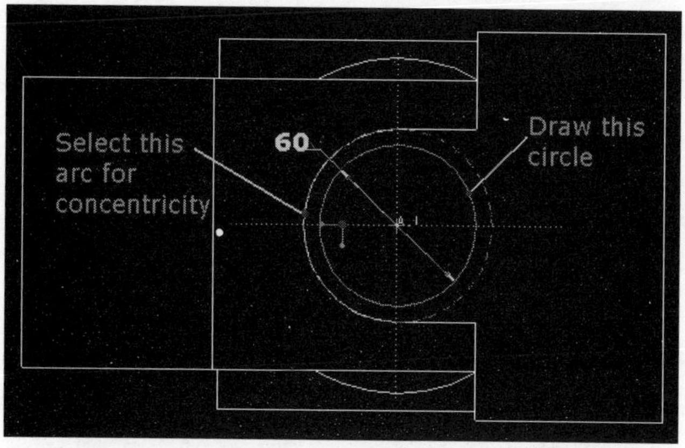

Add dimension to the circle and modify the diameter value to 60

Regenerate the sketch

The system prompts "Regeneration completed Successfully"

Click on done

In depth option select Blind *and click on* done

Enter 2 *and click on* Done

Click on View Default *for default view.*

~~***Feature***~~

~~***Create***~~

~~***Solid***~~

Cut

Extrude

Solid

Done

In attributes option select Both sides *and* done

Select DTM3 as Sketch Plane

Click Ok *to Accept the Direction*

Click on Default *for 2D view orientation*

Click on GeomTools   Offset edge *and Select the Semicircle*

Create a Coaxial hole on the Other side (left side of the block) with diameter as 40 mm and depth as thru next *option*

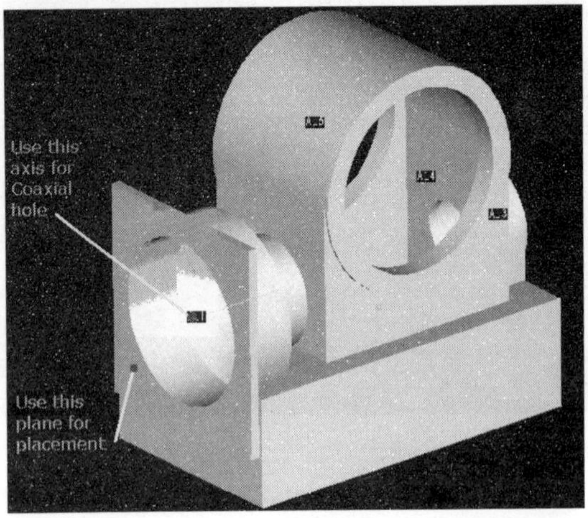

~~Feature~~

~~Create~~

~~Solid~~

Protrusion
Extrude
Solid
Done
attributes option select One side *and* done
Click on Make Datum
In the Datum plane option select the Offset *option and click on* done
Select the plane shown

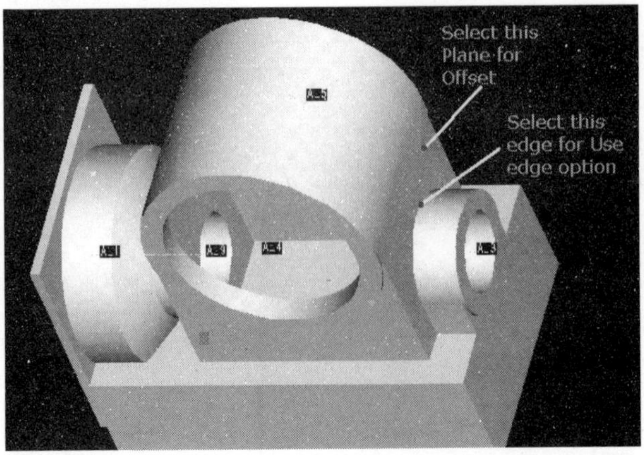

Click on enter value

Enter 3 *(if the arrow points away from the model and –3 if the arrow points towards the model) and click on* Done

The direction of feature creation arrow points away from the component, Flip it to point towards the Component

Click on Ok

Click on Default *for view orientation.*

Click on View Default *for 3D orientation, so that selecting curves will be easy.*

Click on GeomTools Use edge *and select the edge shown*

Now click on sketchview for 2D view orientation

Sketch the lines as shown and trim the curves to form a closed profile

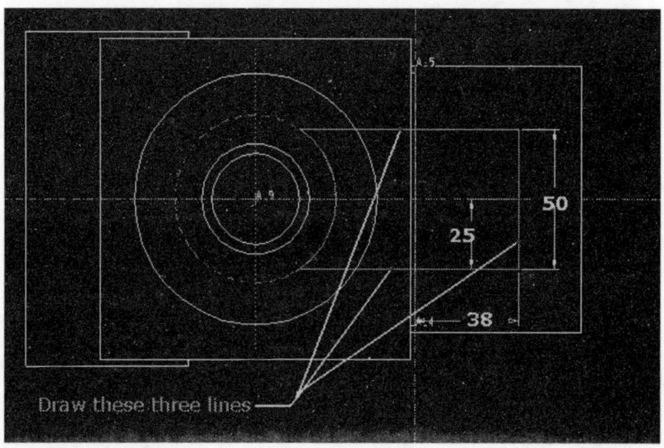

Add and Modify the dimensions

Regenerate the sketch

The system prompts "Regeneration completed Successfully"

Click on done

In depth option select Thru Next *and click on* done

Click on Ok

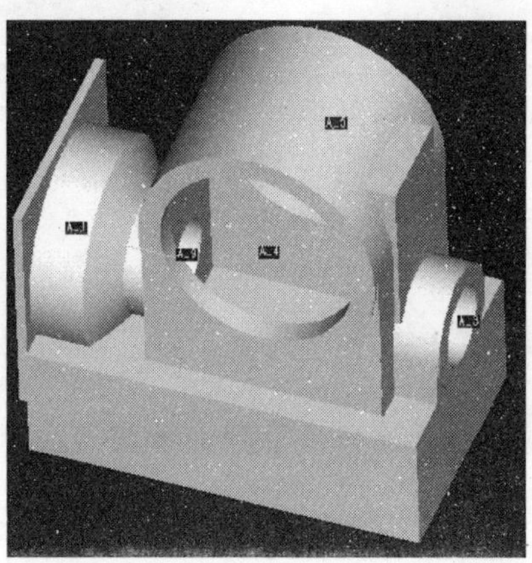

Feature

Create

Datum

Plane

Offset

Select DTM2 (bottom plane)

Click on Done

Select Enter Value

The arrow should point upward

Enter the value as 208

Click on Done

DTM5 is created

~~Feature~~

~~Create~~

~~Solid~~

Protrusion

Extrude

Solid

Done

In attributes option select One side *and* done

Select DTM5 as sketching plane

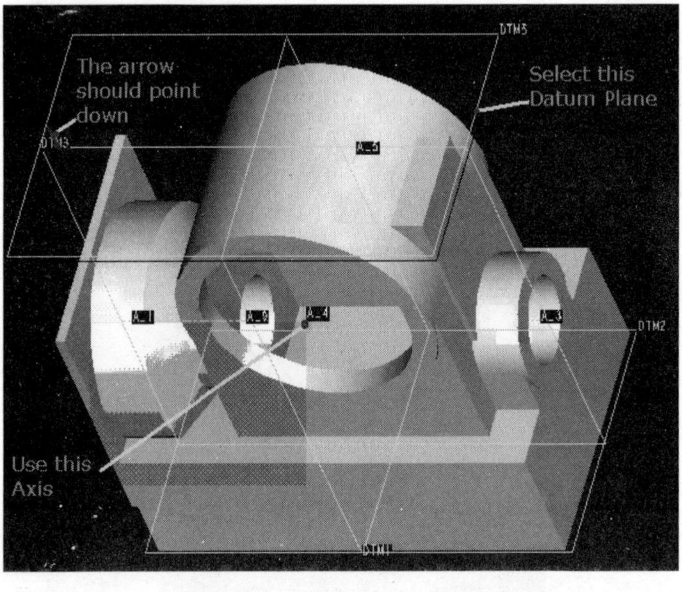

The material direction arrow should be downwards. Otherwise Flip it and click on Ok

Click on Default *for 2D view orientation*

Click on View Default *for 3D view orientation*

Click on GeomTools use edge *and select Axis shown (Axis 4)*

Click on sketch view *to orient back to 2D*

Draw the sketch as shown. The sketch drawn should be on either side of the used axis

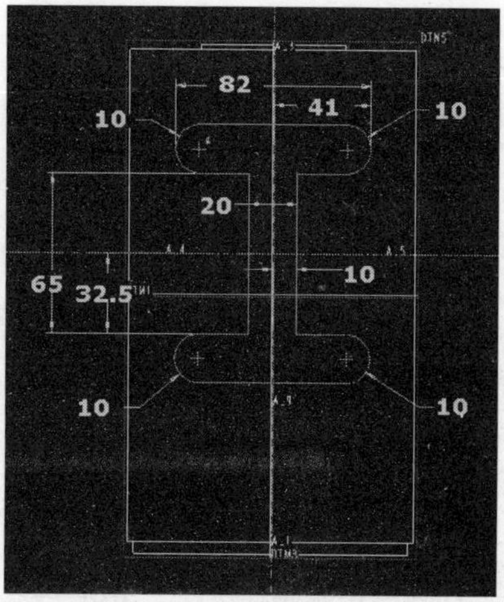

Add and Modify the dimensions

Regenerate the sketch

The system prompts "Regeneration completed Successfully"

Click on view default

Click on done

In depth option select Up to Surface *and click on* done

Select the top surface

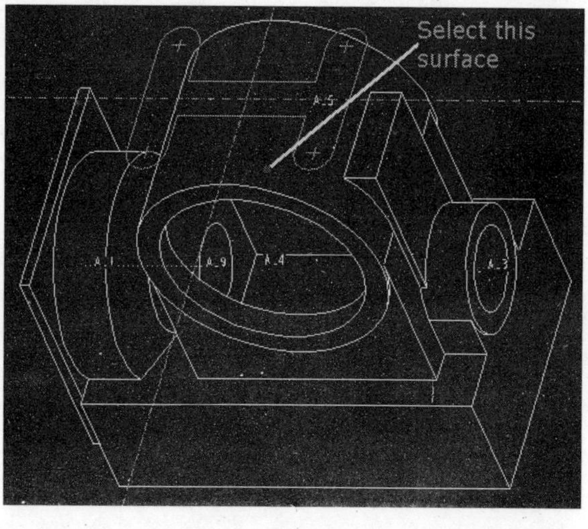

Click on Ok

Feature

Create

Solid

Rib

Select DTM3 as Sketching plane

Click on Default *for 2D orientation*

Draw a slanted line and dimension it as shown

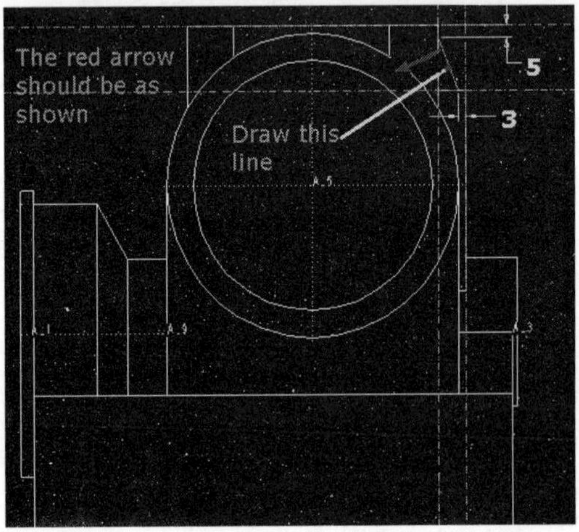

Regenerate the sketch

The system prompts "Regeneration completed Successfully"

Click on done

The arrow should point downwards to add material

Enter thickness as 5

Feature

Create

Solid

Rib

Select Use Prev

The view is oriented to 2D

Click on Geom.Tools Use edge *and select the following curves*

Draw a slanted line and horizontal line as shown

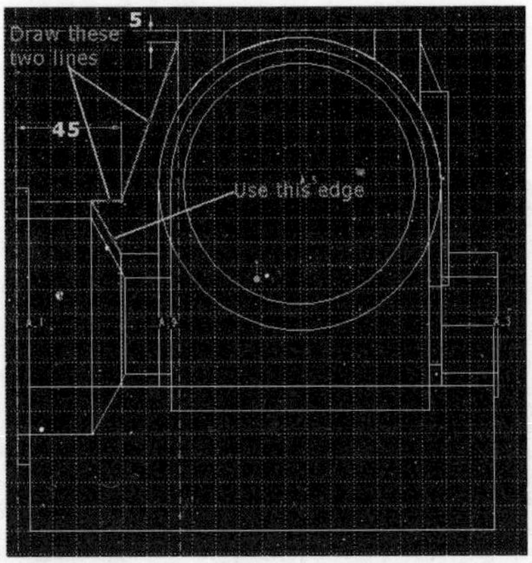

Dimension the curve and modify it.

Regenerate the sketch

The system prompts "Regeneration completed Successfully"

Click on done

The arrow should point downwards to add material

Enter thickness as 5

Feature

Create

Solid

Protrusion

Extrude

Solid

Done

In the attribute option select one side *and click on* done

Select the inner face of the square protrusion

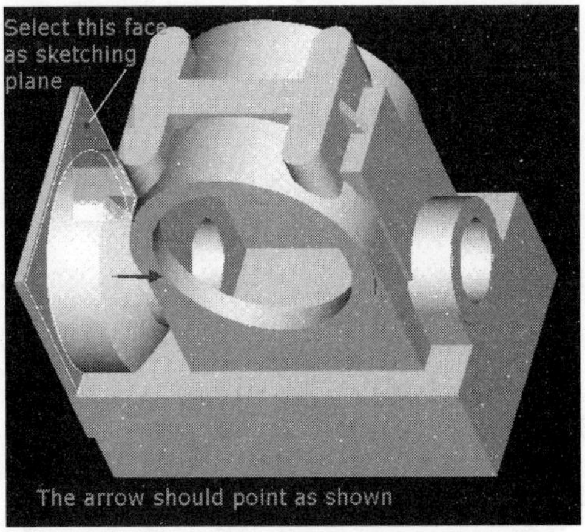

The direction of Protrusion should be towards the component

Click on ok

Click on default *for 2D view orientation.*

Click on GeomTools Use edge *and select the curves shown here*

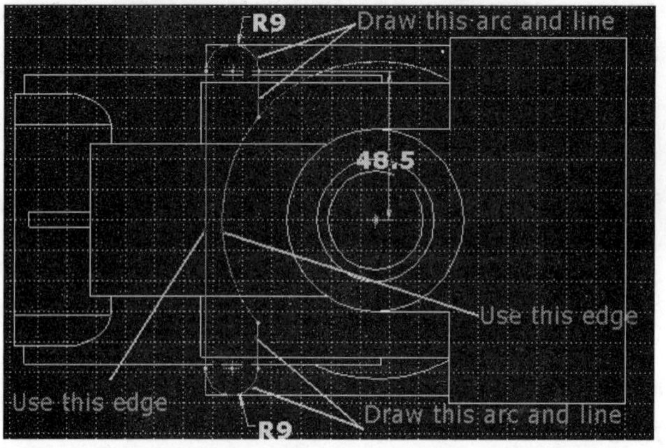

Sketch two arcs as shown and draw Vertical lines to meet the used edge

Trim the curves to get the section as shown

Dimension the curves and modify it

Regenerate the sketch

The system prompts "Regeneration completed Successfully"

Click on done

In the depthoption select Blind *and* done

Enter 5 *as value for depth*

Click on Ok

Feature

Create

Solid

Protrusion

Extrude

Solid

Done

In the attribute option select one side *and click on* done

Select DTM2 as sketching plane

The material dirction should be upwards

Click on default *for 2D view orientation*

Click on GeomTools Offset edge SelLoop Querysel

Select any one line of the outer rectangle

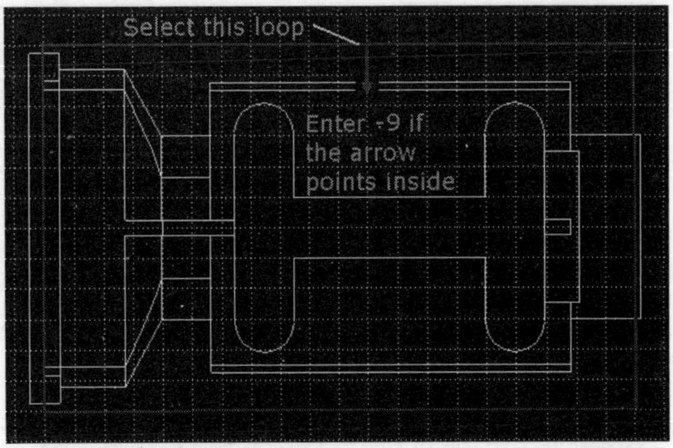

The loop should be rectangular, if any other loop is selected use Next until you get the rectangle

Click on Accept

If the arrow points towards the block, enter the value in negative, if it points away from the block, enter the value in positive

Enter the value as 9

Regenerate the sketch

The system prompts "Regeneration completed Successfully"

Click on done

In the depth option select Blind *and* done

Enter 5 *as value for depth*

Click on Ok

Feature

Create

Solid

Protrusion

Extrude

Solid

Done

In the attribute option select one side *and click on* done

For sketch plane select UsePrev

The material direction arrow should point upward

Click on Ok

Click on GeomTools Use edge

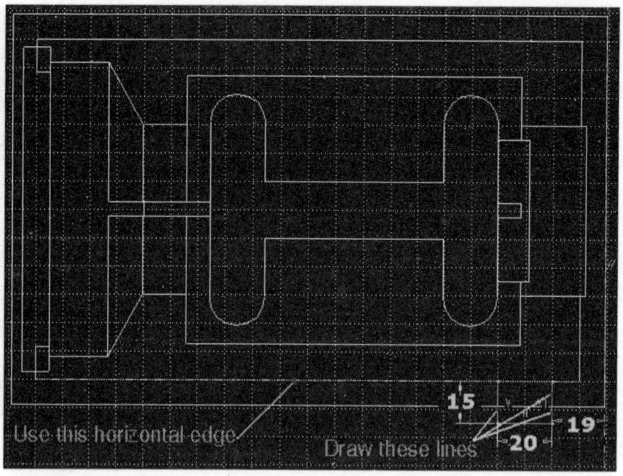

Select the horizontal line of inner rectangular curve

Draw lines to form a small rectangular box (Use Trim if needed)

Dimension the curves and modify it

Regenerate the sketch

The system prompts "Regeneration completed Successfully"

Click on done

In the depthoption select Blind *and* done

Enter 10 *as value for depth*

Click on Ok

Feature

Copy

Move

Select

Independent

Done

Select the leg we created now

Click on done

Click on Translate

The Plane option is selected by default

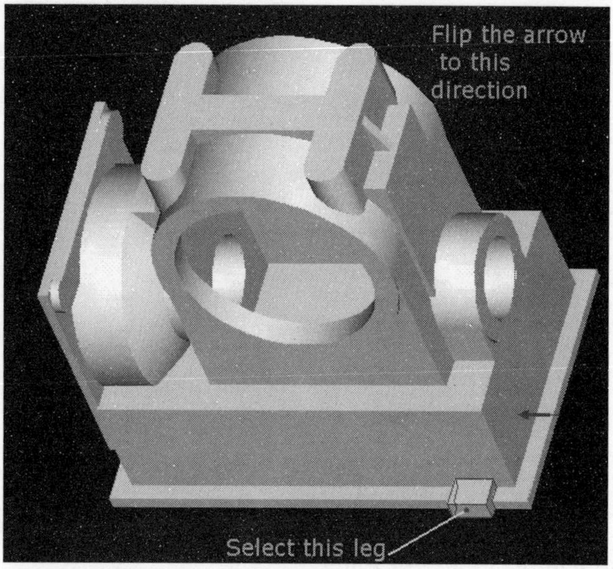

Select the Right plane of the bottom rectangular block

Flip *the arrow to point toward the component*

Click on Ok

Enter the value as 160

Click on DoneMove

Click on Done

Click on Ok

Feature

Copy

Mirror

Select

Independent

Done

Select the First leg we created

Select the second leg we copied

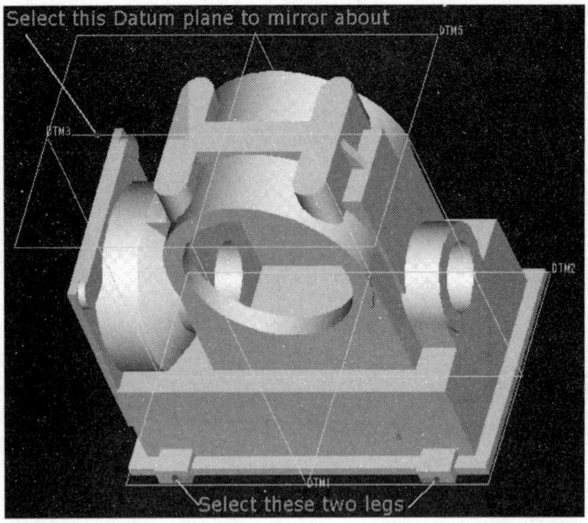

Click on Done

Select DTM3 for the plane to mirror about

Feature

Create

Solid

Cut

Extrude

Solid

Done

In the attribute option select One side *and* done

Select DTM2 as sketching plane

The direction arrow should point upward

Click on ok

Select Default *for 2D view orientation*

Draw a rectangle and add dimension as shown

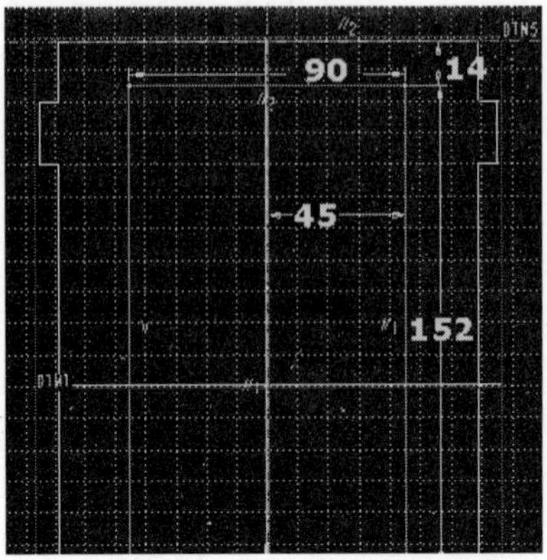

Regenerate the sketch

The system prompts "Regeneration completed Successfully"

Click on done

Click ok for the direction of material to be removed

In the depth option select Blind *and* done

Enter 55 *as value for depth*

Click on Ok

Feature

Create

Solid

Cut

Extrude

Solid

Done

In the attribute option select One side *and* done

Select UsePrev *in the sketching plane option*

Flip *the direction of arrow to point upward*

Click on ok

Click on GeomTools   Use edge

Select the bottom horizontal line of the earlier cut

Draw the lines to form a rectangle

Dimension the curves and modify it

Regenerate the sketch

The system prompts "Regeneration completed Successfully"

Click on done

Click on ok *for material removal*

In the depth option select Blind *and* done

Enter 45 *as value for depth*

Click on Ok

Feature

Create

Round

Simple

Done

Constant

Edge Chain

Done

Click on One-by-one

Select the four corner edges of the base

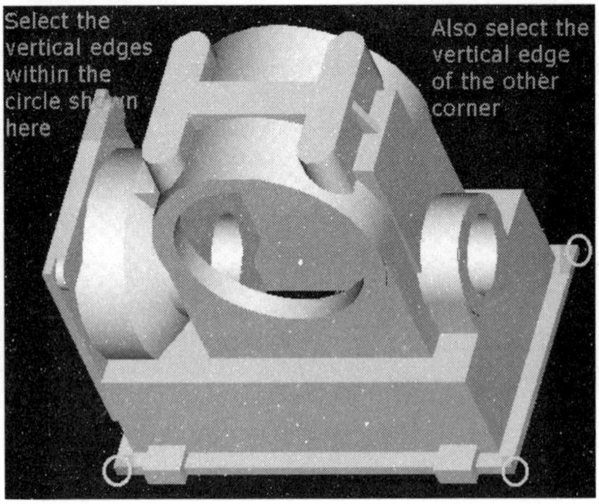

Click on Done

Enter radius as 19

Click on Ok

Feature

Create

Round

Simple

Done

Constant

Edge Chain

Done

Click on One-by-one

Select the four corner edges of the Square Protrusion on the left side

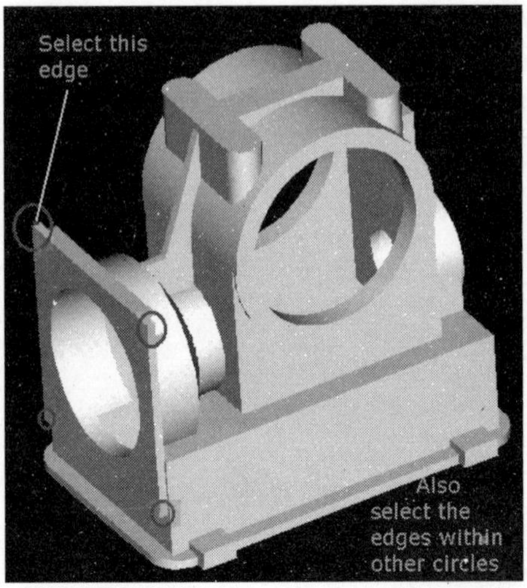

Click on Done

Enter radius as 9

Click on Ok

Feature

Create

Solid

Hole

Straight

Done

Radial

Done

Select the front planar face for placement point (Use Querysel)

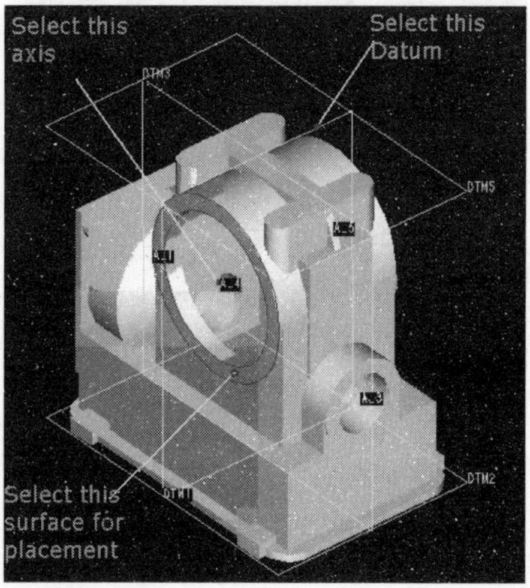

Select the Axis (axis4)

Select DTM1 for polar dimensioning

Enter the value for angle as 0

Select diameter *and click on* Done

Enter the Value of diameter (PCD) as 111

Select One side *and click on* Done

Select Blind *in depth option*

Click on done

Enter depth as 12

Enter diameter (hole) as 6

Click on Ok

Feature

Pattern

Select the last created hole

Select General option

Click on Done

Click on the 0 degree shown

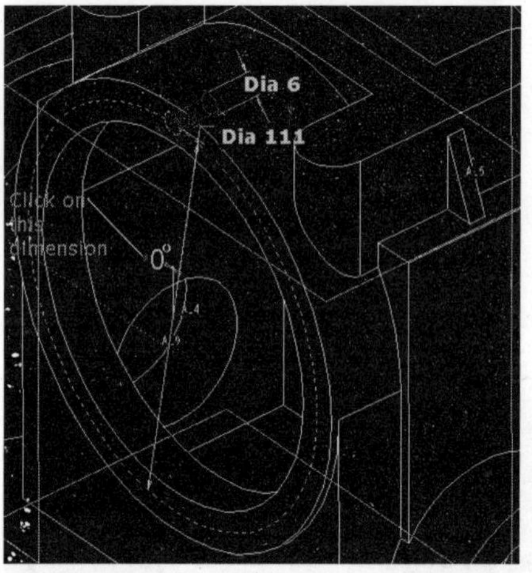

Enter 120 *for value*

Click on Done

Enter 3 *for number of holes*

Click on Done

Feature

Copy

Mirror

Select

Independent

Done

Select the any one hole of the pattern

Click on done

Select DTM3 for plane to mirror about

Feature

Create

Solid

Hole

Straight

Done

Radial

Done

Select the right circular face for placement point (Use Querysel)

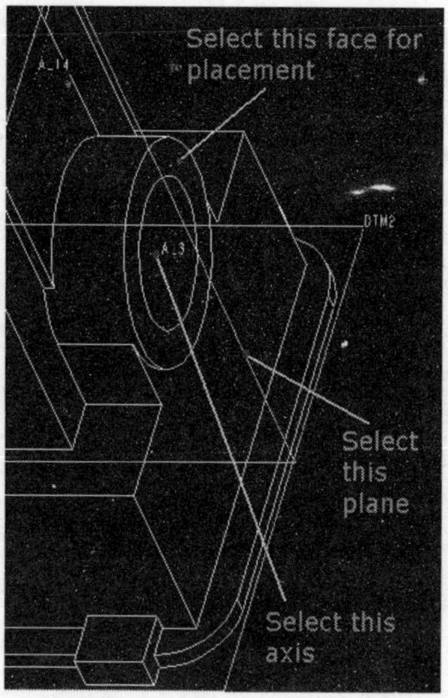

Select the Axis (axis 3)

Select DTM3 for polar dimensioning

Enter 0 *as the value for angle*

Select diameter

Click on Done

Enter value of diameter (PCD) as 50

Select One side *and click on* Done

Select Blind *in depth option*

Click on done

Enter depth as 18

Enter diameter (hole) as 6

Click on Ok

Feature

Pattern

Select the last created hole

Select General *option*

Click on Done

Click on the 0 degree shown

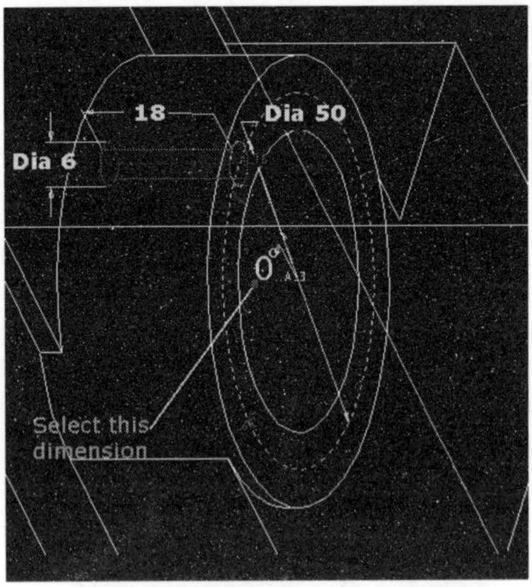

Enter 120 *for value*

Click on Done

Enter 3 *for number of holes*

Click on Done

Rotate the component so that the square protrusion is completely visible

Feature

Create

Solid

Hole

Straight

Done

Radial

Done

Select the left end face of the square protrusion for placement point (Use Querysel)

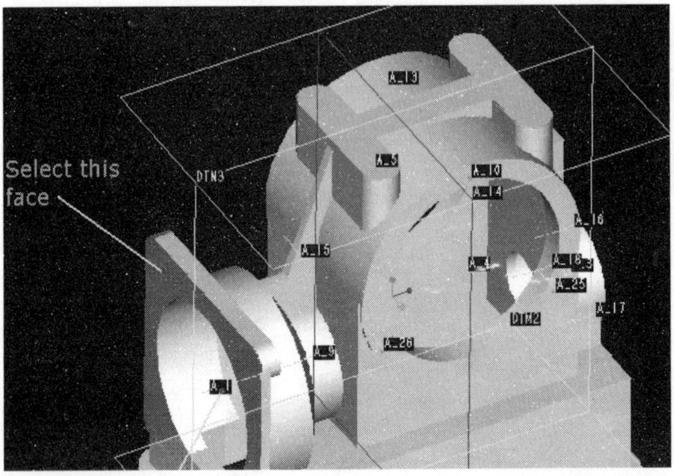

Select the Axis (axis 1)
Select DTM3 for polar dimensioning
Enter 45 *as the value for angle*
Select diameter
Click on Done
Enter value of diameter (PCD) as 138
Select One side *and click on* Done
Select Blind *in depth option*
Click on done
Enter depth as 10
Enter diameter (hole) as 8
Click on Ok
Feature
Pattern
Select the last created hole
Select General *option*
Click on Done
Click on the 45 degree shown

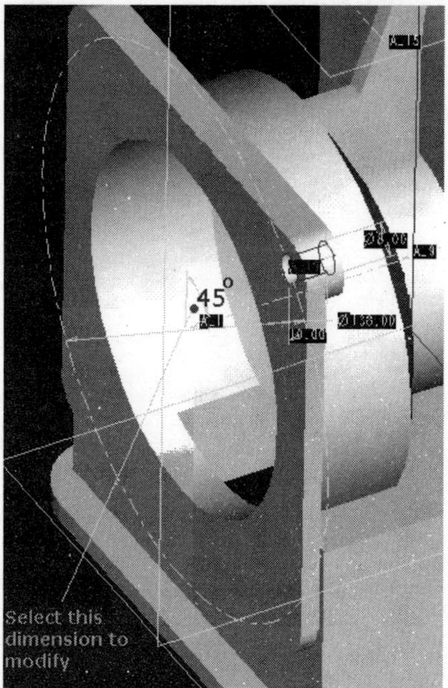

Enter 90 *for value*
Click on Done

Enter 4 *for number of holes*

Click on Done

The finished model is shown below:

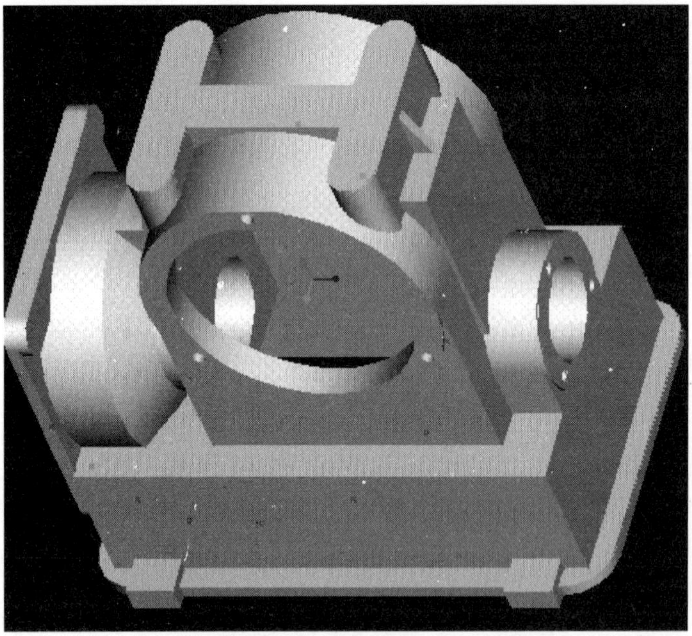

10 PROGRAMMABLE MACHINE CONTROL

Programmable logic controller (PLC) is a core hardware of a CNC Machine. Some CNC systems are built with an integral PLC. The versatility of a CNC machine from the operator point of view depends on the capabilities of PLC. The programmable machine control (PMC) is designed around the PLC. PLC will receive inputs from CNC and various devices like switches and gives output signals to actuate relays, solenoids etc based on the PLC program designed by the machine tool manufacturer. PLC program is designed to ensure proper sequencing of switching functions and interlocking wherever needed.

10.1 INTRODUCTION

The overall control of a CNC machine tool consists of several subsystems as shown in Fig. 1.7 in chapter 1. One of the important subsystems is programmable machine control (PMC). The

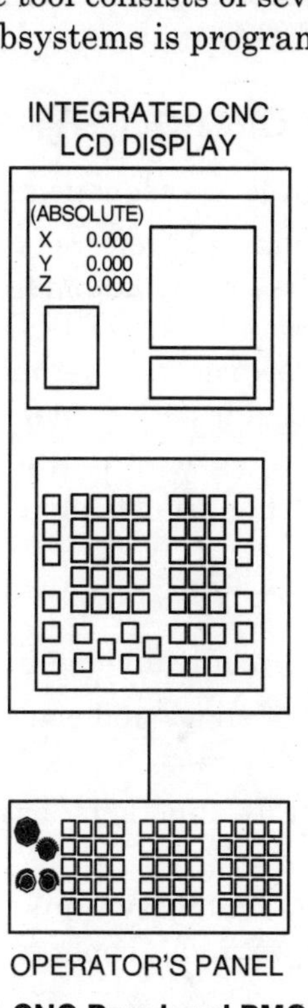

Fig. 10.1 CNC Panel and PMC Panels

control system manufacturers like FANUC, Sinumerik etc provide certain CNC functionalities. However, there are several machine related functions to be integrated with CNC control. Typical functions are motor on/off, motor CW/CCW, coolant on/off, chuck on/off, door open/close etc. There are several switches, solenoids, relays etc have to be operated to synchronize the machine operation. These operations are carried out with the help of several Input/Output (I/O) devices. The input may be from the program or from several proximity, thermal or limit switches fitted on to the machine to sense the machine condition or positioning of slides, chucking of work piece, clamping or closure of door etc. The output may be signals to operate one or more of the several on/off switches, relays, solenoids etc. The programmable machine functions are designed by the machine tool manufacturer. Thus, you may find two distinct control panels n a CNC machine- one designed and supplied by the CNC system manufacturer and the other one designed and fitted by the machine tool manufacturer. Figure 10.1 shows the two panels.

10.2 HIGH PERFORMANCE PMC BASED ON A DEDICATED PMC PROCESSOR

The sequence control in the CNC operation is complex and involves several steps. A separate dedicated processor called PMC processor is often used for the sequence control which enables fast processing. The architecture includes a high-speed window between CNC and PMC to exchange information between the CNC and PMC. Using the window, machine control functions unique to each machine tool can be incorporated by the machine tool builder. A high speed I/O link facilitates high-speed data transfer. The I/O link is an I/O network used to establish a serial I/O connection of PMC with various I/O devices.

Enriched PMC diagnostic functions

The CNC unit incorporates ladder monitoring and editing functions as standard to improve its ease of use. The signal trace function has been improved to allow easy maintenance in the field.

10.3 PROGRAMMABLE LOGIC CONTROLLER (PLC)

PLC is the hardware unit which controls the sequencing operations.

Programmable logic controllers, commonly referred to as PLCs are widely used in industrial automation today. The use of PLCs has made automation flexible. With PLCs the reliability has improved significantly. The modular nature of PLCs enables easy expansion. The cost of the automated system also has come down as PLC permits easy customization. It is also easy to integrate peripheral devices. It also permits both analog as well as digital inputs and outputs.

The following sections deal with PLCs with particular reference to CNC Machines. The concepts discussed can be applied to other industrial automation scenarios also.

10.4 CNC AND PLC

The control of a CNC machine can be broadly divided into two:

(i) Positioning and velocity control of slides and control of main motor in various modes of operation.

(ii) The various switching (ON/OFF) functions associated with the operation of the machine.

The information processing in first category commands is usually coded in G functions. The CNC system will decode the program and generate necessary data for the realization of the commands.

The second category involves switching functions like main motor on/motor off, coolant on/off, tool change, program end etc. These functions are realized through M codes. Many of these functions are to be properly sequenced with appropriate interlocks.

For examples, in a CNC lathe the spindle should not be switched on unless the workpiece is properly clamped and the door of the machine is closed. Each of these actions will generate signals which are then input to the controller. These complex interlocked logical sequences are now performed using a programmable logic controller which receives input from the CNC system as well as various limit switches, proximity switches, pressure switches and other sensors mounted on the CNC machine.

CNC has a programmable machine interface. This interface controls the following:

- Spindle on/off/CCW/CW rotation
- Gear change low/high
- Chucking
- Door/shuttle closing
- Pallet change
- Tool change.indexing
- Coolant and/off
- Chip conveyor on/off

Since the above and many other functions are controlled by PLC in a CNC machine, it is necessary that the reader should have a good understanding of the PLCs. In addition to CNC, PLC's are widely used in industrial automation.

10.5 DEFINITION OF PLC

A PLC is defined as digitally operating electronic apparatus which uses a programmable memory for internal storage of instruction by implementing specific functions such as logic sequencing, timing, counting, and arithmetic to control through digital/analog input/output modules, various types of machines or processes (NEMA). Thus PLC is an electronic interface device used to perform logic operation on input signals in order to generate a set of output signals. Output from a PLC is directed to motors, valves, motor starters, solenoids etc.

10.6 COMPONENTS OF A PLC

PLC is primarily intended to replace relay logic. In this action, the common elements are used in relay devices like switches, relays, timers and counters are discussed.

10.6.1 Switches

A switch either opens or closes a circuit. The switches are classified as:

- locking and non-locking
- normally open/normally closed
- single through/multiple throw
- single pole/multiple pole

Typical switches used in control circuits include:

- Limit switches
- Selector switches
- Push button switches
- Photoelectric switches – non contact
- Proximity switches - non contact
- Pressure switches
- Thumb wheel switches

10.6.2 Relays

A relay is an electromagnetically operated switch.

10.6.3 Counter

A digital counter consists of a count register, an accumulator and a relay contact. The count register holds a pre-assigned count value. The accumulator is used to either increment or decrement a count each time an input pulse is received. Digital counters output in the form of a relay contact when the accumulator value is equal to register value.

10.6.4 Timer

A timer consists of an internal clock, a count value register, and an accumulator. A timer starts operating after receiving a start signal. When a pre-assigned value is reached, it outputs a signal.

10.7 ARCHITECTURE OF PLC

A microprocessor based programmable controller consists of the following parts:

CPU

Power supply

Memory

Input/Output

Peripheral devices

10.7.1 CPU

Current PLC's are microprocessor based systems. CPU scans the status of input devices, examines the control logic to decide what actions to take and then outputs the required response.

10.7.2 Power Supply

The power supply converts the mains AC supply to provide the DC supply required for the internal operation of the PLC.

10.7.3 Memory

The types of memory used in PLC's include RAM, ROM, PROM, EPROM, EAPROM and bubble memory. The memory stores the control program and the status of the peripherals.

10.7.4 Input/Output

The input/output for a PLC is a set of modular plug-in peripherals, which allow the PLC to accept signals from a variety of external devices like limit switches, pressure switches, proximity switches etc. and outputs the control signals based on the logic circuits to out put devices like LEDS, relays etc. The input/output can be both analog and digital signals. Analog inputs can be from flow return, pressure senses, temperature sensor, potentiometers etc.

10.8 PROGRAMMING A PLC

As mentioned earlier, PLC uses ladder logic programming. A ladder diagram is a graphical representation of the program. There are primarily seven types of PLC instructions:

Relay

Timer and control

Program control

Arithmetic

Data manipulation

Data transfer

Sequencers and other elements

10.8.1 Basic Logic Gates

Basic logic gates are discussed in this section from a PLC standpoint. There are six logic gates: OR, AND, NOT, Exclusive OR, NAND and NOR. All gates have one output.

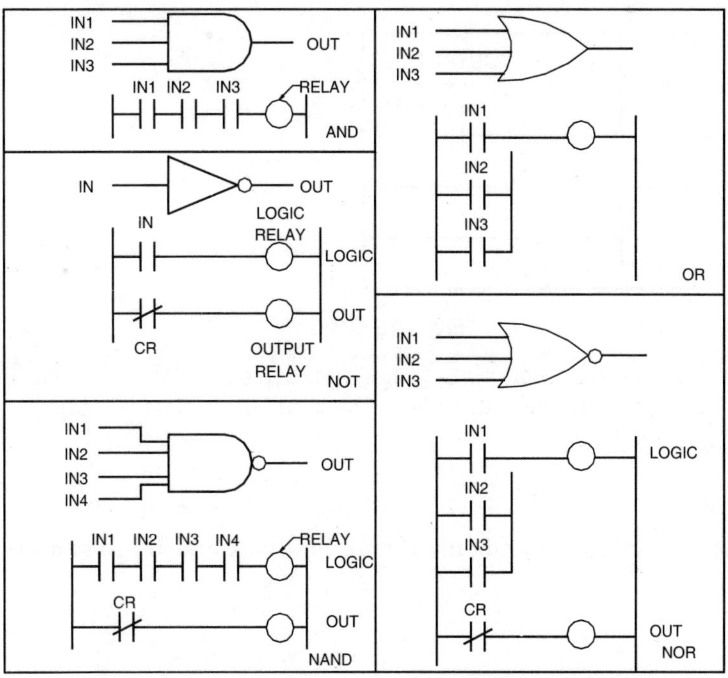

Fig. 10.2 Logic Gates and Their Ladder Equivalents

They are either ON (1) or (OFF) depending on the logic status of their inputs, ON (1) or OFF (0). A gate ON condition is typical when +5 volts DC come out from the output terminal. Off is typically zero volt output. The NOT gate has one input. The EXCLUSIVE OR Gate has usually has two inputs, but can have more. The other four gates can have two to eight inputs and sometimes more. Illustrations of the six logic gates and their PLC ladder equivalents are shown in Fig.10.2.

By using serial and parallel connections, various types of logic can be represented in a ladder diagram. The important logic gates are AND, OR and combined AND and OR.

10.8.2 OR Gate

OR is used when one or more switches out of several are on for the output to be available. An example of OR gate is shown in Fig. 10.3.

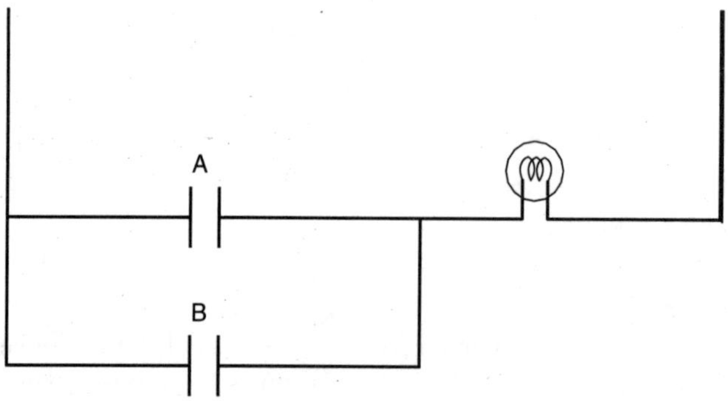

A	B	OUTPUT
0	0	0
0	1	1
1	0	1
1	1	1

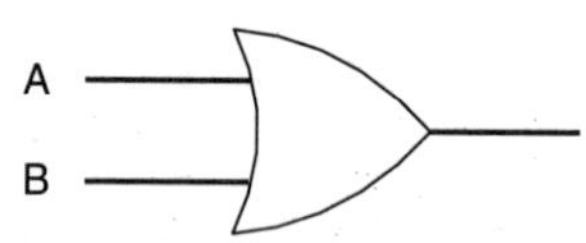

Fig. 10.3 OR Gate

Two switches in normally open (state 0) position are shown in Fig. 10.3. If A or B is closed (state 1) there is output (1). In the example, state 1 indicates that the lamp will be burning. If both are in state 1, the output is 1.

10.8.3 AND Gate

AND gate will yield an output if and only if both inputs A and B are simultaneously present in Fig. 10.4.

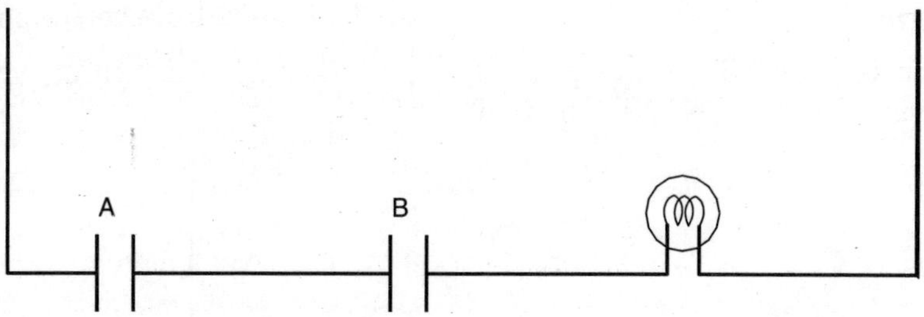

A	B	OUTPUT
0	0	0
0	1	0
1	0	0
1	1	1

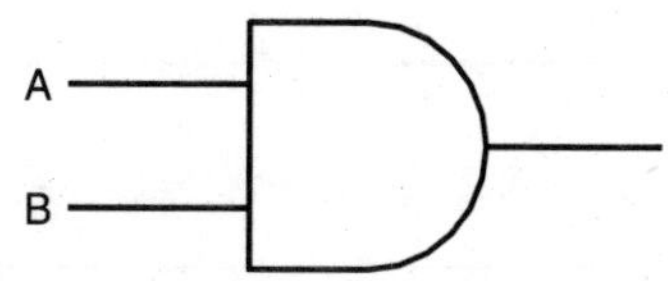

Fig. 10.4 AND Gate

10.8.4 NOT Gate

The logical inversion, or NOT, function can be performed on a contact input simply by using a normally-closed contact instead of a normally-open contact.

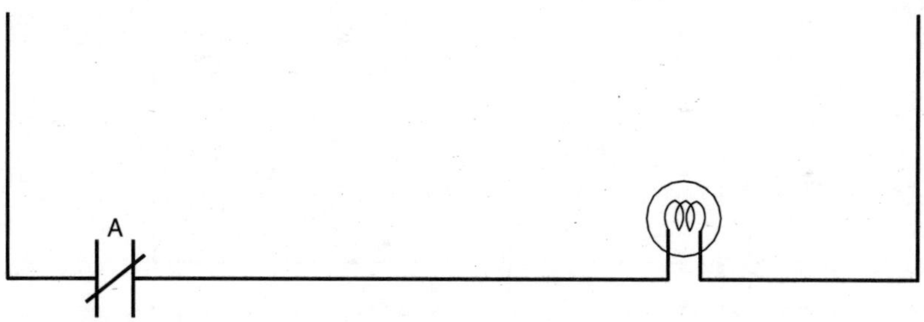

A	OUTPUT
0	0
1	0

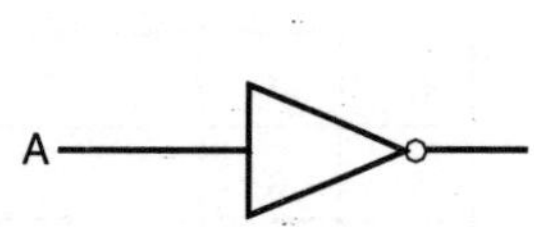

Fig. 10.5 NOT Gate

10.8.5 NAND Gate

If the OR function is inverted i.e. invert each "input" through the use of normally-closed contacts, one will end up with a NAND function.

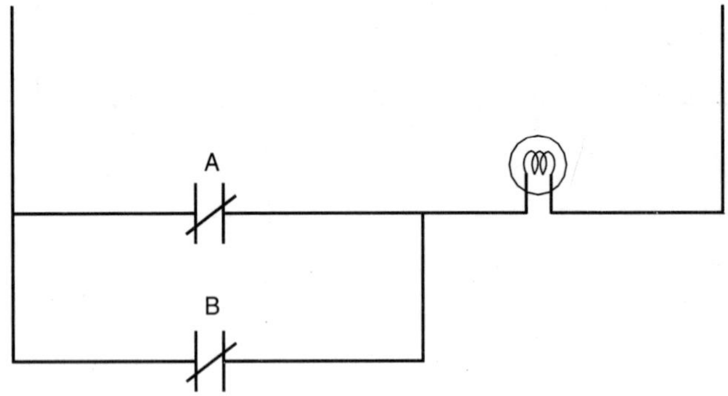

A	B	OUTPUT
0	0	1
0	1	1
1	0	1
1	1	0

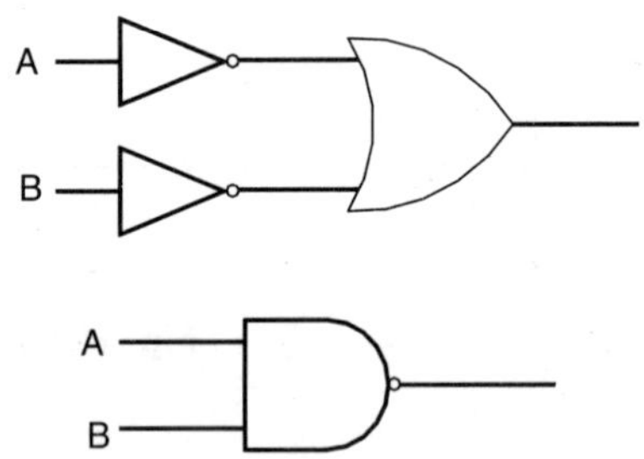

Fig. 10.6 NAND Gate

10.8.6 NOR Gate

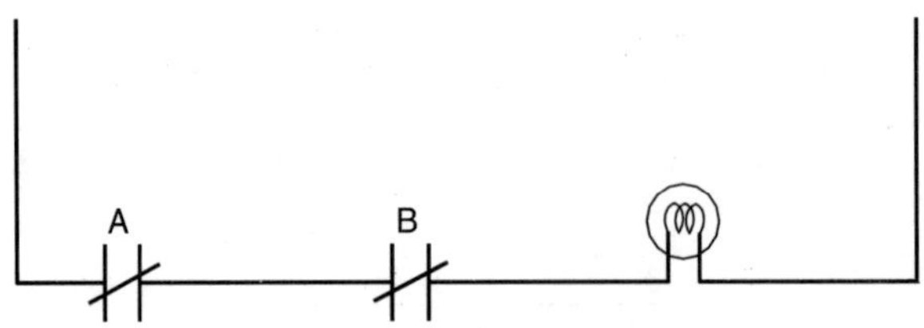

A	B	OUTPUT
0	0	1
0	1	0
1	0	0
1	1	0

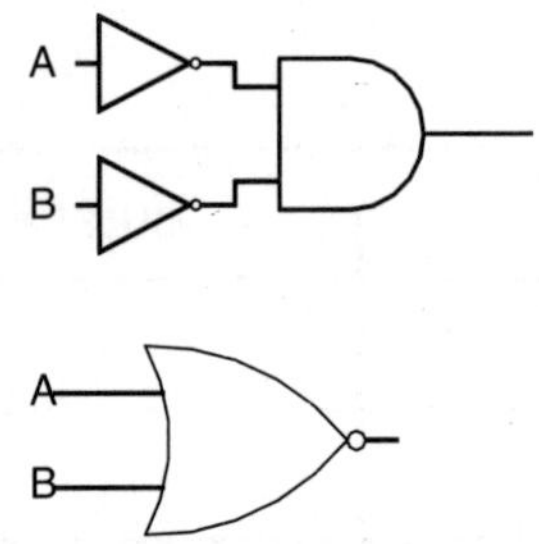

Fig. 10.7 NOR Gate

A pattern quickly reveals itself when ladder circuits are compared with their logic gate counterparts:

- Parallel contacts are equivalent to an OR gate.
- Series contacts are equivalent to an AND gate.
- Normally-closed contacts are equivalent to a NOT gate (inverter).

Combinational logic functions can be built by grouping contacts in series-parallel arrangements, as well. In the following example, we have an Exclusive-OR function built from a combination of AND, OR, and inverter (NOT) gates.

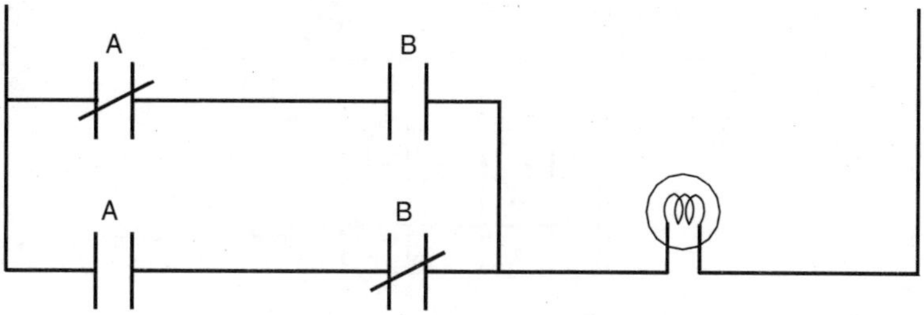

A	B	OUTPUT
0	0	0
0	1	1
1	0	1
1	1	0

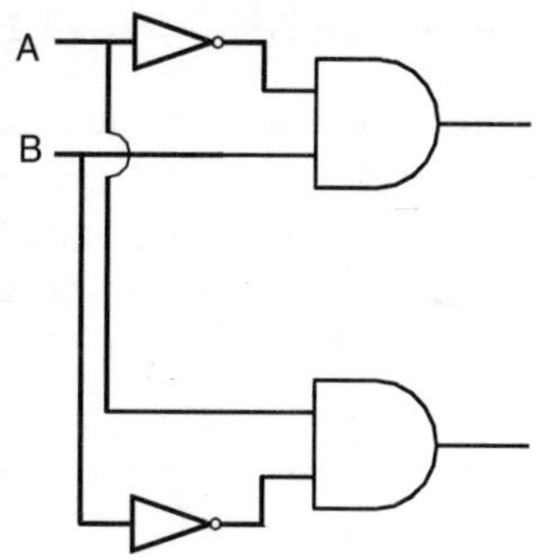

Fig. 10.8 EXCLUSIVE OR Gate

The top rung (NC contact A in series with NO contact B) is the equivalent of the top NOT/AND gate combination. The bottom rung (NO contact A in series with NC contact B) is the equivalent of the bottom NOT/AND gate combination. The parallel connection between the two rungs at wire number 2 forms the equivalent of the OR gate, in allowing either rung 1 *or* rung 2 to energize the lamp.

To make the Exclusive-OR function, it is necessary to use two contacts per input: one for direct input and the other for "inverted" input. The two "A" contacts are physically actuated by the same mechanism, as are the two "B" contacts. The common association between contacts is denoted by the label of the contact. There is no limit to how many contacts per switch can be represented in a ladder diagram, as each new contact on any switch or relay (either normally-open or normally-closed) used in the diagram is simply marked with the same label.

Sometimes, multiple contacts on a single switch (or relay) are designated by a compound labels, such as "A-1" and "A-2" instead of two "A" labels. This may be especially useful if you want to specifically designate which set of contacts on each switch or relay is being used for which part of a circuit.

If we wish to invert the *output* of any switch-generated logic function, we must use a relay with a normally-closed contact. For instance, if we want to energize a load based on the inverse, or NOT, of a normally-open contact, we could do this:

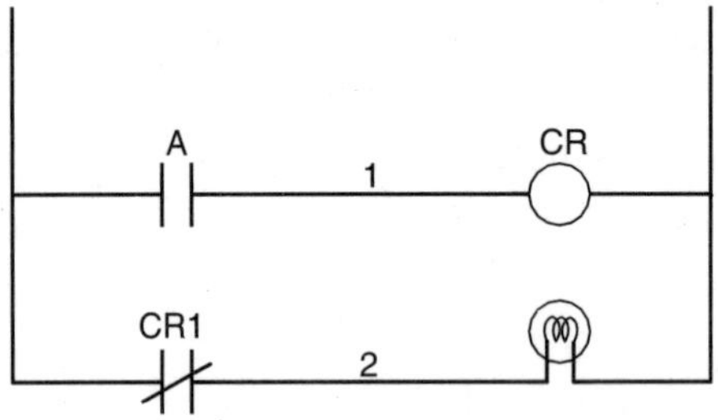

A	CR1	OUTPUT
0	0	1
1	1	0

Fig. 10.9 Use of Control Relay

10.9 EXAMPLE OF STARTING AN ELECTRIC MOTOR

Another practical application of relay logic is in control systems where we want to ensure two incompatible events cannot occur at the same time. An example of this is in reversible motor control, where two motor contactors are wired to switch polarity (or phase sequence) to an electric motor, and we don't want the forward and reverse contactors energized simultaneously:

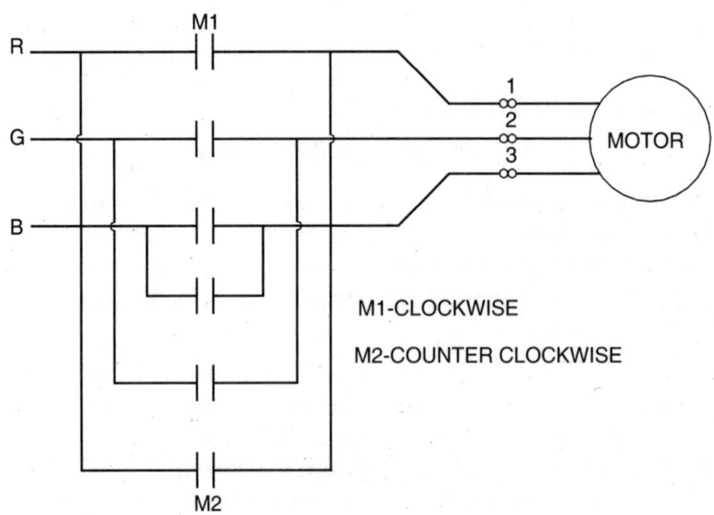

Fig. 10.10 Simple Starting Circuit of a Motor

When contactor M_1 is energized, the 3 phases (A, B, and C) are connected directly to terminals 1, 2, and 3 of the motor, respectively. However, when contactor M_2 is energized, phases A and B are reversed- A going to motor terminal 2 and B going to motor terminal 1.

This reversal of phase wires results in the motor spinning the opposite direction. Let's examine the control circuit for these two contactors:

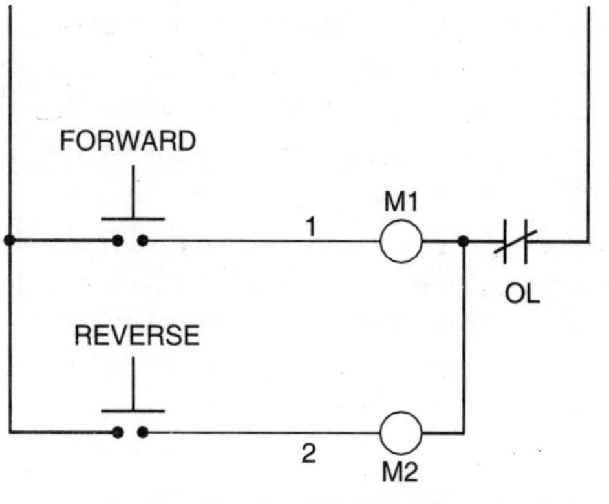

Fig. 10.11 Control Circuit for Contactors

Take note of the normally-closed "OL" contact, which is the thermal overload contact activated by the "heater" elements wired in series with each phase of the AC motor. If the heaters get too hot, the contact will change from its normal (closed) state to being open, which will prevent either contactor from energizing.

This control system will work fine, so long as no one pushes both buttons at the same time. If someone were to do that, phases A and B would be short-circuited together by virtue of the fact that contactor M_1 sends phases A and B straight to the motor and contactor M_2 reverses them; phase A would be shorted to phase B and vice versa.

To prevent this occurrence from happening, we can design the circuit so that the energization of one contactor prevents the energization of the other. This is called *interlocking*, and it is accomplished through the use of auxiliary contacts on each contactor, as such:

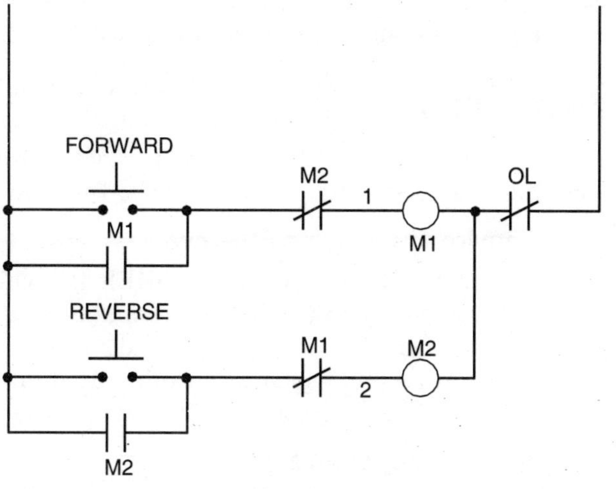

Fig. 10.12 Interlocking

When the "Forward" push button is actuated, M_1 will energize, closing the normally-open auxiliary contact in parallel with that switch. When the push button is released, the closed M_1 auxiliary contact will maintain current to the coil of M_1, thus latching the "Forward" circuit in the "on" state. The same sort of thing will happen when the "Reverse" push button is pressed.

These parallel auxiliary contacts are sometimes referred to as *seal-in* contacts, the word "seal" meaning essentially the same thing as the word *latch*.

However, this creates a new problem of stopping the motor. As the circuit exists right now, the motor will run either forward or backward once the corresponding push button switch is pressed, and will continue to run as long as there is power. To stop either circuit (forward or backward), we require some means for the operator to interrupt power to the motor contactors. This function is performed by STOP switch.

Now, if either forward or reverse circuits are latched, they may be "unlatched" by momentarily pressing the "Stop" push button, which will open either forward or reverse circuit, de-energizing the energized contactor, and returning the seal-in contact to its normal (open) state. The "Stop" switch, having normally-closed contacts, will conduct power to either forward or reverse circuits when released.

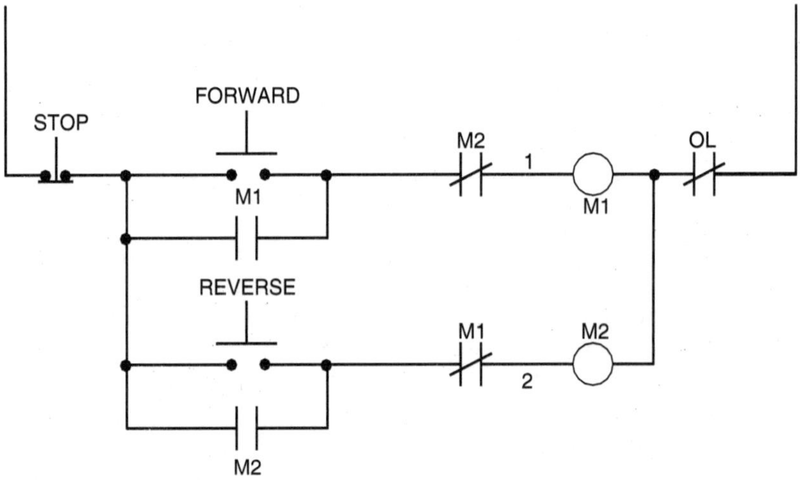

Fig. 10.13 Control Circuit with Stop Switch

10.10 PROGRAMMING OF PLCs

There are many methods of programming PLCs. They are: structured text programming, functional block programming, instruction list, and sequential function chart.

PMC program development environment using Ethernet

By connecting the program development tool FANUC LADDER-III, which runs on a personal computer, with an Ethernet or RS-232-C communication port, ladder programs can be monitored and edited through online remote operation. PMC program development tasks ranging from program creation to debugging can be performed in an integrated environment. The multi-window screen allows development of ladder programs in an efficient way.

Programming methods that facilitate customization

By dividing a large-scale ladder program into modules of functional units using subprogram commands, the program can be designed with parts that can be used in common. By programming with a step sequence function, a complex sequence control procedure can be divided into processes (steps) and transition conditions (transitions) so that it can be described with a flow chart. The movement of the object under control is represented by an easy-to-understand structured flow chart, thereby improving the efficiency of debugging and maintenance.

For advanced customization, programming in C language is possible. A 32-bit C language processor that runs in parallel with the PMC processor for ladder program execution can perform real-time multi-tasking.

10.11 SPECIFICATIONS OF A PLC USED IN CNC MACHINES

The following is a comprehensive list of specifications of a PLC to be used in a machine tool control system.

(A) Hardware Specification

(a) 32 bit Micro-Controller based Controller
(b) Watch Dog Timer
(c) 16 bit Bus Interface for Digital/Analogue Input and Output modules
(d) Operating voltage: 24V DC
(e) Total No. of Digital Inputs: 256
(f) Total No. of Digital Outputs: 256
(g) Total No. of Analogue Inputs: 32
(h) Total No. of Analogue Outputs: 32
(i) EMI/EMC Compatibility
(j) Communication Interface between PC (Personal Computer) and PLC

(B) Digital Input Module

(a) Operating voltage: 24V DC
(b) 8/16/32 Channel configuration
(c) Optical Isolation between 24V DC and 5V DC

(C) Digital Output Module

(a) Operating voltage: 24V DC
(b) 8/16/32 Channel configuration
(c) Optical Isolation between 24V DC and 5V DC
(d) Transistor Output/Relay Output
(e) Sinking Type/Sourcing Type

(D) Analogue Input Module

(a) 4/8 Channel Configuration
(b) 0-20mA, 4-20mA, 0-10V, +/-10V, +/-5V, RTD Input
(c) Isolation
(d) Analogue to Digital Conversion: 50Hz/60 Hz

(E) Analogue Output Module

(a) 4/8 Channel Configuration
(b) 0-20mA, 4-20mA, 0-10V, +/-10V, +/-5V
(c) Isolation
(d) Digital to Analogue Conversion: 50Hz/60 Hz

(F) High Speed Counter Input Module

(a) 16 bit/32 bit Counter

(b) Maximum operating frequency: 200 KHz

(G) Machine Control Panel

(a) 64 Keys/64 LEDs

(b) Keys and LEDs connected in Matrix format

(c) Emergency Stop/FRO/SSO/RTO in Machine Control Panel

(d) Keyboard Controller for Key Scanning and communication

(e) Hardware Debouncing for Keys

(f) Digital communication between Keyboard and PLC

(H) Software Specification

(a) Scan Time: 0.25ms/K of Instructions

(b) Structured Programming (Jump and Call Instructions)

(c) Power On, Time based and Regular Logical Execution

(d) Windows based Application Program Development Software (If PLC Logic is to be edited in Standard PC) and RTOS based Application Program Development Software if Logic is to be edited in CNC controller

(e) Factory Logic/Machine Logic

(f) Instructions

- Arithmetic
- Logical
- Comparison (BCD, Binary, Grey)
- Conversion (BCD to Binary, Binary to BCD)
- Shift
- Rotate
- Exchange
- Move
- Bit/Byte/Word/Double Word Instructions
- Positive/Negative Transition Inputs
- Special Instruction for ATC (Automatic Tool Change)/Turret
- Digital PID Filter for PLC Controlled Axes
- Display Format: Binary, BCD, Hex

(g) Timers (Software)

- ON Delay
- OFF Delay
- Pulse/Extended Pulse
- Variable/Constant Time Value
- Timer Resolution: 1ms
- No. of Timers: 128

- Enable/Preset Inputs
- Maximum Time Value: 32 bit Value x 1ms

(h) Counters (Software)
- Up Counter
- Down Counter
- Up/Down Counter
- No. of Counters: 128
- Enable/Preset/Reset Inputs
- Maximum Count Value: 32 bit Value

(i) Programming Methods
- Ladder Diagram
- Statement List
- Functional Flow Diagram
- Higher Level Languages ('C' Language)

(j) PLC Programming in CNC/Stand-Alone PC

(k) Programming Standard
- IEC61131-3

(l) Editor Software
- Ladder Diagram Editor
- Alarms and Message Editor
- Symbol and Comment Editor
- Statement List Editor
- Functional Flow Diagram Editor
- Text Editor for Higher Level Languages ('C') Programming

(m) Compiler Software for all Programming Languages

(n) Forcing of Inputs/Outputs

(o) Diagnostic Software
- Power Flow Diagram for Ladder Diagram Display
- Status Display of all Inputs and Outputs

(p) Modes of Operation
- Run/Stop/Single Step

(q) Communication (If Logic is built in a Personal Computer)
- To Upload the Logic to PLC Hardware
- To Download the Logic from PLC
- To Monitor the Logic in Power Flow mode

(r) PLC Controlled Axes: Yes
- Maximum No. of PLC Controlled Axes: 2

REVIEW QUESTIONS

(1) Discuss why there are two control panels on a CNC machine tool- a CNC panel and a PMC panel.

(2) What are the functions of a PMC?

(3) What are the functions controlled in the programmable interface of a CNC machine?

(4) What are the components of a programmable logic controller?

(5) Discuss the architecture of a PLC.

(6) Describe the functions of basic logic gates.

(7) How are logic gates implemented in ladder diagrams?

(8) Design a ladder diagram for the following application:

Consider unloading a part from a conveyer to a machine tool in a manufacturing cell. When the part comes near the proximity switch P1, it is scanned by a bar code reader to identify the part. If it is the desired part, a stopper is activated to stop it. The robot then picks up the part and loads on to the machine. The sequence of operations is as follows:

Description	State	Explanation
Micro switch	1	part arrives
Output to bar code reader	1	scan bar code
Input from bar code reader	1	right part
Output robot	1	loading cycle starts
Input from robot	1	loading cycle complete
Output from machine	1	part ready for unloading
Input to robot	1	unloading cycle starts
Output from robot	1	unloading complete
Cycle restarts		

11 ECONOMICS OF MANUFACTURING USING CNC MACHINES

Machining has always been and even today one of the high cost components of the manufacturing process. The manufacturing engineer aims to attain the ideal combinations of production techniques in preparation, handling and the cutting operation, so as to yield minimum cost and maximum production rate.

11.1 INTRODUCTION

The cost involved in carrying out a machining operation can be divided generally into the following groups:

(i) Non-productive cost
(ii) Metal removing cost
(iii) Tooling cost

These are governed by the choice of the machine for the processing.
New machine tools are purchased for specific reasons which may include one or more of the following:

(i) Equipment for a new factory or project.
(ii) Expansion of existing plant for greater output or for a new product.
(iii) Replacement of worn-out or low productivity machines.
(iv) Introduction of new methods to overcome production problems.
(v) The need to improve efficiency and reduce costs.
(vi) To reduce labour.
(vii) To improve quality.

In general it is important that the type of machine tool which is eventually purchased should be the most suitable one for the particular application. CNC machine tools are now one of the important contenders in this process of machine selection. At present, the population of CNC machines in India is significant. The users are now aware of the productivity and quality aspects of the CNC machines. The capital cost of CNC machines is reasonable and CNC machines are now affordable. There is adequate experience and understanding of these machines by the users. Another important reason for the popularity of CNC machines is that operators' skill is no longer the deciding factor in the quality of the component produced or the productivity.

With manufacturing costs continually rising, the economic necessity for cost reduction programmes and the necessity to achieve increased utilization require the correct selection of machines. CNC machine is to be used where it is more economical i.e. to machine complex parts in small batches fast and accurately. The selection of parts to be assigned to CNC operation has a large effect on its pay-off.

11.2 FACTORS INFLUENCING SELECTION OF CNC MACHINES

11.2.1 Labour Skill and Labour Cost

Conventional machines usually need skilled operators. Training and retaining skilled operators are expensive unless the company has the training facility either in the organization or in the nearby training institutions. Labour costs in CNC machines are minimized because of fast machining cycle and employment of operators with practically no machining skill.

11.2.2 Small Batches

If a variety of parts are produced in small batch sizes, the long set-up times and the resultant low utilization of conventional machines will prove to be exceptionally costly. Usually the savings in setup time using presetting technique and tool offsets in CNC machines will outweigh the higher operating costs of CNC compared to conventional equipment. It must be mentioned that CNC machines are being economically used in some large volume production situations also.

11.2.3 Repetition

Repetition of batches on CNC machines is not time consuming, since time required for fixing and clamping the component is less compared to that on conventional machines. Part programs are usually stored in the memory of the CNC system and can be retrieved as and when required. Besides, tools on CNC machines are set on presetting devices and this is an additional time saving factor. There is no need to store bulky and costly jigs and fixtures which are necessary in the case of conventional machines. The saving in tooling has been found to be very substantial in aeronautical and automobile industries.

11.2.4 Complexity

Components of complex configuration, requiring the following attributes, are economically manufactured on CNC machines:

(i) Close tolerances,

(ii) High surface finishes,

(iii) Close inter-related dimensions that are difficult to be machined on conventional machines.

(iv) Components with double curvature surfaces or free-form surfaces.

CNC machines with multi-axis process capability and with continuous speed changing devices enable them to machine any difficult configuration with a very high degree of accuracy.

11.2.5 Large Number of Operations

In the case of components involving large number of complicated and tedious operations, CNC system enables the data in the program to be utilized repeatedly when once the part is satisfactorily programmed and tried out. However, with the conventional machines the complexity continues to be the same for each operation and each component.

11.2.6 Time Lags Between Operations

If a component has got different operations to be carried out on several machines, after each operation it has to wait in the queue for getting the next operation started on the next work centre. The more the number of operations, the more is the time loss due to waiting which contributes to:

(i) High throughput time

(ii) High work-in-progress inventory and

(iii) Large shop area occupation resulting in higher production cost.

CNC machines require less storage space as work-in-progress is less. Since one CNC machine can replace several conventional machines, floor space is further reduced. This can be of considerable importance where the availability of floor space is a major problem.

11.2.7 Ratio of Cutting Time to Non- Cutting Time

The ratio of cutting time to non-cutting time is high in the case of CNC machine. This is one of the important factors where a CNC machine can make a great impact in reducing the machining cost. Generally floor-to-floor time comprises:

(i) Loading and unloading time

(ii) Cutting time and

(iii) Manipulation time

(i) Loading and unloading time: This depends on the lifting and locating the component on machine table and clamping the workpiece in fixture.

(ii) Cutting time: This is the period during which the tool is actually cutting the material. There is not much of a difference between CNC machining time and conventional machining time, since the cutting parameters of the material are almost the same in both the cases. However, since cutting speeds are high, cutting time in CNC is definitely less.

(iii) Manipulation time: This is the period during which non-cutting operations are performed. This includes the times for changing spindle speeds, changing feeds, positioning of slides and in-process inspection. All the movements here are non-productive and still occupy major portion of machining cycles. The available time is most effectively used on CNC machines for productive purpose which otherwise would have been wasted in manipulation of slides etc. The facility for automatic change of speeds and feeds and positioning of slides definitely results in considerable saving of time. There is also practically no need for frequent inspection.

11.2.8 Spare Parts Requirements

CNC machine may be used to provide spare part capability without the actual storage parts or bulky and costly jigs, fixtures and tools even after the product is no longer marketed. Once the part program is stored, on any medium, the part can be produced at any required time conveniently.

11.2.9 Variety

A wide variety of parts dictates frequent changes in the machine set up and requires large tool inventory if machined on conventional machines. Since a CNC machine normally uses standard tools and since it does not usually require jigs and complex fixtures, tool inventory is much less. Set up time on CNC machine is short and changeover is faster.

11.2.10 Sudden Priorities

Sometimes, due to unforeseen circumstances or sudden priorities rush orders for some components will have to be executed. Since the set up time and the machining cycle of CNC machines are small it can be readily used to tide over emergency situations.

11.2.11 Design Change

When design of components undergoes changes normally the costlier jigs and fixtures will have to either undergo modification or in certain cases new jigs are to be designed and fabricated. Since design changes can be incorporated in the part program with relative ease they will hardly have any effect on the production cost involving CNC machines.

11.2.12 Non-Uniform Cutting Conditions

Cutting conditions are non-uniform in the case of facing a large diameter or in the case of profiling a radius or in the case of turning a taper. Here the diameter of workpiece is continually changing and in order to maintain optimum surface speed, the spindle speed should necessarily be continually changing in the correct relationship. Otherwise surface finish will not be uniform and the tool life will be far below optimum. CNC machines provide this continuous changing of spindle speeds even when the tool is in engagement with the work.

11.2.13 Cost of Scrap

A component made out of scarcely available material as in aerospace or defense applications or out of heavy casting or requiring large number of complex operations if scrapped at any stage will turn out to be very costly.
In order to ensure that such a component comes through all the operations successfully, the CNC machines will have the following facilities:

(i) The program can be proved by dry run on the machine or by the tool path simulation, and tool path plotting. The CRT of the CNC system can display the finished component in 11-D with the help of powerful graphic facilities. The program can also be verified before loading in the machine in a CAD/CAM environment.

(ii) Cutting parameters are planned and set by an experienced engineer.

(iii) The CNC machine has built-in process capability of machining to very close tolerances.

11.2.14 Tooling

Normally the CNC machine requires more or less the same cutting tools that are used on conventional machines. Jigs are eliminated here. Number of fixtures are eliminated (or) reduced. Modular tooling can be used to reduce fixture inventory. It can thus be seen that in the long run the tooling requirements and cost is considerably less for CNC machines.

11.2.15 Cost of Set Up of Tools

Set-up time and cost are much less in CNC machine because the cutting tools are preset on a presetting device and whatever be the time required, it does not constitute a part of CNC machine time. The turrets with preset cutting tools are positioned on the turret slide and clamped within a few seconds.

11.2.16 Inspection Time and Cost

Certain components may have:

(a) Too many dimensions to be checked,

(b) Close toleranced dimensions,

(c) Close inter-relationship between dimensions.

In such case, the time required for inspecting dimensions by conventional methods is considerable. Besides, because of close tolerances, highly sophisticated inspection equipment may be required due to which inspection costs will be prohibitively high. If the component is machined on a CNC machine, inspection needs be carried out only at random. Also the component can be inspected on the CNC machine itself. Many CNC machines incorporate facilities for in-process and post-process metrology.

11.3 COST OF OPERATION OF CNC MACHINES

It is often necessary to calculate the cost for producing a component in varying batch sizes by different production methods. These costs are compiled by assessing:

(i) Setting up cost,

(ii) Floor-to floor machining time.

From this information the cost for each component can be calculated for different batch sizes. If this calculation is performed both for the existing method and for a CNC machine, then the savings or the losses that result from using different methods can be established.

In order to arrive at realistic cost figures, it is necessary to assess machines with different capital investments. Most companies have these data as standard figures for costing purposes. Account must be taken of the relevant costs for each machine including capital value, asset value, floor area occupied, capacity usage (in hours) and the annual charges such as interest, depreciation, insurance, lighting and power consumed, tools, repairs, overheads, labour cost etc.

The factors involved in economics of CNC machine tools are:

(i) Increased plant flexibility.

(ii) Introduction of computer techniques in plant operations.

(iii) Reduced lead time.

It should be remembered that CNC will progressively become more economical as labour costs continue to increase while CNC specific costs such as control equipment prices and programming costs go down. CNC machine utilization is improved if tool changes are few. Preset tooling not only cuts idle time, but also lowers tooling storage costs. Multiple use of the same tool is therefore, a significant factor. Another aspect is the elimination of manual checking and workpiece gauging by the operator. The higher the cost of the workpiece, the slower is those operations in conventional working. The factors mentioned above should be taken into account along with the guidelines indicated below:

The total manufacturing cost can be subdivided into 11 major headings as:

(a) Cost of preparing for production.

(b) Production costs (machine hour rate × machining time)

(c) Other related costs.

11.3.1 Cost of Preparing for Production

Before production is begun, preparatory activities have to take place. The extent of these will depend on the magnitude or complexity of the job under consideration.

$$\text{Cost} = \text{Time taken} \times \text{cost/hour}.$$

In assessing the cost of preparatory activities, a proportionate share of the cost of supervision, services, e.g., programmers etc. must be allowed for.

It can be seen that the costs of: (i) Planning, (ii) Programming and (iii) Fixtures will play an important role in this regard.

Programming may need computer facilities. In this case the cost of computer time must be included. The rate per hour for the use of a computer depends on its type and size, but is generally low if CAD/CAM methods are adopted.

11.3.2 Related Costs

The costs under this category occur once every batch e.g., setting time for a machine tool. They are repeated each time a batch passes through the production shops and must be allocated to each component according to the number of components per batch.

11.3.3 Production Costs

Each component must bear the cost of its own machining and this cost is normally based on the production time and the machine hour rate.

$$\text{Machining cost} = \text{Floor-to-floor time} \times \text{machine hour rate}.$$

The machine hour rate includes the costs of all items related to machining. In the interests of accuracy when computing hourly rates, the costs of some items can be isolated and calculated separately. The items which need to be separated in this exercise would be those in which some noticeable difference between costs incurred in CNC and conventional machining would be apparent.

The cost of running a machine tool for one hour is the machine hour rate. The machine tool is the main productive unit on which the output of a factory depends and all the costs of running a productive organization must be recovered in the price at which the product is sold. To achieve this, the costs of the organization are allocated proportionately to the working hours of productive units. This situation requires estimation of the costs of all the services and the fair spreading of these costs over the output of the organization. Some of the services are direct and can be easily related to a particular machine tool. e.g., electricity consumed by the machine. Others are less easily related to particular productive units e.g., the running costs of a purchasing department. The expense of such indirect activities must be spread as equitably as possible over the output. The additional cost which are added to the cost of operating the machine are termed the overheads and must include the following items

(a) Machine depreciation

(b) Allowance for obsolescence

(c) Cost of power consumed by the machine

(d) Machine maintenance cost

(e) Office costs

The calculation of man hour rate is important to estimate the cost of machining. A simple example is given below:

***Example*:**

A job shop purchases a CNC lathe for Rs. 30 Lakhs. The capital was borrowed from a financial institution at an interest of 15% per year. The depreciation is spread over five years.

The cost is calculated as follows:

Cost towards depreciation:	30/5	= Rs. 6.0 Lakhs
Interest per year:		= Rs. 4.5 Lakhs
Cost of operator per year @Rs.1.2 Lakhs/year		
For 2 shift operation		= Rs. 2.4 Lakhs
Cost of programmer/Maintenance person		= Rs. 1.2 Lakhs
Electricity Charges		= Rs. 2.0 Lakhs
Tooling costs		= Rs. 2.1 Lakhs
Total Cost		= Rs.18.2 Lakhs
Assuming 2-shift operation (400 hours/month)		
Cost per hour (approx)		= Rs. 380

11.3.4 Calculation of Cost of Machining

Assume that the machine hour cost of a machining centre is Rs. 800. Given the following costs, calculate the cost of machining:

Machining time per component:	105 min.
Setting up time/component:	15 min.
Total time to produce a component:	120 min. i.e. 2 hours
Machining cost:	800 × 2 = Rs. 1600.

Often, it may be necessary to reduce the cost of machining. This means that the machining time should be reduced. This is best achieved by:

- The use of better tools to increase cutting speed, feed and or depth of cut
- Better process planning
- Machining more components in one set up.
- Use of combination tools
- Reducing idle times

11.4 PRACTICAL ASPECTS OF INTRODUCTION OF CNC

Practical aspects to be considered during introduction of CNC are:

(a) Aspects of control of temperature, humidity and dust:

It is essential that the CNC machine is kept in controlled atmosphere.

(b) Line voltage and frequency fluctuations:

It is important that a voltage stabilizer is installed to safeguard the costly control system and other related equipments, from damage due to fluctuation in electric supply.

(c) Other Aspects to be considered are:

(i) Selection of proper site for machine

(ii) Preparation of foundation

(iii) Provision of services like coolant, current, computer cables, chip disposal, tool and fixture storage etc.,

(iv) Material handling facility

(v) Selection of personnel for machine operation, fixture design, part programming and maintenance.

(vi) Training of personnel

(vii) Design/selection of tools and fixtures

(viii) Preparation for machine installation

(ix) Acceptance tests

(x) Production planning

Finally it is necessary to investigate the return on investment. This can be found out by calculating the cost saving in a year for a particular batch size for one or more components. If the exercise is carried out for a representative range of components, the savings for a fair cross section of typical work will be available and it would be reasonable to suggest that an average of these figures would be representative of the savings that are likely on components produced during a twelve month period.

In short, cost, reductions are affected in three ways:

(i) Less handling between work stations as fewer operations will be required.

(ii) Less handling on the machine because more than one face of the component can be machined at one setting.

(iii) Less handling of finished goods as the result of reduced inspection and fitting requirement.

11.5 TRAINING FOR CNC OPERATION

In order to fully utilize the CNC machines which require heavy investments, properly trained personnel are required.

The training required may be broadly put under three levels:

(i) Operator level

(ii) Programmer level

(iii) Maintenance level

11.5.1 Operator Training

The role of operator is to actually work on the machines. For this the operator must have familiarity with the type of machine with which he is supposed to work. He must also know the capabilities, the limitations and various safety precautions to be taken while operating the machine. Though the above knowledge is not essential, it can have a bearing on output.

The operator is required to be trained in the following areas:

(a) **Training at Console:** The operator must be trained to use the various controls and switches at the console of a particular machine. He must know the correct way of fixing the job and he must be trained as how to enter the Program and how to check whether the program is correct before actually running the machine.

He/she must also know the safe operating range of various parameters such as the hydraulic pressure, the main motor current etc. The operator must know the reference procedure adopted for the particular machine.

(b) **Tools and Tool Coding:** The operator must be trained regarding the different tools that can be used on the machine. He must know the code that has been used in the program for different tools. The different tools that are required for a particular job for which the program has been supplied and the position where each tool has been mounted must be known by the operator. The tool must be changed when its life is over.

(c) **Machine Operation:** The operation of a particular CNC machine is an important concern. The operator is required to know how to start the machine and also, if any pre-start checks are necessary, he must do all these before starting the machine.

The operator must get familiar with various controls of the machine, the various modes of operation, the use of emergency controls and the procedure for switching-off the machine. He must immediately record and report if he finds any abnormality in the functioning of the machine so that the maintenance people can fine out the fault and rectify it.

(d) **Programme Editing:** Usually the operators will be required to use only the correct programs. The program editing at the console will be a costly affair. If there are only simple errors then the operator must know how to correct those errors. In these situations he must know how to edit the program and to make corrections. The operator must run the program in dry run mode and make sure that the program is corrections. The operator must run the program in dry run mode and make sure that the program is correct. He may also have to change offsets to compensate tool wear where automatic correction facilities are not available on the machine.

(e) **House Keeping and Preventive Maintenance:** The operator must be trained to maintain the machine in good condition. Machines should be cleaned at the end of every shift and all the exposed ways should be cleaned thoroughly. The chip tray should be cleaned of coolant and swarf. The operator should be made aware of total preventive maintenance. Training should be given in periodic maintenance, oil and coolant change schedules etc.

11.6 TRAINING OF PROGRAMMERS

Skilled part-programmers are a vital requirement for effective utilization of CNC machine tools. The operational efficiency of these machines and the financial pay-back of the significant investment in these machines themselves, the plants, CNC support facilities and the over-head costs involved depend to a large extent on the programmers.

The principal qualifications for manual programmers are as follows:

(i) **Manufacturing experience:** Programmers must have a thorough understanding of the capabilities of the CNC machines being programmed as well as understanding of the basic capabilities of the other machines in the shop. They must have an extensive knowledge of metal cutting principles and practices, cutting capabilities of the tools, and work holding fixtures and techniques.

(ii) Spatial Visualization: Programmers must be able to visualize the parts in three dimensions, the cutting motions of the machine and possibility of interference between the cutting tool, workpiece, fixture of the machine itself.

(iii) Mathematics: A working knowledge of arithmetic, algebra, trigonometry and geometric operations is extremely important as many of today's CNC systems permit direct programming using these operations. Knowledge of higher mathematics, such as advanced algebra, calculus etc. is not normally required.

(iv) Attention to details: It is essential that programmers be accurately observant and meticulously accurate individuals. Programming errors discovered during machine setup can be very expensive and time-consuming to correct.

(v) Desirable Qualities: Programmers must be able to work effectively with other people. In some instances, another person may be required to check the programs if verification facilities are not available.

Manual programming requires the programmer to have more detailed knowledge of the machine and control, machining practices, and methods of computation whereas computer aided programming relies on considerable built in knowledge base and database.

Computer-aided programming, on the other hand, requires knowledge of the computer programming language and the computer system in order to process that language. In general, manual programming is more tedious and demanding because of the detail involved. In a computer-aided programming system, this detail knowledge is embedded in the computer system (Processor, post processor etc,).

REVIEW QUESTIONS

(1) What are the factors influencing the selection of CNC machines?

(2) How do you justify the purchase of CNC machines?

(3) How is non-cutting times reduced in CNC machines?

(4) A CNC lathe costs ₹ 26 lakhs. It is to be operated for 2 shifts a day. The depreciation period is four years. The connected power is 40kW. Two operators at monthly salary of ₹ 2500/- each and a programmer at a monthly salary of ₹ 11800/- are employed to operate the machine. The tooling cost is estimated at ₹ 1.25 lakhs per year. The interest charges are calculated at 12.5% per annum. Calculate the machine hour rate.

(5) Discuss how you will reduce machining time if a need arises.

(6) Discuss various methods of reducing idle times in CNC operation.

(7) Select a component and compare the economics of manufacture of the component using a CNC machine and a conventional machine.

(8) Discuss the importance of proper training of operators and programmers in the efficient operation of a CNC shop.

(9) What are the aspects one should look into the training of operators and programmers?

12 EFFECTIVE UTILISATION OF CNC MACHINE TOOLS

The unit cost of CNC machine tools is very high. The faster rates of obsolescence make the depreciation costs also high. In order to make the return from investment as maximum as possible, the CNC machine tools must be operated at the maximum level of utilization.

12.1 INTRODUCTION

This chapter deals with some recommendations, issues and the guidelines, which can be used to improve the effective utilization of CNC machines and their related resources. These are versatile enough to be used in all types of CNC machines, individually or in a group. This chapter also introduces indices of production, availability and utilization and establishes a consistent method for the utilization of the CNC resources. The contents of this chapter are selected to help the users of CNC machines to eliminate deficiencies in planning the utilization and to improve the efficiency of production.

12.2 TOOLING RELATED ISSUES

The efficiency in manufacturing depends to a large extent on the tooling, which consists of the following:

(i) Tools

(ii) Fixtures

Chapter 5 has dealt with cutting tools in detail. The manufacturers of special CNC machines like EDM, wire EDM, turret punch press etc often give guidelines on the choice of tools. Since proper selection of tools and operating parameters have significant effect on improving productivity and hence reducing the cost of production this aspect requires careful consideration of process planners in the process definition stage.

12.3 FIXTURES FOR MACHINING CENTRES

Good fixturing is very important to obtain consistently accurate parts. In CNC machine tool operation fixtures play a vital role. Fixture design and manufacture is an essential part of the planning stage for manufacture using CNC machines. When large lot size is to be machined custom-built fixtures can be used. The lead-time and expense required to build such fixtures are difficult to justify when production runs are small and do not repeat on a regular basis.

General purpose work holders such as vises, chucks, and table-mounted clamps are handy for production at short notice; but they are suitable only for small lots of simple parts. Alternative is modular fixturing.

Modular fixtures can be assembled entirely from reusable off- the- shelf components without machining. Many modular components are adjustable and universal. Specially designed tooling plates and blocks with standard grid patterns are the foundation of a good modular system. Modular elements include locating elements, various types of clamps etc.

Modular fixtures are an ideal solution for work holding problems in CNC machines. A modular fixturing system consists of several elements. The desired configuration of the fixture can be built by assembling the individual elements. Once the use is over the fixture can be dismantled and the components can be used for assembling another fixture. When needed, the fixture can be re-built for use in future. Modular fixtures basically consist of the following elements:

Mounting bases

Supporting and locating elements

Clamping elements

12.3.1 Mounting Bases

Mounting bases can be broadly classified into two:

(i) Tooling plates

(ii) Tooling blocks

Tooling plates are basically meant for vertical machining centers. These are available in square, rectangular, round and platform styles. Each plate has a certain number of holes using which they can be accurately mounted on the machine table with the help of locating keys. These are shown in Fig. 12.1. Round tooling plates are particularly suited for indexing tables. Tooling blocks are used mainly in horizontal machining centers. They are either two-sided or 4-sided blocks. Usually one component is mounted on each face. This enables two or four components to be machined in each set up depending on the type. If the components are small, more than one component can be mounted on one face. Figure 12.2 shows tooling blocks.

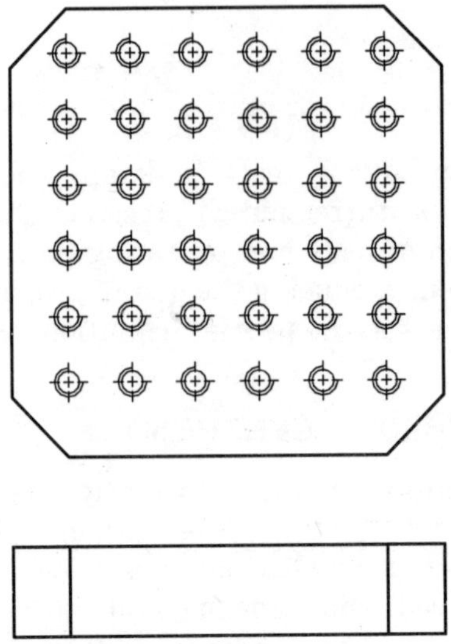

Fig. 12.1 Tooling Plates

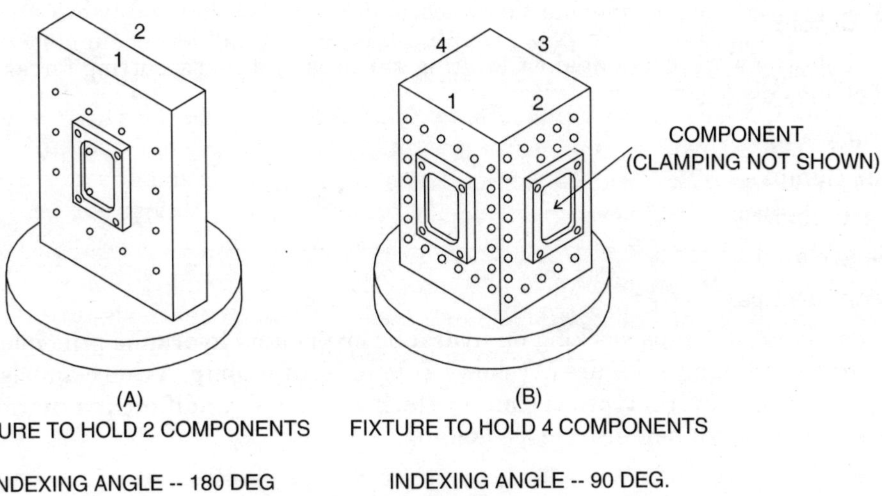

Fig. 12.2 Tooling Blocks

12.3.2 Locating Devices

Main purpose of locating devices is that the workpieces are held on the machine table in the same position in a foolproof manner. The choice of locating method depends on the shape of the workpiece and the type of surface to be located. A workpiece is to be constrained in three mutually perpendicular planes. The locating devices include:

Locating pins and buttons
Adjustable pins and locators
Edge locators
Stops

Locating Pins and buttons are used to support or position the workpieces. Pins are used in horizontal position whereas buttons are used in the vertical position. Adjustable pins and locators are suitable for irregular surfaces. They may be screw type or spring type. Edge locators are used to establish the reference edges on the machine table and are used to locate workpieces. Stops are of two types-fixed type and spring type. They are also used to locate the workpieces. Typical locators are shown in Fig. 12.3.

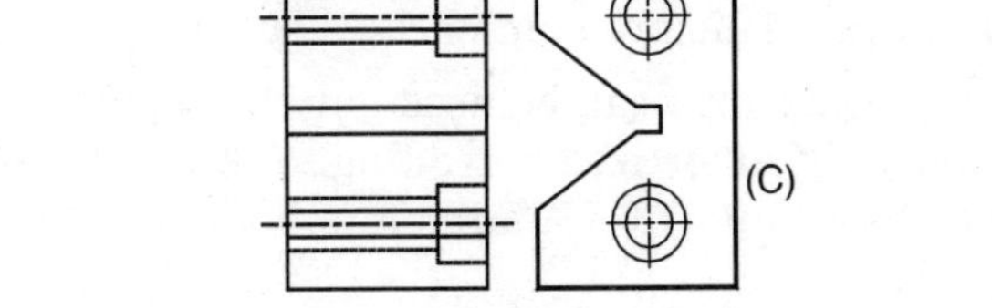

Fig. 12.3 Typical Locators

12.3.3 Clamps

Clamps hold the workpieces against locating surfaces and resist cutting forces. The common type of clamps used is:

Strap clamps

Cam clamps

Toggle clamps

Swing clamp

Wedge clamps

Power clamps (clamps working on hydraulic or pneumo-hydraulic principle). Figure 12.4 shows two typical clamps. Figure (A) shows a simple strap clamp. A cam clamp is illustrated in Fig. (B). There are several types of clamps which are suited for different situations. Clamping methods include down holding or edge holding.

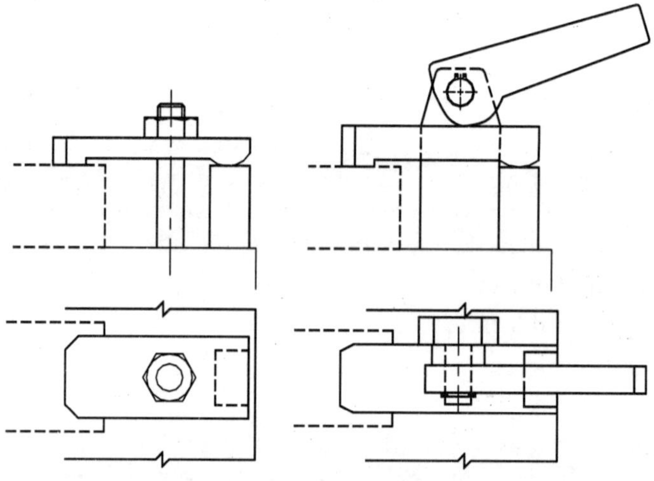

(A) (B)

Fig. 12.4 Typical Clamps

12.3.4 Modular Fixturing

Nowadays it is common practice to use modular fixturing. Fixtures are designed using standard off the shelf components. Since CAD files for these components are readily available, the design involves only drag and drop on the drawing screen. Design hence is very fast. Since the components are readily available, quick fabrication/assembly of the fixture is possible. Once the production run is over, the fixtures can be dismantled and components could be used for another fixture.

The advantages of modular fixturing are summarized below:

(i) ***Economy:*** Custom built fixtures can be used only for a particular component. Hence the cost of the fixture has to be amortized by adding to the cost of parts produced. The cost of modular fixturing is distributed over a large number of components. Hence fixturing cost per component is less.

(ii) ***Lead time:*** Modular fixtures are built using off-the-shelf components and hence the lead-time of fixture production is very little. These are designed for easy assembly and the time required for assembly is small.

(iii) ***Fixture inventory:*** Custom built fixtures requires storing space for future use. Since modular fixtures can be dismantled after use storage space needed is much less.

(iv) ***Design:*** Design of fixtures using modular elements is fast and error-free. In most cases modular fixture kits are supplied with corresponding CAD files. Fixture design is then only an assembly of relevant CAD files. These are available in 2-D or 3-D.These can be directly used in many CAD packages. They are also available in neutral formats like DXF, IGES etc. Hence time taken for drafting a fixture is considerably reduced.

(v) ***Reuse capability:*** Modular elements can be reused any number of times.

(vi) ***Simplicity:*** Modular fixturing is simple compared to custom-built fixtures.

12.4 TWIN SPINDLE MACHINES

Many engineering components carried out in CNC lathes, like impellers, gear blanks, flanges, end covers etc require two operations (or two set ups) for complete machining. The usual practice is to take a batch of say 20 or 50 components in a lot and then set up a machine to carry out the first operation. Then change the tooling to carry out the second operation. This will involve changing the set tools in the turret, changing the corresponding tool offsets and parameters in the memory of the CNC system, removing the chucks and or chuck jaws to refit new chucks and or chuck jaws etc. The latter will involve checking concentricity of operation. Invariably such job changes in a machine will involve time delay, which could be avoided by several innovative means. Twin spindle concept is often employed to improve the productivity in such cases.

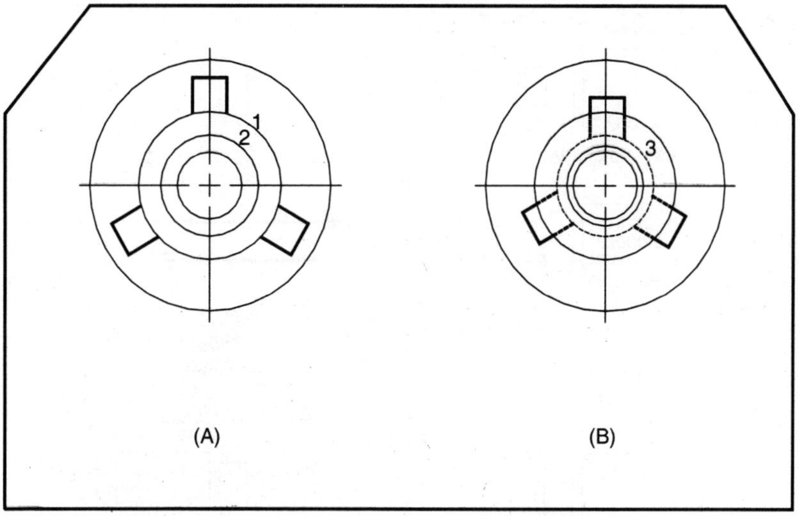

Fig. 12.5 Twin Spindle Machines

A two spindle machine, as the name implies, employs two work holding spindles- one spindle tooled up to carry out the first operation and the second spindle to carry out the second operation. These spindles are arranged parallel to each other in a horizontal position with front-loading or the spindles be positioned vertically. Usually a robot or a special work transfer mechanism is employed for transferring the component from one spindle to another.

The advantage of twin spindle machine is increased productivity. It is found that more than 100% productivity improvement can be achieved by using twin spindle machines. Another advantage is that fully machined components are available for assembly as there is no need for the lot size to be completed in the first operation. The reduction in loading and unloading and tool setting also contributes to increased productivity.

12.5 TURNING MACHINES WITH SUB-SPINDLES

CNC lathes are designed with an addition of sub-spindle to improve productivity in end operations. Two arrangements are discussed in this section.

12.5.1 Machines With Sub-Spindle and One Turret

Figure 12.6 shows the arrangement. The spindle shown on the right is the sub-spindle. The first operation is carried out in the main spindle. At the end of the first operation the turret moves out of the way and the sub-spindle is moved to the left automatically. The jaws on the chuck clamps on to the finished part of the workpiece. It is to be noted that both the spindles are to be rotated synchronously to achieve shock-less transfer. The Main spindle then releases the workpiece and the sub-spindle moves to the right to the working position. The turret moves to the right and the operations in the second set up is carried out.

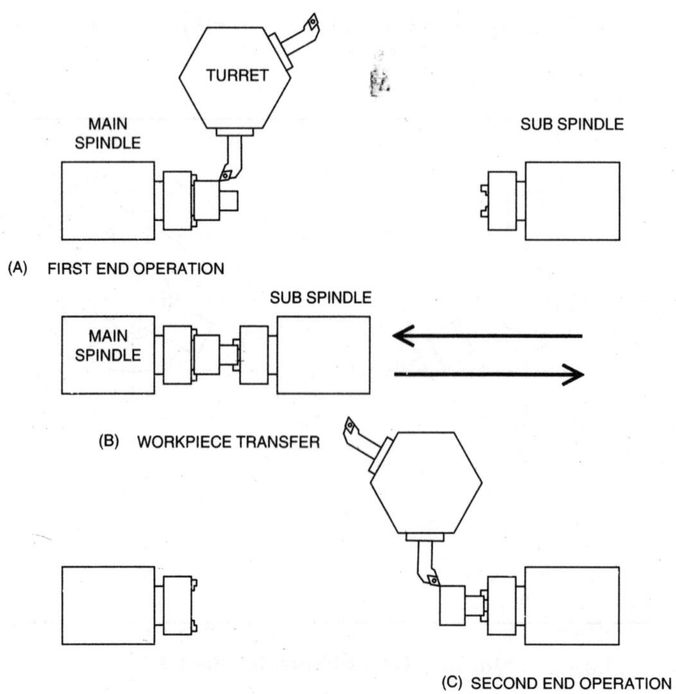

Fig. 12.6 Machine with One Sub-spindle

12.5.2 Machines With Sub-Spindle and Two Turrets

Another variation of the concept discussed above involves two turrets. Here the sub-spindle is fixed and the workpiece transfer is carried out using the turrets. Each turret has a station dedicated to a device to enable work transfer. The procedure is as follows:

As in the previous case the first end operation is carried out with the workpiece mounted in the main spindle. After the first operation in the main spindle is over, turret 1 picks up the workpiece and then indexes through 180 degrees to transfer it to the second turret. The latter indexes through 180 degrees and then moves to the sub-spindle to transfer the workpiece to the spindle. The second operation is then carried out. This arrangement permits almost simultaneous first and second operation resulting in increased productivity. Figure shows the sequence of operations.

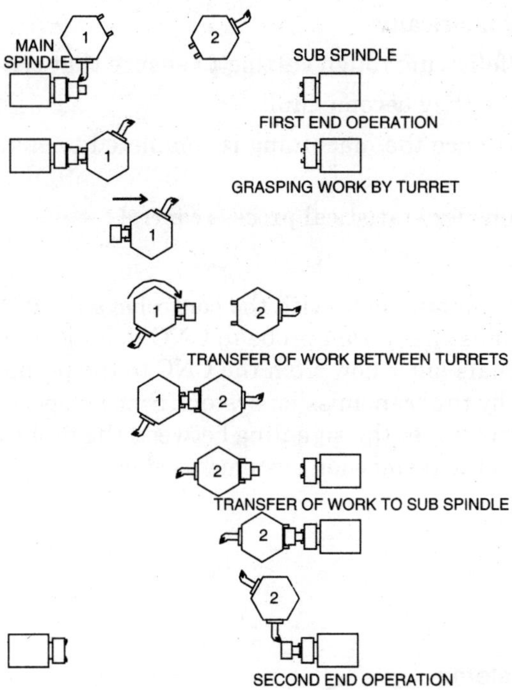

Fig. 12.7 Two Spindles and Two Turrets

12.6 IN-PROCESS METROLOGY

In spite of the built in accuracy and many other features of CNC machines it is likely that there will be deviations in the accuracy of workpieces due to a variety of causes. These causes include tool wear, variability in the mechanical properties of materials, temperature variations, variation in the machining allowance etc. Tool wear is one important reason for variation in the accuracy of parts, the effect of which could be controlled by altering the value of tool offset. This requires frequent measurement of the workpiece. Off-line measurement and manual input of parameters result in wastage of production time. Hence built-in arrangements to gauge the workpieces and comparison with programmed data to calculate the magnitude of the offsets are desirable. This is called in-process metrology.

The probe is mounted on the turret in the case of a CNC lathe or in the tool magazine in the case of the machining center. In the case of grinders the probe can be mounted separately.

Component Setting

The probe identifies the position of the workpiece, automatically updating the work offsets, enabling the parts to be manufactured first time right every time. This can also be used for the following purposes:

- Part identification for FMS systems
- Component location and detection of wrong loading to avoid scrap
- Excess material identification to bring the cutter to the component fast and safely
- In the case of first component inspection in a batch, the idle time involved in waiting for feed back from off-line inspection can be avoided
- Correcting errors automatically
- Measure component following rough cutting to ensure that critical final cuts are correct
- Highlight errors before they become faults
- Inspection of the part once the machining is completed to ensure that the component is within specifications
- Record part dimensions for statistical process control

Transmission Selection

The probe must be able to communicate with the control system (CNC) of the machine tool to which it is fitted. Signals must pass from probe to CNC to indicate the contact of the probe to work or tool. Similarly signals must flow from the CNC to the probe to control its functioning. The signal flow is effected by the transmission system. Since inspection probes are fitted in the tool carousel or on a rotating turret the signaling between the probe and CNC must be remote. There are four main types of transmission systems used between probe and CNC.

- Optical
- Radio
- Inductive
- Direct or hard-wired

Optical Transmission Systems

An optical transmission system uses infrared technology as a means of signal transmission between the probe and the CNC machine. The probe module receives the control signal and transmits the probe status signals. The optical machine module communicates the signals between the control and the probe unit. The machine interface unit converts the probe signal into a form compatible with the controller. Figure 12.8 illustrates the optical transmission system.

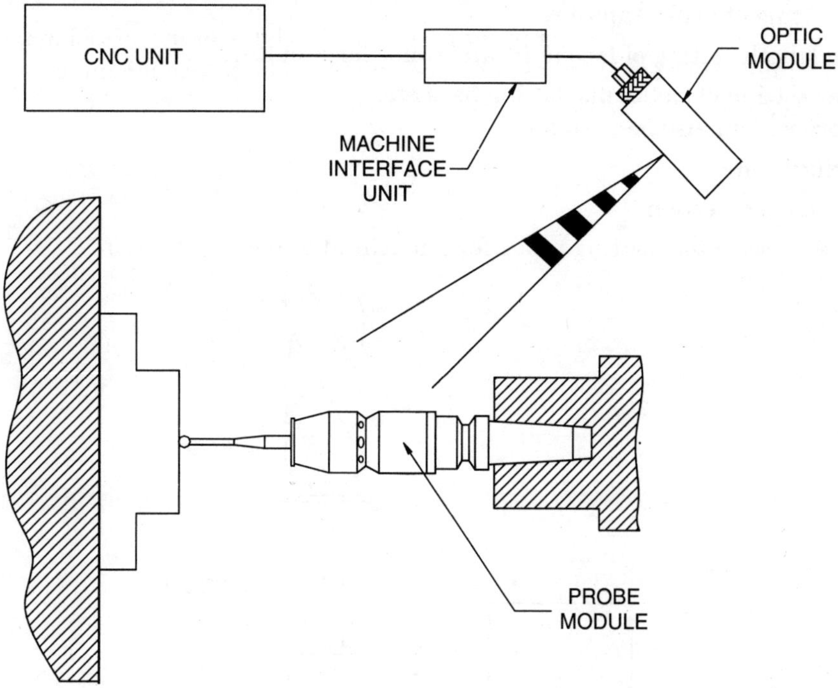

Fig. 12.8 Optical Transmission Systems

Radio Transmission Systems

A radio transmission system provides a long range (up to 15 m) and is non-line of sight means of communication between the probe and the CNC controller. These are suitable for large machining centers and lathes with more than 3 m axis travel.

Inductive Transmission Systems

This method works by passing both power and probe signals across a small air gap between two induction modules. These are suitable for large CNC machines.

Hard-wired System

In this case a signal cable connects the probe and the machine interface unit. This is the simplest arrangement. This is ideal for the following applications:

- Tool setting on machining centers and lathes where the probe remains fixed in one location.
- Inspection on machining centers where the probe is manually placed on the machine spindle.

12.7 TOOLING

Tooling is an area which requires close attention to improve the utilization of CNC machines. The various aspects of tooling are discussed in the subsequent sections.

12.7.1 Tool Setting

A tool setting system automatically determines the tool offset and sends the tool length offset information automatically to the CNC system. Tools are driven against the probe stylus with the tool either stationary or rotating. This is used for:

- Length setting of drills, taps etc.
- Rotating length setting of face mills and other large cutters
- Diameter setting of slot drills, boring bars etc.

Tool setting probes can also be used for:

- Tool verification
- Tool breakage detection

Figure12.9 shows a tool setting probe for a machining center operation

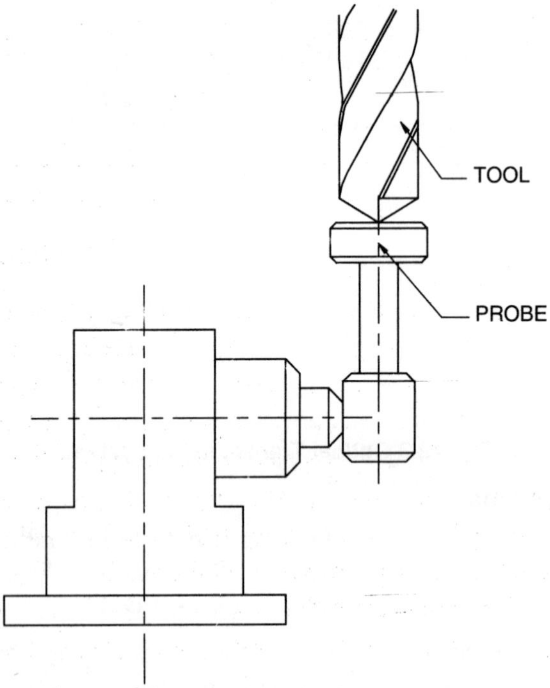

Fig. 12.9 Tool Setting Probe

12.7.2 Tips for Improving Tooling Efficiency

There are several aspects of tooling which are to be considered to improve productivity. Some useful points are discussed in this section. Since the cost of CNC machine is high, right tools will help to reduce not only machining time, but also non cutting time.

(i) First and foremost, the process planner should be knowledgeable about the right tool for a particular operation. With newer and more efficient tools being introduced by tool manufacturers periodically, it is always desirable to consult the tool suppliers before making a choice of tools. This will help in many ways:
  - Reduce tool cost
  - Use of faster cutting conditions
  - Increased productivity
  - Improved quality of parts produced

(ii) Tools should be care fully mounted in tool pockets. In the case of rotating tools there should not be run out. External turning tools should be set slightly above the center height and boring tools slightly below the center height to avoid scoring when the tool is retracted after a cut.

(iii) Chucks and chuck jaws should be checked for run out after remounting. If possible, remounting should be avoided. In the case of first and second operation where the work is to be located on two different diameters, the soft jaw can be designed with two steps- one step for each diameter.

(iv) Careful consideration to be given to the weight and length of tools in machining centers.

(v) In the case of lathes, axial tools should not be located in adjacent pockets.

(vi) Tools should be preferably placed in the same location regardless of workpiece. For example, always place roughing tool in the same pocket, say #1 pocket.

(vii) When certain tool is used to cut for more time, vacant pockets, if available can be used to have an extra tool. This will reduce the number of stoppages to change the tool/index the insert.

12.8 IMPROVING PRODUCTIVITY

Improving the productivity is one of the continuous requirements in manufacturing. This aspect is all the more important in manufacturing using CNC machines. Some tips are given in this section to improve productivity.

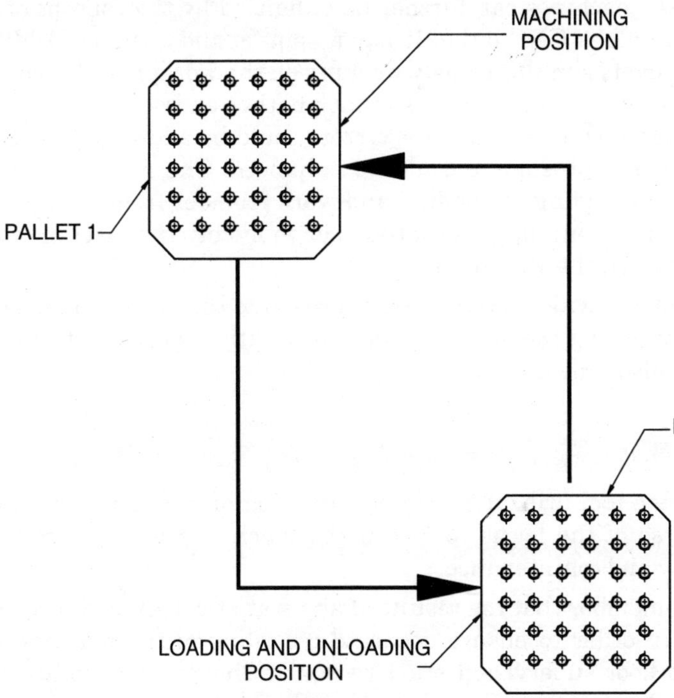

Fig. 12.10 Pallet Changer

(i) Use automatic pallet changers in machining centers. A pallet changer (Fig. 12.9) will help the operator to set up a new workpiece while machining is performed on another. The idle time for changing the workpiece will only be the time for pallet change.

(ii) It is not necessary to employ an operator for every CNC machine. A cluster of machines can be looked after by a single operator.

(iii) Where there are several CNC machines, a DNC program management system will be of advantage.

(iv) In the case of small workpieces to be processed on machining centres, many can be mounted on the table at the same time. Same program with change in work coordinates can be used. This will reduce frequent stoppages for loading and unloading of workpiece. Use modular fixtures and automatically actuated fixture. Even in modular fixtures like tower blocks, more workpieces can be set up if they are small.

(v) Use program simulation and verification before the first piece.

(vi) Analyze each and every element of the process to reduce time.

(vii) Use combination tools wherever possible.

(viii) Use maximum power available in the machine for roughing operations.

(ix) Use constant surface speed option when turning varying diameters.

(x) Use coated carbides and ceramic tools in preference to uncoated carbides or HSS tools.

(xi) Always carry out a cost analysis before finalizing the process and tools.

12.9 RECONFIGURABLE MACHINES

The productivity of CNC machines can further be enhanced by the concept of reconfigurable machines. Take for example, a CNC lathe. It has a spindle and a turret. Addition of another turret will enable two turrets simultaneously working on the workpiece. It is possible to attach one more spindle (sub-spindle) on the ways so that another end operation can be carried out on the same machine itself. One or two more turrets could be added so that the productivity of the operations using the sub-spindle could be enhanced. The machine can be fitted with work handling devices, for loading, unloading and work transfer from one spindle to another. The reconfigurable machine concept enables the user to modify the machine to maximize the productivity depending upon the workpiece.

The following sections provide a systematic approach to the logging of machine utilization data and a method of analyzing the data for proper evaluation. Form that can be used in data logging and analysis is also provided.

12.10 DATA LOGGING

To monitor CNC machine tool utilization, an accurate log of time for each machine must be maintained. The purpose of the log is to record the machine time in four basic categories: production, setup, delay and maintenance.

It is important to remember that the results of any statistical analysis are only as accurate as the data provided. In order to ensure accurate recording of the machine utilization log, management and shop floor supervision must recognize their responsibilities in motivating the staff assigned to the logging task. It is better that the immediate supervisor of the operator may be assigned to the task.

12.10.1 Logging Format

The machine utilization log is used to record start and stop times in the four categories (Production, set up, delay and maintenance). Any degree of details can be achieved depending on whether the log records only the four basic categories. Table 12.1 shows a typical machine utilization log.

Table 12.1 Machine Utilization Log

Machine: CNC Lathe 1

Date	TOTAL HOURS		LOGGED HOURS		TOTAL HOURS LOGGED
	SHIFT 1	SHIFT 2	SHIFT 1	SHIFT 2	
02.08.2011					
03.08.2011					
04.08.2011					
05.08.2011					
06.08.2011					

These four major categories can be used to calculate the utilization indices. It is possible that more than one of these operations may occur simultaneously. For example a malfunctioning shuttle mechanism awaiting repair but the machine remains employed in useful production. In this case the machine time should be logged as production rather than maintenance.

All scheduled times should be logged. All time during which machine is operated or being maintained must be logged, whether scheduled or not. For example maintenance performed after scheduled hours should not be logged.

The time intervals are calculated and entered in the machine utilization log. They are accumulated and total for each category on a monthly basis is calculated.

The percent of logged hours for each of four categories (Production, set up, delay and maintenance) may be useful for identifying problem areas. Also the indices may be calculated for any period of time desired. Also, the indices may be calculated for any period of time desired. Figure 12.10 shows the presentation of data in a bar chart.

It is now possible to acquire the data from the machine itself.

12.10.2 Utilization Indices

Two useful indices can be calculated from the logged data.

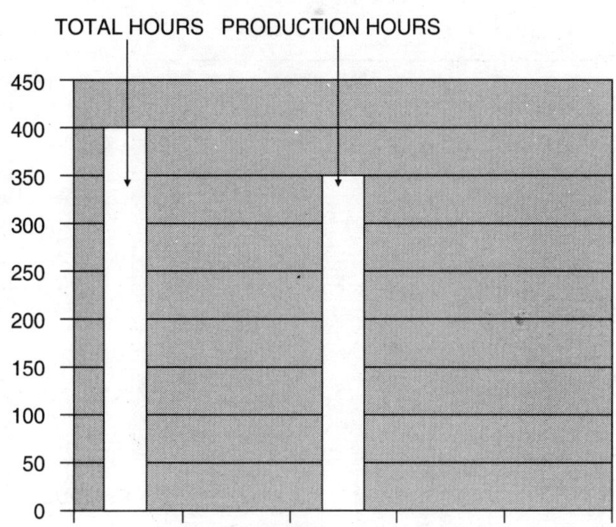

Fig. 12.11 Production Chart

12.10.2.1 Production Index

The production index (PI) is a measure of the effectiveness of the support functions and the reliability of the machine. A low production index indicates extensive set-up, delay or maintenance time:

$$\text{Production Index (PI)} = \frac{\text{Logged Production Hours}}{\text{Total logged Hours}} \times 100$$

12.10.2.2 Utilization Index

The utilization index (UI) is measure of capital equipment usage.

The production and set-up hours are both considered normal functions of machine operation and are added in computing the utilization index. This total is compared to the maximum possible number of hours that the machine could have been used.

$$\text{Utilization Index} = \frac{\text{Logged Production Hours + Logged Setup Hours}}{\text{Total Logged Hours}} \times 100$$

12.10.3 Utilization Charts

Data from the utilization log can be analyzed to determine significant reasons for inadequate utilization of CNC machine tools. Normally, a utilization of 85-90% is suggested. If the utilization falls below this level, the factors contributing to the reduction in utilization need to be identified. A part of the logged hours is utilized for setting up the workpiece and tools. Figure 12.12 shows the utilization of the machine tool for actual production. A detailed study of the process will help in improving the utilization index.

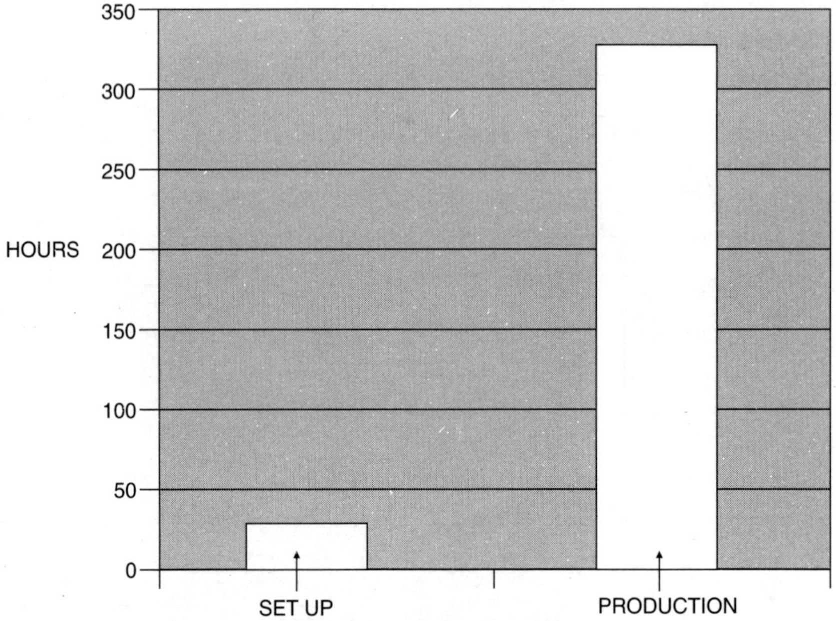

Fig. 12.12 Utilization Chart

12.11 HOW TO MAXIMIZE THE UTILIZATION OF CNC MACHINES

The utilization of CNC machines can be maximized by careful planning. The following factors should be given proper attention:

(i) Availability of jobs
(ii) Planning of programs, fixtures and tools and making them available on time
(iii) Proving the program through off line simulation
(iv) Training of workers on the machining through simulation
(v) Keeping the machine in good working condition by periodic maintenance
(vi) Use modular fixtures
(vii) Reduce set up time by using better fixtures or machining many workpieces in one set up
(viii) Good program management using DNC technique
(ix) Standardize cutting tools used, if possible

REVIEW QUESTIONS

(1) Describe different kinds of mounting blocks used with CNC Machines.
(2) Discuss how set up time per component can be reduced by mounting multiple components in a mounting block.
(3) Figure 12.13 shows two components. Discuss the location and clamping schemes.

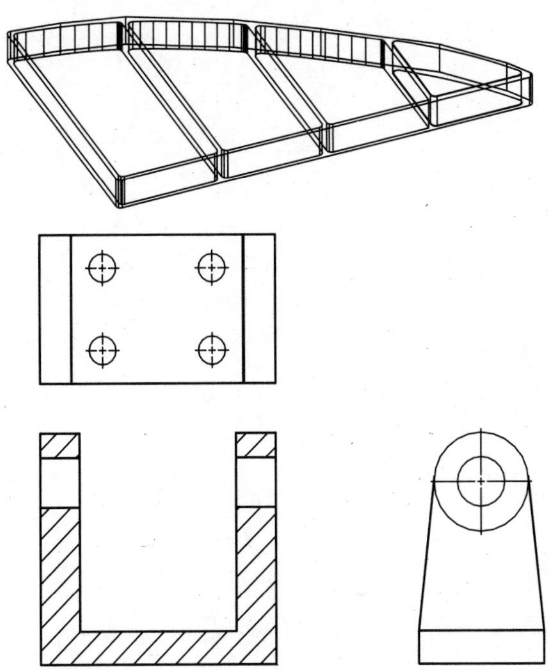

Fig. 12.13 Components

(4) Discuss the benefits of using modular fixture elements.

(5) Discuss a few examples of components which could be economically machined on twin spindle machines.

(6) How will the sub-spindle concept improve productivity?

(7) Compare the working of CNC turning machines with one sub-spindle and two turrets.

(8) What are the advantages of in-process metrology in CNC machining?

(9) Discuss the different approaches to in-process metrology.

(10) How will a tool setting probe improve productivity?

(11) Study the various factors affection the utilization of CNC machines and prepare a bar chart showing the non-production hours as a percentage of total available hours.

(12) Discuss the necessity for achieving a high percentage of utilization of CNC machine.

(13) Describe a typical machine utilization log and explain how the entries are to be made.

(14) Discuss how will a machine utilization log will help to improve effective utilization of a CNC machine.

13 MAINTENANCE OF CNC MACHINES

Proper maintenance of CNC Machines is very critical in ensuring as high availability index as possible. CNC Machines are complex equipment with several subsystems, many of which consist of several hundreds of parts. The break-down of CNC machines will not only upset the production schedule but also will result in huge losses as the machine hour rates of these machines are high. Modern CNC machines incorporate several technological features to facilitate speedy maintenance.

13.1 INTRODUCTION

CNC machines are designed and built to give superior performance when compared to conventional machine tools. Downtime of these machines should be kept to a minimum in order to realize the economic advantages of this technology in full. Repairing CNC Machines is time-consuming and costly considering the following factors:

(i) A substantial amount of spares are not indigenously available.

(ii) Delay in procuring spares.

(iii) Lack of adequate manpower to troubleshoot CNC systems, particularly when the systems are imported.

Breakdown maintenance, therefore, is less preferred than preventive maintenance.

13.2 PREVENTIVE MAINTENANCE

The main objectives of preventive maintenance of CNC machines are to:

(i) Maximize machine availability

(ii) Minimize downtime

(iii) Maintain positioning accuracy

(iv) Increase the service life of the machine.

Generally the manufacturer of the machines will give certain guidelines regarding preventive maintenance. The general emphasis of preventive maintenance is to reduce wear and eliminate malfunctions. Preventive maintenance programmes should include the following:

(i) **Daily schedule:** Oil checks (hydraulic oil, lubricating oil) in various locations are to be carried out daily. It is a good practice to clean the machine ways thoroughly and oil them at the end of the day's work. The hydraulic oil pressure and pneumatic pressure (if used) should be monitored. Hydraulic pressure settings should be checked. Tool changers, turrets, tool probes etc.' should be properly cleaned.

(ii) Monthly preventive maintenance: This may include hydraulic oil cleaning, checking of clamping, hydraulic operation of chucks, tailstocks, steadies, filter changes etc. The schedules for some of the preventive maintenance actions are normally indicated by manufacturers. These include:

(i) Frequency of hydraulic oil change.

(ii) Checking and changing of air filters (for blowers) and oil filters.

(iii) Metering devices in lubricating system.

(iv) Change of brushes in DC servomotors and DC motors.

(v) Checking of backlash in ball screws.

(vi) Alignment of the machine.

(vii) Cleaning of coolant equipment.

(viii) Setting of pressure in pressure switches, pressure regulators etc.

(ix) Checking the battery back-up for parameter storage.

The CNC system may have a provision for saving and display of preventive maintenance information which is very useful. A typical maintenance information screen is shown in Fig.13.1.

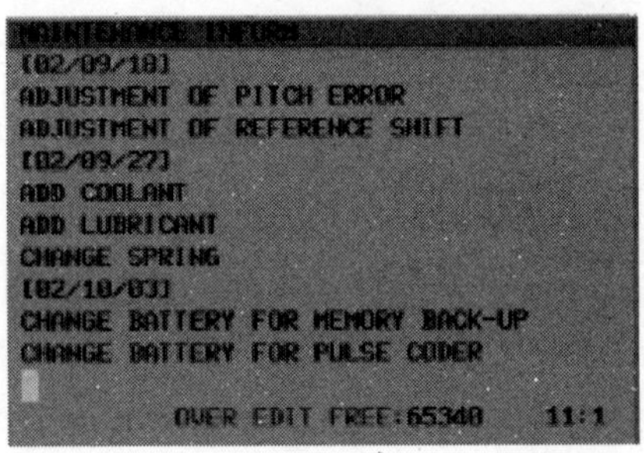

Fig. 13.1 Preventive Maintenance Information Screen

13.3 DOCUMENTATION

Maintenance activities can be well-supported by good documentation. For this purpose machine history cards, maintenance of log books, spare parts inventory etc. are to be properly maintained on standard formats. Documents like machine manuals, assembly drawings, hydraulic circuit diagrams, electrical and electronic circuit diagrams, diagnostics etc. are to be kept in duplicate so that one set can be preserved as a master copy and the other set can be used for reference.

13.4 SPARE PARTS

Inventory of essential spare parts is very important for efficient operation of CNC Machines. Manufacturers often recommend spares for a certain period of operation. In the case of imported machine tools, it will be prudent to order some of the parts like brushes, oil seals, belts, bearings, proximity switches, relays etc along with the ordering of the machine. This is because some of these items may not be readily available in India. Very often a few electrical and electronic items (PCB's) can be included in spares. The cost of spares is reduced if more than one machine of same type is used in the shop. Though it might be probable that all failures cannot be anticipated and some of the spares may not be used at all, still it is wise to keep a small inventory of spares. 5 – 10% of the cost of the machine can be earmarked for initial pack of spares.

Management of consumables and spare parts is a critical activity in CNC operation. It is desirable to know the when some of the critical items need to be replaced. Some of the CNC systems have a facility to display the remaining life time of consumables. This will help proper planning of procurement of spare parts. A typical screen shot is shown Fig. 13.2.

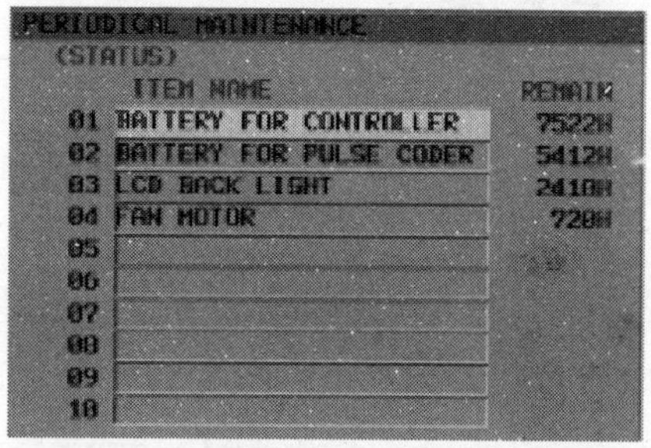

Fig. 13.2 Remaining Life Time of Consumables

13.5 MAINTENANCE FEATURES OF CNC MACHINE

CNC Machines and systems are designed with a high degree of reliability. The mean time between failures (MTBF) of some CNC systems is quoted today at more than hundred months. System failure in such cases is thus a very rare phenomenon. The buyer should always look into this aspect before deciding on the purchase of the machine. Systems with high reliability but higher cost is advisable than low cost systems which are invariably less reliable. Emphasis on cost reduction may often prove costly in the long run. It is also necessary to assess the strengths of the machine tool manufacturer or supplier in the following areas:

(i) Inventory of spares and spare parts support
(ii) Availability of enough persons with the seller to carry out maintenance in electrical, mechanical, hydraulic and electronics hardware
(iii) The time elapsed between the intimation of the failure and response by the machine supplier
(iv) Arrangements made by the supplier to obtain spares from his principals

Diagnostic programs available in CNC machines are a very helpful feature to identify the causes of malfunctioning. The machine manuals give the alarm message and the remedial action. With the help of these a large number of snags in the operation of CNC machines can be rectified by the maintenance staff or even by the operator himself. These diagnostics check the various sections of the system at the time of start up and only if all the systems are working satisfactorily, the "ready" signal is displayed.

In advanced countries, the maintenance of CNC machines are facilitated by connecting the CNC system through telephone cables or Internet to the manufacturer's works so that the experts can check up the machine through remote access and identify the cause for snag. This will avoid unnecessary trips by the service engineers and enable quick despatch of right spare parts or spare boards to the user of the machine.

13.5.1 Diagnostic Features

CNC system incorporates features for self diagnosis. When the machine is switched on, the system undergoes a self check procedure and if any system is malfunctioning, an alarm message is displayed on the monitoring screen. Figure 13.3 shows a typical example. The system can display detailed information regarding an alarm and its diagnosis. The operator can also edit the information and modify the display.

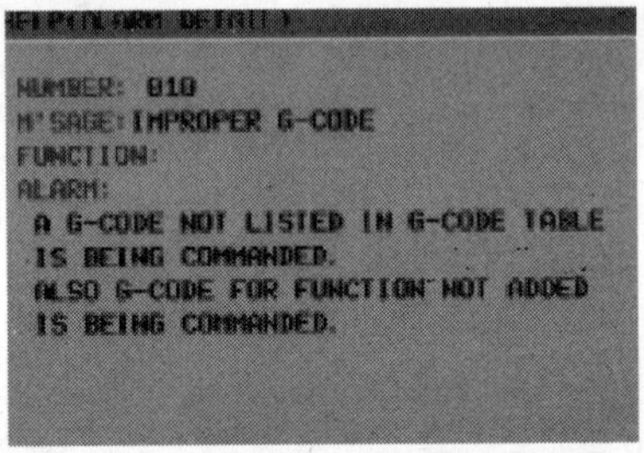

Fig. 13.3 Screen for Alarm Message

In some of the advanced machines conversational diagnostics is available. Fig.13.4 shows a typical dialog screen. Such facilities will improve the speed of trouble shooting.

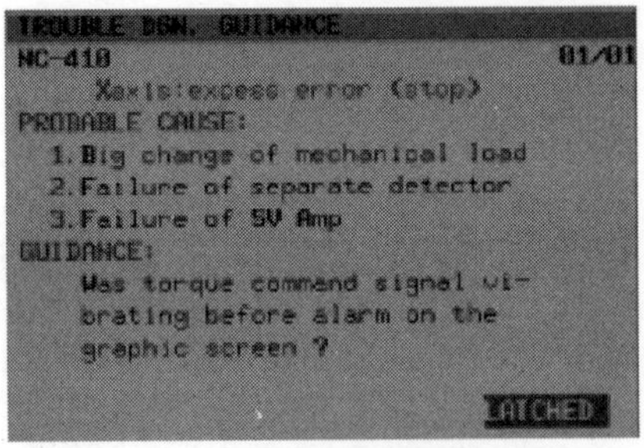

Fig. 13.4 Conversational Diagnostics

Operational history through the alarm monitoring on the screen can also be displayed for servo and spindle alarms. For example, wave form display of servo performance data makes servo adjustment easier. A typical wave form display is shown in Fig.13.5.

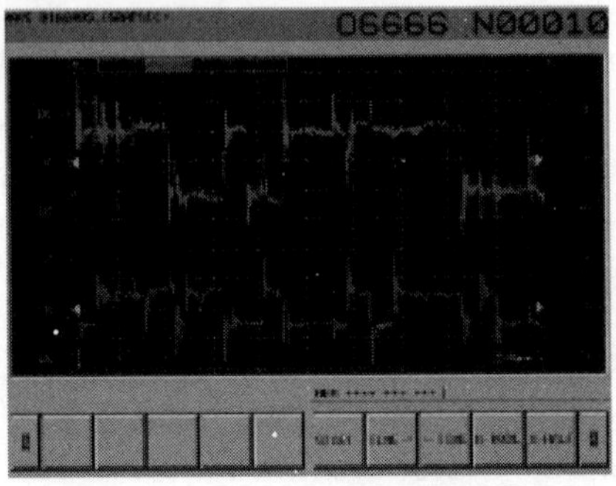

Fig. 13.5 Servo Waveform Display

13.6 REMOTE MAINTENANCE THROUGH INTERNET

In order to facilitate speedy maintenance the CNC system can be directly connected to the factory service centre through Internet. This is illustrated in Fig.13.6. The service centre can sent a diagnostic program to the CNC machine and this program can locate the faults in the machine or system. The service centre can then take immediate corrective action and the machine can be rectified within a short time, resulting in considerable reduction in down time with attendant increase in output from the machine. If a spare parts needs to be airlifted it can be done immediately. If the maintenance can be carried out at the factory by the factory maintenance personnel, appropriate instructions can be passed on to them or the nearest service engineer available can be deputed to carry out the maintenance.

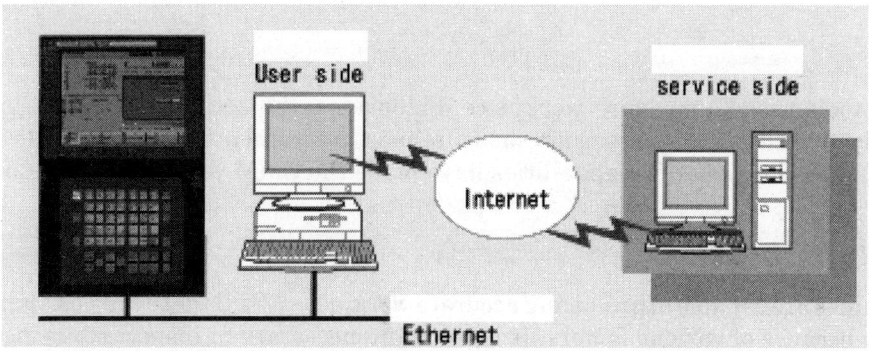

Fig. 13.6 Remote Maintenance through Internet

13.7 TRAINING IN MAINTENANCE

The need for having trained maintenance staff for attending to CNC Machines is to be emphasized. The staff can be trained at the manufacturer's works. Training can be imparted through special programmes organized by system manufacturers or training organizations. The modular design of today's CNC machines enables maintenance to be carried out quickly. As far as PCB's are concerned, maintenance is done by replacing them rather than trying to determine which chip is defective. Similarly the maintenance procedure of hydraulic, mechanical and electrical items is also fairly simple so that persons with good training for a short period can attend to the machines successfully.

REVIEW QUESTIONS

(1) Describe the different types of preventive maintenance programs for CNC machine tools.

(2) Discuss the importance of considering maintenance aspects at the time of procuring CNC machine tools.

(3) Discuss the maintenance features available in CNC machines.

(4) How is remote maintenance through Internet implemented?

14 COORDINATE MEASURING MACHINES

Of all the tools used to measure workpiece dimensions, the coordinate measuring machine is presently the ultimate in precision measurement instruments. Developments in sensors, software and data translation capabilities have made the CMM very versatile equipment.

14.1 INTRODUCTION

CNC machines are capable of producing accurate workpieces. Still there are possibilities of non-conformity because of various factors. It is therefore necessary to inspect components. CMMs work on principles similar to CNC and are fast inspection machines with built- in powerful software capabilities. CMMs collect detailed dimensional data by moving a sensing device called a probe along workpiece surfaces. Most CMMs acquire data using a touch trigger probe that contacts individual points along a workpiece. The single point measurement technique generally can collect data at a rate of about 50-60 points per minute, significantly faster than manual measuring machines. Today there are CMMs that can automatically measure 3D shape and form of workpieces at up to 1000 points per second using current non-contact probe technology. It may go up in future up to 20000 points per second using advanced non-contact sensor technology. These are called scanning CMMs.

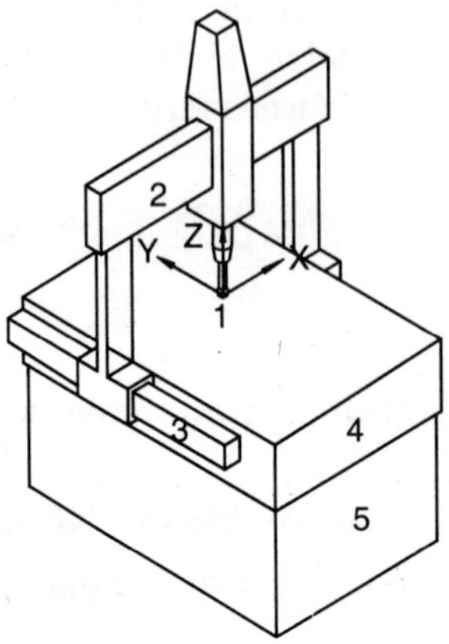

1. PROBE 2. BRIDGE 3.MEASURING SCALE 4. GRANITE TABLE 5. BASE

Fig. 14.1 Bridge Type CMM

Figure 14.1 shows a bridge type CMM. This type of design ensures accuracy and ease of use. The main parts of CMM are:

- A precision surface table, usually of granite material
- A measuring probe attached to the measuring head
- A bridge supporting the measuring head, usually made of granite

The bridge moves in the Y-direction. The measuring head along with the probe can be moved in the Z-direction or can be moved in the X-direction laterally. Each axis is fitted with accurate measuring scales.

The bridge, cross beam, and the measuring spindle are supported on rigid air bearings with exceptional insensitivity to vibrations as the hand lapped spherical air bearing mounts combined with suitable pre-loading arrangement provide maximum dynamic stiffness. These types of slideways reduce friction to a minimum. Air bearings ensure that there is no stick slip. The accuracy of measurement using a CMM is of the order of 0.001 mm.

The granite table is usually provided with a grid of threaded holes, defining clamping locations which facilitate part mounting. The table has a high load carrying capacity and is accessible normally from three sides.

Many types of probes are used with coordinate measuring machines. They may be mechanical, electronic, or optical. The universal touch trigger probes used on most of the machines have the following characteristics:

- Minimization of measuring time as data is acquired at the point of contact
- Piezoelectric sensors for high direction independent probe sensitivity.
- Excellent repeatability
- Very low measuring force, enabling even measurement on foam and similar materials.

Probes can be changed manually or automatically in the case of a CNC CMM.

14.2 TYPES OF COORDINATE MACHINES

There are four major types of construction used in coordinate machines.

(i) **Cantilever type machines:** In this case the probe head is mounted on an overhanging slide. For small and inexpensive CMMs this type of construction is used.

(ii) **Bridge type machines:** This is the most common type of construction of CMMs.

(iii) **Gantry type machines:** Large CMMs used in aircraft and aeronautical industry fall in this category.

(iv) **Robot type machines:** These are built with articulated arms. They are both used for inspection as well as reverse engineering purposes. These can be used to inspect large components which could not be accommodated on conventional CMMs. These are also called portable CMMs. Manufacturers of portable CMM include Geodetics, Faro, Metric Vision, Pixsys, Romer and Northern Digital. These machines are also used on the shop floor to accelerate the manual inspection process. Laser tracker systems like Leica absolute tracker are used for inspection of large parts and structures as well as calibration of robots.

CMMs are also classified on the basis of the level of automation.

(i) **Manual CMM:** These are operated manually. The measuring procedure is facilitated by interactive software. The output of measurement is either noted by the operator or printed out. Probe change is manual. Manual CMMs are manufactured by Accurate,

Brown and Sharpe, CE Johansson, Coord3, DEA, ELM, Helmel, IMS, ITP, Mitutoyo, Mora, Numerex, Poli, Starret, Trimex and Wenzel.

(ii) DCC CMM: These machines, called direct computer controlled CMMs, can be programmed to carry out automatic inspection of components. These can be called flexible inspection centers as they have automatic probe change capability. They can be programmed directly from the CAD model of the component. Softwares like Valysis and Silma are used for generating inspection programs from the CAD model. Some of the manufacturers of DCC CMM include Brown and Sharpe, CE Johansson, Coord3, DEA, ELM, Ferranti, Helmel, IMS, ITP, LK, Mitutoyo, Mora, Numerex, Poli, Starret, Speroni and Wenzel. DCC CMMs are most suitable for large volume production applications.

14.3 COORDINATE SYSTEMS

There are two types of coordinate systems in used in measurement with CMM. One is called machine coordinate system and the other work coordinate system. Figure shows the machine coordinate system. The X, Y and Z-axes refer to the motion of the axes of the machine. The work coordinate system shown in Fig. 14.2 relates to the datums and features of the workpiece. With the software incorporated in the CMM the workpiece coordinate system and the machine coordinate system can be mathematically related. This is called alignment.

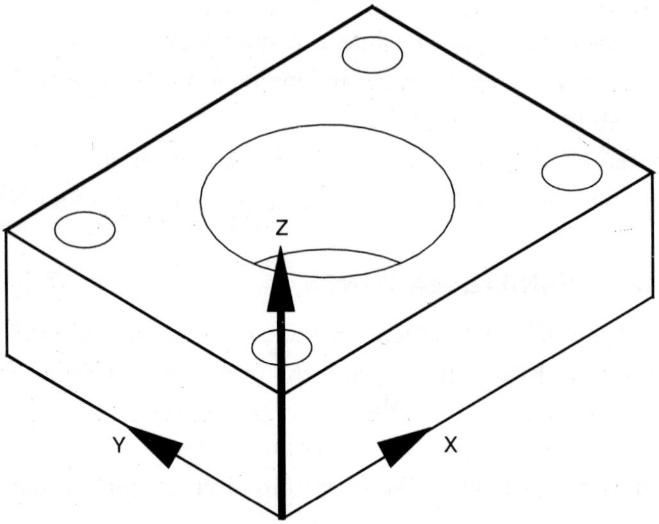

Fig. 14.2 Coordinate System Setting

14.3.1 Measured and Constructed Features

The workpieces consist of features defined by simple geometric elements created by machining or forming. Vertices, edges, planes, circles, cylinders, cones, spheres etc. are some of these elements. The probe of the CMM touches these edges or surfaces with the measuring probe. These are referred to as measured features. There are other features such as distance, symmetry, intersection, angle and projection that cannot be measured but constructed mathematically from the measured features. These are referred to as constructed features. Figure 14.3 shows the machined bore as the measured feature and the pitch circle as the constructed feature. The relationship between one group of features and another feature and group of features is important in manufacturing or assembly. Constructed features are very significant in assembly situations.

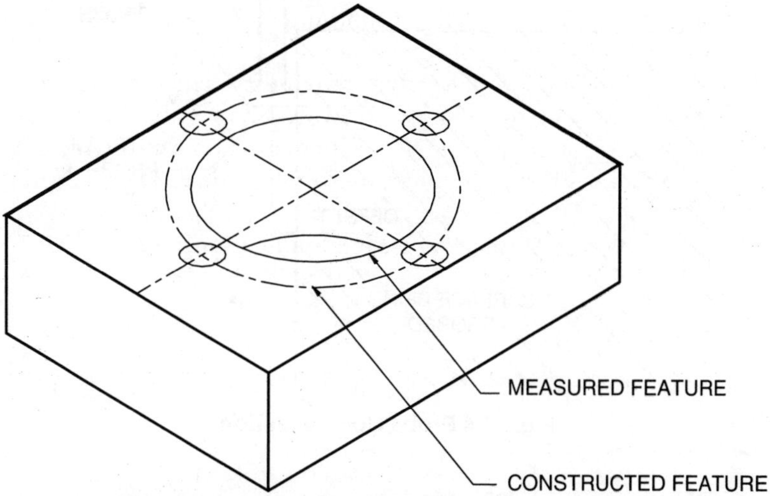

Fig. 14.3 Measured and Constructed Features

14.3.2 Motorised Probe Heads

Motorized probe heads allow the probe to orient in 720 positions in angular increments of 7.5 degrees, allowing the probe to be positioned normal to the work surface. Extension bars upto 300 mm can be used. It is not necessary to re-qualify the probe after every indexing. This automated probe head is very appropriate for volume manufacture.

Volumetric Compensation

The coordinate measuring machines are built to extremely close tolerances. However there can be errors like pitch, roll, yaw, straightness, and squareness and scale errors in their structure and elements. These affect the accuracy of CMMs. The majority of CMMs errors can be corrected automatically through the software. Error mapping is a term used to measure the geometric errors of a CMM. Once error mapping is done, the errors can be eliminated or minimized using the powerful algorithms in the CMMs software. This procedure is called volumetric compensation.

14.3.3 Probe Compensation

Coordinate measuring machines acquire the data by touching the workpiece with a solid probe or electronic touch trigger probe. The probe tip is manufactured accurately. Once the probe is attached to the CMMs measuring axis, the location of the tip with reference to the machine's coordinate system must be determined prior to machining. Since it is the tip's circumference, which touches the workpiece, the probes center and radius are to be determined accurately. Measuring a very accurate sphere does this.

Once the center and the radius of the tip are known, when the tip contacts the workpiece the coordinates of the tip are mathematically offset by the radius of the probe tip to the probe's actual point of contact. This is shown in Fig. 14.4. The direction of the offset is automatically determined by the alignment procedure.

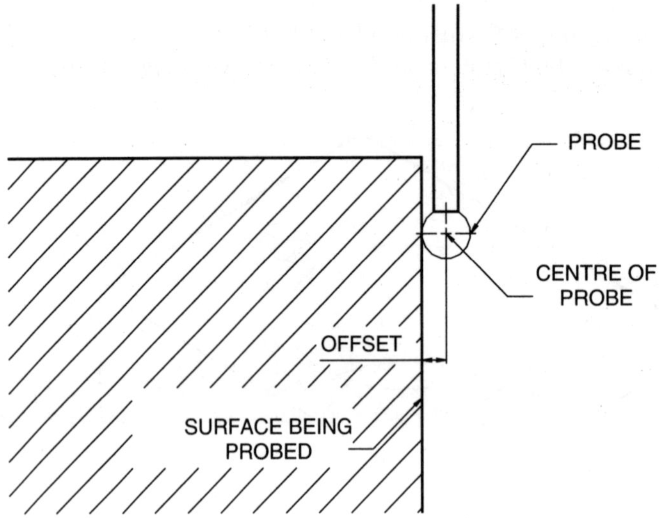

Fig. 14.4 Probe Compensation

14.4 OFF-LINE PROGRAMMING OF CMM

Off-line programming is becoming a necessity for users of CMM mainly for three reasons.

(i) As companies accelerate their move towards paperless manufacturing, 3D surface/ solid modeling is becoming the mode of drawing creation. This has led to the concept of limited dimension drawings. This makes CMM programming from blue prints difficult.

(ii) As product life cycles continue to get shorter product development has to rely more on concurrent engineering. Any manufacturing bottleneck like CMM programming which ties up valuable manufacturing resources like CMM has to be eliminated to compress product development time.

(iii) The use of powerful solid/surface modeling enables the designers to create complex geometries to satisfy critical functional requirements. CMM programming also therefore becomes complex, making it very difficult to carry out manually.

Off-line programming has therefore become a virtual necessity to:

- reduce programming time
- increase utilization of CMM
- improve the quality of inspection
- eliminate errors in interpretation of drawings
- improve consistency

The off-line programming techniques have been developed to meet the following goals:

- Eliminate dry runs
- Quick easy programming
- Natural way of programming
- Compatible with different CMMs

14.5 CAD INTEGRATION

The CMM OLP procedure starts with 3D CAD geometry and tolerance data of the component to be inspected. One method of accessing CAD data is by means of CAD data exchange files. CAD geometry is can be conveniently accessed through any of the data exchange files like IGES, VDA-FS, or STEP. The correct version of CAD files and the right version of data exchange standard should be used. There are however some problems likely to be encountered which are listed below:

Missing tolerance data

Missing CAD geometry

Surface normals may not be uniform or correct

However the recommended approach is through 3D CAD application programming interfaces (API). 3 D CAD APIs provide the best functionality for CMM OLP. The advantage is that APIs can access multiple CAD files and there is no need to have the CAD system. The difficulties associated with the use of data exchange formats particularly version control and tolerance geometry associations.

The next critical component in CAD integration is the 3D CAD engine which is used for extracting features and computing nominal point data on complex geometry of the surface topology which may consist of profiles and surface contours.

14.6 DIMENSIONAL MEASURING INTERFACE STANDARD (DMIS)

DMIS is a standard metrology language for communication of inspection data between computer systems and inspection equipment. This standard was developed more than two decades ago by sophisticated CMM users and major CMM manufacturers so that files could be transferred to and from CAD systems, without translating or reformatting the data. DMIS has been extended in its use as a programming language by vendors like International Metrology Systems. DMIS programs are in ASCII format allowing them to be written and analyzed by humans. DMIS allows the creation of a single CMM part program which can be run on CMMs from different vendors. This gives manufacturers considerable flexibility. Currently DMIS 3.0 (ANSI/ CAM-I 101-1995) is the latest version of the language.

14.6.1 METROLOGY

It is necessary to give the programmer flexibility and full control over the program generation process so that specific metrology practices can be implemented, and the features of the CMM can be fully utilized. Metrology is thus heart of CMM OLP. The characteristics of the metrology technology necessary for CMM OLP are:

- Tools which allow the user to generate CMM part program much more quickly off-line than on-line.
- Post process DMIS part programs to CMM languages
- Program verification including syntax and program structure checking
- Tools that do not constrain or limit the programming process

Object oriented approach is used for programming purposes. This has the following benefits.

- Captures metrology intent without any ambiguity
- On-screen program display

- bi-directional link between text and CAD model
- Real time updating of graphics and program text

14.6.2 Verification

Only a thorough verification process will completely eliminate the need for dry runs on the actual CMM. The only way to succeed with off-line verification is to faithfully reproduce an inspection run on actual CMM in the CMM OLP system The verification needs to:

(i) Simulate continuous motion of all machine axes and probes

(ii) Simulate the entire CMM environment including fixtures, probe changers, and other equipment

(iii) Simulate all CMM program statements

Simulation of the continuous machine motion is the only way to ensure that there is no collision during the inspection process. Another benefit is the calculation of time required to inspect a part. It is also necessary to ensure that output report is complete.

14.7 SCANNING CMM

A coordinate measuring machine with a constant contact scanning probe makes it possible to get complete information about the workpiece features, especially contours. This level of information helps manufacturing shops to improve die making, and die maintenance. With the availability of inexpensive scanning CMMs and the capability to effectively harness the power of massive amounts of dimensional data through CAD/CAM systems, manufacturers today can exercise a level of control over machining processes which was not possible before.

High speed scanning can help to achieve improved process flexibility, adoption of better quality standards, and increase in overall product performance. To achieve high accuracies at high speeds of measurements CMMs incorporate new technologies. The linear encoders used in such machines have a resolution of 0.01 mm with a crystallized glass scale with a linear coefficient of expansion of 0.08×10exp-6 per degree C. The scale installation is done to reduce the hysteresis to very low levels.

Analog probes are used for high speed contact scanning. These act as small, accurate auxiliary 3-axis measuring machines whose readings complement those of the CMM. In the scanning process the probe stylus is in constant contact with the part surface and the measuring machine control system ensures that a consistent gauging force is maintained by detecting any deviations and regulating them immediately. The dimensional data is continuously read off the machine scales and analog probe transducers and sent to the software for analysis. True 3D probe systems are isotropic since they exert the same force in all three measuring axes simultaneously. They are particularly suitable for measuring surfaces of parts like gears, cams, and hobs.

When the characteristics of the part surface are such to make direct probing impractical, non-contact sensors are used . These optical sensors integrate a light source and a photoelectric detector and work on the principle of triangulation. The light source emits a precise focused laser or infrared light beam. When this beam strikes the work surface it forms the image of a spot. The diffused scattered light is then focused on a photoelectric array. Any variation on the surface distance from the sensor results in a change of position of the spot image on the array.

Some non-contact sensors integrate a structured light source that emits a plane of light. When this plane intersects a part, a line forms along the contour of the part. This line is detected by the sensor and is transformed into a measurable digital image. Distance measurements can be obtained, based on the shape and position of this line on the part surface. Non-contact sensors can scan faster than analog probes but has a severe limitation in the accessibility of part features. A combination of analog heads and non-contact sensing is ideal.

14.8 MAINTENANCE OF CMM

It is necessary to keep the CMM clean to maintain the accuracy of measurement. Apart from keeping the CMM in a clean environment, wiping down the machine with alcohol and cleaning the guide ways every day is recommended.

Interim checks are also recommended to assure the accuracy of CMM measurement. For example qualifying the probe tip is one quick test that can be performed on a daily basis. To do this, operators place a precision sphere on the table of the CMM and touch the sphere with the probe. The CMM subtracts out the radius to determine the center of the probe. If it cannot correctly establish the center of the probe it cannot accurately measure the parts. A limited ball bar test involving measurements in four orthogonal positions is recommended once a week.

14.9 CALIBRATION STANDARDS FOR COORDINATE MEASURING MACHINES

Calibration involves adjusting or resetting CMM so that it gives readings that are accurate in comparison to a reference standard. By checking for possible machine errors calibration determines if the machine has remained dimensionally stable and nominally accurate.

The CMM calibration should start with inspecting and cleaning the X, Y, and Z scales. The service engineer should then check all the reader heads with an oscilloscope and adjust them to the proper output. Next the fine adjustment mechanisms in each axis is checked for wear and adjusted if necessary. The parallelism of the beam is checked with respect to the working surface of the CMM. The next steps involve the inspection and adjustment of the perpendicularity or squareness in the XY, XZ and YZ planes. This is followed by the inspection and testing of linearity in the X, Y, and Z-axes. The repeatability in each axis is tested with the electronic touch probe.

A Moore step gauge is also used for calibration purposes.

There are three primary standards used to verify measuring machine performance:

ASME B89.4.1

VDI/VDE 2617

ISO 10360

All these standards evaluate the machine performance but differ in their approach-mainly in the number of tests involved and the way in which performance specifications are written.

The ASME B89 standard, (Methods for performance evaluation of coordinate measuring machines) outlines five basic measurement procedures for assessing CMM performance. In the first procedure multiple measurements are taken of a fixed ball mounted on the machine's table. The range i.e. the difference between the largest and the smallest readings indicates the machine's repeatability. The second procedure assesses linear accuracy. A laser interferometer reading and the CMM reading are compared and the error is entered in the compensation software of the CMM. The third procedure calls for the measurement using a ball bar. A ball bar approximately 100 mm shorter than the smallest dimension of the work zone is recommended. Measurements are taken with the ball bar placed in multiple positions and orientations within the machine's work volume while allowing adequate probing access to both balls. This test indicates the CMMs volumetric performance, with the range of readings providing information on the best and worst cases errors. Ball bars are used in the fourth procedure also. Measurements are taken in four diagonal positions within the work zone of the CMM. In each position the ball bar is checked with two right angle probe offsets, and the difference of measured lengths is determined. The differences are then compared with an offset probe performance specification. This procedure detects Z-axis probe offset errors, which can be important to CMM owners who use articulating probe heads at right angles to the machine's Z-axis. The fifth procedure involves measuring the length of a short gauge block in four orientations. These readings are then compared to a bi-directional accuracy measuring specification.

14.10 APPLICATION OF CMM FOR REVERSE ENGINEERING

Creation of a surface model or a solid model from an existing part or a prototype part is generally called reverse engineering. In the case of parts with straight or regular curved edges (like a circle) this can be carried out using regular measurements. Difficulty is encountered when the components to be reverse-engineered have complex doubly curved shapes. The usual procedure in such cases is to obtain a cloud of points using successive measurements using a CMM and fitting a surface to the measured points. The surface can then be exported to a CAD package to create a regular surface model or solid model which can be used for analysis and manufacturing.

14.11 MEASUREMENT USING CMM

A range of measuring capabilities is built in a CMM. This will depend upon the sophistication of the CMM. A few general capabilities are listed here. The reader is advised to study the working of a CMM and get familiar with the methods of using a CMM for actual measurement.

14.11.1 Setting Up a CMM

The setting up of a CMM include defining the probe, probe calibration , probe change details if required, setting up of coordinate system (Cartesian or Polar), mode setting (incremental or absolute), Reference plane setting, reference axis setting, aligning X-Y plane and setting Z to zero, create origin, axis alignment in X- and Y-axes, determining the position of the workpiece etc.

14.11.2 Measurement of Geometric Elements

The CMM software is designed to measure and evaluate several geometric elements which include point, line, ellipse, circle, sphere, plane cylinder, cone, etc.

14.11.3 Calculations

The CMM software can calculate points of intersection, circle of intersection, straight line of intersection, distance, angle, angle comparison, distance comparison, form tolerances, position tolerances, Parallelism, perpendicularity, angularity, coaxiality, and run out. The statistical evaluations of the measure data can also be carried out.

14.12 INTEGRATION OF CMM IN A MACHINING CELL

Inspection, though a mundane activity is very important to ensure that all components produced in a manufacturing cell meet the design specifications. Automation of the inspection process will ensure consistency of information apart from freeing the skilled operators to do more value added work. A coordinate measuring machine can be easily integrated into a machining cell to automate the inspection process. The following tasks are involved in integrating a CMM with the machining cell. The automatic work handling system or a robot will pull the part to be inspected from the production line, move it to CMM and send a signal to the PLC instructing the measuring software to run the appropriate program. After the inspection is complete, the software signals the measuring interface and PLC of the results of inspection and the PLC directs the part handling system to act accordingly. If the part is good and within allowable tolerance limits, the machine can continue to work. If the part is rejected, next part is also subjected to inspection. If two successive parts are rejected, the machine is stopped for investigation. The selection of the part and frequency of inspection can be predetermined or random. The tasks involved in integrating a CMM in a machining work cell are:

(i) Automate workpiece handling system

(ii) Establish communication between the CMMs software and the PLC of the machining cell. This may require appropriate software interface, usually provided by the manufacturer of CMM.

(iii) Develop and implement appropriate programs in a compatible high level language to integrate the operations, audit the tasks, make relevant decisions, archive information and send appropriate data to the manufacturing execution system.

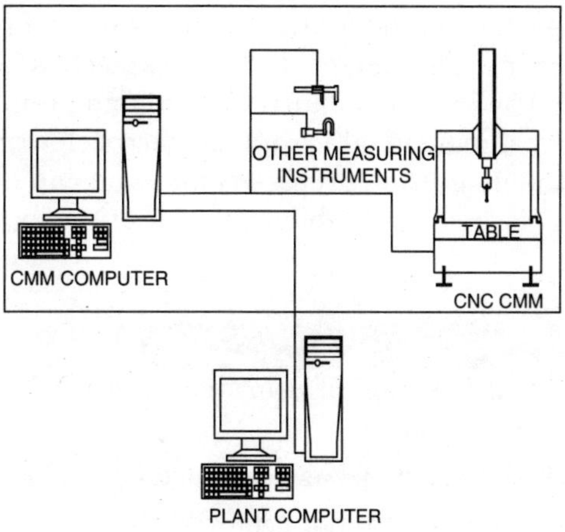

Fig. 14.5 Integration of Metrology in a Flexible Machining Cell

Figure 14.5 illustrates how the metrology function could be integrated into a flexible manufacturing cell. CMM and other measuring instruments can be connected to data acquisition systems and personal computers which in turn can be connected to the plant computer. The software resident in the computer can process the inspection data and take decisions on not only the acceptance or rejection of the part but also provide information on the process control status.

14.13 INTEGRATION OF COMPUTER VISION SYSTEMS IN A MANUFACTURING CELL

Vision systems are also integrated into manufacturing cells. Vision systems are fast and more suitable to detect defects in surface texture, coatings and paintings, casting defects, etc. This will help to eliminate defective parts from the line so that further processing on them can be avoided. A typical arrangement for a vision system is shown in Fig. 14.6. It is also possible to attach a vision system to a robot so that some of the inspection tasks could be carried out by the robot itself.

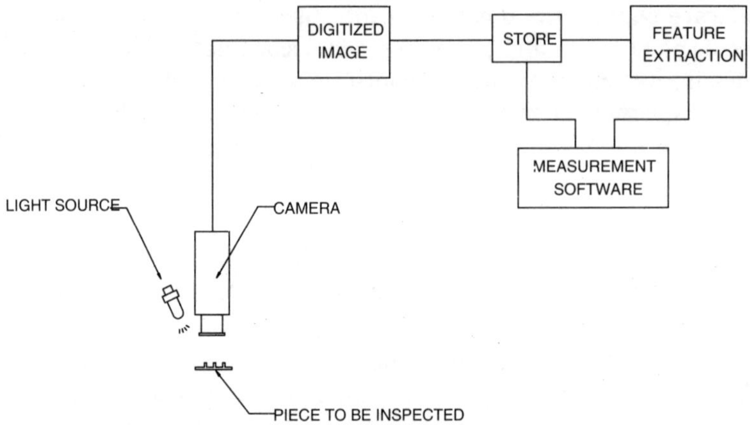

Fig. 14.6

The workpiece to be inspected can be located on a conveyor or a robot can place it in the field of view of the vision camera. The image of the workpiece is acquired by the camera and stored in the frame grabber. The image is digitized and using appropriate software modules, the image can be analyzed for dimensional errors, surface defects, colour etc. The advantage of the vision system is that the inspection process is fast and can be easily integrated into the manufacturing cell. However, issues like ambient illumination should be carefully looked into for reliable results.

REVIEW QUESTIONS

(1) Describe the constructional features of a bridge type CMM and discuss how precision measurement is possible with CMMs.

(2) List the major types of CMMs and discuss the specific applications of each.

(3) What are the special advantages of robot type CMMs?

(4) Why is a CNC CMM superior to a manual CMM?

(5) Compare measured and constructed features with the aid of suitable examples.

(6) Explain the importance of probe heads in ensuring consistent and accurate measurements.

(7) How do you develop inspection program from CAD data?

(8) What is dimensional measurement interface standard?

(9) How can you use a CMM for scanning and reverse engineering applications?

(10) What are the benefits in integrating a CMM in a manufacturing cell?

(11) Discuss the steps involved in feature extraction and dimensional metrology using vision systems.

15 ELEMENTS OF ROBOTICS

A robot is an important manufacturing equipment today in several segments of industry-automobiles, pharmaceuticals, food processing, metal working, painting, welding, coating, semi conductor electronics, materials handling, to name a few. Though robots find their applications in many other fields, the focus of this chapter is manufacturing applications.

15.1 INTRODUCTION

Robots are used in many ways, in many industries. Material handling, palletizing, machine loading and unloading, metal removal, welding, painting, fettling, deburring, cutting, coating, assembly, inspection and material dispensing are just a few of the applications to which robots are put to. The end use often influences the configuration of the robot.

A typical robot used in manufacturing consists of a mechanical arm, an end effector or gripper suitable for carrying out the work, control system, sensors and in most cases a personal computer for supervisory control and programming. Figure 15.1 shows a typical robotic system. In a manufacturing environment, a custom designed work cell is also necessary for the optimum use of the robot.

The credit for coining the word "Robot" goes to Karel Capek, a Czech playwright, who introduced this word in his 1921 play introduced into his play R.U.R. (Rossum's Universal Robots). Robot means "serf" or forced labor (slave) in Czech language. The ISO defines for a robot an automatically controlled, reprogrammable, multipurpose manipulator programmable in three or more axes. According to the Robot Institute of America (RIA) a robot is defined as a reprogrammable, multifunctional manipulator designed to move material, parts, tools, or specialized devices through various programmed motions for the performance of a variety of tasks. A robot can also be defined as an automatic device that performs functions normally ascribed to humans or a machine in the form of a human.

15.2 LAWS OF ROBOTICS

The word 'robotics' was first used in "Runaround", a short story published in 1942, by Isaac Asimov (1940). Asimov is credited with proposing the laws of robotics which are stated below:

Zeroth Law: A robot may not injure humanity, or through inaction, allow humanity to come to harm.

First Law: A robot may not injure a human being, or through inaction, allow a human being to come to harm, unless this would violate a higher order law.

Second Law: A robot must obey orders given it by human beings, except where such orders would conflict with a higher order law.

15.3 HISTORY OF ROBOTICS

Many researchers contributed to early development of robotics concepts. Alan Turing (1950) published computing machinery and intelligence which came to be known as "Turing test" later. The concept of expert system was proposed by Alan Newell and Herbert Simon in 1956. John McCarthy, and his colleagues coined the term artificial intelligence in 1956. The Artificial Intelligence Laboratory (1959) at MIT was started by McCarthy. Heinrich Ernst developed a computer operated hand MH-1 at MIT in 1961.

The credit for development of industrial robots goes to George Devol, an inventor and entrepreneur and Joseph Engelberger, a manufacturing engineer. Devol had earlier patented a playback device for controlling machines. Together they made a serious and commercially successful effort to develop a real, working robot.

Engelberger started a manufacturing company 'Unimation' which stood for universal automation and so the first commercial company to make robots was formed. Devol wrote the necessary patents. Their first robot was nicknamed the 'Unimate' and it was manufactured in 1962. As a result, Engelberger has been called the 'father of robotics.'

The first Unimate was installed at a General Motors plant to extract hot die castings from die in heated die-casting machines. In fact most Unimates were sold to casting machines and to perform spot welding on auto bodies, both tasks being particularly hateful jobs for people. Both applications were commercially successful, i.e., the robots worked reliably and saved money by replacing people. An industry was spawned and a variety of other tasks were also performed by robots, such as loading and unloading machine tools.

Later Westinghouse Electric Company acquired Unimation. Unimation was acquired by Staubli of Switzerland and the company is known as Staubli Unimation.

John McCarthy left MIT and started the AI Laboratory at Stanford University (1963). In 1963 Stanford Research Institute developed Shakey, a mobile robot. The Robotics Institute at Carnegie Mellon University was established in the year 1979.

Several path breaking developments followed. Two notable developments in recent years are the development of AIBO robotic pet by Sony in 1999 and humanoid robot, ASIMO by Honda in 2000.

Our interest here is industrial robots, but it will not be out of place a brief mention is made of other types of robots. Human beings have long been fascinated with the idea of robots and have been a favorite theme with film makers. While in the past humans only fantasized about them, today, many types of robots are a reality. For example, there are industrial robots, toy robots that entertain us, robots used in defense applications, robots that help in space exploration, robots used in nuclear programs for handling radioactive substances and for decommissioning of power plants, robots used in surgery and robots used in agriculture. A new breed of robots are humanoid robots (also called service robots) being created for the service sector, to help with the chores in the home or as caregivers for the elderly and the handicapped. Some of the popular types of robots that are widely used nowadays are described briefly in the subsequent sections.

15.4 TYPES OF ROBOTS

Though initially robots were designed for industrial applications, several new types of robots have been developed during the last few decades. Brief descriptions of these robots is attempted here.

15.4.1 Industrial Robots

Robots today are being utilized in a wide variety of industrial applications. Any job that involves repetitiveness, accuracy, endurance, speed, and reliability can be done much better by robots, which is why many industrial jobs that used to be done by human operators are increasingly being carried out by robots. For example, for the past 30 years or more robots have progressively been employed in the automated production lines of the automobile industry, wherein a chassis of a vehicle is transported along a conveyor belt and is welded, painted, and assembled by a succession of robot stations. Some of the other industrial jobs robots are performing are palletizing and packaging goods, dispensing jobs, laboratory applications, and robots that pick miniscule electronic components from trays or strips and accurately place them on printed circuit boards in the electronics industry. Robots are employed widely in food processing.

15.4.2 Mobile Robots

Mobile robots are used for many manufacturing applications. Manufacturing engineers prefer to call them as Automated Guided Vehicles, or AGVs. These are used for transporting materials over large sized places like factories, container ports, and warehouses. The guidance of these vehicles is by using wires or markers placed in the floor, and lasers, or vision systems, to sense the environment they operate in. An advanced form of the AGV is the SGV, or the Self Guided Vehicle, which can be taught to autonomously navigate within a space, or do it by being given a map of the area. These robots have the ability of performing tasks that are non-sequential and non-repetitive in environments that are complex, hence are called as intelligent robots.

15.4.3 Telerobots or Master Slave Manipulators

These robots are used in places that are hazardous to humans, or are inaccessible or far away. A human operator located at a distance from a telerobot controls its action. Some other examples of telerobots are laparoscopic surgery being done with the help of a telerobot, or doctors using remotely located robots to communicate with their patients, which enables them to treat patients anywhere in the world. This has the potential of patients in remote places of the world, without adequate medical facilities, being able to consult doctors across the world, or even in the next town, and the doctors in turn having the ability to monitor them. Telerobots are also useful in nuclear power plants where they, instead of humans, can handle hazardous material or undertake operations potentially harmful for humans. Telerobots are widely used in space exploration.

Some of the applications in space that are considered include robots used for the maintenance of satellites, manufacturing in space, constructing space ships, etc.

Telerobots and mobile robots are also being increasingly used for military purposes. A typical example is the Unmanned Aerial Vehicles and drones used for reconnaissance, rescue, and surveillance and also to fire at targets. Some of them have even advanced to the level of having the ability to automatically make decisions like choosing the location to fly to, and deciding which enemy target to engage with. Many telerobots and mobile robots are being used by the military in several countries to diffuse Improvised Explosive Devices (IED) or under water vehicles. An advancement of this concept is the unmanned ground vehicle, or UGV, is on the anvil which can carry out military missions independently.

15.4.4 Service Robots

The concept of using robots for service applications is becoming popular of late. Japanese are in the forefront of designing and manufacturing serveral types of robots. These robots can be sub-divided into two main types of robots:

(i) Robots used for professional jobs

(ii) Robots used for personal use

Robots used for the military applications, surveillance, rescue, space exploration, underwater applications and handling hazardous waste fall in the former category.

The rise in the aged population has prompted the development of personal use robots. These are becoming more and more popular, with increased sophistication in artificial intelligence and with them becoming increasingly affordable. The applications include areas like care giving for humans and pets, house cleaning and entertainment. Although it is more expensive and difficult to make highly intelligent and sensitive machines, but service robots designed with minimal intelligence are already fairly common.

Another area where personal use robots are being introduced is in the care for the elderly. In countries where there are increasing numbers of the aged with comparatively fewer numbers of young people to provide them with care, due to low birth rate and increased longevity, such as is the case in Japan and a growing number of western countries, robots are increasingly thought to be the answer. These robots are being designed to provide physical services such as carrying bedridden elderly people (or even the handicapped), or washing or feeding them, and doing various other day-to-day tasks. Android and humanoid robots are no longer a scientific curiosity nor limited to laboratories.

15.4.5 Robots Used in Agriculture

Several robots are experimented for agricultural purposes, such as robots that can pick apples, prune grapevines, transplant seedlings, remove weeds and so on.

15.5 INDUSTRIAL APPLICATION OF ROBOTS

Our interest is manufacturing and robots are used in manufacturing industries to perform a variety of tasks:

Die Casting	Dip coating
Forging	Glass handling
Heat treating	Injection molding
Machine tool tending	Materials handling
Materials transfer	Cleaning, Deburring, Fettling
Press loading	Stacking and Unstacking
Assembly	Welding
Spray painting	Inspection

15.6 CLASSIFICATION OF ROBOTS

An industrial robot is a complex, technological system consisting of several interlinked subsystems operating harmoniously within the robot's physical environment. Each of these subsystems performs its own carefully defined functions and contributes to the overall function of the industrial robot.

Robots are classified on the basis of four factors:

(i) Arm geometry: Cartesian, Cylindrical, Spherical, Articulated, SCARA, Parallel kinematic

(ii) Control: Non Servo and Servo

(iii) Power Sources: Electrical, Pneumatic, Hydraulic or a Combination of these

(iv) Degrees of freedom

15.7 KINEMATIC STRUCTURE OF ROBOTS

A robot arm must be capable of reaching any point in its work space. Different arm configurations have been employed to achieve this. Kinematics refers to the spatial arrangement, according to the sequence and structure, of the axis of movement in relation to each other. There are five basic types of movement that an industrial robot may have: (1) Cartesian, (2) Cylindrical, (3) Polar, and (4) Jointed-arm(5) SCARA.

15.7.1 Cartesian Robots

In a Cartesian robot (Fig.15.1), the robot reaches a point in space by three linear axis movements

Left and Right (X)

Forward and Backward (Y)

Up and Down (Z)

The work envelope of a Cartesian Robot is a cube (Fig. 15.1 (B)).

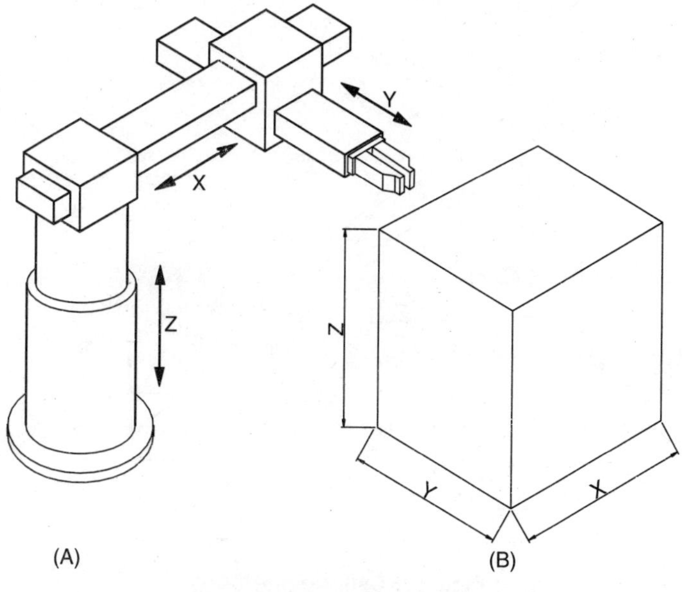

Fig. 15.1 Cartesian Robot

The Cartesian co-ordinate robot has the simplest kinematic arrangement. Basically it consists of a column and an arm. It is sometimes called an x-y-z robot, indicating the axes of motion. The x-axis is lateral motion, the y-axis is longitudinal motion, and the z-axis is vertical motion. Thus, the arm can move up and down on the z-axis; the arm can slide along its base on the x-axis; and then it can telescope to move to and from the work area on the y-axis. The Cartesian co-ordinate robot was developed mainly for arc welding, but it is also suited for many other operations like assembly, machine loading, etc. The gantry robot used in flexible turning centres for loading and unloading is a special case of Cartesian robot.

The Cartesian robots can have large work envelope. An example is the gantry robot used for loading and unloading of workpieces in turning cells. They have higher accuracy and repeatability. Because of their simple structure they are easy to control and program. They have relatively high stiffness and therefore high load carrying capacity. However, in the case of overhead applications, maintenance is difficult.

The applications of Cartesian robots include pick and place, assembly and sub assembly, machine tending, application of adhesives and in some cases welding.

15.7.2 Cylindrical Robot

The cylindrical co-ordinate robot is a variation of the Cartesian robot. This robot consists of a base and a column, but the column is designed to provide rotary motion. It also carries an extending arm that can move up and down on the column to provide more freedom of movement. The cylindrical co-ordinate robot is designed for handling machine tools and assembly.

Cylindrical robots have one rotary axis and two linear axis. These are shown as θ, Z and R in Fig. 15.2. The work space is therefore a partial hollow cylinder as shown in (B). The rotational ability helps rapid positioning. The radial movement enables increased work space. They can carry large payloads and can work in a limited space. The overall rigidity of the cylindrical robot is comparatively less. The repeatability and accuracy in the rotary axis is less if the control system is not sophisticated.

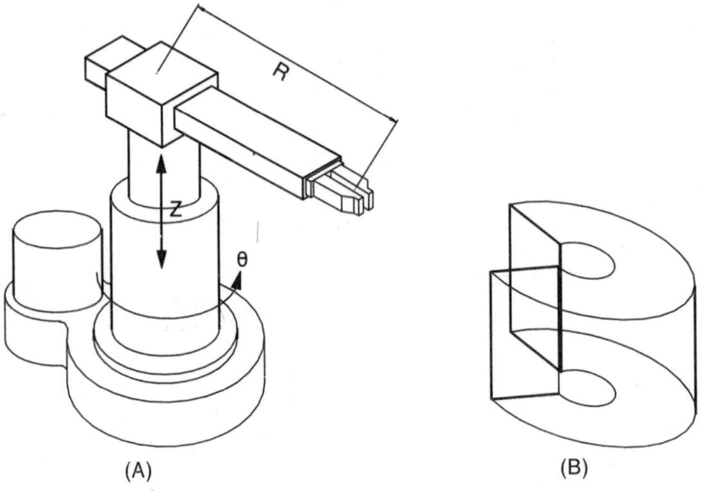

Fig. 15.2 Cylindrical Robot

The applications of cylindrical robots include machine tending, assembly, coating, conveyor pallet transfer, die casting, injection molding, forging and investment casting.

15.7.3 Spherical Coordinate Robot

The polar co-ordinate, or spherical robot consists of a rotary base, an elevation pivot, and a telescoping extend-and-retract boom axis. These robots operate according to spherical co-ordinates and offer greater flexibility. They are used particularly in spot welding.

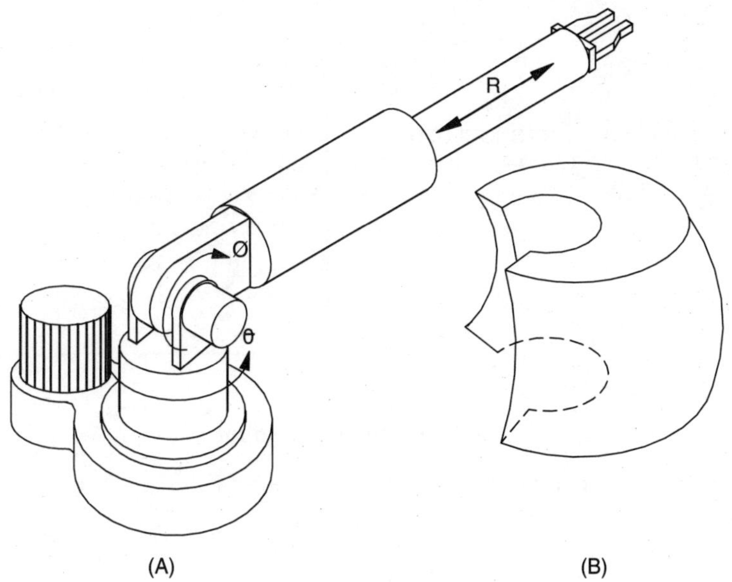

Fig. 15.3 Spherical Robot

A spherical robot has one linear and two rotational movements as shown in Fig.15.3. Because of this configuration the work space is like a part of sphere. The first motion is base rotation about a vertical axis, marked as θ in the figure. The second motion is the elbow movement, marked as φ. The third movement is radial (in and out) movement. The advantage of a spherical robot is its larger work space compared to cylindrical or Cartesian robots. The applications of spherical robots are similar to those of Cartesian and cylindrical robots.

15.7.4 Articulated Robot

Articulated Robot is a popular class of robots which are widely used in many industries. They are very versatile and are popular in automotive industry for assembly, welding, painting etc. They are also used in general engineering industry for many applications. Cleaning, deburring, fettling, etc are some of the other applications of this type of robots. An articulated robot is characterized by a base rotation and two link rotations as shown in Fig. 15.4. The robot shown in the figure has three rotary links (base, shoulder and elbow) and a standard wrist with three movements-pitch, roll and yaw. Thus, there are altogether six degrees of freedom which makes this very dexterous. Depending on the end use, the degrees of freedom may change. This robot is also called jointed arm (because of its construction) or anthropometric robot (because of its similarity to human arm).

The jointed-arm robot resembles a human arm. It usually stands on a base on which it can rotate, while it can articulate at the "shoulder" joint, which is just above the base. The robot can also rotate about its "elbow" and "wrist" joints. With the swiveling and bending at the wrist, six degrees of freedom can be obtained. The jointed-arm robot is the most popular form for a robot and is capable in welding and painting work.

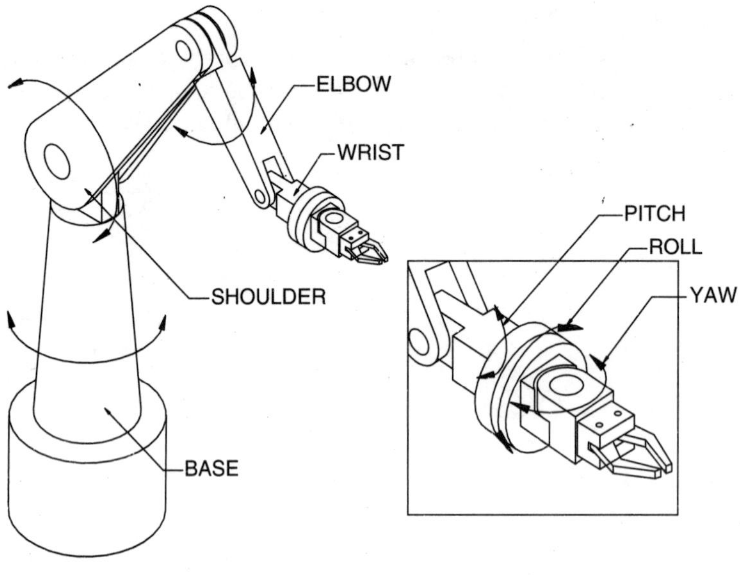

Fig. 15.4 Articulated Robot

Figure 15.5 shows the work envelope of an articulated robot.

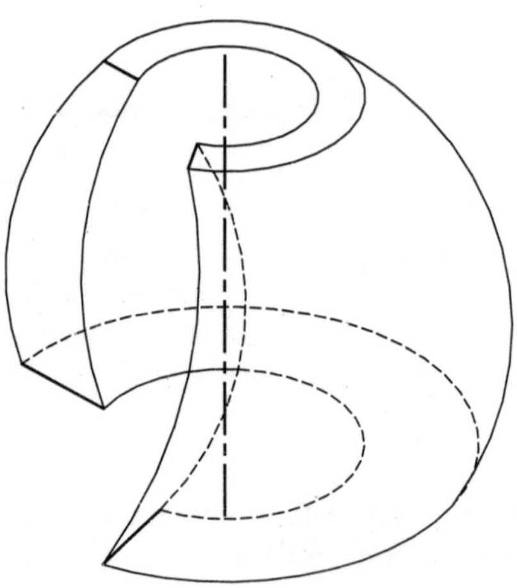

Fig.15.5 Work Envelope of an Articulated Robot

15.7.5 SCARA Robot

SCARA is an acronym for selective compliance assembly robotic arm. This type of robot is characterized by two rotational link movements in a horizontal plane and one or two translational movement along the vertical axis. This robot is primarily meant for assembly operations though can also be used for pick and place operations efficiently.

Figure 15.6 (A) shows a SCARA robot. It has two rotary movements in a horizontal plane and a vertical movement. The gripper is attached to the linear link. This facilitates pick and place and assembly. An additional vertical and/or rotary movement is sometimes provided. The workspace of a SCARA robot is shown in Fig. 15.6 (B).

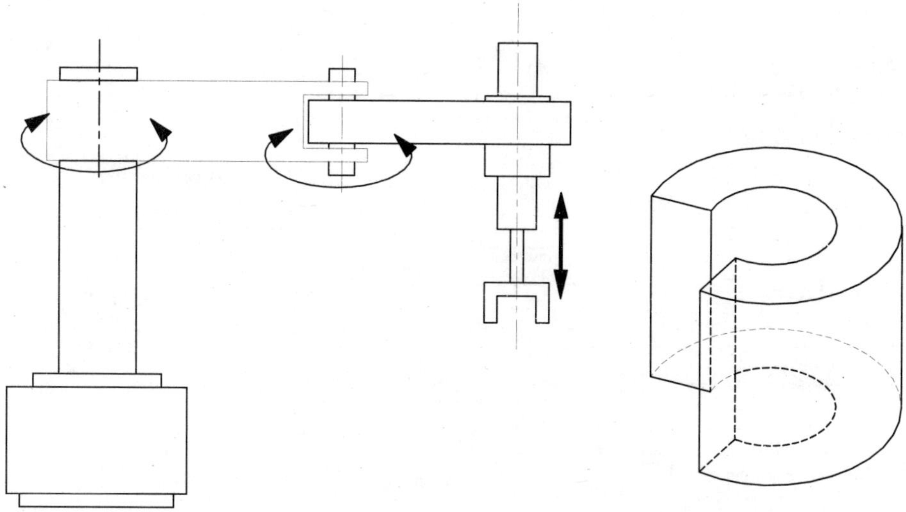

(A) (B)

Fig. 15.6 SCARA Robot

15.7.6 Parallel Kinematic Robots

Parallel kinematic robots have a unique construction. Similar to parallel kinematic machines, parallel kinematic robots are characterized by low inertia and higher accuracy. This class of robots are known to have highest speed of operation and is widely used in packaging and food processing. A typical parallel kinematic robot will have two platforms connected by three sets of linkages. The robot shown in the diagram is a unique design by Adept® and has four sets of linkages. The tool is attached to the lower platform.

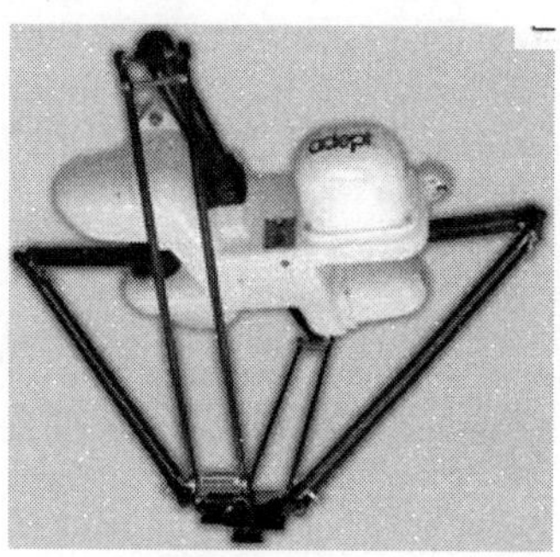

Fig. 15.7 Parallel Kinematic Robot

15.8 TYPICAL ROBOTIC WORKSTATION FOR MANUFACTURING

A typical robotic manufacturing system will consist of the following:

(i) Hardware- actuators, mechanical elements and grippers

(ii) Control system

(iii) Computer
(iv) Sensors
(v) Accessories like conveyors
(vi) Protective fencing

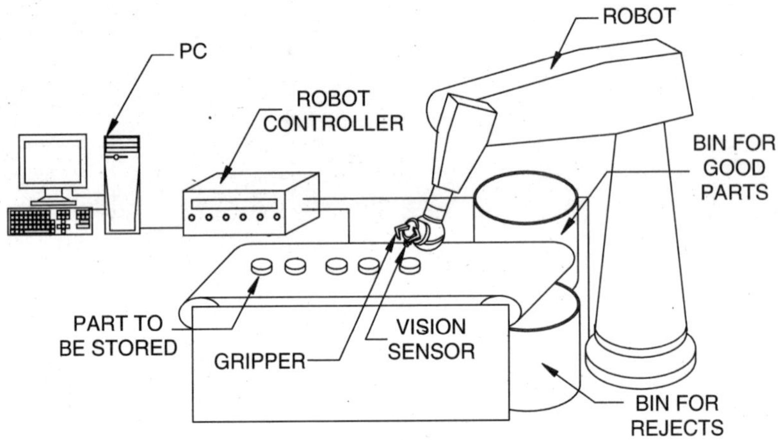

Fig. 15.8 Typical Robotic Workstation

The total system constitutes a robotic work cell. Figure 15.8 illustrates a typical robotic workstation. An articulated robot is used to sort correct parts using a vision system. The parts to be sorted is transferred to a conveyor through a chute (not shown). The vision system captures the image of the part and carries out the calculations required to determine the acceptability of the part. For example, let us assume that the acceptance parameter is the outside diameter. The vision system processes the image of the part and calculates the diameter. If it is within acceptable limits the robot controller sends a signal to orient the gripper to grasp the part, pick it up and deposit in the bin for good parts. If the part is out of tolerance, the conveyor drops the defective part into another bin. Of course, the robot can be programmed to pick it up and deposit into the bin. This is another solution. The conveyor belt moves at a speed in synchronization with the speed of operation of the vision system and the robot. It is desirable to install a suitable fencing to prevent accident to human operators. This is not shown in the illustration.

15.9 HARDWARE ELEMENTS OF ROBOTS

A majority of industrial robots used in manufacture are of stationary type, though mobile robots are also used in some special cases. The elements of robots are:

- Control Systems for Robots
- Mechanical arms or links
- Drives- electric motors for robots, electro-mechanical drives, harmonic drives, cyclo drives, hydraulic and electro-hydraulic drives, pneumatic drives
- Grippers
- Sensors
- Microcontrollers
- Robot work cell

These are discussed in subsequent sections.

15.10 CLASSIFICATION BASED ON CONTROL SYSTEMS

The control systems of an industrial robot determine its flexibility and efficiency, within the limits set beforehand by the design of the mechanical structure. The type of drive used may be the most obvious distinguishing feature of the robot, but just as important, although more subtle, is the degree of control possible over the robot motion. This control is affected by the choice of robot drives, as was seen earlier, but it is not completely determined by the drive. Robot users need to know how much motion control they need for their various applications, because the degree of motion control greatly affects the cost of the robot.

15.10.1 Purpose of the Control System

The control system provides a logical sequence for the robot to follow. The system provides the theoretical position values required for each step and continuously measures the actual position during movement. As the robot operates, the control system evaluates the theoretical/actual difference, together with other measured values and stored data (e.g., theoretical speeds), and produces actuating variables to drive the robot.

15.10.2 Types of Control Systems

There are four basic types of control systems: (a) axis limit (b) point-to-point control system and (c) the continuous path control system (d) line tracking control.

Axis Limit

The least sophisticated and therefore the lowest cost mode of robot motion control is axis limit. This type of control is sometimes called "two-position control" because each robot axis typically has two extreme points. In our description of the pneumatic-powered robots, we saw that the extreme points are usually mechanically adjustable stops.

Users of axis limit robots should have little or no preference for component motion velocities, as these considerations are beyond their control, although a small degree of speed control can be exercised by varying the power source. In addition, pauses can be programmed between robot motions to permit some selectivity in the speed of the overall cycle. The typical application for axis-limit robots is in machine loading and unloading. Axis-limit robots are invariably either pneumatically or hydraulically powered.

Point-to-point

With point-to-point control, the robot records the point where it picks up a part and the point where it releases that part. The robot then determines the best path to take between the two points. The point-to-point system is used when greater repeatability is required, or when the path between endpoints does not matter. Point-to-point control systems work well in loading and unloading applications. A pick and place operation, component insertion, spot welding, mechanical assembly etc are examples of point to point control. Programming of the robot for such applications is simple and straight forward. Simple tasks involving point to point operation with liberal tolerances can be carried out with open loop control.

Some what more versatile than axis-limit control is point-to-point (PTP) control. In this mode, the user can select any point in space in the robot work envelope and move directly to that point. The path and speed of movement enroute to the destination point are generally both uncontrollable. Even if speed is controllable, the robot is point-to-point unless the path enroute is also controllable. PTP control is good for component insertion, hole drilling, spot welding, and simple assembly applications. Machine loading and unloading operations to or from a pallet or tray also require PTP motion control.

Point-to-point motion should not be confused with straight-line motion. In general, even a simple straight-line motion between two points cannot be accomplished by a PTP robot. One exception to this generality is a straight-line vertical lift by a robot of cylindrical configuration. But straight-line movements are not an easy task for robots, especially the articulating robots. Simultaneously, controlled movement in more than one axis is always required to achieve straight-line movement using a fully articulating robot. To counteract this disadvantage, robot manufacturers have developed computer software routines that handle the mathematical mixing of axis voltages, pulses, or valve openings to achieve straight-line movement upon command.

Continuous Path Control System

A continuous path control system is one in which the robot is programmed to follow an irregular path exactly. Inside the control system, the path to be traveled is represented by a large number of points in close proximity. These points are stored in the robot's memory. In the working cycle, the robot follows the points to reproduce the desired path. The system is used for jobs when the robot is required to follow a specific path, such as in seam welding, or painting. Programming is time consuming and requires special skills.

Contouring

As in CNC machine tools, the most sophisticated class of robot motion is the full contouring type. Contouring describes motion in which the entire path is continuously or nearly continuously controlled. When the drive is by stepper motor, the control is not quite continuous but still can be classified as an approximation of contouring if there is a feedback loop to the controller and if in addition the controller is capable of varying the rate of pulses delivered to the stepper-motor drive.

The difference between PTP motion and continuous path contouring is difficult to distinguish, especially by an observer who did not actually program the robot. By detailed and meticulous programming, the programmer can set up a PTP robot to move in a seemingly continuous contour. Sometimes controller software can provide subroutines to relieve the programmer of specifying the myriad points required to simulate the curvilinear motion with tiny straight-line motions. But programming is not the only problem. The execution time of a PTP robot is dependent upon the number of points specified and thus can become too slow to be effective. Continuous contouring motion provides the ability to control not only the position of the robot tool but also the velocity of tool motion in each axis controlled by contouring. Contouring motion control is essential for most spray painting, finishing, deburring, fettling, gluing and arc welding operations by robots.

Line Tracking

One of the most complex contouring motions is called "line tracking" –that is, performing an operation while following alongside a continuously moving conveyor. Line tracking is merely another application of contouring, not a separate class of motion. However, the complexity of line tracking demands intricate programming of the robot controller, especially for robots whose bases are fixed to the floor. Some robots designed specifically for line tracking have a horizontal traverse on a track for the first degree of freedom. The traverse can be adjusted to match the speed of the conveyor, giving such robots a distinct advantage over the fixed-base robots with respect to the task of programming. However, fixed-base robots may be equipped with factory-supplied computer software, which, upon demand, conveniently add the line-tracking feature to the user's program. Therefore, the trade-off between the two types is cost of hardware versus cost of software.

Line tracking has obvious advantages. The product being processed can be transported on a continuous conveyor instead of an intermittent one. Continuous conveyors are much simpler mechanically and thus are less expensive and more reliable. With more reliable conveyor operation and quicker repair time, the continuous conveyor keeps idle time at a minimum, maximizing both production machine usage and robot usage.

Particularly suited to line tracking is the robot application of spray painting. Spray painting generally is applied to all sides of a component as it is transported by a continuous overhead chain. The robot must be directed at all sides of the part, a feat that can be accomplished most conveniently if the part moves continuously past the workstation and if the robot has line-tracking ability. Line tracking is also convenient if multiple operations must be performed by the robot on each part.

15.11 DRIVE

The most distinguishing feature used to describe an industrial robot is its power source. The power source usually determines the range of the robot's performance characteristics and in turn the feasibility of various applications, although there is considerable overlap between types. The four principal power sources are now compared.

15.11.1 Electrical Drive Systems

The electrically driven robot is the most popular drive today for general purpose, commercially available industrial robots. The increasing attention towards applications in automatic assembly have made the electrically driven robot, with its superior accuracy and quickness, the favored choice. Electromechanical drive systems are used in about 60 percent of today's robots. The motors used are servo motors and stepping motors. These motors convert electrical energy into mechanical energy to power the robot. Electric robots are popular for precision jobs because they can be closely controlled and can be taught to follow complicated paths of motion. Though many hydraulic models can have the same features, but sophisticated motion control is more typical of the all-electric models.

DC Motor – The most common type of drive motor used is permanent-magnet, direct-current (PMDC) motors which require only two leads, and use an arrangement of fixed- and electro-magnets (stator and rotor) and switches. These form a commutator to create motion through a spinning magnetic field. These robots invariably incorporate feedback loops from the driven components back to the driver. Thus, the control system continuously monitors the positions of the robot components, compares these positions with the positions desired by the controller, and notes any differences or error conditions. DC current is applied to each motor to correct error conditions until the error goes to zero.

AC Motor - AC motors use the line voltage. AC motors have the advantage of high reliability and robustness.

Stepper Motor - Stepper motors are driven a precise angular displacement for every discrete voltage pulse issued by the control computer interface. The stepper motor movements can be very precise, provided the torque load does not exceed the motor's design limits. Because of this inherent accuracy, the stepper-motor-type robot is sometimes of the open-loop type. The control computer computes the number of pulses required for the desired movement and dispatches the command to the robot without checking whether the robot actually completes the motion commanded. Unfortunately, the robot does not always accomplish the commanded motion because it may encounter an obstacle or for some other reason experience slippage in its mechanical linkage form its drive motors to its mechanical members. When this occurs, the positioning of end effects of open-loop robot is inaccurate and its control computer no longer knows the position of the robot's links.

Stepper motors are like brushless DC or AC motors. They move the rotor by applying power to different magnets in the motor in sequence (stepped). Steppers are designed for fine control and will not only spin on command, but can spin at any number of steps per second, subjected to the maximum limit permitted by the design.

It should be noted that feedback loops can be incorporated into the stepper-motor-type robot also. Optical encoders can be used to monitor the actual angular displacement of the driven component. This information is returned to the control computer, which is programmed to take action to correct any error conditions.

15.11.2 Pneumatic Drive Systems

Some of the least expensive and most practical robots for ordinary pick-and-place operations or for machine loading and unloading are the pneumatic models. The availability of shop air at approximately 5-7 bar is an obvious advantage. Most factories have compressed air piped throughout their production areas, and this can be conveniently employed to power a pneumatic robot.

Pneumatic robots usually operate at mechanically fixed endpoints for each axis. The mechanical stop is similar to those employed on pneumatic actuating cylinders extensively used in automation long before the advent of robots. Each link of robot is powered by individual pneumatic cylinders.

With motion in each axis controlled only at the end points, the programmability of a pneumatic robot is limited to timing and sequencing. This provides infinite variation of possible programmed setups for the pneumatic robot. Adjustment of the mechanical stops, can vary the length of stroke. However, a carefully controlled, continuously varying path is impossible to achieve with a an ordinary pneumatic robot. However, it is possible to realize continuous, controlled motion through the use of differential dithering. Differential dithering applies a series of short pulses of compressed air that can act upon the robot member in either direction, causing it to follow a continuous path under control.

One of the principal advantages of pneumatic robots is their modular construction and the use of standard, off the shelf components. This feature opens up the possibility of manufacturing companies deciding to build their its own robots, sometimes at considerable cost savings.

15.11.3 Hydraulic Drive Systems

The most popular form of the drive system is the hydraulic system because hydraulic cylinders and motors are compact and allow high levels of force and power, together with accurate control. A hydraulic actuator converts forces from high pressure hydraulic fluid into mechanical rotary or linear motion. Hydraulic fluid power is more cost effective for short-stroke, straight-line positioning requiring high forces, controlled acceleration, and repetitive motion. The power to volume ratio of hydraulic system is the highest. Hydraulic drive is ideal for harsh environments and especially suited for heavy duty applications in explosive environments.

Though, hydraulic drives are less popular now, they are still used in the automobile industry. Many of the spot welding robots are hydraulically operated. They are also suitable for handling of heavy forgings and die castings.

15.11.3.1 Mechanical Drives

For completeness, we will include the robots driven by belts, gears, cams and variable speed drives like harmonic drive and cycle drive. They are generally electrically driven. But the power is delivered to the robot arms by mechanical linkages. Two principal advantages of the mechanical linkages are low cost and speed. Since the reader will be familiar with the simple mechanical elements like gear, belt and pulleys, a description of these is not attempted here. However, two mechanical devices capable of providing variable speed drive to robot links are harmonic drive and cycle drive. The advantage is that these are very compact and there by occupy less space.

15.11.3.2 Harmonic Drive

Harmonic drive is popular with many robot designers. The harmonic drive takes advantage of the elastic dynamics of metal. It is generally made up of just three components- a wave generator, a flexspline and a circular spline.

Wave Generator: The wave generator is a component having small ball bearings built into the outer circumference of the elliptical cam. circumference of an elliptical cam. The inside raceway of the bearings is fixed to the cam while the outer raceway is subjected to elastic deformation via the ball bearings.

The wave generator is usually attached to the input shaft.

Flexspline: The flexspline is a thin cup-shaped metal rim component with external teeth. The bottom of the flexspline (cup bottom) is called the diaphragm.

A diaphragm is usually attached to the output shaft.

Circular Spline: The circular spline is a rigid steel ring with internal teeth. The circular spline has two teeth more than the flexspline and is usually fixed to a casing. The harmonic drive is illustrated in Fig. 15.9. The flexspline is deflected by the wave generator into an elliptical shape causing the flexspline teeth to engage with those of the circular spline at the major axis of the wave generator ellipse, with the teeth completely disengaged across the minor axis of the ellipse. When the wave generator is rotated clockwise with the circular spline fixed, the flexspline is subjected to elastic deformation and its tooth engagement position moves by turns relative to the circular spline. When the wave generator rotates 180 degrees clockwise, the flexspline moves counterclockwise by one tooth relative to the circular spline. When the wave generator rotates one revolution clockwise (360 degrees), the flexspline moves counterclockwise by two teeth relative to the circular spline because the flexspline has two fewer teeth than the circular spline.

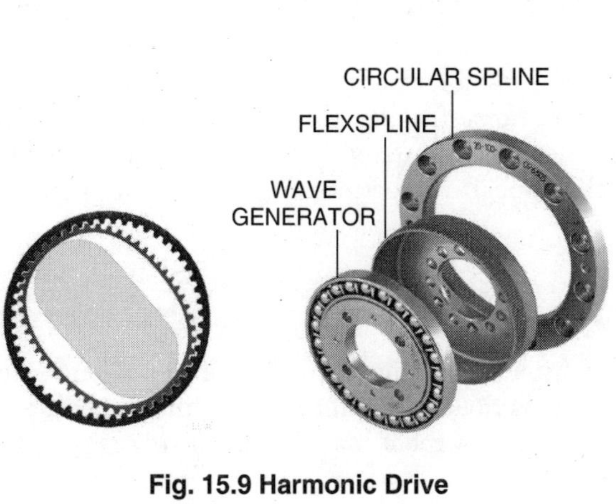

Fig. 15.9 Harmonic Drive

Advantages of harmonic drive are high reduction ratio, no backlash, precision, fewer number of components, small size, light in weight, high torque, ease of assembly, high efficiency and noise free operation. These are briefly explained in the following sections.

(i) **High-speed reduction ratio:** A harmonic drive has high single-stage coaxial reduction ratios of 1/30 to 1/320. This is why the harmonic drive provides high efficiency gearing without using complex mechanisms and structures.

(ii) **Free of backlash (lost motion):** Different from the ordinary tooth-with-tooth mating mechanism, the harmonic drive operates with very little -- nearly zero -- backlash, which is an essential characteristic for motion control.

(iii) **High precision:** With the harmonic drive, high positional/ rotational accuracy is assured because a) it has many simultaneous-mating teeth built-in, and b) because these teeth mate with one another in two symmetrical positions at 180 degrees. This means influences of tooth pitch errors and accumulated pitch errors on rotational accuracy are equalized to assure high positional/ rotational accuracy.

(iv) **Small numbers of components and ease of assembly:** Effective speed reduction ratios are possible with only three basic components, and since all three components are co-axially aligned, the harmonic drive can be easily built into component-assembled products, allowing for simple configurations.

(v) **Small size and light weight:** Robots can be made smaller and lighter because the harmonic drive provides the same levels of torque and speed reduction ratios as conventional gearing mechanisms, while being less than 1/3 the size of conventional products in terms of capacity and less than 1/2 the weight.

(vi) **High torque capacity:** The flexspline is made of special steel with a higher resistance to fatigue. Different from the typical driving force transmission apparatus, every tooth is subjected to very little force yet provides a high torque capacity. Because a) the number of simultaneously mating teeth in the flexspline accounts for some 30% of the total number of teeth, and b) these teeth come into contact with one another face to face, every tooth is subjected to a minimum of force while providing a maximum of torque.

(vii) **High efficiency:** The mating portion of each tooth is subjected to very little sliding motion. Therefore, motion loss due to friction is reduced substantially, enabling the harmonic drive to maintain a high level of efficiency, and allowing driving motors to be made smaller.

(viii) **Quiet, vibration-free operation:** With the harmonic drive, quiet and vibration-free operations are possible because the teeth do not come into rolling contact with one another, and as the circumferential speed of each tooth is low, the teeth provide a well-balanced force.

15.11.3.3 Cyclo Drive

A cycloidal drive is sometimes used for obtaining variable speeds in a robot. This drive is also compact, durable, robust and noise free. In this drive a high speed shaft turns a cycloid disk around the internal circumference of a fixed ring gear. In each turn the cycloid disc advances a distance of one lobe in the opposite direction of the ring gear. This results in the slow motion of the output shaft.

15.12 MECHANICAL ARMS/LINKS

A robot is designed usually for a specific payload. The term payload refers to the maximum load it can handle. For example a payload of 50 kgf means that the robot can manipulate an object with a maximum weight of 50 kgf. A robot may consist of several links connected by joints.

There are mainly four types of joints that are found in robot manipulators:

- Revolute, rotary or pin joint (R)
- Prismatic or sliding joint (P)
- Spherical or ball joint (S)
- Helical or screw joint (H)

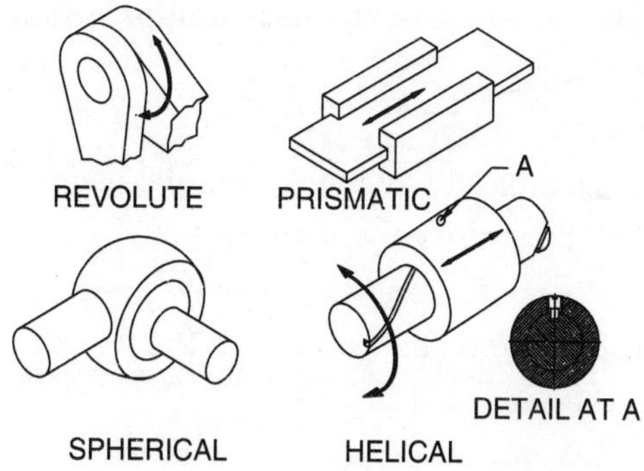

Fig. 15.10 Typical Robot Joints

The revolute joint allows a rotation between the two connecting links. The prismatic joint allows a pure translation between the two connecting links. The spherical joint between two links allows the first link to rotate in all possible ways with respect to the second. The helical joint allows a helical motion between the two connecting bodies. A simple helical joint is shown in Fig. 15.10.

Translational joints will provide linear motion between elements where as rotary joints will facilitate rotational displacement. For example, an articulated robot may consist of only rotary joints whereas a cylindrical robot may have both rotary and translational joints.

The kinematic structure of the robot arm allows to position its end point at any (x, y, z) location in the 3D space (within the robot's working space). In order to provide for the proper orientation of the hand or end effector the robot arm should have *a wrist*. Typically a robot wrist provides the same 3D rotations as a human hand: roll, pitch, and yaw. A wrist where the three axes of rotation intersect is called a *spherical wrist*. These have the advantage that the mathematical model used to calculate the wrist joint angles from their position and orientation in space is soluble.

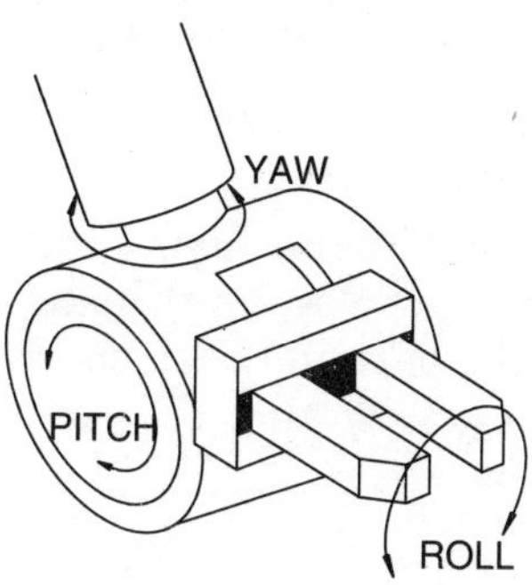

Fig. 15.11 Wrist

One problem in achieving spherical wrist design is the physical difficulty of fitting all the components into the available space. The size of the human wrist is small because the muscles which power it are located in the forearm, not in the wrist. Wrist design is a complex task, involving conflicting goals. Desirable features of a wrist include:

- small size
- axes close together to increase mechanical efficiency
- tool plate close to the axes to increase strength and precision
- solvable mathematical model
- no singularities in the work volume
- back-driving to allow programming by teach and playback
- decoupling between motions around the three axes
- actuators mounted away from the wrist to allow size reduction
- paths for end effector control and power through the wrist
- power proportionate to the proposed task
- rugged housing.

15.13 ROBOT TOOLING

Although this chapter frequently refers to robot grippers, most robots do not come equipped with such devices unless ordered alongwith robots. Programmability and versatility are hallmarks of the modern industrial robot. The robot manufacturers' strategy is to leave the choice of the end-of-arm tooling to the user or a system integrator. Many robots are programmed to use a variety of tools or grippers in a single setup, automatically selecting and changing tools according to a prescribed sequence.

15.13.1 Grippers

Robot gripper selection is a critical design decision to be made by the automation engineer. This decision can be as important to the success of the application as the selection of the robot. The engineer must be mindful of the conditions of use of the robot gripper and remember that the workplace environment may not be the same as that of the laboratory in which the robot application was tested. Heat, for instance, can cause the grippers to expand, burn, or melt, depending upon the materials used. Abrasive workpieces can cause wear, especially considering the thousands of repetitive operations the robot may be called upon to execute. Perhaps most critical of all is the question of what may happen to the robot gripper if the workpiece is not properly aligned and a collision occurs. Collision also frequently occur when the robot is programmed improperly.

Grippers come in a wide variety of configurations and are often designed by the customer to fit a particular application. Most grippers close on the part to be picked up, but a large number of them insert their fingers inside the part and then open to grip the part. Many grippers are fashioned to work effectively either way so that the choice is up to the programmer. Figure 15.12 illustrates a variety of grippers.

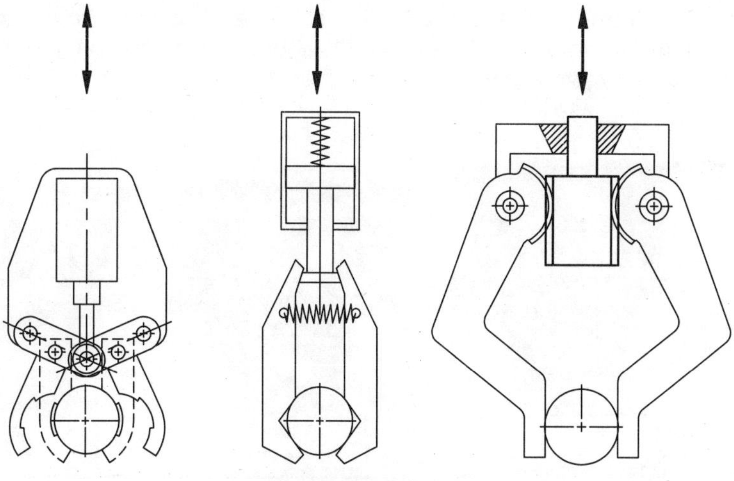

Fig. 15.12 Grippers

Some applications require a variety of grippers in the same setup, so some type of facility is needed to enable the robot to change grippers or to change form a gripper to a special purpose end effector. For many applications, a double-handed gripper is more efficient than a single-handed gripper. This is typically true of machine loading and unloading, as the robot is able to both unload and load a given station without moving between stations. This saves much time that would otherwise be wasted in repetitious motion in the principal axis (normally base rotation). Base rotation is typically the slowest axis on the robot.

15.13.2 Appliances

Besides the common gripper used for piece-parts handling, tool heads of various types can be attached to the end of the robot arm. The wide variety of these end-of-arm tools sets the robot apart from ordinary material handling devices.

Welding heads are the most common type of robot tool, excluding grippers. Spot welders are the most common, but arc welding robots are growing in importance. Spray painting heads, mentioned earlier in this chapter are an important type of robot tool. Related to spray painting heads are glue applicators. Both of these tools are useful because of the precision and repeatability of the robot. An unusual tool is a dispenser for electric cable. This tool is used in the programmed assembly of electrical wire harnesses for aircraft and other large equipment.

15.13.3 Part Compliant Tooling

A tiny misalignment of a piece-part or robot tool can result in complete failure of the process and perhaps damage to the product or to the robot hand. The usual method to avoid the effect of misalignment problems is to mount the gripper with a flexible connection that allows the gripper tool to yield a little when it encounters the object to be picked up. This approach is often referred to as part-compliant tooling.

One sophisticated type of part-compliant tooling is called remote center compliance (RCC). The concept is illustrated in Fig. 15.13. In Fig. 15.13 (a) , the robot is attempting to insert a pin into a hole, but there is lateral misalignment. The chamfer helps, but with rigid tooling the pin still may not enter the hole. A less rigid tooling still might not deliver the desired result because the lateral component of force at the chamfer will tend to rotate the pin about its flexible center of compliance. The assembly in Fig. 15.13 (b) projects the center of compliance to the leading end of the shaft, which is a remote center of compliance point. The important consequence of this projection is that the pin shifts laterally instead of rotating about its top end.

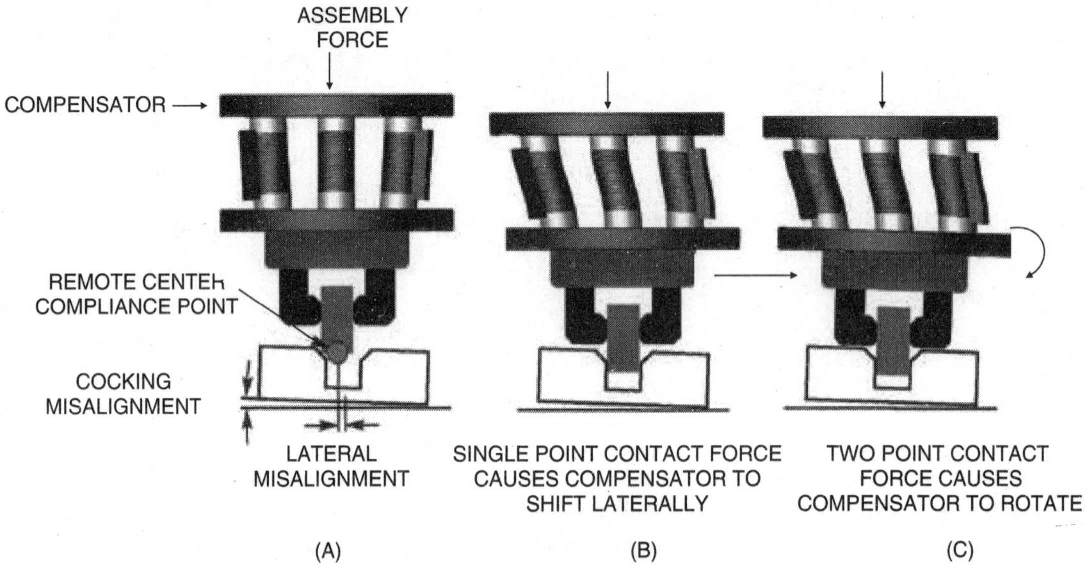

Fig. 15.13 Remote Centre Compliance

Figure 15.13 (c) presents a correct lateral alignment, but an error in angular alignment. Note that this time the pin makes contact with the hole at two places. Lateral components of force on the pin are parallel and opposite each other, but these parallel, opposite forces do not act in the same line because the lateral force from the left acts on a point higher on the pin than the lateral force from the right. This causes a moment to act on the pin. The physical appearance of RCC device is illustrated in Fig. 15.14.

Fig. 15.14 RCC Device

An even simpler strategy that works in some cases is to use rubber or nylon in the construction of the fingers themselves so that a soft, compliant touch not unlike that of human fingers is used to pick up the object. Any such flexible pickup method can be considered part-compliant tooling. The principle is so simple and practical that it would seem to be an obvious solution to gripper alignment problems.

15.14 Sensors

Sensing capability on a robot can have widely ranging degrees of sophistication in addition to a variety of sensing media. For instance, optical sense capability can vary from a simple photoelectric cell to a complex, three-dimensional vision system. Various sensing categories will now be described, beginning with the simplest and most practical and proceeding to the most advanced systems available.

Robots react according to a basic temporal measurement, requiring different kinds of sensors. In most systems a sense of time is built in through the circuits and programming. For this to be productive in practice, a robot has to have perceptual hardware and software, which is updated quickly. Regardless of sensor hardware or software, sensing and sensors can be thought of as interacting with external events. The sensor measures some attribute of the world. The term transducer is often used interchangeably with sensor. A transducer is the mechanism, or element, of the sensor that transforms the energy associated with what is being measured into another form of energy. A sensor receives energy and transmits a signal to a display or computer. Sensors use transducers to change the input signal (sound, light, pressure, temperature, etc.) into an analog or digital form capable of being used by a robot.

Logical Sensors: One powerful abstraction of a sensor is a logical sensor, which is a unit of sensing or module that supplies a particular percept. It consists of the signal processing, from the physical sensor, and the software processing needed to extract the percept.

Proximity Sensors: Proximity sensors are used to sense if an object is within a specified distance.

Infrared (IR) Sensors: Another type of active proximity sensor is an infrared sensor. It emits near-infrared energy and measures whether any significant amount of the IR light is returned.

Bump and Feeler Sensors: Another popular class of robotic sensing is tactile, or touch-based, done with a bump and feeler sensor. Feelers or whiskers are constructed from sturdy wires. A bump sensor is usually a protruding ring around the robot consisting of two layers. The sensors used for collision avoidance in AGVs are of this type.

15.14.1 Gripper Pressure Sensing

The most elementary sense capability on a robot is probably the ability of the gripper to detect gripping force between its fingertips. In its simplest form, the grip sensor consists merely of a limit switch that trips when a given preset grip pressure is reached. Such a limit switch is a practical safeguard against over closure of the gripper in case of either program error or payload dimensional variability. But the disadvantages go beyond this safeguard because the limit switch can be used to gauge thickness by simply closing its gripper in a gauging operation. Thus, a robot can be used to gauge thickness by simply closing its gripper upon an object. This feature of a robot is inexpensive to apply, and accuracy surpassing that of human fingers is easy to achieve.

Sometimes grip pressure and grip closure are in fact the same operation. This can be achieved, for instance, by using "tendon technology" – that is, the actuation of the axes by cables leading to motors mounted on the robot base.

15.14.2 Vision Sensors

A large number of robots, nowadays are fitted with vision sensors. The vision sensor is very useful for pick and place, sorting or inspection. It is also useful for seam tracking during welding. Vision sensors can be widely used inspection of automobiles in body in white condition. The main advantage is that vision sensing is fast and the robotic system can be carried out to inspect a large number of features concurrently. The only limitation is the field of vision of the sensing camera. The vision sensor can guide the gripper to grasp an object based on the orientation of the object. It is useful for sorting based on geometrical features, color etc.

15.15 MICROCONTROLLERS

Microcontrollers (MCUs) are intelligent electronic devices used to control robots. They deliver functions similar to those performed by a microprocessor (central processing unit, or CPU) inside a personal computer. MCUs are slower and can address less memory than CPUs, but are designed for real-world control problems. One of the major differences between CPUs and MCUs is the number of external components needed to operate them. MCUs can often run with zero external parts. There are four basic aspects of a microcontroller—speed, size, memory, and architecture. Speed is designated in clock cycles, and is usually measured in millions of cycles per second (Megahertz, MHz). The use of the cycles varies in different MCUs, affecting the usable speed of the processor. Size specifies the number of bits of information the MCU can process in one step-the size of its natural cluster of information. MCUs come in 4-, 8-, 16-, and 32-bits. MCUs count most of their ROM in thousands of bytes (KB) and RAM in single bytes.

Microcontrollers includes features such as a dedicated input device that often (but not always) has a small LED or LCD display for output. A microcontroller also takes input from the device and controls it by sending signals to different components in the device. The program counter keeps track of which command is to be executed by the microcontroller.

15.16 OPEN SOURCE CONTROL OF ROBOTS

OROCOS (Open Robot Control Software) is an effort to start up an open source robot control software project. Goals of the OROCOS project are to develop robot control software with the following characteristics:

- Under open source and/or free software license(s),
- As modular as possible,
- Of the highest quality (from both technical and software engineering perspectives),
- Independent of (but compatible with) commercial robot manufacturers,
- For all sorts of robotic devices and computer platforms,
- Localized for all programming languages, and
- Featuring configurable software components for kinematics, dynamics, planning, sensing, control, hardware interfacing, etc.

The goal of the OROCOS project is to develop shareable libraries, stand-alone components (sometimes referred to as software agents), and a configurable run-time environment from which to eliminate and control all distributed robotics systems. These types of projects are useful in several ways:

- For re-using code,
- For use as an independent sub-system,
- For copying their organizational structure,
- For learning from the experience of managing an open source project, and
- For designing and developing extensible and reusable software.

15.16.1 Open Source Matrix Libraries

There are several open source matrix libraries that satisfy the above-mentioned requirements.

GNU Octave - GNU Octave is a high-level language, primarily intended for numerical computations. It provides a convenient command line interface for solving linear and nonlinear problems numerically, and for performing other numerical experiments using a language that is mostly compatible with Matlab. It is easily extensible and customizable via user-defined functions written in Octave's own language, or using dynamically loaded modules written in C++, C, Fortran, or other languages.

GSL (GNU Scientific Library) - GSL is an ongoing effort to develop a modern extensive and ANSI C library for numerical computing. The GNU Scientific Library (GSL) is a collection of routines for numerical computing. The routines are written from scratch by the GSL team in ANSI C, and are meant to present a modern Applications Programming Interface (API) for C programmers, while allowing wrappers to be written for very high level languages. GSL is free software. It is distributed under the terms of the GNU General Public License.

Real-Time Linux (RTLinux) - RTLinux(TM) is a real-time operating system that handles time-critical tasks and runs Linux as its lowest priority execution thread. In RTLinux, the kernel shares one or more processors with standard Linux. This allows the system to run accurately timed applications performing data acquisition, systems control and robotics, while still serving as a standard Linux workstation.

15.17 ROBOTIC WORK CELL

Robots are used for automating a manufacturing operation. In order to make the best use of robots it is necessary to have the following additional equipment:

- End effectors suitable for the intended use
- Equipment for feeding the workpieces like conveyors, bowl feeders, pallets etc
- Equipment for handling the workpieces like lift and turntables
- Equipment for manipulating and presenting the workpieces to the robot. These positioners determine how the part is presented to the robot for operations like welding. Typical positioner types include stationary tables, turntables, headstocks, tailstocks and Ferris wheel types
- Fixtures to hold the part to proper tolerances for welding. Unique to each automation project, fixtures are only as good as the quality and innovation the systems integrator puts into them.
- A common base platform, which the systems integrator designs and constructs, connects all components. It is also a base for controls, flash screens, barriers and safety components
- Dispensing cells for adhesives, paints, or other materials
- Programmable logic controller and computer
- Operator Interface is the final component of the work cell. Simple push buttons, or a touch-screen panel, are often recommended interfaces
- Safety guards and interlocking arrangements to ensure that no human is within the working zone of the robot.

All these forming parts of a robotic work cell should be properly engineered by a system integrator for optimum performance. The total cost of the work cell may be sometimes equal the cost of the robot itself. It is advisable to design a proper work cell for efficient operation. There could be multiple options and the system integrator is the right person to tender proper advice to the user of the robot. Some integrators offer pre-engineered or standard work cells. These systems provide out-of-the-box affordability, but are not always the right solution when customization is required. Integrators with flexible, modifiable work cells can provide a cost-effective solution tailored to the application. The systems integrators should conduct a risk analysis and then design and adjust systems for the safest operation that meets or exceeds all plant, state and local codes. These safety measures include fence barriers, gate interlocks, floor safety switch mats, photo-cell and light curtains, fixed guards, emergency stop hardware and software, as well as frames and screens to protect workers from injurious environment like welding arc flash.

15.18 PROGRAMMING OF ROBOTS

The usual method of programming a robot is teach in and play back. The robot is taken through the appropriate link movements to perform a task. This is usually done by the operator with the aid of a teach pendant. The teach pendant will have buttons with appropriate symbols so that the operator can take the robot through the required movements of the arm and the end effector. The movements are stored in the memory of the robot. Subsequent operations can be performed in the play back mode. Some advanced robot systems will have the capability to optimize the movements. Many robot manufacturers provide necessary instructions to program a robot without using an off line programming language.

Use of a programming language helps to carry out off line programming and simulation of the operation of the robot. There are several programming languages used in robotics. The robot manufacturers supply user friendly interactive programming systems along with the robot, eliminating the need for mastering a complex programming language. However for the sake of information details of some programming languages are given in this section.

There are two approaches for robot programming. One is robot oriented programming and the second is task oriented programming. In robot oriented programming the various links of the robots are moved to desired positions so that a work is performed. Task oriented programming is more complex. For example let us consider a mechanical assembly operation in which a part has to be inserted into another part. A typical example is the insertion of an IC on to a printed circuit board. The gripper has to orient properly to grasp the IC. This is done with the aid of a vision system and appropriate image processing software and gripper orientation program. The gripper has to approach the IC, orient itself, decelerate, grasp the IC with appropriate means, move to the socket, decelerate, insert the IC and retract. The programming in such cases will have to be done carefully.

RoboML (Robotic Markup Language) - RoboML is used for standardized representation of robotics-related data. It is designed to support communication language between human-robot interface agents, as well as between robot-hosted processes and between interface processes, and to provide a format for archived data used by human-robot interface agents.

XRCL (Extensible Robot Control Language) - XRCL (pronounced zircle) is a relatively simple, modern language and environment designed to allow robotics researchers to share ideas by sharing code. It is an open source project.

Open System Architecture for Controls within Automation Systems (OSACA) - OSACA is a joint European project that aims to improve the competitiveness of the manufacturers of machine tools and control systems in the world market. The main goal of the project is to specify system architecture for open control systems, which is manufacturer independent.

15.19 RESOLUTION, ACCURACY AND REPEATABILITY OF ROBOTS

An industrial robot is often used for applications requiring very high positioning accuracy. As in the case of CNC machines and coordinate measuring machines, manufacturing engineers are concerned with the accuracy and repeatability of robots.

15.19.1 Resolution

The resolution of a robot is a feature determined by the design of the control unit and is mainly dependent on the position feedback sensor. It is important to distinguish the programming resolution from the control resolution. The programming resolution is the smallest allowable position increment in robot programs and is referred to as the basic resolution unit (BRU). The control resolution is the smallest change in position that the feedback device can sense. For example, assume that an optical encoder which emits 7200 pulses per revolution of the shaft is directly attached to a rotary axis. This encoder will emit one pulse for each of 0.05° of angular displacement of the shaft. The unit 0.05° is the control resolution of this axis of motion. Angular increments smaller than 0.05° cannot be detected. Best performance is obtained when programming resolution is equal to control resolution. In this case both resolutions can be replaced with one term: the system resolution.

15.19.2 Accuracy

Accuracy refers to a robot's ability to position its wrist end at a desired target point within the work volume, and it is defined in terms of spatial resolution. At first accuracy depends on robot technology and how closely the control increments can be defined for each of the joint motions, excluding for the moment. The mechanical inaccuracy depends on the quality of manufacture of the robot. Let us consider considering the case where the target point is directly between two control points Theoretically the accuracy is equal to one-half of the control resolution (Fig. 15.15). For more realistic consideration we have to include mechanical inaccuracies with a statistical distribution as shown in Fig. 15.16 in that case accuracy is defined as one-half of the spatial resolution.

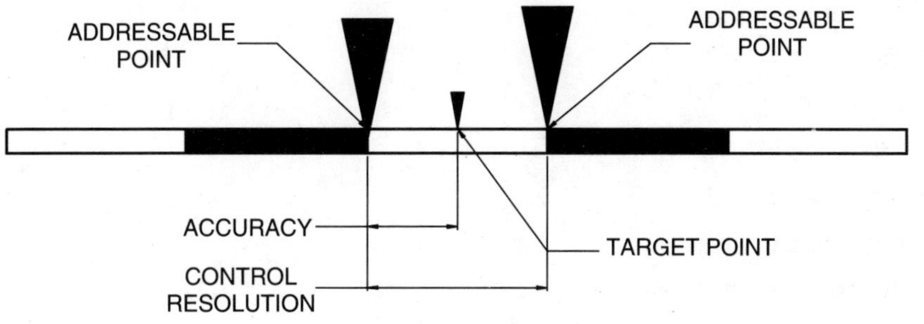

Fig. 15.15 Accuracy

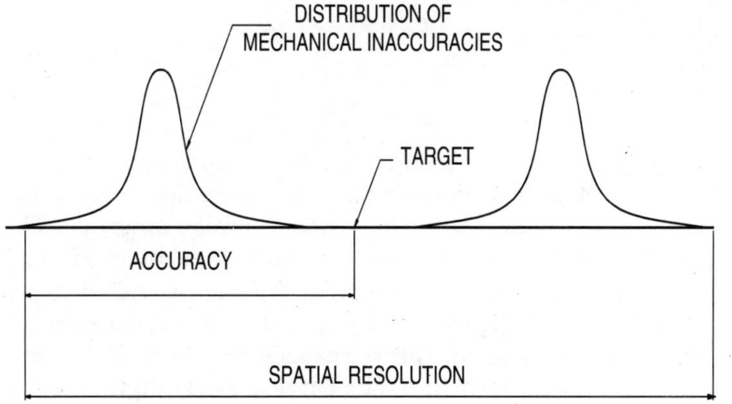

Fig. 15.16 Accuracy and Spatial Resolution with Mechanical Inaccuracies

The term accuracy in robotics is often confused with the terms resolution and repeatability. The final accuracy of a robotic system depends on its mechanical inaccuracies, the computer control algorithms, and the system resolution. The mechanical inaccuracies are caused mainly by backlash in the manipulators joints and bending of the links. The backlash exists in gear mechanisms, in lead screws, and in actuators of hydraulic drives. The minimization of the link deflection is the main design requirement for the link, as any deflection of the link due to the load at the robot's end causes position errors. A higher rigidity of the links, however, should not be achieved by a substantial increase in their mass. A larger mass causes an increase in the time response of the arm. Control algorithms might cause position errors due to round-off errors in the computer. Computer round-off errors might be significant if a robot controller uses scaled integer representation of Cartesian and angular coordinates. If the computer uses floating point representation, then the round-off errors will probably be insignificant.

Different definitions of robot accuracy exists, for example system inaccuracy due to resolution is considered to be 1/2 BRU **(Basic Resolution Unit)**. The reason is that displacements smaller than 1 BRU can be neither programmed nor measured and, on the average, they count for 1/2 BRU. A realistic accuracy system is determined in the following relationship:

Robot accuracy = (BRU + mechanical accuracy)/2

The definition currently used is the ISO 9283 definition (ISO/TC 154/SC 2/ WG 2). It considers errors in three dimensions.

Errors in robots can be due to:

Control System Errors

Position error

Resolution of measuring system

Clock speed

Natural frequency

Type of drive

Mechanical Errors

Compliance of the links

Manufacturing tolerances

Thermal deformation

Flexibility of transmission system

Play in bearings

Backlash

Friction

Accuracy is affected also by external factors. As torque is becoming more important on the wrist point with the fully extended configuration, accuracy decreases within the work volume, from the closer position of the arm to its base, till the work envelope. The term error map is used to characterize the level of accuracy possessed by the robot as a function of location in the work volume. Accuracy is improved if the motion cycle is restricted to a limited work range, while it decreases if the load being carried by the robot becomes important Position accuracy depends on the position of gripper in the workspace envelope. The sources of position error that affect accuracy can be grouped into four categories: a) digitization error, b) calibration error, c) deterministic kinematic error, d) stochastic kinematic error.

As the assembly robots axes are often vertical, accuracy is slightly better because it is less affected by external factors and mechanical inaccuracies; but this is not enough to perform some parts mating applications as peg-in-hole without problems.

15.19.3 Repeatability

Repeatability is a statistical term associated with accuracy, it describes how a point is repeated. If a robot joint is instructed to move by the same angle from a certain point a number of times, all with equal environmental conditions, it will be found that the resultant motions lead to differing displacements as shown in Fig. 15.17. Although a target is always missed by a large margin, if the same error is repeated, then we say that the repeatability is high and the accuracy is poor. Repeatability does not describe the error with respect to absolute coordinates. System repeatability is the positional deviation from the average of displacements.

Most robot manufacturers provide a numerical value for the repeatability rather than the accuracy of their robots. The reason is that the accuracy depends upon the particular load that the gripper carries. A heavier weight causes larger deflections of the robot links and larger load on the joints, which degrade the accuracy, while the repeatability value, however, is almost independent of the gripper load.

The repeatability of robots will usually be better than the accuracy, it is normally measured in hundredths of a mm. Repeatability definition which is currently used is the ISO 9283 definition (ISO/TC 154/SC 2/WG 2).

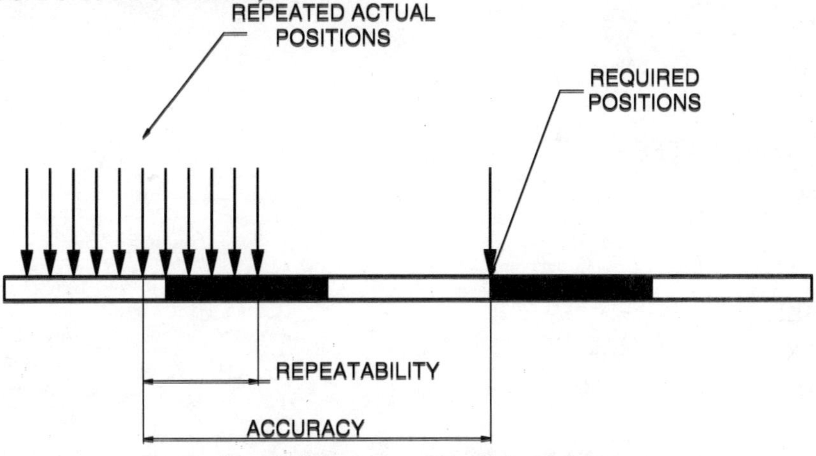

Fig. 15.17 Accuracy and Repeatability

15.20 MANUFACTURERS OF ROBOTS

There are a large number of robot manufacturers. Some of them are listed below:

ABB
ADEPT
AMERICAN ROBOT CORPORATION
ANGELUS RESEARCH
ARRIK ROBOTICS
BEUMER
COMAU

CYBERMOTION
DENEB
DENSO
EPSON
EROWA
ESAB
FANUC
FKI LOGISTICS
iROBOT
JANOME
K-TEAM SA
HYUNDAI
KAWASAKI
KUKA
LINCOLN
MILLER
MOTOMAN
NACHI
OKURA
OTC
RIXAN ASSOCIATES
PANASONIC
SEIKO
SONY
STAUBLI
VENTAX
YAMAHA

15.21 SPECIFICATIONS OF ROBOTS

A number of parameters are to be considered while selecting a robot.

(i) Type of robot-Cartesian, cylindrical, spherical, articulated, SCARA etc.
(ii) Drive-electrical, electromechanical, electro hydraulic, electro pneumatic etc.
(iii) Number of axes and travel in each axis
(iv) Load capacity
(v) Reach (work envelope)
(vi) Application (welding, painting, assembly, dispensing (gluing, filling, sealing), assembly, inspection, materials handling, machine tending, cutting, deburring, marking, drilling, punching, packaging, pharmaceutical, medical, etc.
(vii) Special mounting-ceiling, wall, portable, mobile etc.

Axis Movement Specifications:

(1) **Axes:** The individual segments of each robot manipulator are connected with mechanical joints-each serves as an axis of movement. The most common industrial robots have six axes of movement. The number and placement of axes determines the flexibility of each model. Check out our industrial robot axes FAQ for more information.

(2) **Robot Motion Range**: Robot axes have limits to each movement. Every axis has a specific scope of motion. On a typical specifications sheet, the degree of movement shows up as positive or negative degree of movement from the center base position of each axis.

(3) **Robot Motion Speed:** Each axis moves at a different speed. They are listed as degrees traveled per second. Focus on this criterion when you need to match certain speed specifications for your application.

(4) **Repeatability:** Industrial robots are known for their accuracy. But this ability to return to an exact location again and again, known as a robot's repeatability, can vary with each model. More precision-driven applications will require tighter repeatability figures. Repeatability is listed as a millimeter of alteration plus or minus from the point.

Robot Specifications for Weight:

(1) **Payload**: The weight capacity of each robot manipulator is its payload. This is a critical specification and includes the tooling weight as well.

(2) **Robot Mass**: Every robot has a specific weight or mass. This number only indicates how much the robot manipulator weighs. It does not include the weight of the robot's controller.

Specifications and Work Envelope:

(1) **V-Reach**: A robot's vertical reach specification refers to the height of the robot when it extends upwards from the base. Use this to determine whether or not a model is tall enough for your application and location.

(2) **H-Reach**: The horizontal reach measures the distance of the fully extended arm-from the base to the wrist. Some applications will require a wider work envelope with a big reach, others are satisfied with a contained, short horizontal reach.

REVIEW QUESTIONS

(1) What is the significance of the laws of robotics?

(2) Describe different types of robots based on application.

(3) Discuss the classification of robots based on arm geometry.

(4) Sketch the work envelope of an articulated robot.

(5) What are the elements of a typical robotic workstation?

(6) Discuss point to point and continuous path control of robots.

(7) What is line tracking?

(8) Describe different solutions for driving the links of robots.

(9) What are the advantages of electric drives for robot arms?

(10) Compare hydraulic and pneumatic drives for robot arms.

(11) Discuss the working principle of a harmonic drive.

(12) How do you determine the speed ratio of a harmonic drive?
(13) What are the advantages of harmonic drive?
(14) Discuss common types of joints used in robots.
(15) What are the desired motions in a typical robot wrist?
(16) Discuss two designs of grippers.
(17) What is meant by remote centre compliance?
(18) Sketch and explain a typical RCC device.
(19) What is the significance of using a sensor with robots?
(20) Why do we go for gripper pressure sensing in some applications?
(21) Why is a vision system usually an integral part of the robot?
(22) Discuss the common sensors used in robots.
(23) What are the typical controllers used in robots?
(24) What approach is adopted for open source control of robots?
(25) Discuss the significance of designing a robotic work cell.
(26) What is the difference between robot oriented programming and task oriented programming?
(27) Compare the features of two robot programming languages.
(28) Give an example of programming a robot using VAL programmimg language.
(29) Distinguish between resolution, accuracy and repeatability.
(30) What are the factors contributing to inaccuracy in the operation of a robot?
(31) How do you determine the accuracy and repeatability of a robot?
(32) How do you specify a robot?

16 KINEMATICS OF ROBOTS

Many manufacturing operations using robots like welding and painting require complex programming involving kinematics, dynamics and control of robots. Programming of robots requires the knowledge of the position of the end effector and its orientation. This chapter gives an overview of the kinematics of industrial robots.

16.1 INTRODUCTION

A robot can be modeled as an open loop articulated chain of several links connected in series. As discussed in the last chapter, the connection can be usually either a revolute or translational joint driven by an actuator. One end of the chain is fixed to the ground (base of the robot) and the other end carries the tool which performs the intended task. The tool has to be oriented and positioned in space to carry out the tasks.

Kinematics of robots deals with the analytical study of the motion of a robot arm with reference to a fixed coordinate system. The forces or moments that cause the motion are ignored in kinematic analysis. There are two fundamental approaches in robot kinematics.

(i) Given specific displacements for each robot link, obtain the position and orientation of the tool or end effector. This is called direct kinematics or forward kinematics.

(ii) Given the position and orientation of the end effector, determining the individual displacements of each one of the links that will result in the desired position and orientation. This is called inverse kinematics.

Figure 16.1 illustrates both kinematic approaches. The difference between forward and inverse kinematics is clear from the diagram. In forward kinematics, the programmer determines the final position and orientation of end effector for specified displacements of the links whereas, in inverse kinematics, the programmer has to work backwards. Programming a robot using a teaching pendant is an example of direct kinematics. In inverse kinematics the desired position is known and the objective is to determine individual link displacements to achieve the desired position. This is a mathematically complex task, the complexity increasing with increase in the number of degrees of freedom of the robot. In some cases there may be more than one solution in which case the programmer needs to search for an optimum solution. The singularities in the solution often create difficulties. In some cases there may not be a feasible solution at all. Obviously direct kinematics is much simpler than inverse kinematics.

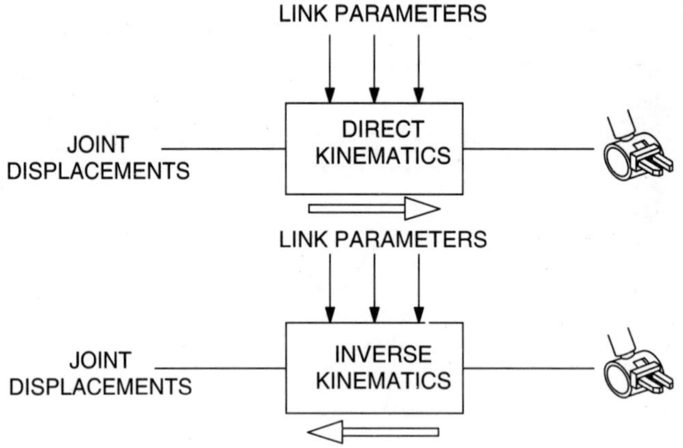

Fig. 16.1 Approaches to Robot Kinematics

16.2 APPROACH

The links of a manipulator rotate or translate with respect to a reference coordinate frame. The total spatial displacement of the end effector is therefore the sum total of all the link displacements. A systematic approach to represent the spatial geometry of the links with reference to a fixed coordinate frame was proposed by Denavit and Hartenberg (DH) in 1955 to solve forward (direct) kinematics. A 4×4 homogeneous transformation matrix is used in D-H method to describe the spatial relationship between two adjacent links. This chapter gives a brief description of the DH method. The inverse kinematic problem is solved by iterative, geometric or algebraic methods.

16.3 FORWARD KINEMATICS

Forward kinematics problem is developed using the concept of a body attached coordinate frame for each link which is illustrated in Fig. 16.2.

Usually, any tools or handling devices of a manipulator can be described with the help a constant homogeneous transformation, if related to the last, outermost link of the robot.

In this tool frame, environmental objects can be easily located relative to the tool tip or gripper. It is quite simple to find relative motions necessary for the tool tip in order to handle objects.

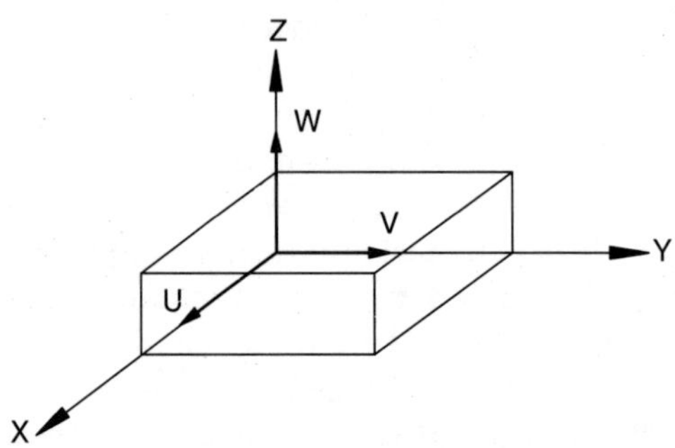

Fig. 16.2 Body Attached Coordinate Frame

However, to really achieve the related joint motion to move the tool tip appropriately, the necessary motion trajectory of the tip with respect to the base frame has to be calculated. The resulting base frame description can then be used to solve the inverse kinematics problem that is to find the related joint coordinates.

Multiple coordinate frames are also useful in traditional robotics. For example, consider the simple robot arm depicted in Fig. 16.3. If we want to have the gripper pick up a part off of a table, then we need to figure out the part's location. We can use a camera to initially determine the location of the part (in camera coordinates). We might need to transform that location into world coordinates to evaluate if it is accessible to the robot and to gripper coordinates to determine when we should close the jaws of the gripper.

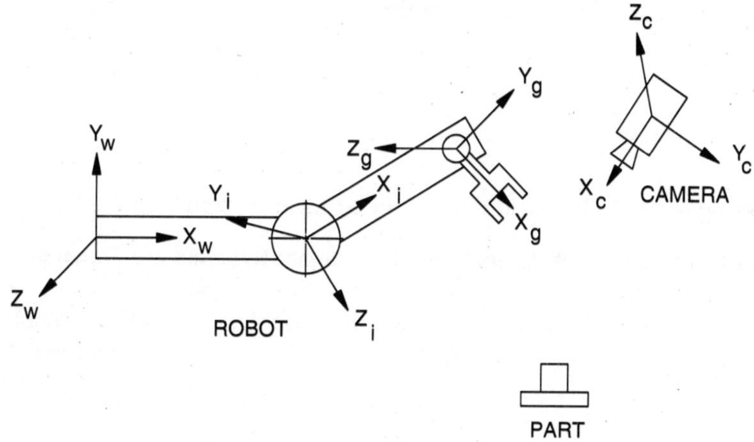

Fig. 16.3 Simple Robot Arm

Let us assume that the location of a point in one coordinate frame (for example, gripper coordinates) is known and we want to know its location in another frame (for example, world coordinates). We will start with a very simple case considering the two coordinate systems, world coordinates and robot coordinate frames, shown in Fig. 16.4.The only difference between the two coordinate frames is that the robot frame has been translated by 5 units along the y axis from the world coordinate frame. The origin of the robot frame is located at (0, 5, 0) with reference to world coordinates. We can represent this as $[0\ 5\ 0\ 1]^T$. Similarly the origin of the world coordinates is $[0\ -5\ 0\ 1]^T$.

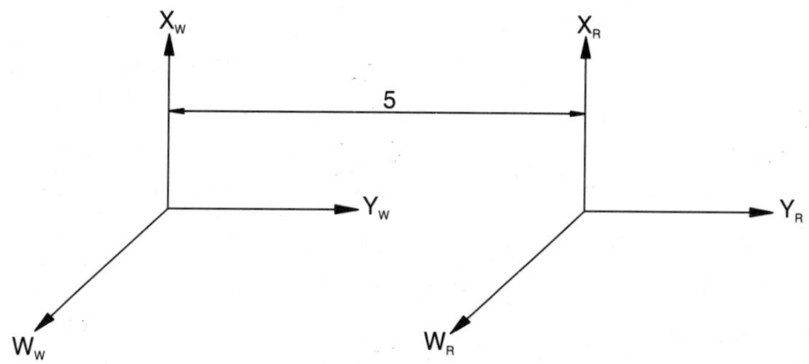

Fig. 16.4 Translation of Coordinates

Consider an arbitrary point in the world coordinates. Its location with respect to robot coordinate will be:

$$\begin{bmatrix} 0 \\ -5 \\ 0 \\ 1 \end{bmatrix}$$

Similarly, a point on the robot coordinate system with respect to world coordinate eill be:

$$\begin{bmatrix} 0 \\ 5 \\ 0 \\ 1 \end{bmatrix}$$

In general, the location of points can be specified as shown in Table 16.1

Table 16.1 Location of Points When Coordinate Systems are Translated

Location of a point in world coordinates	Location of a point in robot coordinates	Pre-multiplying the coordinates in the world coordinates by $\begin{bmatrix} 1 & 0 & 0 & 0 \\ 0 & 1 & 0 & -5 \\ 0 & 0 & 1 & 0 \\ 0 & 0 & 0 & 1 \end{bmatrix}$
$\begin{bmatrix} 0 \\ 0 \\ 0 \\ 1 \end{bmatrix}$	$\begin{bmatrix} 0 \\ -5 \\ 0 \\ 1 \end{bmatrix}$	$\begin{bmatrix} 1 & 0 & 0 & 0 \\ 0 & 1 & 0 & -5 \\ 0 & 0 & 1 & 0 \\ 0 & 0 & 0 & 1 \end{bmatrix}\begin{bmatrix} 0 \\ 0 \\ 0 \\ 1 \end{bmatrix} = \begin{bmatrix} 0 \\ -5 \\ 0 \\ 1 \end{bmatrix}$
$\begin{bmatrix} 0 \\ 5 \\ 0 \\ 1 \end{bmatrix}$	$\begin{bmatrix} 0 \\ 0 \\ 0 \\ 1 \end{bmatrix}$	$\begin{bmatrix} 1 & 0 & 0 & 0 \\ 0 & 1 & 0 & -5 \\ 0 & 0 & 1 & 0 \\ 0 & 0 & 0 & 1 \end{bmatrix}\begin{bmatrix} 0 \\ 5 \\ 0 \\ 1 \end{bmatrix} = \begin{bmatrix} 0 \\ 0 \\ 0 \\ 1 \end{bmatrix}$

In general to convert k coordinate frame to j coordinate frame, one has to:

- translate k's X axis by a
- translate k's Y-axis by b
- translate k's Z-axis by c

This implies that every coordinate in the j coordinate frame to k coordinate frame, the point must be pre-multiplied by:

$$\begin{bmatrix} 1 & 0 & 0 & a \\ 0 & 1 & 0 & b \\ 0 & 0 & 1 & c \\ 0 & 0 & 0 & 1 \end{bmatrix}$$

Figure 16.5 shows two coordinate frames, world coordinate frame on the left and robot coordinate frame on the right. To transform the robot coordinate frame to the world coordinate frame, one needs to translate 50 units along X-axis, 70 units along Y-axis and 15 units along Z-axis.

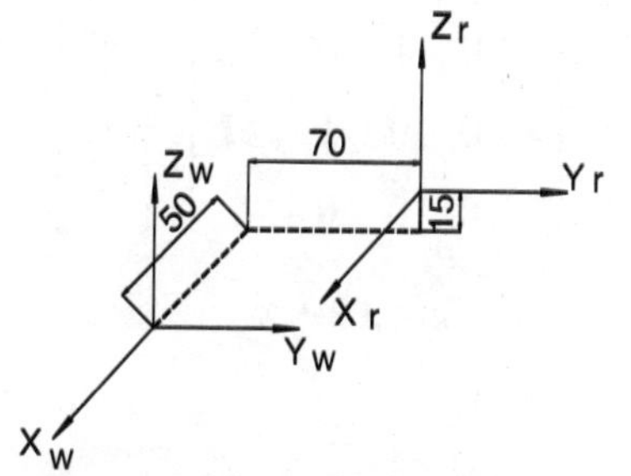

Fig. 16.5 Two Coordinate Frames Differing only by Translation

Thus to take a point on the world coordinates and transform that into robot coordinates, one needs to pre-multiply that point by the matrix:

$$\begin{bmatrix} 1 & 0 & 0 & 50 \\ 0 & 1 & 0 & 70 \\ 0 & 0 & 1 & 15 \\ 0 & 0 & 0 & 1 \end{bmatrix}$$

Example:

Consider a Cartesian robot shown in Fig.16.6. Joint J_1 and J_2 are translational joints with link lengths of L_1 and L_2. The coordinate of J_1 are (x_1, y_1, z_1) and coordinates of J_2 (x_2, y_2, z_1) respectively.

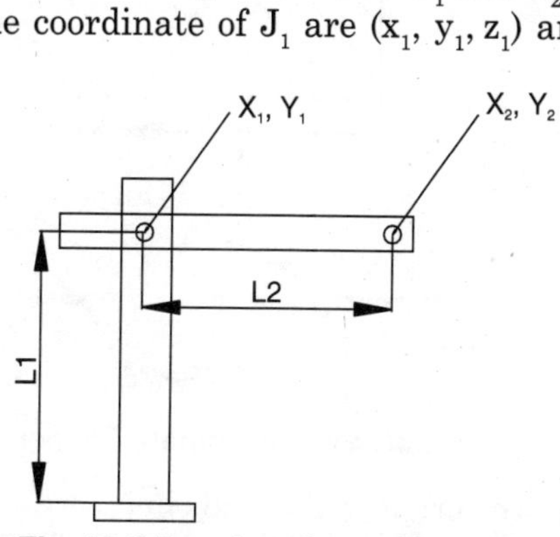

Fig. 16.6 Two Arm Cartesian Robot

Point J_2 can be obtained by:

$$\begin{bmatrix} x2 \\ y2 \\ z1 \\ 1 \end{bmatrix} = \begin{bmatrix} 1 & 0 & 0 & L2 \\ 0 & 1 & 0 & 0 \\ 0 & 0 & 1 & 0 \\ 0 & 0 & 0 & 1 \end{bmatrix} \begin{bmatrix} x1 \\ y1 \\ z1 \\ 1 \end{bmatrix}$$

$$X2 = T1 \cdot x_1$$

The end effector point is represented by (x, y, z_1)

$$\begin{bmatrix} x \\ y \\ z1 \\ 1 \end{bmatrix} = \begin{bmatrix} 1 & 0 & 0 & 0 \\ 0 & 1 & 0 & L2 \\ 0 & 0 & 1 & z1 \\ 0 & 0 & 0 & 1 \end{bmatrix} \bullet \begin{bmatrix} x2 \\ y2 \\ z1 \\ 1 \end{bmatrix}$$

$$x = T2 \cdot x_2$$

Therefore, $x = T2 \cdot T1 \cdot x_1$

16.4 ROTATION MATRICES

16.4.1 Coordinate Frames that Differ by a Rotation about one Axis

Consider two coordinate frames J and K shown in Fig. 16.7. They differ only by rotation about the Z–axis. To transform J coordinate frame to K coordinate frame we perform a rotation about K's Z–axis by –90°. By looking at Fig.16.6 we can observe that $X_k = Y_j$ and $Z_k = Z_j$ and $X_j = -1 * Y_k$

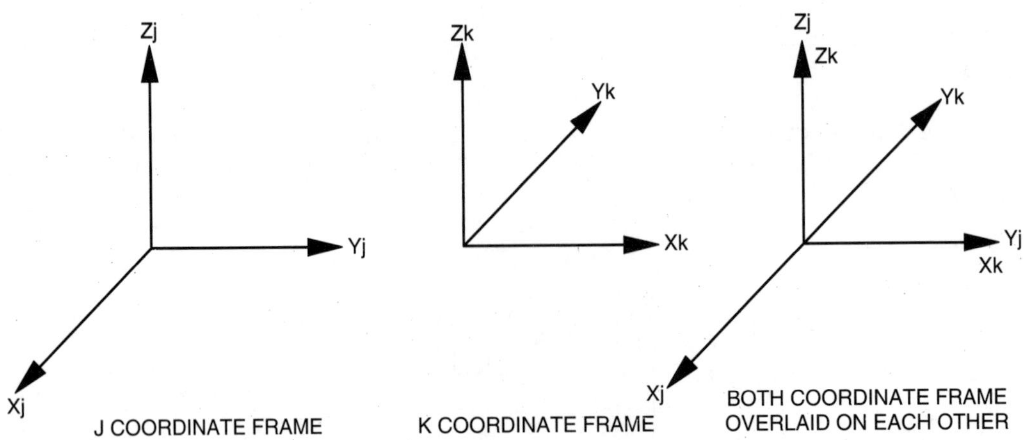

Fig. 16.7 Rotation of Coordinate Frames

Let us look at a few examples. The origin of the j axis in j coordinates: the point $[0 \quad 0 \quad 0 \quad 1]^T$ is the same as the origin of j axis in k coordinates $[0 \quad 0 \quad 0 \quad 1]^T$. The point $[a \quad b \quad c \quad 1]^T$ in j coordinates is located at $[b \quad -a \quad c \quad 1]^T$ in k coordinates. If to transform j coordinate frame to k coordinate frame $F^j{}_k$ you rotate about Z axis by θ, then you can pre-multiply a point in j coordinates by the matrix $\begin{bmatrix} \cos\theta & -\sin\theta & 0 & 0 \\ \sin\theta & \cos\theta & 0 & 0 \\ 0 & 0 & 1 & 0 \\ 0 & 0 & 0 & 1 \end{bmatrix}$ T^{k}_{j} to get the location of the point in j coordinates.

In our example, θ = –90°. Hence sin –θ = –1 and cos –θ = 0. So the matrix becomes

$$\begin{bmatrix} 0 & 1 & 0 & 0 \\ -1 & 0 & 0 & 0 \\ 0 & 0 & 1 & 0 \\ 0 & 0 & 0 & 1 \end{bmatrix}.$$

If we multiply this matrix by T, we get . $\begin{bmatrix} b \\ -a \\ c \\ 1 \end{bmatrix}$

16.5 HOMOGENEOUS TRANSFORMATION MATRIX

The homogeneous transformation matrix is a 4 × 4 matrix which maps a position vector expressed in homogenous coordinates from one coordinate system to another. A homogeneous transformation matrix can be considered to consist of three sub matrices representing rotation (3 × 3), translation (3 × 1) and perspective (1 × 3).

$$\begin{bmatrix} r1 & r2 & r3 & \Delta x \\ r4 & r5 & r6 & \Delta y \\ r7 & r8 & r9 & rz \\ 0 & 0 & 0 & 1 \end{bmatrix}$$

16.6 ROBOT KINEMATICS

Kinematics is the study of motion without regard to the forces which cause it. Within kinematics one studies the position, velocity and acceleration, and all higher order derivatives of the position variables. The kinematics of manipulators involves the study of the geometric and time based properties of the motion, and in particular how the various links move with respect to one another and with time.

Using kinematics to describe the special configuration of robots gives us two approaches:

(i) Forward or direct kinematics: Forward kinematics is concerned with the determination of the position and direction of the end effector if each link is assigned specified displacements or rotation.

(ii) Inverse kinematics: Inverse kinematics is used for the determination of joint angles or displacements for a given orientation and position of end effector. Inverse kinematics problem is difficult as there may be multiple solutions. Solution becomes more and more tedious as the number of degrees of freedom increases. Sometimes, there may not be a solution at all.

16.7 COMBINED TRANSFORMATIONS

The previous sections dealt with the procedure to create the matrix that will compute the coordinates of a point in one coordinate frame given the coordinates of that point in another coordinate frame, subject to the following condition: the two frames may only differ by a translation (along the 3 axes), or by a rotation about one axis. It is indeed possible to convert points between two coordinate frames that differ, perhaps by two translations or by a rotation then a translation and then another rotation.

The key to understanding how to do this is to understand that there are two ways to view any sequence of translations and rotations. The first way we will call "moving" coordinate systems. In moving coordinate systems, each step happens relative to the steps that have come before it.

The alternative approach is the "fixed axes" approach. In this technique, all the moves are relative to the original world coordinate frame.

Table 16.2 gives a summary of transformation matrices.

Table 16.2 Summary of Transformation Matrices

To convert the k coordinate frame into the j coordinate frame F^j_k	Then to convert a point in j coordinates into a point in k coordinates, pre-multiply that point by T^j_k	Transformation
Translate along k's x axis by a, along k's y axis by b, along k's z axis by c	$\begin{bmatrix} 1 & 0 & 0 & a \\ 0 & 1 & 0 & b \\ 0 & 0 & 1 & c \\ 0 & 0 & 0 & 1 \end{bmatrix}$	Trans (a,b,c)
Rotate k's x axis by θ	$\begin{bmatrix} 1 & 0 & 0 & 0 \\ 0 & \cos\theta & -\sin\theta & 0 \\ 0 & \sin\theta & \cos\theta & 0 \\ 0 & 0 & 0 & 1 \end{bmatrix}$	Rot x(θ)

Rotate k's y axis by θ	$\begin{bmatrix} \cos\theta & 0 & \sin\theta & 0 \\ 0 & 1 & 0 & 0 \\ -\sin\theta & 0 & \cos\theta & 0 \\ 0 & 0 & 0 & 1 \end{bmatrix}$	Rot y(θ)
Rotate k's z axis by θ	$\begin{bmatrix} \cos\theta & \sin\theta & 0 & 0 \\ \sin\theta & \cos\theta & 0 & 0 \\ 0 & 0 & 1 & 0 \\ 0 & 0 & 0 & 1 \end{bmatrix}$	Rot z(θ

16.8 DENAVIT HARTENBERG REPRESENTATION

Typical robots are serial-link manipulators comprising a set of bodies, called links, in a chain, connected by joints. Each joint has one degree of freedom, either translational or rotational. For a manipulator with n joints numbered from 1 to n, there are n links, numbered from 0 to n. Link 0 is the base of the manipulator, generally fixed, and link n carries the end effector. Joint i connects links i and i+1. Figure 16.8 shows two successive links and the link parameters.

A link may be considered as a rigid body defining the relationship between two neighbouring joint axes. A link can be specified by two numbers, the *link length* and *link twist*, which define the relative location of the two axes in space. The link parameters for the first and last links are meaningless, but are arbitrarily chosen to be 0. Joints may be described by two parameters. The *link offset* is the distance from one link to the next along the axis of the joint. The *joint angle* is the rotation of one link with respect to the next about the joint axis.

To facilitate describing the location of each link we affix a coordinate frame to it —frame i is attached to link i. Denavit and Hartenberg proposed a matrix method of systematically assigning coordinate systems to each link of an articulated chain. The axis of revolute joint i is aligned with z_{i-1}. The x_{i-1} axis is directed along the normal from z_{i-1} to z_i and for intersecting axes is parallel to z_{i-1}x z_i. The link and joint parameters may be summarized as:

link length, a_i the offset distance between the z_{i+1} and z_i axes along the x_i axis;

link twist, a_i the angle from the z_{i+1} axis to the z_i axis about the x_i axis;

link offset d_i the distance from the origin of frame i+1 to the x_i axis along the z_{i+1} axis;

joint angle θ_i the angle between the x_{i+1} and xi about z_{i+1} axis.

For a revolute axis q_i is the joint variable and d_i is constant, while for a prismatic joint d_i is variable, and q_i is constant. In many of the formulations that follow we use generalized coordinates, q_i, where:

$$q_i = \begin{cases} \theta_i \text{ for revolute joint} \\ d_i \text{ for prismatic joint} \end{cases}$$

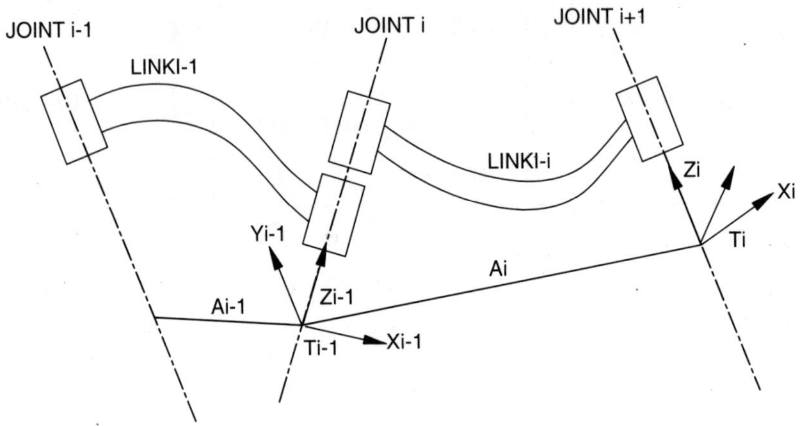

Fig. 16.8 DH Representation

The Denavit-Hartenberg (DH) representation results in a 4×4 homogeneous transformation matrix:

$$^{i-1}Ai = \begin{bmatrix} \cos\theta & -\sin\theta i\cos\alpha i & \sin\theta i\cos\alpha i & ai\cos\theta i \\ \sin\theta i & \cos\theta i\cos\alpha i & -\cos\theta i\sin\alpha i & ai\sin\theta i \\ 0 & \sin\alpha i & \cos\alpha i & di \\ 0 & 0 & 0 & 1 \end{bmatrix}$$

representing each link's coordinate frame with respect to the previous link's coordinate system. That is:

$$^0T_i = {}^0T_{i-1}\, {}^{i-1}A_i$$

16.9 EXAMPLE OF FORWARD KINEMATICS

Consider the robot arm given in Fig. 16.9 (A). This arm has two links of length L1 and L2 and one joint which can rotate about its Z axis. There are 3 coordinate frames, world coordinates, joint coordinates, and gripper coordinates. Figure 16.9 (B) is the illustration of the same arm with the joint rotated by θ degrees about its y axis in the clockwise direction.

Now look at the object to be gripped in both figures. It should be clear that the world coordinates of the object do not change between Figures (A) and (B), but the location of the object in link coordinates and gripper coordinates changes.

There are two points in this image whose locations do not move in any frame as the joint moves i.e. the base point A and joint B. The gripper coordinates change when the link L2 is rotated. Usually, any tools or handling devices of a manipulator can be described with the help a constant homogeneous transformation, if related to the last, outermost link of the robot.

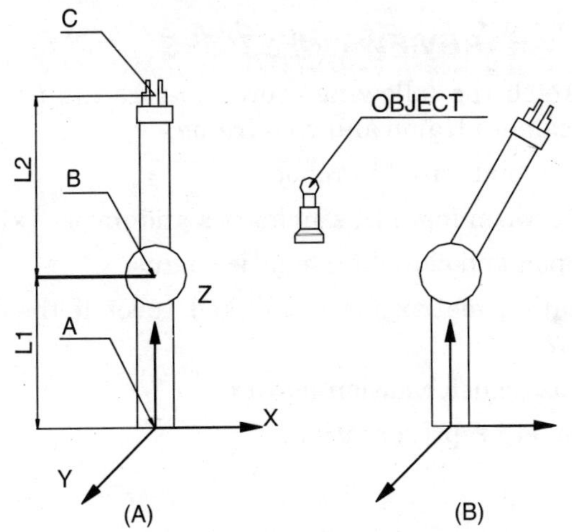

Fig. 16.9 Two Link Robot Arm

In this tool frame, objects to be manipulated can be easily located relative to the gripper. With reference to Fig. (a) it is quite simple to find relative motions necessary for the tool tip in order to handle objects. The point located at the very centre of the base of the link L1 is always at world coordinates (0, 0, 0). The coordinates of joint B in world coordinates is (0, 0, L1). The coordinates of the gripper in world coordinates is (0, 0, L1 + L2). The coordinates of the joint with respect to the gripper is (0, 0, -L2).

Now consider Fig. 16.9 (b). Suppose that we want to convert between gripper coordinates and world coordinates, as a function of the angle of the joint, θ. To move the reference frame from world coordinates to gripper coordinates, it is necessary to translate a distance of L1 along the Z axis, and then rotate by 30 degrees as in Fig. (b).

$$\begin{bmatrix} 1 & 0 & 0 & 0 \\ 0 & 1 & 0 & 0 \\ 0 & 0 & 1 & L1 \\ 0 & 0 & 0 & 1 \end{bmatrix} \times \begin{bmatrix} \cos(\theta) & 0 & \sin(\theta) & 0 \\ 0 & 1 & 0 & 0 \\ -\sin(\theta) & 0 & \cos(\theta) & 0 \\ 0 & 0 & 0 & 1 \end{bmatrix} = \begin{bmatrix} \cos(\theta) & 0 & \sin(\theta) & 0 \\ 0 & 1 & 0 & 0 \\ -\sin(\theta) & 0 & \cos(\theta) & L1 \\ 0 & 0 & 0 & 1 \end{bmatrix}$$

The reference frame from joint coordinates to gripper coordinates can be done by a simple translation of [0, 0, L2].

$$\begin{bmatrix} 1 & 0 & 0 & 0 \\ 0 & 1 & 0 & 0 \\ 0 & 0 & 1 & L1 \\ 0 & 0 & 0 & 1 \end{bmatrix} \times \begin{bmatrix} \cos(\theta) & 0 & \sin(\theta) & 0 \\ 0 & 1 & 0 & 0 \\ -\sin(\theta) & 0 & \cos(\theta) & 0 \\ 0 & 0 & 0 & 1 \end{bmatrix} \times \begin{bmatrix} 1 & 0 & 0 & 0 \\ 0 & 1 & 0 & 0 \\ 0 & 0 & 1 & L2 \\ 0 & 0 & 0 & 1 \end{bmatrix}$$

16.10 SUMMARY

This chapter introduced some basic ideas about the robot kinematics. The reader is advised to refer to books dealing this topic in detail in order to carry out path planning for the applications discussed in the next chapter.

REVIEW QUESTIONS

(1) Explain with a neat sketch the following coordinate frames used in robot kinematics: link frame, tool frame, camera frame and goal frame.

(2) Discuss different kinds of joints used in robots.

(3) Discuss the difference between forward kinematics and inverse kinematics.

(4) Differentiate between open and closed kinematic chains.

(5) Develop the transformation matrix for a 2-linked robot if the links are extended by displacements L1 and L2.

(6) Discuss the homogeneous transformation matirx.

(7) Explain Denavit-Hartenberg representation.

17 APPLICATIONS OF ROBOTS IN MANUFACTURING

Robots are widely used in several manufacturing applications. Robots are preferred in hazardous environments as well as to carry out mundane repetitive tasks. This chapter briefly reviews some of the important manufacturing applications of robots. Competitive manufacturing of the future will increasingly depend on the progress of robotics technologies and the availability of safe and cost-effective robotic products and related services.

17.1 INTRODUCTION

Industrial robots have wide range of applications for the aerospace, automotive, consumer goods, food, metal fabrication, medical, pharmaceutical, solar panel, and many other industries. Today, robotics affects a broad sector of economic activities from automotive and electronics industries to food, recycling, logistics, etc. Up to now however, robot automation technologies have mainly been deployed in capital-intensive large-volume manufacturing, resulting in relatively costly and complex robot systems, which often cannot be used in small and medium sized manufacturing. New branches of robot automation that emerge nowadays such as food, logistics, recycling etc. require radical new designs of robot systems.

Automobile industry is a major beneficiary of introduction of robots on the shop floor. Technological advancements in the late 1970s and early 1980s brought a new outlook to the automobile industry. Automotive industries, as the key application driver in terms of cost, technology and services robotics industry are subject to fierce global competition. The development of the robot for manufacturing marked the beginning of change in this booming industry. Robots opened a world of possibilities for manufacturing plants. These machines could assemble cars and car parts at a much greater rate of precision and at a much faster speed than the average human. From the company's standpoint, robots could significantly cut down on labour costs by requiring fewer employees. Since production efficiency is constantly in the interest of a company, the use of robotics provided the perfect solution for large automobile manufacturers. Typically prime areas of application for robots in car manufacturing are welding, assembly of body, motor and gear-box, and painting and coating.

Apart from automobiles other industries are chemical, rubber and plastics manufacturing, aerospace, electrical and electronics, food stuff and beverage manufacturing, glass, ceramics and mineral production, printing, die casting and wood and furniture manufacturing.

Advantages of using robots in manufacturing are:

(i) **Cost Effectiveness:** A robot can work twenty-four hours a day without a break, and continuously perform the same mundane tasks over and over again virtually non-stop.

(ii) **Job Efficiency:** Barring any computer errors, robots will almost always get the job done quicker and more efficiently than a human possibly could.

(iii) **Safety:** Robots are able to withstand exposure to extreme heat, chemicals in the air, and general physical contact with parts and structures.

(iv) **Accuracy:** Robots can be programmed to perform precise intricate duties at much faster speeds than any human could be expected to.

(v) **Physical Capacity:** Robots are not limited like humans when it comes to performing many assembly jobs like painting, finishing, welding, riveting, and installation. Robots also do not have restrictions with moving heavy objects or issues of fatigue.

Industrial robots used for the following tasks:

- Arc Welding
- Spot Welding
- Assembly
- Cutting
- Die casting
- Dispensing
- Machine Tending
- Machining
- Packaging
- Painting
- Palletizing
- Part Transfer
- Polishing/Finishing
- Press/Forming
- Product Inspection

The following sections give detailed description of the above applications.

17.2 ROBOTS FOR WELDING

Robotic welding has been extensively used in automobile and industrial applications like boilers, structures etc. Both articulated and Cartesian robots are used for welding applications. Welding of body in white involves both spot welding and arc welding. While spot welding requires only point to point positioning, arc welding often requires contouring ability.

17.2.1 Arc Welding

Cartesian robots fitted with a wrist are used for welding. Apart from the X, Y, Z movements the wrist movement allows rotation of the welding torch. Articulated robots fitted with a wrist are used for contoured welds. A robotic welding system may perform with higher repeatability than a manual welder because of the monotony of the task. However, robots may necessitate regular recalibration or reprogramming.

Many factors need to be considered when setting up a robotic welding facility. Robotic welding needs to be engineered differently than manual welding. Some of the considerations for a robotic welding facility are listed below:

- Accuracy and repeatability
- Number of axes
- Reliability
- Welding Fixtures
- Programming
- Seam tracking systems
- Maintenance

Accuracy and repeatability are specified based on the application. Robots should have the number of axes necessary to permit the proper range of motion. The robot arm should be able to approach the work from multiple angles. Robotic welding systems are able to operate continuously, provided appropriate maintenance procedures are adhered to. Continuous production line interruptions can be minimized with proper robotic system design. Proper welding fixtures will ensure that deformation after welding is reduced to a minimum. Contoured welds may require complex programming involving multiple axes. In order to ensure accurate and quality welds seam tracking systems are integrated with the welding systems. Complex welding applications require weld positioners to manipulate the part and present the portion to be welded to the torch. Part transfer depends on the application. In the case of body in white application, the chassis moves from station to station using some kind of conveyor system.

17.2.2 Spot Welding

Spot welding, a resistance welding technique, connects two pieces of sheet metal. Two copper electrodes compress the sheets, conducting electricity through the metal, which resists the current. A weld forms at this spot - the resistance heat melting and joining the sheets by forming a weld nugget at the interface of the sheets where the pressure is applied.

Automatic welding imposes specific demands on resistance welding equipment. Often, equipment must be specially designed and welding procedures developed to meet robot welding requirements. The spot welding robot is the most important component of a robotized spot welding installation. Welding robots are available in various sizes, rated by payload capacity and reach. A spot welding gun applies appropriate pressure and current to the sheets to be welded. There are different types of welding guns, used for different applications, available. An automatic weld-timer initiates and controls the duration of current. During the resistance welding process the welding electrodes are exposed to severe heat and pressure. In time, these factors begin to deform (mushroom) the electrodes. To restore the shape of the electrodes, an automatic tip-dresser is used. One problem when welding with robots is that the cables and hoses used for current and air etc. tend to limit the capacity of movement of the robot wrist. A solution to this problem is the swivel, which permits passage of compressed air, cooling water, electric current and signals within a single rotating unit. The swivel unit also enables off-line programming as all cables and hoses can be routed along defined paths of the robot arm.

The welding gun usually will have 6-axis capability. Some of the welding machines employ servo spot welding which uses an additional servo motor and encoder (7th axis) of the robot to drive and control the clamping force of the welding electrodes. Using a spare robot axis to actuate the weld gun gives added benefits than a pneumatic weld gun. First, a wider range of clamping pressures can be controlled for different materials and thicknesses. Reduced cycle time can be achieved by having full control of the stroke of the weld gun. Along with this, it gives a low impact condition when contacting the workpiece at the beginning of a weld sequence. This gives a longer life span of the electrodes. Another benefit would be that it is much quieter than a pneumatic weld gun. Collision detection is another option usually providing on welding equipment.

17.3 ROBOTS FOR ASSEMBLY

Assembly robots are widely used in mechanical and electronic assembly situations. Robotic assembly has expanded production capabilities in the manufacturing world by increasing production rate and reliability. The assembly process is faster, more efficient and precise than ever before. Robots have released workers from tedious and dull assembly line jobs, and increased production and savings in the process.

Advantages of Robot Assembly:

Robotic assembly has several distinct advantages.

- **No Fatigue:** An assembly robot can work every day, every hour without pause.
- **More Output:** The consistent output of a robotic system along with quality, and repeatability are unmatched even with the most challenging of applications.
- **Better Performance:** Automated systems provide precise, exact assembly performance. Many of them are equipped with vision technology to aid in production.
- **Savings:** Robot assembly systems create savings by eliminating downtime and labour costs, while increasing production and performance. With automation, the return of investment (ROI) is high.

17.3.1 Robots in Electronic Manufacture and Assembly

Robots have been used in manufacturing electronic components and semiconductors for a long time. Robots are used in electronic assembly where they mount microchips on circuit boards. As the trend towards ever smaller electronic devices continues along with the requirement for cleanliness, the need for robots will increase in these applications.

Robotics finds interesting applications in assembly in electronics industry. Fast, accurate and high repeatability robots are ideal for tasks such as PCB manufacture, mobile phone assembly and hard disc production as well as other pick and place functions in electronics applications. Semiconductor assembly generally uses SCARA robots due to their simple design and inherent cleanliness. Another reason for automating is a desire to bring down costs. For instance, Selectively Compliant Articulated Robot Arm (SCARA) is one of the most popular types of robot preferred for electronic assembly. Higher speeds of assembly can be achieved by employing delta type robots. Use of small articulated robots also has been reported in some specialized applications. Dual-arm robots have humanlike movement and dexterity and are ideal for electronics assembly. Another popular robot type is seven-axis robot which can be mounted virtually anywhere to tend machines, load parts, assemble components and transfer parts between stations. Vision systems can be integrated with the robots to provide enhanced capabilities for part location and inspection.

As technology changes products containing semiconductors, along with the way these products are manufactured, the semiconductor industry has developed a set of standards for communications among production equipment. These standards, promulgated by the Semiconductor Equipment and Materials International (SEMI) help manufacturers that use robots to conform to a global protocol when producing cutting-edge products such as photovoltaics, flat panel displays, LEDs and other emerging products for both military and consumer electronics. SEMI's Equipment Communications Standard (SECS I and II) and Generic Equipment Model (GEM) delineates a universal communication standard for automated semiconductor manufacturing equipment, including robotics.

17.3.2 Mechanical Assembly Using Robots

Assembly is one of the fastest growing industrial applications of robotics. There are many applications of robotics in mechanical assembly. Automobile assembly is a typical example. In fact the assembly effort is jointly by robots and workers. It requires higher precision than welding or painting and depends on low-cost sensor systems and powerful inexpensive computers. Present day manufacture of automobiles is heavily dependent on the use of robots.

The typical car or truck is constructed from the ground up. The frame forms the base on which the body rests and from which all subsequent assembly components follow. The frame is placed on the assembly line and clamped to the conveyer to prevent shifting as it moves down the line. From here the automobile frame moves to component assembly areas where complete front and rear suspensions, gas tanks, rear axles and drive shafts, gear boxes, steering box components, wheel drums, and braking systems are sequentially installed.

An off-line operation at this stage of production mates the vehicle's engine with its transmission. Workers use robotic arms to install these heavy components inside the engine compartment of the frame. After the engine and transmission are installed, a worker attaches the radiator, and another bolts it into place. Because of the nature of these heavy component parts, articulated robots perform all of the lift and carry operations while assemblers using pneumatic wrenches bolt component pieces in place.

Generally, the floor pan is the largest body component to which a multitude of panels and braces will subsequently be either welded or bolted. As it moves down the assembly line, held in place by clamping fixtures, the shell of the vehicle is built. First, the left and right quarter panels are robotically disengaged from pre-staged shipping containers and placed onto the floor pan, where they are stabilized with positioning fixtures and welded.

The front and rear door pillars, roof, and body side panels are assembled in the same fashion. The shell of the automobile assembled in this section of the process lends itself to the use of robots because articulated arms can easily introduce various component braces and panels to the floor pan and perform a high number of weld operations in a time frame and with a degree of accuracy no human workers could ever approach. Robots can pick and load roof panels and place them precisely in the proper weld position with tolerance variations held to within .025 of a mm. Moreover, robots can also tolerate the smoke, weld flashes, and gases created during this phase of production.

As the body moves from the isolated weld area of the assembly line, subsequent body components including fully assembled doors, deck lids, hood panel, fenders, trunk lid, and bumper reinforcements are installed. Although robots help workers place these components onto the body shell, the workers provide the proper fit for most of the bolt-on functional parts using pneumatically assisted tools.

In the final assembly area, robots are used for windshields and seats, but operator assist devices facilitate the mounting of heavy and bulky elements such as the wire harness and cockpit. The painted shell proceeds through the interior assembly area where workers assemble all of the instrumentation and wiring systems, dash panels, interior lights, seats, door and trim panels, headliners, radios, speakers, all glass except the automobile windshield, steering column and wheel, body weather strips, vinyl tops, brake and gas pedals, carpeting, and front and rear bumper fascias.

Next, robots equipped with suction cups remove the windshield from a shipping container, apply a bead of urethane sealer to the perimeter of the glass, and then place it into the body windshield frame. Robots also pick seats and trim panels and transport them to the vehicle for the ease and efficiency of the assembly operator. After passing through this section the shell is given a water test to ensure the proper fit of door panels, glass, and weather stripping. It is now ready to mate with the chassis.

The chassis assembly conveyor and the body shell conveyor meet at this stage of production. As the chassis passes the body conveyor the shell is robotically lifted from its conveyor fixtures and placed onto the car frame. Assembly workers, some at ground level and some in work pits beneath the conveyor, bolt the car body to the frame. Once the mating takes place the automobile proceeds down the line to receive final trim components, battery, tyres, anti-freeze, and gasoline.

17.4 CUTTING WITH ROBOTS

Robots can be used to cut sheets and plates of different materials on the shop floor. The tools used can be oxy-acetylene flame, plasma, laser or water jet. A six axis articulated robot is best suited for cutting applications. Cutting application requires accurate, high-performance robots featuring payloads from 6-50 kg, a wide range of reaches and work envelopes, brakes on all axes, and floor-, wall- and ceiling-mounted configurations.

Parts can be flame cut using robots which provide tremendous flexibility combined with accuracy and high production rates.

Plasma cutting is a process which uses a high velocity of ionized gas delivered from a constricted orifice. This high velocity ionized gas, the plasma, conducts electricity from the torch of the plasma cutter to the workpiece. The material is heated and melted by the plasma. The high velocity stream of ionized gas mechanically blows the molten metal away, severing the material. Plasma cutting is used to cut steel or a non-ferrous material of about 25 mm or less. Robotic plasma cutting is easy to use and offers higher quality cuts at faster travel speeds.

Robots are used in water jet cutting. Because of considerations of safety robot is ideal to be used to manipulate the water jet. Many non metallic materials and difficult to cut materials can be cut or drilled using this process. Robots used for this application would have to have a high acceleration capacity and great flexibility.

Laser cutting is a very useful manufacturing process to cut different types of materials including paper, wood, plastic, and metal, by melting the material in the beam path. It cuts out complex shapes, which are used to assemble a larger object. Laser cutting is used primarily by manufacturers to cut metal and plastic parts. Laser cutting by robots is employed in the manufacture of automotive body panels, body bumpers, exhaust assemblies, contoured exhaust pipes, radiator supports, vehicle frames to name a few applications.

17.5 APPLICATIONS OF ROBOTS IN DIE CASTING

Die cast products comprise the bulk of mass produced items manufactured by the metal working industry. Robots are used automate die casting which involves complex handling and gap-free spraying of all areas of the special casting molds. This is done through the use of six-axis jointed-arm robots. Failure to achieve the required repeatability during the spraying of the parting agent would result in sections of the casting becoming stuck in the mold.

After the solidification a robot uses three-pronged gripper to take the blank from the hot casting mold of the machine. Because the robot always grips the casting on its sprue, it is able to handle a wide variety of products. The robot then positions the casting in front of sensors, by means of which the controller checks whether it is complete. If the casting is acceptable, the robot then immerses it in a quenching bath of about 30°C (the temperature of the casting is between 300°C and 350°C) and then taken out and places it on the trimming press. Rejected castings are removed by placing them on a slide leading to a separate container.

Robots used in die casting should be built with heat resistant materials. The material of the end effector should also be made of heat resistant material as this has to handle hot castings.

As soon as one robot unloads the casting, another robot sprays the mould of the die-casting machine with water-soluble parting agent under high air pressure, thus ensuring that the next casting will also be easy to remove.

17.6 DISPENSING

Dispensing jobs require materials to be moved from one location to another. The consistent, accurate movements of industrial robots make them well suited for dispensing. From pouring liquids to picking and placing objects, robots are the most reliable, cost-effective dispensing solution. Robots offer several advantages for use in dispensing applications. Robots can dispense materials with great accuracy. They do not make mistakes so that material and time are not wasted. Robots dispense materials with a specified level of consistency and assured throughput. Robots with their inherent flexibility are also capable of sufficient reach. High payload capacity of robots enables them to lift huge vats. Many materials to be dispensed are hazardous and robots are eminently suitable for such tasks.

17.7 MACHINE TENDING

Loading and unloading of workpieces on machine tools is a common application of robots. Articulated, Cartesian, spherical, cylindrical and gantry robots are used for machine tending. Gantry robots are popular with flexible turning centres. The productivity can be increased by designing the work cell such that a robot can service two or three machines in the cell.

Press tending used to be a taxing, dangerous job. Loading and unloading parts from a press, operating the machine, and maintaining consistency with every part proved tedious work. Robots have changed this. They have taken over the job of placing blanks into press machines the same way every time. They are faster, more productive, and less likely to make mistakes.

Robot press tending goes beyond simply moving parts in and out of machines. Robots can move parts around to three or four dies within the same press. Robots are also useful in rotating, flipping, tilting a part between press operations.

17.8 MACHINING AND MANUFACTURING

Robotic machining technology has advanced to where it poses a serious alternative to metal cutting applications on more traditional machining centers. With the latest robotics equipment and related software, automation suppliers and robotic system integrators are gaining some traction using robots in many material-removal applications previously done only with machine tools.

Rigidity and accuracy remain the major obstacles to widespread use of robots for metal material-removal jobs, making robotic milling of harder metals difficult. However, robots have been widely deployed in material-removal applications, including deburring, deflashing, trimming, polishing, and grinding. Robots can be used for milling of softer materials, including foam, plastics, wood, sand castings, and aluminum. Parallel kinematic machines (robots) have special advantages in machining because of its unique structural design which yields higher stiffness.

Robots could have the functionalities of a CNC machine tool, including full 5-axis contour surface-machining capabilities, and it could be programmed quickly to work on any 3- or 5-axis workpiece. Robots could provide a low-cost alternative to machining centers and routers for secondary part operations and could eliminate the work-envelope constraints of those machines when dealing with large components.

Robots have been successfully used in layered manufacturing and deburring.

17.9 PACKAGING

Packaging robots are becoming popular with manufacturing companies because they are user friendly, cost efficient, flexible and fast. Types of robots used for packing are gantry robots, poly-articulated robots, delta and SCARA robots. High speed robots are generally used and items to be packed include food items, cases, crates, trays, and totes. During the past few years, the use of robotics in the area of food packaging has increased and new applications come up very frequently. The standard uses for robots in the food manufacturing environment are in packaging—such as for top loading wrapped articles into cartons, or case-packing, and palletizing, as well as high-speed pick and place applications - and will continue to grow. Robots have become simpler to use, cost less and the technology has evolved to apply to a much wider range of applications today. Developments in special end-of-arm-tooling, vision technology and the controller technology expanded the application of robots for packaging.

17.10 PAINTING

Painting can be efficiently carried out using robots. Painting of automobile is a typical and most apt example.

Prior to painting, the body must pass through a rigorous inspection process in, the body in white operation. The shell of the vehicle passes through a brightly lit white room where it is fully wiped down by visual inspectors using cloths soaked in hi-light oil. Under the lights, this oil allows inspectors to see any defects in the sheet metal body panels. Dings, dents, and any other defects are repaired right on the line by skilled body repairmen. After the shell has been fully inspected and repaired, the assembly conveyor carries it through a cleaning station where it is immersed and cleaned of all residual oil, dirt, and contaminants.

As the shell exits the cleaning station it goes through a drying booth and then through an undercoat dip—an electro statically charged bath of undercoat paint (called the *E-coat)* that covers every nook and cranny of the body shell, both inside and out, with primer. This coat acts as a substrate surface to which the top coat of coloured paint adheres.

After the E-coat bath, the shell is again dried in a booth as it proceeds on to the final paint operation. In most automobile assembly plants today, vehicle bodies are spray-painted by robots that have been programmed to apply the exact amounts of paint to just the right areas for just the right length of time. Considerable research and programming of robots has gone into the dynamics of robotic painting in order to ensure the fine wet finishes. Typically eight painting robots per car, select a paint cylinder the size of a large water bottle. A whirling disk at the end of the robot arm flings out a mist of top-coat paint. When a car is painted the paint cartridge is set back down, and a freshly filled cartridge is selected by each robot. This method helps to paint cars in different colours without time delay or loss of paint.

Once the shell has been fully covered with a base coat of colour paint and a clear top coat, the conveyor transfers the bodies through baking ovens where the paint is cured at temperatures exceeding 135 degrees Celsius.

17.11 PALLETIZING

Palletizing refers to the operation of loading the object such as a corrugated carton and a workpiece for welding on a pallet or a device like that in a defined pattern. Depalletizing refers to the operation of unloading the loaded object in the reverse pattern.

Many factories, food processing plants and palletizing plants have automated their application with a palletizing robot. Robotic palletizing technology increases productivity and profitability. Robotic palletizing systems allow for more flexibility to run products for longer periods of time.

A robot control system with a built-in palletizing function makes it possible to load and unload an object without spending a lot of time on teaching. Robotic work cells can be integrated towards any project. With current advancements in end of arm tooling (EOAT), robot palletizing work cells have been introduced to many factory floors.

17.12 PART TRANSFER

Part transferring was once done entirely by human labour. It was tedious, exacting work for workers. Robots are changing this part of production. Part transfer is faster, more cost-effective, and efficient with customized robots. Robots do not experience fatigue, or strain. They work at the same rate, increasing production and accuracy.

Recent technological advancements in robot end of arm tooling and vision systems are making robotic part transferring even more attractive to companies.

17.13 POLISHING AND FINISHING

Polishing is the process of refining surfaces until they are smooth and shiny. A wide variety of products require polishing to look their best. Polishing is a repetitive, tedious job, ideally suited for speedy robots. Polishing requires consistency and precision-both of which are achieved in a fraction of the time by using robots. With robots, products emerge evenly and thoroughly polished. Robots are programmed to apply just the right amount of pressure and move in just the right direction, making for faster, more effective performance. With robots, cycle times are shorter and breaks unnecessary. Robots save workers from both the drudgery and safety hazards associated with polishing. Polishing robots are unharmed by fumes and dust. Plus, robotic polishing is better for the environment because dry abrasive wheels are used instead of chemical solutions.

17.14 INSPECTION ROBOTS

These robots fall under the category of service robots that take over dangerous and monotonous work for humans in difficult to access areas such as sewer systems, facades, tanks and wind energy converters. Robots are used for inspection of welds in pipes, in order to check their condition, locate leakages, and clean the ventilation systems. A typical robot, pipe crawler is a flexible robot, well suited for carrying out inspections on pipe systems, especially those that have a large number of bends, vertical sections and pipe branches. Robots can also be used for inspection in nuclear installations where human beings cannot have access due to radiation.

These robots are mainly used in the nuclear power industry, refineries, chemical plants, petrochemical plants, the offshore industry, gas pipelines, the beverage industry and all types of pipe lines. Another robot in this category is a power line inspection robot. As power-transmission lines age, preventive maintenance and inspection become more important.

17.15 SUMMARY

Robots perform varieties of operations on the shop floor. This chapter gives a brief overview of several applications that are possible with robots.

REVIEW QUESTIONS

(1) Why are robots widely used in:
   (i) Automobile industry
   (ii) Nuclear Industry
   (iii) Food Processing Industry
(2) List the common applications of robots.
(3) Why are robots preferred over workers in welding and painting?
(4) Discuss the various applications of robots in automobile manufacturing.
(5) Why are robots preferred in loading and unloading in presses?
(6) Why are robots preferred in dispensing applications?
(7) Discuss some examples of robots in materials handling in flexible manufacturing cells.
(8) Discuss the use of robots in die casting and plastic injection moulding.
(9) Why are robots used in packaging and palletizing?
(10) Discuss the use of a robot for inspection on shop floors.
(11) A robot could be used for machining to a limited extent. Discuss.

18 CNC AND MANUFACTURING AUTOMATION

Computer Numerical Control (CNC) opened up tremendous opportunities in expanding manufacturing automation. With the development of CNC, it has been possible to integrate the machine tools into an overall system of Computer Integrated Manufacture.

18.1 INTRODUCTION

Manufacturing is one of the many activities carried out in a factory. The other manufacturing related activities are design, materials management, process planning, production planning and control, materials handling, storage, assembly and inspection. Today, computers are used to aid engineers in carrying out every one of these tasks. Integration of these activities has been tried by many companies and software houses.

This chapter discusses some of the important developments related CNC to achieve the above integration.

18.2 DIRECT NUMERICAL CONTROL (DNC)

The technology of direct numerical control was developed in 1960's itself. The early attempts were to send the NC data directly to the machine control by-passing the tape reader. This way, it was possible to control the NC machine tool directly by the computer, hence the name direct numerical control (DNC). Since the computer has large processing capability, it was possible to connect a number of NC machine tools to a single computer. Figure 18.1 shows the block diagram of an early DNC system.

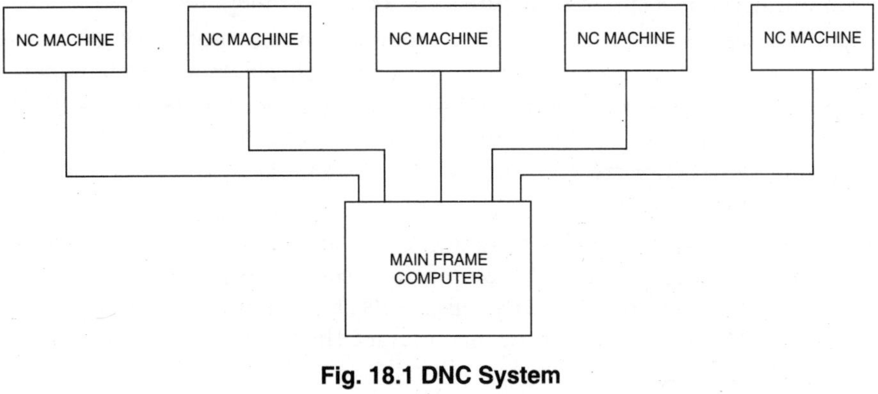

Fig. 18.1 DNC System

The DNC system offers a number of advantages:

(i) A single computer can serve a number of NC machine tools. The computer can process the NC programs using APT or other high level NC programming languages, and transfer the required data to the appropriate machine tool, whenever data is required by the machine tool. The multi tasking capability of the main frame computer can be used to service several machines on the shop floor simultaneously. The computer can store several programs required for different NC machines and different programs for each machines can be processed. This bypassed the tape readers of the early generation of NC machines improving the reliability of the systems as the mechanical tape readers were liable to malfunction. The computer added to the processing capability of the NC systems.

(ii) The computer can be used in addition to handle the following tasks:

  (a) Design

  (b) Production Planning

  (c) Process Planning

  (d) Inventory Control

(iii) Shop floor monitoring and data acquisition.

The computer can also be used for a variety of other tasks like preparation of purchase order generation, bill of materials processing, order follow-up, inventory control, design analysis, payroll preparation, report generation related to management information systems etc.

Early DNC systems not only eliminated the less reliable tape reader but also represented an important step towards total manufacturing automation.

Today, DNC is still used but the scope of DNC has considerably widened. It is more appropriate to call today's DNC systems as distributed numerical control systems, as a number of computers are involved in the processing of information.

With several CNC machines on shop floors to day program management is an important task. DNC software facilitates efficient program management. A dedicated DNC computer stores all the CNC programs and feed the CNC machines with appropriate programs depending on the machining requirements.

Modern DNC systems are based on client server architecture. A part library folder is given access under the part name or number to information such as setup sheets, tooling data, drawings and part programs. DNC sôftware incorporates multi-level security as it applies to DNC administrators, operators and machine tools. An operator can be restricted to a single machine or given access to any number of machines on the network. Administrators are given access to communication setup parameters as it applies to machine tools.

Most of the present generation DNC systems have the capability of showing real-time status of machine tools on the shop floor. An opto-isolated monitor/modem is that can be installed in the machine control to monitor one or more digital points. The state of the machine is monitored in real-time by a DNC hub and made available on the PCs connected to the network running the DNC software. Figure 18.2 shows a typical DNC system connected to a hierarchical system of computers.

Some DNC systems incorporates remote call feature that enables the machine operator to upload and download part programs at the machine control. A part program is identified by its file name on the server. Directory information can also be obtained using remote call. This feature eliminates the need for a separate PC or terminal for the operator to call up part programs.

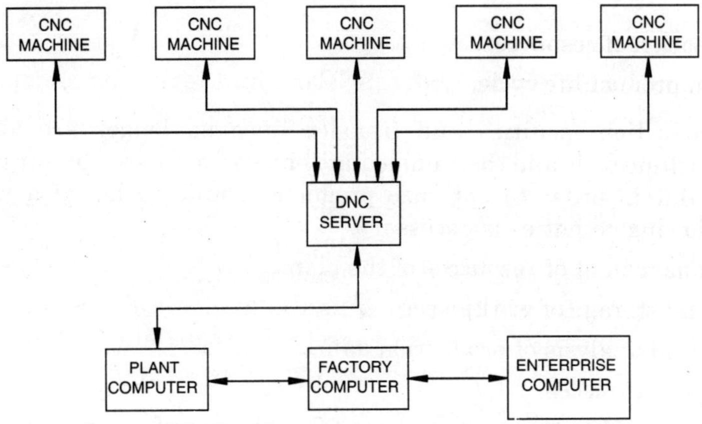

Fig. 18.2 Modern DNC System

The CNC machine tool is the lowest element in to-day's DNC hierarchy. The CNC program can either reside in the memory of the computer or in the shop floor computer to which a number of machines are linked. The plant computer (shop floor computer) can process programs or can access the factory computer or the host (Mainframe) computer for more involved programming tasks. The shop floor computer acts as a supervisory computer and monitors the shop floor data. The factory computer carries out a number of tasks related to manufacturing management and shares some of the tasks with the mainframe. The data bases with the plant computer and the main frame can be accessed by the computers at lower levels of hierarchy. The factory computer can also be used for several other tasks related to manufacturing and management. Instead of a single plant computer a number of minicomputers can be used in a networked environment. Similarly, the CNC machines and the computer nodes on the shop floor can be linked to the plant computer. The factory computer can be linked to the enterprise server or main frame computer so that manufacturing information can be accessed from any locations of an enterprise.

18.3 REQUIREMENTS OF MODERN BATCH PRODUCTION

While DNC technology tried to approach manufacturing automation through the integration of various activities linked to the computer, the challenge to manufacturing during late seventies and eighties necessitated new technologies using CNC. Intense competition in the market for mechanical parts manufactured on machine tools is forcing manufacturers to reduce delivery time and quote competitive prices ever for relatively small orders. This has led to a system of manufacture based on just-in-time (JIT) principle. The requirements a modern batch manufacturing facility has to meet are:

(i) High productivity for all batch sizes, large or small.

(ii) Shorter throughput times.

(iii) Lower storage costs.

(iv) Reduced personnel costs.

(v) Trend towards smaller orders.

(vi) Greater variety of products and product versions.

(vii) Reduction in stocks.

(viii) Better utilization of resources.

(ix) Reduction in product life cycle.

Conventional production facilities and transfer lines no longer are able to meet these requirements. Machine tools and their immediate environment are already automated through CNC and PLC. But in order to optimize production, automation of a wider environment including the following activities is necessary:

(i) Efficient management of resources of the plant.

(ii) Transport and storage of workpieces.

(iii) Acquisition and analysis of production data.

(iv) Inspection of workpieces.

The above factors led to the development of flexible manufacturing cells.

18.4 CONCEPT OF FLEXIBLE MANUFACTURING

Flexibility means the ability to produce reasonably priced customized products of high quality that can be quickly delivered to customers. Flexibility can be interpreted in different ways depending on the perspectives of manufacturers and end users. As far as manufacturing is concerned flexibility is the capability for producing different parts without major re-tooling. This enables quick change over when new products are to be manufactured. This also facilitates many variations of parts or products, quick change of production schedules, handling of multiple parts etc. From the operational perspective, this helps in manufacturing highly customized products to meet the specific needs of customers which are strategically advantageous. Customers are happy because of shorter delivery times. Flexibility also provides the ability to rapidly increase or decrease production levels or to shift capacity quickly from one product to another.

18.5 FLEXIBLE MANUFACTURING CELLS (FMC)

The concept of Flexible Manufacturing Cells (FMC) was evolved to meet the challenges outlined above. FMC combines a number of CNC machines both mechanically and in terms of data processing, into a linked manufacturing unit. This way, highly automated manufacturing cells are created which are capable of handling a number of different workpieces. Manual monitoring and correction facilities are usually kept to a bare minimum. Apart from production machines, a manufacturing cell may include service machines like washing machines, inspection machines and transport system for workpieces and tools. The cell computer simultaneously controls automatic manufacture of workpieces of either the same or different designs within the manufacturing cell. Figure 18.3 shows a typical flexible manufacturing cell. This consists of two turning centres, two horizontal machining centres, two robots for loading and unloading of workpieces, an optional automatic storage and retrieval system for storing of raw materials and finished parts. The supervisory control function is carried out by a programmable logic computer and a cell control computer. The latter can be connected to a supervisory computer if the cell is to be connected to other cells in the shop floor. The FMC software performs system generation and parameterization, system initialization, collection of data, monitoring of cell functioning and display of error messages etc.

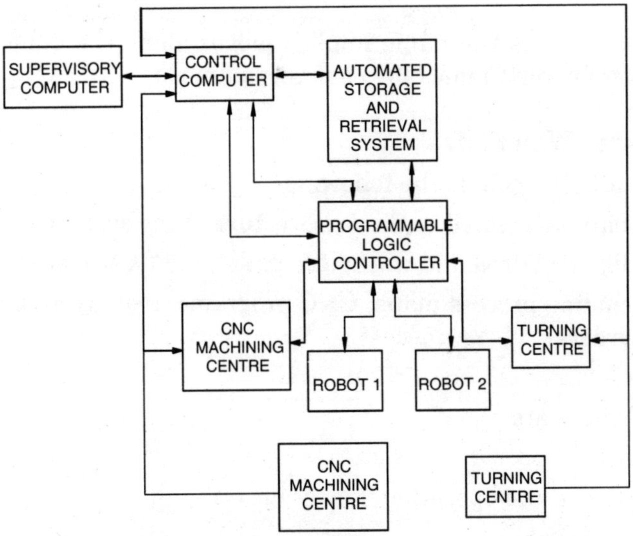

Fig. 18.3 Typical Flexible Manufacturing Cell

Instead of using robots for loading and unloading purposes, a rail guided vehicle can be used for loading and unloading workpieces from the machine tools. A modified form of FMC using rail guided vehicle is shown in Fig. 18.4. An additional fixture with a rotating table is needed for transferring the workpiece from the rail guided vehicle to the table of the machine tool.

Desirable additional features in a flexible manufacturing cell will include:

- A Palletizing station
- Tool pre-setter
- Workpiece washing/cleaning station
- Inspection station

These can also be integrated into the cell.

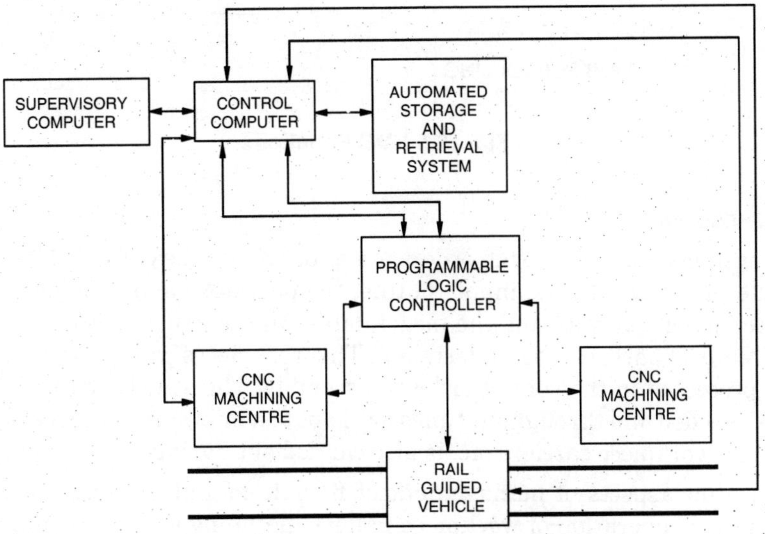

Fig. 18.4 FMC Using a Rail Guided Vehicle

The rail guided vehicle, as the name implies moves along the guides. It can be used to transport workpieces from and to machines as programmed.

18.5.1 Data Associated With FMC

Data associated with a FMC include the following:

(i) System specific data associated to the architecture of the system
(ii) Resources data like tool data and workpiece pallet and fixture data
(iii) Control data including process plans, CNC programs, tool layouts, work schedules, and manufacturing orders
(iv) Plant status data
(v) Material availability data
(vi) Diagnostics data
(vii) Manufacturing status and operational messages
(viii) Alarm messages, alerts
(ix) Tool specific messages like tool breakage and end of tool life

Figure 18.5 shows a block diagram of FMC functions.

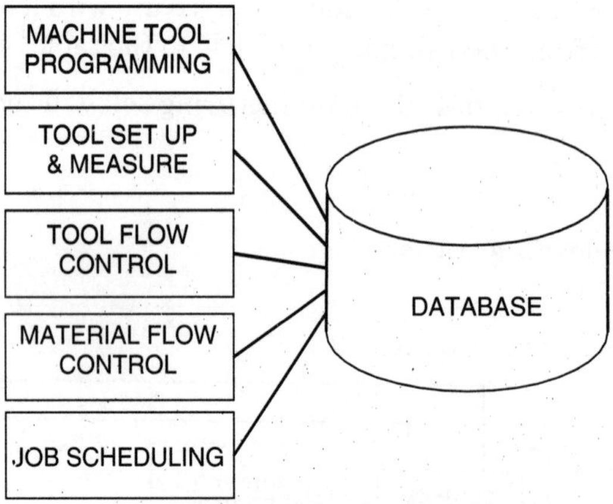

Fig. 18.5 FMC Functions

18.5.2 Job Scheduling

In many FMC systems, manufacturing orders are entered into the cell computer by the operator using a dialogue procedure. In the input routine, the operator enters the job number, the part number, the production quantity and the target dates. Manufacturing orders can be taken up in batch mode or a mix of parts can be undertaken. The workpieces can be processed in such a way that parts are processed in the correct order of assembly. The scheduling is done to use as few work carriers as needed and throughput times are kept to a minimum. A check on the availability of CNC programs, workpiece carriers etc. is also carried out during the scheduling process.

Other important aspects of management of flexible manufacturing systems include tool planning, planning of operation of workpiece pallets, clamping and unclamping of workpieces, material flow control, CNC program supply, and tool control and cell simulation.

18.6 FLEXIBLE MANUFACTURING SYSTEMS (FMS)

A number of Flexible Manufacturing Cells can be integrated into a Flexible Manufacturing System (FMS). FMS is an integrated approach to automating a production operation. They are much more complex than a flexible manufacturing cell, which typically includes between one and three machines. The primary characteristic of an FMS is that it is a computer-controlled manufacturing system that automates production machines, in process inspection and program correction, material storage and retrieval, tool management and materials handling equipment in an integrated manner. FMS is designed to be flexible so that it can fabricate a variety of different products of relatively low volumes. There are three major automated subsystems in an FMS.

(a) Computer-controlled production equipment (e.g. numerically controlled machine tools, CMM, automated production machines etc)

(b) Devices like AGV, RGV, ASRS etc for automated materials handling covering storage, transport, and transfer.

(c) Manufacturing execution and control system

Some FMS's may have additional subsystems. For example, in a machining application there may also be systems for storing and retrieving tools and disposing of chips and cutting fluids. These subsystems must be integrated with the main system.

Although FMS was initially developed for machining, the concept has subsequently been used in a variety of other manufacturing applications, such as:

Assembly

Semiconductor processing

Plastic moulding

Sheet-metal fabrication

Welding etc.

Such systems have proved to be practical and economical for applications with the following characteristics:

Similar types of equipment and processes

Families of similar parts

A moderate number of tools and process steps

Low to medium quantities of parts

Moderate precision requirements

FMS thus represents an automated approach to batch manufacturing operations. It is an alternative that fits in between the CNC and hard automation represented by transfer lines. FMS is best suited for applications that involve an intermediate level of flexibility and quantities whereas CNC is best suited for very small quantities of many different types of parts. Hard automation with dedicated equipment is best suited for the production very large quantities of identical parts as in automotive manufacture. A large portion of the manufacturing industry which deals with the intermediate level of batch operations lends itself to the FMS application.

18.7 ADVANTAGES OF A FMS

The major advantages of FMS are:

Reduced cycle time

Reduced scrap and rework

Lower Work-in-Progress (WIP) inventory

Low direct labour costs

Ability to change over to different parts quickly

Improved product quality due to improved consistency

High utilization of equipment

Reduced space requirements

Ability to optimize throughput of machines

Expandability for additional processes or added capacity

Reduced number of tools and machines required

Motivation for designers to increase variations and features.

Some of these advantages can lead to significant savings. Direct labour can be eliminated almost entirely. Cycle time and WIP can be reduced to a fraction of what is normally required in a manual operation. A FMS is designed to have the production machines working most of the time rather than standing idle. An automated material handling system and a computer-based production scheduling system are needed to keep the machines fed with parts. FMS uses computer automation techniques to lower the overall cost of production operations.

18.8 SUBSYSTEMS OF FMS

FMS consists of a number of subsystems. Each of the major subsystems performs a number of functions and is dependent on the others to make the entire system work. These functions will vary, depending upon the type of equipment and manufacturing operations involved.

(i) **Production Machinery:** FMS typically has a number of machining centres and turning centres apart from other production equipment to provide a wide variety of machining capabilities. Machining centres offer the greatest flexibility, since they can perform many different machining operations (i.e. milling, drilling, boring, reaming and tapping). This is made possible by the tool magazine and an automatic tool changer that are part of the machining centre. Similar facilities can be provided in turning machines also. Automatic offset determination takes care of likely variation in tool lengths. A part can, therefore, undergo multiple machining processes at a single workstation. Other types of machines may also be included in the FMS to perform operations like gear cutting, grinding etc. The family of parts which the FMS is designed to produce will determine the specifications required from the machine tools like accuracy, size and power.

(ii) **Support Equipment:** Automated machine tools typically required several systems to support their operation. The tools required to perform the multiple processes of a machining centre may be stored in pallets or bins at each machine or in a central tool room. Local magazines provide fast access as well as backup capability, but in a large FMS a central tool facility may be more efficient. Centralization not only permits the total number of tools to be minimized but also provides the opportunity to perform additional functions automatically. There are:

Monitoring tools for wear

Presetting of tools

Tool maintenance and repair

Replacement of broken or worn tools

Many CNC machine tools have built-in systems to monitor tool wear and detect tool breakage. They may use probes or non-contact techniques such as acoustic emission. Tool life can be programmed and stored in the memory of the system. When a tool needs replacement, the computer can signal the tool magazine for the delivery of a replacement. The replacement can be performed by a number of methods.

Automated machining operations also need to have the chips cleaned off the workstation and the workpiece. This may be performed by robots or special washing stations. Cleaning may involve turning the workpiece over, vacuuming, and washing. A centralized coolant system can be another support facility.

(iii) Materials Handling: Materials handling does not add value to the product and hence needs to be eliminated as much as possible. However, some amount of material handling cannot be avoided. One of the methods to improve the efficiency of a manufacturing operation is to automate the handling of the product and materials involved. In traditional manufacturing processes, the product spends most of its time waiting rather than being worked on. This is due to inefficiencies in the movement and handling of materials and the scheduling of machines. By using advanced materials handling techniques, one can make substantial reductions in this waiting time, which results in lower WIP inventory and shorter manufacturing cycle times. These techniques include approaches to automating each step in the process that requires the movement or handling of the product or materials (e.g. machine loading and unloading, machine-to-machine transfer, in-line movement of WIP, and storage).

A variety of materials handling technologies are used in such applications, and they all lend themselves to the use of computers for control. The loading and unloading of machines is often the simplest application and can use traditional hard automation approaches or programmable robots. Materials can be moved between machines and process steps by a variety of techniques, including conveyors, transport systems, transfer lines, carousels, and automatic guided vehicles (AGVs).

The materials handling system includes:

(i) A transport system to move workpiece into and out of the FMS (e.g. conveyors, RGV's, AGV's)

(ii) A transport system to move workpiece between machines within the FMS (e.g. gantry equipment, conveyors, carts, AGVs)

(iii) A buffer storage system for queues of workpieces at the machines (e.g. conveyor loops).

(iv) A transfer system to load and unload the machines (e.g. robots)

For these systems to work effectively they must be synchronized with the machine operations. The location and movement of workpieces must be tracked automatically. This is done by using sensors on the materials handling system and workstations. These may be either contact devices (e.g. switches) or non-contact devices (e.g. optical or proximity devices).

(iv) Automatic Guided Vehicles (AGV): AGV is one of the widely used types of material handling device in an FMS. These are battery-powered vehicles that can move and transfer materials by following prescribed paths around the manufacturing floor. They are neither physically tied to the production line nor driven by an operator like a forklift truck. They can take several different forms, but they are typical vehicles whose movements are controlled either by following guide paths buried beneath or painted on the floor, or by radio transmission. Such vehicles have on-board computers and controllers that can be programmed for complicated and varying routs as well as load and unload operations. The computer for the materials handling system or the central computer provides overall control functions, such as dispatching, routing, traffic control, and collision avoidance. AGVs usually complement an automated production line consisting of conveyor or transfer systems by providing the flexibility of complex and reprogrammable movement around the manufacturing shop.

(v) **Automated Storage and Retrieval Systems (ASRS):** A key part of any materials handling systems is storage. Major advances have been made in recent years to automate the storage and retrieval of product and materials by employing sophisticated materials handling machines, high-density storage techniques, and computer control Such systems come in a variety of forms and sizes depending on the materials handling and storage job that has to be done. They often take the form of automated warehouses, conveyors, and computers to control the materials handling machines and to track and control the inventory. The characteristics of such warehouses include:

(a) High-density storage (in some cases, large, high-rise rack structures)

(b) Automated handling systems (such as elevators, storage and retrieval machines and conveyors).

(c) Materials tracking systems (using bar code, RFID, optical or magnetic sensors).

In such a storage system, the computer can keep track of a large number of different parts, products, and materials and can assign bin locations to optimize the use of storage space. When such a system is integrated into the production control system, parts and materials can be replenished as they are consumed on the factory floor, keeping the WIP to a minimum.

(vi) **Control Computers:** An FMS must be under the control of an integrated computer system that includes:

(a) CNC Controllers

(b) PLC's

(c) Controllers for materials handling system

(d) Devices for monitoring and sensing

(e) Data collection and communication system

(f) Supervisory computer

This control system must also interact with other computer systems which may exist in the factory. It needs access to data form other systems and provides data to them. In particular, the FMS system must communicate with the following systems:

(a) The process planning system which generates numerical control (NC) programs for the machine tools

(b) The shop floor control systems which schedules loading and routing of the work

(c) The MIS system which provides management reports on the performance of the system.

The FMS computer system and the hierarchical manufacturing control system integrate all the pieces of the FMS. Without the ability to integrate the various controllers and exchange information between systems, such an automated operation would not be possible.

18.9 APPLICATION OF FMS

Following are some approaches which should be considered in order to optimize the overall efficiency and effectiveness of FMS:

(i) Minimize the process cycle time
The number of different jobs must be minimized in order to reduce changeovers.

(ii) Maximize the utilization of each machine
This can be done by balancing the work load in the system.

(iii) Use automated storage systems to keep work ready for machines to process
This can include loading the system for automated operation on off-shifts and week-ends.

(iv) Provide for the detection of errors or problems
This includes the detection of the presence and absence of parts, jams tool wear, machine failures, non-conforming parts and so on.

(v) Build in backup capabilities
The system should be able to run even when failures occur (e.g., use spare tools, isolate machines, have alternative materials transport paths, have additional machine capacity.

(vi) Include automatic measurement and Inspection techniques
These control the process and assure product quality

(vii) Use identification marking techniques
This permits automatic tracking of workpieces and too using bar codes or RFID tags.

18.10 INTEGRATION OF MANUFACTURING SYSTEMS

It has been explained at various sections in this book that automation can be introduced into all phases of manufacturing activity. It can take the form of automating the operation of an individual machine tool, or it can be a complex FMS. Although these and other examples of automation can be productive and beneficial to manufacturing, they do not represent a computer-integrated factory. The concept of integrated manufacturing systems goes beyond implementing "islands of automation" in the factory. It integrates all the design and manufacturing systems together into an overall factory management system. An integrated system is larger, more complex, and broader in scope than FMS.

When systems are not integrated, they cannot exchange data automatically. If there is a need to exchange information between systems, it must be done manually. This requires data collection, entry, analysis, and interpretation. Each of these steps is subject to inefficiencies and error. When paper is involved in this process, it limits the amount of information that can be transferred, as well as its accuracy and efficiency. When automated systems are tied together into integrated manufacturing systems, several benefits can be realized. These typically include:

(i) Reduced labour requirements (for both direct and indirect activities)
(ii) Reduced lead times in both the development and manufacture of products
(iii) Increased flexibility in production capacity and scheduling
(iv) Reduced levels of inventory in materials, WIP, and finished goods
(v) Increased utilization of resources (e.g. equipment, facilities, and labor)
(vi) Improved ability to respond to changes (e.g., product design, demand, product, mix)

18.10.1 Tasks to be Automated in a FMS

An integrated manufacturing system must link together the basic tasks involved in the manufacturing process. These tasks fall into three major areas:

(i) **Product Design:** Data for manufacturing is generated through the design process. This includes conceptual design, detailed design, and preparation of part and assembly drawings as well as the bills of materials for products. Design process continues throughout the manufacture of a product. Engineering changes are made to correct, modify, and improve designs after they have been introduced into production. This design information is, therefore, a key source of the data.

(ii) **Manufacturing planning:** Before a product can be manufactured, a great deal of activity is required to plan manufacturing activities. This must start with planning the manufacturing line itself, including defining the processes, tools and capacity required as well as the arrangement of the line. The production must then be planned, which results in schedules, process routings, operator instructions, and tool control programs. Like design, these are dynamic elements. They will continue to change as the product, process, and tools change.

(iii) **Production:** The most visible part of a manufacturing system is the actual production. The tasks involved here are primarily some form of control. The processes, tools, and production schedules must all be controlled by technical and logistical data systems. In addition, the performance of the manufacturing operation must be monitored and measures. This involves data collection and reporting activities.

These are the general areas of activity that one finds in any manufacturing operation. There are many detailed tasks below this level as well as activities that may be unique to a particular type of manufacturing. It is the sum total of these activities that must be tied together to achieve an integrated manufacturing system.

18.11 TOOLS FOR MANUFACTURING IN FMS

In this book you have been introduced to the application of microprocessors to automate machining tasks. An integrated manufacturing system is possible if these tools are applied wisely and planned so that they can ultimately be integrated together. The major types of computer tools available for manufacturing to use are:

(i) **Computer Hardware:** Computer hardware includes I/O devices, personal computers, minicomputers, mainframe computer systems and supercomputers and also includes a wide range of software, from large operating systems to programming languages and application programs. An important link in system integration is data communications. This requires the use of communication controllers and networks (MAP, LAN etc). Other essential ingredients are database management systems such as relational database. An emerging computer technology that can be used to perform many tasks in manufacturing is artificial intelligence (AI). In the most general terms, this includes sensors, machine vision, voice recognition systems, adaptive control, natural language processing, logic programming, and expert systems.

(ii) **Computer Aided Engineering (CAE) Tools:** These use computer graphics technologies to perform engineering tasks. They include computer aided design (CAD) techniques such as geometric modeling, finite element analysis (FEA), and mechanism analysis. Software also includes process simulation tools and production line modeling tools.

(iii) Automation Technologies: Computer based technologies can be used to automate both the data and physical operations in production. CNC is, of course, a popular computer technology for the automation of manufacturing processes. Materials handling techniques can be used to automate the physical movement of parts and products through the line. Data collection can be automated with a variety of computer-based methods. In addition, robotics has emerged as a key technology for providing flexible automation in manufacturing.

(iv) Management Systems: These are applications of computer systems to automate the management tasks involved in manufacturing such as group technology, part family manufacture, enterprise resource planning (ERP) and product life cycle management (PLM).

Since many of these systems need to use the same data, it should be desirable to link them. These computer tools automate the tasks that people and machines perform. In a traditional factory, these tasks would be integrated by an organizational structure. In an automated factory, the tasks must be integrated in a computer-based structure.

18.12 FUNCTIONS IN A MANUFACTURING SYSTEM EMPLOYING FMS

The functions of an integrated manufacturing system can be thought of in terms of the levels of control that it performs, the types of data that it manages, and the information that it provides:

(i) Hierarchical Structure: In a hierarchical structure, each level of the system is responsible for performing a different type of control. This is similar to the structure of an organization in which each level of management deals with a different scope and level of business decisions. Such a division of responsibilities can be thought of as a four-level system structure as shown in Table 18.1.

The lowest level controls the operation of machines. This involves machine tool and process control functions as well as data collection.

Table 18.1
Hierarchical Structure of Control

Manufacturing activity		Control functions
Level 4	Plant management	Production planning Resource planning Database management
Level 3	Supervisory	Production scheduling Performance tracking
Level 2	Group of machines	Machine loading Materials handling Monitoring
Level 1	Machine	Tool and process control

The next level controls a group of machines. This may be a manufacturing cell or line. The control functions include materials handling, machine loading, and monitoring the status of the operation of the production line.

The third level performs supervisory functions over the production operations. It generates production schedules and tracks manufacturing performance. It is also usually the source of operational data that is needed by the lower level systems (e.g. routings, CNC programs).

At the highest level, the control functions are focussed more on planning than on the operational aspects. This includes forecasts and resource plans. Central data processing functions may also be performed at this level, such as data base management and data communications control. It also serves as the source for major common databases, such as engineering design information and production plans.

(ii) Manufacturing Data: An integrated manufacturing system must provide a wide variety of data to the production operation and support functions. This data generally falls into many categories, including information about the product design (e.g., geometry, specifications, bills of materials), production plans (demand and supply), and resource plans (e.g. labour, capacity) and data used by manufacturing like CNC programs, production schedules, and process control parameters.

(iii) Manufacturing Information System: The manufacturing system must provide reports on the performance of the production operation. These may be real-time feedback to production operators, daily operational reports to supervisors and MIS reports. The types of information typically reported include:

(i) Production status (e.g., shipments, back orders, WIP)

(ii) Manufacturing performance (e.g., cycle time, production rates, labour utilization)

(iii) Equipment performance (e.g., availability, utilization, throughput)

(iv) Costs (e.g., expenditure, unit costs, inventory)

18.13 SUMMARY

This chapter deals briefly several issues related to integrated automation. The cell type manufacturing systems employed in several tier1 and tier 2 automotive ancillary factories use many of the techniques discussed in this chapter effectively. Though fully integrated FMS has not been very popular of late, FMC's are widely employed in several industries. The key components in all these, is the Computer Numerical Controlled Machines and the CNC Technology.

REVIEW QUESTIONS

(1) Discuss the principle of Direct Numerical.

(2) What are the advantages of Direct Numerical Control?

(3) What are the requirements of the batch manufacturing to adopt just-in-time philosophy?

(4) Describe the elements of a typical flexible manufacturing cell.

(5) What are the various data associated with FMC?

(6) Discuss the various functional units of a flexible manufacturing cell.

(7) Describe the concept of a flexible manufacturing system.

(8) What are the subsystems of a FMS?

(9) What are the advantages of FMS compared to hard automation?

(10) What are the tasks to be automated in FMS?

(11) What are the techniques and equipment used for handling materials in a flexible manufacturing system?

(12) How does an automatic storage and retrieval system operate?

(13) How will you optimize the efficiency of FMS?

(14) What are the issues involved in the integration of manufacturing systems?

(15) What are the different levels of control in computer integrated manufacturing?

INDEX